The Purposeful Argument:
A Practical Guide

D1556785

Third Edition

Harry R. Phillips

Patricia Bostian

Central Piedmont Community College

All Illustrations by iStock.com/A-digit

CENGAGE

Australia • Brazil • Canada • Mexico • Singapore • United Kingdom • United States

The Purposeful Argument:
A Practical Guide, **Third Edition**
Harry Phillips, Patricia Bostian

Product Team Director: Catherine Van Der Laan

Product Manager: Nancy Tran

Learning Designer: Leslie Taggart

Senior Content Manager: Kathy Sands-Boehmer

Product Assistant: Tran Pham

Art Director: Lizz Anderson

Digital Delivery Lead: Matt Altieri

Manufacturing Buyer: Karen Hunt

Intellectual Property Analyst: Ann Hoffman

Senior Intellectual Property Project Manager: Betsy Hathaway

Executive Marketing Manager: Kina Lara

Associate Marketing Development Manager: Camille Beckman

Production Service: MPS Limited

Text Designer: Shawn Girsberger

Cover Designer: Lizz Anderson

Cover Image: iStock.com/A-digit

Compositor: MPS Limited

For product information and technology assistance, contact us at **Cengage Customer & Sales Support, 1-800-354-9706** or **support.cengage.com**.

For permission to use material from this text or product, submit all requests online at **www.cengage.com/permissions**.

Library of Congress Control Number: 2019911091

Student Edition:
ISBN-13: 978-0-357-13866-3
ISBN-10: 0-357-13866-3

Loose-leaf Edition:
ISBN: 978-0-357-13867-0

Cengage
200 Pier 4 Boulevard
Boston, MA 02210
USA

Cengage is a leading provider of customized learning solutions with employees residing in nearly 40 different countries and sales in more than 25 countries around the world. Find your local representative at **www.cengage.com**.

To learn more about Cengage platforms and services, register or access your online learning solution, or purchase materials for your course, visit **www.cengage.com**.

Instructors: Please visit **login.cengage.com** and log in to access instructor-specific resources.

Printed at CLDPC, USA, 10-20

BRIEF CONTENTS

Preface xv

PART 1 **How to Approach Argument in Real Life   1**
   1   Argue with a Purpose   2
   2   Explore an Issue That Matters to You   21

PART 2 **How to Establish Context Through Research   51**
   3   Develop a Research Plan   52
   4   Evaluate and Engage with Your Sources   80
   5   Read Critically and Avoid Fallacies   110
   6   Work Fairly with the Opposition   136

PART 3 **How to Plan, Structure, and Deliver an Argument   155**
   7   Explore an Issue   156
   8   Consider Toulmin-Based Argument   187
   9   Consider Middle-Ground Argument, Rogerian Argument, and Argument Based on a Microhistory   205
  10 Build Arguments   241
  11 Support an Argument with Fact (*Logos*), Credibility (*Ethos*), and Emotion (*Pathos*)   273

PART 4 **How to Take Ownership of Your Argument: A Style Guide   299**
  12 Enhance Your Argument with Visuals   300
  13 Develop and Edit Argument Structure and Style   319

PART 5 **An Anthology of Arguments   353**

PART 6 **MLA and APA Documentation Systems   479**

   Glossary   518
   Index   523

TABLE OF CONTENTS

Preface   xv

PART 1   **How to Approach Argument in Real Life**   1

1   **Argue with a Purpose**   2

What Argument Is and What Argument Is Not   3
Excerpt from "The Price of Admission," by Thomas Frank   4

Recognize Where Argument Is Appropriate in Real Life   6

Argue about Issues That Matter to You   7

Establish Local Context via the Research Process   10
Determine Your Audience   10
Establish Local Context for Your Issue   11
Connect Local and Global Contexts   13

Recognize Why Arguments Break Down   15
Arguments Break Down When They Do Not Persuade an Audience   15
Arguments Break Down When There Is a Lack of Balance in the Support   15
Arguments Break Down When the Audience Is Poorly Defined   15
Arguments Break Down When They Contain Fallacies   16
Arguments Break Down When They Do Not Fairly Represent Opposing Views   16

Match Argument with Purpose   16
Toulmin-Based Argument   17
Middle-Ground Argument   18
Rogerian Argument   18
Argument Based on a Microhistory   19

2   Explore an Issue that Matters to You   21

Determine What Matters to You and Why   23
    School/Academic   23
    Workplace   24
    Family/Household   24
    Neighborhood   25
    Social/Cultural   25
    Consumer   25
    Concerned Citizen   26

Choose an Issue within a Topic   27

Pre-Think about Your Issue   29
    Brainstorming   29
    Freewriting   30
    Mapping   30
    Move from Boring to Interesting   30

Define and Target Your Audience   32

Stake, Defend, and Justify Your Claim   34
    Develop a Claim, Reasons, and Qualifiers   34
    Argue with a Purpose   36

Vary the Types of Support You Bring to an Argument   37
    Support Based on Fact   37
    Support Based on Your Character   37
    Support Based on the Emotions of an Audience   38
    Working with a Target Audience: Two Examples   38

Argue at the Right Moment   46

Getting Started   47

iStock.com/A-digit

PART 2   How to Establish Context Through Research   51

3   Develop a Research Plan   52

Use Reference Works, Encyclopedias, and Topic Overviews Profitably   54
    Read an Overview of Your Topic   54
    Gather Search Terms   55

Use Search Engines to Find Internet Sources on the Surface
Web and on the Deep Web   57
    Search the Surface Web   57
    Search the Deep Web   60

Perform Keyword Queries   61

Find News Sites and Use RSS Feeds to Receive Updates   63

Find and Use Databases in Libraries   65

Find and Use Primary Sources   69
  Find and Use Government Sources   71
  Find and Use Multimedia Sources   72

Find Books   75
  Find Books in Libraries   76
  Find Books on the Internet   77

4   Evaluate and Engage with Your Sources   80

Take Notes, Read Critically, and Evaluate Internet Sites   81
  Critically Read Material on the Internet   82
  Evaluate Internet Sites   83

Take Notes, Read Critically, and Evaluate Articles   84
  Read Articles Critically   85
  Reading Strategies for Longer Articles   86
  Evaluate Articles   90

Take Notes and Read Books Critically   90

Take Notes and Evaluate Primary Sources   91

Introduce and Comment on Sources   92

Quote and Cite Quotations   95
  Quoting Material Quoted in the Original Source   98
  Alter Quoted Material   99

Summarize and Cite Summaries   100

Summary Checklist   100

Paraphrase and Cite Paraphrases   101

Avoid Plagiarism   105

Documentation: Works Cited Page   107

5   Read Critically and Avoid Fallacies   110

Define Fallacies   111

Identify and Avoid Fallacies   112

Avoid Fallacies of Choice   114
  Blanket Statement   115
  False Dilemma, Either–Or, and Misuse of Occam's Razor   116
  Slippery Slope   117

Avoid Fallacies of Support   119

Circular Argument   *119*

Hasty Generalization and Jumping to Conclusions   *120*

Faulty Causality: Post Hoc, Ergo Propter Hoc   *120*

Non Sequitur, *Red Herring, and False Clue*   *121*

Straw Man Argument or Argument Built on a False Fact or Claim   *122*

Avoid Fallacies of Emotion   124

Ad Hominem   *124*

Testimonials and False Authority   *125*

Bandwagon   *126*

Ad Misericordiam   *126*

Scare Tactics   *126*

Avoid Fallacies of Inconsistency   128

Moral Equivalence   *129*

Material Equivalence   *129*

Definitional Equivalence   *129*

Inconsistent Treatment (from Dogmatism, Prejudice, and Bias)   *130*

Equivocation   *130*

False Analogy   *131*

6   Work Fairly with the Opposition   136

Why the Opposition Matters   138

Resist Easy Generalizations   139

Listen to Local Voices   140

Summarize Other Voices Fairly   141

Value Expertise over Advocacy   145

Avoid Bias When You Summarize   146

Find Points of Overlap   148

Identify Common Ground with the Opposition   *148*

Respond to Other Views   151

PART 3   How to Plan, Structure, and Deliver an Argument   155

7   Explore an Issue   156

Use Definitions   157

Seven Types of Definition   *160*

Discover Causes or Consequences   164

Present Comparisons   168

Propose a Solution   170
    Section A: Exploring the Problem   171
    Section B: Different Types of Exploration   173
    Section C: Exploring Implementation   178

Evaluate Your Claim   181

Write an Exploratory Essay   183
    Sample Exploratory Essay   184

iStock.com/A-digit

8   Consider Toulmin-Based Argument   187

Construct an Argument to Fit Your Purpose   189

Terms of Toulmin-Based Argument   189
    Claim   191
    Reasons   191
    Support   191
    Warrant   192
    Backing   192
    Rebuttal   192
    Qualifiers   193

Map a Toulmin-Based Argument   194

Student-Authored Toulmin-Based Argument   198

9   Consider Middle-Ground Argument, Rogerian Argument, and Argument Based on a Microhistory   205

Middle-Ground Argument   207
    Make a Middle-Ground Position Practical   207
    Recognize Where Middle-Ground Arguments Are Possible   208
    Map a Middle-Ground Argument   209

Student-Authored Middle-Ground Argument   214

Rogerian Argument   219
    Listen Closely to the Opposition   219
    Identify Common Ground   221
    Map a Rogerian Argument   223

Sample Rogerian Argument   227

Argument Based on a Microhistory   228
    Focus on the Local and Specific   228

Make Room for Local Histories   229
Work with Primary Materials   231
Subjects and Materials for Microhistories   232
Map an Argument Based on a Microhistory   233

Sample Argument Based on a Microhistory   236

10   Build Arguments   241

How a Claim Functions   243
Claim: The Center of Your Argument   243
Connect Claim with Purpose   245

Five Kinds of Claims   246
Claim of Fact   246
Claim of Definition   248
Problem-Based Claims   250
Claim of Evaluation   251
Claim of Cause   253

Use Reasons to Support Your Claim   254

Build Body Paragraphs around Reasons   257

Use Qualifiers to Make Your Argument Believable   259

Justify Your Claim with a Warrant   261

Use Your Audience to Construct a Warrant   262
Know What Your Audience Values   262
Let a Warrant Bridge Claim and Support   263

Use Backing to Support a Warrant   265
Let Your Audience Determine the Extent of Backing   266
Make Backing Specific   267

Respond to Audience Reservations to Make a Warrant Believable   269

11   Support an Argument with Fact (*Logos*), Credibility (*Ethos*), and Emotion (*Pathos*)   273

Field-Specific Support   274
Find Support for the Physical Sciences   275
Find Support for Education, History, and Social and Behavioral Sciences   277
Find Sources for the Humanities and the Arts   279

Use All Three General Kinds of Support   281

Use Support Based on Facts and Research (*Logos*)   282
Facts and Opinions   282

iStock.com/A-digit

Statistics   284

Scholarly Articles   288

Use Support to Create Credibility (*Ethos*)   289

Use Support to Create Emotion (*Pathos*)   292

Anecdotes   293

Photographs   294

Using Humor in Your Arguments   294

PART 4   **How to Take Ownership of Your Argument: A Style Guide   299**

12   Enhance Your Argument With Visuals   300

What Are Visual Arguments?   301

Understanding and Using Visual Arguments   303

Reading Photographs and Illustrations   308

Using Photographs and Illustrations in Your Argument   311

Reading Graphs and Charts   312

Using and Creating Graphs in Your Argument   314

Reading Advertisements   316

13   Develop and Edit Argument Structure and Style   319

Consider Your Argument's Claim   320

Introduce Your Claim   320

State Your Claim   323

Position Your Claim   326

Introduce Your Counterarguments   329

The Counterargument Is Incorrect   330

The Counterargument Is Correct, But . . .   330

Create Strong Introductions   331

Anecdote   332

Misdirection   332

Conflict   333

Suspense   334

A Seeming Impossibility   335

Write Memorable Conclusions   336

Broadening Out   336

Opposition   337

Circling Back   338

Edit and Organize Your Argument's Support   339
Edit Support   339

Organize Your Support   342

Three Organization Samples of Body Paragraphs   343

Supply a Strong Title   346

Participate Effectively in a Peer Review Session   348
Your Role as a Reviewer   348

Your Role as a Reviewee   350

PART 5   An Anthology of Arguments   353

Intersections   Contemporary Issues and Arguments   354

Anthology 1: School and Academic Community   354

Jennifer A Mott-Smith, *Bad Idea About Writing: Plagiarism Deserves to be Punished*   354

Jon Marcus and Holly K. Hacker, *The Rich-Poor Divide on America's College Campuses is Getting Wider, Fast*   358

Keith Ellison, *The Argument for Tuition-Free College*   366

Katie Reilly, *Record Numbers of College Students Are Seeking Treatment for Depression and Anxiety—But Schools Can't Keep Up*   368

Anthology 2: Workplace Community   374

Gar Alperovitz and Keane Bhatt, *Employee-Owned Businesses Ignored by Mainstream Media*   374

Tim Kastelle, *Hierarchy Is Overrated*   376

Jan Edwards and Molly Morgan, *Abolish Corporate Personhood (Thinking Politically)*   380

Rich Meneghello, *Solutions at Work: When Love Enters the Workplace*   386

Anthology 3: Family and Household Community   390

Sue Ferguson, *Leaving the Doors Open*   390

Jewel, *Street Life Is No Life for Children*   393

Richard Louv, *Introduction from Last Child in the Woods*   396

Dahr Jamail, *A Morally Bankrupt Military: When Soldiers and Their Families Become Expendable*   399

Anthology 4: Neighborhood Community   405

Barbara Nichols, *Airbnb is Crashing the Neighborhood*   405

Eleanor Novek, *You Wouldn't Fit Here*   408

James Q. Wilson, *Bowling with Others*   413

Noah Smith, *The Poor Don't Deserve Toxic-Waste Dumps in Their Backyards*   420

Anthology 5: Social/Cultural Community   423

Daniel J. Solove, *Why "Security" Keeps Winning Out Over Privacy*   423

Vince Dixon, *The Case Against Tipping in America*   426

Ronald Davis, *My Truth About Being A Black Man And A Black Cop*   433

Jeff Yang, *Killer Reflection*   436

Anthology 6: Consumer Community   441

Judith Simmer Brown, *A Buddhist Perspective on Consumerism*   441

Matt Stannard, *Seizing the Public Banking Moment*   445

Andy Kroll, *How the McEconomy Bombed the American Worker: The Hollowing Out of the Middle Class*   449

Dali L. Yang, *Outsourcing Compromises the Safety and Quality of Products*   453

Anthology 7: Concerned Citizen Community   460

Harry Binswanger, *The United States Should Adopt Open Immigration*   460

James L. Dickerson, *Climate Change Could Cause Disease Resurgence*   465

David Howard, *Automatic Voter Registration: A Rational Solution to an Irrational Problem*   469

David Kelley, *Private Charity Should Replace Welfare*   473

Anthology 8: Classic American Arguments   MindTap

Susan B. Anthony, *On Women's Right to Vote*

Mary Antin, *Have We Any Right to Regulate Immigration?*

Alexander Hamilton, *The Federalist No. 6*

Thomas Jefferson, *In Congress, July 4, 1776*

H. L. Mencken, *The Penalty of Death*

Judith Sargent Murray, *On the Equality of the Sexes*

Leo Szilard And Cosigners, *A Petition to the President of the United States*

Sojourner Truth, *Ain't I a Woman?*

Booker T. Washington, *Atlanta Compromise Address*

PART 6   MLA and APA Documentation Systems   479

APPENDIX A   MLA Documentation and the List of Works Cited   480

APPENDIX B   APA Documentation and the Reference List   500

Glossary   518

Index   523

Purpose

This third edition of *The Purposeful Argument* delivers the essentials of argumentative writing in accessible, student-friendly language. The textbook allows writers to recognize where argument fits in their lives and how it can be a practical response both to the issues in everyday life and to academic and intellectual problems encountered in the classroom. In this way, the text meets student writers on their own terms, in their own lives, and demands that they determine what they argue about. Changes to this new edition reflect the suggestions of our students and those of veteran teachers of argument, who are sensitive to what makes a textbook genuinely useful.

The philosophical center of *The Purposeful Argument* rests with John Dewey's notion that public education can best serve a democratic culture when it connects classroom with community and by thinking of the class-room as a laboratory for intelligent democratic activity. Building on this idea, those who argue competently can become the lifeblood of local action and change. Put another way, a nation, state, or community that does not engage purposefully in regular discussion and informed argument cannot fulfill itself.

Accessibility is central to the purpose of this project, and this third edition includes a streamlining of many features of the textbook. From many students' perspectives, some current argument texts are dense and filled with examples apart from their worlds. In response to these concerns, *The Purposeful Argument* relies less on discussion via traditional academic language to get across a concept and more on cogent definition, explicit example, and practical exercises that guide student writers through the process of assembling an argument. Examples of student, local, and professional writing are in many cases annotated and color-coded so as to identify elements of argument structure.

From another perspective, *The Purposeful Argument* puts in place the groundwork for student writers to create possibilities for themselves in a culture that demands more and more from its citizens. When so much of what we encounter has to do with the lure of consumption, and when so much of our national discourse is riveted to economic conditions, job security, and terror and intervention, it can be tough for freshman writers to think of themselves as agents capable of meaningful change. But at its core, *The Purposeful Argument* argues this very position. In its purest moment, this guide enables student writers to establish rhetorical places for themselves that ideally can reinvigorate our democracy via responsible citizenship. Because communication is less local in advanced industrial nations, this project invites a return to a more traditional form of democratic participation with its attention to local engagement. And local engagement can begin with a writer's commitment to the idea that the private responsibility to argue is essential to the public good.

With this emphasis on local engagement, we have noticed stronger, more focused arguments in the past several years. In general, when students are encouraged to honor and respond to issues that matter to them, their investment becomes evident and their writing, purposeful. This kind of ownership, we believe, results from an approach that steers writers into issues originating in the larger worlds of political, economic, and social issues as well as into their own worlds and concerns. With some students, this means arguing on issues that are solidly academic and intellectual in nature; with others, it means tackling issues of immediate concern in everyday life. Thus, compelling writing has emerged on issues as varied as the U. S. Supreme Court's ruling on corporate personhood, student loan requirements, China's behavior at the climate change conference in Copenhagen, favoritism in the workplace, recent health care reform and its implications for students, social networking and employment, religious values and curriculum design in Texas, and American consumers' role in the mining of "conflict minerals" in the Republic of the Congo.

A central focus of *The Purposeful Argument* is our intention to write to our specific audience—first-year writers—and this means delivering the fundamentals of argument to many nontraditional students, to nonnative speakers of English, to parents, to students who work one or more jobs, often in excess of the traditional work week, and to students who may or may not have experience with conceptual material and its application in their academic careers. This book is structured to accommodate our students and the diverse life experience they bring to our classrooms. Following are features of *The Purposeful Argument* that, in our view, distinguish it from the many excellent argument textbooks currently on the market—textbooks that may, however, fall outside the lines of accessibility and usefulness to many college students.

Organization and Chapter Flow

Part One of this guide attends to how effective arguments work. Chapter 1 introduces readers to essential features of argument and their interrelatedness. The chapter's sections move students into thinking about argument as a practical response to both everyday and academic issues and briefly introduce them to the types of argument found in the book. In Chapter 2, the crucial need to separate issue from topic is treated early. As a way to recognize issues and where they arise, this chapter identifies communities we belong to and some issues within these communities. The chapter offers numerous prompts and strategies for exploring an issue, such as prewriting activities that help students make a topic they might initially see as "boring" interesting to them and their readers. Audience focus, emphasized throughout the chapters, is introduced here, and students are presented with practical ways to determine appropriate audiences for their arguments. Arguing at the right time and establishing credibility fill out this chapter.

Part Two begins with the essential work of building clear context for an issue, the focus of Chapter 3. It is here that students are introduced to sources and how to access and use them. We choose to bring in the research process earlier rather than later because building a knowledge base often can enlarge the way we think about an issue, and this can influence what a writer claims and the way an argument is structured. Chapter 4 is geared toward the important work of using resources and how to read and evaluate them critically. As well, this chapter is a primer for working responsibly with borrowed material and ideas. Learning how to recognize and avoid fallacies is the center of Chapter 5. This chapter organizes fallacies—common in advertising and politics—into categories of choice, support, emotion, and inconsistency. Chapter 6 is devoted to the opposition, why it matters, how to work responsibly with it, and finding points of overlap. This chapter, we feel, adds to conventional approaches to opposing points of view.

Part Three treats the how-to of argument building. Chapter 7 helps students develop their argument strategies based on definitions, causes or consequences, comparisons, solution proposals, and evaluations, concluding with a rubric for preparing an exploratory essay. Discussion of Toulmin-based argument makes up Chapter 8. Chapter 9 introduces Rogerian argument, in addition to two less traditional approaches to argument in American classrooms: Middle Ground and Microhistory. We are enthusiastic about students learning to argue from a middle-ground perspective, as this approach insists on a close knowledge of audience and opposition. The middle-ground approach has, in the past few years, been popular among writers looking to escape either–or thinking and instead craft practical positions on complex issues. We are equally enthusiastic about a fourth kind of argument discussed in this chapter—an argument based on a microhistory—where writers work with primary documents and then forge a position apart from conventional understanding of the period in which these documents originate. Chapter 10 is about building arguments. It is example-rich and orients writers to the building blocks of argument—claims, reasons, qualifiers, support, the warrant, backing, and audience reservations. We view this chapter as one writers will use frequently during the drafting process. We elaborate in Chapter 11 on how to use support effectively, and this involves establishing writer credibility, specific appeals to audience, and a rubric for evaluating support brought to an argument.

Part Five is centered in the ideal of ownership, that is, in ways writers can make arguments distinctly their own. Chapter 12 is a discussion of how writers can vary their approaches to an audience using visuals. And Chapter 13 is devoted to writing style and editing. While material in this final chapter is typically relegated to textbooks designed for earlier writing courses, we present this material in the context of argument writing as what we feel are necessary refreshers.

All chapters in Parts One through Four begin with a narrative that describes a real-life issue and conclude with a "Keeping It Local" exercise, pointing out that argument is a practical way to negotiate purposefully issues in everyday and academic life.

Part Five is an anthology of arguments written by everyday people who have stakes in local issues and by professional writers whose commentary on a given issue can provide a larger critical frame. Arguments are followed by questions tied to argument structure, audience, comprehension, and ways to connect concerns in the local community with the broader geopolitical culture. Another level of questions prompts students to acknowledge issues in their own lives that are the same or similar to issues found in the readings.

Part Six is devoted to MLA and APA documentation systems. For each system, guidelines and examples are provided. The important work of documenting carefully material borrowed from other writers and sources is addressed in this section.

New Features

- Many new essays in the anthology, Part Five, demonstrate how contemporary writers build arguments in response to specific issues affecting the seven communities addressed in *The Purposeful Argument*: school, the workplace, family, neighborhood, social-cultural, consumer, and concerned citizen.
- Part Six, MLA and APA Documentation Systems, now contains a complete APA student essay to accompany the annotated MLA student essay.
- Classic American Arguments anthology has been moved to the e-book/MindTap.

Key Features

- Writers are encouraged to argue in response to issues in their everyday and academic environments—school, the workplace, family, neighborhood, social-cultural, consumer, and concerned citizen—and thus learn how argument can become an essential negotiating skill in their lives. This book emphasizes local and intellectual issues throughout and provides a methodology for connecting the local with global trends. Importantly, this allows writers to build a strong understanding of an issue by generating broad context.

- Argument structure is presented in practical, how-to ways, complete with exercises, charts, and real-life examples. Ways to organize an argument—Toulmin-based, Rogerian, Middle Ground, and Microhistory options—are fully defined and demonstrated.
- Simplified text format and page layout improve upon conventional argument textbook design by making information direct and accessible.
- Checklists throughout *The Purposeful Argument* provide support for writers as they craft their own arguments.
- Annotated examples of effective arguments illustrate strengths and weaknesses.
- "Your Turn" exercises consist of questions and prompts so that writers can apply argument structure to arguments they are building. "Internet Activity" prompts direct writers to online investigations that connect to the research process.
- "Tips" panels typically are clues for ways of thinking about a feature of argument during the planning process.
- Key terms are bolded throughout the text. A Glossary related to practical argument provides an alphabetized reference for these and other terms found in *The Purposeful Argument*. A term is defined with regard to its function and placement in an argument.

The Online Program

MindTap English for Phillips/Bostian, *The Purposeful Argument,* is the digital learning solution that gives you complete control of your course—to provide engaging content, challenge every individual, and build students' confidence. MindTap increases student engagement via peer modeling of critical thinking and writing practices, tutorials on four types of arguments, and immediate feedback on students' responses to auto-graded activities.

MindTap gives you complete ownership of your content and learning experience. You can add your own comments to the e-book and your own materials to the learning path. You can move, rename, and delete content to ensure that your course is exactly how you want it. An easy-to-use paper management system helps you prevent plagiarism and allows electronic submission, grading, and peer review. Visual analytics track your students' progress and engagement.

MindTap extends the instruction in the book/e-book with end-of-chapter activities, brand-new tutorials on four types of argument, videos of students working through argument assignments, and additional student and professional readings.

- **New "Argument Tutorials" on Toulmin, Rogerian, Middle-Ground, and Microhistory arguments.** The extensive tutorial on Toulmin argument includes four short video presentations of concepts, interspersed with auto-graded activities that give students step-by-step help in applying Toulmin. Students can use the "Grade It Now" function in the auto-graded activities to get immediate feedback on their responses. Every activity includes three versions in order to give all students the opportunity to succeed. Slightly shorter tutorials on the other three types of argument follow the same pattern.

- **New "Students Working on Arguments" videos.** Nine new videos showcase reading critically, investigating the rhetorical situation, developing an argument, synthesizing diverse perspectives, revising logical fallacies, using research in argument, investigating the source of information, evaluating a format to determine if a source is "fake news," and determining the expertise of an author.

- **New "Collaborative Activities" after every chapter.** Each activity for pairs, groups, and the whole class is followed by a Reflection question that individual students can submit in order to demonstrate what they have learned.

- **Revised "Review Activities" after each chapter.** These auto-graded activities provide a comprehension check and a first opportunity to apply chapter concepts. Immediate feedback is available, and each activity includes three versions to give students the best chance to succeed.

- **New "Annotated Student Readings with Discussion Questions."** Nine student papers are annotated to demonstrate aspects of argument; they are followed by discussion questions.

- **New "Professional Readings with Discussion Questions."** To supplement the professional readings in Part 5 of the book/e-book, 18 additional readings on contemporary topics are provided. Discussion questions follow.

- **"How-to Research Video Activities."** 50 video activities on particular aspects of the research-writing process.

- **"Auto-Graded Activities."** 75+ auto-graded activities on the writing process, essay structure, documentation, grammar, and more.

- **"Just in Time Plus,"** a set of tutorials that provide extra help on 21 foundational topics. Each topic includes a video tutorial, two to four pages of textual instruction, and an auto-graded activity. A diagnostic test helps you determine who needs instruction on specific topics and which topics to discuss in class. A posttest allows you to evaluate students' progress at semester's end.

- **"Resources for Teaching"** provides support materials to help you plan and teach your course. A video demonstrates how to customize your MindTap course. In the Instructor's Manual, author Patricia Bostian shares sample syllabi, assignment rubrics, chapter-by-chapter resources, and questions to jump-start discussions. An Educator's Guide demonstrates how to use activities in MindTap to enrich your course.

Empower your students to accelerate their progress with MindTap.

- The instructor's manual provides course-specific organization tools and classroom strategies, including sample syllabi, designs for mapping the course, assignment flow, ways to utilize the book, suggestions for teaching the course online, and ways to best use electronic resources. The center of the guide is a series of rubrics and exercises that can be adapted to an instructor's work with each chapter.

In sum, *The Purposeful Argument* is a student-centered approach to argument. It is a guide that lets students determine how they can use argument in life and equips them with a concrete, how-to approach. It lets instructors play to their strengths by letting writers work with their strengths—their investment in issues that matter to them in daily and classroom life. From the beginning, the text presents argument in ways that can empower and enable writers to publicly validate what most concerns them.

The Purposeful Argument is designed to complement and not overwhelm. The language of *The Purposeful Argument* is friendly and direct. Short, concise paragraphs are the rule; paragraphs are followed immediately by real-life examples, checklists, charts, rubrics, exercises, and sample student writings.

Competent, informed argument is as important today in American life as it was during other crucial periods in our history. It was and is a way to be heard and, when conditions permit, to be granted a seat at the discussion table. While public memory has shaped the way we view extraordinary moments in our past—indigenous peoples' fate at the hands of colonizers and an aggressive government, debates over sacred and secular ideals, arguments for political independence, the rhetoric of abolition and women's rights movements, the voice of labor, and the Civil Rights Movement—it is crucial to remember that, in addition to the arguments of accomplished writers, activists, and orators associated with these moments, a turbulence of voices was audible. These were the sounds of everyday people moving the culture forward. Without their contributions, the figures we celebrate now would be footnotes only. The voice of the individual *does* matter. If we choose not to speak up, others will make decisions for us.

ACKNOWLEDGMENTS

We are grateful to the many individuals at Cengage for their help with this edition: Nancy Tran, Product Manager; Leslie Taggart, Learning Designer, Anne Alexander and Breanna Robbins, Subject Matter Experts; Kathy Sands-Boehmer, Content Manager; Lizz Anderson, Designer; Tran Pham, Product Assistant; Ann Hoffman, IP Analyst; Betsy Hathaway, IP Project Manager; Camille Beckman, Associate Market Development Manager; and Kina Lara, Marketing Manager.

The astute reviewers for the third edition helped us identify ways to improve our online program. We are grateful for their insight:

Kerry L. Beckford
Tunxis Community College

Conrad A. Davies, Sr.
University of Kentucky

Ana de La Serna
California State University,
  Dominguez Hills

Lisa M. Russell
Georgia Northwestern Technical
  College

We'd also like to thank reviewers from previous editions:

James Allen
College of DuPage

Marsha Anderson
Wharton County Jr. College

Lynnette Beers-McCormick
Santiago Canyon College

Laura Black
Volunteer State Community
  College

Mary Chen
Tacoma Community College

Kathleen Doherty
Middlesex Community College

Cassie Falke
East Texas Baptist University

Karen Golightly
Christian Brothers University

Nate Gordon
Kishwaukee College

Lauren Hahn
DePaul University

Betty Hart
The University of Southern
  Indiana

Erik Juergensmeyer
Fort Lewis College

Lindsay Lewan
Arapahoe Community College

Theodore Matula
University of San Francisco

Mandy McDougal
Volunteer State CC

Gary Montano
Tarrant County College

Elizabeth Oldfield
Southeastern Community
  College

M. Whitney Olsen
Arizona State University

Amy Ratto Park
University of Montana

Deborah Ruth
Owensboro Community and
  Technical College

Dan Sullivan
Davenport University

Robert Williams
Grossmont College

We also wish to thank members of the Advisory Review Board and more than 65 reviewers and focus group participants who contributed steadily to the first edition. Their thoughtful feedback allowed us to refine and improve a range of chapter-specific features of this textbook.

Susan Achziger
Community College of Aurora

Kara Alexander
Baylor University

Steve Anderson
Normandale Community College

Sonja Andrus
Collin College

Joseph Antinarella
Tidewater Community College

Brad Beachy
Butler Community College

Evelyn Beck
Piedmont Technical College

Jeff Birkenstein
Saint Martin's University

Carol Bledsoe
Florida Gulf Coast University

David Bockoven
Linn-Benton Community College

Ashley Bourne
J Sargeant Reynolds Community
  College

Michael Boyd
Illinois Central College

Marty Brooks
John Tyler Community College

Shanti Bruce
Nova Southeastern University

JoAnn Buck
Guilford Technical Community
  College

Carol Burnell
Clackamas Community College

Anthony Cavaluzzi
Adirondack Community College

Mary Chen-Johnson
Tacoma Community College

Scott Clements
Keiser College, Melbourne
  Campus

Jennifer Courtney
University of North Carolina at
  Charlotte

Susan Davis
Arizona State University

James Decker
Illinois Central College

Tamra DiBenedetto
Riverside Community College

Connie Duke
Keiser University

Keri Dutkiewicz
Davenport University

Sarah M. Eichelman
Walters State Community College

Gareth Euridge
Tallahassee Community College

Jane Focht-Hansen
San Antonio College

MacGregor Frank
Guilford Technical Community
  College

Richard Gilbert
Benedictine University of Illinois

Nate Gordon
Kishwaukee College

Virginia Grant
Gaston College

Valerie Grey
Portland Community College

Annette Hale
Motlow State Community College
  (McMinnville Center)

Pamela Herring
Southwest Texas Junior College

Cheryl Huff
Germanna Community College

Sue Hum
University of Texas at San
  Antonio

Rachel Key
Grayson County College

Jill Lahnstein
Cape Fear Community College

Charlotte Laughlin
McLennan Community College

Gordon Lee
Lee College

Michael Lueker
Our Lady of the Lake University

Anna Maheshwari
Schoolcraft College

Jodie Marion
Mt Hood Community College

Sarah Markgraf
Bergen Community College

Melinda McBee
Grayson County College

Randall McClure
Florida Gulf Coast University

Jeanne McDonald
Waubonsee Community College

Jim McKeown
McLennan Community College

Richard Middleton-Kaplan
Harper College

Gary Montano
Tarrant County College

Jennifer Mooney
Wharton County Junior College

Vicki Moulson
College of the Albemarle

Andrea Muldoon
University of Wisconsin-Stout

Mary Huyck Mulka
Minnesota State University
  Moorhead

Lana Myers
Lone Star College

Marguerite Newcomb
University of Texas–San Antonio

Troy Nordman
Butler Community College

Eden Pearson
Des Moines Area Community
College

Jason Pickavance
Salt Lake Community College

Paula Porter
Keiser University

Jeff Pruchnic
Wayne State University

Esther Quantrill
Blinn College

Maria Ramos
J. Sargeant Reynolds Community
College

Arthur Rankin
Louisiana State University at
Alexandria

Simone Rieck
Lone Star College

Jeffrey Roessner
Mercyhurst College

Ron Ross
Portland Community College

Jennifer Rosti
Roanoke College

Karin Russell
Keiser University

Debbie Ruth
Owensboro Community &
Technical College

Jamie Sadler
Richmond Community College

John Schaffer
Blinn College

Dixie Shaw-Tillmon
The University of Texas at San
Antonio

Suba Subbarao
Oakland Community College

Daniel Sullivan
Davenport University

Susan Swanson
Owensboro Community and
Technical College

Paul Van Heuklom
Lincoln Land Community College

Angie Williams-Chehmani
Davenport University

Will Zhang
Des Moines Area Community
College

Traci Zimmerman
James Madison University

Harry Phillips would like to thank Aron Keesbury, formerly acquisitions editor at Thomson Publishing for his steady encouragement and insightful feedback during the early stages of this project.

Patricia K. Bostian would like to thank her wonderful family for their generous support, particularly her husband Brad for his many wonderful textbook ideas, and her children Wyndham and Rhiannon for allowing her to talk about her ideas with them.

Finally, we want to acknowledge the steady interest our students have shown in argumentative writing over the last 15 years. In truth, it was their authentic interest in the course and their recognition that argument could serve them in daily life that fueled original interest in this project. As teachers, the course inspired us to regularly refine our approaches and, mostly, to listen closely to student writers who sensed, perhaps for the first time, that their private concerns could influence public thinking and decision making. In particular, we are grateful to Linda Gonzalez, Blaine Schmidt, and Ben Szany, among other students, for their willingness to contribute arguments to this textbook.

Harry R. Phillips

Patricia Bostian

CHAPTER 1 Argue With a Purpose

CHAPTER 2 Explore an Issue that Matters to You

PART ONE

How to Approach Argument in Real Life

All Illustrations by iStock.com/A-digit

Argue With a Purpose

Learning Objectives

By working through this chapter, you will be able to

- define argument.
- explain the purposes of argument.
- identify context for an issue via the research process.
- identify why arguments break down.
- determine an appropriate argument type for an argument's purpose.
- form an argument about an issue that matters to you.

This text introduces you to argument and how to use it in response to everyday issues—at school, in the workplace, at home, in your neighborhood, with people who matter to you, in the swirl of community politics, and on a national or global scale. You will be able to use the tools in the following chapters to build practical arguments that make your voice clear and direct on issues in which you have a stake. Skills in argument will help you in your life as a student, a member of the local labor force, a consumer, a concerned citizen, and perhaps a parent and homeowner; in fact, argument can help you address all of the many issues associated with life in these communities.

This chapter is an overview of the nature and purpose of argument. Later chapters address the apparatus of argument—how to craft a claim, build support, work with the opposition, and build other structural elements. Think about argument as a set of tools that lets you negotiate your world with clarity and purpose. The skills you take away from this text,

All Illustrations by iStock.com/A-digit

and the work required to complete a class in argument, can transfer to the real world. You may simply be responding to short-term assignments, but in doing so, you will learn to build sound arguments—a skill that will be useful long after your final class project is turned in.

What Argument Is and What Argument Is Not

You are arguing when you claim a point of view on an issue, defend your claim with different kinds of support, and respond fairly to those with differing points of view. Argument is useful when you want to persuade others (decision-makers, fellow classmates, coworkers, a community agency or organization, a special interest group, elected representatives, business leaders, or an individual) to take seriously your point of view; when you want to find out more about something that matters to you; and when you want to establish areas of common interest among different positions. With nearly all arguments, it is essential to establish a clear context for your issue and to have a target audience.

Argument is not about putting yourself in uncomfortable, win–lose, either–or situations. It is not about fighting or trying to shame someone who holds a different point of view. Some people associate argument with anger, raised voices, and emotional outbursts. But when these people behave in competitive, angry, and overly emotional ways, communication is often sealed off and the people involved become alienated from one another. This is not the aim of argument. Argument creates a space where we can listen to each other.

The following essay by Thomas Frank is excerpted from "The Price of Admission." The full essay appears in the June 2012 issue of *Harper's*, a magazine that began publication in 1850 and today treats a wide range of issues in literature, politics, culture, finance, and the arts. In the essay, Frank includes a claim, various levels of support, and efforts to build his credibility as one taking a position on the issue of college tuition. Missing from the excerpt, but present in the longer essay, are attention to the opposition, reasons that support the claim, and a warrant, that is, attention to the values that motivate the writer to argue on this issue. The essay is accompanied by an editorial cartoon by R.J. Matson (see Figure 1.1).

Excerpt from "The Price of Admission"

by Thomas Frank

Figure 1.1 Editorial cartoon by R.J. Matson

Massive indebtedness changes a person, maybe even more than a college education does, and it's reasonable to suspect that the politicos who have allowed the tuition disaster to take its course know this. To saddle young people with enormous, inescapable debt — total student debt is now more than one trillion dollars — is ultimately to transform them into profit-maximizing machines. I mean, working as a schoolteacher or an editorial assistant at a publishing house isn't going to help you chip away at that forty grand you owe. You can't get out of it by bankruptcy, either. And our political leaders, lost in a fantasy of punitive individualism, certainly won't propose the bailout measures they could take to rescue the young from the crushing burden.

What will happen to the young debtors instead is that they will become *Homo economicus*, whether or not they studied that noble creature. David Graeber, the anthropologist who wrote the soon-to-be-classic *Debt: The First 5,000 Years*, likens the process to a horror movie, in which the zombies or the vampires attack the humans as a kind of recruitment policy. "They turn you into one of them," as Graeber told me.

Actually, they do worse than that. Graeber relates the story of a woman he met who got a Ph.D. from Columbia University, but whose $80,000 debt load put an academic career off-limits, since adjuncts earn close to nothing. Instead, the woman wound up working as an escort for Wall Street types. "Here's someone who ought to be a professor," Graeber explains, "doing sexual services for the guys who lent her the money."

The story hit home for me, because I, too, wanted to be a professor once. I remember the waves of enlightenment that washed over me in my first few years in college, the ecstasy of finally beginning to understand what moved human affairs this way or that, the exciting sense of a generation arriving at a shared sensibility. Oh, I might have gone on doing that kind of work forever, whether or not it made me rich, if journalism had not intervened.

It's hard to find that kind of ecstasy among the current crop of college graduates. The sensibility shared by their generation seems to revolve around student debt, which has been clamped onto them like some sort of interest-bearing iron maiden. They've been screwed — that's what their moment of enlightenment has taught them.

As for my own cohort, or at least the members of it who struggled through and made it to one of the coveted positions in the knowledge factory, the new generational feeling seems to be one of disgust. Our enthusiasm for learning, which we trumpeted to the world, merely led the nation's children into debt bondage. Consider the remarks of Nicholas Mirzoeff, a professor of media at New York University, who sums up the diminishing returns of the profession on his blog: "I used to say that in academia one at least did very little harm. Now I feel like a pimp for loan sharks."

Analyze this Reading

1. What is the writer's claim, the position the writer takes in response to the issue of student debt?
2. Identify examples the writer uses to support his claim.
3. How does the writer establish his credibility; that is, how does he build trust with readers regarding his competence to take a stand on this issue?

Respond to this Reading

1. The writer contends that political leaders won't make the effort to bail out today's college students from debt. Do you favor a legislative bailout? Explain, and if you don't favor such a bailout, what claim would you make to address the student debt problem?
2. What is your relationship to education and debt? What examples would you use to demonstrate this relationship?
3. If you were to argue on this issue, at what target audience would you aim? Would your audience be officials at your college, your state legislators, your peers, or the members of your community? Explain.

Recognize Where Argument Is Appropriate in Real Life

You'll get to know this guide as a student in a class, one class among many that you need to complete as you move toward your degree, but there is another, equally important way to think about your work with argument—the set of skills you'll acquire and take with you when class is over. Make these skills serve what matters to you, in and beyond the classroom. Whether it's a small group of coworkers, the author of a scholarly article, your local parent–teacher organization, the editor of an online magazine, a car mechanic, or the billing agency for your cell phone or broadband service, you'll have a better chance of being taken seriously when you support your point of view with credible information delivered through a variety of logical, ethical, and emotional appeals.

Vital issues in our lives occur both in the academic world and in the swirl of everyday life. When you have a clear point of view (a claim) about the quality of cafeteria food at your child's school and then justify your claim with effective support, thereby establishing your credibility as a concerned parent, your audience will listen. Similarly, if a teacher in one of your classes asks you to claim a position on the status of immigration reform in your state and you respond by drafting a claim based on thorough research, your argument is likely to fare well when it is evaluated. This is especially true when you come across as well-informed and sensitive to those who might differ from you. And if conditions at work start to resemble positions that were recently outsourced, you're more likely to get the attention of your boss or coworkers when you present a balanced, fair-minded argument that takes into account those who view the issue differently.

In your life as a student, are there issues that involve tuition, lodging, the accessibility of your teachers, course policies, conflicts with your job, and loan opportunities? Are there also intellectual issues in your life as a student that you are asked to respond to, such as genetically engineered food, climate change, and representative government as practiced in our country? And outside the classroom, if your street lacks adequate storm-water facilities, if earlier public-school start times are proposed by the school board and you know that this will affect your family's schedule, or if a family member has a contrary idea about what makes a sensible budget, a well-crafted argument allows you to move away from emotional arguments (a trap for many) and into the realm of reason, common sense, and community. An emotional argument, on the other hand, lacks the support of a rational approach to an issue and puts in jeopardy your credibility with your target audience. The exact change you want is never a guaranteed outcome of a good argument, but at the very least you will have made your voice audible before an audience that matters to you.

From another perspective, you affect and diversify the particular community you address with an argument. A well-organized argument gets you a seat at the discussion table, whether in the classroom or before your city council. This means that your position on an issue can matter in the local decision-making process (see Figure 1.2). If we say nothing, others will speak for us or make assumptions about us that conflict with who we are and what we value.

Argue About Issues That Matter to You

Argue about what matters to you as a student and in everyday life. Some people associate argument with dry, abstract issues that may or may not directly affect their lives, but this is an attitude to stay away from. Good writing, and similarly, good argument, spring from the same place—from the effort of everyday people struggling to define and solve problems. A good argument will touch the reader in many ways: logically, because you provide real-life support for your point of view; emotionally, because you touch on something that the reader cares about; and ethically, because you establish your credibility as an informed community member whom your audience can trust.

One way to think about argument is as a practical tool for the regular challenges we face. For example, would it be helpful to know how to present your

Figure 1.2 Speaking up in response to issues that matter to us is the heart of argument. In this photo, the figure speaking is responding to a workplace issue.

point of view to city and county politicians when repairs on your street are neglected while streets in other areas are taken care of much sooner? Might it be helpful to compose an argument in the form of a letter to a son, daughter, parent, or in-law regarding an important family matter? Do you have an idea about how certain parts of your job can be improved, and would a logical, well-researched proposal directed to a supervisor be a reasonable first step? Do parking problems and a smoking ban at school disturb you, and do you want to find out more about these issues and formulate a claim that is reinforced by careful research? If you answer "yes" to these or similar everyday issues, then this guide can be useful as a way to represent yourself with integrity.

Let's look, for example, at the issue that begins this chapter and one that nearly all college students contend with these days—increasing tuition rates. Some of us may be compelled to argue on this issue because we're forced to work more hours during the week to pay for this semester's tuition, forced to take out loans that mean years of debt after college, and disturbed that our college seems to endorse lending practices that unfairly burden students heading into the world after graduation. A carefully arranged argument gives us the chance to claim a strong position on tuition rates, conduct research on the nature and history of the problem, listen to other points of view, and then propose a way to address the problem reasonably. After choosing to argue on this issue, a reasonable first step would be to establish context and determine your target audience, tasks discussed in the next section.

Another way to think about argument is as a practical tool for the intellectual and academic work you are asked to complete as a student. The steps in developing a good argument are the same, whether you are writing for a class assignment or about an issue in daily life. In both contexts you will need to evolve a precise point of view and then defend it. Successful arguments about the origins of our national debt, same-sex marriage, interpreting constitutional amendments, health-care policy, and the federal government's relationship with the banking industry are built on the same foundations as arguments responding to the everyday issues of life.

In fact, one measure of good arguments on issues like these is their ability to connect local and global contexts. So much of what comes to us through mainstream news—issues in the fields of medicine, technology, health care, and geopolitics, for example—has its origins beyond our immediate lives and communities. You can of course apply the tools of argument to these issues, and with good success, but arguments on these issues can and should be connected to local contexts, too. The list below is a small sampling of large issues that have local impact.

Standardized testing
Gun laws
LGBTQ adoption rights
Racial equity and food systems
Promotion practices in the nursing
   profession

Bullying in schools and in the
   workplace
Choice and public schools
Taser guns in public schools

Immigration reform and local business

Big box construction and local business

Confederate monuments

Living wage proposals

High school dropout rates

Opoids

Local job outsourcing

Local transit

The elderly and nursing home care

Crowded classrooms

Eminent domain and home owners

Sex offenders in the community

Fossil fuels

Climate crisis

Sexual harassment

Photo-ID voting requirements

Campaign finance reform

Locally-grown food

Returning veterans and health-care

Energy rate hikes

Health-care and non-native speakers

Election cybersecurity

Health insurance

Gentrification and evictions

Payday lending

In today's world, we all face multiple demands as we move through our day. Combine this busyness with the sheer scale of many of the issues we face—the climate crisis, the wealth gap, health care, surveillance, data confiscation, immigration, and military intervention—and it can be tough to believe that articulating our point of view on an issue is worth the effort or makes any difference. But it *can* make a difference, and building a good argument is a way to exercise some control over your life and establish your influence in the community. When your well-planned argument articulates your view on an issue in a thorough and compelling manner, you can generate confidence in yourself and respect from your audience. A sound argument does not, of course, guarantee that your issue will be resolved or that substantial change will result, but you can define for yourself exactly where you stand. For a democracy to remain healthy, it must function in large part by individuals responding to the forces that global environments put in our way.

Well-crafted argument is a way to represent yourself publicly with dignity and in an informed, fair, and open-minded way. Learn these skills now, and you'll have them forever.

your turn 1a GET STARTED Acknowledge Issues That Matter to You

Make a list of issues that concern you today. Include issues in your personal life, your workplace, your school, your church, a group you belong to, your neighborhood, and your town or city. As you make your list, consider also national and global issues that affect your life, such as conflicts in other countries, environmental concerns, or fuel costs. As a way to narrow your focus to issues most important to you, respond to the following questions.

1. Identify a major issue in your life or a position a teacher asks you to take in response to an academic issue.
2. When did this issue begin, and why does it continue to be a problem?
3. Identify a second issue that concerns you. If in question 1 you identified an academic issue, identify a more personal issue here.
4. When did this issue begin, and why does it continue to be a problem?

Establish Local Context via the Research Process

The important work of establishing local context for an issue involves aiming your argument at an appropriate audience, conducting research so as to generate a history for your issue, and when possible, connecting your local issue to broader, even global, conditions. These essential features of building local context are described in the following section.

Determine Your Audience

Recognize a practical audience for your argument; that is, direct your argument to those you most want to inform and persuade. Once you identify your audience, make a close study of them. An audience can be as small as one person, especially appropriate for an argument in a letter format, or your audience can be as large as your community or a block of undecided voters in a statewide election. Other audiences can include the following:

- Your class or certain members of a class
- Members of your church or parents in your neighborhood or school district
- The local school board, city council, county commission, or state legislators
- Family members, friends, or a partner
- A teacher or school administrator
- A supervisor at work or coworkers
- Readers of a zine, blog, listserv, special interest newsletter, or your local or school newspaper

Your audience may or may not agree with your point of view. In addition, an audience may not be as fully aware of the issue as you are, and in these cases you'll need to inform readers in order to get your claim across. Your job is to persuade an audience to think seriously about your point of view, and this means that you must know what your readers value. It's vital that you listen closely and get a sense of *why* they feel the way they do. What is it about their histories and values that make them see the issue differently from you? While you may deviate from your audience on a given issue, your argument will be much stronger and more concrete if you take the time to listen charitably—that is, without judgment and with an open mind—as you attempt to understand their viewpoints.

With regard to the tuition issue, one practical approach might be to target your city or town council and ask members to approve a resolution that you and other students have drawn up calling for a moratorium on tuition hikes.

Your argument will become more persuasive as you find overlapping points of view with your audience. Determine what you have in common with your audience—what values, beliefs, expectations, and fears you share. Move away from oppositional thinking, the "I'm right/you're wrong" approach. In the real world, when you work to identify common ground, you're more likely to get others to listen to you and move toward consensus.

your turn 1b ▸ GET STARTED **Identify a Target Audience**

Begin thinking about a practical audience for an argument by responding to the following questions.

1. Who might be interested in hearing what you have to say about the issues in your life today? Why?
2. Is there a specific person or group who could benefit from your perspective, affect an issue, or resolve it or modify it in some way? Explain.
3. How will you learn more about this target audience?
4. What tempting assumptions about this audience may prove inaccurate?

Establish Local Context for Your Issue

No man is an island! When English poet John Donne delivered this idea in a 1624 meditation, he claimed that, while isolation may be a part of living, we are all connected to the continent, to a community. We do not live separately from our communities, although sometimes it may feel as if we're living on their margins. The point is that when you decide to claim a position on an issue that matters to you, gather plenty of information so that you're fully aware of the **context**, the past and present, of your issue. An issue materializes in the swirl of local events and occurs because folks disagree—about its cause, what should be done about it, the terms that define it, whether or not it actually exists, and/or how it should be evaluated. So if you feel hemmed in by an issue, find out through research what others think and how they're responding.

You have many ways to find out where your issue originates. For an issue occurring at work, look into what created it. You may already know the answer, but asking fellow workers their understanding of the issue can fill in gaps. You may also want to gather information about your employer's past to get a sense of how the issue evolved. If you work in a large industry, you can read up on the deeper roots of this issue and how it is handled elsewhere in the state, country, or world. If your English teacher requires that you develop an argument in response to a character's behavior in a short story or poem, or if your history teacher asks you to evaluate the term *American exceptionalism*, plan to gather online and print sources as a way to inform yourself of the context in which your issue occurs and what scholars have to say about it.

When you argue in response to an issue on local or neighborhood politics, access the archives of your local newspaper and study the history of your issue. Newspapers often are available for free via online databases. For issues involving a family member and a health problem, for example, there are a number of databases available that house articles and essays on health-care issues, and your school may subscribe to these databases. Building local context can also involve interviews with knowledgeable professionals or those who have been invested in the issue over time. You can also design and administer a survey that will add to your information base.

Returning to the tuition issue, this problem has a significant and well-documented local and national history. Scores of students, faculty, and social justice activists have responded to regular tuition hikes since they began. From the perspective of your school's administration, funding priorities may prevent immediate action, but during an interview you may learn a great deal from a school official who defends the hikes but is sympathetic with your desire to succeed with your education. And often you can count on there being a knowledgeable reporter in local media who can provide a larger frame for this issue as well as links to factual information. These are resources that can help you build local context for this issue.

Creating this kind of context does two important things for your final argument: It lets you argue with a strong sense of local history, and it sends a direct message to your readers that you've done your homework, that you've thought deeply about your issue, and most importantly, that you should be taken seriously.

Facundo Arrizabalaga/EPA/Newscom

Figure 1.3 Protestors respond to tuition hikes and other issues important to their local context.

internet activity 1a **Exploring**

Conduct an informal Internet search to look for general background information on an issue, perhaps one that you identified in the Your Turn 1a activity. Begin by accessing the online archives of your local newspaper; continue by using the academic databases your school provides and other online sites that your teacher recommends. Answer the following questions:

1. Has your search produced answers to some of your questions? Explain.
2. What kind of additional information do you want to gather?
3. As you begin to gather information, is your perspective changing; that is, does learning more about your issue let you see the issue in different and perhaps broader terms? Explain.

Connect Local and Global Contexts

When you write specifically about a local issue, like tuition hikes, plan to connect the issue with a context beyond your community. This makes a positive impression on readers because it shows that you're able to frame your issue in broad terms. It reveals that through your research you recognize that your issue is influenced by trends in regional, national, or global cultures. This will also allow your audience to think more critically about the issue, and it will likely make your argument more persuasive.

For example, escalating tuition rates in this country, Canada, and England, among other countries, reflect economic realities and corporate decision-making outside our communities (see Figure 1.4). When you argue about having to pay more for your education, you must bring to your argument a broad context for tuition hikes so as to orient readers to the origins of this issue. Similarly, when the outsourcing of certain jobs— like those in manufacturing, web design, accounting, and customer support—affects the local economy, trace this outsourcing to the global economic climate in order to form a larger picture for your audience. In addition, issues associated

Figure 1.4 Editorial cartoon by Rob Rogers

Richard Levine/Alamy Stock Photo

Figure 1.5 Connecting a local issue to a broader context can be powerful.

with food in local markets—the conditions in which it's produced and harvested, transportation, health concerns, pricing, and availability of certain items—typically lead to issues in another part of the country or world. Standardized testing, according to some researchers, can be traced to the presence of a business model in many of our public schools; learning about this aspect of the issue—and about the values and motives for this kind of testing—can fill in important background for this arguable issue. If you are motivated to write on local environmental matters like air and water quality, you'll want to read up on the influence of local development and regional energy production to get a sense of what causes these problems.

Whether the local issue that concerns you is in the area of health care, education, politics, work, family, or a retail industry, there likely are larger, often global, forces shaping the issue. When it's a trend you can trace beyond our national borders, we might use the term **glocal** to connect local and global contexts. When you look at what sustains us—air, water, food, transportation, education, and electronic communication—it won't be difficult to connect local issues with broader contexts. And when you look at what we desire materially—dwellings, cars, fashion, and so on—and begin examining American consumer culture, you should be able to make some revealing connections that will enlighten readers and move your argument along.

The key to connecting local and global contexts is found both in your own good sense of how things work and in your ability to research thoroughly in order to familiarize yourself with the history surrounding an issue. Your research process is vital to the success of your argument.

> **your turn 1c** ➤ **GET STARTED** Connect the Local and Global
>
> Answer the following questions to get a sense of how local issues can have global effects.
>
> 1. Identify a single *glocal* issue that concerns you, and describe its local effects.
> 2. How do these effects have an impact on your life and the lives of others?
> 3. In general terms, explain how economic and political ripples from a global or national issue may spread and affect the lives of others across your region, state, and community.

Recognize Why Arguments Break Down

Arguments can succeed when a writer has something to say, knows to whom it should be said, and knows how to present supporting information in persuasive ways. But arguments can also fail, especially when the essential steps needed to build good arguments are not given thorough treatment. Following are some of the major reasons why arguments don't succeed.

Arguments Break Down When They Do Not Persuade an Audience

Sometimes writers summarize and explain rather than argue. This can occur when a discernable issue is not separated from the larger topic. For example, by deciding you want to write on problems in your workplace, you've identified a good *topic* but not an arguable *issue*. There are numerous issues under this big topic—hiring practices, the politics of promotion, compensation, environmental impact, benefits, working within a hierarchy, discrimination, communication, and so forth—and it is vital that you choose a single issue on which to argue. When you fail to narrow and instead stay with the big topic, your writing lapses into summary and general statements, and this is death to persuasive writing. By focusing on the big topic, problems in your workplace, you'd be treating important issues only superficially. Each of these sub-issues is worthy of a full argument. Narrow your topic to a single issue that affects you, and you will be able to dig deeply and avoid spreading out generally.

Arguments Break Down When There Is a Lack of Balance in the Support

By loading body paragraphs with facts and logical appeals only, your argument will lack a cooperative, humanizing feel. The idea is to place ethical appeals (in which you establish your credibility through personal experience and the testimony of experts) and emotional appeals (in which you touch readers with emotionally charged examples) in balance with logical support. When you tilt too much in the direction on one kind of appeal, readers lose interest. After all, we're complex beings, and we want to be convinced in a variety of ways. Experts tell us that logical appeals should dominate in most arguments, comprising some 60 to 70 percent of an argument's support. When you focus your arguments in this way, you earn the opportunity to address your readers ethically and emotionally. They must know that you've done your research and that you write from experience; then, you can broaden your argument with different types of appeals.

Arguments Break Down When the Audience Is Poorly Defined

Nearly 2,500 years ago, Aristotle explained that a target audience is essential to competent argument. Early in the writing process, you should decide precisely whom you want to persuade. This will allow you to focus closely

 tip 1a

Embrace the Glocal!
Remember that you are a local resident *and* a global citizen. Things are so interconnected today that it's hard to define ourselves and the conditions we live in without recognizing forces—economic, political, and environmental—that originate beyond our communities.

on an audience whose values you understand. Knowing these values lets you build a bridge to the audience, which is necessary if you are to persuade them. This is what warrant and backing are about. You can design a good argument when you know what an audience expects, what touches it, and what kinds of appeals are likely to be effective. For example, if you want to argue for a moratorium on tuition hikes in your school or in all public colleges in your state, consider your target audience. To rally immediate support, your audience might be students, but to work toward real change, your target audience might be state lawmakers who have the decision-making capacity to enact legislation.

Arguments Break Down When They Contain Fallacies

Fallacies, often found in an argument's claims and reasons, weaken an argument because there are mistakes in logic and can involve unfair treatment of others. Fallacies are common in the many advertisements we take in every day. For example, ads for a certain brand of car, clothing, food, or medication, may promise that if we purchase the product, prestige, attractiveness, taste satisfaction, and health will be ours. These ads contain fallacies because the promise cannot be kept. In an argument, fallacies are statements that mislead due to poor or deceptive reasoning. For example, if you claim that third parties are the only way to restore true democracy to our political system, you have committed a fallacy based on a hasty generalization. Some readers of your argument may agree that third parties are needed to restore democracy, but some may claim that campaign finance reform, term limits, and citizen activism are also needed. The hasty generalization backs you into a corner.

Arguments Break Down When They Do Not Fairly Represent Opposing Views

The rebuttals and differing views you bring to your argument should not be brief and superficial: They should attend to what the opposition claims, how it supports a position, and what it values. This easily can require several full paragraphs in an argument. When you respond to a rebuttal after having treated the other side fairly, you are in a position to thoroughly counter or build on another view. When full treatment of another view is neglected, however, writers tend to profile and stereotype, and this can offend perceptive members of an audience.

Match Argument with Purpose

After you decide what you want to accomplish with an argument, you can choose the kind of argument that fits your purpose. This guide helps you choose from four kinds of argument, all of which are treated in detail in Chapter 8,

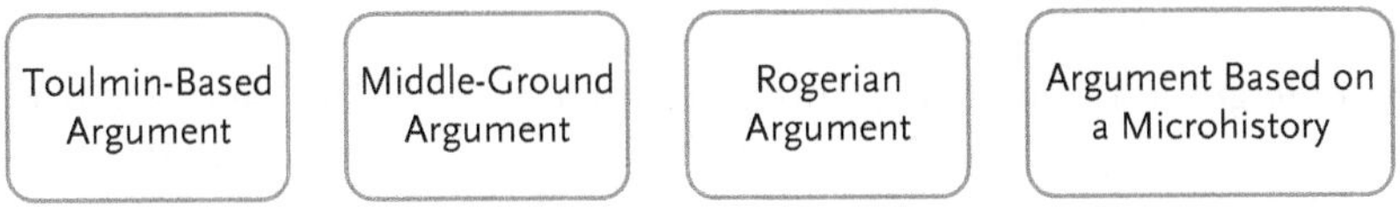

Toulmin-Based Argument	Middle-Ground Argument	Rogerian Argument	Argument Based on a Microhistory

Figure 1.6 Four kinds of arguments

"Consider Toulmin-Based Argument" and Chapter 9, "Consider Middle-Ground Argument, Rogerian Argument, and Argument Based on a Microhistory."

For example, an issue that received a lot of attention in North Carolina a few years ago concerned the attorney general's recommendation that children of illegal immigrants be barred from pursuing degrees in the state's community colleges, a recommendation that the president of the community college system chose to follow. The issue generated much discussion across the state based on the news media's regular attention to it. A writer's decision to argue in response to this issue would require choosing the kind of argument practical to the arguer's goals with a specific target audience.

The following paragraphs describe how different kinds of arguments might be applied to the issue of barring children of illegal immigrants from attending the state's community colleges. These paragraphs provide an overview of four kinds of arguments (see Figure 1.6). Think about how these approaches to argument can fit with issues you plan to address in argument.

Toulmin-Based Argument

Using a Toulmin-based approach, a writer would focus closely on his audience—in this case, the State Board of Community Colleges—and what it values. He knows that individuals on this board are committed to workforce training, economic development, and service to local communities. With this in mind, the writer can develop convincing support by using many examples of children of illegal immigrants succeeding in community colleges and going on to hold good jobs and contribute to their communities. Examples can include statistics, scholars analyzing the community college as a resource for the children of illegal immigrants, and firsthand student accounts. This varied support will honor values held by the board. Additionally, the writer can elaborate on why training, business, and service are important to the state's quality of life. And because the board is charged with carrying out the policies of the state's community colleges, the writer could craft a problem-based claim and ask that the board permit children of illegal immigrants to pursue degrees. Rebuttals brought to the argument would focus on the opposition's concerns with legality and citizenship. Central statements in the argument, such as the claim and reasons, would include qualifiers that keep writers away from making absolute, and unrealistic, points.

Middle-Ground Argument

A middle-ground argument on this issue would view the "for" and "against" positions as extreme and argue instead for a practical position in the middle. Each extreme position would be analyzed in terms of why it fails to offer a practical perspective. Based on the reasons listed previously, those who favor barring children of illegal immigrants from seeking degrees could be analyzed as extreme because this position fails to note the many contributions immigrants make to their communities, the taxes they pay, the contributions they make to the workforce, and the long delays they endure with regard to immigrant legislation. Those on the other side of this issue could be considered impractical because they lump all immigrants together and thus do not take into account the very different experiences of the various immigrant groups living in the United States. For example, the immigrant group often getting the most attention today is from Mexico, and its experience in American culture is in some ways quite different from that of groups from various Asian, Caribbean, and Latin American countries. Over-generalizing about diverse groups plays to a limited understanding of the varying immigrant experiences in the United States, and arguments built on such over-generalization can be considered impractical for this reason.

Several middle-ground positions are possible with this issue, and each has been argued over the course of the debate. One such position argues that the "for" and "against" reasoning described previously ignores the reason that many immigrants move to the United States—jobs—and that until local businesses enter the debate (because of their practice of hiring illegal workers), nothing will change. Another position argues that this issue should be moved into the courts and that in the meantime community colleges should remain open-door institutions, admitting all who apply regardless of citizenship status. While those holding these positions may consider them moderate and middle ground, each position must be proven to be a practical and logical choice between two extreme positions.

Rogerian Argument

In a Rogerian argument, the writer would aim to create a space for positive back-and-forth discussion between his view and one or more different views. To do this, the writer would need to present other views with respect and accuracy, emphasizing the values embedded in these views. Having established this respectful tone, the writer is now in a position to introduce his view by looking for areas where values on all sides overlap. This is the common ground that makes Rogerian argument a practical choice when parties are far apart on an issue.

If the writer opposes barring immigrant students from attending community college, he would pay close attention to the opposition and focus on its values and reasons for supporting the regulation. The writer notices strong emphasis on values of citizenship, employment, education, and rights. While the writer may differ in how these values can be extended to the children of illegal immigrants, he shares with the opposition a deep commitment to these values and their importance in community life. This is the common ground that the writer would hope to create. On the surface, the views are far apart, but underneath the sides share strongly held values. There is of course no guarantee that the writer of this argument and his opposition will now or in the future see eye to eye on this controversial issue, but the writer has made the effort to listen to and honor the opposition. Because an audience may acknowledge his objectivity and sense of fair play, he is in a position to earn some measure of credibility, a necessary condition to the success of any argument that seeks to create common ground.

Argument Based on a Microhistory

An argument based on a microhistory can be a practical approach to this issue because an arguer could provide specific history relevant to the recommendation to bar children of illegal immigrants from community colleges and then offer a claim. This kind of argument could be used to look closely at one feature of this issue—for example, the reaction of a student, parent, teacher, or concerned citizen. Studying the response of a prospective community-college student affected by the recommendation could bring in from the margins of this issue a voice that media and the general public do not hear, an aim of the microhistory. Primary materials needed to prepare such a microhistory could include interviews with the prospective student or something the student has written. The center of the microhistory would be the ways in which the student's life will be affected by having the opportunity to attend college withdrawn and how this student's experience reveals something about our culture and what it values. Additionally, the arguer will need to provide context for the student's experience, and this must include an overview of this issue in the state, region, and country. Having provided extensive information about the student and the history of the issue, the arguer is then in a position to offer a claim that an audience may view as credible based on the arguer's extensive research. Arguments based on microhistory focus an argument in the commonplace and everyday, perspectives that many mainstream and conventional approaches to history often neglect.

Reflect and Apply

Directions: The following questions ask you to step back and reflect on the concepts delivered in this chapter. You should think about the questions that conclude each chapter and apply them to your own writing. We encourage you to think about how the various pieces of an argument fit together and why they're all necessary.

1. In your own words describe what an effective argument does. Include in your description how you think about argument now contrasted with how you thought about argument before reading this chapter.

2. Early sections of this chapter encourage you to use skills associated with argument both inside and outside the classroom. Explain how these skills would be of value in everyday life.

3. Clarify why a target audience is essential to a good argument. Include in your response what an argument would look like with a vague or unspecified audience.

4. Define the term *context*. Describe its place in an argument in terms of your credibility as an arguer.

5. Identify the reasons why arguments break down. Which of these reasons will you need to pay close attention to so that your arguments don't break down?

CHAPTER 2

Explore an Issue
That Matters to You

Learning Objectives

By working through this chapter, you will be able to

- identify the communities of which you are a part.
- identify issues associated with each community.
- examine issues within topics on which you may want to write an argument.
- identify your audience for a specific argument.
- use reasons and evidence to support your claim.
- demonstrate an argument that considers cultural, social, and historical context.
- deliver your argument at a time when it is most likely to be taken seriously.
- respond to practical prompts to brainstorm ideas for your argument.

Seven weeks into the semester, you're between worried and anxious about next week's midterm exam in your online "Early American Literature" class. At a coffee shop on campus, you run into a pal you met in a class last year, and the two of you begin talking. A minute into your conversation, you confess your anxiety about the exam and suddenly realize that you're both in the same class and that your friend is also worried about the exam. You share the concern that the instructor does not participate regularly on the discussion board, takes too long to answer email messages, and sometimes does not respond to messages at all. He has made it clear from the beginning that he'll respond to messages "time permitting." The first two units in the course include much tough

All Illustrations by iStock.com/A-digit

COMMUNITY

School-Academic

Workplace

Family-Household

Neighborhood

Social-Cultural

Consumer

Concerned Citizen

TOPIC: Life in the Online Classroom

ISSUE: Teacher–Student Interaction

AUDIENCE: Director of Distance Learning

CLAIM: Clear standards for teachers' commitment to interacting regularly with students should be stated in the introductions to online English courses.

reading, and there have been times when you wanted honest and prompt feedback, especially as to your comprehension of the challenging readings. The instructor has informed the class that the exam will include a section on analyzing passages, and this makes you even more anxious. The two of you gather yourselves and decide to meet for a study session over the weekend.

An argument is a practical response to a pressing question, problem, or concern that generates differing points of view, such as the issue described above. An argument works best when you are invested in an issue, like online instructor response time, and when you feel that what you want to achieve is being hampered. For example, if you feel you're being paid unfairly at work in comparison with other workers of similar experience and seniority, you have an arguable issue. Or, if you feel strongly about stem cell research, about credit card marketing campaigns targeted at you and other college students, about accusations of racial profiling by local law enforcement, about the quality of food at your child's school, or about toxic coal ash, you can construct an effective argument that fully represents your point of view, your claim, on such an issue. But first you must assess current issues in your life and determine those that genuinely matter to you. This is the vital first step in the argument process. This chapter guides you through the process of choosing issues for argument.

Determine What Matters to You and Why

All of us belong to many different communities—school, workplace, family neighborhood, social–cultural, consumer, and concerned citizen—and our individual worlds are defined, at least in part, by the issues we encounter in each of our communities. Some of these issues are the results of external forces acting on our lives (a directive from a supervisor at work, a public ordinance that permits one kind of gathering but not another, an assignment from a teacher) while other kinds of issues are of our own choosing (who we vote for in an election, our decision to become active in response to a community or national issue, decisions we make about parenting). And the issues you choose to write about, whether you argue for something to change or simply want your audience to reflect on your point of view, should originate with what is most important to you. Your arguments become compelling to readers when you write in an informed way about something that deeply concerns you. So, while you will learn how to build arguments in structured, logical ways, *what* you argue on should begin with issues that stir your emotions and that motivate you to speak out, as in the case of the mother speaking in Figure 2.1. Consider the communities you belong to and some, but not all, of the topics that can affect each community.

A **community** is a group of individuals that share common experiences, interests, needs, and expectations. Students in your classes, the general college community, people you work with, your neighbors, and citizens with a stake in local politics are examples of communities. Review the following communities and some of the issues associated with each community.

School/Academic

As a member of your academic community, what issues affect your goals of acquiring knowledge, learning new skills, and earning a degree so that you can move on to the next phase of your life? Consider some of the following topics that affect your life as a student.

AP Images/The Laramie Boomerang, Barbara J. Perenic

Figure 2.1 Compelling arguments become possible when individuals argue about what matters most to them. In this photo, a mother speaks to a group of University of Wyoming students about her son, and seven other students, who were killed in a car crash caused by a drunk driver, the man to her right in the yellow shirt.

Loan repayment
Degree requirements
Life in the real-time
    classroom
Teacher attitudes
Time management
Free speech
Diversity and tolerance
Student services

Curriculum design
Life in the online
    classroom
Issues in your field of
    study
Personal responsibility
Academic integrity
Privacy and
    surveillance

Campus safety
Transportation
Blogging
Fairness
Plagiarism
Grade inflation
Extra credit

Workplace

At many points during our working lives, we face conditions that affect our motivation, engagement, and sense of fair play. Other times the workplace offers opportunities that are welcome challenges. What are your conditions at work? By what are you challenged? Consider the following list of topics as a way to identify issues that most matter to you.

Job expectations
Balancing work and life
Bureaucracy and red
    tape
Pay scale
Benefits
Commuting and
    telecommuting
Gender bias
Organizing and
    negotiation

Dispute resolution
Training
Bullying and
    harassment
Corporate social
    responsibility
Daily conditions
Stress
Downsizing and
    layoffs
Unions

Privacy and
    surveillance
Advancement
Discrimination
Leadership
Favoritism
Job security
Rankism
Team building
Office politics

Family/Household

This community refers both to a traditional family unit—parents (or parent) and children—and to any group of individuals sharing a home and its responsibilities. Issues can spring from relationships within and across generations, from economic and purchasing concerns, and from household maintenance arrangements, among many others.

Toy safety
Financial planning
Landscaping
    and grounds
    maintenance
Children and online
    safety
Home buying and
    mortgages

Home owners
    associations
Food safety
Diet/food
    consumption
Health-care planning
Home improvement
Furniture and
    appliances

Product safety
Neighbors
Parenting
Same-sex marriage
Pet care
Senior care
Wills and trusts

Neighborhood

Neighborhoods are distinct geographical areas. Some neighborhoods comprise a three- or four-block square within a city or urban area. Other neighborhoods comprise only a single block or even a single complex of dwellings. People living in a neighborhood frequently are affected by residential and commercial development, by local government decisions, and by activities such as local parades or events, school closings, or rezoning.

Street improvement	Storm drains	Property alterations
Rezoning ordinances	Sidewalks	and additions
Graffiti	Economic development	Safety
Erosion	and housing	Gangs
Yard maintenance	Water and sewage	Noise
Neighbors with special	Waste collection	Traffic
needs	Parking	Crime
The digital divide		

Social/Cultural

Some communities link us to people we'll never meet, yet we share with them features that are central to our self-concept. Based on your religious, sexual, and political preferences, are there issues before you? And based on the racial or ethnic group you identify with, the virtual environments you spend time in, or the friendships and loyalties you keep, are there concerns that might motivate you to argue?

Profiling and	Relationships	Friendship
stereotyping	Local government and	Loyalty
Sex and sexuality	the individual	Gender
Public space	Racial and ethnic	Education
Political preference	identity	Economics
Virtual environments	Training and	Fake news
Class status	opportunity	Religion

Consumer

We live in a consumer-oriented society, one in which advertisements from competing companies and producers rain down on us every day. We regularly make decisions about what we eat and wear, how we transport ourselves, how we stay warm, what we purchase for our children, and how we entertain ourselves. Are there issues important to you as a consumer that fall under these and other topics?

Prescription drugs	Electronics and	Utilities/energy
Local lending	communication	Food security
practices	Consumer fraud	Insurance
Identity theft	Shopping at home	Investing
Telemarketing	Landlord/tenant	Credit
Home repairs	relations	Advertising
Transportation	Demographic profiling	

Concerned Citizen

While much of our focus concerns the local and the personal, many of us—as concerned citizens living in a democratic culture—naturally pay attention to politics, economic trends, and social concerns that extend beyond our communities; in other words, we pay attention to what we can term the *glocal* environment. Arguments deriving from some of the topics below, and many more, are vital to our commitment to democratic life, because democracy means speaking up about what matters to us; if we don't speak up about our issues, we may be left out of the conversation completely. What issues come to mind when you investigate some of the broad topics below?

Environment	Automatic voter	Animal research
Agricultural practices	registration	Alternative energy
National security and	Private corporations and	Individual rights and
surveillance	the public interest	counterterrorism
Substances and	Public schools	Scarcity and abundance
regulation	Immigration reform	Globalization
Prisons	Science/technology	Voter suppression
Health-care reform	and ethics	Military intervention
Class division	High school graduation	Digital access/privacy
Phone culture	rates	Homelessness
Genetically modified	Information	Air and water quality
foods	distribution	Climate disruption
Professional behavior	Criminal justice	Censorship

Communities and topics listed above should get you thinking about what matters to you at this point in your life. These lists are not intended to be comprehensive; rather, they are intended to help you identify issues in the various communities to which you belong, especially issues that motivate you to argue.

tip 2a

Listen to Your Emotions
As you note issues in your life, pay close attention to your emotional responses. Are there some issues that make your heartbeat faster? This is often where good arguments are born. While this guide will steer you through logical approaches to practical arguments, it is often these emotional and intuitive moments that signal the beginning of a strong argument.

your turn 2a ▶ GET STARTED **Focus on Communities**

For each community above, identify two or three topics that concern you, and then answer the following questions.

1. What issues within these broad topics most concern you?
2. Overall, what two or three issues matter to you most? Why?

Choose an Issue within a Topic

The categories listed previously help you identify the communities to which you belong and the important issues in your life—not that you necessarily need reminders of what's most pressing for you. Nevertheless, completing the "Your Turn 2a" exercise should get you thinking about what motivates you to argue, and it will likely affirm your sense that life is quite complex and varied these days. This section asks you to begin the argument process by narrowing your focus to a single, arguable issue.

iStock.com/RossHelen

Figure 2.2 This writer is gathering information from print sources for a single issue. Narrowing your focus to a specific issue, rather than writing generally about a topic, lets you write about a precise set of conditions and thus appeal to an audience more directly.

An argument will fail if its focus is too broad. For this reason, it is essential that you distinguish between a topic and an issue. A **topic** is a category—such as local politics, gender bias, neighborhood security, race relations, or family planning—that contains numerous issues. Topics are places from which issues and arguments are derived. In contrast, an issue is a specific problem or dispute that remains unsettled and requires a point of view and sometimes a decision. It always occurs within a larger topic and within a precise context, or set of conditions.

A good argument results from a process of narrowing from a broad topic to a specific, arguable issue. For example, as a concerned citizen, if you state that you want to argue about America's military presence in the Middle East, you'd be taking on a big topic, one that might require book-length treatment with chapters devoted to separate issues. This topic actually includes dozens of issues, and your job as arguer would be to narrow your focus and choose one specific issue. Instead of spreading out and writing generally about America's military presence in this region, choose a single issue and write very specifically about it. Any argument you build will be more effective when you focus on a single issue. This will give your argument depth and precision, features difficult to include when writing about a big topic in a relatively short argument.

The topic of our military presence in Middle Eastern countries includes, among many others, the following specific issues: the cost of wars; the wars' effects on economic growth; the spike in oil prices, the wars' effects on ethnic populations in Iraq, Afghanistan, and other countries; the decision to begin a preemptive war; concerns about weapons of mass destruction, diplomacy, reconstruction and humanitarian efforts; democracy and governance in these countries; the U.S. Constitution and the War Powers Resolution; returning

 tip 2b

Narrow to a Single Issue

To make sure you are focused on an issue and not a topic, make a list of the reasons you intend to use to support your argument. Do some reasons seem substantial enough to become full arguments in themselves? If yes, consider refocusing on one of these issues.

Immigration Reform
• Border security
• Citizenship
• U.S. Intervention
• Local business
• Guest worker programs
• Worker verification systems
• Effects on citizen workforce
• Workplace enforcement
• Green cards

Office Politics
• Communication
• Gender bias
• Taking credit
• Rankism
• Sexual harassment
• Trust
• Dispute resolution
• Fair treatment

Diet/Food Consumption
• Racial equity
• Working conditions
• Pay scale
• Transportation and greenhouse gases
• Processing and packaging
• Genetically engineered food
• Food deserts
• Obesity and advertising
• Advertising and customer perception
• Environmental impact, biodiversity loss, and excessive pesticide use
• Global trends and local effects
• Regulating imports

Life in the Classroom
• Disruptions and tardiness
• Plagiarism
• Assignments
• Teacher performance
• Course organization
• Teacher availability
• Relevance of course
• Hybrid courses

veterans and their treatment; and the duration of the wars. Choosing one of these issues will make building your argument more manageable and more realistic.

The following section provides four topics, each from a different community, along with some of the many issues found within each topic. As outlined, immigration reform, office politics, diet/food consumption, and life in the classroom are broad topics containing many issues; if you're compelled to write within one of these categories, narrowing your focus to a single issue can result in a powerful, focused argument. Again, the issues identified for each topic are but a small sampling of the many issues related to each.

The work you do at this point—narrowing your focus to a single, arguable issue—can be the most important effort you make as you pull together an argument. Focus on a community, narrow your broad topic down to a single issue, probe the issue fully, and then determine where you stand and what you want to accomplish.

Pre-Think about Your Issue

Whether your topic has been assigned or self-selected, your argument will be much more successful if you are able to find an approach that is grounded in your own interests. It often happens that a topic is assigned and may not be one you wish to argue. As you work on your argument, at any stage before and after collecting your research, you should take some time to pre-think. Pre-thinking is a low-stakes process of thinking and writing about your issue. There is no right or wrong way to go about pre-thinking; its function is to give you time to reflect on your argument as it comes together. All pre-thinking methods do not work for all people. Some writers find freewriting provides them with the most ideas; some look at a blank page and freeze. Some love lists; others hate outlines. Find a process or method that works for you, but do spend time pre-thinking. During this process you may find an angle to your argument you had not expected, or you may be able to anticipate potential problems to avoid. The purpose of reflective thinking/writing at different points along the argument process is to allow you to see what you know so far versus what you still need to know, to question your assumptions, and to better explore your understanding of the audience.

There are some standard methods of pre-thinking that may already be familiar to you: brainstorming, mapping (or clustering), and freewriting. These are covered in this section, along with a more nontraditional method, "moving from boring to interesting."

Brainstorming

Brainstorming is one of the easiest prewriting techniques to use. Although you can brainstorm by yourself, it works best with several people. By yourself, you list as many topics that you can think of that relate to your topic, not bothering with connections, continuity, or practicality. The increased effectiveness of this technique when used with a group is apparent. As one person thinks of an idea, it prompts another person to think of another one, and a true storm of ideas can occur. Here is an example of a brainstorming session about an argument on wastewater assigned in an Urban Studies course.

• gray water	• chemicals	• cooking
• pollution	• household cleaners	• doll-making
• groundwater runoff	• white-water rafting	• gardening

As you can tell, some terms likely inspired others (chemicals—household cleaners) and others are less obviously connected (pollution). Once a list is generated, you can begin seeing if there are any individual terms that may be a starting point for more brainstorming or a more focused argument topic. You may also find that there are terms that can be grouped together to make for a focused topic.

Freewriting

Freewriting is a technique made popular by Peter Elbow in his 1973 *Writing Without Teachers*. This technique shuts off the inner censor and frees you to write down all of your thoughts about a topic—random or focused. What do you know about your topic so far? What do you find interesting or boring about the topic? Can you find a personal connection to the topic? Some people time themselves or set a page limit, which forces them to produce material. When you have reached your time or page goal, you will no longer be faced with a blank page, and you may even have some ideas among the free-wheeling thoughts that could help you get started. An example passage of freewriting (on the same topic used for the brainstorm above) may look like this:

What can I say about wastewater? I don't think I have ever even thought about where the water from my toilet or sink goes. I have heard that some people use the water from their showers in their gardens. Is this even safe in a vegetable garden? But how safe is our water anyway? In a history course I learned that water from factories used to be directed into the rivers that people drank from. And people fuss about fluoride in their drinking water?

As the writer looks over the passage, she may find the idea of gray water a good starting point. Maybe the safety issue could lead to another round of freewriting to think more about those ideas.

Mapping

Mapping, also known as *clustering*, is a more focused form of brainstorming in which the writer consciously attempts to make connections between terms. In Figure 2.3, the term to be mapped is in the center circle, and the circles radiating from the center follow subterms.

Move from Boring to Interesting

One of America's best-loved authors, Ray Bradbury, loved to write and enjoyed his writing career immensely. The author of dozens of science fiction stories, Bradbury talked about the worst essay he ever wrote—a piece magazine editors asked him to write about life on other planets. Although he loved science fiction, he wasn't really interested in the assignment. Bradbury forged ahead and tinkered endlessly with the piece. He researched the topic to death and wound up producing a dead piece of writing. It took several editors to bring the article back to life. Bradbury, best known for his science fiction stories about life on other planets, was embarrassed. Bradbury's advice, and ours, is to write about what you are interested in, a topic that means something to you.

Angry at your city council for refusing to do anything about the graffiti problem near your child's school? Write a letter. See a problem at work? Send a memo. Have an assignment that seems boring? Find your own angle into the topic. Become engaged, and your writing will be engaging as well.

Writing about real-life situations rarely leads to boring arguments, but trying to write about an instructor-assigned topic can. How can you take a boring topic and find an interesting way to write about it? We call our method for addressing this problem "moving from boring to interesting."

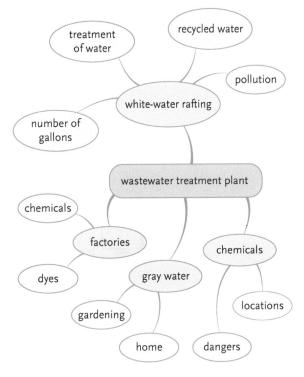

Figure 2.3 An example of mapping or clustering

This method can be applied to any topic. Let's say that in your Urban Studies course, you are assigned the topic of wastewater treatment plants, perhaps not the most exciting of topics. Can you really find something interesting to say about treating wastewater? Try this: list all the things you are interested in; it doesn't matter if they appear to have nothing to do with clean water.

Now try to make a connection between each of these topics and the one assigned: wastewater treatment plants.

- Where does the water come from for the new artificial white-water rafting course in town? How is it treated?
- Cooking grease going down the drains—how does it get cleaned out of the water?
- How did the old process of draining dyes from nineteenth-century fabric manufacturers into rivers change the way water is treated today?
- Can gray water be used safely for gardens?

GET STARTED Use Boring to Interesting **Strategies**

For each of the following topics, make a connection to a topic that is of interest to you:

- Circadian rhythms
- The fall of the Roman Empire
- *Moby Dick*
- Rural health care

internet activity 2a **Exploring**

Based on the issues of concern you identified in "Your Turn 2a," conduct an informal Internet search for each issue. Use the academic databases your college provides, the online sites your teacher recommends, and the recommended websites described in Chapter 3, "Develop a Research Plan."

Define and Target Your Audience

A **target audience** is the group or individual at whom your argument is aimed; you want them to accept or at least acknowledge your position on an issue. Your audience initially may be opposed to your position, undecided about it, or lean toward accepting it. You may want audience members to take immediate action, to reflect on your argument, or to rethink their own points of view.

Aristotle, a founding father of what we know today as argument, encouraged his students to know their audiences before delivering arguments. As you choose issues on which to argue, make sure you know the people you plan to address. Are they inclined at first to accept or reject your claim? What are the ages and occupations of your audience? Are most people in your audience wealthy,

Jetta Productions/Iconica/Getty Images

Figure 2.4 When you make an argument, choose your audience carefully and work to understand that audience as fully as possible.

struggling financially, male, female? Use the following exercise to understand your audience. The work you do to understand your audience and its values will make it easier to craft a practical claim and find the best support to produce a solid, persuasive argument.

your turn 2c ⟩ **GET STARTED Define Your Audience**

Your argument must be aimed at a specific target audience. To ensure that you're focused on a specific audience, answer the following questions about an issue and its relationship to your audience. Remember that you will argue before an audience that is as invested as you are in the issue at hand.

1. Who is the group or individual you want to persuade? List the reasons you want to target this audience. Be careful to avoid arguing to a general or neutral audience. Remember that you are writing to individuals with whom you may share certain values, goals, and expectations.
2. What are the physical characteristics, or demographics, of your audience? Consider these criteria as you make this determination: occupation, family size, age, gender, marital status, political leaning, religion, race or ethnicity, education, income, and geographic location.
3. Does your audience already have a position on your issue? Is your audience undecided about your issue? Is it likely to accept or reject your claim? Or does your audience occupy an extreme position? Explain.
4. What are the biases and limitations of your audience?

your turn 2d ⟩ **GET STARTED Reach Your Audience**

Answer the following questions to identify the most practical ways to build an argument that is effective for your audience.

1. What sources will you use to establish full context for your issue? How will you research your issue so that you have a sense of how important the issue is to your audience? See Chapter 3, "Develop a Research Plan," for a guide to researching issues.
2. What kind of language makes your audience comfortable? Is it formal and academic, is it the language of political debate, is it the language of mainstream media, or is it informal language? Whatever language makes your audience comfortable, plan to use it in your argument.
3. How will you demonstrate respect for your audience?
4. Can you find common ground with your audience based on what audience members' values, experiences, loyalties, and likely emotional responses are? Explain.

5. Because establishing credibility with an audience is so important, what values and beliefs do you share with your audience?

6. What precisely do you want to accomplish with your audience? Do you want your audience members to question your issue, to learn more about it, to convert to your point of view, or simply to examine their current thinking on the issue?

7. To what extent will you need to inform your audience so that it can accept your argument? Based on what you know about your audience members, what can you assume they already know versus what they need to know in order to accept, but not necessarily agree with, your claim?

8. What will your audience permit you to claim; that is, what are the practical limits of your ability to persuade this particular audience? What is the range of perspectives audience members will accept regarding your issue? To determine the answers to these questions, you will need to know, at least generally, the beliefs and attitudes your audience holds on your issue. Guard against assuming that others share your views and values to keep you from "preaching to the choir," that is, addressing those who feel as you do about an issue.

Stake, Defend, and Justify Your Claim

Fully supporting your claim—your point of view on an issue—is vital to building a successful argument. And before you bring in specific information to defend your claim, it's essential that you use reasons in support of a claim. Many body paragraphs in effective arguments begin with reasons and then bring in specific support. Qualifiers, as noted in the second example below, make your claims and reasons more realistic and more practical.

Develop a Claim, Reasons, and Qualifiers

A claim is the most important part of your argument. Claims use precise language to let your audience know your point of view. For example, writing on the issue of bullying at your child's school requires orienting the reader right away to your point of view. Your claim organizes and centers an argument. Choose the kind of claim you want to use as the basis for your argument.

Working with Claims, Reasons, and Qualifiers: Three Examples

Each of the following three examples contains a sample claim and an explanation of that claim. Attention is also paid to the necessary elements of reasons and qualifiers, which are used to support the claim.

Claim: "Bullying at my child's school continues because school administrators refuse to thoroughly respond to this problem."

Discussion: The arguer has centered her argument in a clear claim that indicates cause and effect. The rest of the argument will be devoted to proving the accuracy of this claim. She'll need to be sure that readers understand the nature of school bullying and its effects, by defining the term *bullying* in specific language. The writer will also need to provide reasons that directly support her claim, and this will mean digging into the reasons administrators are failing to address the problem.

Ted Soqui/Corbis Historical/Getty Images

Figure 2.5 Defending a claim thoroughly with reasons and support is essential to a successful argument, especially when you have the attention of an audience. In this photo, the arguer is defending his claim to others who are also concerned about the issue.

Claim: "Most people in our state favor giving tax breaks to new companies able to produce alternative energies, but many of our elected representatives seem to be working against this kind of incentive."

Discussion: The arguer can use this claim of fact to articulate the priorities that separate voters and representatives based on the factual information he brings in. He must prove that his claim is factual by bringing in support—examples, studies, testimony from experts, and so forth. Staying with this issue but centering his position around a claim of value, the claim might look like this: "It is unfair that the representatives we voted for are working against our calls to produce more alternative energy in the state." The word "unfair" makes this claim one of value; he has judged his representatives for overlooking popular interest. In the rest of the argument, the writer must prove precisely how the situation is unfair. Note the qualifiers "most," "many," and "seem" in the writer's claim. While the writer believes that numerous representatives have differing agendas on this issue, he avoids claiming that *all* representatives differ from *most* people. Qualifiers make claims more believable.

Claim: "Start times for local high schools should be moved back one hour."

Discussion: A few years ago, a parent made a compelling argument about the issue of start times for local high school students. Reasons were something like this: The parent was motivated because her kids had to get up early and were not at their best during the school day, and early start times and rescheduling transportation caused problems at home for everyone. She used a problem-based claim because she wanted something to change.

Choose the kind of claim that works best for what you want to accomplish in your argument. Choose the kind of claim that will put you in the best position to persuade your audience. Chapter 10, "Build Arguments," discusses claims and how they can serve your purpose in an argument.

Argue with a Purpose

Make the claim in your argument match the intensity of your purpose by asking yourself what, exactly, you want to accomplish. When you land on an issue that matters to you, you're in a position to argue with a purpose and strength. From there, you must ensure that everything you bring to your argument relates to your purpose.

Do you want readers to understand your issue more clearly and in terms that differ from its mainstream representation? Do you want to argue that something should change? Do you want to redefine a term or terms that in your view need clarification? Do you want to argue what causes an issue? Or do you want to respond to an issue through the lens of your own strong values or beliefs? Answering these questions will let you narrow your focus and choose the kind of claim that matches your purpose, thus letting you argue more persuasively. The kinds of claims described in Chapter 10, "Build Arguments"— fact, definition, evaluation, cause, and problem-based—give you the chance to build an argument around the kind of claim that best matches your purpose.

If extra-educational problems at school (for example, lack of parking, financial aid services, or academic advisers) interfere with the deeply held belief that your education will afford you opportunities for future success, then you have a purpose and a center to an argument. The reasons, varied support, and attention to the opposition you bring to such an argument will anchor your purpose and provide readers the concrete evidence needed to defend your claim.

---

your turn 2e   GET STARTED Identify Your Purpose

Focus on two current issues in your life, one academic and one personal, and answer the following questions.

1. What would be your purpose in building an argument for each issue?
2. What is the claim you want to make for each issue?
3. What reasons come to mind as you reflect on each issue?
4. Can you bring to your argument personal experience with each issue? Explain.

Vary the Types of Support You Bring to an Argument

Our understanding of how support functions in an argument begins with the work of Aristotle, a Greek philosopher who used the terms *logos, ethos,* and *pathos* to categorize the ways in which an audience can be persuaded to accept a claim. Aristotle knew that the impression the arguer makes on an audience often can determine whether an argument will be taken to heart; he theorized that a conscientious audience wants to be assured that you appeal to it in three essential ways—through practical evidence grounded in reason (*logos*), through your good character (*ethos*), and through emotional appeals that touch the audience's values (*pathos*). While a sound argument is typically a blend of these appeals, good writers often devote 60 to 70 percent of their support to rational appeals. Use all three kinds of appeals in order to build the credibility of your argument and make it more believable. Following is an overview of these three kinds of support, all of which are covered in more depth in Chapter 3, "Develop a Research Plan."

Support Based on Fact

Factual support, or *logos*, includes verifiable information gathered from your research and experience. Arguing before your local school board for or against end-of-grade testing, for example, you'll want to do much of your persuading with facts, statistics, a range of documents, and other kinds of rational evidence. Documented reports from other school districts, for instance, are a kind of rational appeal. They can be studied and evaluated as part of the problem you're attempting to solve.

Support Based on Your Character

This kind of support, which Aristotle termed *ethos*, establishes your credibility. It is your job to present yourself as knowledgeable and, just as important, honest and fair-minded. Doing this thoroughly can build trust with your audience, essential to a successful argument. On the other hand, if your audience senses that you have an unstated motive or that you're not representing other views fairly, then trust is usually impossible. To earn credibility with your audience, be informed, make smart use of your own experience, bring in

iStock.com/PeopleImages

Figure 2.6 This arguer is building a research base for an argument by drawing on the work of experts. By presenting her research in a fair, open-minded way, she can build trust with an audience, vital to any competent argument.

the testimony of experts, respect readers by making your language accessible, and reveal your motives. Bring in your child's experience with end-of-grade testing, for example, to provide an insider's perspective on testing issues. Balance your personal viewpoint by bringing in the findings of bipartisan and independent professionals who have studied your issue.

Support Based on the Emotions of an Audience

Using emotional appeals, or *pathos*, is effective when you know what your audience members value and the emotions that may sway them to accept your claim. Examples from your life or from the lives of others in your community are especially useful. When you let readers identify with an emotionally engaging example, you create a positive connection. If your neighbor believes that end-of-grade testing narrows what's taught and does not encourage intellectual curiosity, you can bring that perspective into your argument as a way to touch other parents who agree with the neighbor's perspective. This kind of appeal can also build a sense of community between you and your readers, adding to the momentum of an argument.

your turn ▶ **PRACTICE Vary Your Support**

Practice working with support for a claim by answering the following questions, based on an issue you are considering for argument:

1. What kinds of facts can you offer?
2. How can you establish your credibility on the issue so that your audience will trust you?
3. Identify emotional connections you can create between your audience members and yourself that will allow readers to identify with your issue.

Working with a Target Audience: Two Examples

When you are motivated to argue on an issue, aim your argument at an audience willing to listen, rethink the issue, and perhaps act on your claim. Targeting the right audience can determine the success or failure of an argument. Review the following sample issues and arguers' efforts to target appropriate audiences.

EXAMPLE 1

Develop a Claim and Target an Audience
The explanations in this first example walk you through the process of determining a practical claim and audience for the issue of teacher workload. As you can see, there are important choices an arguer must make before the drafting process can begin.

TOPIC: Working Conditions

ISSUE: Workload

AUDIENCE: Readers of local newspaper

CLAIM: Current teacher workloads at our college limit the quality of education that students receive.

COMMUNITY:	Workplace
TOPIC:	Working conditions
ISSUES:	Salary
	Job description
	Interview and hiring protocol
	Benefits
	Workload
	Professional development opportunities
	Union representation
	Equal opportunity employment
	Dispute resolution policies
AUDIENCE:	State community college system officials
	College board of trustees
	State legislature
	College president
	Student body
	Coworkers
	Local government
	Readers of local newspaper
CLAIM:	Current teacher workloads at our college limit the quality of education that students receive.

Much thought has gone into this claim. Because it reveals an important issue in the lives of the arguers and because their purpose is to persuade, careful planning is needed when determining an appropriate audience. Review the following planning process regarding claim and audience for this "workload" issue.

Why this issue?

The workplace, a community nearly all of us belong to, is full of arguable issues. For example, we are authors of this text on purposeful argument, and we are workers in a labor force. As teachers we have issues, among them a deep concern about the number of classes we are required to teach each term. We feel that this issue of workload affects our job performance, our professionalism, and importantly, our ability to serve students. We plan to aim our argument at a specific audience and to prove our claim with specific kinds of support.

Why this audience?

This argument will target readers of our local newspaper and thus will appear both in print and online formats. We chose this audience because its members' tax dollars in part support our publicly funded college, because members of our community expect quality services, because individual readers of the argument (and perhaps their family members) have attended our college, and because the integrity of the local workforce is dependent on the graduates of our college and their training. We feel that other audiences may view our issue from different perspectives and may be less likely to be swayed by our claim.

Why this claim?

We will work with a claim of cause because our intention is to inform readers how teacher workload compromises our ability to meet students' expectations, the mission of the college, and the school's service to the community. We are not calling for immediate action; rather, the purpose of the argument is to let readers know in specific terms about the issue and to suggest that they reflect on it. As a first step in acting on this issue, we hope to generate interest and awareness. A follow-up argument would be aimed at a different audience, one with decision-making power, and may require a problem-based claim in which we argue for a reduced workload. But for now our goal is to raise awareness of this workload issue. (For descriptions of kinds of claims, see Chapter 8, "Consider Toulmin-Based Argument," and Chapter 9, "Consider Middle-Ground Argument, Rogerian Argument, and Argument Based on a Microhistory.")

We assume that many of our audience members know the services our college provides, but that many may not be aware of teacher workload and how it affects delivery of the expected services. Accordingly, the support we bring to the argument, especially specific examples drawn from our experiences, will be vital to fully informing our audience. Because the college has served the community for many years, we can expect some immediate "permission" from our audience to argue our claim, but based on our research, we also know that there has been some persistent grumbling in the past two election cycles over bond proposals that, if passed, would earmark money to the college, and we will need to fully acknowledge and respond to this concern in one of our rebuttals.

EXAMPLE 2
Map an Argument for a Target Audience

TOPIC: The Online Classroom

ISSUE: Teacher–student interaction

AUDIENCE: Director of Distance Learning

CLAIM: Clear standards for teachers' regular interaction with students should be stated in the introductions to online English courses.

When you settle on a claim and a target audience, it can be helpful to rough out most of an argument. This example presents a preview of a Toulmin-based argument, typically the most common kind of argument used in academic writing. (Toulmin-based and other kinds of arguments are discussed in Chapter 8, "Consider Toulmin-Based Argument," and Chapter 9, "Consider Middle-Ground Argument, Rogerian Argument, and Argument Based on Microhistory.") The example picks up on the issue that opens this chapter. This will give you a sense of how the parts of an argument work together. All parts of an argument are fully discussed in chapters that follow.

COMMUNITY:	School/Academic
TOPIC:	The online classroom
ISSUES:	Course navigation
	Clarity of course objectives and expectations
	Online courses and ADA requirements
	Teacher–student interaction
	Grading policies

	Teacher feedback
	Accessibility of course materials
	Course technologies
	Student support services
AUDIENCE:	Teacher
	Department chair
	Other online students
	College dean
	Readers of your local newspaper
	Director of distance learning
	College president
CLAIM:	Clear standards for teachers' regular interaction with students should be stated in the introductions to online English courses.

Why this issue?

Of the many issues that fall under the topic of the online classroom, teacher-student interaction is the most compelling in the online course experience of this writer. Writing about distance learning in general is much too broad, and a writer is sensible to choose a single issue that can be argued in depth. Other issues listed may be of concern, but for this writer they are not as pressing as the need for clear guidelines regarding the interaction with and availability of instructors of online courses.

Why this audience?

The writer plans to aim this argument at her college's director of distance learning in the form of a substantial letter. While there are other possible targets for this argument, the director of distance learning may be the most practical choice because the director is invested in the integrity of the college's distance learning program and capable of acting on the writer's concern for regular interaction with her online teachers. Other audience choices are not as directly tied to online course concerns. Additional practical reasons to target this audience may include the director's ability to suggest options that address the writer's concern, such as disseminating to teachers online course templates that model effective student interaction; designing workshops for teachers; and producing comprehensive student opinion surveys where students' concerns about contact with teachers can be documented.

Because the director is the most important person associated with online instruction at this school, the writer can assume the director knows the importance of student–teacher interaction in online environments. Additionally, the director likely has training in current theoretical approaches to distance learning and thus is in a position to hear the arguer's concern. Writing to a department chair, dean, or college president would add another administrative layer and probably would require considerable explanation of the claim.

As the audience for this argument likely shares the writer's goal of supporting student success in online courses, the director of distance learning may find reasonable a claim for establishing clear standards; in addition, these changes are well within the director's decision-making limits. This kind of "permission" from an audience is essential.

Research

The writer would be wise to research the goals of the college's distance learning program and its commitment to students. This information should be available on the college's website and in the print catalog. However, a quick review of several institutions that offer online programs shows that the schools' websites offer little information about teacher–student interaction standards for online courses. The University of Illinois's online catalog, for example, describes the kinds of lectures that may be offered by its online faculty but suggests that students contact faculty for specifics about how the courses will be managed. And many community colleges in the state offer no information about expectations for student–teacher interaction in online courses.

Why this claim?

The writer is clear in her claim that she wants her audience to respond to this argument by way of direct action. In this case, the writer strongly implies that she wants the director to respond to her point of view and take action that will result in improved interaction with her online teachers. This kind of claim, where a writer is arguing for something to change, is a problem-based claim.

Other possible claims

The five kinds of claims available to a writer arguing on a particular issue are discussed in Chapter 10, "Build Arguments." The following types of claims represent those a writer might consider specifically when arguing the issue of student–teacher interaction in the online classroom.

- Teaching effectively in the online classroom includes interacting regularly with students. (This is a **claim of definition**, where the writer will center an argument by defining a key word or term and then provide reasons for the definition. In this example, the writer would define the phrase "teaching effectively in the online classroom.")

- Regular interaction with teachers is essential for success in online courses. (In this example, the writer would use a **claim of fact** and prove in the argument that it is a fact that succeeding in online courses requires regular interaction with teachers.)
- The absence of clear standards regarding student–teacher interaction in online classes is unfair to students. (A **claim of evaluation** involves the writer making a judgment or evaluation. In this example, the writer will be responsible for proving that it is unfair to students when they enroll in online courses that are missing clear standards for student–teacher interaction.)
- Regular student–teacher interaction in online courses will often result in better grades and better understanding of course content. (A **claim of cause** argues that one thing causes another. In this example the writer would argue that regular interaction in the online classroom can lead to better student grades and a better grasp of course content.)

When you are fully motivated to argue a point of view on an issue important to you and are realistic in the audience you target, you can begin building your argument. Continuing with the issue of student–teacher interaction in the online classroom, this is how the writer might outline the remainder of her argument before beginning work on a first draft.

Warrant/Justification   This term is discussed fully in Chapter 8, "Consider Toulmin-Based Argument," and refers to a deeply held value, belief, or principle you share with your audience. To make a successful argument, your audience must, in a sense, grant you permission to make your argument based on a shared value, such as the belief that students should succeed in online courses. In this argument, a successful warrant might be: "Student success in online classes means that students will complete their educations and the college will fulfill its mission to educate students."

Reasons   Reasons, similar to topic sentences, are used to support your claim. They are followed by more specific kinds of support. Here are reasons this writer might use in building her argument:

- Specific turnaround times for responses to email messages and graded assignments will guarantee feedback for my questions and performance on my assignments.
- Regular teacher participation on the class discussion board means that all members of a class benefit from the teacher guiding us through challenging parts of the course.
- Trust and teamwork in a class are more likely to develop when the teacher is prompt with feedback.
- Teachers can and should model practical ways to interact online.

Support   Specific kinds of support the writer can bring to these reasons fall into logical, ethical, and emotional categories (discussed in more depth in Chapter 11, "Support an Argument with Fact (Logos), Credibility (Ethos), and

Emotion (Pathos)." This writer certainly can rely on personal experiences in online classes, refer to experts in the field of distance learning and the experience of other students, and use examples that will appeal to readers' emotions.

Backing and Reservations Backing is the support you bring for your warrant. In this argument, examples of student success will provide effective backing that, overall, the college does fulfill its mission. A reservation is a statement that cautions readers that the warrant does not apply in certain circumstances. For example, a reservation in this argument might be: "But if online students do not have the chance to evaluate teachers' abilities to interact with students during a course, then standards may not be effective."

Rebuttals and Differing Views A writer brings rebuttals and differing views to an argument to acknowledge and respond to other points of view on an issue. Some objections to this writer's claim might include the following: online courses are more time consuming than real-time courses for teachers and thus there is limited time to interact with students; many online teachers feel that students should use online resources instead of depending on teacher feedback; and teacher–student interaction in online courses is not part of a teacher's annual review and therefore is not considered, by many teachers, to be important. The writer must answer, or counter, each rebuttal. Differing views on this issue may not argue directly against this writer's claim but may approach the issue from different perspectives. The writer may choose to build on and extend these views or to demonstrate their shortcomings.

Qualifiers Qualifiers make an argument more practical because they involve words and terms like "in most cases" or "often" that replace words like "only" and "always." For example, would the second reason given above—"Regular teacher participation on the class discussion board means that all members of a class benefit from teacher guidance through challenging parts of the course"—be more believable if a qualifier were added and read, "Regular teacher participation on the class discussion board means that *many* members of a class would benefit from teacher guidance through challenging parts of the course"? Qualifiers should be used throughout an argument and are discussed in Chapter 10, "Build Arguments."

> **your turn 2g** ▸ PRACTICE **Map an Argument**
>
> Based on the overview of the argument process this chapter provides, identify a pressing issue in your life and perform the following tasks:
>
> 1. Write a first draft of a claim.
> 2. Identify the values you share with your audience.
> 3. Draft reasons and outline support for your claim.
> 4. Establish backing to address audience reservations.
> 5. Identify opposing viewpoints and rebuttals.
> 6. Use qualifiers to make your claim and reasons practical.

Argue at the Right Moment

The essential work you must do in planning an argument—determine an issue important to you, identify a practical target audience for your argument, and map your argument—requires another vital consideration: arguing at the right time. This means delivering an argument at a time when it is most likely to be heard and responded to. As a perceptive arguer, take advantage of current local and intellectual interest in an issue to energetically deliver an argument, something the individuals in Figure 2.7 are prepared to do.

An argument can be effective when you deliver it at the right time, what in classical rhetoric is known as *kairos*, or timeliness. This means having a strong understanding of your audience and how ready it is for your claim. It also means having a sense of the issue's urgency. For example, if your audience is your colleagues—your fellow students—when might be the best time to argue about the issue of increased student fees? You may decide that early in the semester is best—a time when registration, textbook fees, and parking fees are fresh in the minds of other students *and* a time before projects are due or major exams are looming.

If, on the other hand, your aim is to inform readers of your local newspaper or community forum (via a substantial letter to the editor or post) that construction of a natural gas pipeline will not benefit the local economy, you may determine that the best time to make your argument is when local media are reporting on this issue and when community interest is high. Likewise, an argument on the issue of air quality will have more currency during the run-up to an important policy decision on toxic emissions than after such a decision.

When you sense that the time is right to deliver an argument, take full advantage of the momentum surrounding your issue. This is good timing. Delivering an argument before an audience is ready for it or when an issue's urgency has passed can render the argument, and your efforts, ineffective. So how can you determine the right time to make your argument? Determine how an issue is affecting an audience. For example, if you're concerned about how returning soldiers are being treated, and you know that local and national news media are reporting on this issue, you may decide to target your state's U.S. senators as your audience and let them know that legislation should be proposed based on this current problem. You can also keep your focus closer to home and target veterans' groups and area veterans' affairs hospitals. Deliver your argument when public exposure and interest in an issue have created an

iStock.com/track5

Figure 2.7 Deliver an argument to an audience when there is genuine and immediate interest in an issue. In this political rally, individuals are responding with genuine interest to the issue of health-care reform.

opening for change so as to ensure that your argument has currency and that your voice will be part of the conversation.

What might be the best times to argue the sample issues discussed previously? The writer who claims the need for clear standards of interaction with her online teachers may choose to deliver the argument toward the end of the academic term, a time when she will have established her credibility with her audience as a serious student wanting more from her online course and also a time when the director of distance learning may take seriously the need to implement new policies for the next term. Concerning our goal of raising local awareness of the workload issue at our college, we plan to deliver the argument to our local newspaper in October, approximately a month before voters decide on a bond proposal that would direct money to our school. We also note local and national media reporting on the trend of more students electing to complete their first two years of study at two-year and community colleges, as tuition cost in those institutions is substantially lower than at four-year colleges. With both issues, arguing at appropriate times will be crucial to attracting the immediate interest of an audience.

your turn 2h ▸ **GET STARTED Argue at the Right Moment**

Answer the following questions about your claim or one of your claims. Is it a good time to argue your claim with this particular audience? If not, how can you either adjust your claim so that it is timely or target a different audience that you determine is the right one to hear your claim right now?

1. Are you arguing at a time when your audience is aware of and invested in your issue? Explain.
2. Are you confident in your claim and prepared to defend it? Explain.
3. Describe the ways your audience can benefit from reflecting on or acting on your claim.
4. Are conditions such that your audience is willing to tolerate differing views on your issue? If yes, describe how you will take advantage of this time in an informed way in your argument.

Getting Started

After you decide on an issue, target an audience, map your argument, and decide on the right time to deliver your argument, use the following prompts to get started. These prompts are designed to move you deeper into your feelings about an issue and help you determine whom you want to persuade, what you want to change, and how accepting your claim can benefit the audience you're targeting. Answering these prompts can give you insight into the direction an argument should take.

 tip 2c

Read the Signs!
To determine if an argument will carry weight with an audience, make a list of the indications, or signs, that the time is right to craft and deliver your argument. This list can include conversations you participate in and overhear, articles in the local media, and references to the issue that you find in blogs, magazines, and websites.

your turn 2i   GET STARTED **With an Argument**

Address the questions below.

1. What topics *not* included in the earlier section "Determine What Matters to You and Why" might you be interested in addressing?
2. Thinking in terms of both your personal life and your academic life, what issues concern you the most?
3. What are the two or three most pressing issues for you both inside and outside the classroom?
4. What is the single issue on which you are most motivated to argue? Explain.
5. In response to question 4, what makes you sure that you are taking on a manageable issue and not a broad topic?
6. In addition to your own position on this single issue, briefly describe other points of view.

your turn 2j   GET STARTED **Target the Right Audience**

With regard to the issue you have identified as motivating for you, describe your target audience by answering the following questions.

1. What are the two or three most practical target audiences for this argument?
2. How do you want your audience to respond after taking in your argument?
3. Based on how you want your audience to respond, what is the most practical target audience for your argument?
4. What is it about the demographics of your target audience that suggests it is a practical choice?
5. What are the values and beliefs you share with your target audience?
6. In practical, everyday terms, why do you want to persuade this target audience?

your turn 2k   GET STARTED **Draft the Right Claim**

Respond to the following questions as a way to determine whether a claim is appropriate for your argument.

1. By accepting your claim, how will your target audience benefit?
2. Of the five kinds of claims described under "Example #2: Map an Argument for a Target Audience," what kind of claim is most appropriate for your audience? Explain.

your turn ➤ **GET STARTED Research an Issue**

As a way to begin your research process, respond to the following questions.

1. So as to fully inform an audience about your issue, what sources will you consult first?
2. Based on the issue you plan to argue on, why will it be necessary to gather compelling evidence to defend your claim and reasons?
3. Are there particular biases and limitations that could get in the way of your target audience accepting your claim? If yes, what are they?
4. What opposing points of view do you feel should be included? How will you respond to them?
5. Why is now a practical time to argue on your issue? Explain why your target audience will have a natural interest in this issue.

Reflect and Apply

Answer the questions that follow to ensure that the argument you plan to build is a practical response to an issue that matters to you.

1. Explain why the issue you're working with is important to you now. Why is it more important than other issues in your life?
2. Discuss how you'll focus on a single issue in an argument and thus avoid the kind of general writing that results from a focus that is too broad.
3. Who is your target audience? What are its values? What research will you pursue to better understand this audience?
4. Discuss how the parts of an argument mentioned in Example #2—warrant/justification, reasons, support, backing and reservations, rebuttals, and qualifiers—will be treated in the argument you plan to build.
5. Of the types of claims discussed in this chapter, which one seems the most practical for the issue you're addressing? Explain.
6. Defend the timeliness of your argument; that is, explain why now is a practical time to build and deliver it. Refer to successful arguments, in either public or private life, that have been delivered at the right moment.

KEEPING IT LOCAL

POWERFUL, compelling arguments often begin in very private, personal moments with issues that present a struggle for you. Pay close attention to these moments. Writing an argument gives you a structure to dignify what you're feeling and to influence an audience. Choosing to write on issues that matter to you can clarify how argument fits into your life and how sound arguments can serve your short- and long-term goals. When you make your point of view on an issue known, you also contribute to democratic life in your specific and broader communities.

The writer who argued about the need for better interaction with her online instructor forged a clear, purposeful claim and wanted immediate action taken in response. After all, in practical terms, she won't be a student at her college much longer, and she's speaking up with the hope that she will not run into this problem in another online course. The anxiety she felt about her upcoming exam and her desire to be prepared for it made the problem she had with her instructor an issue that mattered to her. The issue evolved from a community (school) in which she invested much time and money. Because she wanted her issue to be addressed with action, her argument moved beyond the status of class assignment and into real life. This is how argument can be a practical skill for everyday living. The writer targeted her argument at the director of distance learning at her college, an official who could be motivated to act in response to the issue. In this case, arguer and audience overlap in their concerns for effective student–teacher interaction, prompt delivery of services, and higher education as an essential step in meeting career goals. Furthermore, delivering her argument at the right time—during her college career and during a course in which teacher response time needs to improve—also makes her argument practical. This student wasn't getting what she needed from her online instructor and did something about it. Mapping her argument carefully, she supported a strong claim and aimed the argument at an audience likely to take it seriously. Her efforts are proof that argument can serve what matters to us.

● ▬ ▬ ▬ ▬ ▬ ▬ ▬ ▬ ▬ ▬ ▬ ●

In the last few weeks or months, what is the most compelling argument you've encountered? From what community in the arguer's life did it spring? What got your attention and what made it compelling? Describe how an issue in your own life can match the intensity and purpose of the argument you identify.

CHAPTER 3 Develop a Research Plan

CHAPTER 4 Evaluate and Engage with Your Sources

CHAPTER 5 Read Critically and Avoid Fallacies

CHAPTER 6 Work Fairly with the Opposition

PART TWO

How to Establish Context through Research

All Illustrations by iStock.com/A-digit

CHAPTER 3

Develop a Research Plan

Learning Objectives

By working through this chapter, you will be able to

- locate topic overviews using credible reference works.
- list appropriate search terms to be used in database and Internet research.
- identify reliable Internet and print sources to find information for a research project.
- perform keyword queries when searching databases and Internet sources for a research project.
- subscribe to sources such as RSS feeds for the purpose of receiving research updates.
- gather research through the use of vetted library databases.
- name examples of primary, government, and multimedia sources.

You always arrive a few minutes early to your office to check your personal email at your desk. Then, about midmorning, when your colleagues are taking a smoke break, you log on to the Internet to check the scores for last night's baseball games. When things get a little slow after lunch, you sometimes play a couple of hands of solitaire on the computer. At your yearly evaluation, you are surprised to receive not only poor comments but also a reprimand that you are wasting company time by misusing your computer. How did your boss know what you were doing at your desk? Electronic surveillance. Can your company watch what you are doing on your computer? Is it legal for the company to "spy" on you? You head back to the computer, the one at home, and begin researching employee monitoring. You're surprised at what you find.

All Illustrations by iStock.com/A-digit

TOPIC: Computer Usage

ISSUE: Privacy and Computer Use

AUDIENCE: Business Ethics Professor

CLAIM: Workplace electronic monitoring practices should be revealed to employees through company policies.

Research is the backbone of much of the writing you will do in school and in the workplace, and there are many ways to conduct research—via print sources, the Internet, interviews, and so on. These sources have to be integrated with your own ideas to create a researched essay or report that follows a certain format appropriate either for your academic classes or for your workplace. The whole process can become overwhelming, particularly with the additional burden of avoiding plagiarism.

In Chapter 1, "Argue with a Purpose," you learned how argument can work for you, its purpose, and some argumentative strategies. You discovered the process of choosing an issue to argue in Chapter 2, "Explore an Issue that Matters to You." The focus of this chapter is on introducing the various types of resources available and how to find them. Chapter 4, "Evaluate and Engage with Your Sources," will focus on how to evaluate and read the various types of resources and how to incorporate and cite information from those sources into your writing. "Appendix A: MLA Documentation and the Works Cited Page" and "Appendix B: APA Documentation and the References Page" cover how to create a works cited page for your researched report or essay in MLA and APA format.

Throughout Chapters 3 and 4 you will follow the progress of Hal, a college student who is writing a researched argument on computer surveillance of employees for his Business Ethics course. Whether you have two weeks or two months, the strategies in these chapters should help you tackle any project.

Once you have your issue in mind, and at any other stage of the argument–writing process when you need more information, it is time for serious research. The types and number of sources available are seemingly endless. Google, the most popular Internet search engine, searches billions of pages of information. Many libraries now subscribe to thousands of newspapers, journals, and magazines through databases. These databases also offer reference and scholarly books that can be read online. Large libraries house thousands of books and other print media. If you plan on finding any needles in this enormous information haystack, you will need a research plan. Begin with setting up a basic library of reference tools that can answer questions and provide facts.

Use Reference Works, Encyclopedias, and Topic Overviews Profitably

Although they are not considered acceptable sources to include in college-level arguments, reference works and encyclopedias are extremely useful for fact checking and providing issue context. Many of these sources, such as the *CIA World Factbook*, the *Infoplease Almanac*, dictionaries, and encyclopedias, are available on the Internet or through public and college libraries. Find them and bookmark them so that they are literally at your fingertips when you need them. Infoplease (http://www.infoplease.com) provides quick facts through a world atlas and almanac, the *Columbia Encyclopedia*, *Brewer's Dictionary of Phrase and Fable*, information on U.S. politics, world rulers, and much more.

Here is a good list of sites to bookmark:

- The CIA's *The World Factbook*: https://www.cia.gov/library/publications /the-world-factbook
- General Reference Internet Source is a site compiled by the United States of the Interior with links to several dozen general reference sites organized by type, including almanacs, careers, style manuals, and various dictionaries: https://www.doi.gov/library/internet/General-Reference-Sources
- The U.S. Census Bureau's Quick Facts: https://www.census.gov/

Read an Overview of Your Topic

What do you know about your topic? Often you will be familiar with topics assigned in class: the Battle of Appomattox; the id, ego, and superego; teenage suicide; *The Scarlet Letter;* Russian propaganda posters. Familiarity, though, is not enough of a foundation for a written argument. Too many writers skip making themselves familiar with their topics and rush to gather sources.

At the beginning of your research, find an overview article, brochure, or reference work about your topic. This is the one time in the research process to find an encyclopedia article. Encyclopedias are a great, yet often misused, resource for writers. Even though you may not use material from an overview or general reference work or encyclopedia in an academic argument, these sources are invaluable for two things: (1) providing an understanding of the background and context of your issue and (2) offering a list of search terms. Encyclopedias offer background information in a brief outline, listing key people and events involved in the issue and providing a list of search terms that will be of great value when you begin your more sophisticated searches. Your library will have at least one encyclopedia, usually electronic, and often more than one. Encyclopedias can be found on the Internet as well.

The most frequently used Internet encyclopedia is Wikipedia. This resource accepts contributions from anyone who cares to write on a topic. While scholars are working to produce stronger and more research-driven articles, Internet encyclopedia articles have their fair share of errors. They are still excellent sources for compiling search terms, bibliographies, and links to other sites. Some of these articles are well written and supported with sources; others are not. You must use some caution and some common sense to avoid information that is misleading and erroneous. Looking at articles on your issue in more than one encyclopedia will provide you with even more information to get you started. You may not cite from any encyclopedia, print or online, in academic writing.

To return to our example, Hal was interested in an overview of electronic surveillance of employees in the workplace, so he began a search with *Funk & Wagnall's New World Encyclopedia*. He tried several search terms, including *electronic surveillance* and *email privacy*, but had no luck. He then tried *Wikipedia* and found a lengthy article on surveillance that included privacy issues and links to legal resources. An article on email privacy netted him even better results. One of the valuable terms he gathered was the Electronic Communications Privacy Act and a link to the legal case of *Smyth v. Pillsbury*, in which "a reasonable expectation of privacy" was not found to extend to emails sent from company computers. This helped Hal to understand what has been done on the issue so far.

Other overviews can be found by simply typing some of the following words, along with your topic, into an Internet search engine:

- Overview
- Context
- Background
- History
- Introduction

Hal tried the word "overview" along with "Internet privacy" and retrieved a Congressional Report that provided an overview and the most current legislation on the issue.

Gather Search Terms

To find information more efficiently, keep a thorough list of search terms. Once established, a list of search terms can be plugged into as many search engines as you care to use. Be as concise with your terms as you can, but be prepared to broaden your terms if you are not receiving any hits.

 tip 3a

List Search Terms and Vocabulary
As you conduct your research, keep track of words and phrases that apply to your issue. When you conduct searches on search engines and in databases, having a list of search terms will make your searching more effective.

Hal came away from his overview reading with a number of search terms that he found:

- Internet privacy
- e-Government Act
- Email tracking
- Employee privacy
- Electronic surveillance
- Electronic communication
- Employee privacy rights
- Email privacy

As Hal reads, he will add more terms to his list.

Notice that some of these terms seem very close to each other, and some are actually synonyms. It is important to think of all the ways a topic may come up so that you are not cutting off avenues of research because your selected search term does not match the one used by the creators of the search engine. For example, if you are searching for statistics about car buying trends, you should use both the terms *car* and *automobile*. The more terms you use, the less likely you are to miss potentially useful sources.

Background Research

- ☐ 1. Check reference sources for basic facts.
- ☐ 2. Consult encyclopedia or reference book overviews for context, search terms, and links to articles.
- ☐ 3. Develop list of search terms.

internet activity 3a **Read Encyclopedia Articles or Other Overviews on Your Issue**

Find at least two introductions to your issue, and answer the following questions about each:

1. What is the background of your issue?
2. Who is involved?
3. What are some of the search terms you can use when conducting further research?
4. How do the articles compare with each other? Are there any incidents of personal opinion or bias in the articles? Do the articles seem objective and fact oriented?

Use Search Engines to Find Internet Sources on the Surface Web and on the Deep Web

Armed with a better understanding of the history of electronic privacy, Hal prepares to conduct an Internet search. This process will take place many times throughout the research and writing process, as new information is needed or new ideas elicit new searches. Many people content themselves with visiting their favorite search engine and using whatever sources appear on the first page of hits. This may be fine if you are looking for football scores (though there are better ways to find even that information), but if you are looking for sources suitable for academic writing, you'll need to dig further.

Not all search engines produce the same search results. Most people are familiar with Google, Ask.com, and Yahoo!, but there are many more search engines available that do different things. Even if you are happy with Google, you are probably not using all of the powerful research tools it has to offer. We will learn some of its features throughout this chapter.

Search the Surface Web

You are likely already familiar with **search engines,** vehicles for finding material on the World Wide Web. What you may not know is that search engines are not all the same. Type in the same query at each of the engines listed below, for example, and you will get different results from each. The way they each search, collect, and rank hits is different.

Some consistently useful search engines include:

- Google   http://www.google.com
- Yahoo!   http://search.yahoo.com
- Ask.com   http://www.ask.com
- Bing   http://www.bing.com

A very thorough list of free search engines is available on Wikipedia: https://en.wikipedia.org/wiki/List_of_search_engines.

Hal used the same search term ("electronic privacy" + work) in four different search engines: Ask.com, Bing, Yahoo!, and Google (see Figure 3.1). You can see that the search results and their organization are very different from one site to the next. In addition, three search engines offer additional search terms to use and one doesn't. Find a search engine that retrieves results in a method that makes sense to you.

Hal began a new search on Google using the phrase "workplace privacy" (see Figure 3.2). The sites highlighted in purple are the ones Hal visited. Notice that the ending of the URL (the website's address) for these three sites is ".org." This indicates that the site is maintained by an organization, although the rules for determining "organizational" status seem to be flexible. By visiting the Privacy Rights Clearinghouse, the Electronic Privacy Information Center, and the American Civil Liberties Union, Hal was able to come away with several views of the issue of workplace privacy.

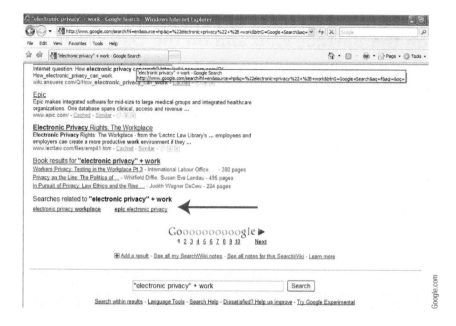

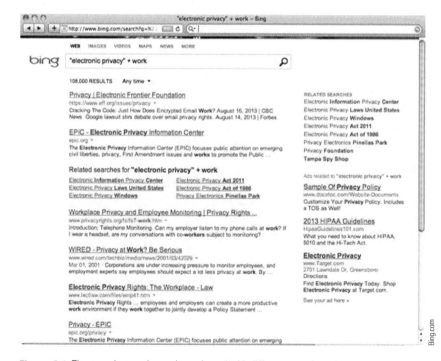

Figure 3.1 The same keyword search conducted with different search engines

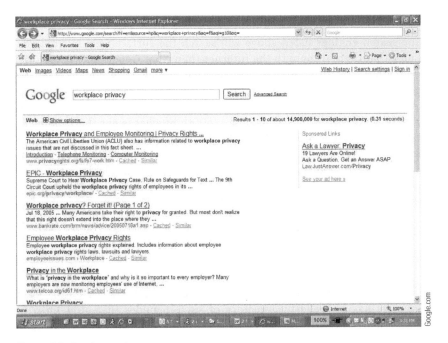

Figure 3.2 Google search screen

Other than .org domains, a URL can end with the following extensions:

- .com   a commercial site
- .edu   an educational site, such as a school or university
- .gov   a government site, for example the Library of Congress or the White House
- .int   not so common, but refers to an international site
- .mil   extension used by U.S. military organizations such as the Army or Navy
- .net   used as a generic extension for many types of sites
- .org   used by an organization

internet activity 3b Compare Search Engines

Select several search engines and conduct a quick basic search to see what hits are returned and how they are organized. Which search engine appeals the most to you based on page layout, number of hits, and organization?

Search the Deep Web

The search engines listed above will search the surface web, but did you know that there is more to the Internet than what Google and Yahoo! can find? There are thousands of sources that cannot be easily accessed by general-purpose search engines. This information is called the "deep web," or sometimes the "invisible web." Some studies indicate that what we can generally access on the Web is only 1/500th of what is out there. Some of this information is password or firewall protected, but much of it is just in formats that do not make it easy for the search engines to find. Many databases housing scholarly or scientific information are available in the deep web, and there are search engines and database sites developed to access much of it.

- LibrarySpot.com (http://libraryspot.com): Particularly useful are the site's link to scholarly journals that can be accessed online and its link to museum sites. The World Digital Library, for example, offers thousands of images from many countries.
- Academic Info (http://www.academicinfo.net/subject-guides): This site has a wonderful directory of subject guides that offer links to resources. The link to Afghanistan News and Media, for example, offers links to Afghan newspapers, documentaries, and materials from the State Department.
- Videolectures.net (http://videolectures.net): Another great site for video material is Videolectures.net. This site contains lectures from many venues, including university guest lecturers and speakers from international conferences. The videos are organized by topic and range from art to the social sciences.
- DOAJ (https://doaj.org/) is a great site to search for even more journal articles from journals around the world, many in English.

Another search engine to use is Surfwax and there are a few other sources that will be discussed in the section on using primary sources in this chapter: USA.gov., Science.gov., and the Library of Congress. Try them all to see what you can find on your issue. As you can probably tell, research is not a one-stop activity. The broader you cast your net, the more likely you will find sources that are reputable and pertinent to your issue.

Keep this template (and all the other publication information templates typed in red in this chapter) available as you collect sources. Not all information will be available on every website; record what is available. You may want to be careful about sites that do not have authors that you can find out more about.

 tip 3b

Using a Bibliography File

Always collect publication information for an electronic source. If you do not have this information when you write your report, you will not be able to use the source. And trying to relocate an Internet source can be exceedingly frustrating and time consuming.

A bibliography file is a great way to keep your sources organized. You may not have a use for a particular article once you've completed your assessment, but you may change your thesis at a later date, and a previously useless article may now be useful.

Source Information: Template

Author, if one is listed: _____

Title of the specific web page: _____

Name of website (italicized): _____

Name of website sponsor: _____

Date it was posted: _____

URL: _____

Note that if you find a source that is actually an article from an online periodical, you will need to gather the complete periodical publication information in addition to the site information.

---

internet activity 3c Explore the Deep Web

The deep web is a great place to explore. Take your time playing with the search engines and databases, and mark the ones that include material on your issue for future searches.

Perform Keyword Queries

Now that you are familiar with some of the available search engines and database sites that will look for information on the Web, you should read the following instructions on basing keyword queries on the vocabulary lists you created during your basic fact and encyclopedia reading so that your searches will be more effective and efficient. Remember when Hal typed in the query "electronic privacy" + work? He was using a **search string** to tell the search tool what he was looking for. You can use Boolean search operators (*not, and,* and *or*) between your search terms to tell the search engine exactly what to look for. Boolean logic can be tweaked endlessly, whereas using + and − signs will only add or subtract terms from your search. The following chart lists the basic kinds of search strings you can use and what they mean.

Search String	What You Are Asking For
electronic privacy	Pages that have both the words *electronic* AND *privacy* somewhere on the page
"electronic privacy"	Pages that have both words next to each other
"electronic privacy" AND work	Pages that have both words next to each other AND include the word *work* somewhere on the page
"electronic privacy" + work	Same as above
"electronic privacy" NOT surveillance	Pages that have both words next to each other and do NOT include the word *surveillance*
"electronic privacy" − work	Same as above
"electronic privacy" 2010...2014	Pages that have both words next to each other AND only pages that have material between the date range of 2010 and 2014
site: .edu	Pages from educational websites only

You will need to gather the following publication information for articles found on the databases. Record all available information—not every site will have all the elements listed.

> **Source Information: Article from Website (Basic)**
> Author of article: _____
> Title of article: _____
> Title of periodical (italicized): _____
> Publication information of periodical: _____
> And then,
> Author(s) of web page: _____
> Title of web page: _____
> Name of website (italicized): _____
> Name of website sponsor: _____
> Date originally posted: _____
> URL: _____

MLA no longer requires the URL, but recording it is helpful in finding the site again.

 internet activity 3d **Perform Internet and Internet Database Searches**

Using one of the search engines or database sites listed previously, find three Internet sources pertaining to your topic. Use the advanced search feature for your search engine, or use the search strings above to limit your results to .edu domains for the past three months only.

Find News Sites and Use RSS Feeds to Receive Updates

Hal also decides to take advantage of the archives that newspapers and other news sources provide. Although the issue of privacy in the workplace is a longstanding one, the constant development of communication technology makes this issue particularly current. News search engines are a good place to search for information about current issues. The following is a good beginning list:

- CNN   http://www.cnn.com
- CBS News   http://www.cbsnews.com
- ABC News   http://abcnews.go.com
- Google News   http://news.google.com
- Reuters   http://www.reuters.com
- BBC News   http://news.bbc.co.uk
- The Associated Press   http://www.ap.org
- *The Wall Street Journal* http://online.wsj.com/home-page
- *The New York Times*   http://nytimes.com
- National Public Radio   http://www.npr.org
- *Slate Magazine*   http://www.slate.com
- Yahoo! and Google also search for news and have searchable news archives

Play with the various sites to learn how the news is organized on each site and to use their search functions. When you find a news article you like, collect the following publication information for later use:

> ## Source Information: Article from News Site
> Author(s) of article: _____
>
> Title of article: _____
>
> Title of periodical or web page (italicized): _____
>
> Original publication date: _____
>
> URL: _____

internet activity 3e Perform a News Search

Visit two of the news search sites listed previously and find information on the same stories. How is the material treated differently by the different news sites? Which appeals the most to you based on design and organization? Which seem to have the most links to your issue?

If you find sites that consistently provide you with information you find useful on your issue, subscribe to the RSS feed at that site and you can receive updates on your issue as news becomes available. Many websites now offer RSS feeds to their readers. You will often find one of the two icons shown in Figure 3.3 on a site, which you can click on to subscribe to a feed. Sometimes you will see the RSS in a box.

Soland/Dreamstime.com

Tamilsna/Dreamstime.com

Figure 3.3 Look for one of these two icons to subscribe to a feed.

Subscribing to a feed can be a big time saver if you are following a changing story or if you are tracking several sites and don't want to have to keep visiting over and over to see if new information has been posted.

An **RSS feed** delivers updates on your issue to you, either through a reader that you can access online, to your email account as alerts, or to a mobile unit, such as your phone. These feeds are free to subscribe to, and so are most **newsreaders,** also known as "aggregators," which are needed to read the feeds as they come to you. Different newsreaders work differently, so you'll have to play around to see which may work best for you. Yahoo! offers links to many of the most popular newsreaders on its directory.

With newsreaders, you can control how often you receive updates: hourly, as they happen, or weekly. With a good search query, you can sit back and let the computer do some of the leg work for you.

Find and Use Databases in Libraries

Databases that you access through your library (Opposing Viewpoints, MasterFILE Premier, ERIC, etc.) are collections of articles from various publications gathered in one place to make research easier. Instead of subscribing to hundreds of journals for which they have little physical space, libraries now subscribe to databases so that journals can be searched electronically. Some databases are field specific. For example, ERIC is a clearinghouse of education sources. There are databases specifically for newspaper articles, for business sources, for medical articles, and so on. Most of the time, though, a general database like Opposing Viewpoints will work for you.

Searching a database is not so different from searching the Internet. You have choices such as date ranges, publications, and document type that can make your searching more efficient. Most libraries offer connections to their databases that you can reach from your home computer. Hal accessed Opposing Viewpoints through his library's remote connection. When you use databases on the deep web, some of the search screens will look a lot like the ones described here; others, though, will have their own idiosyncrasies for searching. Most database sites have tutorials that will walk you through the search process, and the results will be worth it—lots of articles you can use in academic writing.

Hal narrowed his date range to two years and selected the Full Text check box so that the results generated by his search would include available full-length articles only (see Figure 3.4). This step is necessary unless you have time to request through interlibrary loan articles that are not available in the database. Most professors will not allow you to cite from article abstracts alone; you must have access to the full-text article. Most databases will provide hits sorted by source type: newspaper, journal, video, etc. (see Figure 3.5).

Documents accessed through a computer database such as EBSCOhost will appear in one of two formats: PDF or HTML. A **PDF document** requires that you have Adobe Acrobat Reader on your computer. If you do not, you can download Adobe Acrobat Reader free from the Adobe website.

An article in PDF format is simply a photocopy of the original article—page breaks, images, and so forth are maintained, and reading the article is no different than it would be if you were turning pages in a print journal. The publication information is usually found at the top or bottom of the journal pages (see Figure 3.6). When you cite from an article you accessed in PDF

tip 3c

Use RSS Feeds
Other sources you can use to gather information about your topic are RSS feeds to newsgroups, discussion boards, and blogs.

tip 3d

Verify Citations
Before you end your database search session, verify that you have all of the article's publication information. Some databases will also help you generate a complete citation (see arrow in Figure 3.7).

Patricia Bostian

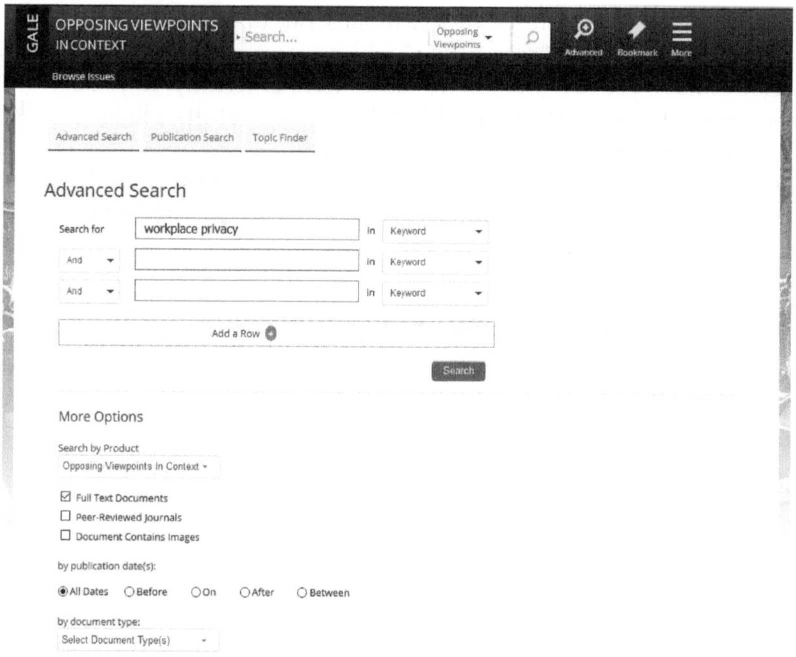

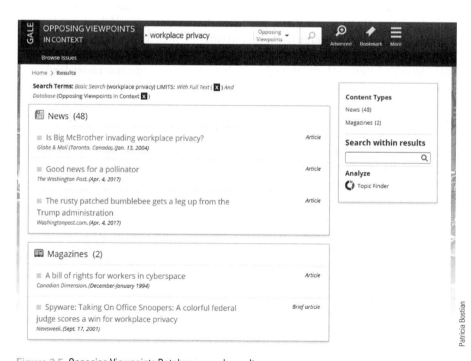

Figure 3.4 Opposing Viewpoints advanced search screen.

Patricia Bostian

Figure 3.5 Opposing Viewpoints Database search results

MARKET SEGMENTATION

Because all customers do not have the same needs, expectations, and financial resources, managers can improve their pricing strategies by segmenting markets. Successful segmentation comes about when managers determine what motivates particular markets and what differences exist in the market when taken as a whole. For example, some customers may be motivated largely by price, while others are motivated by functionality and utility. The idea behind segmentation is to divide a large group into a set of smaller groups that share significant characteristics such as age, income, geographic location, lifestyle, and so on. By dividing a market into two or more segments, a company can devise a pricing scheme that will appeal to the motivations of each of the different market segments or it can decide to target only particular segments of the market that best correspond to its products or services and their prices.

Managers can use market segmentation strategically to price products or services in order to attain company objectives. Companies can set prices differently for different segments based on factors such as location, time of sale, quantity of sale, product design, and a number of others, depending on the way companies divide up the

PRIVACY, PRIVACY LAWS, AND WORKPLACE PRIVACY

Privacy, privacy laws, and workplace privacy are issues of major concern to individuals and organizations in the modern world. Privacy violation and encroachment have become a norm as a result of the surveillance capabilities of the new and emerging electronic gadgets and information technology (IT) systems. This trend has prompted many countries to pass laws that govern the handling and collection of personal information of individuals and organizations with the use of electronic instruments.

WHAT IS PRIVACY?

What constitutes an encroachment to an individual's or an organization's rights to privacy? In legal terms, privacy simply refers to the accepted standards of related rights that safeguard human dignity. Definitions of privacy vary according to the environment, the participating interests, and the contextual limits. In many countries, the concept of data protection is included in the definition of privacy to achieve an interpretation that views privacy in terms of boundaries to an individual's personal information or an organization's data.

Figure 3.6 Page from a journal article in PDF format

format, you can refer to specific page numbers as they appear, just as you normally would with a print document.

An **HTML document** appears as a continuous page, generally with no page breaks or images. The publication information you will need appears

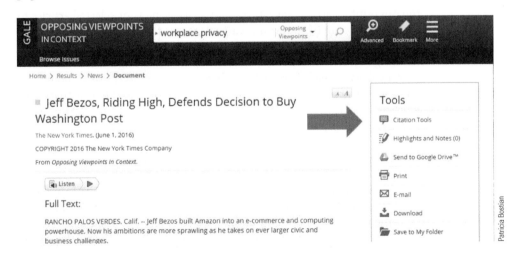

Figure 3.7 Some databases help you generate a complete citation.

either at the beginning of the article or at the very end of the article. You cannot refer your readers to specific page numbers when you cite from an article in HTML format, as HTML documents do not contain page numbers. A reader would, however, be able to easily perform a search of the original article for cited material.

The publication information you need to gather for a journal, a magazine, or a newspaper article is as follows:

Journal	Magazine	Newspaper
Author(s)	Author(s)	Author(s)
Title of article	Title of article	Title of article
Title of journal	Title of magazine	Title of newspaper
Volume and issue numbers	Publication date (month/week + date/year)	Publication date (day, month, and year)
Year of publication (sometimes includes season—e.g., Fall)	Page numbers of article (if available)	Page numbers of article (if available)
Page numbers of article (if available)	Title of database	Title of database
Title of database	DOI Digital Object Identifier or permalink Date database accessed	DOI or permalink Date database accessed
DOI or permalink		

You can print an article, save it to a flash drive, send your selected articles to your email account (if you are on campus), or save them to your personal computer (if you are working from a remote location). Because Hal has the option of saving any articles that look interesting and reviewing them more closely later, he doesn't read them as he finds them. When he is ready, though, he will skim the articles looking for certain information, deciding at that point which articles he wants to read more closely and which he can delete from his research folder.

your turn 3a ▶ **GET STARTED** **Use Library Databases**

Access your campus or public library's journal databases and conduct a search for your topic. Find two articles that have been published within the past two years. Copy all information that you would need to find the article again, including the database in which you found the article.

Find and Use Primary Sources

Using primary sources can help you get closer to the heart of an issue. Whether your argument is concerned with historical issues or current ones, whether you are arguing in the classroom or in the community, asking questions that can be answered by interviews, surveys, court transcripts, letters, photographs, raw statistics, or congressional hearings will put you in closer contact with the real people behind the issue. It is easy to fall into the trap of looking for the "truth" of an issue, looking only for hard facts to support your rational argument, when, in fact, there is rarely only one truth involved in any issue. People are rarely factual, nor do they usually operate on strictly rational lines of thought. Real people are motivated by a variety of reasons, which are not always based on the relevant facts of an issue. Determining the facts that are relevant to your issue is without a doubt extremely important. However, it is how these facts are interpreted by the stakeholders, the real people involved in your issue, that will determine how successful your argument ultimately will be.

We've already covered some of the many sources to choose from when you are researching your issue. Will newspaper or journal articles answer your research questions, or do you need to conduct interviews or gather statistics? **Secondary sources** are those that analyze or explain some aspect of your topic. A magazine article evaluating the dangers of factory emissions would be a secondary source. **Primary sources** are original documents or information gathered from firsthand research—yours or someone else's. An interview with a resident of a neighborhood affected by factory emissions would be a primary source.

Primary Sources

- Historical newspapers
- Public records
- Government documents
- Interviews
- Surveys
- Statistics
- Historical documents
- Diaries
- Letters
- Advertisements
- Maps
- Documentaries
- Archives

Secondary Sources

- Most articles from current newspapers
- Articles from magazines and scholarly journals
- Books

Some of the general issues in evaluating primary sources are determining the purpose of a document, evaluating its validity or accuracy, and determining what was important to the author of the source, especially in the case of diaries or letters.

The U.S. Library of Congress has an amazing website that offers links to hundreds of sites housing primary sources in every area from literature to history to sociology (https://www.loc.gov). Here you can explore photographs, diaries, videos, links to statistics, interviews, maps, and so on.

Here are more sites that may help in your search for primary sources:

- U.S. Census Bureau—Data tables and maps presenting census data, plus materials to help use census information https://www.census.gov/.
- Survey Research—The Writing Center at Colorado State University presents this guide to conducting survey research and reporting on results (https://writing.colostate.edu/guides/research/survey/index.cfm).
- Public Agenda Online—Polling data on a wide array of topics and issues (https://www.publicagenda.org).
- National Criminal Justice Reference Service—Data, reports, and links from the Department of Justice on topics related to criminology and corrections (https://www.ncjrs.gov).
- National Opinion Research Center—This center at the University of Chicago indexes studies on a wide variety of topics from aging to energy consumption to substance abuse (http://www.norc.uchicago.edu).
- Pew Global Attitudes Project—This ambitious project from the Pew Research Center presents the results of more than 90,000 interviews in 50 countries (https://pewglobal.org).
- Population Reference Bureau—Articles, datasheets, and lesson plans on topics related to the study of population (https://www.prb.org).
- Federal Government and Statistical Agencies (https://nces.ed.gov /partners/fedstat.asp)—This site has links to a large number of government statistic sites.
- First Measured Century—This companion website to a three-hour PBS special with Ben Wattenberg presents information on social trends in the twentieth century (http://www.pbs.org/fmc/index.htm).
- Institute for Social Research—Results of research studies done at this center at the University of Michigan. Topics range from attitudes toward cell phones, to why some women don't enter careers in math and science, to how wealth influences people's experiences in their last year of life (https://www.isr.umich.edu).
- U.S. Vital Record Information—Allows you to access certain public records (https://usvitalrecords.org).

Your college or university library may also have special collections of primary sources, particularly those related to the school, its surroundings, and famous people in the area.

👉 **tip 3e**

Primary Source Citations

There so many types of primary sources that it is often difficult to determine what publication information you need to gather. Part VI, "MLA and APA Documentation Systems," of this text covers quite a few primary sources you are most likely to come across in your research.

internet activity 3f **Find Primary Sources**

Visit a number of the sites for primary sources listed previously, and play with the search features to find sources relating to your issue. What kinds of material do your selected sites search? Historical? Literary? Legal? Business? Medical? What sites best meet your needs for your issue?

Hal decides to use several primary documents in his research project: (1) laws governing employees' rights to privacy; (2) a survey of employers completed by the American Management Association; and (3) interviews with both employees and supervisors at his company. He found several transcripts of court cases at the Electronic Frontier Foundation and one at Find Law, which covered the 2003 ruling against a Nationwide Insurance employee's complaint about invasion of his workplace privacy.

Find and Use Government Sources

These days it is very easy to find government-printed brochures and guides, copies of Senate and House reports, and bills. Don't be intimidated by the format of these documents. Most are searchable for keywords even though they can be tricky to cite. You can search for particular documents by title on any search engine, but visit the following sites to browse and conduct deeper searches.

- USA Government (https://www.usa.gov) is the U.S. Government's official website with access to consumer brochures, information on taxes, family care, and Internet security, among dozens of other categories. You can also find historical documents, statistics, maps, and links to various government agency libraries, including the Pentagon's.
- The Library of Congress https://www.congress.gov offers links to bills, the Congressional Record, treaties, and other government research.
- The Catalog of U.S. Government Publications (https://catalog.gpo.gov) provides access to and information about government publications. Many of the documents are online, but the search features are not easy to use. You'll need to follow its search tips for the best results.
- The White House website (https://www.whitehouse.gov) offers links to many primary sources as well.
- The U.S. National Archives website (https://www.archives.gov) houses 80 years' worth of government documents including naturalization and war records.

Gathering publication information for government publications can be difficult. These documents are often written without a clear indication of author, title, publisher, or copyright date. Look for available clues, and give as much information as possible, including the URL and date accessed. In general, cite what you can find, in the order listed here. Not all government sources will have all of these items.

Source Information: Government Document

Name of government: _____

Name of agency: _____

Document title (italicized): _____

If applicable, number and session of Congress; type and number of publication: _____

Title of publication: _____

Name of editor or compiler of publication: _____

Publisher, date of publication: _____

Pertinent page numbers (if available): _____

Title of online collection (italicized): _____

Date of posting or most recent update (if available): _____

Name of project or reference database (italicized): _____

Name of sponsoring institution (e.g., Lib. of Congress): _____

Electronic address: _____

---

internet activity 3g Find Government Sources

Using the sites given above, perform keyword searches for government sources relating to your issue.

Find and Use Multimedia Sources

From audio transcripts of a president's inauguration speech, to videos of protestors in Iran, to podcast lectures of a professor at Stanford, to blogs of newspaper columnists, to the latest images of Mars craters, there is a host of valuable resources online that goes beyond print. Millions of viewers use YouTube to find serious lectures, music, and film clips, along with silly videos and instructional videos. Websites such as NPR and PBS have archives of video, and as of this printing, PBS is offering full-length episodes of some of its programs. Many libraries also subscribe to full-series PBS programs. The Library of Congress's (LOC) American Memory Project (http://memory .loc.gov/ammem/index.html) houses audio and video interviews with former slaves, documentary footage of Thomas Edison at work, and many other marvels of early film and recording technology.

The U.S. National Archives (https://www.archives.gov) has its own YouTube channel. Movies Found Online (http://www.makeuseof.com/dir /moviesfoundonline) offers access to free public-domain documentaries as does the Internet Archive (https://archive.org/), which also provides millions of books, software, and other resources. Of course, news services such as BBC and CNN have live news feeds featuring breaking news around the world. FreeDocumentaries.org offers full viewing documentaries.

You will need to gather the following publication information for videos found on the Internet covering topics from slavery to animal activism.

Source Information: Video Clip

Author's last name, first name OR corporate/institutional author name, if available: _____

Title of document or file: _____

Document date OR date of last revision: _____

Title of larger website in which clip is located: _____

Name of hosting library or agency (if appropriate): _____

URL: _____

In Chapter 12, "Enhance Your Argument with Visuals," you will learn about the power that visual images can add to your argument. There are many repositories of photographs, drawings, artwork, and maps on the Internet. Be sure to document your images properly (see the discussion in Chapter 12 and Appendices A and B). Some wonderful sources of images are:

- Digital History (www.digitalhistory.uh.edu). A link to images is provided.
- Image searches at Google (https://images.google.com), Bing (https:// www.bing.com/), and Yahoo! (https://images.search.yahoo.com). Try them both as they offer different advanced search options based on color, size, date, and so on.
- National Geographic Photography (https://nationalgeographic.com /photography).
- The New York Public Library Digital Gallery (https://digitalcollections .nypl.org).
- Pulitzer Prize winners for photography (https://pulitzer.org/prize -winners-categories).

You will need to gather the following publication information for an image:

> ### Source Information: Image
> Artist name: _____
> Title of the work (italicized): _____
> Date it was created: _____
>
> *For artworks, include*
> Dimensions of the work: _____
> Repository, museum, or owner: _____
> City or country of origin: _____

Also, include all information for the web page on which your image was found.

Podcasts of all sorts are popular on the Internet. Podcast Alley (http://www .podcastalley.com) is one of the sources that can help you find podcasts on dozens of topics from the arts, to politics, to the news, which you can download to your smartphone or listen to on your computer. Some of the most reputable podcasts are those that come from syndicated shows such as *Face the Nation* and the news sites. You can subscribe to many podcast feeds as well. You can also perform a keyword search with your search engine as follows: inurl:podcast "your keyword." Hal tried this search with the keywords "workplace privacy" and found several podcasts covering the workplace privacy debates in California.

You will need to gather the following publication information for a podcast:

> ### Source Information: Podcast
> Name of author, host, or producer (if available): _____
> Title of podcast: _____
> Date of podcast: _____
> Podcast series: _____
> Title of podcast show (if different from title of podcast): _____
> Title of larger site (if available): _____
> URL: _____

Blogs are online journals that focus on any topic imaginable. Many news columnists have blogs affiliated with their news sites. For example, the *New York Times* has blogs covering Afghanistan, Pakistan, and Iraq reportage; the arts scene; business mergers and acquisitions; medical science; the latest techno-logical trends; and photographic, visual, and multimedia reporting (http://www.nytimes.com/interactive/blogs/directory.html).

Although many blogs are useful and entertaining, you will need to be care-ful about what blog information you use in your argument. Do you care what the man on the street in Anchorage thinks about the cost of college tuition? You might, but whether you want to cite information from his blog will be determined by the scope of your argument.

You will need to gather the following publication information for a blog entry:

Source Information: Blog Entry

Author: _____

Title of the entry: _____

Title of the blog (italicized): _____

Name of the blog host: _____

Date:_____

URL: _____

---

internet activity 3h Find Multimedia Sources

Find images that will support your issue. Find audio and video links of speeches, press conferences, or breaking news. Finally, find a blog that discusses your issue. How reputable do these sources feel? In Chapter 4, "Evaluate and Engage with Your Sources," you will learn how to evaluate Web content, but for now, base your response on how the host site is organized, how neutral the coverage of events are, how the words are or the speech is presented, or how the tone of the blog feels. Would you use these sources in your argument? Why or why not?

Find Books

It may seem odd that books are listed last in this chapter. It's not that we don't think books are important; it's just that, for most issues, your readers are look-ing for the most current, up-to-date information. It can take years from con-ception to printing to make a book available. An issue can change a lot in a few years. For very current issues, books may not be the way to go. For issues that have a history or that will always be on the table (child care, human and animal rights, some environmental issues, etc.), older books can still be useful in establishing a context or background for the reader. In this section, we will cover how to find books in brick-and-mortar libraries and in virtual libraries.

Find Books in Libraries

Most libraries have similar catalogs. You can search for books by title, author, or subject. Hal's next step is to look for books in his school's library. He will perform the same search in his local public library as well. Hal is looking for books that are fairly current.

Hal decides to search by subject and types his search term "workplace privacy" into the library catalogue. This term doesn't yield any results, so he tries the more general term "privacy" (see Figure 3.8). His library has 18 titles on the subject of the right of privacy, not so many that he needs to narrow his search further. He clicks on the subject "Privacy, Right of" and scans the titles for books that meet his criteria of being predominantly about privacy in the workplace and specifically about emails and Internet usage.

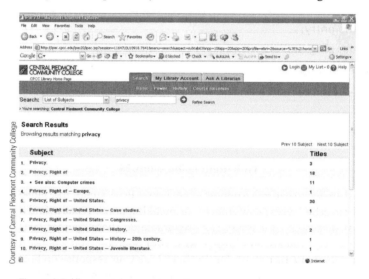

Figure 3.8 Library catalog search results

Hal finds a couple of sources, and depending on how much material he feels is useful in each one, he either photocopies the useful pages or checks out the book to review later.

You will need to gather the following publication information for books:

Source Information: Book

Author(s) or editor(s): _____

Title of the book (italicized): _____

Edition (if applicable): _____

Name of publisher: _____

Year published: _____

If you are using an essay from a book, collect the following publication information:

Source Information: Essay from Book

Author(s) of the essay: _____

Title of the essay (in quotation marks): _____

Title of the book (italicized): _____

Editor(s) of the book: _____

Edition (if applicable): _____

Name of publisher: _____

Year published: _____

Page numbers of essay: _____

---

your turn 3b ▶ **GET STARTED** **Find Books in Libraries**

Find two books on your topic. Make sure that they have been published within the past five years. Copy all information that you would need to find the book again, including the call number, which indicates where on the shelves to find the book.

Find Books on the Internet

Even large colleges may have limited library space. Students can find ebooks in the library catalog and have access to many databases with more current information that is frequently updated. The number of books available electronically is growing rapidly, which is great for libraries with space limitations. Library resources such as the *Opposing Viewpoints* database allow readers to access chapters and essays from hundreds of titles covering every issue imaginable.

The *Opposing Viewpoints* database houses a collection of articles, book chapters, and other types of documents organized by subject. The title is a bit misleading: The articles are wide ranging, not just pro-subject and con-subject. Your professors are not looking for you to find material supporting only your side and the opposing side; this structure implies that there are only two sides to each issue, which, of course, is nowhere near reality for most argumentative issues.

your turn 3c ▶ **GET STARTED Find Books in the Opposing Viewpoints Database**

Access your library's *Opposing Viewpoints* database or any other database available to you to find books or book essays on your issue. Find as many viewpoints as possible.

Most libraries require a library card to access their **ebooks.** Ebooks are just like print books, except they can be searched and read online. Many times, you cannot copy from them, though, and must take notes manually.

Books can also be found on the Internet, the majority of these titles being out of copyright. Project Gutenberg (https://www.gutenberg.org) and ManyBooks.net (http://manybooks.net) offer thousands of books that can be downloaded or read online. The Internet Sacred Text Archive (http://www.sacred-texts.com) houses full-text books on every religion imaginable. For more recent scholarship, though, you can read significant chunks of some current titles at Google Books.

Research can seem daunting. There are so many resources available to us that this wealth of riches can seem more of a curse, and it is tempting to rely on Google and the first few hits that match our search terms. But take the extra time to go beyond the first page of search engine hits or Wikipedia entries. By searching for types of sources that you may not normally consider, such as blogs, documentaries, or news feeds, you will open your research up to paths that will provide you with many rewards.

Reflect and Apply

1. In what ways can you use encyclopedias and basic reference sources to help orient you to your issue and its parameters, vocabulary, and viewpoints?

2. Much of Chapter 3 is devoted to finding sources through Internet searches. How are you using primary sources to gain insight into different facets of your issue? What sources are you using to find secondary material that is academically acceptable?

3. How are you using your school's research databases? Are there databases that seem to be consistently useful in researching your issue?

4. How will you manage your materials as you find them? What organizational system are you using to efficiently track your notes from print sources?

5. How are you keeping track of bibliographic information as you find it? How are you managing image, video, and audio sources along with their publication information so you can access it all readily?

KEEPING IT LOCAL

Playing a game of solitaire on your computer during work?
Scanning social media in between responding to text messages?
Sending personal emails from your office?

ALL OF THESE activities can be monitored by your boss and can get you fired. Whether you work in a small local company or a sprawling national or even global firm, you need to know your rights as an employee. Not asking can get you in trouble. But performing better on your job requires work on your part as well, work that includes knowing where to look for answers. Knowing how to develop a research plan and how to find the sources you need to answer questions about your privacy rights and anything else that pertains to your employment is crucial to your job success. Books, journals, Internet sites, and libraries all have valuable information, if you know where and how to look for it.

Research is at the heart of your argument. Your credibility and support rest on the thoroughness of your research strategies. Unlike some college skills, research is one skill that you will use in every part of your life: at school, at work, and even while addressing the needs of your community. What research sources will work for your needs? Can you use multimedia sources to help you address a problem at work? Will newspapers provide the support you need to solve a neighborhood dispute?

CHAPTER 4

Evaluate and Engage with Your Sources

Learning Objectives

By working through this chapter, you will be able to

- critically analyze a reading.
- take effective notes.
- critically evaluate Internet sites, articles, and books.
- evaluate primary sources.
- effectively incorporate sources into a writing.
- properly cite quotations.
- effectively summarize and paraphrase sources.
- properly cite summaries and paraphrases.

This morning you sat down to read the newspaper while you ate break-fast. An article in the financial section about employees' rights caught your attention. The author of the article made some claims that didn't seem accurate to you. Later in the day, you tried to find sources that supported the author's claim but couldn't find anything. One database search uncovered several studies that seemed promising. As you began reading, however, you realized that one study used so much jargon that you couldn't understand it at all. Another report was 50 pages long. Although the title looked promising, you just didn't have time to read the entire report. Frustrated, you gave up.

All Illustrations by iStock.com/A-digit

COMMUNITY

School-Academic

Workplace

Family-Household

Neighborhood

Social-Cultural

Consumer

Concerned Citizen

TOPIC: Computer Usage

ISSUE: Privacy and Computer Use

AUDIENCE: Business Ethics Professor

CLAIM: Workplace electronic monitoring practices should be revealed to employees through company policies.

Chapter 3, "Develop a Research Plan," focused on introducing the various types of resources available to you and on how to find them. Chapter 4 will focus on how to evaluate and read the various types of resources. You will also learn how to incorporate information from those sources into your writing and how to cite them appropriately. For full information on creating a works cited page for your researched report or essay in Modern Language Association (MLA) and American Psychological Association (APA) formats, see Part VI, "MLA and APA Documentation Systems."

As you find materials, you will need to evaluate their accuracy and their usefulness for your argument.

Take Notes, Read Critically, and Evaluate Internet Sites

In Chapter 3, "Develop a Research Plan," we followed Hal's research strategies as he found a wealth of information on electronic privacy in the workplace on the Internet. Finding material, though, is only the beginning. Now he must evaluate the sources and determine what he needs to use in his argument. Internet sources are easy to find but not always as easy to evaluate as print sources.

Hal's method of note-taking for Internet sources is a good one. He pastes the information he finds useful into a document he saves as "Workplace Privacy Notes." Hal is careful to keep track of information he copies verbatim so that he does not accidentally plagiarize it. His favorite method is to leave all verbatim sources in a different font color so that he does not forget that the material is not his original wording. He will keep all of the research he gathers from electronic sources in a folder he saves on his computer. He will also keep a folder for print sources that he photocopies and for newspaper clippings, brochures, and so on.

There are also online services that allow you to save links to web pages. Some of these tools even allow you to clip, highlight, and write comments on your clippings, gathering them all in one spot. There are many online organizational tools that can help you keep track of your research, for example, Zotero.org.

As he gathers electronic sources, Hal makes sure to comment on *why* he saved this material and *how* he thinks he may use it. Of course, how and why may change over the course of his research, but always determining the reason for keeping a source will keep him from gathering material that will not be of any use. Hal also remembers to copy any publication information that he will need later to document the sources he uses in his paper. Remember to keep track of links to websites.

Critically Read Material on the Internet

Narrowing his search still left Hal with thousands of results, but the first one he looked at, "E-Mail Privacy in the Workplace," seemed promising. Now he had to decide not only if the information provided on the site was useful but also if it was **credible**. We all know that, along with the wonderfully useful information on the Web, there is also a lot of garbage. Reading critically will help you sort through it all. The first step Hal took when he accessed the site was to determine its credibility.

Figure 4.1 Critically reading content on the Internet is the first step you can take when determining credibility.

Hal asked himself a few questions about the article "E-Mail Privacy in the Workplace." The first step Hal took was to determine who sponsored the web page. By clicking on the "About" link, he found that the authors of the site are concerned with providing accurate information to those working in the security industry. They provide only articles that are well-researched, so that decisions based on their material would meet current security laws. Hal felt that this site, although not geared toward employees of companies, had solid, trustworthy information about employees' rights to email privacy, so he marked the site for further reference.

When you are accessing unfamiliar websites, it is best to evaluate them using a series of questions like the ones below. Taking this precaution will ensure that you have credible material to use in your argument.

Evaluate Internet Sites

The following checklist provides some important questions you should ask about Internet sources before you use them.

Internet Evaluation Checklist

☐ **Author of Page/Site**

Who is the author of the page or source? Can you contact them or is there an "About Us" tab with author details? Is the author credible? Have they published other material on the topic or are they considered experts in their field?

☐ **Extreme Bias**

Chapter 5, "Read Critically and Avoid Fallacies," will discuss bias further, but ask if the bias exhibited in the web source exceeds what you feel comfortable with. In other words, is there evidence of racism, sexism, or extreme political or religious views?

☐ **Up to Date**

When was the site or source last updated? Are there links to the latest publications or sites?

☐ **Navigation**

Do all links to other sites work? Do images and files open quickly? Are there any dead links or dead ends in the site itself?

internet activity 4a **Evaluate Internet Sites**

Using the Internet Evaluation Checklist, evaluate one of the sources you found for Internet Activity 3d. Is it a credible source? Why or why not?

Take Notes, Read Critically, and Evaluate Articles

The Computer Age has made research worlds easier than it was even 20 years ago. Along with the advantages of researching and writing with computers are some disadvantages that can cause headaches. There are still many sources, particularly older ones, that are not accessible either through library databases or on the Internet. Let's address journal articles that you have accessed in print (paper) journals on the library shelves that you cannot find online or in your library's databases.

The better way to take notes is to photocopy the article you want, making sure that all the needed publication information is printed somewhere on the photocopied pages, and to write your notes directly on the article itself. Highlight those passages that you think are useful, writing notes in the margins about how to use this material or making note of questions you need to ask, words to look up, or other sources to gather. Keep these photocopies in a folder, so that they will be available when you are ready to write the report.

So that's easy enough. You'd think, then, that taking notes on articles you have downloaded to your own computer would be even easier. After all, there is no retyping to do—you can use your computer's cut-and-paste function to copy material from the original article to your own document.

But there are several errors that writers can make during this process, some of them costly. To avoid errors while taking notes on computer documents, follow the steps in the following "Careful Note-Taking Checklist."

Careful Note-Taking Checklist

- ☐ Have you made sure to differentiate your own ideas from the ideas you have borrowed? When pasting material from the original source, remember to highlight this material in some way to indicate to yourself later that this material is not based on your own ideas or words. Some people, like Hal, type all their original ideas in a different color or font to separate them from the information borrowed from an article. Forgetting to give credit to borrowed material, whether intentionally or accidentally, will be viewed as **plagiarism**, cheating by using the work of others as your own. (See the tips for avoiding plagiarism at the end of this chapter.)

- ☐ Have you commented on your sources? Writers frequently paste information into their own document and then later have no idea what this information means or why they saved it. Always make comments on the copied material, discussing what its function will be in the argument and why it is important. For example, will it support your own claims or provide an illustration of an opposing viewpoint?

- ☐ Have you included documentation for all sources? Another costly error is neglecting to include documentation for where you retrieved the material. A simple note in parentheses as to the origin of the source will save you time tracking down a source later, and sometimes saves you from having to leave out a source because you cannot document it.

Read Articles Critically

Articles, whether accessed through an online database or elsewhere, are originally published in academic journals, magazines, or newspapers. Understanding the differences between the sources can help you better understand the articles they contain. Although magazines and journals share similarities, a journal differs from a magazine in several ways. Both types of periodicals can be directed toward a particular audience. For example, the 2012 issue of *IUP Journal of Chemistry* includes the article "Arsenic Removal from Potable Water Using Copolymer Resin-III Derived From P-Cresol." The article's abstract offers the following:

Copolymer was synthesized by condensation of p-Cresol (p-C) and Adipamide (A) with Formaldehyde (F) in the presence of 2M HCl as catalyst with 4:1:5 molar ratios of reacting monomers. Water is the most important constituent of our body. Thus, its quality should be good and perfect because it directly affects our health. Water pollution due to arsenic leaching is one of the biggest problems all over the world. Ion-exchange studies of this purified copolymer resin were carried out for As^{3+} ions. 'A' proved to be a selective chelating ion-exchange copolymer for certain metals. Chelating ion exchange properties of this copolymer were studied for As^{3+} ions. Batch equilibrium method was employed to study the selectivity of metal ion uptake involving the measurements of the distribution of a given metal ion between the polymer sample and a solution containing the metal ion. The study was carried out over a wide pH range and in media of various ionic strengths. The copolymer showed a higher selectivity for As^{3+} ions.

Compare the language from the technical journal to that used in a magazine aimed at the general reader in the article about arsenic in the drinking water, "Textile Dyeing Industry an Environmental Hazard," in the magazine *Natural Science*.

Color is the main attraction of any fabric. No matter how excellent its constitution, if unsuitably colored it is bound to be a failure as a commercial fabric. Manufacture and use of synthetic dyes for fabric dyeing has therefore become a massive industry today [. . .] Synthetic dyes have provided a wide range of colorfast, bright hues. However their toxic nature has become a cause of grave concern to environmentalists. Use of synthetic dyes has an adverse effect on all forms of life.

Kant, Rita. "Textile Dyeing Industry an Environmental Hazard." *Natural Science*, vol. 4, no. 1, 2012, pp. 22–26.

You can easily see the difference—the *IUP Journal of Chemistry* article is more technical, using **jargon**, language that is used in a specific field and may be unfamiliar to those outside the field. Besides the language difference, journal articles are written by scholars or industry experts. The journals themselves are often peer reviewed, which means the articles are reviewed by other experts in the field before they are printed. Journals are also usually sponsored by a university or organization.

Magazines, on the other hand, are written for the everyday reader. Even someone with little familiarity with the topic of drinking water contamination would be able to read and understand the magazine article published in *Natural Science*. Less technical in nature, magazine articles are often written by freelance writers with little experience in the area about which they are writing. Your project may include information from both journal and magazine articles, depending on the assignment's requirements.

Finally, newspapers are usually produced daily. Those with online versions often provide updates during the day. They feature articles on crime and politics, along with human interest stories. Editorials and opinion pieces express the views of individuals, whereas the news stories themselves are mainly reportage of events.

None of these three types of periodicals are free of bias. **Bias** refers to the particular viewpoint or slant that an author or a publication leans toward. Bias is neither good nor bad, as readers can choose to read a publication or not depending on their own interests, beliefs, and values. A good researcher/writer understands that biases exist and is careful to select sources that are not bigoted, misleading, or downright false.

Reading Strategies for Longer Articles

A few reading strategies will make your time spent reading longer articles both more efficient and successful. At this stage, you are trying to quickly determine if an article is useful to you. Use the following questions to aid you in making that determination.

Initial Assessment Checklist

- ☐ Is there an **abstract**? An abstract is a brief overview of the author's argument, usually outlining the article's thesis and main points of support. Reading the abstract is no substitute for reading the full article, but the abstract will tell you at a glance if the article fits your needs.

- ☐ If no abstract exists, can you determine what the author's argument is? Although critical articles are longer than essays you may write, there still should be a clear beginning (with a thesis statement within the first one to three paragraphs), a body with supporting ideas, and a conclusion. Read the introduction and the conclusion for the main idea—in a critical article, the author's argument should be in one if not both places.

☐ Scan the article subheadings and any graphics (tables, charts, etc.). Being aware of how the author has organized the material into sections can help you both navigate and understand the article more easily. Tables and other graphic organizers can also help you understand the article's material.

☐ Is there a bibliography or footnotes? Although you should not necessarily reject an article that does not have a works cited page or a bibliography of further reading, the appearance of one is a bonus, as it gives additional avenues of research.

☐ Look up all words that keep you from understanding the article. Most journals are trade or field specific. They are not written for the general reader but for those already in the field; the vocabulary, therefore, can be a stumbling block. The language and vocabulary of a scholarly article may be unfamiliar to you, but the writing should not be so dense that you cannot read it at all. If you cannot comfortably read *most* of an article, then reject it in favor of an article that is easier to comprehend.

That may look like a lot of steps to take before you actually read an article, but following them will save you a great deal of time. After assessing your article, you will be able to determine if it is right for your purposes instead of reading 20 pages only to come to the same conclusion.

Using the Initial Assessment Checklist, the first step Hal takes when he is ready to review his journal articles is to look for an abstract. The article on email privacy does not have an abstract, so Hal continues to the second step and reads the introductory paragraphs and conclusion. At the end of the second paragraph, he finds the article's claim: "This article examines the employer/employee workplace privacy relationship, identifies the existing federal and state law governing workplace privacy, and discusses the rapidly developing monitoring software market."

Hal's next step is to scan the article subheadings and any graphics (tables, charts, etc.). At the end of the article is a list of references and a brief biography of the author, including contact information. The inclusion of references and author contact information is reassuring to Hal as is the easy-to-read format and language of the article. This one is a keeper. Hal decides that this article is worth reading and adds its publication information to his bibliography file.

But where do you find the elements to help you assess a journal article? Pages 87–88 include examples of these elements—Abstract, Key Words, Conclusion, and Works Cited—from an article in a humanities journal. The annotations in the margins identify key parts.

The Carnivalesque in Nathaniel Hawthorne's *The Scarlet Letter*

by Hossein Pirnajmuddin and Omid Amani

ABSTRACT: This study sets to examine the applicability of Bakhtin's theory of the carnivalesque to Nathaniel Hawthorne's *The Scarlet Letter*.

Abstracts are useful for identifying the central claim of the author's argument and often provide an explanation of how the claim is going to be supported. They can also set the context for the claim.

Along with the abstract, some journals require a list of keywords. Pay attention to these keywords as they not only help you grasp the scope of the article, but can also help you when you are performing your own searches.

The canonical novel of the American literature published in the middle of the nineteenth century portrays the genesis of the American Puritan culture, while the polyphonic nature of the novel, it is argued, exposes the rifts of and the grotesqueness of this culture.

Key Words: Nathaniel Hawthorne, *The Scarlet Letter*, Bakhtin, Carnivalesque, Polyphony, Heteroglossia, Grotesque

Conclusion

The conclusion of most arguments in the humanities often restates the initial claim.

Nathaniel Hawthorne's *The Scarlet Letter* deftly addresses the Puritan culture of the seventeenth-century America as, to use Bakhtin's terms, a "monological culture." Hawthorne's novel is, among other things, the fact that laughter and the spirit of carnival cannot be totally repressed even in the most ideological and monological cultures. Although the writer apparently creates a Romantic grotesque, that is, one of dark, gloomy monstrosities, to intimate the distorted nature of the society he portrays, the implication is that the Bakhtinian conception of the grotesque, one associated with "light", with the carnivalesque, capable of subverting the rule of 'darkness,' 'decrowning' it, is in the background too (Bakhtin 41).

Works Cited

Adamson, Joseph. "Guardian of the 'Inmost Me': Hawthorne and Shame." *Scenes of Shame: Psychoanalysis, Shame, and Writing.* Eds. Joseph Adamson and Hilary Clark. State U of New York P, 1999. pp. 53–82.

Arac, Jonathan. "Hawthorne and the Aesthetics of American Romance." *The Cambridge History of The American Novel.* Eds. Leonard Cassuto et al. Cambridge UP, 2011. pp. 135–150.

A works cited, references, or bibliography can provide additional sources, and depending on the format of the source, even links to other materials that can help you write your argument.

> **your turn** 4a ▸ **Conduct an Initial Assessment of Your Articles**
>
> Using the Initial Assessment Checklist, find a source and determine if it is right for your argument. Which of the steps helped you make a decision?

The next set of questions will help you make sense of articles you have determined will be useful. You need to be able to find the author's main argument(s) and the examples being used to support the argument(s). You should also be able to determine the article's strengths and weaknesses. Use these steps to find the main ideas and examples.

Reading Checklist

- ☐ Look for the main idea. If the thesis cannot be found on the first page, write the main idea at the top of your photocopied or saved article for easy reference. (If you do find the thesis on the first page, simply highlight it.)

- ☐ What evidence is the author offering to support his or her argument(s)? If an article is very long, there may be subsections, titled or not, that indicate movement from one example (or argument, if the author has more than one) to another. Look for these. Skim quickly, reading only the first and last sentences of each paragraph as you look for ideas and arguments. When you find something particularly useful, read the entire paragraph to make sure you are not reading anything out of context.

- ☐ Make notes throughout. Highlighting a passage is great, but if there are no comments made next to the passage, chances are good that, when you are ready to write your paper, you may not remember what struck you as important when you highlighted it.

- ☐ What are the article's strengths and weaknesses? Skim through several articles, reading the bibliographies and noting which sources are mentioned frequently. These are the sources you should definitely read. They will serve as touchstones by which to gauge the arguments of the articles you've selected. This is not to say that all of your articles need to agree with your touchstone articles. However, the touchstone articles will give you some idea of the general trends of thought concerning a topic, and they will allow you to judge if your selected article is too far off base to be reasonably considered.

- ☐ Come to a conclusion about the author's arguments. Do you agree or disagree? Do you see how the article can be used in any part of your own essay? Do you agree wholeheartedly and therefore can use the article as support for your own thesis? Do you disagree and want to use the article as an argument you wish to rebut (destroy)? Is the author's idea useful but limited? Maybe the author doesn't take an idea as far as you would like to take it?

your turn 4b ▸ **Read the Articles You've Selected**

Using the Reading Checklist, skim quickly through the article you evaluated from Your Turn 4a, or if that article did not work, select a new one. What is the author's claim? What support is provided by the article? What are the article's strengths and weaknesses? What is your final opinion of the article? Is it one you can use effectively in your argument? Why or why not?

Evaluate Articles

Before you add information from that article to your argument, make sure that you have determined that it is credible. Is your source actually an essay from a college student? A graduate student may have written a solid researched argument on homelessness, but your professor is undoubtedly looking for material that is more expert in scope. Research the author of the article, whether it is in a magazine, a website, or a scholarly journal. Answer the following questions before using any article:

Article Credibility Checklist

- ☐ Who is the author? Conduct a quick Internet search to determine if the author has published anything else on the topic. With whom is the author affiliated (an academic institution, or an industrial or business institution, for example)? Is there any scandal surrounding the author's integrity that may throw suspicion on his or her work?
- ☐ What is the reputation of the venue (periodical or site) in which the article is published?
- ☐ How current or reputable is the information cited in the article? A bibliography is not always necessary, particularly if original research is being conducted, but it helps to see what sources the author uses to support his or her argument.

Take Notes and Read Books Critically

So now, like Hal, you've completed your review of the library's catalog and you've got a long list of books you think may be useful in your research project. You gather them and set them all out on a table in front of you. Now what? Well, what you shouldn't do is take them all home with you. Do a cursory inspection of their tables of contents and their indexes; read a bit of the authors' prefaces or introductions. Make sure that you are not aggravating your tennis elbow unnecessarily by lugging 15 pounds of books to your car. Select books that seem promising. Are there any chapters or essays specifically on your topic, or at least near enough? Do your search terms appear in the index? Is the book's age appropriate? For some projects, older books may be fine, but for others more current material is preferable. Once you've made your selection, save yourself a great deal of time by using the FLOI method, discussed next.

The **FLOI method** will help you investigate books in a consistent manner and will save you time.

First: Read the author's introduction or preface. Read the first chapter looking for a thesis or a main argument.

Last: Read the final chapter to find out the author's conclusion and to make sure it is summarizing what you thought was going to be proven.

Outside: Look at those materials that are outside the text. The table of contents and the index will direct you to supporting examples and illustrations of the book's thesis. The dust jacket can be very helpful, providing a brief overview of the author's intent. Skim through any maps, appendices, glossaries, tables, or charts.

Inside: At this point, you can take one of two steps. If you have plenty of time, or the book appears to warrant it, you can read the entire book. Most of the time, however, it will suffice for you to skim the text carefully, looking for words and phrases that pop out—you'll notice that the things that catch your attention are the good examples, things that are interesting to you that you can use in your report.

> **your turn 4c** ▶ **GET STARTED Use the FLOI Method to Skim a Book**
>
> Use one of the books you found for Your Turn 3b, and skim it using the FLOI method.
>
> 1. First: Skim the preface and any other introductory material, and record the author's claim or main point.
> 2. Last: Read the last chapter. How does the author conclude the argument? Are you surprised by the conclusion? Is it what you thought it would be based on the preface?
> 3. Outside: Skim through the table of contents and the index. List any of your search terms or additional topics of interest that are covered. Flip through the book looking for graphs, charts, or illustrations. Are they clear and easy to understand? Do they offer any insights into your topic?
> 4. Inside: Does the book warrant your time reading it, will skimming suffice, or is the book not a good match for your subject?

Take Notes and Evaluate Primary Sources

Hal gathered a large number of primary sources, including interviews, documentaries, acts, and laws. Before he uses any of them, he asks himself a series of questions to determine who produced the source, why, for what audience, and under what circumstances.

Primary Sources Checklist

- ☐ Who created the source and why? Was it created through a spur-of-the-moment act, a routine transaction, or a thoughtful, deliberate process?
- ☐ Did the recorder have firsthand knowledge of the event? Or did the recorder report what others saw and heard?
- ☐ Was the recorder a neutral party, or did the creator have opinions or interests that might have influenced what was recorded?
- ☐ Did the recorder produce the source for personal use, for one or more individuals, or for a large audience?
- ☐ Was the source meant to be public or private?
- ☐ Did the recorder wish to inform or persuade others? (Check the words in the source. The words may tell you whether the recorder was trying to be objective or persuasive.)
- ☐ Did the recorder have reasons to be honest or dishonest?
- ☐ Was the information recorded during the event, immediately after the event, or after some lapse of time? How large a lapse of time?

Source: Questions for Analyzing Primary Sources, Library of Congress https://www.loc.gov /teachers/usingprimarysources/guides.html.

internet activity 4b Evaluate Primary Sources

Select one primary source you gathered in Internet Activity 3f. Answer the eight questions above about your source to determine its credibility.

Introduce and Comment on Sources

One of the more difficult aspects of writing any sort of research report is smoothly incorporating your own ideas on a subject with ideas you've gathered from other sources, such as newspaper articles, books, a television documentary, or a web page. It's very important to be clear about what material in your report is yours and what comes from an outside source. You must make sure that any ideas you use, whether you are quoting a source verbatim or paraphrasing, are attributed to their original author.

Three steps should be followed when using source material, either quoted or paraphrased:

1. Introduce the source, also known as *source attribution*.
2. Provide the source.
3. Cite the source.

It is often best to introduce the author of your source material, especially if you are paraphrasing and likely to confuse source material with your own original ideas. The phrases used to introduce sources are called **attributive phrases or statements**. An attributive statement tells the reader who is being cited. It may indicate the author's name and credentials, the title of the source, and/or any helpful background information. Here are some examples of attributive words:

accepts	*considers*	*explains*	*rejects*	*acknowledges*
affirms	*argues*	*asserts*	*contradicts*	*adds*
contrasts	*criticizes*	*declares*	*interprets*	*shows*
defends	*lists*	*states*	*believes*	*denies*
maintains	*stresses*	*cautions*	*describes*	*outlines*
suggests	*claims*	*disagrees*	*points out*	*supports*
compares	*discusses*	*praises*	*concludes*	*emphasizes*
proposes	*verifies*	*confirms*	*enumerates*	*confutes*

The first time you introduce a source, you should provide the first and last name of the author you are citing. It is also helpful to give the author's credentials.

> David Solomon, the leading critic of Ira Levin's novels, argues . . .

> In *Rosemary's Offspring*, David Solomon's recent book of essays on Levin's novels, he explains . . .

In subsequent references to the author, you may just use the last name.

> Solomon defends . . .

If there is no author, you should introduce the source by a title.

> According to the "Food and Nutrition" page on the USDA website, nutrition is . . .

> The article in *The New York Times*, "Fowl Play on Chicken Farms," states . . .

Never include website addresses within the text of the paper; these will appear on the Works Cited page.

your turn 4d ▸ PRACTICE Introduce Sources

Select three passages from this excerpt from "Notification, an Important Safeguard against the Improper Use of Surveillance" by F. Boehm and P. de Hert. Introduce the sources properly, using the list of attributive words or other words or phrases.

1. Introduction

The surveillance of individuals and the resulting collection of information are regarded by the security community as an effective tool to locate terrorists and other criminals. In addition to the establishment of crime-fighting databases, the travel behaviour of citizens is recorded, and telecommunication and internet data are required to be retained for possible use in investigations. Databases and information systems containing such data exist at both national and EU levels. Personal data are increasingly collected, analyzed and interlinked. This article examines the importance of the right of citizens to be informed that their data has been collected, or that they have been the subject of surveillance, by reference to current laws. It first provides a brief overview of the increasing surveillance measures at EU level, then analyzes the current notification requirements existing in the EU, and discusses the right of notification in the framework of the Council of Europe and the case-law of the ECtHR. With the proposed changes to EU data protection law in mind, an overview of potential future regulation in this field is then essayed.

2. Increased surveillance at EU level

Before discussing existing and potential notification rules, a brief impression of the current databases and systems of surveillance within the EU is instructive. Post 9/11 policy concepts, such as proposed in the Hague and the Stockholm programme led to an increase of systems developed to control various parts of our daily life. Surveillance thereby takes place at different levels: On the initiative of the EU, Member States implement the data retention directive to reinforce their police and secret service activities. At EU-level, so called anti-terrorism measures are increasingly often initiated: travellers are comprehensively checked when they enter EU territory and EU databases and information systems serving multiple purposes are installed to collect and analyze information (see further, Boehm 2012). In addition to databases serving police purposes (the Europol Information System) (EIS), the Schengen Information System (SIS) and the Customs Information System (CIS), databases initially installed to facilitate border control such as the Visa Information System (VIS) and Eurodac are increasingly used for surveillance purposes. In fact, almost all existing databases have multiple functionalities. The SIS for instance is a database in the framework of law enforcement and immigration control and collects data of third state and EU nationals. The CIS serves customs control purposes but also contains personal data of individuals suspected of illicit trafficking activities. The VIS serves the purpose of the exchange of visa data and entails information of third state nationals who apply for a visa to enter the EU. Plans to give law enforcement access to the VIS are under consideration. Eurodac stores fingerprint data of asylum seekers and should prevent that asylum seekers make multiple asylum applications in different Member States of the EU. The EIS and Eurojust's database entail data of criminals, but also of suspects, victims and witnesses. Frontex is the EU's border agency and collects data of third state nationals trying to pass the external borders.

The rise of techniques and databases developed in recent years touches therefore on different aspects of the daily life of citizens. Not only traditional criminals are targeted by such measurers, but also individuals not suspected of having committed a crime. A shift towards the preventive entry of citizens in databases serving police but also other purposes can be observed. The rights of individuals affected by such measures do not always keep up with this fast developing field of different surveillance techniques (Van Brakel and de Hert).

Source: Boehm, Franziska, and Paul De Hert. "Notification, an Important Safeguard against the Improper Use of Surveillance—Finally Recognized in Case Law and EU Law." *European Journal of Law and Technology*, vol. 3, no. 3, 2012.

Quote and Cite Quotations

When you use an author's exact words in your own writing, you are **quoting**. There are certain rules to follow to properly introduce, quote, and cite material that you take directly from a source.

First, you want to use direct quotes very sparingly—it is almost always better to put original material into your own words (see the discussion of paraphrasing below).

Occasionally, though, using a quote is the way to go. Save quotations for those times when there is no better way to say things, or for when you are citing laws, definitions, or comments that are best quoted in full to avoid confusion or misrepresentation.

Let's use the following excerpt from an Internet source as an example. The highlighted text is what Hal wants to use in his paper on privacy in the workplace.

Internet Privacy in the Workplace: The Grey Areas Between Monitoring and Private Virtual Spaces

Similarly in the corporate workplace, a 2007 survey by the American Management Association and the ePolicy Institute found that two-thirds of employers monitor their employees' website visits in order to prevent inappropriate surfing. And 65% use software to block

connections to websites deemed off limits for employees. This is a
27% increase since 2001 when the survey was first conducted.

Source: Chin, Eugenia. "Internet Privacy in the Workplace: The Grey Areas between
Monitoring and Private Virtual Spaces." *IS1103 Group 306*, 3 Mar. 2013, https://blog
.nus.edu.sg/2013is1103group306/2013/03/03/internet-privacy-in-the-workplace-the-grey
-areas-between-monitoring-and-private-virtual-spaces/

The paragraph that includes the desired material has survey results for
employer monitoring. Hal wants to use just the first item, and he decides to
quote it directly. Here is that highlighted information included in a paragraph
as a direct quote.

DIRECT QUOTE[1]

In 2007, the American Management Association and the ePolicy Institute
conducted a survey on the use of monitoring practices of employers.
The survey found that "two-thirds of employers monitor their employees' website visits in order to prevent inappropriate surfing" (Chin).
These results seem extremely high and indicate the widespread use of
monitoring software used in the workplace.

Notice how he introduces the quote by indicating that a survey was conducted by the American Management Association (AMA) and the ePolicy
Institute. He leads into the quote with the attributive "the survey found."
Then he begins his quote with the words "two-thirds" and ends where the
original sentence ends. Note that the quotation marks only surround the
quoted material, not the citation information in parentheses (highlighted).

After the quote, Hal comments on the information, helping the reader to
understand the importance of the quoted material to his argument. Never
just drop a quote into a paragraph without any explanation. Provide commentary that explains the cited material. Does it provide an illustration of
a point you've made? Does the quote represent confirmation of or disagreement with a point that you've made?

When you use an outside source, either as a direct quotation or as a paraphrase, you need to provide readers with information that tells them the origin of that source. This is done both internally and in a reference list at the
end of the paper. This reference list is usually called a **Works Cited** page and
includes only those sources that you have actually used in your report. To cite
the quote that Hal used from the previous Internet source, he will have to
put in parentheses at the end of the quoted material where that information
can be found. This information should be the same as it appears on the works
cited page; for the sample here, Hal's source had an author. But what if there
is no author to cite?

---

[1] These examples are in MLA format; both an MLA and an APA formatting guide is found in Part 6 "MLA and
APA Documentation Systems," of this text.

See the following sample works cited page:

Works Cited

Chin, Eugenia. "Internet Privacy in the Workplace: The Grey Areas between Monitoring and Private Virtual Spaces." IS1103 Group 306, 3 Mar. 2013, https://blog.nus.edu.sg/2013is1103group306/2013/03/03/internet-privacy-in-the-workplace-the-grey-areas-between-monitoring-and-private-virtual-spaces/

Lazar, Wendi S., and Lauren E. Schwartzreich. "Limitations to Workplace Privacy: Electronic Investigations and Monitoring." *Computer & Internet Lawyer,* vol. 29, no. 1, 2012, pp. 1–16. *ProQuest,* http://ezproxy.cpcc.edu/login?url=https://search.proquest.com/docview/912479753?accountid=10008.

"New Jersey Supreme Court Rules in Favor of Employee Privacy." *Electronic Privacy Information Center,* EPIC 30 Mar. 2010. https://www.epic.org/privacy/workplace/

The third source, which is highlighted, has no author. In his citation, then, Hal should include as much information as the reader needs to be directed to the source on the "Works Cited" page:

There are some court cases that have gone in favor of the employee. The New Jersey Supreme Court "ruled in favor of a female employee whose employer read emails that she sent while using Yahoo Mail on a company-owned laptop" ("New Jersey Supreme Court").

Because this source does not have an author, it is alphabetized on the "Works Cited" page by the first word of its title: *New.* When you provide article titles in parentheses, as done here, you may shorten lengthy titles to the first few words.

There is no page number included in our example because the source is from a website. If there are page numbers (from a book, print copy of a periodical, or from a document in PDF format), then the page number(s) from which the cited material comes is included; for example, (Lazar and Schwartzreich 9). Notice that the quotation mark ends after the last word in the quote. The citation is considered part of the sentence, and the period comes after the parentheses. The excerpt in Figure 4.2 is from the third item on Hal's "Works Cited" page (the Lazar and Schwartzreich article) and includes page numbers.

If authors are introduced in the attribution, their names do not need to be repeated in the parenthetical citation; only the page numbers are necessary, if there are any.

In a study of workplace privacy conducted by Wendi S. Lazar and Lauren E. Schwartzreich, the authors found that the courts must be able to "balance a business's need to protect data and proprietary information against individual rights and freedoms" (9).

Hal introduced the authors in the preceding example, so he only included the page number of the quoted material in the parenthetical citation. Notice, too, that the authors' first and last names in the body of the paragraph are in the normal order—reverse the order of the first author's name only in the "Works Cited" page for alphabetization purposes.

Privacy

---

false light invasion of privacy (*e.g.*, for online misrepresentations about employees, such as statements made by managers on social networking sites like LinkedIn),[115] intrusion of seclusion,[116] or tort claims arising out of workplace cyberstalking.[117] It may also be possible to bring a tortious interference with contract claim against an employer that requires an employee to authorize employer access to a social networking site profile by claiming that this act violates a service agreement or that doing so violates public policy concerns.[118]

International Trends in Workplace Privacy Protections

Unlike the United States, many countries have had strong privacy policies in place since World War II, in both the public and private workplace. In fact, in many countries such as Chile, France, and Mexico, the right to privacy in regard to emails in the workplace is an unwaivable right.[119] In most European Union (EU) countries this was a direct reaction to the holocaust and widespread civilian collusion with the Nazi regime.[120] In certain Asian countries and in parts of South America, data privacy and other individual privacy rights in the workplace are protected by statute and in some countries they are constitutional rights.[121] In the global workplace, however, all of these countries, much like the United States, share an increased sense of urgency in dealing with the technological revolution in the workplace and its resulting lack of employee privacy.

Specifically, in many European countries, monitoring, gaining access to employees' computers, and video surveillance are void *ab initio* or circumscribed by statute.[122] In 2007, the European Court of Human Rights held, under Article 8 of the European Convention on Human Rights, that employee email messages are protected communications.[123] More recently, the EU released a plan to revise European data protection rules based on the Commission's position that an individual's ability to control his or her information, have access to the information, and modify or delete the information are "essential rights that have to be guaranteed in today's digital world."[124] Increasingly, individual EU nations are poised to enact more stringent privacy laws. For instance, Finland recently introduced a statute expanding employee privacy rights,[125] and Sweden is expected to follow suit.[126] Within the last year, Germany (a country that instituted strong data privacy and anti-monitoring laws after the holocaust) also approved a draft law amending its Federal Data Protection Act, which prohibits employers from disciplining employees for their private online activities, to provide even broader protections.[127]

Even outside the EU, other countries continue this trend toward protecting employee privacy rights. In the Middle East, the Israeli National Labour Court issued a decision in February 2011 that severely limits the extent to which employers can monitor their employees' emails. According to the opinion, employers must now create an understandable policy for employee use of communications systems at the workplace. This policy must be clearly communicated to all employees, and must be written into their contracts.[128]

Conclusion

The changing forms of technology and their vast access to information will undoubtedly continue to dictate operational realities and expectations of privacy in the workplace. The challenge for courts is that they must continuously monitor these changes and balance a business's need to protect data and proprietary information against individual rights and freedoms. In the wake of *City of Ontario v. Quon*, and facing the risk of sacrificing overbroad constitutional rights, courts may consider the societal role of the particular electronic communication at issue and refrain from issuing rulings based solely on the language of a standardized privacy policy. In *Quon*, the Supreme Court recognized the increasing importance of technology in workers' lives, noting that "[c]ell phone and text message communications are so pervasive that some persons may consider them to be essential means or necessary instruments for self-expression, even self identification."[129] As the Court explained, the more pervasive and essential or necessary an electronic tool becomes for an individual's self-expression or identification, the "[stronger] the case for an expectation of privacy."[130] As new technologies become the norm of everyday life and employees' private lives intertwine with their work lives, the law will have to respond accordingly with safeguards that prevent employers from abusing and interfering with their employees' everyday communications and recognize that workplace privacy is a value worth protecting.

Notes

1. Social media sites are "a popular distribution outlet for users looking to share their experiences and interests on the Web," which "host substantial amounts of user-contributed materials (*e.g.*, photographs, videos, and textual content) for a wide variety of real-world events of different type and scale." Hila Becker, Mor Naaman, & Luis Gravano, "Learning Similarity Metrics for Event Identification in Social Media," Proceedings of the third ACM international conference on Web search and data mining, WSDM '10, 291–300. This umbrella term encompasses social networking sites such as Facebook, LinkedIn and MySpace, and microblogging information networks, such as Twitter. *See* Lisa Thomas, Comment," Social Networking in

The Clute Institute

Figure 4.2 Source material from a PDF article including page number

A study of workplace privacy found that the courts must be able to "balance a business's need to protect data and proprietary information against individual rights and freedoms" (Lazar and Schwartzreich 9).

In this second example, Hal needs to include the authors' names in the parenthetical citation because they do not appear in the introduction to the quote.

Quoting Material Quoted in the Original Source

Occasionally you will want to quote material that your source itself is quoting (see Figure 4.3).

In this excerpt from the Schatt article, an item is quoted from a source in which the author was quoting another source. To use quoted material, you do not need to track down the original source. (Note that in the parenthetical documentation in Figure 4.3 there is an author's last name, year, and page. The article's authors are using APA style, which is covered in full in

Motivation is the foundation for human achievement. A psychological construct, "motivation is considered both a catalyst for learning and an outcome of learning" (Hurley, 1993, p. 17). Without motivation little can be achieved, but with the appropriate inspiration, substantial growth may occur. A study by Cattel, Barton, and Dielman (1972) noted that nearly 25% of student achievement might be attributed to motivational elements. Asmus (1994) suggested that estimates of student achievement that were due to motivation ranged from 11 to 27 percent in the literature. Experienced educators may believe that this percentage is even higher yet.

"Achievement Motivation and the Adolescent Musician: A Synthesis of the Literature." Research & Issues in Music Education 9.1 (Sept 2011).

Figure 4.3 Quoted material in original source

Part VI. In MLA, you would use the author's last name and a page number, with no comma separating them.) You need only indicate that the material you are using is a quote from another source:

> There are several definitions of motivation, according to Hurley, that have to do with learning and music: one is "motivation is considered both a catalyst for learning and an outcome of learning (qtd. in Schatt 4).

"Qtd." is the abbreviation for "quoted." The use of it here indicates to the reader that, although the quoted material appeared in the Schatt article, this author got that information from Hurley.

Alter Quoted Material

Here is an example of quoting a quote, where the original material was altered slightly to fit the sentence into which it is to be inserted.

> The court explained: "If [an employee] had left a key to his house on the front desk at [his workplace], one could not reasonably argue that he was giving consent to whoever found the key, to use it to enter his house and rummage through his belongings. ..."

In the original material that Lazar and Schwartzreich cited, the material in the brackets [ ] was in the plural form—"employees" and "their workplaces." The authors needed these terms to be in the singular form to fit the rest of their paragraph. It is acceptable to alter quoted material so that it fits grammatically with your sentence as long as you indicate changes by using the brackets. If you remove material, you would use an ellipsis where words are missing.

your turn 4e ▶ **PRACTICE Quote a Source**

Use the first page of Wendi S. Lazar and Lauren E. Schwartzreich's "Limitations to Workplace Privacy: Electronic Investigations and Monitoring" to write a paragraph on workplace privacy. Incorporate two quotations from the article in your paragraph, making sure (1) to introduce the quote, (2) to quote the original using quotation marks, and (3) to include a parenthetical citation. The passage below is from page 1 of the article.

As cell phones, the Internet, and social media continue to define personal and professional communication, federal and state laws are redefining and, in many ways, broadening the concept of workplace privacy. For years, employers in the private sector paid little attention to concerns over workplace privacy, as few laws prevented employers from monitoring employees and employees had greater control over their personal communications. As technology developed, however, employers quickly obtained resources to conduct sophisticated searches of employees' or prospective employees' backgrounds, to monitor employees in and outside the workplace, and to track and access employees' Internet usage. Most recently, employers have begun to demand access to employees' personal communications through third-party service providers, such as wireless cell phone providers and social networking sites.

Over the last decade, courts and legislatures have responded to these developments by applying existing laws in ways that protect employees' privacy rights and enacting new laws to provide a remedial effect. Nevertheless, private sector employees continue to face many challenges to their workplace privacy.

Lazar, Wendi S., and Lauren E. Schwartzreich. "Limitations to Workplace Privacy: Electronic Investigations and Monitoring." *Computer and Internet Lawyer*, vol. 29, no. 1, 2012, pp. 1–16. ProQuest, http://ezproxy.cpcc.edu/login?url=https://search.proquest.com /docview/912479753?accountid=10008.

Summarize and Cite Summaries

Sometimes you will want to summarize the contents of an article, its main ideas or arguments. In summarizing, you do not need to explain secondary ideas, details, or tangents. It sounds easy, but it takes skill to summarize effectively. Follow these guidelines when you need to summarize the contents of a source.

Summary Checklist

☐ Provide the title of the source and the author, if available.

☐ In your own words, explain the source's thesis (i.e., claim or main idea) in one sentence.

☐ Make sure that you are not using any phrases from the original; if you decide to use a phrase, maybe a special term the author has created, put that phrase in quotation marks.

☐ Answer as many of these questions as are relevant: who, what, where, when, how, and why.

☐ Do not include any opinions or first-person commentary.

☐ Do not include details or examples.

You will introduce your summary as you would any other source, by author or title.

Paraphrase and Cite Paraphrases

It is tempting to use only quotations in your writing as it is easier to avoid plagiarizing. After all, you only have to put quotation marks around the borrowed material and put any additional information in the parenthetical citation and you're finished. But a collection of quotes does not make a research paper. You are being asked to incorporate your research with your own ideas, and this involves reading and digesting your sources and connecting ideas into a cohesive argument. This can best be accomplished with paraphrasing: putting source material into your own words. Let's look back at Hal's source on employee monitoring again.

Internet Privacy in the Workplace: The Grey Areas between Monitoring and Private Virtual Spaces

Similarly in the corporate workplace, a 2007 survey by the American Management Association and the ePolicy Institute found that two-thirds of employers monitor their employees' website visits in order to prevent inappropriate surfing. And 65% use software to block connections to websites deemed off limits for employees. This is a 27% increase since 2001 when the survey was first conducted.

Source: Taylor, Raymond E. "A Cross-Cultural View Towards the Ethical Dimensions of Electronic Monitoring of Employees: Does Gender Make a Difference?" International Business & Economics Research Journal, May 2012.

Hal also could have incorporated the same material by putting it into his own words, as shown in the following example.

Eugenia Chin finds in a survey conducted by the American Management Association and the ePolicy Institute that two-thirds of employers monitor the computer usage of employees to prevent surfing of nonwork-related sites. And 65% use software to block connections to websites deemed off limits for employees. This is a 27% increase since, 2001, when the survey was first conducted.

Source: Chin, Eugenia."Internet Privacy in the Workplace: The Grey Areas between Monitoring and Private Virtual Spaces." IS1103 Group 306 Blog, 3 March, 2013, https://blog.nus.edu.sg/2013is1103group306/2013/03/03/internet-privacy-in-the-workplace-the-grey-areas-between-monitoring-and-private-virtual-spaces/ . Accessed 11 June, 2019.

This is called **paraphrasing**. As you can see, the paraphrase is very different from the wording of the original, yet it conveys the same meaning. You can still tell the difference between Hal's words and the words of the source. Even though Hal may put the survey information in his own words, the ideas have been borrowed from a source—they are not his—and he must provide a citation to that source material in the same way as if it were quoted.

Hal avoids plagiarism by carefully paraphrasing material from the article "A Cross-Cultural View Towards the Ethical Dimensions of Electronic Monitoring of Employees: Does Gender Make a Difference?" published in the May 2012 issue of *International Business & Economics Research Journal*. Hal's first task was to decide what parts of this article he could use as source material. He came up with three items he wanted to use:

1. A summary of the author's argument
2. A paraphrase of the criticisms of electronic monitoring
3. A quote from one of the author's research questions

After Hal reads "A Cross-Cultural View," he decides he wants to offer a summary of the main points of the article. For our purposes, a passage from the article's introduction is provided here, in which the author states the purpose of his article:

> In developing partnerships between Chinese and foreign companies, it is important to be sensitive to the mindsets of both parties, especially when merging organizational policies. With this in mind, this article presents the results of a study examining the attitudes of Taiwanese and American study participants regarding the ethics of electronically monitoring employees (Taylor 529).

Hal's summary of the article may appear in his paper in this way:

> "A Cross-Cultural View" offers a good overview of some of the issues involved in electronic monitoring in the workplace in Taiwan. Raymond E. Taylor feels that to establish sound partnerships with Taiwanese businesses, the different attitudes of the Taiwanese and Americans need to be examined. To understand ...

Notice that Hal summarizes the article's main ideas, or at least those that are relevant to his essay (the ethics of electronic monitoring). Use only what you need from a source. Too often writers include information that is not needed, cluttering a paper and diluting its strength with unneeded material. Also note that Hal did not cite any page numbers. This is because he is not citing anything specific from the article; he is only summarizing the article's contents. He does, however, mention the authors' names and the title of the article.

Next, Hal is interested in the passage in Figure 4.4. The article offers many criticisms of electronic monitoring, and he is interested in discussing a few of these. In doing so, he must be careful to put the material in his own words and not to include any phrasing that too closely resembles the authors' words. He also needs to be careful when citing materials from an APA-formatted journal article in an MLA-formatted essay, particularly when citing sources the author of the article is citing himself.

> Business executives have always monitored their employees' behavior. Electronic monitoring may be especially useful in training and improving productivity (Blylinsky, 1991, and Laabs, 1992). However, critics of electronic monitoring suggest that the more obtrusive forms of electronic monitoring can lead to elevated levels of stress, decreased job satisfaction and quality of work, decreased levels of customer service and poor quality (Kallman, 1993). Electronic monitoring, by imposing excess control over employees' behavior, can alienate employees and develop a feeling of working in a modern "sweatshop" (Kidwell and Bennett, 1994). Employers have the legal right to electronically monitor their employees (Kelly, 2001). The question is not whether or not employers can electronically monitor their employees, but rather "how should it be done?"

The Clute Institute

Figure 4.4 Passage from "A Cross-Cultural View"

Original Source

Hal's first attempt at paraphrasing the passage did not go well:

> Electronic monitoring by imposing excess control over employees' behavior, can alienate employees and develop a feeling of working in a modern "sweatshop" (Kidwell and Bennett).
>
> In this case, Hal has cited authors that the author of the article has cited. He has included a parenthetical citation including the authors Kidwell and Bennett, 1994, just as the source appeared in the original APA article.

PARAPHRASE

> Kidwell and Bennett argue that imposing excess control as a means to monitor employees' behavior makes people feel they are working in a modern sweatshop (qtd. in Taylor 539).

Now Hal has introduced the source cited by Taylor and has then added the information that the source was quoted in Taylor along with the page number. You can see that many of the phrases of Hal's paragraph come directly from the passage. Even though Hal has indicated that the material came from an article and even cited the authors' names and page number, he is indicating that he has put all of the material into his own words when in fact he has not done so. This is an example of plagiarism.

Plagiarism is, of course, using materials produced by someone else as if they are yours. This includes a range of infractions extending from the accidental omission of a citation to passing off an entire essay as your own. In this case, Hal has used much of the authors' wording and indicates by his lack of quotation marks that the material is in his own words.

SECOND ATTEMPT AT PARAPHRASING

> Kidwell and Bennett argue that the use of electronic monitoring is detrimental to employees' morale and creates an unhealthy environment where their every action is monitored to make sure they are constantly working (qtd. in Taylor 539).

The concept of the sweatshop, a place where employees are closely watched to make sure they meet their work quotas, is still there, but it is now in Hal's own words.

Sometimes it is just easier to quote, and as suggested earlier this is often the case when citing policies and laws: these materials usually need to be presented in their original form. The author of this article provides two research questions, and Hal wants to include one of them. A direct quote would be appropriate here as well.

ORIGINAL SOURCE

Does "giving notice" versus "secretly monitoring" make a significant difference in the ethical dimension of electronic monitoring?

Notice that in this example there are quotation marks around certain words. When Hal cites this research question, he needs to turn those double quotation marks into single quotation marks to indicate a quote within a quote.

HAL'S USE OF THE SOURCE

Taylor provides two research questions for his study. The first one, "Does 'giving notice' versus 'secretly monitoring' make a significant difference in the ethical dimension of electronic monitoring?" (530). The importance of determining the ethics of monitoring employees' computers and cell phones hinges on whether they know such monitoring is going on.

Hal does a few important things here.

1. He introduces his quote; it is not just dropped in via parachute to land where it will. He sets up the quote for the reader.
2. He begins and ends his quotation with quotation marks. The marks indicate that everything inside of them comes directly from an outside source. Note that the quotation marks end after the quote, not after the parenthetical citation.
3. Hal takes into account the fact that, in the original, the phrases *giving notice* and *secretly monitoring* were in quotation marks. Hal follows the rule for reducing the quotation marks to 'single' quotes and using "double" quotes around the entire quotation.
4. After Hal ends his quote, he comments on why the material is important.

Following these techniques when summarizing, paraphrasing, or quoting will save you a lot of grief and help you avoid charges of plagiarism.

Avoid Plagiarism

The definition of plagiarism is using the work of others as if it were your own without proper attribution. To most readers (instructors, bosses, etc.), there is no difference between accidentally forgetting to cite a passage and deliberately presenting outside material as your own. How to avoid a failing grade (or a job dismissal)? Avoid plagiarism by following these guidelines.

Avoiding Plagiarism Checklist

☐ Cite all outside material whether you have quoted it or paraphrased it.

☐ Use introductory phrases with sources, such as "author says" or "according to author," followed by the cited material, and then comment on the cited material. This will help the reader distinguish between your own ideas and the ideas that you have cited.

☐ When pasting material from a source into your paper, make sure to mark it in some way (e.g., by using boldface type, by using a different font color or size, by highlighting), so that you will remember that the words are not yours. Then go through your document thoroughly to make sure you have cited all the highlighted material correctly.

☐ Always include the source publication information in your bibliography file or on your photocopies. If you do not have author or publication information when you are ready to use the source, you cannot use it.

your turn 4f   PRACTICE Paraphrase Properly

Read the following article on some of the costs of delaying comprehensive immigration reform legislation, an issue in 2008, when the essay was first published, and for today's U.S. Congress as well. Write a paragraph about immigration reform and include paraphrasing of two passages from the article by following the tips to avoid plagiarism and citing them correctly.

I'm Not Dangerous

By Danny Postel

The past six months have seen three of the largest workplace immigration raids in U.S. history. In May [2008], the rural Iowa town of Postville was convulsed when 900 Immigration and Customs Enforcement (ICE) agents stormed a kosher meatpacking plant and arrested 389 workers. In August, ICE agents descended on an electrical equipment factory near Laurel, Mississippi, detaining nearly 600 workers. And in October, the scene was repeated in Greenville, South Carolina, where 330 workers were swept up at a chicken-processing plant.

The humanitarian costs of the raids, according to a statement issued by the U.S. Conference of Catholic Bishops Committee on Migration, were "immeasurable and unacceptable in a civilized society." Children were separated from their parents for days. Those arrested were not immediately afforded the rights of due process. And local communities were, in the words of John C. Wester, bishop of Salt Lake City and chairman of the Committee on Migration, "disrupted and dislocated." These raids, he said, "strike immigrant communities unexpectedly, leaving the affected immigrant families to cope in the aftermath. Husbands are separated from their wives, and children are separated from their parents. Many families never recover; others never reunite."

The bishop called on the Department of Homeland Security, of which ICE is an agency, on President George W. Bush, and on then-candidates John McCain and Barack Obama to "reexamine the use of worksite enforcement raids" as an immigration-enforcement tool. He noted that immigrants "who are working to survive and support their families should not be treated like criminals."

Having visited Laurel after the ICE crackdown, I must report that is exactly how the workers there have been treated and made to feel. The majority of the immigrant workers caught up in the raid were taken immediately to a holding facility in Louisiana. ICE released a number of women, some of them pregnant, on "humanitarian" grounds. But many of them were shackled with ankle bands equipped with electronic monitoring devices. Several expressed their humiliation and shame—not to speak of their physical discomfort—at having been branded this way. For days, one of them told me, she avoided going out in public or to the grocery store. "It makes me look like a criminal, like a dangerous person," she lamented. "I'm not dangerous."

This woman told me she had come to the United States out of sheer desperation. She said she was unable to feed her children in her home village in Mexico. Now, with deportation imminent and no means to pay her bills, she and her coworkers were facing a further harrowing fate.

Immigration raids, even large, media-covered ones, are selective and symbolic in nature. They are orchestrated to send a political message that the government is willing and able to enforce the law. But why penalize the least among us—hardworking people who earn very little and endure some of the harshest conditions in the American workplace? The Postville and Laurel plants both have long histories of taking advantage of their workers. Iowa's attorney general recently filed charges against the Postville meatpacking plant for more than nine thousand labor violations. In July, religious and labor leaders joined more than a thousand marchers in the town to show solidarity with those seized in the ICE raid.

Indeed, religious communities have been playing a pivotal role in the aftermath of these raids. Catholic parishes have been safe havens for families scrambling to feed their children amid the turmoil. Immaculate Conception Church in Laurel and Sacred Heart Catholic Church in Hattiesburg worked virtually round-the-clock to feed and provide for the affected families.

To remedy what the U.S. bishops call "the failure of a seriously flawed immigration system," they "urge our elected and appointed officials to turn away from enforcement-only methods and direct their energy toward the adoption of comprehensive immigration reform legislation." That is now up to the new administration and to Congress.

Documentation: Works Cited Page

One of the most tedious aspects of writing research reports of any type is the documentation. You must supply publication information for every source you use in your report. This information must appear in a standardized format or style sheet dictated by your company or instructor.

- In the humanities (fine arts, literature, and history), the most common format is MLA—the Modern Language Association.
- Fields such as sociology, anthropology, education, psychology, and business often require writers to document sources in APA—the American Psychological Association.
- The Council of Science Editors' manual (CSE) is used for the natural sciences, such as biology and geology.

All of these style guides are similar in *what* information you should provide for a source, but they vary in *how* that information is presented. For example, see how a book is cited for MLA, APA, and CSE side by side:

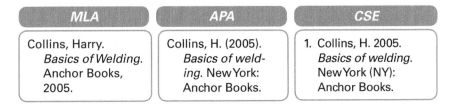

MLA	APA	CSE
Collins, Harry. *Basics of Welding.* Anchor Books, 2005.	Collins, H. (2005). *Basics of welding.* New York: Anchor Books.	1. Collins, H. 2005. *Basics of welding.* New York (NY): Anchor Books.

The complete guides to MLA and APA can be found on the Internet at a variety of sources. If you do not have access to the manuals themselves, a very reliable Internet source for both is The Online Writing Lab at Purdue University:

MLA https://owl.purdue.edu/owl/research_and_citation/mla_style/mla _formatting_and_style_guide/mla_formatting_and_style_guide.html

APA https://owl.purdue.edu/owl/research_and_citation/apa_style/apa _formatting_and_style_guide/general_format.html

In Part VI, "MLA and APA Documentation Systems," we will cover how to cite sources in both MLA and APA format, how to use the hanging indent function, and the strengths and weaknesses of citation-generating software.

your turn 4g ▶ **Integrate a Source**

Once you have found the information you want to use, follow Hal's example and (1) introduce your sources. Explain to the reader why you have selected this source. Why this author? Then (2) paraphrase the source, putting it entirely in your own words. Your argument should not be a string of quotations. Quotations should be used sparingly. And finally (3), comment on the source. Do you agree with the author's points? Is this a source you disagree with? Do you have more to say on the subject or point the author raises?

Reflect and Apply

1. As you are collecting your sources, how are you evaluating them for unacceptable biases?

2. How are you maximizing your time as you determine which sources are the most useful for you? As you read through your sources, how are you taking notes that pull from material at the beginning, middle, and ends of them in order to avoid using material out of context?

3. How are you determining the value of any primary sources you are finding on your issue?

4. When you use research material, in what ways are you making sure the reader knows why you are using that particular source at that particular time?

5. How are you guaranteeing that all source material in your argument is properly paraphrased and cited, eliminating accidental plagiarism?

KEEPING IT LOCAL

THE WORLD IS SHRINKING, or expanding, depending on how you view the changes in technology. We have access, even in small towns, to vast amounts of published research from all over the world. We can access blogs written by experts in every field imaginable. We can also access blogs written by anyone who wants to write one on any subject, whether they are an expert or not. We can read articles published by highly credible sources in distinguished journals. We can also learn that those same experts are guilty of plagiarism, making all their work suspect. It is important, now more than ever, to use the Internet wisely to learn as much as we can about the authors of any material we plan on using to support our arguments. Embrace all that the world of technology offers, but do so with great caution.

Approach the sources you have selected for your argument by assessing their usefulness. How many sources are still useful after your initial assessment? Do you need to find more sources that fit your argument better? Take the remaining sources and assess their credibility. Do you feel the articles are credible once you have assessed them? Finally, read the sources, making sure you have identified the authors' claims and all supporting and opposing views. Answer these questions: Who is the author? What is the claim? What are the supporting views? What are the opposing or alternate views addressed?

CHAPTER 5

Read Critically and Avoid Fallacies

Learning Objectives

By working through this chapter, you will be able to

- define fallacies.
- identify fallacies of choice.
- identify fallacies of support.
- identify fallacies of emotion.
- identify fallacies of inconsistency.
- write without using fallacies.

Once again, you receive an email request from your boss to donate to a large national charity. Because of recent misappropriation of the charity's funds in particular and the downturn in the economy in general, the charity is receiving fewer donations. It's not that you have anything against the charitable organization, and you recognize that it does great work. You feel pressured, however, to give to an organization that you have not chosen. Your boss has sent several emails encouraging donation, emails that ask employees not to leave children without proper meals or winter clothing. You don't want to be the only bad guy, so you write a check.

Later, you are approached by a coworker to buy Christmas wrapping paper as a fundraiser for her son's fourth-grade fieldtrip. If enough money isn't raised, the children won't be able to go, and then they won't be able to compete for future opportunities with the kids at the more affluent schools because they won't have the same background experiences. Again, you reach for your checkbook.

All Illustrations by iStock.com/A-digit

COMMUNITY

School–Academic

Workplace

Family–Household

Neighborhood

Social–Cultural

Consumer

Concerned Citizen

TOPIC: Workplace

ISSUE: Peer/Employee Pressure

AUDIENCE: Fellow Employees

CLAIM: Employees should be free from solicitations for donations or purchases in the workplace.

It is difficult to sort through the arguments that seem logical on the surface or that stir your emotions. Which arguments or causes are valid, and which are meant only to part you from your money? Which arguments contain fallacies to get you to do things you don't want to do? In Chapter 5, you will learn how to identify the four major categories of fallacies in the arguments of others and learn to eliminate each type of fallacy from your own arguments.

Define Fallacies

Very often when we are listening to a speaker's argument or reading an argument in a magazine or newspaper, it is easy to get caught up in the speaker's excitement and overlook the fallacies in his argument. **Fallacies** are errors in an argument, whether accidental or deliberate, that serve to draw attention away from the problems in the argument's claim or support. They can be the result of a poor understanding of the subject, or they can be deliberate manipulations of the argument to misdirect readers. The difficulty with fallacies is that they are often hard to spot, in your own writing and in the writing of others.

Detecting fallacies in arguments is a component of reading well. How well do you know how to read? "I can read just fine," you say. But there is a type of reading that many struggle with—critical reading. **Critical reading** is a more active form of engaging with a text, be it a newspaper article, a politician's speech, or a note from your son's teacher. For example, what is really being said in that politician's speech? You are hearing her words, but are you really listening to what she is saying? The two actions are not the same thing. The best-sounding arguments can fall to pieces when examined closely by a reader who is actively responding to them, rather than passively receiving them.

Figure 5.1 Information overload can make us feel that we are always a step behind.

We are bombarded daily with an overwhelming amount of information. We must sort through emails; phone messages; and newspapers and news programs, which now have 24-hour-a-day updates. You can even subscribe to sites so that updated news on certain topics can be emailed to your computer or sent to your phone. Then there are all of the other sources of information you encounter: reading for your courses; updates to the Operations and Procedures Manual at work; and the buzz about the latest movies, television shows, music, and fashion trends. Miss one day's information due to a cold, and you feel you have fallen behind a week. This anxious feeling is called **information overload**—the sense that you are always one step (if not more) behind.

Spotting fallacies can be difficult, but it is not impossible. The more tools you have at hand, the easier your job of cracking someone's argument will be. In Chapter 4, "Evaluate and Engage with Your Sources," you learned that there are some methods that will help you get to the heart of any argument, whether the argument is presented in print (such as a book, an article, or an Internet posting) or orally (such as a speech or an advertisement). In this chapter, you will learn to demand of authors that they convince you that their claims and support are valid. By learning to identify fallacies in the arguments of others, you will also learn how to avoid using them in your own arguments. Let's tackle the most common forms of fallacies.

Identify and Avoid Fallacies

Many arguments can sound good until you begin to follow them closely. All of a sudden, those high-flying words seem to be saying very little. You begin to suspect that the writer is trying to trick you. And you may be right. Dishonest arguers often use fallacies to direct the reader's attention away from the real issues or to hide their real purposes. Just as frequently, though, inexperienced writers use fallacies because they don't know any better. Fallacies are errors in a writer's argument—not errors in fact, but errors in reasoning.

In a recent class, a student writer argued, "I think we should stop spending so much money on the space program because people are starving here on Earth." Other students disagreed, but they were not sure what to say to counter the argument. One traditional way of arguing is to learn to recognize specific fallacies and then see if the argument you disagree with contains one of these errors in logic. Is this an *ad hominem* or an *ad misericordiam*? Is the argument a *post hoc* fallacy, a *com hoc* fallacy, or maybe a *tu quoque* fallacy? One thing is certain: if you take this route, you may be studying fallacies *ad nauseum*—which means "on and on and on . . . ."

The good news is there is a far easier way. All fallacies boil down to four categories. There is overlap between types, and you could argue that a fallacy can fall into more than one category, but in general the four categories are as follows:

1. Fallacies of choice
2. Fallacies of support
3. Fallacies of emotion
4. Fallacies of inconsistency

In the argument against the space program, the fallacy happens to be a false choice, an either–or argument that tries to force you into supporting either feeding the hungry or exploring space. This is a smart move. Of those two choices, what ethical person would ever choose space exploration over feeding people who are starving? But there is also inconsistency. The arguer is assuming that there is only enough government money to do one of two things: (1) feed the hungry or (2) explore space. But, of course, that same arguer drives over roads paid for by government money, lives in a country defended by a military, and will someday retire and receive Social Security benefits from the government. In fact, there are lots of programs she doesn't propose to sacrifice in order to feed the hungry, so why should she pick on the space program? She is being inconsistent. The problem is that she is not directly articulating the inconsistency. Some fallacies are obvious, but most require you to dig a little deeper into the arguer's assumptions. Luckily, you don't need to know the name of each fallacy in order to find the inconsistency.

Keep in mind that even a fallacious argument can be right—just as a stopped clock is right twice a day. We shouldn't just accept fallacious arguments any more than we should tell time by a stopped clock. In each case, further investigation is warranted. How else might it be? Maybe the clock is working after all, and we just looked at it wrong. Or maybe we can fix it; it might just need a new battery. And maybe it's telling the right time, even though it won't be in just one minute from now. The goal is not understanding all of the types of fallacies but learning how to recognize when someone is being inconsistent. Every time you want to test the strength of an argument, look closely at what it is saying and what it assumes.

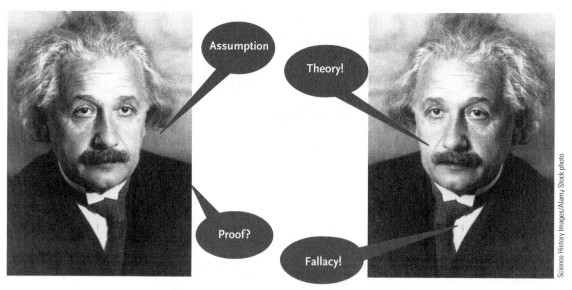

Figure 5.2 Albert Einstein

Before we go any further, let's discuss bias. Say you're writing a paper with the following claim: the study of extrasensory perception (ESP) deserves equal funding with stem cell research. One obvious assumption (warrant) the claim makes is that ESP is real. Another is that it is worth studying. It is impossible to write any argument without some fallacies, especially bias, since we are all biased. The very fact that we are making a certain claim and dismissing alternatives to that claim is evidence of our bias toward our own claim. We also tend to give short shrift to competing evidence and make leaps of logic that may not be warranted.

The heart of critical thinking is asking, "How else might it be?" Looking for fallacies involves a search for answers to that same question. If I use a blanket statement and say, "Everyone is born with paranormal powers," I am dismissing the possibility that some people are born without any extramental powers, that they can't read minds, tell the future, or move objects simply with the power of thought. The first category of fallacies involves making bad or unwarranted choices about what to believe.

Avoid Fallacies of Choice

Fallacies of choice ask you to make the wrong choice by limiting your view of what the future holds or what the choices are. They put things into simplistic terms that don't allow for positive alternatives. They tell you that only the choice they want is possible or worthwhile. You will see how this overlaps with scare tactics and other emotional fallacies.

Blanket Statement

Blanket statements use the language of absoluteness. They use words like *all, always, never, no, every,* and *none*. They are fallacies as soon as someone can think of an exception. If someone claims that all dogs have tails, you could go home and chase your dog around with a pair of scissors, trying to prove that person wrong. (See Figure 5.3.)

Figure 5.3 The Schipperke is a tailless dog

Some people take the sixth commandment to mean that a person should never kill. But, of course, people kill to live by eating plants and animals. And people kill to defend themselves, or to serve their country in times of war, or to mete out punishment for murder. To say that we should never kill is a blanket statement. If you believe that killing is sometimes okay, then you have found an exception and turned the blanket statement into a fallacy. Some examples of blanket statements include:

- Cell phone use in the classroom is *always* inappropriate.
- The *only way* to understand the increasing high school dropout rate is to study the lack of student motivation.

Both of these claims use unqualified terms (*always, only way*) that can easily be rebutted. Of course there are times when it is appropriate to use a cell phone in the classroom—calling security, for example. Students drop out of school for many reasons, not just lack of motivation. Avoid absolutes. Blanket statements hinge on the following terms and terms like them. Be careful to qualify these **absolute terms** in your own writing. Also note that plural nouns can imply absolutism (for example, using the word *students*, implies "all students"). You can modify these terms using the qualifiers in Chapter 10, "Build Arguments."

Absolute Terms			
all	no	none	100 percent
every	always	never	must
has to	can't	won't	only

Photo credit (vertical): GROSSEMY VANESSA/Alamy Stock Photo

False Dilemma, Either–Or, and Misuse of Occam's Razor

False dilemma/either–or thinking suggests that only one thing can happen—either A or B. As in the sample claim that the space program can exist only at the expense of the poor, arguers who make this type of mistake state that there are only two choices in the argument.

> So much of the food I eat, the fuel I expend, and the clothing I wear work against the idea of sustainable living. Why should I even bother to try?

This student's claim suggests that there are only two choices available to the speaker. He can either (a) live a lifestyle that is completely geared to sustainable living, from food to fuel, or (b) not even try to make any efforts at sustainability. A critical reader will ask, "Does it have to be either–or?" This author has created a false choice, a dilemma that is not really there. A person may not be capable of living in a totally green way, but most people agree that anything done to help the planet is a good thing.

Occam's razor is a philosophical point of view that argues that the simplest solution is usually the correct one. If it walks like a duck, looks like a duck, and quacks like a duck, chances are very good it is a duck. Most of the time, using Occam's razor to cut through far-fetched and overly complex theories is the way to go. But this chase for simplicity can be misused.

The following story is an example of public officials finally breaking out of fallacious false choice/either–or thinking. For many years, suicidal people had been leaping to their deaths from the Golden Gate Bridge, yet nothing had been done to stop it. Partly the inaction was born from a desire to maintain the landmark beauty of the structure by not cluttering its profile with high fencing. Partly the inaction stemmed from the fallacy of thinking that any suicide prevented at the bridge would simply take place elsewhere. There were, the doubters argued, only two choices: either keep letting people kill themselves and leave the bridge unchanged, or force depressed people to kill themselves elsewhere by marring the beauty of the bridge with new barriers. In this view, nothing could be done about suicides, because anybody who wanted to kill themselves enough to jump off a bridge would simply find another way to do it. Either people wanted to keep living or they didn't, in which case there was nothing anyone could do to stop them. Because it was impossible to prevent all suicides, the decision was made to prevent none. Any other choice, such as the plan recently adopted, was considered impossible.

In fact, suicide is often preventable, and it's also an act of opportunity. No sane person would hand a suicidal individual a loaded gun. Why? Because it would be giving the person an opportunity. Because it could *change the person's behavior*. Therefore, it stands to reason that removing opportunities for suicide might also change behavior. At last, bridge officials decided to break free from their loop of fallacious thinking by adding nets below the bridge's surface. This solution prevents suicides at the bridge, while damaging the bridge's landmark profile very little. As a result of breaking through the either–or thinking, a solution that considered both sides of the argument was reached.

Slippery Slope

A **slippery slope (or staircase)** argument is one of the easiest fallacies to recognize. You will often hear people say that, if we let one thing happen, then that will cause some other thing to happen, which in turn will lead to something bad, which then will cause chaos. If we take that first step, then we will fall all the way down the slippery slope to chaos or evil, as illustrated by Figures 5.4 and 5.5.

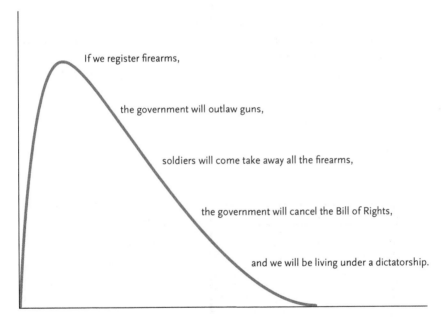

If we register firearms,

the government will outlaw guns,

soldiers will come take away all the firearms,

the government will cancel the Bill of Rights,

and we will be living under a dictatorship.

Figure 5.4 A slippery slope argument

But events do not always follow the predicted slope. For example, in contrast with common gun-control arguments, some societies have taken away guns without becoming dictatorships, or they took them away for a while and ended up giving them back later on. A good history lesson often reveals that the "slippery slope" in an argument is actually an unlikely series of events. A better description for most such cause–effect chains might be a "staircase" because we usually can move up the slope and down the slope. Sometimes it is a slippery staircase, but it's rarely inevitable that if we take the first step, we will slide all the way down.

internet activity 5a

Use the Opposing Viewpoints database or another available database to find arguments about gun control. Read through these arguments and see if you can find slippery slope fallacies. What makes them fallacious? Where do they start, and where do they end?

Signs that you may be reading or writing fallacies of choice include:

☐ Support for extreme positions: we *must* do something (e.g., bomb, invade, kill, torture, outlaw, silence, close a factory, fire an employee, censor objectionable material).

☐ The language of certainty: all, every, 100 percent, never, none, each, always, everywhere, there is just no reason to go to Mars, I can't think of a single benefit of joining the military.

☐ Hard, even impossible choices: it's either this or that, my solution or your hellish problem, my way or the highway.

☐ Surprising conditionals: if we don't do X, we'll face Y; if we do A, the sky will fall; if we do A, we'll reach nirvana; if we do A, then B will happen, and B will naturally lead to C, which in turn . . .

☐ Support for a decision already made: that page was already written; we're going to do X, it's just a matter of how; one way or another we have to . . .

Figure 5.5 This cartoon uses the slippery slope fallacy to make its point.

your turn 5a **PRACTICE Identify Fallacies of Choice**

Here is a paragraph from the paper on ESP. See if you can spot the types of fallacies. Match the numbered fallacies with the correct box below.

The study of extrasensory perception (ESP) deserves equal funding with stem cell research. ❶ We can recognize this fact, or we can continue to waste the opportunities such funding represents. ❷ No medical treatment comes without a price in terms of research funding. ❸ It's hard to think of treatments that didn't involve some government-funded research; therefore, it's safe to assume there aren't any. ❹ If we continue ignoring this potentially valuable source of knowledge, we can expect to begin ignoring other valuable types of innovation, and after that, what's next? Like any species, human beings survive and prosper by constantly learning and adapting to a changing environment. Without ESP funding, we may well face extinction.

Which numbered sentence in the paragraph best represents each type of fallacy? Fill in each box with a different number.

☐ Blanket Statement   ☐ False Dilemma/Either–Or

☐ Misuse of Occam's Razor   ☐ Slippery Slope

Avoid Fallacies of Support

Fallacies of support involve making connections and conclusions that aren't warranted. If Michelle had two ducks and someone gave her two more ducks, no one would suggest that she now had five ducks. Yet this often is exactly what people do with the logic of their arguments. They support their claim with their claim. They jump to conclusions based on very little evidence. They make superstitious connections between events, build arguments on falsehoods, and support their claims with facts that aren't even relevant.

Circular Argument

A **circular argument** is simply one that ends up relying on its own claim for support. In this way, it seems to chase its own tail. A person who doesn't agree will tend to see the arguer as trapped in her own logic. The arguer is caught in the circle of her own prior beliefs. For example, she may assume that God exists and is all-powerful. Anything less than God's full existence would violate her assumption of God's full existence. That's the circle. (See Figure 5.6.) Other arguers might believe in other, equally powerful beings. Do they all have to exist? Only to someone trapped in that particular circle of logic.

We need to drill more for oil. Why? Because gas prices are high. Why? Because we need more oil than we have available to us. Why? Because we haven't drilled enough oil wells.

Courtesy of the Harry Phillips

Figure 5.6 A circular argument that uses its claim as its support

This kind of argument ignores all other possibilities, such as conservation, alternative energy sources, or simply letting shortages raise prices to the point that we only use the oil that is absolutely necessary, a kind of conservation that would be enforced by the marketplace laws of supply and demand. The argument also ignores any balancing of costs and harm from more oil drilling and simply treats it as a good thing that we may or may not do, instead of a complex thing that may do as much harm as good, for example, by continuing global warming.

Hasty Generalization and Jumping to Conclusions

The fallacy of **hasty generalization** involves taking a single case and generalizing from it. Your friend takes a ride in a vintage automobile from the 1930s and the axle breaks, causing an accident that breaks your friend's leg. Now, you refuse to ride in anything older than last year's model. Or your grandmother smoked cigarettes and lived to be 90. Therefore, smoking must be harmless and all this talk about lung cancer and early deaths is just a scare tactic.

Faulty Causality: *Post Hoc, Ergo Propter Hoc*

Post hoc, ergo propter hoc: This Latin phrase sounds complicated, but it's really simple, and it represents a fundamental process in animal thought. The entire phrase can be translated as "After this, therefore because of this." When two events happen one after the other, we naturally tend to think the first event caused the other event. We kick the sleepy copy machine, it starts working, and we assume it was our kick that did the trick. In fact, maybe it had just then finished its warm-up cycle. This is how superstitions get started. A baseball player forgets to change his underwear, and he pitches a no-hitter. Well, no way is he changing that underwear. No, he's going to wear the same pair every time he pitches until the magic finally wears off.

Parents should not have to vaccinate their children because vaccinations cause autism.

A classic case of *post hoc* fallacy presents itself in arguments that claim vaccinations cause autism. We don't yet know what causes autism, but we do know that it exists. A certain percentage of children will be diagnosed with autism at a young age. If virtually all young children are given, for example, the MMR (mumps, measles, and rubella) vaccine, it is certain that, soon after, some of those children will develop autism. If none of the children are vaccinated, it is equally certain that, soon after, some of those children will develop autism. After all, the MMR vaccine is given to children at 12 to 15 months of age. Autism is usually diagnosed around three years of age. Therefore, MMR almost always comes before a diagnosis of autism, making it is easy for parents to assume a causal connection, even if there isn't one.

The fallacy comes into play when parents assume that the vaccine caused the autism, even though they would never assume that the lack of a vaccine would cause autism, though the evidence is the same in both cases. That is the inconsistency at the heart of the *post hoc* fallacy: just because one thing happened after the other doesn't mean the first thing caused the second thing. The MMR vaccine comes before autism, but often so does potty training. Could potty training be the cause of autism? Could baby formula? The fact is, we don't know exactly what causes autism. It might be a genetic disorder. It could be caused by hormones while the fetus is in the womb. It could be a result of exposure to common household materials or chemicals. The fact is, we don't know, although research is getting closer to showing what the cause might be.

Many errors in arguments come from making mistakes in causality. You may believe that a chain of events exists where it doesn't. You may believe that one event is caused by another. You may believe that only one cause is responsible when there may be a combination of causes leading to an effect.

Fallacies in causality are not easy to spot. Keep your eyes open, and do some investigating on your own about claims of causality that seem too easy or are not well supported.

> Some people have claimed that the city council's decision to again postpone its discussion of homelessness is only increasing the number of homeless in our community.

Here, it cannot be proven that the city council's inaction has anything to do with the increase in homelessness. More research would need to be done.

Non Sequitur, Red Herring, and False Clue

Authors of murder mysteries are famous for planting false clues, otherwise known as red herrings. They force the detective and the reader to follow a scent that doesn't lead anywhere or leads to the wrong conclusion. A false clue in a murder mystery is simply one that doesn't support our attempt to identify the real killer. But false clues appear in all kinds of arguments. So do statements that don't follow what came before, that are out of order, or that might sound good but don't actually relate.

In Latin, *non sequitur* means "it does not follow." Often, an arguer will write or say something that doesn't seem to belong, that suddenly shifts the focus or the argument, or that makes a conclusion that doesn't seem justified from the evidence that has been presented.

Some of these *non sequiturs* are accidental. A writer might suddenly change the subject or make a point that comes from out of the blue. Or the writer might even force in a point that doesn't belong, simply because he likes it. This is known as "shoe-horning," after the old metal scoops that people used to use to guide their feet into tight leather shoes. Two other metaphors you may hear to describe these pet arguments are "hobby horse," named after the rocking horses that go back and forth, but never forward, and "having an axe to grind," meaning a fixation on an idea, springing from a desire for vengeance.

If a writer's claim is that diet can help to prevent diabetes, discussion of issues not related to diet or diabetes may seem like *non sequiturs*. Discussion of illness prevention in general could be risky, in that it could seem like it's off topic. Or it might simply be an example of broadening out the claim to include other kinds of disease prevention besides diet or diabetes prevention. In the following passage, however, the writer goes way off the track.

> Diet can help prevent type 2 diabetes. A new study published in *Diabetes Care* compared the glycemic control (blood sugar levels) of patients on traditional American Diabetes Association diets with a low-fat vegan diet. Patients on the vegan diet did roughly twice as well in reducing their glycemic index. This goes to show that the Texas beef producers were wrong for suing Oprah Winfrey for her 1996 anti-beef comments. When it was pointed out that cows were being fed to other cows, Oprah said, "It has just stopped me cold from eating another burger!"

Sentence 4 came out of left field, didn't it? The writer shifted suddenly from discussion of diabetes prevention to a lawsuit concerning a statement by a celebrity.

Some *non sequiturs* represent conscious efforts on the part of the arguer. The intent might be to change an unpleasant subject. A politician who is unpopular for her handling of a state's economy might take a strong interest in creating harsher penalties for child molesters. A skeptic of global warming might bring up the subject of government conspiracies in hopes that an audience upset about the possibility of too much government control might forget all about potential harm from changes in the climate.

Straw Man Argument or Argument Built on a False Fact or Claim

Straw man arguments are those that are based on incorrect information, whether the intention is to deliberately misrepresent an opponent's claims or because the facts that are being used are plainly incorrect. For example, someone might claim "One piece of the solution to homelessness in our community is more affordable housing." You would be committing a straw man fallacy if you said "My opponent says that we can end homelessness just by building cheap apartments." The misrepresentation of that position makes it easy to dismiss.

Signs that you may be reading or writing fallacies of support include:

- ☐ Making the same point in two places in a chain of reasoning: the economy is bad because the housing market fell, which happened because wages were not rising fast enough for people to afford the higher prices, which resulted from a weakening economy.

- ☐ Support based on a single case, anecdotal evidence, or making too much out of a few cases: back in 1979 . . . , reports of similar occurrences indicate . . . , this incident shows that . . .

- ☐ The language of time or events happening after each other: then, after, when, preceded by, I'll never get a flu shot—my aunt and uncle got a flu vaccine and then they came right down with the flu.

- ☐ Sudden or unexplained shifts in topic.

- ☐ Unquestioned assumptions: everything hinges on . . . , the key is that . . .

- ☐ Statements that put words in someone else's mouth instead of quoting them in context.

your turn 5b **PRACTICE Identify Fallacies of Support**

Here is a paragraph from the paper on ESP. See if you can spot the types of fallacies. Match the numbered fallacies with the correct box below.

❶ Whenever researchers take ESP seriously, they document many more cases, which shows that the first step toward unlocking paranormal powers is simply to look for them. ❷ In one case, the paranormal researcher herself began reporting the ability to move objects without touching them, showing that if she, a trained, hardened scientist can do it, anyone can. ❸ According to that researcher, Dr. Ruth Bandylegs, ESP could even lead to an increase in religious faith and consequently better our world in that way too. ❹ However, paranormal powers are not taken seriously by most scientists, most likely due to their bias toward traditional science. In traditional science, the emphasis is placed on the known laws of physics, but ESP must work based on physical laws that are unknown. Otherwise, traditional science would have taken it seriously by now, and those laws would be recognized. ❺ Since paranormal research has been shown to increase both incidents of ESP and also its importance in religious faith, an increase in funding is definitely warranted.

Which numbered sentence in the paragraph best represents each type of fallacy? Fill in each box with a different number.

- ☐   Circular Argument
- ☐   Hasty Generalization/Jumping to Conclusions
- ☐   Straw Man Argument
- ☐   Faulty Causality/*Post Hoc*
- ☐   *Non Sequitur*/Red Herring

Avoid Fallacies of Emotion

Appeals based on emotion are those that evoke sentiment, fear, desire, and so on. But wait a minute, we said in earlier chapters that emotional appeals are a good thing. Can they also be fallacies? Well, not in theory, but in practice they can be. Whenever we rely too much on any one kind of support, we can run into trouble because we are giving it more weight than another kind of support and, therefore, being unbalanced. Many people would claim that in the end, everything we believe comes down to emotion. Perhaps this is true; even when an argument is based on scientific evidence, at some point we accept that evidence because we like it. In other words, we accept it not because it fits the definition of good scientific evidence, but because it's a definition that we like. Fallacies of emotion are a problem because they completely replace evidence with feelings. They play on the heart strings and the fears of the audience. They name-call, they poison your view of things, they make you feel left out, and they use famous people to vouch for things they know very little about.

Ad Hominem

Ad hominem simply means "to the person." It is the fallacy of arguing based on the arguer's personality or character, credibility, or authority. It's the opposite of shooting the messenger because you don't like the message. Here, you shoot the message because you don't like the messenger.

> We cannot believe she will follow through on her plans to funnel more money toward charities. Can we trust a former alcoholic?

The inconsistency of *ad hominem* fallacies is that we dismiss arguments from people we dislike but accept the same arguments from people we admire. Another way to say it is that, when we do like the arguer or when we do not have an emotional response one way or the other, we generally judge an argument as good or bad on its own merits. To be consistent then, when we don't like the arguer, we should still judge the argument on its own merits.

Testimonials and False Authority

The opinions of people with authority can provide valuable support to an argument, but only if the **testimonials** come from true experts in the relevant subject area. Otherwise, the arguer is guilty of using **false authority**.

Consider this the flip side of an *ad hominem* attack. Here, instead of attacking the messenger instead of the argument, we embrace the argument because we like the messenger. This often means giving someone unwarranted credibility. If Einstein said that whales should wear velvet waistcoats to hit home runs, should we believe it? We love Einstein, and he was a genius. But what did he know about baseball, or marine biology, or fashion design?

Commercials are a source of testimonials, often by celebrities. Some of these endorsements seem to be supported by the celebrity's career. For example, Olympic swimmer Michael Phelps endorsed Under Armour, a brand of sportswear. Since he is an athlete, the endorsement makes sense. The entertainer Rihanna has also endorsed a brand of sports apparel—Puma. Should we care more about what an entertainer says about athletic wear or what an Olympic swimmer says? Testimonials like these don't represent a fallacy. However, they still should be balanced against the bias that comes from the "expert" being paid to represent a product.

Former U.S. Vice President Al Gore and U.S. Senator James Inhofe are both famous for their views on global warming. Gore has spent decades calling for action, and he even won the 2007 Nobel Peace Prize for his work. Inhofe has long been a denier who has called global warming the "greatest hoax ever perpetrated on the American people." What are their grounds for authority? Senator Inhofe has a bachelor's degree in economics and has worked in business and insurance. Gore got a bachelor's degree in government and has also studied law, divinity, journalism, and English. Neither is a climate scientist. If they have any authority at all, it has come from studying the work of those scientists who do the actual research and who are the actual experts.

In some cases, the fact that a person is an anti-authority actually makes the case stronger. President Ronald Reagan famously opposed funding for AIDS research, thinking that AIDS patients were responsible for having the disease. After he left office, he made a television commercial pleading for Americans to give money for AIDS research. He said, "You see, sometimes old dogs can learn new tricks."

Sometimes, even a true authority can be used in a fallacious way. Email and the Internet are often used to spread stories or warnings on the basis of fraudulent information or testimony. In one such case, the Apollo moon landings were argued to be a hoax staged by the National Aeronautics and Space Administration (NASA). One piece of "evidence" offered was a statement by Stephen Hawking that humans could not survive a trip through the Van Allen radiation belt. Stephen Hawking is a renowned physicist, so he could be trusted as an authority on this issue. The problem is he never made such a statement.

Bandwagon

A **bandwagon fallacy** means that since everybody believes it, I should too. This is the fallacy of following popular tastes, or accepting a claim simply because other people do.

There is a clichéd response to this fallacy that clearly shows the inconsistency: "If everyone jumped off a bridge, would you do it?" This type of fallacy involves people basing an argument on the popularity of the claim or proposal, rather than its merits. "Everybody is getting tattoos, so you should get a tattoo" is an example of a bandwagon argument. But if everyone says "Hey, I really like that Hitler—he really has some good ideas," is it then okay to jump on the Hitler bandwagon and accept those Nazi arguments? Of course not, because to be consistent, we need to consider every argument on its merits, rather than accepting the ones we like and denying the ones we don't.

> There must be something to that Kennedy assassination conspiracy, or why would so many people believe it?

There is power and peril in group thinking. The power is that we can rely on other people to get there ahead of us, to discover things we don't have time or resources to discover. Other people blaze the trail. We just follow along. That's also the peril. If the trail they blaze leads to a cliff, then we can find ourselves in big trouble, believing things that don't make sense, or that are even harmful. In the case of the John F. Kennedy assassination, so many different kinds of people have raised questions about the lone gunman theory that it feels like "Where there's smoke, there's fire." All those theories with all those points of evidence can't be wrong—can they? The fact that many people believe something is not, by itself, evidence.

Ad Misericordiam

Ad misericordiam is an appeal to pity. Users of this fallacy are trying to win support for their argument by manipulating the audience's feelings of guilt or pity. As instructors, we are frequently on the receiving end of this type of fallacy: "Please let me take the exam. My dog died, I lost my job, and I think I have the flu. Please don't make me fail school as well!"

Governments often use gut emotions like fear, revenge, or pity to motivate their citizens in time of war. This poster from World War I show the extent to which our government used images portraying Germans as barbarians, animals, and rapists terrorizing innocent women and children. Did our government do the same after 9/11 in the war with Al Qaeda?

Scare Tactics

When all else fails, frighten your audience. Fear is a powerful emotion. Fear of homosexuality, fear of Islam, fear of MRSA, fear of other races: humans have a long history of acting poorly when they are afraid. Scare tactics capitalize on poor economies, war, and any other controversial issue to persuade their audiences to act or not act in a way that is beneficial to the arguer.

A common advertising technique is the use of scare tactics in order to sell products or encourage people to vote or act in a certain way. (See Figure 5.7.) Either the audience acts in the desired way, or it will suffer some terrible fate. Don't buy our brand of teeth whitener? Your dates will draw back in horror when they see your yellow teeth. Use our competitor's vacuum cleaner? It actually manufactures toxic dust that will quickly fill your rooms to the depth of your ankles. Scare tactics always work to create this kind of either–or choice.

Is an emergency always an emergency? On February 15, 2019, President Donald Trump signed a spending bill to prevent a second government shutdown in as many months, and promptly declared a State of Emergency to fund the border wall that he was advocating. He stated, "So I'm going to be signing a national emergency . . . We're talking about an invasion of our country with drugs, with human traffickers."

This move has plenty of political and legal implications, but whether or not the declaration is allowed to stand by Congress or the courts, the president's support is a clear use of scare tactics. Scare tactics are a kind of straw man argument: arguing on the basis of a falsehood or an exaggeration designed to scare people into agreeing. Invasions, drugs, and human trafficking are three frightening things that almost everyone would want to stop. However, with

Everett Historical/Shutterstock.com

Figure 5.7 Posters from World War II encourage the viewer to feel a strong bond against the enemy

illegal immigration at a thirty-year low, what constitutes an invasion? And since drugs and human trafficking have been with us for decades or longer, what makes them an emergency in 2019? The answers would require nonfallacious thinking in the form of serious research and analysis.

The best way to avoid being taken in by scare tactics is simply not to react. It's best to react when a bus is flying toward you down a hilly street. When there is no immediate danger and someone argues that there is, that's a good time to pause, and do nothing except examine the situation more closely.

Signs that you may be reading or writing fallacies of emotion include:

- ☐ Discussion of someone's background or life, or of aspects unrelated to their argument
- ☐ Reasoning based on what the crowd is doing: mention of high or increasing popularity; discussion of how new something is
- ☐ Off-topic testimonials: for example, a baseball player used as support for a type of plant fertilizer; celebrities touted for their opinion, not their expert judgment
- ☐ Emotionally charged language: worry, hope, fear, desire; that would be a disaster; such a thing should worry any sane person

your turn 5c ▶ PRACTICE **Identify Fallacies of Emotion**

Here is a paragraph from the paper on ESP. See if you can spot the types of fallacies. Match the numbered fallacies with the correct box below.

> *If it led to breakthroughs in the practice of ESP, a full-fledged research program could help us tackle some of the world's biggest problems.* ❶ *Right now, countless children in the Third World are going to bed without their supper; millions of thinking, feeling animals are being mistreated in factory farms; and far too many women are suffering the torments of oppression and domestic abuse.* ❷ *In a world with so many problems, we simply can't afford to neglect any possible avenue for solutions, and we do so at our own peril.* ❸ *We also can't afford to miss the boat, as France, Belgium, and Botswana have each set up their own state-of-the-art government-funded research facilities.* ❹ *No less than the Royal Prince of England has called for similar efforts in his own country.* ❺ *It seems clear that anyone who would refuse to explore such promising opportunities for advancement just isn't thinking straight.*

Which numbered sentence in the paragraph best represents each type of fallacy? Fill in each box with a different number.

☐ *Ad hominem* or other inappropriate negative personal argument

☐ Testimonials, false authority, or other positive personal argument

☐ Bandwagon

☐ *Ad misericordiam*

☐ Scare tactics

Avoid Fallacies of Inconsistency

All fallacies boil down to an inconsistency, but some arguments are blatantly inconsistent. One obvious but all too common kind of inconsistency is a **double standard**. Someone might say, "I like Chairman Gripspike because he is vocal and really speaks out for what he believes, but Chairwoman Leadpocket sure got on my nerves; she was so pushy and opinionated." A common complaint women leaders make is that, when men assert themselves, they are considered strong and capable, but when women assert themselves, they are considered difficult to work with. Anyone with a strong enough bias will use this kind of inconsistency, often without realizing they are doing so. To a white racist, a white criminal is simply a bad egg, an exception, but a black criminal is one more bit of evidence to show that black people are thugs. A black racist might see a wealthy black business person as a hero to be admired and emulated, while seeing a wealthy white business person as a typical selfish oppressor who only looks out for himself.

Sometimes instead of treating similar things inconsistently, people will treat different things as if they are the same. This is a fallacy of false consistency, or false equivalence, treating things as the same when they really aren't the same.

Moral Equivalence

In this fallacy, two very unequal things are balanced against each other *morally,* as if they are equally bad or good. Your boss catches you leaving the office with a company pen on the same day she fired your coworker for embezzling thousands of dollars from the company advertising account. She confronts you and says you are just as guilty as your coworker and need to be fired. Technically, stealing is stealing, but are these two acts really morally equivalent?

Material Equivalence

Here, two very unequal things are equated, or balanced against each other as if they are *materially* equivalent. If an apple a day keeps the doctor away, does it matter if the apple is a red one or a green one? An apple is an apple, right? Well . . .

Sweet gum trees give off gases that, when mixed with automobile emissions, can contribute to ozone pollution. Trees also take in carbon dioxide and give off oxygen. Someone might say that these two things balance out, that the material effects of a tree cancel out so completely that cutting down trees will neither help nor harm the environment. President Reagan was famous for his statement that trees pollute more than cars, so we shouldn't complain or worry when they are cut down. In reality, trees suck in carbon dioxide, a principal greenhouse gas responsible for global warming, and they also give off oxygen. Until we actually weigh trees' beneficial effects against their harmful effects, we don't really know if the material evidence is equal. And it turns out, trees do far more good than harm, so we should not cut them down.

Definitional Equivalence

In *definitional* equivalence, two things are defined as being the same, whether they are or not. Often, before we can tell if two things are morally equivalent or have equivalent material effects, we first have to know what the things are. Do they even belong to the same category? The abortion debate centers around the definition of personhood. Is a fertilized egg a human life? Is a fetus a person? The U.S. Constitution defines a citizen as someone born or naturalized in the United States. What does science say? What do the courts say?

Life is so diverse that scientists can't agree on a single definition of what a species is, so more recently they have begun using a combination of definitions. These kinds of arguments sound pretty esoteric, but in fact they can matter in the real world. Suppose a population of foxes is threatened by a home builder's development activity. If it represents a separate species, it could be protected under the Endangered Species Act. If it is defined as simply a subgroup of a common fox species, it might be exempted from any protection. A developer could lose big money, and people might not be able to buy homes where they'd like, or a species might disappear from the earth. A definition, then, can seal the fate of an animal.

Inconsistent Treatment (from Dogmatism, Prejudice, and Bias)

Often this fallacy shows itself in the way an arguer supports a claim. Arguers look for facts to help their side of the argument but ignore facts that work against their side.

One infamous case of inconsistent treatment involved voting laws. Various poll taxes were levied and literacy tests adopted to make it harder for black Americans in Southern states to vote. Many black citizens in the early twentieth century were poor and so could not pay the tax, or they would have had trouble answering detailed written questions about the U.S. Constitution. They were effectively disenfranchised when they went to the polls to cast their vote. Poor and illiterate white citizens were often waved through or given easier questions to answer.

Even strictly equal treatment can be considered unequal when the audience is unwittingly biased and looks for treatment that favors their own point of view. The issue of media bias is a good example. During any election cycle, watch the letters to the editor. Democrats write to complain of bad pictures and negative stories about their Democratic candidates, while Republicans write to complain about similar treatment of the candidates they favor. Truly unbiased studies that could find true cases of bias are rarely done. When they are done, they are often attacked for using biased criteria to measure bias. For instance, next time there is an election, gather an equal number of friends from different political sides (say, Democrat, Republican, and Independent). Set some criteria that you can all agree are unbiased (number of minutes spent on a story about a candidate or issue, number of words, pictures with a smiling or frowning candidate), and start counting to see if your own impression of bias holds true.

Equivocation

Good thinking requires us to look at various sides of an issue and consider contradictory evidence. Or we might consider various sides because we are trying to explore a subject, or even come to a compromise. In that case, it would be okay to consider contradictions without resolving them.

In a traditional persuasive argument, however, it is considered a fallacy to make contradictory claims. People call it "arguing out of both sides of your mouth." A cliché line of attack in a courtroom is to catch a witness making two opposite statements and then to ask the witness, "So which is it, Mr. Knucklepump, were you lying then, or are you lying now?" Equivocation occurs in a context, and that context is crucial. For example, equivocation undercuts an argument because, if the arguer can't even agree with her own argument, why should we agree with her? But in a more exploratory situation, equivocation can actually help build trust with an audience, to establish a spirit of going forward together in order to find enough evidence to form a conclusion.

Equivocation often happens because we keep arguing a claim we like, regardless of the support. If one reason fails, we try another, and so we set one reason against another. The war in Iraq could be considered representative of this type of equivocation. It was first presented as a means of defending the world against weapons of mass destruction. Later it was declared to be about fighting terrorism by Al Qaeda. When resistance by Saddam Hussein's armies collapsed, a banner was raised that said "Mission Accomplished." Later, the U.S. Government claimed that a premature end to the Iraq war would be disastrous. This example of equivocation shows how the seeds of doubt in an argument can be sown. That is why they are considered fallacious.

False Analogy

An analogy is a comparison between two things or a claim that two situations are similar. A good analogy can help people think about things in a new way by pointing out parallels. A **false analogy** occurs, however, if an arguer says the situations are comparable but they really aren't.

Arguers use many analogies to support a position, and often those analogies don't hold up because the situations are more different than they are alike. In other words, analogies do not always present fallacies; often an analogy does hold up, and the situations are alike in some essential way. The Bush administration argued that we could help a defeated Iraq become a democracy because after defeating Japan and Germany in World War II, the United States helped them become democracies. It is a judgment call whether or not that is a worthwhile or a false analogy. One strike against the argument may be that both Japan and Germany were homogenous societies, whereas Iraq is divided into several ethnic and religious groups, making a transition to a working democracy difficult if not impossible.

All fallacies boil down to an inconsistency of one kind or another. We're almost always inconsistent when we argue because we have our own point of view. We have values and beliefs. We want to believe certain things, and we want to support those beliefs. Intentionally or unintentionally, these factors sometimes leads us to argue inconsistently, favoring our view of things.

Even though fallacies are to some extent inevitable, they are a matter of degree. We can be as fair as possible, including and weighing other views along with our own. We can be somewhat fair, acknowledging other claims, or we can purposely try to manipulate our audience by ignoring evidence that supports another side of things.

Signs that you may be reading or writing fallacies of inconsistency include:

- ☐ Unbalanced discussions: 90 percent of the support falls on one side of an argument.
- ☐ Undeservedly balanced discussions: 50 percent of the support falls on each side of an argument (33 percent with three sides), with no real justification.
- ☐ Language of contradiction: but, however, on the other hand, still, while at the same time.
- ☐ Language of equivalence: this is like, just as, in the same way that, similarly.
- ☐ Comparisons that don't sound right: being a president is a lot like being a restaurant owner.

your turn **PRACTICE Identify Fallacies of Inconsistency**

Here is a paragraph from the paper on ESP. See if you can spot the types of fallacies. Match the numbered fallacies with the correct box below.

> ❶ *Perhaps those who dismiss paranormal research are thinking straight; maybe they just don't know the facts.* ❷ *They might not realize that not funding ESP is essentially the same as using Jewish prisoners in dangerous medical experiments.* ❸ *It's just as unethical, too.* ❹ *Perhaps they don't know that, just as the hard sciences have their flagship institution, the Massachusetts Institute of Technology (MIT), paranormal research also has had its flagship in the Institute for Parapsychology at Duke University, an equally prestigious institution, albeit that the university broke ties with the Institute in 1965, when its founder retired.* ❺ *The advancements of the paranormal sciences should receive exactly the same funding as the natural sciences; nay, they should in fact receive more, to make up for the funding inequities of the past. If we do these things, we will likely ensure a better future for our children, and isn't that what it's all about?*

Which numbered sentence in the paragraph best represents each type of fallacy? Fill in each box with a different number.

- ☐ False analogy: Moral equivalence
- ☐ False analogy: Material equivalence
- ☐ False analogy: Definitional equivalence
- ☐ Equivocation
- ☐ Inconsistent treatment (from dogmatism, prejudice, or bias)

To be able to identify fallacious strategies in the arguments of others is a great asset to being a stronger reader and thinker. To be able to avoid these same fallacious strategies in your own arguments makes you a stronger writer.

your turn 5e ▶ PRACTICE **Identify Four Types of Fallacies**

In the following passage, try to spot the fallacies from all four groups:

- Fallacies of choice
- Fallacies of support
- Fallacies of emotion
- Fallacies of inconsistency

> *We should get rid of our current male president and put a woman in the White House. Every bad thing that has happened in this country has happened under a male president. We had slavery, the Civil War, the Great Depression, Pearl Harbor, and the defeat in Vietnam all under male presidents. Therefore, a woman president could only do a better job. There is nowhere to go but up.*
>
> *Furthermore, little girls all over this country have grown up with no presidential role model. The damage of this injustice has been devastating to the psyche. We might as well have shackled these girls and tied them to a ball and chain. There is no doubt that this lack of inspiration has held women back.*
>
> *One perennial problem that traditionally faces this country has been budget deficits, yet this is an area a woman president is uniquely qualified to handle. For centuries, women have successfully managed home finances, keeping a budget, spending their limited incomes wisely to keep their families fed and clothed. A woman would bring that same kind of efficient money management to the White House.*
>
> *Women have run countries before. Margaret Thatcher was widely considered to be an excellent prime minister of the United Kingdom. That proves that women in general can lead and lead well. Men, on the other hand, are worthless as leaders. Consider recent history. We elected Richard Nixon, and we lost the Vietnam War. We elected Jimmy Carter, and we had an oil crisis. We elected Ronald Reagan, and the stock market crashed. We elected Bill Clinton, and the White House was used for sleazy activities. If we keep electing male presidents, the country will keep falling. If the country keeps sliding into corruption and moral decay, we may soon find ourselves a mini-power instead of a superpower. We could end up last among nations. And keep in mind that Hillary Clinton would have beaten John McCain in a head-to-head match-up.*
>
> *It may be true that the gender of a candidate has no bearing on how effective a leader he or she may be. On the other hand, the famous musician Gidget Snotbrackler has said that we need now more than ever to "Go pink." For the sake of our little girls, can we afford not to?*

Reflect and Apply

1. As you read your sources, what steps are you taking to evaluate them for fallacious information?

2. As you write your argument, what are you doing to ensure that you are not including fallacies? Do you have a way to identify these fallacies as you review your argument?

3. If you are using emotional support, how are you preventing your images or anecdotes from becoming fallacies of emotion?

4. As you include material from multiple points of view in your argument, how are you avoiding fallacies of inconsistency?

5. What is the harm in selecting sources only because they support your own views, or because they espouse views that are easy to dismiss? Which type of fallacy is involved in doing so?

KEEPING IT LOCAL

YOU LIKE YOUR COWORKERS and want to get along with them all, but you don't like feeling pressured to participate in every fundraiser that comes along; you would like to be able to pick the fundraisers that seem to support the most important causes or that are selling products in which you are truly interested. The same holds true for donations. Many charitable causes are legitimate and do a lot of good work. But again, you don't want to have to donate to causes that you have not selected.

The biggest obstacle to taking a stand is that so many of the arguments your coworkers give seem so persuasive. "If we don't raise enough money, the Tigers bowling team will be disbanded and these children will never learn to work as a team." "How can you look at the faces of these poor hungry people and not contribute to hunger relief?" "Everyone else has already placed an order for doughnuts." These are fallacies—each and every one of them. Ask questions, dig deeper, and find out more before you pull out your wallet. Maybe you will be perceived as heartless, or maybe you will be seen as the department hero.

Detecting fallacies in the wide variety of sources you read, view, or listen to can be difficult. But actively asking questions about each source and each claim can keep you from passively accepting illogical or manipulative arguments. Look for fallacies of choice, of support, of emotion, and of inconsistency in the sources you are using in your argument. Secondarily, can you turn your critical focus on your own writing and detect any fallacies in your own writing? Doing so will make you a stronger reader, writer, and thinker.

CHAPTER 6

Work Fairly with the Opposition

Learning Objectives

By working through this chapter, you will be able to

- recognize bias and generalizations made toward opposing arguments.
- find credible local and scholarly sources on an issue.
- summarize opposing arguments fairly and accurately.
- identify areas of overlap between arguments.
- respond critically to opposing viewpoints.

For the past few months, you have been aware of a neighbor whose health and well-being seem to be suffering. From others in the neighborhood, you learn that the neighbor, John, lost his job and health insurance earlier this year and has complained about not being able to afford his medical bills and that this has discouraged him from visiting his doctor as often as he needs to. Additionally, family members are unable to stop by regularly, and it is increasingly difficult for John to visit friends because the closest bus stop is nearly a half mile away. John is a proud man, and while he appreciates the efforts of you and others on your block to check up on him, he wants more control over his life and his health. John's monthly unemployment check, modest as it is, puts him on the outside of a health-care system on which he has become dependent. Your frustration with John's situation increases as you realize, uncomfortably, that family and neighbors are not enough to supply John with what he needs, and your thoughts, like the thoughts of many associated with folks in John's circumstances, turn to our health-care

TOPIC: Health care

ISSUE: Universal Health care

AUDIENCE: State and Federal Representatives

CLAIM: Universal health care should be a right guaranteed to all American citizens.

system and how it might better serve John. And among your very first thoughts is the awareness that we are sharply divided about whether to continue to keep the health-care system as it is, reform it, or change it entirely.

We build arguments to articulate positions on issues that matter to us, like the one described above, and knowing who disagrees with us and why is vital to the success of any argument. This chapter is devoted to strategies useful in responding to those who argue positions different from your own. When you conduct your research thoroughly and understand what motivates an opposing argument and how this argument is supported, you are in a position to interact with respect and fair-mindedness. This will earn you credibility with an audience.

When we plan and deliver an argument, we're nearly always in conversation with others. It's important to remember that those opposed to a claim we make are equally invested in the issue at hand—but from different perspectives. Treat the opposition respectfully and as fellow members of the community tied to your issue. Acknowledge the values that motivate an opponent. Send the message to your audience *and* your opponents that you can accurately identify and summarize positions other than your own. In an argument, it is your job to remain critical and fair-minded at the same time. This chapter offers guidelines for working with the **opposition**, guidelines that will be helpful when you construct various kinds of argument—Toulmin-based, Middle Ground, Rogerian, and the Microhistory—all of which are discussed in Chapter 8, "Consider Toulmin-Based Argument," and Chapter 9, "Consider Middle-Ground Argument, Rogerian Argument, and Argument Based on a Microhistory."

Why the Opposition Matters

Opposing points of view on an issue matter. Like you, your opponents are part of a conversation on an area of life important to them. In most cases, you'll learn more about an issue when you study the opposition. For example, based on how an opponent supports a position, you can:

- Acquire new context.
- Learn to see the issue from another perspective.
- Recognize the values that motivate an opponent.
- Familiarize yourself with a body of specific support different from yours.
- Recognize what you have in common with your opponents.

Suppose you plan to argue on free universal health care for Americans, both a national and a local issue. Based on your experience with your neighbor, you feel compelled to encourage your state's senators and representatives in Washington, D.C., to move beyond the Patient Protection and Affordable Care Act, commonly referred to as "Obamacare," and to support free universal health care. From your research, you know that the issue is complex in terms of its many well-supported positions. For example, various opponents claim that universal health care would undermine the insurance industry, that higher taxes would result, that the government bureaucracy would mean long delays for patients in need, that consumers would no longer be able to shop for their best health-care values when government replaces

Figure 6.1 Paying close attention to points of view that differ from your own builds credibility with an audience.

free-market competition among providers, and that health-care standards may erode with a single provider. These differing positions matter. If your view on free universal health care is to be taken seriously by your audience, you must negotiate your way through these different views. As you do so, you'll learn about the strengths and weaknesses of arguments competing for the attention of your audience. This can make all the difference to an audience—your willingness to study the opposition thoroughly and to present it in both fair and critical terms.

your turn 6a ▶ **GET STARTED Size up the Opposition**

Based on an issue you're working with, respond to the following questions and prompts:

1. On what issue do you plan to argue?
2. What motivates you to argue on this issue?
3. Based on your general awareness of this issue, identify two or three positions different from your position.

Resist Easy Generalizations

Oversimplifying an opponent's position weakens your argument. Different positions on an issue endure because they are built on solid foundations that appeal to people. Your task in an argument is to resist **easy generalizations** of other views and instead summarize them in dignified, respectful terms. This means reading the other position closely so that you can identify and put into your own words its claim, warrant, reasons, and support. This method will get you away from generalizing another position in just a sentence or two. Plan to devote a substantial paragraph to each differing view you bring to an argument.

In your background reading, you likely note a persistent opposing claim arguing against universal health care for Americans. Principal reasons supporting this claim include problems in other countries where universal health care is provided: long waits in doctors' offices, frequent cancellations of appointments, and the pain that patients often must endure while waiting for health-care services. This opposing argument brings in effective support, including data that reveal the number of Canadians (Canada's universal health-care system is often suggested as a model for an American system) who have died or suffered heart attacks while waiting for health-care services. Other data suggest that an alarming number of Canadians perform their own medical and dental procedures instead of waiting. Additionally, examples of the suffering of some individuals make for compelling support. This view also holds that universal health care in Canada is unfair to many everyday people. The argument is thoughtful and well structured. Your aim in working with this opposing view, or rebuttal, is to summarize it accurately. Doing so will set a respectful tone of fairness.

internet activity 6a **Exploring**

Conduct an informal Internet search, and identify two or three differing positions on your issue. For each opposing view that you might include in your argument, answer the following questions.

1. What, exactly, does each differing position claim?
2. What reasons support each differing claim?
3. What effective support—such as particularly compelling facts and data, personal examples, and research from experts—does each differing position use to support its claim?
4. What makes these other positions valid and arguable? Is your perspective on your issue getting broader based on familiarity with these other views? Explain.

Listen to Local Voices

Before beginning your formal research into scholarly sources on an issue, there are many ways to get a sense of why an issue is important to people in your community and your peers in the classroom. Conversations with colleagues, friends, and family are one way. Another is your local media. Many online sources, like news sites, information sites, and opinion blogs, can provide useful glosses of an issue. Your local and regional newspapers can also be helpful, and most online editions of newspapers contain a search feature that allows you to read past articles and thus get a sense of the history of an issue in your area. Refer to Chapter 4, "Evaluate and Engage with Your Sources," for specific information on gathering online sources.

Listen closely to **local voices**. This will allow you to craft an argument that becomes part of a local conversation on an issue that means something to you and your neighbors, coworkers, or classmates. Whether you take in differing perspectives on an issue over coffee with friends, in conversation with coworkers, during a class discussion, at the dinner table, from your local news, or by interacting on Facebook or a favorite blog, open yourself to the range of attitudes on an issue. Familiarizing yourself with this local knowledge will make your argument more focused and immediate; it will also let you appeal to your audience with specific information.

As we know, the issue of health care in our country can elicit strong points of view. If you happen to be in conversation with a health-care professional—a nurse, doctor, or emergency medical technician—you may run across the view that a universal health-care system might limit earning power, as government-assigned fees would be less than what market value is now and that this would in turn reduce the number of trained professionals entering the health-care field. Additionally, many argue that burnout would occur when the government overloads doctors with patients. Another conversation might avail you of the financial hardships a family endures because of rising costs and that free health care is necessary. Still another conversation puts you in touch with the view that free health care would eliminate the advantages of a com-

Figure 6.2 Take advantage of informal, local moments as a first step in familiarizing yourself with the opposition.

petitive, free-market system, a system that many feel is responsible for innovation and efficiency in the medical field. Listening with an open mind and heart to these and other views can sensitize you to others and their investment in the issue. Your fair acknowledgement of their views in your argument will make positive impressions on your readers.

 your turn 6b **GET STARTED** **Listen to Local Voices**

Answer the following questions as a way of acknowledging local views on an issue you plan to argue.

1. What individuals in my community are most deeply invested in this issue?
2. What, in their personal and professional lives, motivates them to speak out?
3. What reasons do they give for their positions on the issue?
4. What solutions do they propose?
5. After listening to others invested in my issue, what do I know about this issue now that I did not know before?

tip 6a

Access Local Voices
Your local newspaper may have a search engine that allows you to search past articles and issues. Find the link to this search engine on your newspaper's home page, and then type in keywords connected to your issue.

Summarize Other Voices Fairly

To earn the trust of your audience, it is important that you treat your opponents fairly, and this means withholding judgment of opponents' views when you introduce them in your argument. Your evaluation of differing views can

iStock.com/bobbieo/Bobbie Osborne

Figure 6.3 To a target audience, fairness is often measured by how an arguer treats those holding opposing views. It is essential that the arguer makes the effort to summarize the other side fairly.

and should occur *after* you summarize them in a neutral tone. In many cases, those holding other views are just as determined as you are to be heard and to influence local thinking. Review the following examples of writers' treatments of differing positions and the analysis that follows each summary.

Summary #1: By Linda Gonzalez

This writer is responding to the issue of illegal immigrants in the United States having driver's licenses and claims that immigrants should be allowed to obtain licenses under certain conditions. In the paragraphs that follow, the writer summarizes a view opposing her claim.

Another point of view is the one held passionately by opponents of giving driver's licenses to illegal immigrants. These opponents argue that driving is a privilege and not a right. For instance, Republican Sue Myrick of Charlotte, North Carolina, says, "Our feeling is that a driver's license is a privilege for citizens and legal aliens and it shouldn't be something given to somebody who broke the law" (qtd. in Funk). Backers of Myrick agree by saying that issuing driver's licenses to undocumented people would attract more illegal immigrants to the country and it would then be easy for terrorists to come to the United States. Considering driving as a privilege, many politicians are completely against a plan that would allow illegal immigrants to obtain a driver's license. They believe that because people who have entered the country illegally have broken the immigration laws, they should not be allowed to receive any kind of benefits in this country. Moreover, a driver's license allows a person to be able to work, drive, and open a bank account; all these things make life easier for undocumented people in this country.

Additionally, the government is taking stricter ways to keep the nation safe. One effective way is to not issue driver's licenses to illegal aliens so they cannot enter federal buildings, board airplanes, or use it as identification to give the impression of being legal. An illustration of this in their favor is that 8 of the 19 men in the terrorist attacks on September 11, 2001, got licenses in Virginia (Lazo).

Another example of illegal immigrants threatening the nation's safety is that there are drug dealers and criminals looking for easy ways to get licenses. "Driver's licenses are as close as we get to a national ID," says John Keely of the Center for Immigration Studies, a group in Washington that advocates limited immigration (A5). "While the overwhelming majority of immigrants don't pose a national security threat, I don't think issuing driver's licenses to them affords protection to Americans, but hurts the efforts to shore up national security" (Johnson 3). Authorities against a plan to provide driver's licenses to illegal immigrants do not take into consideration that undocumented people are not going to go away just because they do not have driver's licenses and that they will drive with or without it. Certainly, the arguments in favor of and against issuing driver's licenses to noncitizens are so strong that it is difficult to imagine an alternative position.

Funk, Tim. "Myrick [R-NC]: N.C. Must Halt Illegal Driver Licenses (Bill Would Cut off $870 Million to N.C.)." *Charlotte Observer*, 9 Nov. 2005. http://www.freerepublic.com/focus/f-news/1519066/posts

Lazo, Luz. "Virginia to Begin Issuing Driver's Licenses That Will Be Required for Air Travel in 2020." *The Washington Post*, 28 July, 2018. https://www.washingtonpost.com/local/trafficandcommuting /virginia-to-begin-issuing-drivers-licenses-that-will-be-required -for-air-travel-in-2020/2018/07/27/5f723820-8b65-11e8-85ae-511bc 1146b0b_story.html?noredirect=on&utm_term=.eb99bc0f5960

Discussion

This is a fair-minded summary of a position different from the writer's. The writer maintains a respectful, neutral tone in reference to her opponents. The writer identifies the opponent's claim of driver's licenses being a privilege of citizenship in the second sentence. Views of Myrick, Johnson, and Keely appear without judgment. The writer briefly disagrees with her opponents in the next-to-last sentence of the final paragraph, and her final sentence hints that her claim and support will occur later in the argument. The summary avoids brief, superficial treatment of opponents, and the writer is in no rush to dismiss them. This summary appears in a middle-ground argument, as the last sentence suggests, where the writer will offer a practical position between what she views as two extreme positions. See Chapter 9, "Consider Middle-Ground Argument, Rogerian Argument, and Argument Based on a Microhistory," for a full treatment of middle-ground argument.

Summary #2: By Brittney Lambert

This writer is responding to the issue of whether students on college campuses should be allowed to carry concealed weapons. She claims that students should be granted this right. She begins her paragraph by identifying a view opposed to hers.

One argument against the right to carry concealed weapons on campus is that students' protection and safety should be left to the police. This is because police have gone through four to five months' worth of training, but citizens who carry licensed concealed weapons have only gone through about a day of training. First of all, adults with concealed handgun licenses can protect themselves in most "unsecured places" already; they just lose that right when they step on campus. Secondly, police officers cannot be everywhere all of the time. In a study by the U.S. Secret Service, 37 school shootings were researched. According to "Common Arguments against Campus Carry," of the 37 school shootings, "over half of the attacks were resolved/ended before law enforcement responded to the scene. In these cases the attacker was stopped by faculty or fellow students, decided to stop shooting on his own, or killed himself. The study found that only 3 of the 37 school shootings researched involved shots being fired by law enforcement officers" ("Common").

"Common Arguments against Campus Carry." *Students for Concealed Carry*, 2012. https://concealedcampus.org/common-arguments/

Discussion

Although the writer has written an otherwise strong argument, there is room for improvement in her coverage of the opponent's position. This summary is not as strong as it could be because only the first two sentences of the paragraph address the opponent's position. The opponent's claim is clear, that campus safety is the responsibility of the police, but only one reason is given, that campus police have undergone training. The student's argument could have been stronger if she had included support for the opponent's claim-quotations, facts, or specific examples. Sometimes when an arguer glosses over an opponent's claim, it can strike an audience as unfairly brief, especially when the remainder of the paragraph is devoted to countering the opponent. By devoting only two sentences to another view, the writer might appear dismissive and unwilling to treat the opponent fairly. With some adjustments, this essay could become a strong, Toulmin-based argument, a kind of argument discussed in Chapter 8, "Consider Toulmin-Based Argument."

Summary #3: By James Guzman

In the following summary, the writer focuses on health care and whether it should remain privatized or change to a system with free services to all Americans. He argues a middle-ground position and claims that the answer to the health-care question is to reform the present system. Prior to the paragraph below, the writer summarized the view of those opposed to free health care. He is now summarizing what he considers to be a second extreme position on health care.

On the other side are those who believe that our country should provide universal health care to all American citizens. The 46 million uninsured citizens are a disgrace on our country that is thought of as the land of opportunity for all. It's their opinion that this number alone is reason enough to warrant universal health care. It is hard to brag about equal opportunity when there are a huge number of low-income families that do not have a doctor or receive the necessary medical attention to maintain their health. Every other wealthy country has found it unacceptable to have portions of the populations uninsured and have implemented universal health care. Of all things that the government provides, health is surely up there with education and police protection in importance. It is true that this huge number of uninsured is alarming, but is it really *society's* responsibility to take care of those who choose not to buy health insurance? If a person truly is a hard-working citizen, we have tax credits designed specifically for those who buy their own health care. This argument could be easily interpreted as class envy. If this is another weapon in class warfare, then it would no doubt turn out to be another wealth-transfer system designed to punish the successful.

Discussion

This summary has both strengths and weaknesses. The first half of the summary identifies a claim and then refers to very clear reasons that support this claim. Brief support is included in the form of "46 million uninsured citizens" and "every other wealthy country." Yet this support would be even more compelling and trustworthy if documentation as to where the writer gathered this information were given. Proper documentation, examples, quotations, and other specific support for this opposing view would strengthen the summary and move the writer closer to earning credibility with his audience.

In your own arguments, include the strengths and avoid the weaknesses in the preceding summaries. Each of these writers crafted strongly worded claims and reasons and brought plenty of effective support to his or her argument, but only the writer of the first summary was fair and thorough in her treatment of an opposing view.

> your turn 6c **GET STARTED** Evaluate Summaries of Differing Positions

Based on your treatments of opponents in an argument you are building, answer the following questions.

1. What does each opposing position claim? What reasons and support for opposing positions do you include in your summaries?
2. Do you document in parentheses the source of quoted and summarized material?
3. Is your audience likely to believe that you achieve a tone of fair play and mutual respect in your summaries of other positions? Explain.
4. In your view, would those holding the differing positions you summarize approve of these summaries? Would they feel they've been treated fairly and with respect? Explain.

Value Expertise over Advocacy

Make every effort to include opponents who support their claims with clear reasons and thorough support. In addition to local sources, bring to your argument opposing views found in scholarly journals and periodicals gathered from academic databases and from search engines that allow access to scholarly and professional material. Avoid sources that are purely ideological, overly emotional, brief, and general. Referencing an advocate for or against universal health care, for example, who argues on primarily emotional grounds will weaken your argument. Your audience will have difficulty taking such an advocate seriously, and this will reflect on your willingness to

**Search Thoroughly
to Avoid Shallow
Summaries**
Many of us tend to default
to mainstream search
engines as a way to begin
researching an issue. Avoid
this habit! Instead, consult
the academic search engines
and databases to which your
school subscribes, some of
which are devoted specifically
to particular fields, such
as medicine, environment,
education, government,
business, and specific
academic disciplines like
English, history, and computer
science. See Chapter 4,
"Evaluate and Engage with
Your Sources," for additional
sources housing scholarly
material.

treat the opposition fairly. On the other hand, when you refer to an opposing view that is full of effective support and grounded in strong values, your argument becomes more credible and, importantly, challenges you to make your argument equally compelling in view of a well-informed opposition.

For example, during a prewriting activity in class you choose to share with your group a neighbor's complaint that universal health care is merely "welfare for the uninsured" and "rewards the lazy." The neighbor appears to offer no support for these claims. This is the kind of opposing view to avoid in an argument. Without substantial support, such claims become fallacies only. See Chapter 5, "Read Critically and Avoid Fallacies," for a full discussion of fallacies and how to avoid them in your writing.

internet activity 6b Connecting

Working with the online materials you gather for an argument, answer the following questions.

1. What specific research will you bring to your argument? How does this research go beyond mere advocacy along ideological grounds for a position and use facts and credible information as support?
2. While another position may include emotional appeals, is the position centered in primarily rational support? Explain.
3. Are the opposing views you bring to your argument found in reputable publications that include current facts and statistics? What are these publications?

Avoid Bias When You Summarize

Summarize positions of your opponents accurately, in your own words, and without a hint of judgment or evaluation. Your summaries should be so accurate that opponents approve of them. Consider the following paragraphs and the two summaries: one brief, inaccurate, and full of **biased language,** and the other accurate and objective. The paragraphs are from the article "Universal Healthcare's Dirty Little Secrets," by Michael Tanner and Michael Cannon, well-informed opponents of universal health care.

> Simply saying that people have health insurance is meaningless. Many countries provide universal insurance but deny critical procedures to patients who need them. Britain's Department of Health reported in 2006 that at any given time, nearly 900,000 Britons are waiting for admission to National Health Service hospitals, and shortages force the cancellation of more than 50,000 operations each year. In Sweden, the wait for heart surgery can be as long as 25 weeks, and the average wait for hip replacement surgery is more than a year. Many of these

individuals suffer chronic pain, and judging by the numbers, some will probably die awaiting treatment. In a 2005 ruling of the Canadian Supreme Court, Chief Justice Beverly McLachlin wrote that "access to a waiting list is not access to healthcare." (qtd. in Tanner and Cannon).

Everyone agrees that far too many Americans lack health insurance. But covering the uninsured comes about as a byproduct of getting other things right. The real danger is that our national obsession with universal coverage will lead us to neglect reforms—such as enacting a standard health insurance deduction, expanding health savings accounts and deregulating insurance markets—that could truly expand coverage, improve quality and make care more affordable.

Summary #1

Michael Tanner and Michael Cannon, both from the Cato Institute, argue the same tired conservative position we have heard for years. They provide only negative evidence from countries with free health care and want us to think that many people die before getting treatment because delays are so long. They view a competitive, free-market approach as better than guaranteeing that everyone receives health care.

Discussion

This brief summary is biased and inaccurate. Using words like "tired," "conservative," and "negative" establishes a narrow, judgmental tone. The summary ignores the factual support the writers bring to their argument. It also ignores the writers' call for specific reforms and their attention to those Americans who are now underserved. In general, the summary is not effective because it misleads and includes biased language.

Summary #2

Michael Tanner, Director of Health and Welfare Studies at the Cato Institute, and Michael Cannon, Director of Health Policy Studies at the Cato Institute, provide substantial data to argue against universal health care. They refer to other countries with established universal health-care systems—Great Britain, Sweden, and Canada—and claim that large numbers of citizens have to suffer through long delays for hospital service and for operations. In Sweden, for example, the authors claim that some patients will die while waiting for heart surgery and hip replacement. Tanner and Cannon agree with their opponents that "far too many Americans lack health insurance," but they feel that reforming our present system is a more practical approach to this issue. Specifically, they want to see a deduction built into health insurance policies, an emphasis on health savings plans, and expanded deregulation of the health insurance industry.

Tanner, Michael D., and Michael F. Cannon. "Universal Healthcare's Dirty Little Secrets." *Los Angeles Times*, 5 Apr. 2007, https://www.latimes.com/la-oe-tanner5apr05-story.html.

tip 6c

Peer Edit Summaries
As a check against offering biased summaries, ask a peer to evaluate your summaries of differing views on the issue you're working with. Pay close attention to these peer responses, as they can point out biased language that can block fair representation of other views.

Discussion

This is a fair-minded, objective summary of an opposing viewpoint. The opposition's claim (first sentence), selected support (sentences two and three), and warrant (sentence four) are noted. The summary is free from biased language.

your turn 6d **GET STARTED** **Avoid Bias**

Based on your research of opposing views on an issue you're working with, answer the following questions.

1. Have you avoided judgmental or emotionally loaded language in your summary that could mislead an audience? Explain. What words might you replace to assure your audience that your summary is accurate and fair?

2. Are your summaries mostly in your words with only occasional quotations? Would your opponents agree with your summary of their positions, and would you feel confident presenting your summaries to your opponents? Explain.

3. When quoting or paraphrasing an opponent, do you document in parentheses appropriate page or paragraph numbers?

Find Points of Overlap

Although you may differ with your opponents, there likely are points in your argument where you overlap and share certain concerns and values. For example, you favor free universal health care and others oppose it, but in closely studying other views you'll probably observe that some of your values and the values of opposing views are quite similar. Often the best place to find shared values is at the level of the warrant in an argument, that is, the moral grounding on which an argument is based. For example, all players in the free health-care debate may agree that:

- Quality health care should be available to those in need.
- Delivery of health care should be timely.
- Health-care services should be run efficiently.

These shared values make rational communication possible and create a positive bridge between you and others at the discussion table. This bridge becomes possible because of your willingness to take in without judgment the views of others.

Identify Common Ground with the Opposition

The following issues are controversial because they elicit strong and often emotional responses. On the surface, it may seem that finding **common ground**

Marmaduke St. John/Alamy Stock photo

Figure 6.4 Acknowledging shared concerns and values is a strength in an argument.

would be impossible. But when you dig beneath attitudes and proposed solutions to our most controversial problems, you may uncover core beliefs, values, and principles that reveal some common ground. To make these revelations possible, be diligent in your research process and keep an open mind to those who differ from you.

Example #1

Issue   Should water be publicly held or privately owned?

Description   This is a full-fledged issue in several western states and in numerous countries. Proponents of classifying water as a privately held commodity argue that, although water is a basic need, access to it should not be a legally guaranteed right. This side also reasons that private companies are better at protecting water than the government, that innovation in the water industry springs from privately owned water companies, and that competition among companies can drive down the price of water for the consumer. On the other side, those who favor public ownership of water claim that water is too essential for survival to let it be distributed by companies. This side also argues that the government is needed to ensure that water resources are conserved, that water remains safe, and that it is not subject to changes in an economic market, as this can work against its availability to consumers.

Common Ground   Shared values among opposing sides on this issue may include the recognition that, in recent decades, many water sources have diminished and become tainted and that efforts to purify our water are essential, that apparatus for distributing water be efficient, and that any realistic assessment of our future must include water availability.

Example #2

Issue   Does homeschooling threaten American democracy?

Description   Many critics of homeschooling claim that homeschooled students may succeed as students but not as citizens. They reason that homeschoolers are trained to be more concerned about themselves than their communities, that they are subjected to educational agendas grounded in religious or ideological beliefs, and that the social isolation in which homeschooled students learn steers them away from civic involvement. On the other hand, many proponents of this movement argue that homeschooled students in fact make better citizens than students educated in public schools. As studies emerge following the first generation of homeschooled students in recent American history, these supporters note that homeschoolers contribute to democratic culture in greater percentages than graduates of public schools in the following areas: support of political parties, membership in civic organizations, voting, speaking out on public issues, and community service work.

Common Ground   Opponents in this issue may overlap in their belief that children deserve an education that prepares them for active citizenship and that this includes participation in civic and political activity.

tip 6d

Recognize Shared Values

Like yours, an opponent's public position on an issue and his or her problem-solving apparatus rest atop a set of values and core beliefs. This is where you can look to find common ground when none is immediately evident. Sometimes the opposition will spell out in direct language his or her values and beliefs; at other times, these values are implied or stated only indirectly. When researching other positions, remember to read carefully for the values that underlie a position.

Example #3

Issue   Is it fair to make birth records unavailable to adopted children?

Description   States vary in the laws that prohibit, limit, and allow access to the birth records of adopted children. Many claim that it is unfair to prohibit access to records on grounds that medical information of birth parents can reveal conditions that may affect adopted children and future generations. Another argument on banning access involves the regret and sense of loss that some women later feel after giving up their children for adoption, often at a young age. Others feel that laws protecting the privacy of biological parents should be honored, especially with regard to women who chose to give up their children with the understanding that confidentiality would be assured. Additionally, this side argues that the privacy of the adopted family would be compromised were adopted children given access to birth records.

Common Ground   Both sides on this issue have in common deep concern for the welfare of adopted children. This value alone can make communication possible when differing views are treated respectfully. Building on this shared value, this issue can reveal the importance of precisely crafted claims, those that avoid all-or-nothing approaches. For example, given that both sides want the best for adopted children, qualifiers can be built into claims that allow for access to birth records under certain conditions based on the needs of birth and adopted parents.

GET STARTED Find Common Ground

Based on your understanding of views different from yours on an issue, answer the following questions.

1. What values and principles do you share with your opponents?
2. What reaction can you anticipate from your audience based on the shared values and common ground you establish with your opponents? How will audience reaction help your argument?

Respond to Other Views

This chapter is devoted to opposing points of view on an issue and how to present them fairly. But you should also plan to respond to differing views, and in general there are three approaches. First, based on your careful evaluation of another position, you may find yourself in disagreement with it, and your argument will be stronger if you spell out precisely why you disagree. Second, you may agree with another position, and this means that you should state why you agree. This view may not directly oppose your position, but it may approach your issue from a different perspective and bring in different reasons and support. Explaining the grounds on which you agree will add momentum to your argument. And third, you may choose to work with another view that you both agree and disagree with.

Whether you disagree, agree, or agree only in part with another view, it is essential that you respond immediately after summarizing the different view. This can occur in the same paragraph with your summary of another view or in the paragraph immediately following the summary.

Use the prompts in your turn 6f, 6g, and 6h to practice disagreeing, agreeing, and both agreeing and disagreeing with other views.

PRACTICE Disagreeing with Another View

To respond to a view you disagree with, answer the following questions. This will put you in a position to explain in specific terms the basis of your disagreement.

1. What are the limitations of this view; that is, what does it fail to acknowledge about the issue at hand and how do these omissions affect its credibility?
2. Does this view include overly general statements that do not stand up to close investigation? If yes, what research will you bring in to reveal the weaknesses in these statements?
3. Does this opposing view include the elements of good argument? For example, is support effective and free from fallacies, and does it include fair treatment of the opposition?

4. Is sufficient context part of this opposing view, and is the presentation of this context fair and objective?

---

your turn 6g   PRACTICE **Agreeing with Another View**

To respond to a view you agree with, answer the following questions.

1. Are there values in this view with which you overlap? If yes, what are they, and why are these values appropriate in an argument on the issue at hand?
2. How does research validate this view?
3. What makes this view a practical approach to this issue? In your answer, identify how readers can benefit in practical ways by reflecting on this view.
4. In what ways does this view move beyond popular, less-informed responses to this issue?

---

your turn 6h   PRACTICE **Agree and Disagree at the Same Time**

To respond to a view you both agree and disagree with, answer the following questions.

1. On what specific points do you agree with this view?
2. What keeps you from fully accepting this view?
3. How, precisely, does your view improve on, or add to, this view?
4. To what extent will you recommend this view to your readers?

Reflect and Apply

1. Based on an argument you plan to build, what opposing views will you include and how, specifically, will you be thorough and fair in presenting them?
2. What sources will you draw from as you gather research for your argument? Explain why an audience would consider them credible.
3. What common ground are you finding with other views in your argument? How will you make use of this common ground?
4. Your turn 6f, 6g, and 6h list ways of responding to other views in an argument. How will you respond to each differing view you bring to your present argument?

KEEPING IT LOCAL

AS DISCUSSED IN CHAPTER 1, "Argue with a Purpose," and Chapter 2, "Explore an Issue that Matters to You," an issue exists because people have different points of view on something that affects them. Views different from yours need to be acknowledged. After all, if you want a seat at the discussion table in your community and in the classroom, it's essential that you acknowledge and validate others at the table. When you bring in differing views on an issue and do so with accuracy and a sense of fair play, you strengthen your argument and move yourself closer to winning the respect of an audience.

Returning to the matter that begins this chapter—a writer's concern with her elderly neighbor—you should now see why it's important to make plenty of room for the opposition in an argument; additionally, the exercises in the chapter provide you with a methodology for proceeding with others in a thorough, fair-minded way. The writer recognized that rallying those on her block to look in on John would not be enough. At this point, she began looking at her issue in broader, systemic terms, a choice that led her to advocate for free health care. The student who prepared this argument still looks in on John. The debate over free versus private health-care systems continues. But because this student crafted an argument responding to a neighbor's circumstances and took in a range of other perspectives, she earned the right to be heard. A solid argument does not ensure change, but it does let us speak up on issues that matter to us and puts us in touch with others equally invested in local and, in this case, national issues.

● — — — — — — — — — — ●

Based on the argument you're working with now, how will you make sure that your treatment of opposing views is fair and thorough? And if your issue affects the local community, how will you identify various positions that respond to the issue? Your answers to these questions will be the foundation for a major piece of your argument. Keep in mind as well that your treatment of the opposition can build your credibility with your target audience.

PART THREE

How to Plan, Structure, and Deliver an Argument

CHAPTER 7   Explore an Issue

CHAPTER 8   Consider Toulmin-Based Argument

CHAPTER 9   Consider Middle-Ground Argument, Rogerian Argument, and Argument Based on a Microhistory

CHAPTER 10   Build Arguments

CHAPTER 11   Support an Argument with Fact (*Logos*), Credibility (*Ethos*), and Emotion (*Pathos*)

All Illustrations by iStock.com/A-digit

CHAPTER 7

Explore An Issue

Learning Objectives

By working through this chapter, you will be able to

- develop an argument strategy.
- write an effective exploratory essay.

As you stand in line to order a soda at a local fast-food restaurant, you notice a young mother with three children taking their food to a table. The trays Mom is juggling are piled with burgers and fries, even though healthier kids' meals are offered by the restaurant. You're puzzled. If healthy options are offered, why hasn't this mother taken advantage of them? You begin to think that maybe the mother just doesn't know any better. By offering healthy choices for children, fast-food restaurants are doing their part. But is there more that can be done?

You think about the family while you develop ideas for a nutrition course paper and wonder what your claim should be. Should you argue the causes of childhood obesity or the effects of children eating a fast-food diet? Should you work to discover the problems underlying childhood obesity and offer a solution? Along the way you will need to define terms and evaluate any solutions you propose. How can you use similar situations, maybe involving food served in school cafeterias, to compare with food served in fast-food restaurants?

All Illustrations by iStock.com/A-digit

TOPIC: Food Consumption

ISSUE: Fast Food and Health

AUDIENCE: Fast-Food Restaurant Owners

CLAIM: Fast-food restaurants should move beyond just offering healthy foods to encouraging children to eat healthier.

There are many argumentative writing tasks you may be asked to perform in your college writing career. In a business course, you may be assigned an evaluative essay that asks you to determine the feasibility of a new project. In a political science course, you may be asked to compare the governmental systems of two countries. Most frequently, you will be asked to argue a position. In Chapter 8, "Consider Toulmin-Based Argument," and Chapter 9, "Consider Middle Ground Argument, Rogerian Argument, and Argument Based on a Microhistory," you will learn about formal types of argument (e.g., Toulmin, Rogerian). Here we will discuss the practicalities of presenting definitions, evaluations, causes and consequences, comparisons, and solution proposals.

Chapter 7 is designed to help you explore your issue from different angles, further solidifying your claim so that the argument's organizational structure becomes clear.

Use Definitions

Use a **definition** when an argument may benefit from an in-depth discussion of the terms involved. Throughout your college career (and very frequently in your professional career as well), you will be asked to define terms. Maybe you are developing a brochure for your clients and want your services to be clear. You would define each one. Maybe you are debating the outcome of a battle in a history course. Who won? That depends on the definition of *winning* that you use. Sometimes you will need to define terms within a paper in conjunction with other types of support; other times the definition will be the point of the paper.

Figure 7.1 Images like the above may inspire you to explore the issue of childhood obesity.

Defining terms can be a useful way to begin your argument. But please do not begin every essay with "According to *Webster's Dictionary* ... " Supply a definition only under these circumstances:

- Your definition of a term is very different from that normally provided.
- There is a controversy surrounding the definition of the term, and it is important for your audience either to know about this controversy or to understand why you have settled on the definition you are using.
- Your term may have a multitude of meanings, and you need to clarify how you are using the term.
- Your term is often misunderstood.

For example, Brandon is working on an argument for his political science course. He is interested in the debate surrounding genetically modified foods, or biotech foods that are derived from genetically modified crops or organisms (GMOs). Brandon wants to argue that GMOs are safe, but will need to define some terms, particularly *GMO*, in order to specify how he is going to be using the terms. Here is his claim and two supports that provide two different definitions: one from the Food and Drug Administration (FDA) and another from an anthropologist. These are then presented as an introduction and two body paragraphs.

CLAIM: GMO foods are safe because they meet the standard of being substantially equivalent to their natural counterparts.

SUPPORT ONE: The FDA's definition of *substantial equivalence*.

SUPPORT TWO: The anthropologist's definition of *natural foods*.

The term *GMO foods* refers to foods that are made from genetically modified organisms. Specifically, this means organisms modified through the use of genetic engineering, or intentional manipulation of the organism's genetic material, its genes, or its DNA. Organizations that regulate food health worldwide use the concept of substantial equivalence to determine whether or not GMO foods are safe. If the modified food is substantially equivalent to its natural counterpart, it can be considered safe. Piet Schenkelaars, a biotech consultant, explains that the original definition of the term *substantial equivalence*, created in 1993 by the Organisation for Economic Co-operation and Development, was that the GMO food in question "demonstrates the same characteristics and composition as the conventional food."

Some studies have found that genetically modified foods have more or less of certain important nutrients, therefore calling into question the idea that these foods are substantially equivalent. The whole usefulness of this safety standard depends on how we define the term *substantial*. Does it make a substantial difference if we eat soybean products that contain more lectin but less choline? The FDA specifically looks for substances that are new to the food and for different levels of allergens, nutrients, and toxins.

It may help to define *substantial equivalence* by making comparisons. There will always be differences between GMO foods and their natural counterparts. However, how great are these differences compared to the differences between other kinds of foods and their natural counterparts? After all, most of the foods we eat were genetically modified using traditional mutation and breeding techniques. A study by Cheng et al. argues that these other differences were greater than those found in GMO soy. If we accept some differences between the foods we eat and their natural counterparts, why should differences in GMO foods be especially worrisome?

Another issue is the context behind the definition of the term *natural foods*. No two varieties of conventional foods share the "same characteristics and composition," yet we readily accept these differences. In addition, virtually all of the foods we eat are very different than the original wild varieties. An anthropologist might define *natural foods* as those that human beings evolved to eat or those that were cultivated long ago. In prehistory and throughout our agricultural history, humans have selected and bred the plants that we preferred.

Through this process of human intervention, the original ears of the teosinte plant have been transformed from the size of a slender finger to the foot-long ears of corn we know today. According to *Corn: Origin, History, Technology, and Production,* corn (officially "maize") allowed civilizations like the Mayans and Aztecs to flourish and is currently one of the most important food crops in the world (Smith et al. 9). Which variety—conventional maize or the original teosinte—should be used as the "natural counterpart" for comparing with GMO maize to see if it is substantially equivalent? Are GMO strains natural counterparts of the foods we eat today, which have been created through techniques like mutation and selective breeding? Or should the GMO foods be compared with the original wild varieties that human beings evolved to eat, but which most of us have never seen, let alone eaten? These questions should be a part of any discussion of GMO food safety or the issue of substantial equivalence.

Works Cited

Cheng, K. C., et al. "Effect of Transgenes on Global Gene Expression in Soybean Is Within the Natural Range of Variation of Conventional Cultivars." *Journal of Agricultural and Food Chemistry,* vol. 56, no. 9, 2008, 3057–67. doi: 10.1021/jf073505i.

Smith, C. Wayne, Javier Betrán, and E. C. A. Runge, Smith, C. Wayne, et al., editors. *Corn: Origin, History, Technology, and Production.* Wiley, 2004.

Vahl, C. I., and Q. Kang. "Equivalence Criteria for the Safety Evaluation of a Genetically Modified Crop: A Statistical Perspective." *The Journal of Agricultural Science,* vol. 154, no. 3, 2016, pp. 383–406. *ProQuest,* http://ezproxy.cpcc.edu/login?url=https://search.proquest.com/docview/1768537417?accountid=10008, doi:http://dx.doi.org/10.1017/S0021859615000271.

Discussion: Notice that there are two definitions included in Brandon's supporting material: the definition of *GMO* and the definition of *natural foods.* Both definitions support the larger question of how to define *food safety.* His argument will undoubtedly include more terms to be defined because his audience will need to understand these terms in order to agree with his claim that GMOs are safe. In his argument, he will need to support each of these definitions with research.

Seven Types of Definition

There are many definition strategies that you can use in your academic writing. They may be combined as needed. An overview of seven of the types (Scientific, Metaphoric, Example, Riddle, Functional, Ironic, and Negation) follows.

Define with Science (Descriptive, Factual)

In this type of definition, whether the subject is scientific or not, you are answering questions such as, "How big?" "What color?" and "How old?" You are describing the subject systematically. Usually, you are describing those characteristics that make the subject what it is—a mammal, a poem, a weapon, a disease.

Bees are insects with six legs and two pairs of wings. Bees vary in size from roughly four millimeters to well over four centimeters in length, and weigh anywhere from ....

> **your turn 7a** ▸ **Define with Science**
>
> Define an issue that you are working on in terms of science. What are its component parts? Describe it accurately.

Define with Metaphor (Comparison)

Metaphors are not just useful in poetry and fiction. Metaphors provide a new way of looking at a subject and comparing it with other things. You may use metaphors and similes, and you might also include analogies and list synonyms for your subject term. Metaphorical definitions are very common. The following examples explain how metaphors can be used to define terms:

- A new diet, technology, or government program might be referred to as "a panacea." The real Panacea was a Greek goddess of healing. Now any time something seems like a cure-all, it will invariably be called a panacea.
- To convey that something is a burden, you might call it an "albatross." Here the reference is to the bird (an albatross) that was tied around a sailor's neck as a punishment in a poem by Samuel Taylor Coleridge.
- If you are defining something as a "red herring," you would be saying that it is irrelevant and out of place, like an actual red herring would be.
- An "anchor tenant" is a retail business that, like the anchor on a ship, provides stability for a shopping center or a mall. It consistently draws in customers who may or may not also shop in the smaller satellite stores. A store would be defined as a satellite if it is peripheral to the anchor tenant the way a satellite orbits the periphery of the earth.

> **your turn 7b** ▸ **Metaphorical Definitions**
>
> Metaphorical definitions can be very effective in introductions. Write an introduction in which you define your term using a metaphor. What does this metaphor add to your introduction?

Define by Example

With this method, the writer provides examples that exemplify members of the category being defined. What are some examples of great athletes, poor drivers, early mammals? By describing the features of the individuals in the group, you will be defining the group as well.

> A great writer is someone like William Chaucer, Jane Austen, or Theodor Geisel, better known as Dr. Seuss.

your turn 7c Define by Example

Use examples to define your issue. Why are these examples good representations of the category into which your issue falls?

Define with a Riddle

Riddles work well in introductions. The definition is given, but the reader has to guess what is being defined.

> If we allow these people to be integrated into the military, they will cause great harm to morale and discipline. They will cause dissension in the ranks and destroy unit cohesion. If unit cohesion goes, so will military readiness. If we lose military readiness, the defense of our country will be at risk. Our very survival is at stake. We must keep these people separate.
>
>   Who are we talking about? Homosexuals? No. Women, then? No. This is a great example of misdirection. Keep going back in time to the first people the military tried to keep from integrating. Of course, the remainder of the argument can use any of the other definition methods to expand upon the answer to the riddle.

your turn 7d Define with a Riddle

Write an introduction that poses your issue as a riddle. If you can mislead your reader, all the better. How is a riddle an effective strategy for introducing your issue?

Define by Function

When you are looking at your subject's function, you are explaining what it can (or cannot) do. The function of the space program is what? The function of a sphygmomanometer is what? The function of war is what? The essay then discusses these functions.

Functional definitions define things by what they do. To some people, a religion becomes different from a philosophy when it plays a psychological or sociological role. The social and legal definition of *family* was once bio-logical, but that is now giving way to a functional definition.

- A family is a group of people who act as a family, with the bonds of family, or the behaviors or living arrangements of a family.
- A vegan is someone who doesn't eat any animal products.
- Functional definitions also help to classify things. Illicit drugs are classified according to their harmful effects on people. Whenever the government finds that people are using a substance to significantly alter their mood, no matter how natural that substance is, some officials will invariably call for that substance to be defined as a drug and outlawed. (The more harmful the substance, the higher its classification, with "A" indicating the most dangerous class of drugs.)

your turn 7e **Define by Function**

Define your issue in terms of its functions. Identify at least three functions related to your issue. Which may be the most important function and why?

Define with Irony

In an ironic definition, you are arguing that something is not necessarily what it seems, or you are arguing that it is something other than it seems, usually the least likely possibility. You are using ironic definition when, for example, you define a forest fire as the bringer of life. This statement seems counterintuitive, going against reason; after all, so much is destroyed in a forest fire. However, there are many important benefits that come from the destruction. One benefit is that the high temperatures of a fire allow certain pine cones to release their seeds.

your turn 7f **Define with Irony**

Irony is related to tone, so you do not want to push your irony to the point of sarcasm and put off your argument. Again, an introduction is a good place to provide an ironic definition. Write an introduction that defines your term in an ironic way.

Define by Negation

When you define a subject by what it isn't, you are setting up an interesting essay. For example, you could define *education* as NOT merely recall. You can use negation with description, example, function, and so forth.

Philosophers say that you cannot define anything by using only negatives, but in fact, negative definitions are often quite useful.

- A virgin is a person who has not yet had sex.
- Parallel lines are a pair of lines on a plane that do not meet or cross.
- Candidate A is nothing like Abraham Lincoln. (Political candidates are often defined by negatives—that is, they lack a certain quality, such as integrity, or they lack a qualification, such as military experience.)
- A manx is a certain breed of cat that originated on the Isle of Man, but it is also a cat without a tail.

your turn 7g ▸ **Define by Negation**

Sometimes it is easier to define your issue by what it is not, particularly if you are trying to highlight how your issue is lacking or approached differently in a different culture or situation. For example, you may define *democracy* by describing a country where democracy is not the standard way of life. Take a moment to define your issue in terms of what it is not.

Discover Causes or Consequences

A thorough examination of the causes or consequences of your argument (both good and bad) can help you select the best evidence to support your claim. What good would come if your argument is accepted? What bad? What might happen if your argument is not accepted? **Consequences (or effects)** look to the future; **causes** look back at the past. Together they create a chain of evidence that can be very convincing (as shown in Figure 7.2).

Figure 7.2 Causes and Consequences (simple)

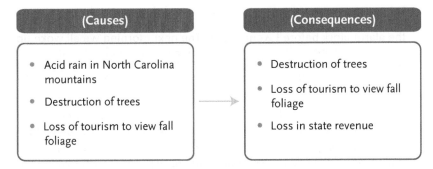

Figure 7.3 Causes and Consequences (complex)

Are you interested in arguing based on causes or consequences (effects)? If you need to explain how something came about, you are arguing causes. Do you want to argue what the outcomes of a particular event will be? Then you're interested in presenting evidence of effects. But it's not as simple as it appears. In the example posed in Figure 7.2, we can see that a few of the causes of air pollution are on the left and some of the effects of air pollution are on the right. Air pollution is an issue that can be approached using both cause and effect. The effects themselves can go on to be causes of future events (as shown in Figure 7.3).

Claim: Several factors are responsible for the acid rain destroying North Carolina's mountain trees.
Causes: Factory smoke and car emissions cause acid rain.
Claim: Acid rain in the North Carolina Mountains results in the loss of state revenue.
Consequences: The destruction of trees will discourage tourists from visiting the mountains in North Carolina to view the fall foliage.

As you can see, each effect in turn becomes the cause of something else. And each one of these effects could be argued as being caused by factors other than the ones selected. Cause and/or consequence support can be useful, but very tricky. How far back do you need to research before you feel comfortable that you have reached the earliest cause? How far do you need to project into the future to feel confident that you have anticipated all reasonable consequences? Can you differentiate between primary causes and secondary causes?

A **primary cause** is the one that immediately precedes the effect. It can be very difficult to determine the primary cause of an event. As a humorous example of causal narrative, review the following student example:

 tip 7a

Difference between *Affect* and *Effect*

One is a noun:
The _effect_ of cutting back on welfare payments is that single mothers have to pay more for childcare.
One is a verb:
This _affects_ their budgets adversely.

> This morning I broke my arm. This is how it happened. Last night my husband and I had an argument. Because I was so angry, I forgot to set the alarm clock before I went to bed. The next morning we all woke up late, so we were rushing around. As I went to leave, I realized I could not find my glasses. Figuring it was too late to search for them, I rushed out of the door and, to my dismay, stepped on the skateboard my son had left on the front steps. I fell and broke my arm.

The scenario may be silly, but an analysis of cause is not. Can we determine the primary cause of the student's broken arm? Was it the fight with her husband? Not wearing her glasses? The skateboard being in the wrong place? Actually, we could say that the primary cause of the injury was the contact of the cement steps with her arm bone! It is the one cause about which there can be no dispute. Concrete usually wins out over unprotected bone.

But what about secondary, sometimes called "peripheral," causes of the accident? **Secondary causes** are contributing factors. The list of factors contributing to the broken arm is quite long: an unset alarm clock, missing glasses, and a misplaced skateboard. How far and wide should the net be cast when exploring secondary causes? It depends. Here are a couple of examples. The first is real, the second hypothetical.

> **Claim:** The rubella outbreak in the mid 1960s resulted in closed-captioning television.
>
> **Causes:** 1964–1965 rubella outbreak ⟶ high numbers of deaf children ⟶ as these children grew, they demanded closed-captioned TV.

Discussion: The link between the cause and effect could leave many scratching their heads. During the 1964–1965 worldwide rubella epidemic, an estimated 12.5 million cases of rubella occurred in the United States, resulting in 20,000 infants born with congenital rubella syndrome (CRS), a condition that includes deafness. These children were born to mothers who had contracted the rubella virus while pregnant. As these children became adults in the early 1980s, they (along with other hearing-impaired individuals) demanded equal access to television programming. Closed captioning was developed in 1980 and spread quickly through the industry. At first, the claim—that the rubella outbreak led to the development of a technology that allowed deaf people to access television programming—seems unlikely. Yet, through a presentation of contributing factors, the connection is clear. Links such as these must be established with a chronology of events connecting the cause to the effect.

This next example involves a hypothetical plane crash. Note the different claims that are put forth by different participants in the scenario. The participants are

- Attorneys for crash victim's families
- Attorneys for the airline
- Attorneys for the Fancy School of Aviation Mechanics (FSAM)

Claim One (made by attorneys for crash victims' families): A stress fracture (*effect*) in the plane's wing was the result of poor inspections by the airline (*cause*).

Support: The inspectors were poorly qualified.

Claim Two (made by attorneys for the airline): The stress fracture was missed (*effect*) because the inspectors were poorly trained by FSAM (*cause*), an accredited school from which we have been hiring inspectors for years.

Support: Inspectors are trained by FSAM, not the airline.

Claim Three (made by attorneys for FSAM): A lack of funding (*cause*) has led to the loss of quality instructors (*effect*).

Support: FSAM's president embezzled millions of dollars affecting the school's budget.

Discussion: Plane crashes are always investigated, but not always for strictly humanitarian reasons. The primary cause of a crash can often be determined fairly quickly: a wing fell off, a bomb was detonated, the controls jammed, the pilot ignored the air traffic controller. The secondary causes, however, are often messier, and uncovering them is often a more protracted task. To determine the reason, blame has to be assessed. Who is at fault, and therefore, who must pay the cost of lost lives, cleanup, and so on?

How far back can we go to find contributing factors of a plane crash? Would it be unreasonable for the airline's attorneys to argue that the cause of the crash was the embezzlement of millions of dollars of school funds by the FSAM president? Follow the flowchart in Figure 7.4 to see how such a chain of evidence could evolve.

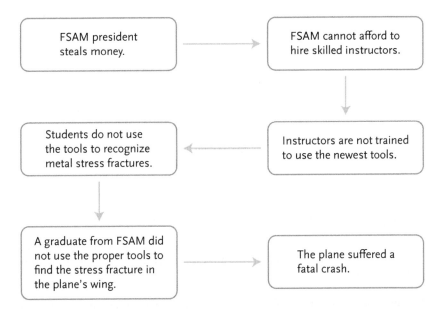

Figure 7.4 This flowchart depicts a chain of evidence.

Claim Four (made by the attorneys of the families): Because the airline hired the inspectors, the airline is responsible for the plane crash (*cause*).

Consequence: The airline must pay restitution to the victims' families (*effect*).

Discussion: Obviously it is in the airline's best interests to argue that the cause of the plane crash originated elsewhere. After all, if the airline is held liable for the crash, all sorts of consequences could arise, including loss of revenue due to loss in reputation and millions of dollars lost in insurance claims. The immediate, primary cause of the plane crash may have been the wing falling off of the plane, but the secondary causes are more important in this argument. Most important in determining cause is to find the right one for the effect. Too often, arguments are based on flimsy cause–effect relationships, resulting in arguments that are not persuasive.

How far in both directions (toward causes and toward consequences) do you need to go to be comfortable in supporting your claim?

your turn 7b   **Explore Causes and Effects**

Cast your claim in terms of causes. What is the primary cause of your claim? What are at least two secondary causes? Which of these causes would be most persuasive to your audience? What about effects? List at least three effects of your claim. Are they positive? Negative?

Present Comparisons

Comparisons can be very useful for establishing precedence and examining how similar situations have been handled. Perhaps your claim is one that is often lumped in with other topics. You may want to argue that compared with the other topics, your claim is significantly different and should be examined separately. Or you may be arguing that your claim is similar to other claims made and should be addressed in the same way.

Claim: Stop signs need to be installed at the intersection of Beadle and Poppin Streets, which is surrounded by a shopping center and a large neighborhood.

Support: The intersection of East and West Streets, similarly situated between a neighborhood and a shopping center, has benefited from traffic signs.

Discussion: It can be useful to compare the intersection to another one in town that has the same shopping center/neighborhood configuration. Why does location B have a light, but location A does not? What is similar about the locations? What is different? Are the differences significant enough to allow B to have a light, but not A?

> **Claim:** The intersection of Beadle and Poppin Streets is being denied a traffic signal because it is in a lower income section of town.
>
> **Support One:** Of the requests for any improvements (roads, sidewalks, lights, etc.) in upscale Mayfair neighborhood, 80 percent are being granted; yet only 10 percent of requests from lower income Saxony neighborhood are being granted.

Discussion: What if there is no closely related situation? Then you should look for a situation that has similar characteristics. This type of comparison is larger in scope than an obvious comparison, such as one intersection and another, but it is helpful in shoring up your argument.

You can look for historically similar situations as well. This is called **precedence** and is one of the tools used by lawyers and judges in evaluating court cases. What past cases (in this town or in other towns) have been similar to this one? How were they handled? Knowing how previous problems were solved may be useful in arguing how the new problem can be solved. (See "Propose a Solution" in the section that follows.)

For example, a similar case of seeming discrimination was handled in Atlanta by the establishment of a citizen's group, which investigated all requests and routed them on to the correct departments after the investigations were complete. This group was composed of individuals from all areas of the city and therefore less likely to discriminate or show favoritism. Can such a solution be effective in Saxony? You may argue that it could.

One of the most frustrating experiences you can have in doing research is not finding anything on your particular subject. You know your issue is important, but you are just not finding any support that relates directly to it. Let's look at the issue of including extreme sports in the Olympic Games. We'll narrow the issue even further to target the inclusion of skateboarding. You have spent hours online and in the library but have found nothing really useful on skateboarding and the Olympics. Perhaps you need to do some historical research.

Maybe you can answer the question, "When were women first allowed to compete in the Olympics?" or the question "Why were women not considered athletic competitors in the first place?" Another question to research is "How did an obscure sport like curling become part of the Olympics?" Based on the answers to these questions, you may be able to argue by **analogy**. An analogy is a type of comparison. What about the history of curling is similar to the history of skateboarding? Can the same arguments for including one sport be extended to including the other? How can the answers to questions about including women and curling in the Olympics relate to including skateboarding, an activity that some people do not even consider a sport?

> **your turn** 7i **Look for Comparisons**
>
> In support of your claim, what can you use for comparison? How are the two situations similar? How are they different? Are there enough similarities that your audience would agree to entertain the comparison you are making?

Propose a Solution

As you continue to develop your argument, it may be useful to think in terms of problems and solutions. There are 13 exploratory steps that we suggest you consider in proposing a solution to a problem. You may find that you need to look at all 13 steps for your issue, or you may need to examine only a few. For example, you may already know the problem, such as when an instructor has assigned you a particular issue to research. Your goal may then be to find support for your claim, Section B. Or maybe you have a great solution but are not sure how to implement it; Section C would be the most useful for you. The chart below offers an overview of the 13-step problem–solution exploration process.

Section A: Exploring the Problem	1. Preparation and Persistence 2. Understanding the Problem 3. Ethical Considerations
Section B: Conducting Different Types of Exploration	4. Historical Exploration 5. Process Exploration 6. Creative Exploration 7. Critical Thinking Exploration 8. Metaphorical and Analogical Exploration
Section C: Exploring Implementation	9. Selecting Solutions 10. Implementing Solutions 11. Communicating Solutions 12. Evaluating Solutions 13. Future and System Considerations

These steps need not be followed in order, but by considering all of them, you will develop a clearer idea of what your argument is actually about, and you will know how to creatively find ideas and solutions that may elude you otherwise. As you skim over the list, you can see that it can lead you to ideas you had not considered, or that it may help you in solving a problem or implementing a solution (Section C). You may find that you are reinventing the wheel because you have not looked at how a particular problem has been solved historically (Section B). What has been done before and why did it not work? Or maybe you have to consider the ethical nature of a problem in determining fair and equitable solutions (Section A).

At the heart of this process is creative thinking. Ask yourself the question, "How can I approach my topic in a more creative way?" A wonderful book about creative thinking is Robert and Michèle Root-Bernstein's *Sparks of Genius* (Houghton Mifflin, 2001). The authors researched ways that creative people in varying fields and disciplines came up with ideas. They found, for instance, that a physicist might get ideas by listening to a Bach concerto. A sculptor might discover a new technique by meditating. An engineer might find a solution to a problem while rowing a sea kayak in a storm. Creative thinking refuses to shut out possibilities and embraces ideas that can be found in all avenues of life. The most creative people do not close the door to ideas; instead, they find them in unexpected areas.

Figure 7.5 Using the science behind obesity and nutrition can help identify a process solution.

Our 13 items reflect many of the ideas that the Root-Bernsteins developed in their research. These steps are meant to be practical tools you can use to come up with ideas that strengthen your arguments. Let's follow the progress of a student, Lise, as she works through all 13 steps to develop a solution to the persistent problem of unhealthy fast-food meals and their link to childhood obesity.

Section A: Exploring the Problem

The steps in this section are very basic. What exactly is the problem at hand? Very often, problems can be challenging to solve because the exact cause is not clear; it can be difficult to find the causes of the problem, who it affects, and who is responsible for it. Moving through these steps can help you address these initial considerations.

1. Preparation and Persistence

What do you need to solve the problem? What are the necessary resources? Do you have enough assistance and persistence? Do you have the time, money, strength, and faith to continue toward a solution? Thomas Edison said that "Genius is one percent inspiration, ninety-nine percent perspiration." It is easy to be inspired, but it takes hard work to complete a task. What do you need to complete your task?

- Do you need to talk to people in relevant fields?
- Do you need research help from librarians?
- Do you need to start all over from scratch?

Lise's issue is one that she is arguing in her college health course, so the possibility of getting a high grade contributes to her motivation to find a solution. However, because she is studying to be a dietician, her motivation is professional and personal as well. Issues such as fast food and childhood obesity relate directly to her chosen career. In addition, she genuinely wants to help people eat better. A strong database of medical articles is available to her, making research easy. Lise's college's health program is linked to the local hospital which means she has access to faculty at the hospital as well. She envisions interviews with doctors at the hospital along with traditional library research.

2. Understanding the Problem

What exactly is the problem? Identify it. Define it. Define it scientifically; descriptively; metaphorically; by example; define the solution without naming it; define the problem by its function; ironically; by its negation; using elaboration; using evaluation.

- What exactly is the problem?
- Is it made up of several smaller problems?
- For whom is it a problem? For whom is it not a problem?
- What caused the problem?

Answering this set of questions will ensure that you are arguing about the real problem. In the student sample below, the problem is not the quality of the product, but the public's perception of the cost.

What does Lise really know about the problem of childhood obesity? Lise's reading so far indicates that there are both controllable reasons (e.g., diet and exercise) and uncontrollable reasons (e.g., genetics) for childhood obesity. Which of the controllable reasons are the biggest culprits for weight gain in children?

- Fast-food diets
- School lunches
- Lack of exercise at school and at home
- Too many unhealthy snacks

Lise will have to decide which problem to tackle. After witnessing the family ordering burgers and fries at the fast-food restaurant (as discussed in this chapter's first pages), she is leaning toward writing about the problem of fast-food diets.

3. Ethical Considerations

What are the rights and wrongs of solving your problem? In other words, how will solving your problem be right and wrong, and for whom?

- Should this problem even be solved?
- What will solving it do to the people involved?
- What will solving or not solving the problem do to the main purpose or core business of the problem-solver?
- What happens if the problem is not addressed or solved?

Solutions require us to expend resources, and they also affect future decisions and operations. Is solving the problem worth the costs, and to whom? Always consider the main purpose of the problem-solver. At our college, our main purpose is to serve students and our community. We consider our decisions ethical if they're good for students and good for our community.

But issues of right and wrong are often complicated. For instance, my purpose is to make a good living for my family. If the state of North Carolina raises instructors' salaries, where will the money come from? Higher taxes on other families who are already struggling with the economic downturn? Ethics can be a cloudy area.

> Lise is convinced that it is extremely important to solve the problem of unhealthy fast-food products being targeted at children. She feels restaurants have a moral obligation to improve their nutritional options for children and to provide encouragement and education through marketing programs or brochures. If the problem is not solved, those families who—by lack of better nutritional options or lack of education—frequently eat fast food will be raising an unhealthy generation of children who will develop health problems that will strain our medical system.

your turn ⟩ **Explore the Problem**

For Steps 1–3 above, explore your own issue, following Lise's example.

Section B: Different Types of Exploration

Now that you know what the problem is, where can you look for solutions?

4. Historical Exploration

Historical exploration answers the question, "How have similar problems been solved in the past?" Past cases and examples generate solutions. There is no sense in always starting from scratch. If we know how similar problems have been solved in the past, we may be able to adapt those solutions to fit our current needs. Looking to the past is often a very productive step toward a solution. Always start here.

- What have been some of the historical solutions to the problem?
- Why have they failed?
- Did they fail because the solution was a poor one or because it was not implemented correctly?
- Can an historical solution be used and improved upon with some newly available modifications?

> Of course there have always been overweight children, but studies show that the number of children considered overweight in this country is increasing at an alarming rate. In the past, most childhood weight gain was due to overeating and lack of exercise. The solution was considered simple: eat less and exercise more. Today, though, the childhood obesity problem is complicated by families eating out more, by the increased availability of cheap fast-food options marketed to children, and by skyrocketing food prices that encourage parents to buy cheaper, usually less healthy, foods. If families are having to cut back and are going to be eating out frequently, then one solution is to make sure fast-food restaurants have healthier options and that families know how to choose nutritious foods.

5. Process Exploration

How does the problem work? How do possible solutions work? When we explore processes, we are looking at how things work in order to generate solutions. Areas of exploration can be laws, policies, rules, or psychological and scientific theories. For example, advertisers market their products to younger people, even though older folks buy more products. The reason? They know that the older we are, the less likely we are to change brands, and that getting consumers to change brands is one main purpose for advertisements. Advertisements, then, target the audience that is most likely to be responsive. The idea is that if we know how things work, we can use known processes, theories, tendencies, and behaviors to help craft solutions.

Some processes are informal and more likely to change; they aren't written in stone. Whenever a new president comes into office or a new manager comes into a business, the staff has to figure out what the new person likes, dislikes, tolerates, expects, and so forth. These changing processes may depend on the new leader's personality, but the effect they have on people's lives is every bit as real as the law of gravity or criminal statutes.

- What processes are at work in relation to our problem?
- What are the existing theories in this field or area of activity?
- Which sciences are involved, and what do the experts tell us about our problem?
- What are some predictable behaviors surrounding our problem and its possible solutions?

How did fast-food restaurants begin serving such bad foods to children? When did kids' meals become popular? Lise suspects that fast-food advertising during Saturday morning cartoons began the craze for kids' meals and the toys they contain. By including toys that relate to popular movies, the restaurants and the kids' meals become even more attractive to children. Who makes the choices at the local level about what restaurants serve? For example, McDonalds has locations all around the world, and different foods are served in different places. To some extent, local decisions must determine which products are sold in each location; Lise needs to learn the processes that governs who makes these decisions.

6. Creative Exploration

This process allows you to explore and answer questions such as, "How else might the situation be?" and "What could we add to it or put in its place?" As important as it is to research historical solutions to similar problems, it is also important to use creative free-range thinking. For this step, ignore processes, past examples, and assumptions. If you could wave a wand to come up with any solution you like, what would that solution be? Then, once you've imagined the solution, no matter how far-fetched it is, work backward to see how you might get there. Freeing yourself from logical thinking can often have amazing results. Perhaps you had a good idea all along, but your fears of looking foolish prevented you from committing the idea as a solution. Through creative exploration, you may discover that the idea may actually work! Here are some examples of creative problem-solving:

- When the Japanese invaded Okinawa, in 1607, the locals were forbidden to carry weapons, so they developed a form of open-hand combat called karate.

- According to legend, Irish step-dancing came about because dancing was outlawed but people wanted to dance anyway. They held their arms still and moved only their legs, which allowed them to dance behind stone walls without appearing to be dancing at all.

- When parents are desperate, they find creative ways to motivate their children to get good grades. Some of them even pay their children money for grades.

People have a long history of coming up with creative solutions to difficult problems. Climb out of the box for solutions. Read books or articles about topics that seem different from yours in order to see how other problems have been solved. For example, if your company has tried unsuccessfully to motivate employees with bonuses, try reading trade journals in other fields to see how different kinds of businesses motivate their employees.

Creativity shows up in the restaurant business frequently. "Thinking outside the bun" led to the creation of tortilla wraps. The focus on low-carb eating resulted in the introduction of ethnic cuisines, such as lettuce wraps.

In the best of all possible worlds, children would be able to eat hamburgers and French fries that would actually be healthy for them. Fast-food restaurants are missing an opportunity to think outside the box about what healthy eating means. If a father insists on feeding his children a steady diet of burgers, then the burgers should at least be healthy. There are dozens of vegetarian versions of burgers that kids love. Potatoes are not inherently unhealthy, but frying is, so the fries could be baked instead. Apples can be served instead of apple pie; low-fat yogurt with granola can be served instead of full-fat yogurt with candy sprinkles. Problems that seem impossible at first can often be addressed with a little creative thinking.

7. Critical Thinking Exploration

How else might the situation be? What could we take away from the problem or from each possible solution? Question your basic assumptions to generate solutions.

- Do you even need to solve the problem?
- Are the rules governing the problem mandatory?
- Did past solutions work for the reasons you thought they worked?

At a local pizza shop, customers who pay with plastic have a long wait-time. In order to process credit card transactions, the cashier has to ring up the order at the register, swipe the card, walk across the store and around a shelving unit, wait to gather the receipt once it prints, come back, and only then complete the transaction. The manager's explanation of the problem was, "Our credit card machine runs through the computer, which is across the store." Hasn't she considered moving the systems closer together? A little critical thinking could make credit card processing more efficient.

It often pays to ask, "What if the accepted 'truth' is not actually true?" What if there really is no gravity? What if we don't have to die? What if the earth *isn't* round? The weird people who ask these odd questions end up discovering new things. In fact, our latest theory of gravity (Einstein's) is being questioned and may soon be replaced with a new theory. In fact, science may find a solution to the dying process in your lifetime. In fact, the earth is bulgy, not round.

Is fast food really the problem? Isn't lack of exercise just as important a factor in childhood obesity? The assumption is that children are getting too many "bad" calories from burgers and chicken fingers, but do we know that is true? Perhaps the number of times a week a family stops at Burger Barn is a bigger factor than what is actually consumed. Lise asks questions that seem obvious but need to be addressed. She also needs to examine the products that popular fast-food chains actually offer children. Have the restaurants tried to provide healthy options in the past? Were these attempts profitable? What could they do to increase the profitability of healthy options?

8. Metaphorical or Analogical Exploration

Metaphorical thinking asks us to see the connections and similarities between seemingly different things. Analogies involve seeing similarities between seemingly different situations. It can be helpful to think more creatively about your issue. For example, Lise was having difficulties untangling all the threads of her issue to determine which one to present as her claim. She could concentrate on fast-food advertising, the types of kids' meals restaurants serve, the types of families that eat in fast-food restaurants frequently, and the cost of the food. Until the image of a tree with branches came to her, Lise couldn't see that her argument had one "trunk" and that the different areas of her argument could be organized into "branches." Her metaphorical thinking yielded an organizational format that she couldn't see before: one main problem with smaller problems branching off from the main trunk.

- What is the problem like?
- What are possible solutions like?
- Can a metaphor be created?
- Is an analogy better?

Example of Metaphor:

Let's say I sell used cars and I'd like to double my sales. I can cast about in my mind to answer the question, "What else doubles?" and come up with the answer, "Bread dough." "How?" "Yeast." "What's the yeast in sales?" "Energy, charisma, good looks, manipulation, reciprocity, value, compassion—whatever is needed." One of these ideas might prove to be an important part of the solution, no matter what an expert consultant might say. My car lot might well need sprucing up. Or my cars might not seem to have much value. Or my staff might smell bad. Textbook solutions (historical and scientific) are wonderfully important in many cases, but in this case the metaphor might be useful because thinking of my sales as bread dough sent me looking for the "yeast" that might be missing.

Example of Analogy:

I had a problem keeping all of the leaves and debris out of my pool. I live in the country, surrounded by nature's abundance, and a lot of stuff gets in the pool. It is almost an everyday affair to keep it cleaned. I could clean it myself, but doing so would take up immense amounts of my time and energy. While I was watching a show about animals whose teeth and bodies are cleaned by other animals, I thought of my pool-cleaning problem. In order to clean themselves, the animals would expend energy and time, just as I would do if I cleaned my own pool. They would have the impossible task of growing new appendages, just as I would have the impossible task of creating more time. I decided to invest in an automatic pool cleaner—just as the animals have "automatic" teeth and body cleaners.

If a solution has been found to a problem that is similar to yours, perhaps you can apply or adapt that solution.

What object, issue, or situation does the problem of childhood obesity resemble? The more Lise read, the more the issue seemed to branch off into other issues. Before long, her issue had become as tangled as tree branches. The metaphor of a tree worked for Lise. She could see the different types of problems (poor nutrition, lack of family time, the low cost of fast food) as branches of a tree (fast food). Chopping the tree down is not an option, but leaving it alone only allows it to continue growing wildly in any direction it chooses. Lise started to think about ways that the branches could be pruned and shaped so as the tree continues to grow, the branches (the issues) will be directed. How can specific foods offered by fast-food restaurants be modified to become healthier?

your turn 7k   **Look for Creative Answers**

For Steps 4–8 above, explore your own issue, following the student models of Lise.

Section C: Exploring Implementation

Maybe your problem is not coming up with solutions, but identifying which potential solution would be the best choice. Or maybe you have settled on a solution but don't know whom to address in your claim or how to implement your solution.

9. Selecting Solutions

Which proposed solution should be chosen? Often, a given problem will have several potential solutions. Deciding which one to choose is difficult. If it's your problem, you have to satisfy yourself, right? What if it satisfies you but makes your family mad? Or your boss? Or what if you can't afford it?

- Which is the best solution?
- Which is the simplest solution?
- Which solution best fits your goals?
- Which solution is the most ethical?
- Which solution is the cheapest?
- How will you decide which solution to propose?

As Lise continued her research, she saw solutions that companies in other industries had used, and she began thinking of how to apply those solutions to the problem of fast-food meals for children. But which of these solutions should be present in her argument? Some solutions would be expensive because they would involve introducing new products, and passing this cost on to the consumer would drive lower-income parents to search out cheaper types of fast food. Some solutions would involve developing clear nutritional guidelines for kids' meals. Some of the less expensive solutions might not offer the same degree of success. Cost and effectiveness were the two variables that Lise decided to use as her guide in crafting solutions that would please both fast-food restaurants and families.

10. Implementing Solutions

How can the solution best be implemented?

- What resources will the solution entail?
- What process should we put in place?
- Will it involve monitoring and enforcement?
- Who should do the implementing?

I went to a discount store the other day and encountered a problem. When I asked the cashier to ring up six bags of dirt, she told me I needed to go outside and make sure it was there. I said it was probably there and asked her to go ahead and ring it up. She was very nice but refused to let me pay for the dirt until I had gone personally to verify that it was in stock. I looked at the long line behind me and left the store. The store had a problem: How could they make their products convenient to buy? In other words, how could they save their customers time and money? The first solution they tried didn't work in my case: they wanted employees to remember what the store had in stock and not ring-up anything else. This solution relied too much on training employees to remember which products were in stock.

The next time I purchased dirt at the discount store, a new solution was in place. The manager had checked the stock and covered the bar codes on the scan sheets to show items not in stock. That way no one could ring up something they didn't have. The second solution was easier to implement, a lot cheaper than training, and a lot more reliable than a busy clerk's memory. The solution had been possible all along, they just hadn't identified it.

Lise comes to realize that fast food causes big problems for children struggling to maintain a healthy weight. When children eat a steady diet of fast food, they do not thrive physically. Issues contributing to the problem were food cost and fast-food convenience. Lise decides that issues of time and money are not as easily addressed as food quality. Since restaurants can be required to provide nutritional information for the foods they sell, then surely they can be required to provide nutritious food for children. School lunch programs have become healthier by providing options that do appeal to children; fast-food restaurants can do the same.

11. Communicating Solutions

Very often, solutions are devised at the very top of an organization, and the steps required to implement the solution are communicated quite efficiently throughout the organization. Unfortunately, the reason for those steps often does not filter down, diminishing the effectiveness of the solution. How, then, can the solution best be communicated?

> Lise's argument has to be presented as a researched paper to a college professor. However, if she were working for a particular restaurant desiring to provide healthier foods, she would probably have several choices in how to communicate her findings to her boss. Here are two of her choices:
>
> • A formal report may be the best choice in response to a request by the boss for a study of the issue
> • A memo may be appropriate if she is the one bringing up the topic with her boss and wants to do so informally

12. Evaluating Solutions

How can the effectiveness of the solution be evaluated? Was it really the best solution? Although it is most often thought of as occurring after a solution is implemented, evaluation is actually part of every step: before, during, and after implementation. At each of these stages, the key to good evaluation is to understand the real values we need to measure the results against.

> To determine whether a solution is effective, Lise will have to implement it and develop a tool to evaluate its effectiveness. What would such a tool look like? To whom should she propose her solution and how might it be implemented? Lise's research led her to believe that in addition to submitting her argument to her professor, she could pitch her problem–solution argument at the fast-food restaurant in her neighborhood, a locally owned eatery. She develops a new policy to encourage children to lose weight and get fit using a "fat-to-fit" program that will result in increased sales. She now has a narrower perspective on the issue, and this narrows the type of research she needs to do. A narrow angle can really benefit an argument by allowing the writer to focus on specifics.

13. Future and System Considerations

Now that we've solved the problem and evaluated the effectiveness of the chosen solution, what is the next step?

• Should we consider the process closed? Or has our solution created another problem to solve?
• Has the solution eliminated our argument's reason for being?
• Has it changed the nature of our core business?
• What are the unintended consequences of the chosen solution?
• How has the solution changed the internal or external organizational system?

A positive example of evaluation of a solution is provided by the G.I. Bill. After World War II, huge numbers of young men came back from the war and enrolled in college using money from the G.I. Bill. That gave them the skills they needed to compete for good-paying jobs. In turn, that boosted our economy, which in turn helped people make more money and buy houses and pay more in taxes, so that the government had even more money to give the next generation of soldiers to go to college. It helped the whole system.

After using the problem-solving process to evaluate her topic, Lise now has a claim that she can research and a solution she can propose. She may even be able to evaluate the solution if it is implemented in her community. If successful, a change in a small local restaurant may spark interest in the larger chains, prompting them to implement similar changes. Lise is ready to tackle her research in earnest, and her argument will be more effective and focused, using specifics instead of abstractions.

your turn 7 ▸ **Implement Your Solutions**

For Steps 9–13 above, explore your own issue, following the student models of Lise.

Evaluate Your Claim

An **evaluation** should be used when you are attempting to persuade your audience that one thing is better (more efficient, more feasible, etc.) than another. As long as you clearly explain your evaluation criteria, evidence that provides an evaluation of your problem and solution can be important in persuading your audience. When presenting your evaluation, you will sometimes be asked to offer a single solution or to offer several solutions and indicate which is best based on the indicated criteria. For example, in a humanities course, you may be asked to which category, genre, or movement a work of art, a text, or a piece of music belongs.

The Problem: *Madonna and Child with Angels and St. Jerome* by the Italian artist Parmigianino (see Figure 7.6), is an example of what style of art?
    The Solution: *Madonna and Child with Angels and St. Jerome* is an example of Mannerist art because ...
    The Criteria: ... it exhibits the following characteristics of Mannerism:

- Elongated figures and forms
- Garish color combinations
- Exaggerated body positions

Parmigianino's painting is an example of Mannerist art because it exhibits all three characteristics of that art style.

Madonna with the Long Neck, 1534–40 (oil on canvas), Parmigianino (Francesco Mazzola) (1503–40)/Galleria degli Uffizi, Florence, Italy/Alinari/The Bridgeman Art Library

Figure 7.6 Parmigianino, *Madonna and Child with Angels and St. Jerome*

In an evaluation, you will:

- Select the criteria or characteristics that you will use to evaluate your subject.
- Discuss your selection of criteria.
- Present an evaluation of your subject based on that criteria.

your turn 7m ▸ **Evaluate Your Solution**

From your exploration of your issue from the 13-step problem–solution perspective, evaluate the solution you decided upon. Make sure to select the criteria you will use, and evaluate the solution based on those criteria. Alternatively, develop three solutions and use your criteria to determine which solution best fits the problem.

Write an Exploratory Essay

An exploratory essay is a useful way to examine both (a) what you know about your topic so far, and (b) what directions you may still need to pursue before putting your argument together.

What do you know about your issue? An exploratory essay usually is undertaken after you have completed some research on the issue, maybe after you have worked through some of the prewriting methods or the problem-solving items. Don't narrow your research too soon. At the beginning, read enough on the subject to be conversant with the players involved, about the problems and different points of view. You can then sift through your materials and decide what parts of the issue you are now comfortable with. What you do know may include:

- Historical or cultural background on the issue.
- The players involved in the issue.
- What claims you may want to make.

Once you have seen what you do know, it is time to examine what elements about your issue that are confusing or that require further research. As you tackle what you do know, you may often find more questions that need to be answered.

What you don't know may include:

- Support for your claims.
- Where to look for materials such as statistics, interviews, articles, and so on.
- Possible solutions.

Your essay should present the reader with a clear idea of what your questions are, what you have learned so far, and what you still need to do to complete your argument.

Exploratory Essay Checklist

Have you included the following elements in your exploratory essay?

- ☐ Claim
- ☐ Background that includes context and all those involved
- ☐ What you know so far (research and common knowledge)
- ☐ What you still need to research
- ☐ Types of support you will need (see Chapter 11, "Support an Argument with Fact (Logos), Credibility (Ethos), and Emotion (Pathos)")

Sample Exploratory Essay

Below is Lise's exploratory essay, along with her instructor's comments.

Lise Holt

Health 232

Professor Smith

4 September 2013

Exploratory Essay

What is the specific claim to be made? What organizational strategy would best be employed?

Fast-food restaurants have been around for quite a while now. They have not traditionally been known for their healthy foods; they are popular for their ability to get hungry, busy people in and out fast. Can't the two goals, health and speed, be combined? In particular, can't healthy foods and a healthy eating program be combined to help families eat healthier? I am arguing that fast-food restaurants should add nutrition-education programs, using their websites and brochures, to explain their healthier kids' menus. My primary strategy will be to offer a solution with a fat-to-fit program at Mama Maya's Italian Eatery in town. The program will be both healthy and cost effective.

Who are the players involved in this issue?

Who is involved in the issue? Families with children who eat at fast-food restaurants are the focus of my claim; they would be the beneficiaries of any educational programs and the improvements that restaurants make to their kids' menus. The restaurant owners themselves are the second interested parties. Their motivation is keeping businesses. How would they be motivated to change their menus? Are they receiving any complaints now? If not, what would be their motivation to offer education and new menu selections?

By selecting a topic that generates personal interest, Lise will be able to begin forming opinions about the issue and selecting research that is more focused on her particular claim.

I became interested in this topic when I was standing in line at Mama Maya's ordering dinner. It occurred to me after seeing several parents ordering food for their children that they were ignoring the healthier options on the menu. In my health class, we are currently debating the issue of obesity in children and I immediately thought of the kids at the restaurant.

What is there still to be done? Lise has now identified a claim that will help her direct her research and gather appropriate support.

My next step will be to research the argued causes of childhood obesity. I will also need to find out why some restaurants have begun offering healthier options for kids and others haven't. Finally, I will develop a fat-to-fit program to accompany Mama Maya's menu.

your turn 7n **Write an Exploratory Essay**

Address these items in an exploratory essay about a topic you are researching.

- What is the historical or cultural background to the issue?
- Who are the players involved in the issue?
- What tentative claims do you want to make?

Include what you do not know that needs more research. What you don't know may include:

- Support for your claims.
- Where to look for materials (statistics, interviews, articles, etc.).
- Possible solutions.

Reflect and Apply

1. As you explore your issue, you will need to make some choices about how to arrange your argument. Explain your decision to use one of the following organizational strategies: define, compare, evaluate, or evaluate causes and effects. Why did you select your organizational strategy? How would your argument be different if you selected a different strategy?

2. Once you have identified which sections of the exploration process you need to apply to your issue, work through them carefully. Explain what these processes add to your thinking about your issue. What solutions do these processes suggest?

3. Your exploratory essay is an opportunity to take a step back from your issue and consider what you have discovered and what more needs to be done. How are you articulating your ideas to your reader in your exploratory essay? Are there any questions that your reader may still have after they read your exploratory essay? How would you answer those questions?

KEEPING IT LOCAL

IN EVERY TOWN there is at least one popular local restaurant that everyone flocks to after football games, soccer practice, even church on Sunday. For as diverse a culture as we have in the United States, the offerings of these restaurants are surprisingly similar. Most menus will include hot dogs, hamburgers, fried fish or shrimp, chili, ice cream or shakes, and cakes and pies. Even those eateries that offer veggie plates usually fry their okra or boil their field peas with fat back. If we want our children to eat better, we cannot rely on fast-food restaurants to magically begin putting healthier foods on the menus. By using different argument strategies, we can compare restaurants' offerings in parts of the country where people are considered healthier with those in parts of the country where people are not so healthy. We can define what healthy food choices mean to us and outline processes to meet these definitional goals. We can campaign against bad food choices based on their effects on our children's lifestyles and health. By examining the restaurant issue, or any other issue important to us, through multiple lenses, we can discover powerful methods of developing solutions to seemingly insurmountable problems.

● — — — — — — — — — — — ●

What issue is important to you? Start the exploration process by asking yourself the questions in the "Propose a Solution" section. Where are these questions taking you? Sometimes you may find that these questions are opening avenues that you had not considered. Are you ready to go down those avenues and learn something new?

CHAPTER 8

Consider Toulmin-Based Argument

Learning Objectives

By working through this chapter, you will be able to

- organize a Toulmin-based argument to fit your purpose.
- apply the features of Toulmin-based argument to an issue.
- map a Toulmin-based argument.

During a class activity, a student spoke intently about the political climate at our community college. He was born in the United States, and his native language is English. His parents moved to the United States from another country 25 years ago, bringing his two sisters—who were very young at the time—with them, so that he and his siblings could enjoy more opportunities and the promise of better lives. Ever since he can remember, his parents have contributed to the civic and religious life of our community. Both hold full-time jobs, and his mother has been promoted several times at work. This student has earned top grades, and his sisters plan to attend the same college in the next few years. But last spring, just after the end of the semester, our state—North Carolina—became the first in the country to recommend that children (who do not have lawful immigration status) of illegal immigrants be barred from attending community college. While the student will complete his degree next semester, he worries about his sisters not being able to attend community college, which will mean that college will be delayed for them. He reveals that he is caught in a swirl of emotions and is not sure what to do. Motivated by concern for his sisters and others in the community who had planned to take advantage of the reasonable tuition and convenience of the local community college, he wants to make his point of view known on this important issue.

All Illustrations by iStock.com/A-digit

COMMUNITY

School-Academic

Workplace

Family-Household

Neighborhood

Social-Cultural

Consumer

Concerned Citizen

TOPIC: Children of Illegal Immigrants in the Community College System

ISSUE: Admission Policy for Children of Illegal Immigrants

AUDIENCE: State Board of Community Colleges

CLAIM: Children of illegal immigrants should be allowed to attend community colleges.

The student decides to contact two instructors at the school and ask if they would be interested in supporting him. Together, the three decide to aim an argument at the State Board of Community Colleges, an organization in a position to ensure that the community college system continues its original open-door policy.

This chapter introduces you to Toulmin-based argument and the ways this structure can serve your purpose as you argue an issue that matters to you. As discussed in Chapter 2, "Explore an Issue that Matters to You," an argument should be a practical response to an issue, especially when you have a good sense of your audience, what it values, and why this issue is important to this audience. In the example that opens this chapter, the writers have made a practical decision to target the State Board of Community Colleges as the audience for their Toulmin-based argument.

You should construct an argument so that all its pieces serve your purpose. If your purpose is to convince an audience of the rightness of your own claim, as opposed to differing claims on an issue, then working with a Toulmin-based approach can serve your purpose. As you'll see in Chapter 9, "Consider Middle Ground Argument, Rogerian Argument, and Argument Based on a Microhistory," there are other argument structures that may be appropriate for your purpose. For example, if your intention is to argue for a practical position between two extreme positions, then a middle-ground strategy can serve your purpose. But if your purpose is to create productive dialogue and common ground on a testy issue with an individual or group whose perspective differs sharply from your own, then a Rogerian approach is practical. And if your purpose is to examine closely a largely forgotten individual, place, or event from the past, then an argument based on a microhistory can work for you.

Construct an Argument to Fit Your Purpose

Once you've decided what you want to accomplish with a Toulmin-based argument, make sure you (as discussed in Chapter 2, "Explore an Issue That Matters to You"):

- Deliver your argument at a time when your audience is invested in the issue at hand.
- Center your argument in what is practical and possible.
- Know what your audience values.
- Let your audience know what it has to gain from your argument.
- Earn credibility early in the argument by establishing your knowledge of the issue and by defining your relationship to your audience.

For example, the narrative that opens this chapter addresses an issue getting a lot of attention in our state. The issue originates with the attorney general's recommendation at that time that children of illegal immigrants be barred from pursuing degrees in the state's community colleges, a recommendation that the president of the community college system has chosen to follow. Because this student attends a community college and because his coauthors teach at the same college, writers of this argument have firsthand knowledge of this issue, and this may establish their credibility with their audience. The issue is generating much discussion across the state based on the news media's regular attention to it. Thus, the argument will be delivered at a decisive moment in the state's struggle with the immigrant presence in schools and other publicly funded institutions. The writers' decision to use a Toulmin-based approach is practical for their purpose—to convince their audience that "children of illegal immigrants should be allowed to attend community colleges." Consider how an argument centered in this issue might take shape using a Toulmin-based approach.

Terms of Toulmin-Based Argument

Contemporary British philosopher Stephen Toulmin has shaped the way we think about argument today. Where classical argument is centered in a three-part structure called a syllogism (major premise, minor premise, and conclusion), Toulmin renames these terms, adds three additional terms to the model, and moves argument from an exercise in logic to a practical scheme geared toward audience acceptance. Toulmin's six terms can be used as a checklist for writing effective arguments when your purpose is to persuade an audience of the rightness of your position. Those terms, defined in the following section, are *claim, support, warrant, backing, rebuttal,* and *qualifier.*

When you build an argument based on the Toulmin model, it's helpful to think of each term as a question that you must answer. With regard to the term *claim,* the question you must answer is, "What is my point?" or "What am I trying to prove?" For the term *support,* the question is, "How will I prove

Ozgurcankaya/E+/Getty Images

Figure 8.1 Close attention to audience and what it values is the hallmark of a Toulmin-based argument. The need to convince an audience of the rightness of a claim depends in large part on the range of support, or evidence, the arguer brings to an argument.

my point?" For the term *warrant*, the questions are, "Will my audience believe me based on values we share?" and "How can I justify my claim?" For the term *backing*, be prepared to answer the question, "What additional support for my warrant will I need in order to persuade my audience?" The term *rebuttal* requires that you ask, "What points of view different from mine should I bring to an argument?" And for the term *qualifier*, you must ask, "How can I modify the language in my argument, especially with reference to my claim and reasons, to make an argument more acceptable?"

But we must add a seventh and vital term to the Toulmin model, and this term is *reasons*. A reason falls between a claim and the specific support you bring to an argument. A reason supports a claim, and in turn, a reason requires support to make it believable. For example, focusing on the issue of children of illegal immigrants being barred from attending community colleges, if you claim that children of illegal immigrants should be allowed to enroll, you will need to provide reasons in support of this claim. One reason the coauthors can address beyond moral or financial arguments is that a skilled workforce is better for the state's economy. This reason requires specific support. So, while the term *reasons* is not among the terms usually used to develop a traditional six-part Toulmin argument, this seventh term is important, especially when you use a Toulmin approach to build a practical response to an issue affecting you.

Claim

A **claim** organizes your argument. It is the single statement to which every-thing else in an argument connects. It focuses your audience on what you want to achieve. It's the point you want to make. For example, a few years ago, a student new to her city made this claim in her first argument: "Links to websites that promote dangerous, antigay propaganda should not be posted on official community websites." Her online search for gay organizations at one point led her to a site stating that same-sex relationships were mor-ally wrong and that counseling was available for those struggling with their sexual identity. The fact that a link to the site appeared on the Chamber of Commerce website motivated her to argue.

Key Questions:
What is my point? What am I trying to prove?

Reasons

Reasons are direct support for your claim. Reasons often function as topic sentences, which you studied in earlier writing courses: they many times begin paragraphs and announce a paragraph's main idea or focus. As a way to begin working with reasons in an argument, think about immediately following a claim with the word *because*. Thus, the claim "Links to websites that promote dangerous, antigay propaganda should not be posted on official community websites" was supported with these reasons:

Key Question:
What comes after *because?*

- Because sites that promote "recovery" from homosexuality are just as harmful as explicitly hateful sites, such as "godhatesfags.com," a site promoting lies and cruelty
- Because not only is the information from such "recovery" sites harmful, but it is also inaccurate
- Because the dangers of antigay propaganda are vast, the most visible occurring in antigay battery and assault

Support

Bring in specific **support** to defend your reasons. As we will see in Chapter 11, "Support an Argument with Fact (Logos), Credibility (Ethos), and Emotion (Pathos)," support can be logical (e.g., facts, statistics, data), ethical (e.g., scholarly articles, credible publications, examples from your own and oth-ers' experiences), or emotional (e.g., examples and startling information that can cause an audience to react emotionally). Vary the support you use, but remember that logical support is proof to an audience that you've done your research and that you're prepared to defend your claim on rational grounds. In most arguments, your goal is to have your audience accept your claim, and the thoroughness of supporting evidence is often what sways an audience. Consider the support this writer brings to her argument.

Key Question:
How will I prove my point?

- Logical support includes numerous examples drawn from antigay web-sites; the FBI's *Uniform Crime Report*, which reveals the annual number of hate crimes based on victims' sexual orientation; and an academic study focused on gay teens and suicide.

- Ethical support includes quoted and paraphrased commentary on homosexuality from the American Psychiatric Association (APA) and the dean of the Georgetown University Medical Center, along with examples—from the writer's experience and those of her friends— of antigay violence, including slurs, bullying, beatings, and property damage.

- Emotional support includes reference to Matthew Wayne Shepard, a gay man beaten and left for dead in Wyoming (an example that opens the argument) and personal examples of her experience with those in her new community who offer "love and guidance" as "solutions" to her sexual orientation.

Warrant

Key Questions:
Will my audience believe me based on values we share? How can I justify my claim?

Use a **warrant** to identify the values and beliefs you share with an audience. The warrant grants you permission to address your audience with your argument because you share at least some moral principles. A warrant justifies a claim; as a writer, you must make clear to your audience that the moral principle in your warrant justifies your claim. This is the warrant the writer used to argue against antigay websites: "I do not want any person to suffer the harm and injustice that so many GLBT (gay, lesbian, bisexual, transgender) persons suffer on a daily basis." This writer connects warrant and claim. The principle in her warrant—not wanting people to suffer harm and injustice—justifies her claim of not wanting her local Chamber of Commerce, a publicly funded organization, to support an antigay website.

Backing

Key Question:
What additional support for my warrant will I need in order to persuade my audience?

Backing supports a warrant. Bring in backing when you sense that an audience will need additional convincing of your warrant. In support of the warrant that centers on the need to avoid harm and injustice, the writer explains why sexual orientation should not be cause for discrimination. She brings in compelling examples from individuals who have suffered harm and injustice as well as examples from individuals who live in communities where sexual orientation is not an issue.

Rebuttal

Key Question:
What points of view different from mine should I bring to my argument?

A **rebuttal** argues against a claim. It presents a different or opposing point of view on your issue. It is helpful to anticipate objections to an argument for several reasons. First, when you summarize a differing view fairly, you become credible to your audience—because you can be trusted to describe without bias another view. Second, countering a rebuttal to your claim gives you the chance to demonstrate to an audience that your claim (or solution) is more practical than the one proposed by the opposition. A rebuttal needs to be countered, with an eye toward why an audience might consider a position different from yours. In the issue we're working with, the writer brings in two rebuttals. One claims that choosing a gay lifestyle is abnormal and unhealthy. The second argues that homosexuality is "wrong, immoral, and dangerous" and should be corrected. The writer counters both rebuttals by claiming that sexual orientation is not about choice; rather, she explains, sexuality is a "precognitive aspect of personality developed even before language skills." Additionally, she counters both rebuttals by referring to the American Psychiatric Association and the scientific view that homosexuality is not a psychiatric illness and that the only disorder in this context has to do with not accepting one's sexuality.

Qualifiers

The great strength of Toulmin's system is its focus on audience. A claim is your position on an issue, a position that must be delivered to an audience open to hearing it. The support you bring to an argument will be of three kinds—logical, ethical, and emotional—and each kind should appeal to your audience in a practical way. Your warrant ties you to your audience based on shared or similar values, beliefs, and feelings. Backing allows you to elaborate on your warrant in order to appeal more specifically to your audience's value system. A rebuttal (or rebuttals) in an argument lets you anticipate audience objections to your claim, objections that you can then counter. **Qualifiers** prevent you from making absolute statements because they involve words such as *often, typically,* and *in most cases* (instead of words like *always, only,* and *for certain*). Collectively, wise application of these qualifying terms centers an argument in practical—rather than idealistic, unrealistic—appeals.

As you can see, Toulmin-based argument is about arguing before an audience that is invested in your issue and therefore willing to listen to what you have to say. This kind of argument is also about each part of an argument supporting another part—a warrant that supports a claim, backing that supports a warrant, specific support that strengthens reasons, and reasons that support a claim. The seven strands of a Toulmin argument are knit together to form a single garment, a single argument. Each part serves the next with no room for filler. With reference to any single strand, a question helpful in building a Toulmin argument can be, "How does this part of my argument move my audience closer to accepting my claim?"

Key Question:
How can I modify the language in an argument, especially with reference to my claim and reasons, to make an argument more believable?

your turn 8a **GET STARTED A Toulmin-Based Argument**

Answer the following questions as a way to begin working with the Toulmin model.

1. What issue will you argue on? Why is it important to you? What might you claim?
2. What reasons can support your claim?
3. What support will you use to prove your reasons? Specifically, what kinds of logical, ethical, and emotional appeals will you use with your audience?

4. What values and beliefs connect you to your audience? Explain how you will build on this connection during your argument.
5. Describe the rebuttals you'll bring to your argument. How will you counter these differing views?
6. In addition to your claim, would other statements in your argument benefit from the addition of qualifiers? If yes, what are the statements, and what qualifiers will you use?
7. Bring to class an example of a Toulmin-based argument. Find this argument in an online or print newspaper or magazine.

Map a Toulmin-Based Argument

Below are outlines for two arguments that use the Toulmin system. Figure 8.2 on page 197 provides a visual reminder of the way Toulmin argument works. Note that the term *reasons* is given separate treatment and lies between *claim* and *support*.

COMMUNITY
School-Academic
Workplace
Family-Household
Neighborhood
Social-Cultural
Consumer
Concerned Citizen

TOPIC: Food Consumption
ISSUE: Traditional vs. Fair Trade Bananas
AUDIENCE: Church Social Action Group
CLAIM: Consumers should buy organic, fair trade bananas because of the high humanitarian and environmental costs of marketing traditional bananas.

Reasons

- Most workers on traditional banana plantations labor under unsafe conditions.
- Low wages prevent the majority of workers from improving their living conditions.
- The absence of child labor laws means that children, many of whom are more susceptible to dangerous pesticides than adults, are often made to work on these plantations.
- Workers who do manage to organize and strike for better conditions often are threatened with violence if they do not return to work.

- Many banana producers blatantly violate environmental laws.
- Local ecosystems can suffer due to the intensive use of pesticide and antifungal chemicals.

Support
- Logical support includes facts, figures, statistics, and commentary that describe the banana trade and conditions for workers, as well as definitions for the terms *organic bananas* and *fair trade practices*.
- Ethical support can include scholarly articles and research drawn from credible online and print sources that focus on conditions of banana production and marketing. It can also include personal examples that motivate readers to buy fair trade bananas.
- Emotional support can focus on your decision to switch to organic, fair trade bananas; descriptions of working conditions; and examples drawn from the experience of workers, families, and children associated with traditional banana production.

Warrant
The fair treatment of workers and good stewardship of the environment are important for the global economy.

Backing
Support for this warrant can include examples of the increasing number of importers that will buy bananas only from companies that guarantee worker rights and environmental standards. It can also include the commentary of economists who view fair trade as essential to the global economy.

Rebuttals
The following rebuttals will need to be countered.

- Major banana exporters argue that they comply with the "Social Accountability 8000" labor and human rights standard.
- Major exporters also claim 100 percent compliance with the Rainforest Alliance's "Banana Certification Program," designed to protect workers from excessive exposure to pesticides and to protect the environment from pollution and deforestation, among other requirements.

Qualifiers
Note that in the first reason, the qualifier *most* is used, and that in the second reason the phrase *the majority of* functions as a qualifier. The third reason includes the qualifiers *many* and *often*; the fourth reason also uses the qualifier *often*; and the final reason uses the qualifier *can*.

COMMUNITY

School-Academic

Workplace

Family-Household

Neighborhood

Social-Cultural

Consumer

Concerned Citizen

TOPIC: Relationships

ISSUE: Online Dating Sites and Advertising Practices

AUDIENCE: Members of My Writing Class

CLAIM: Some high-profile online dating companies use extreme and unfounded claims to attract clients.

Reasons

- Some companies, though they do not openly deny access to gays and lesbians, nevertheless deny options for people seeking same-sex matches.

- Other companies seem to require a religious preference and will not pursue matches for clients falling outside this invisible guideline.

- As a way to lure clients, a number of companies create false profiles representing potential matches; then, after the prospective client pays the joining fee, the enticing profiles disappear.

Support

- Logical support can include factual information from online dating companies, such as questionnaires, application materials, and promotional language and images; statistics drawn from scholarly articles; and surveys conducted by reliable sources and by you.

- Ethical support can include personal experience with online dating; the experience of others with online dating; the use of credible, agenda-free research on online dating companies; and proper documentation of your research, including quoting and paraphrasing.

- Emotional support can include brief, powerful anecdotes drawn from your experience with online dating; the testimony of others with regard to online dating; and examples drawn from your research that appeal to your audience's values and emotions.

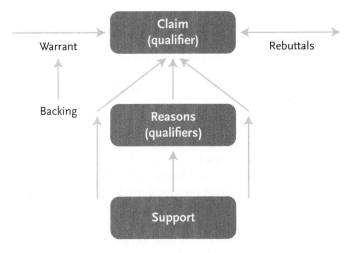

Figure 8.2 The Toulmin model of argument

Warrant

What I want to stress most is that no one should become a client of companies that discriminate.

Backing

- Everyone deserves to be happy and find special love, regardless of faith, sexual orientation, or race.
- These companies need to reevaluate their policies and realize that today gay couples raise families and in most cases experience no ill will from their communities.

Rebuttals

- If these complaints about online dating companies are taken seriously, it can lead to overregulation of a successful industry, and this will damage profits.
- Many companies have successful histories matching their clients.

Qualifiers

Note the qualifiers used in the claim and reasons above. Do they make these statements more believable than if they were left out? Note also the absence of qualifiers in the warrant and backing. Are these statements acceptable as they are, or would they benefit from qualifying language?

your turn 8b **PRACTICE Map a Toulmin-Based Argument**

Map a Toulmin-based argument for each of the following five issues. Specifically, in response to each issue, draft a claim, two reasons that support this claim, two or three specific examples supporting each reason, and a warrant. Then identify one or two rebuttals you might encounter.

1. The term *food dumping* refers to the practice of industrialized countries providing free food to developing countries. Some critics claim that this practice hurts rather than helps, because the injection of free product into local markets causes small farmers in developing countries to go out of business and thus fall further into poverty.

2. Promotions and higher pay at your job are based strictly on seniority. In your view, your job performance exceeds the performance of some coworkers with more seniority.

3. Because of increasing development and gentrification in your community, air and water quality have declined. Laws are in place to monitor and respond to these declines, but local officials claim that hiring an adequate number of trained inspectors will raise local taxes.

4. Pharmaceutical companies defend targeting their research at markets that will generate profitable returns. Returns from drugs for Alzheimer's, male enhancement, and cancer, for example, allow research to continue. Some argue that pharmaceutical companies are without social conscience for neglecting the many devastating tropical diseases that affect poor people.

5. The prevailing attitude of many local school board members is that the history of slavery, especially as it concerns the treatment of the enslaved, is an inappropriate subject for public school students.

tip 8a

Use Visualization with Toulmin-Based Argument

Visualize yourself as an attorney defending an unpopular client. Know that your case must be painstakingly researched, that you must answer the opposing attorney's claims, and that you must use varied appeals to sway the jury.

Student-Authored Toulmin-Based Argument

In the following example, a student is using a Toulmin-based approach to advocate for a school voucher system in his community. As a home-schooled student, the writer is intent on proving the advantages of an education apart from public schools. His audience includes members of his writing class, especially those who defend public schools and regard home-schooling as ideological and prescriptive. Strengths of this argument are the writer's application of the Toulmin approach, his effective research, and his inventiveness to offer and defend an original idea. Note: For essays that demonstrate correct formatting, please see Appendix A for MLA style and Appendix B for APA style.

Ben Szany

ENG 112-04

Professor Phillips

March 18, 2019

Vouching for Our School System?

Our public school system is our country's biggest and most inefficient monopoly, yet it keeps demanding more and more money.—Phyllis Schlafly

A monopoly is defined as exclusive control of a product or service. Public schools may not possess exclusive control of education in Charlotte, but for low-income families there are no real alternatives. Private schools cost several thousand dollars a year per child. Home-schooling is very difficult to nearly impossible in single-parent households or in situations where both parents must work. The problem would be lessened if the public schools provided a good education. However, in 2011, only 72.2% of Charlotte-Mecklenberg high school students earned a diploma (Chesser, 2011). How can we give families more options for their children's education? By giving parents vouchers for education, we can create an opportunity for parents to send their children to the private school of their choice. The Charlotte-Mecklenburg School system and local government must allocate vouchers—which can be exchanged at public schools, private schools, and homeschools—to parents.

In a school voucher system, the money follows the student. A month before school enrollment opens, families would receive a voucher for every school-aged child in their family. Each student could only redeem a voucher in his or her name. Vouchers could not be stockpiled, saved from year to year, or reused. When the time came to enroll in school, the student could redeem the voucher for a given amount of money at any qualified private school and receive a credit toward the cost of enrollment. At a public school, the cost of enrollment after a voucher would always be $0, just as the cost of enrollment in public school is currently $0. If used toward a private school, the voucher's value would vary based upon income of the family. Poorer families or children with disabilities would receive vouchers worth more than vouchers for children of the middle or upper classes. This would make private school significantly more affordable for lower-income families. For those parents who home-school, the vouchers would have a value dependent upon the income of the family. Home-schooling families would turn in the vouchers when filing their taxes; the money would be given in the form of a tax refund. The amount would be worth 15% of the voucher's value at a private school. If the voucher was worth $1,600 because of the family's income level, they would receive $240 if they home-schooled. This money could be spent on school books, supplies, computers, or other educational items.

All families, regardless of income, can benefit from a school voucher program. Lower-income parents gain access to a wider range of educational

Although the title does suggest the subject of the argument, opening with a question often is not effective. An assertive title, one that hints at a writer's claim, is a good strategy.

The quotation orients the reader as to what will follow and sets a decisive emotional tone.

A qualifier, such as *some* or *many*, in front of *parents* would make the writer's assertion more believable.

The final two sentences of the first paragraph are the writer's warrant and claim. The warrant is grounded in values of "opportunity" and "choice."

The paragraph opens with a reason that directly supports the writer's claim.

options. Often these parents are forced to leave their children in failing or low-performing schools. As Harvard University Professor Paul E. Peterson explains in the video *The Case for Vouchers*, "I would say the results on parent satisfaction are overwhelmingly conclusive. If parents are given a choice, they're very happy. They're much happier with their private schools" (Peterson, 2000). A school voucher program would greatly aid these parents, who are desperate to give their children the educational opportunity to succeed. Wealthier families' tax dollars would continue to fund the public school system as they do now, and they too would receive educational savings from the vouchers if they choose to enroll their children in private schools or home-school, although these savings would be modest at best. Thus, the vouchers do not ignore the needs of the poor nor do they swindle the wealthy; they are fair to both.

Making private schools and home-schools more affordable offers another advantage to parents; it forces the public school system to become more competitive. Currently in Charlotte, the public schools have something of a monopoly, especially regarding the education of children from lower-income families. By providing the opportunity for these parents to more easily remove their children from the public school system, we level the educational playing field. The Charlotte-Mecklenburg school system will have no alternative but to improve performance in schools that consistently score below average. If they do not, children will leave the failing schools in favor of local private schools. This has already happened in Milwaukee, a voucher-using city that is comparable to Charlotte in both population and ethnic diversity. According to Stossel (2007), after 11 years of the voucher program, a study conducted by Harvard's Caroline Hoxby showed increased scores from children who used the vouchers to enroll in private school and from the children in local public schools. Public school test results jumped by 8.1% in math, 13.8% in science, and 8% in language (pp. 135–136). The number of private schools in Milwaukee had increased to meet the demand of parents who opted out of the public schools (Koch, 1999, p. 296). "The public schools," wrote Stossel (2007), host of ABC's *20/20*, "didn't want to lose their students to voucher schools, so they tried harder. They did a better job" (p. 136). There is no reason why a school voucher program in Charlotte would not provide a similar improvement in results.

There is some concern that a school voucher program would greatly weaken Charlotte's public school system. Sandra Feldman, president of the American Federation of Teachers, stated, "[School vouchers mean]: Give up on public education in America; stop investing in it, siphon off as much funding as you can" (as cited in Koch, 1999, p. 286). A school voucher system would lessen the public school's monopoly on education, but it would not mean abandoning the public school system. The Charlotte-Mecklenburg school system would still be expected to teach a majority of local students. Presently, public schools are responsible for the education of 90% of American children. With a universal school voucher program, that number is estimated to drop

---

This clearly worded reason links directly to the writer's claim and announces the purpose of the paragraph.

In terms of its persuasiveness, this is the most effective paragraph in the argument—because the writer documents his idea about vouchers with factual information, which is vital to readers who are undecided about an issue.

The final sentence makes a dangerous guarantee, a problem that would be avoided by the use of a qualifying phrase to replace "There is no reason."

This opposing view and the opposing view in the next paragraph need fuller treatment so that (1) readers understand what drives Feldman's comment and (2) so that the writer demonstrates a willingness to work with the opposition fairly.

to 60% or 70% (Hood, 2007). Despite this shift, Charlotte schools would be able to spend more money per pupil than without a voucher system. How is this possible? In Milwaukee, the average cost per voucher is $4,894 (Koch, 1999, p. 292). That figure is several thousand dollars less than the $8,523 that Charlotte schools spend per pupil ("How," 2018). In other words, if the Charlotte school system would spend $8,523 to educate a child for one year, and that child instead uses a $4,894 voucher to go to a private school, the public school system nets $3,629 per voucher, which can then be spent on other students. "What's more," said then Virginia Governor Tim Kaine, "for every few hundred students who accept vouchers, the district saves itself the expense—tens of millions of dollars—of building a new school to accommodate rising enrollment" (as cited in Hinkle, 2015). It isn't just theory. In 2001, Greenberger, wrote "In Milwaukee, which has the nation's oldest and largest voucher program, even voucher opponents now acknowledge that no public school has been decimated by a loss of money or pupils. Furthermore, many public school principals and teachers here say the voucher program has pushed them to improve." A school voucher program would not signal abandonment of the public school system but a desire within the community to improve the educational system as a whole.

Opponents of a Charlotte-Mecklenburg school voucher system claim that such a program would be unconstitutional because many private schools have religious affiliations. Elliot Mincberg, of People for the American Way, argues, "Voucher programs that include sectarian schools grossly violate the constitutional separation of church and state" (as cited in Koch, 1999, p. 297). However, children are not ever required to use the voucher at a religious private school. Only their parents can decide where they go to school. In other words, if a parent does not want their child in a religiously oriented setting, there is nothing that can force their child into such a school. The decision is entirely up to the family. Koch points out that it must also be noted that public funds often support students in religious schools. Students receiving federal grants are free to attend sectarian universities such as Brigham Young University (Mormon) or Notre Dame (Roman Catholic) (p. 290). Federal child care funds can be used by parents to send their toddlers to religiously affiliated day care centers. Finally, the Wisconsin Supreme Court ruled that Milwaukee's school voucher program was well within the bounds of both the state constitution and the U.S. Constitution (p. 288). A voucher system that permits enrollment in religious schools does not violate the rights of any citizen, and the decision to send a student to such a school can only be made by that student's parents.

The Charlotte-Mecklenburg school system holds a monopoly on education in Mecklenburg County. Breaking this stranglehold with a school voucher program would give parents more educational options and force the public and private schools to compete. This healthy competition would provide a better and more fruitful learning experience to students currently stuck in the public school system.

This conclusion can be stronger. Ideas in the writer's claim and warrant are repeated, but some attention here and earlier in the argument is needed to address why this competition would be "better and more fruitful" for students. Backing for the writer's warrant would be effective.

References

Chesser, J. (2011, November 2). The highs and lows of high school graduation rates. *UNC Charlotte Urban Institute*. Retrieved from https://
ui.uncc.edu/story/highs-and-lows-high-school-graduation-rates

Greenberger, S. S. (2001, February 26). Voucher lessons learned. *Boston
Globe*. Retrieved from http://ezproxy.cpcc.edu/login?url=https://search
.proquest.com/docview/405375821?accountid=10008

Hinkle, A. B. (2015, June 10). The case for school vouchers: Why choice
should trump coercion, *Reason*. Retrieved from https://reason.com
/archives/2015/06/10/the-case-for-school-vouchers

Hobbs, T. D. (2018, January 28). Do school vouchers work? Milwaukee's
experiment suggests an answer. *Wall Street Journal*. Retrieved from
https://www.wsj.com/articles/do-school-vouchers-work-milwaukees
-experiment-suggests-an-answer-1517162799

Hood, J. (2007). Spend a lot to teach a little. *The (NC) Laurinburg Exchange*.

How is CMS funded? (2018). *Charlotte-Mecklenburg Schools*. Retrieved from
http://www.cms.k12.nc.us/mediaroom/budget/Pages/HowisCMSfunded
.aspx

Koch, K. (1999, April 9) School vouchers. *CQ Researcher*, *9*, 281–304.
Retrieved from http://library.cqpress.com/

Monopoly. (n.d.) In *Dictionary.com*. Retrieved from https://www.dictionary
.com/browse/monopoly

Peterson, P. (Producer). (2000, May 3). *The Case for Vouchers*. UNC-TV.
Retrieved from https://www.pbs.org/wgbh/pages/frontline/shows
/vouchers/choice/provouchers.html

Stossel, J. (2007). *Myths, lies, and downright stupidity: Get out the shovel—
why everything you know is wrong*. Hyperion.

Reflect and Apply

Answer the following questions as a way to review the purpose of a Toulmin-based argument.

1. Based on the argument you're presently building, why is or isn't a Toulmin-based argument appropriate to your purpose?

2. Map a Toulmin-based argument based on an issue you're struggling with in daily life. Where would you place the rebuttal and how would you respond to it?

3. Stephen Toulmin believed that argument should have a practical function and that an effective argument could be modeled, in part, on sound courtroom practice. Given a Toulmin-based argument you intend to build and with a courtroom setting in mind, how will you balance the support you bring to your argument; that is, will you balance evenly logical, ethical, and emotional support, or will you emphasize some kinds of support more than others? Explain.

KEEPING IT LOCAL

THE COMPELLING NARRATIVE that begins this chapter responds to a local and personal issue with a Toulmin-based argument. It is the kind of argument the writers consider most practical when they want to prove the rightness of their position and when they want action taken in response to their claim. The student bringing this issue to the table is motivated by deep concern for his siblings, by his parents' efforts to create opportunities for their children, and by others in his community who happen to be children of illegal immigrants. Had this writer elected not to respond to the state's recommendation to bar children of illegal immigrants from attending community colleges, then the public debate over this issue would be missing the informed position of a stakeholder in this important controversy. When we fail to speak up on an issue that matters to us, we let others make decisions for us, and this means that our position on an issue may be left out of the conversation. And because the writers want immediate action taken on this issue, they aimed their argument at the State Board of Community Colleges, an audience in a position to act. They are careful to identify values they and board members share and then build their arguments based on these values. Toulmin-based argument gives these writers, and us, a way to respond to important personal issues. This kind of argument and the kinds of argument discussed in Chapter 9, "Consider Middle Ground Argument, Rogerian Argument, and Argument Based on a Microhistory," are created using practical skills that can be deployed before audiences we want to influence and inform. Learn these skills and you'll be in a position to represent yourself with integrity and with a sense for what is practical on issues that matter to you.

● ‒‒ ‒‒ ‒‒ ‒‒ ‒‒ ‒‒ ‒‒ ‒‒ ‒‒ ●

As you work through your argument, consider the following questions: At what audience will you aim your Toulmin-based argument? How did you narrow to this audience?

A common complaint about arguments is that they're too theoretical and not practical enough. What, exactly, will make your Toulmin-based argument practical?

Consider Middle-Ground Argument, Rogerian Argument, and Argument Based on a Microhistory

Learning Objectives

By working through this chapter, you will be able to

- distinguish between middle-ground arguments, Rogerian arguments, and arguments based on a microhistory.

A couple of your coworkers were recently detained by police for remaining in the lobby of the local utility offices after being told to leave. After a good conversation with your coworkers, you understand the issue and why they were willing to be arrested. You learn that your local utility is actually a monopoly across the state and that it recently announced plans to ask a state regulatory agency for permission to request regular rate hikes. You also learn that the utility is stuck on a model of generating nearly all its electricity from coal, nuclear, and natural gas, and that this means continued dirty air, economic risk, and hydraulic fracturing. You were vaguely aware of these issues in the past, but you now view them as threats to the local quality of life. Further research informs you that the utility is backing a law that would effectively reduce the opportunities for public comment on proposed rate hikes and that it wants ratepayers to finance construction of new nuclear plants—whether or not these plants reach completion.

You decide that the state Utilities Commission is the most practical audience for your argument because it is the organization with the power to regulate the powerful utility. More specifically, the commission can approve, reject, or call for modifications on the utility's policies and activities. This choice of audience seems practical because the Utilities

COMMUNITY

School-Academic

Workplace

Family-Household

Neighborhood

Social-Cultural

Consumer

Concerned Citizen

TOPIC: Utility Company's Proposed Rate Hikes and Other Potential Dangers

ISSUE: Regulation of utility company

AUDIENCE: State Utilities Commission

CLAIM: The Utilities Commission should announce a moratorium on requests from the utilities for rate hikes and changes to public hearing requirements.

Commission is charged with being on the look-out for any economic hardship that the utility might cause citizens of your state. The stated values of the Utilities Commission must overlap considerably with the values of ratepayers like you who may suffer from rate hikes and other utilities-related issues.

The chapter introduces you to three approaches to argument: Middle-Ground, Rogerian, and Argument Based on a Microhistory.

Each of these approaches is uniquely different from Toulmin-Based Argument, the focus of Chapter 8, "Consider Toulmin-Based Argument." Collectively, the four kinds of argument provide you with options when you approach a given issue.

To distinguish in a general way among these approaches, it can be helpful to think about audience. In a Toulmin-based approach, the idea is to persuade an audience of the rightness of your position by using convincing support and effective handling of the opposition, much like the arguments created by competent trial attorneys. A middle-ground approach allows you to offer an audience a reasonable middle position between two relatively extreme positions. A Rogerian approach challenges the arguer to demonstrate common ground among sharply divergent positions on an issue; Rev. Martin Luther King, Jr. takes up this challenge in "Letter From Birmingham Jail" (excerpted in sections that follow). Finally, an Argument Based on a Microhistory lets you step into the shoes of a historian as you work with primary sources: in this kind of argument, you are making sense of the past in a new way, one that can let an audience view a particular event, for example, from different perspectives. Let the approach you choose to work with complement your goals with your audience.

Middle-Ground Argument

A **middle-ground argument** argues a moderate, practical claim between two extreme positions (see Figure 9.2). Middle-ground arguments often are used with political, business, religious, and even personal issues and can provide a practical position when two sides of an issue are far apart. When aimed at an appropriate target audience, the middle-ground approach offers a practical, more moderate alternative to two more extreme positions. When an audience is uncertain, unaware, undecided, or silent on an issue, arguing for a practical middle position—or what you *perceive* to be a middle position—can be an effective strategy.

Make a Middle-Ground Position Practical

Importantly, a middle-position approach is used when you believe your solution to be between two extreme positions, but you still must *prove* that your middle-ground position is practical. Do this by discussing why the other positions are extreme and by providing your audience with persuasive reasons and support for your position. As with a Toulmin approach, you will include a claim, reasons, support, warrant, backing, and qualifiers. But compared with the Toulmin approach, middle-ground argument requires much more attention to the opposition, or the two extreme positions you argue against. In Toulmin argument, attention to the opposition is called "rebuttals."

A sensible approach to Middle-Ground arguing is first to introduce an issue and explain why a middle position is appropriate at this time. This introduction can then be followed by substantial and accurate summaries of each extreme position, with special emphasis on what makes each position impractical. These summaries first should be accurate and objective; second, each summary must be followed by your evaluation of each position, in

Kablonk/SuperStock

Figure 9.1 Middle-Ground argument means arguing for a position between two extreme positions. This photo reveals a thoughtful third party who may be ready to argue for a more practical solution to an issue.

which you identify the shortcomings of each view. The remainder of your argument should prove why your position is more practical than the two positions you have identified as extreme. In contrast with the Toulmin structure, you will devote up to half of your argument to the opposition before you get to your own position. (See Chapter 6, "Work Fairly with the Opposition," for tips on presenting the opposition fairly.)

> your turn 9a   PRACTICE **Recognize When a Middle-Ground Approach Is Practical**
>
> Respond to the following questions as a way to begin thinking about how a middle-ground approach can offer practical choices on tough local and global issues.
>
> 1. Identify three issues—a personal issue, a community issue, and a global issue—that are polarizing or that set two clear positions against one another. For each issue, describe the two positions.
> 2. Focusing on one of these issues, does each group seem extreme or impractical in its position? Why?
> 3. What middle-ground position can you offer? Why would your position be more practical than either of the other positions?

Recognize Where Middle-Ground Arguments Are Possible

Consider the following three issues, the two extreme positions for each, and then the claims that argue for middle-ground solutions. With each issue, the two extreme positions are far apart; this can open the door to a more practical middle position.

Issue #1: "Brain drain" of health-care workers from poor to rich countries

- Extreme Position A: Doctors and nurses from poor countries have the right to pursue opportunities in rich countries.
- Extreme Position B: Doctors and nurses from poor countries have an obligation to serve people from their home countries.
- Middle-Ground Position: Groups such as Human Rights Watch should recommend that doctors and nurses from poor countries serve people in their native countries for a minimum five-year period.

Issue #2: Flying the Confederate flag in our community's public cemeteries

- Extreme Position A: The Confederate flag should be flown daily as a way to honor our ancestors who died during the Civil War.

- Extreme Position B: The Confederate flag should not be flown at all because it symbolizes a way of life that kept many of our ancestors oppressed.
- Middle-Ground Position: The Confederate flag should be flown on national holidays only.

Issue #3: Reducing carbon emissions in our state

- Extreme Position A: The best way to reduce carbon emissions in our state is to make a complete switch to alternative fuels in the next 10 years.
- Extreme Position B: Because laws are now in place to protect our air and water quality, we simply need to hire more inspectors and regulators.
- Middle-Ground Position: The governor needs to appoint a committee that allows consumers to work with public policy experts and energy companies in order to create a realistic plan to lower carbon emissions.

Let's say that the arguer targets students in her nursing classes as an audience for the "brain drain" issue. For the Confederate flag issue, the arguer aims at readers of the local newspaper. And for the carbon emissions issue, the governor is the target audience. Because there are strong views on all of these issues, it will be vital that arguers offer middle-ground positions that appear reasonable and well-thought-out. But remember that the audience might not agree with the arguer's opinion that the middle position offers a compromise or that it presents the Middle-Ground between two extreme positions. Your best chance at having your middle position accepted is to know what your audience values and then craft appropriate appeals based on these values. Because writers of middle-ground positions regard other positions as extreme, they will need to specify why the extreme positions are less practical than the proposed middle position. Furthermore, while the writer's middle-ground position differs from the other positions, the writer must nevertheless respect the differing views and acknowledge points of overlap. It may be that underneath the differences all groups want a similar outcome, but the methods each extreme position advocates are less practical than your approach. In general, you will need to earn credibility from your audience by appearing fair-minded in your summaries and critical in your evaluations. Use Your Turn 9c as a guide to setting up middle-ground arguments.

Map a Middle-Ground Argument

An outline for a middle-ground argument addressing the contentious issue of extra credit work and whether it should be allowed in college classes appears in the following section. To many students and teachers, extra credit is an important issue because it touches one's sense of fairness. In fact, the following positions, labeled "extreme" by many, may not seem extreme to readers of the college newspaper, the writer's intended audience. If the middle-ground position is to be convincing, it surely must acknowledge—and, when possible, honor—the range of school newspaper readers and their values. This will be challenging work for this writer because research demonstrates that most students favor the chance at extra credit work, especially when their grades are low or some of their required work is missing. The support this writer uses with his reasons must be compelling and reveal the practicality of his position.

EXTREME POSITION #1: No! It's unethical.

CLAIM: Extra credit work rewards students for being irresponsible; therefore, it is unethical.

Reasons

- Extra credit work rewards students for failing to learn course content, as reflected in poor exam scores.
- Final course grades should reflect performance only and not be based on extra credit work.
- Extra credit usually is not available in the real world, especially in the workplace.
- Extra credit opportunities are unfair to responsible students.

EXTREME POSITION #2: Yes! It's practical.

CLAIM: With so much pressure on students to complete a college degree and transition into the workplace these days, teachers should allow extra credit opportunities.

Reasons

- Extra credit gives students a second chance.
- Denying extra credit can be a roadblock to success.
- Demands of family and job get in the way of preparing for class.
- Extra credit rewards effort.

MIDDLE-GROUND POSITION: Yes, extra credit work should be allowed, but only when it leads to deeper knowledge of the content area.

CLAIM: Extra credit should be allowed for students who want to pursue a question or problem that falls outside requirements of a course but within the content area.

Reasons

- Extra credit assignments can be designed to create deeper familiarity with course content.
- Extra credit is one way to encourage research and critical-thinking skills.
- This kind of extra credit is a way to reward genuine effort beyond what is expected.
- Establishing and maintaining a single standard for extra credit work is one way to keep grading policies consistent and without exception.

COMMUNITY

School-Academic

Workplace

Family-Household

Neighborhood

Social-Cultural

Consumer

Concerned Citizen

TOPIC: Grading Policies

ISSUE: Extra Credit

AUDIENCE: Readers of School Newspaper

CLAIM: Extra credit should be allowed for students who want to pursue a question or problem that falls outside requirements of a course but within the content area.

Based on the middle-ground position this writer will defend, Position #1 is considered extreme because it shuts the door on the possible benefits of extra credit work. It makes a dangerous assumption that extra credit work encourages irresponsible behavior. It does not allow for the chance that some students may want to pursue deeper work with a topic. It ignores the conditions for extra credit that some teachers set, such as limits on how extra credit can affect a final grade or that all required coursework must be completed before extra credit assignments can be pursued. This position also assumes that students seeking extra credit did not put forth effort in a class. Finally, it neglects to consider circumstances such as illness and family duties, which can get in the way of a student's preparation for exams and assignments.

Position #2 assumes that students need second chances in order to succeed. The argument assumes that teachers—not students or the circumstances of students' lives—can be roadblocks to student success. Implicit in the reasons for this claim is the attitude that students are naturally under duress and unable to keep up with requirements of their courses.

With these extreme positions summarized for the audience, the writer must now aggressively support his claim and prove that his middle position is more practical. The writer is a teacher who has struggled during his career with the idea of extra credit. For the past five years, he has settled on the position defended below. Claim and reasons were noted in the previous section under "Middle-Ground Position."

Support

Support will be drawn primarily from the writer's experience with extra credit work over a 20-year teaching career. References to published scholarly research addressing extra credit in the college classroom will also be included.

Warrant

Providing opportunities for students to pursue a problem or topic connected to course content rewards intellectual curiosity.

Backing

- Intellectual curiosity is important because it complements critical-thinking skills, a core competency at our college.
- Intellectual curiosity is important because it respects a student's interest in a course and the questions that follow from this interest.

Qualifiers

The claim does not make extra credit work available to all students under unspecified conditions; instead, it limits extra credit work to students who want the chance to pursue a question or topic not covered in class. Reason number one includes the qualifier *can*; reason number two includes the qualifier *one way* (as opposed to *the only way*); reason number three includes the qualifier *a way*, and reason four includes the qualifier *one way*.

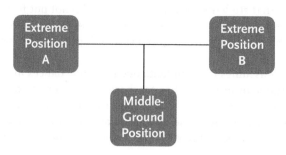

Figure 9.2 The middle-ground model

your turn 9b ▶ **PRACTICE Middle-Ground Thinking**

Based on the following descriptions of six different issues, along with the two extreme positions noted for each, write a claim for each issue that offers a middle position. Below each claim you offer, list two or three reasons that support your claim.

1. Executive compensation—salaries and bonuses paid to executives in American companies—has come under fire recently. Some argue that a top executive in a company should not be allowed to earn more than 25 times what the lowest paid employee in the company earns. Others believe that attractive compensation packages are needed to attract top talent and should not be regulated.

2. Plagiarism occurs in our schools and colleges at alarming rates. One possible response is to institute a campus-wide honor code that mandates a single standard: expulsion. Another view claims that a more practical approach would be for writing classes to provide more comprehensive attention to the issue of plagiarism and how to avoid it.

3. Undocumented workers in the United States are the subject of a long-standing debate. The center of this debate is whether or not penalties should be levied on employers hiring undocumented workers. Several political action groups have formed to protest the hiring of undocumented workers, arguing that these jobs should belong to American workers and that penalties should be levied on employers. Another side claims that most American workers don't want these low-paying jobs and that employers are left with little choice other than to hire undocumented workers.

4. *Digital divide* is a term that refers to the gap between people who have access to the Internet and people who do not. Some people believe that Americans whose annual income falls below the poverty line should be given inexpensive laptops and access to the Internet. Others hold that this provision is unnecessary because Internet technology has become available to almost everyone through schools, libraries, and a range of social programs.

5. The local newspaper's recent series of stories on poultry processing plants revealed horrific worker conditions that have resulted in many chronic injuries. Some concerned parties advocate for union representation for workers; others argue that laws are already in place to protect workers and that hiring more inspectors to enforce these laws is the solution.

6. Tipping in local restaurants, a concern for servers whose income depends on tips, generates two extreme positions: first, that a mandatory 15 percent tip should be noted on restaurant menus; or second, that tipping should be at the discretion of customers, who presumably base the tip amount on the professionalism of the server.

tip 9a

Identify Local Models of Middle-Ground Positions

In many ways, we are trained to look to leaders beyond our immediate communities for practical solutions to pressing issues. But this need not be our first line of inquiry. Identify practical middle-ground positions offered to address local issues. These solutions might be offered by friends, fellow students, coworkers, or family; they might also be found in the local newspaper, on your favorite blogs, or on social networking sites. What makes the middle-ground positions more practical than the extreme positions?

your turn 9c ▶ **GET STARTED Set Up a Middle-Ground Argument**

Answer the following questions to set up a middle-ground argument.

1. Identify the issue you plan to address and describe the specific context you bring to your argument. How far back in time will you need to go to reveal the roots of this issue? What are these roots?
2. Why, exactly, is this issue deserving of our attention now? What specific present conditions make this issue important?
3. What does each extreme position claim? What is the history of each group with regard to this issue? Why is each group so deeply invested in its position?
4. How does each group justify its position? What is the warrant for each group's claim? What support does each group use?
5. What values and beliefs do you share with each group?
6. What are the limitations and potential damages you see with each position?
7. What is your claim on this issue? Why is it more practical than other positions?
8. What reasons will you use to support your claim? What major examples, statistics, and personal experiences will you use as part of your support?
9. What does your audience have to gain by accepting your position? How will the community benefit?

Student-Authored Middle-Ground Argument

Illegal immigrants, mostly Hispanics, are employed extensively in the community in the construction, landscaping, and food and beverage industries. The writer of the following argument is responding to the issue of whether illegal immigrants should be eligible for driver's licenses. This issue has been a matter of public concern for several years and is reported on regularly by local media. The writer perceives the need for a more practical approach, so she has chosen to write a middle-ground argument, one that (in her view) offers a practical middle position between two positions that the author considers extreme. The writer's purpose is to generate awareness of the importance of driving privileges for illegal immigrants in the community. Her audience is her writing class, most of whom are U.S. citizens. The first paragraph introduces the issue, the next two paragraphs present the two extreme positions, and the fourth paragraph presents the writer's claim. The remaining paragraphs support the claim with reasons and plenty of support, as shown in the Works Cited. Note: For essays that demonstrate correct formatting, please see Appendix A for MLA style and Appendix B for APA style.

Linda Gonzalez

Professor Phillips

English 112

March 5, 2019

Driving to a Reasonable Solution: The Middle Ground
of Undocumented Drivers

Millions of undocumented, illegal immigrants live in the United States. Most of them drive to work every day without a driver's license. Before 9/11, illegal immigrants in North Carolina could get a driver's license with a foreign legal document presented to the Department of Motor Vehicles (DMV). Some of the documents accepted at the time were passports, birth certificates, voting cards, and driver's licenses from the applicant's country of origin. Then, the DMV stopped accepting foreign documents and asked for a document issued by the U.S. government. The Individual Tax Identification Number (ITIN) is used by undocumented immigrants in order to pay their taxes. They also used this document to obtain driver's licenses. Today, Maryland is one of the states that still issues driver's licenses without asking for migratory status. According to the Maryland Department of Transportation, Motor Vehicle Administration, undocumented immigrants are eligible to apply for a non-compliant driver's license or identification card ("Non-Compliant"). Some state authorities want to adopt a plan to issue driver's licenses to undocumented immigrants while others are totally against it.

Those in favor of providing driver's licenses to undocumented immigrants think the roads would be safer and would get people out of the shadows. There are many drivers who drive without insurance due to the lack of a driver's license. The proponents' plan is to issue driver's licenses that would distinguish undocumented immigrants from citizens of the United States. This driver's license would be strictly for driving purposes only and would be labeled with the driver's migratory status. In addition, the carrier would not be able to board airplanes or enter federal buildings with it. In any state in the United States, in order to get a driver's license, one must pass a written test and a driving test. Undocumented immigrants would need to read the driver's handbook, which would ensure the driver's knowledge of the road rules and would lower the possibilities of committing a traffic violation. Immigrants would be able to get insurance and low insurance rates at the same time as other drivers.

According to The National Immigration Law Center, New York's State Department of Insurance estimates that expanded license access would reduce the premium cost associated with uninsured motorist coverage by 34 percent, which would save New York drivers $120 million each year ("Toolkit").

Even though the American Civil Liberties Union sued Arizona on behalf of a group of DACA recipients who were denied driver's licenses saying that states are prohibited from making distinctions among different classes of noncitizens ("Trump") what they fail to see is that undocumented immigrants would not want to have a labeled driver's license that would let people and the police know they are not legal residents. They fear being deported; therefore, many would prefer to remain without a license.

Another point of view is the one held passionately by opponents of giving driver's licenses to illegal immigrants. They argue that driving is a privilege, not a right. Brian Quinn reviews concerns about New York state's bill to provide undocumented drivers with licenses. Genesee County Clerk Michael Cianfrini raises some of the issues that opponents have regarding driver's licenses for undocumented immigrants, the biggest concern being that of identification verification. Everyone who applies for a driver's license has to provide verification of identity through birth certificates. Cianfrini argues that an illegal immigrant would present a foreign birth certificate or passport, which country clerks would have no way of checking (A11). Because they have no other verification, such as a social security card, the argument is that since an American citizen has to present a social security card, then the illegal immigrant receives a driver's license that an American citizen could not if he or she did not have a card. Considering driving as a privilege, many politicians are completely against a plan that would allow illegal immigrants to obtain a driver's license. They believe that people who have entered the country illegally have broken the immigration laws and therefore should not be allowed to receive any kind of benefits in this country. Moreover, a driver's license allows a person to be able to work, drive, and open a bank account; all these things make life easier for undocumented people in this country. The argument is also made that the driver's license then seems to confer on the recipient the status of citizen because with a driver's license, one can vote.

Additionally, the government is seeking stricter means to secure the nation's safety. One effective way for them is not issuing driver's licenses to undocumented aliens so they cannot enter federal buildings, board airplanes, and use the licenses as identification to give the impression of being legal. Virginia began issuing a new driver's license in fall of 2018, designed to tighten security requirements for state-issued identification. This action was taken based on a recommendation of the 9/11 Commission when it was discovered that 18 of the 19 9/11 terrorists had obtained their driver's licenses in Virginia, explains Luz Lazo.

Another example of undocumented immigrants threatening the nation's safety is that there are drug dealers and criminals looking for easy ways to get licenses. For example, Sean Hannity says illegal immigrants account for up to 75 percent of federal drug possession convictions (Selby). Limiting driver's licenses, the argument goes, would cut down on this number. Authorities against a plan to provide driver's licenses for undocumented immigrants do not take into consideration that undocumented people are not going to go away just because they do not have driver's licenses and that they will drive with or without them.

Certainly, the arguments in favor of and against issuing driver's licenses to non-citizens are so strong that it is difficult to imagine an alternative position.

However, there is another position, one that is held just as passionately. Many people think that driver's licenses should be given to illegal immigrants. If that cannot be accomplished, the ones that were able to obtain them at one point without legal status and have no major traffic violations should at least be able to renew them. Individuals who hold this point of view say that issuing driver's licenses to illegal immigrants would help the police do their job better. In addition, they believe immigrants would help the economy from those paying taxes, and it would lower the use of false documents. The job of the police would be easier by being able to verify the identity of a driver in case of a traffic violation. The DMV database would have names, addresses, dates of birth, and countries of origin for every driver's license holder. When there is no driver's license, there is no way of knowing if there is any criminal record and if the name given is the real name of the driver. "Driver's Licenses Make It Easy for Law Enforcement to Identify Illegal Aliens," by Ronald W. Mortensen, argues that although criminals can be more easily tracked through driver's licenses, others fear that ICE agents use state motor-vehicle data to "identify immigration enforcement targets."

The Daily Record explains that driver's licenses would ensure both consistent standards of driving competence and more insured drivers ("Driver's Licenses"). Furthermore, undocumented immigrants would help the police by reporting crimes and assisting local law enforcement in community policing activities. Erin Cox reports that an audit of Maryland's Motor Vehicle Administration (MVA). Over 820 driver's licenses were issued using counterfeit documents. Many of the fraudulent licenses were obtained using false home addresses, so that MVA was unable to track down and confiscate these licenses. Additionally, issuing driver's licenses to undocumented immigrants would help reduce identity theft. Having a legitimate driver's license would allow immigrants to use their real personal information, keeping safe the personal information of other drivers.

Taxes would be another benefit for the nation by allowing undocumented aliens to obtain driver's licenses. Supporters of undocumented immigrants say that they work hard and make valid contributions to the community as taxpayers. The *Immigrants Rising* website provides statistics on the number of undocumented immigrants living in the United States. In its "Overview of Undocumented Students," they state that there are 11 million of all ages and 1.2 million of these are between the ages of 18–24. Sales taxes are one way, property tax paid through a rent fee is another, and many immigrants use their W-7 to file tax returns in the hope of creating a paper trail to show the government that they are willing to pay their share. CNN's Octavio Blanco explains that undocumented immigrants pay their taxes for many reasons, not the least to provide a paper trail of their efforts to be good citizens. Magaña-Salgado, a policy attorney at the Immigrant Legal Resource Center, says that judges tend to look more favorably on immigrants in court cases when they have paid their taxes. "Filing taxes helps to build a record of existence here in the United States if they are facing permanent deportation hearings" (Blanco). Moreover, because most undocumented immigrants use a fake Social Security number in order to work, they will not collect any benefits later. Having an ITIN allows people to pay their taxes, which builds the tax base. According to "The Facts About the Individual Tax Identification Number (ITIN)," the IRS reported that in 2015, 4.35 million people paid over 13.7 billion in net taxes using an ITIN.

Let's take into consideration that undocumented immigrants are not the only ones driving on the road without licenses. There are many American citizens who have revoked licenses due to traffic violations and still drive cars, and some teenagers who do not have the legal age to drive one but still do it anyway. As a society, we must accept the fact that the United States is a multicultural country. People come from everywhere looking for the American dream. That includes being able to obtain a driver's license that allows them to drive to work every day to support their families. National security is definitely a high priority Immigration reform would correct not only the issue of driver's licenses, but also most issues regarding undocumented people, including national security. Those who are driving without licenses are human beings too; the fact that many people prefer to ignore them does not mean they are not around. People should have a decent way of living, and that includes legal and illegal inhabitants of the United States.

Works Cited

Blanco, Octavio. "Why Undocumented Immigrants Pay Taxes." *CNN*, 19 April, 2017, https://money.cnn.com/2017/04/19/news/economy/undocumented-immigrant-taxes/index.html. Accessed 3 June 2019.

Cox, Erin. "Maryland Issued Hundreds of Fraudulent Drivers Licenses Based on Counterfeit Documents, Audit Says." *The Baltimore Sun*, 1 December, 2017, https://www.baltimoresun.com/news/maryland/politics/bs-md-mva-audit-20171201-story.html. Accessed 3 June, 2019.

"Driver's Licenses for Illegal Immigrants." *Daily Record*, 2 February, 2019. *ProQuest*, http://ezproxy.cpcc.edu/login?url=https://search.proquest.com/docview/2175032111?accountid=10008.

"The Facts About the Individual Tax Identification Number (ITIN)." *American Immigration Council*, 2 January, 2018. https://www.americaimmigrationcouncil.org/research/facts-about-individual-tax-identification-number-itin.

Lazo, Luz. "Virginia to Begin Issuing Driver's Licenses that Will Be Required for Air Travel in 2020." *Washington Post*, 28 July, 2018. https://www.washingtonpost.com/local/trafficandcommuting/virginia-to-begin-issuing-drivers-licenses-that-will-be-required-for-air-travel-in-2020/2018/07/27/5f723820-8b65-11e8-85ae-511bc1146b0b_story.html?utm_term=.74db346ebee6. Accessed 3 June, 2019.

Mortensen, Ronald W. "Driver's Licenses Make It Easy for Law Enforcement to Identify Illegal Aliens." *Center for Immigration Studies*, 3 May, 2017, https://cis.org/Mortensen/Drivers-Licenses-Make-It-Easy-Law-Enforcement-Identify-Illegal-Aliens.

"Non-Compliant Driver's Licenses & ID Cards." *Maryland Department of Transportation, Motor Vehicle Administration.* http://www.mva.maryland.gov/announcements/non-compliant-driver-license-ID-cards.htm.

"Overview of Undocumented Students." *Immigrants Rising*, 2019, https://immigrantsrising.org/wp-content/uploads/2018/09/Overview-of-Undocumented-Students.pdf.

Quinn, Brian. "County Clerk Criticizes 'Green Light' Legislation." *Daily News*, 10 May, 2019, p. A11, *NewsBank*, infoweb.newsbank.com/apps/news/document-view?p=AWNB&docref=news/17371E8ADA4B75E8. Accessed 3 June 2019.

Selby, Gardner W. "Sean Hannity Says Illegal Immigrants Account for up to 75 Percent of Convictions for Selected Crimes." *Politifact Texas*, 2 September, 2016, https://www.politifact.com/texas/statements/2016/sep/02/sean-hannity/sean-hannity-says-illegal-immigrants-account-75-pe/.

"Toolkit | Access to Driver's Licenses." *National Immigration Law Center*, 2017. https://www.nilc.org/issues/drivers-licenses/dlaccesstoolkit5/

"Trump Criticizes his Justice Department for not Joining Fight over Arizona Driver's Licenses for 'Dreamers'." *Washingtonpost.com*, 21 March, 2018. *Opposing Viewpoints in Context*, http://link.galegroup.com/apps/doc/A531829088/OVIC?u=centralp&sid=OVIC&xid=8ccf4f8b.

Rogerian Argument

Rogerian argument is a way to establish **common ground** between a position you hold and positions that one or more other parties hold on an issue. It is a kind of argument built on fair, compassionate presentation of differing views, and it highlights the strengths of each, along with points of overlap with your view.

Listen Closely to the Opposition

Rogerian argument is centered in good listening and in close, respectful consideration of points of view different from your own. It is an argument strategy adapted from the work of psychologist Carl Rogers, who was interested in factors that help or hinder good communication. He theorized that good communication requires that each position on an issue is fully acknowledged—without judgment. Rogers believed that a careful, empathic listener can clarify differing positions and create space for productive interaction. This approach to an issue asks that a writer listen and respond with charity in order to create common ground based on shared values and a shared sense of purpose. Rogers

Figure 9.3 Taking in fully another view and then presenting it fairly is at the center of the
Rogerian approach.

believed that, although on the surface of a contentious issue the sides may
seem far apart, on a deeper level warring sides may in fact share some values
and beliefs. However, before such commonalities can be identified, we must
first take the time to cool our emotions and really listen to each other.

For example, when Martin Luther King, Jr. reaches out to white clergymen
in his famous "Letter from Birmingham Jail," he refers to his audience—the
same clergymen who helped put him in jail—as "men of genuine good will,"
and as "Christian and Jewish brothers." In addition, throughout the letter he
emphasizes their common faith and adherence to religious principles. In this
letter, King responds to a moment of intense racial and political separation
by studying with compassion the values of his opposition, who vigorously
oppose the nonviolent demonstrations supported by King and the Southern
Christian Leadership Conference. He identifies a desire on both sides for
negotiation, but he also embraces the need for a "constructive, nonviolent
tension which is necessary for growth."

Over the years, many students have claimed that Rogerian argument is a
practical approach to controversial issues, especially in the workplace and in
local politics where compromise is essential. They reason that when things
need to move forward—for example, a company's projects, production, and
sales; decisions affecting local schools; help for the increasing number of
homeless people; crime prevention in the community—it becomes essential to listen closely to individuals deeply invested in their positions. While
resolution of every issue cannot be guaranteed, many businesses practice
Rogerian methods, simply because when a positive dialogue is created production and efficiency improve. Dispute-resolution programs used by large

community organizations, such as local post offices and city governments, value Rogerian strategy because it emphasizes listening and mutual respect, allowing disputing parties to better understand each other. And when understanding and respect are built, better communication often follows.

Writers of a Rogerian argument are similar to mediators, people who facilitate settlements among two or more disputing parties. In a closed mediation, a mediator often asks each party to restate the other party's position; in this way a sense of understanding and trust can begin to develop. Sometimes a resolution of the issue can result; almost always, parties understand each other better. Your job as a writer is to adapt this process of close listening to a written argument as you respectfully and accurately present positions that differ from yours. Usually during the second half of a Rogerian argument the writer steps out of the mediator role and brings in his or her claim and support for an issue, creating common ground with other views.

Rogerian strategy replaces rebuttal of opposing views with efforts to understand them. Because the foundation of Rogerian argument is an accurate, bias-free description of an opposing view, make sure you restate accurately for readers other positions on issues you address. Strategies for fairly negotiating with the opposition are discussed in Chapter 6, "Work Fairly with the Opposition."

In brief, Rogerian argument requires the arguer to see an issue from other points of view, emphasizing points of overlap, or common ground, among differing positions. (See Figure 9.4 for a representation of Rogerian argument.) A successful Rogerian argument allows your audience to judge for itself whether or not your claim is practical. And along the way you do much to earn credibility with an audience through your compassionate and accurate restatement of opposing views.

Identify Common Ground

The following two issues recently were addressed successfully with a Rogerian approach. Note the common ground that each writer creates.

Issue #1: Living at home while attending college

This writer fully acknowledges her parents' position that, because she has completed high school, living at home is no longer an option. Her parents content that they can no longer afford for her to live at home, that they plan to downsize to a smaller home, and that she should take on the responsibility of paying for things herself. The writer honors her parents' position by describing it fairly and without judgment. She offers these reasons for wanting to remain at home: she will be able to devote more time to her courses and earn her degree sooner, she won't have to work a second and possibly third job to cover costs of living on her own, and she will be there to help with chores around the house. But before delivering her reasons, the writer first creates common ground with her parents by identifying certain shared values and beliefs tied to this issue. For example, both parties value the importance of a college degree, professional competence, financial independence, and the ability to provide for one's family.

In this example, the writer's audience (her parents) is also her opposition. To earn credibility with this audience, the writer completes the two essential steps in Rogerian writing: she describes without bias her opponent's position and locates common ground. Rogerian strategy is more about reaching into opponents' camps and representing their views fairly; it is less about achieving a desired outcome. Rogerian argument extends the olive branch of peace and fair play.

Issue #2: Homelessness in the community

With the recent downturn in the economy, the number of homeless people in the community—including children who attend local public schools—is increasing. Area shelters provide beds for less than 25 percent of the homeless population, and it is uncertain when new shelters will be available. At a recent county commission meeting, a coalition of local organizations working with homeless people rolled out a 10-year plan to end homelessness in the area. The plan was unanimously approved by commissioners, but more than a year later, no funding has been approved. Last week your teacher invited the volunteer coordinator from the city's largest shelter, along with an expert on affordable housing, to speak to your class, motivating you to act. You want to argue that funding the 10-year plan is the community's best hope for addressing the homelessness crisis. Based on what you learned during the presentations, you know that your opposition is not a single individual or a single group but an attitude that is held by many local citizens who would rather not deal with the issue because it is uncomfortable and without a clear solution. Additionally, many people in this silent majority believe that homeless people do not make the same kind of effort as those who work hard to pay for their homes and that the homeless are gaming a system that will allow them to get by without assuming the responsibilities of citizenship.

You choose as your audience members of your communications class, and you plan to deliver your argument as a speech due in this class in a few weeks. You choose a Rogerian approach because you know that if the 10-year plan has any chance of being funded those on opposite sides of this issue must begin listening to each other. You identify and honor values of citizenship that you share with those reluctant to fund the plan: making positive contributions to the community, paying taxes, sustaining employment, and renting or owning a home. These points of overlap become clear when you converse with your opposition. You are now in a position to build on the common ground you have created by paying close attention to another perspective on homelessness. Because you have established this common ground and validated your opposition, you can argue your claim without rebutting.

Furthermore, you now have a chance to provide some education on the issue of homelessness. You recognize that many citizens opposed to funding the 10-year plan may not have a clear sense of the causes of homelessness, such as mental illness, physical disability, job loss, natural disasters, divorce or break up, and a full range of unforeseen events that throw an individual off balance. By listening closely to your opposition, you have earned the chance to deliver your argument on homelessness. Whether your claim is accepted is another matter, but you have put your best foot forward by building your argument on a foundation of shared values and beliefs.

The issues discussed above—one personal and the other local and national—involve parties that at first are far apart and aggressive defending their positions. Toulmin-based arguments might produce rhetorical victories, but a Toulmin approach would miss the common ground of the disputing parties. Similarly, a middle-ground approach would miss chances to work with shared values and instead emphasize the failures of the opposition on these important issues. Rogerian argument, however, can bring sides closer together. Its aim is to identify values that the disputing parties share. In turn, these shared values can make clear for all sides a common ground, where strategies for resolving issues can be discussed openly and without fear of judgment.

your turn 9d ▶ **PRACTICE Rogerian Thinking**

For each of the following issues, provide your claim and one or two claims made by differing points of view; then identify common ground. Plan to research issues with which you are not familiar.

1. Campaign finance reform in your state: This movement seeks to limit the amount of monetary contributions that can be made by individuals and groups to the campaigns of political candidates.
2. Affordable housing and homelessness: The term *affordable housing* refers to housing that does not exceed 30 percent of the household or family income. The term is often used in the discussion of homelessness in the United States.
3. Stem cell research focuses on scientists' ability to reproduce cells from living organisms. Some argue that this kind of research has important medical and reproductive benefits for humans; others feel it unfairly manipulates human life and that it can be used for cloning.
4. Course evaluation and instructor performance surveys are common in U.S. colleges. They are often used as a performance measure during an instructor's annual review.

Map a Rogerian Argument

The earlier examples about living at home and homelessness, both rooted locally, suggest ways to build arguments based on Rogerian strategy. The key to the success of this kind of argument is your ability to understand and honor differing views. The following section presents a fuller treatment of another local issue, this one related to the workplace. The writer is frustrated with a pay scale based on seniority; her supervisor is the audience for her argument.

Supervisor's View

CLAIM: Increases in salary should remain tied to the seniority
                          system.

Reasons

- The seniority system has been in place for many years and has been proven to help with employee morale.
- A clear standard for pay raises supports consistency and prevents favoritism.
- Our company values employee loyalty and years of service, and the seniority system is a way to reward employees who share these values.
- Many of our senior employees are hard working and productive.

SUPPORT: Because the supervisor has been at the company for
                          many years, she can attest that few complaints have
                          been filed with regard to the seniority system, loyal and
                          productive employees, or the company owners' com-
                          mitment to fair treatment.

WARRANT: The seniority system is effective because it maintains
                          an ethical standard that employees are aware of from
                          the beginning of their employment.

Backing

- Consistency and fair play are important in the workplace.
- A predictable reward system can mean fewer complaints from employees and greater worker satisfaction.

Writer's View

COMMUNITY

School-Academic

Workplace

Family-Household

Neighborhood

Social-Cultural

Consumer

Concerned Citizen

TOPIC: Compensation

ISSUE: Pay Scale and Seniority

AUDIENCE: Supervisor

CLAIM: Our company should award salary increases based on production and efficiency.

Reasons

- Efficient, productive employees can generate more profit for this company.
- Regular effort and productivity should be rewarded with regular salary increases.
- Pay raises based on productivity can elevate morale and foster loyalty to the company.

SUPPORT: Much of this writer's support should be drawn from her experience as a productive, hard-working employee. Examples can reveal her contributions to company expectations and beyond. Additionally, research drawn from professional and academic journals can reinforce her pay-based-on-productivity request. Personal examples can also speak to the writer's ability to maintain good work habits while pursuing her college degree.

WARRANT: Ethical standards should be maintained in the workplace.

Backing

- Consistency and fair play are important in the workplace.
- A fair, predictable reward system can lead to increased worker satisfaction.

COMMON GROUND: Listening closely to her supervisor, the writer is able to pin down common values and goals. They include shared concerns for employee morale, avoidance of favoritism, company loyalty, and hard work and productivity. In the summary of her supervisor's position, the writer can validate these concerns and then build on them as she delivers her argument. Often, common ground among disputing parties is established at the level of the warrant, and this should be clear in the mapping of this argument. Ethical standards, consistency, a sense of fair play, and predictable rewards are common values the writer shares with her supervisor.

Note that the writer avoids at every turn rebutting her supervisor. From her experience with this company, it likely would be easy to rebut with plenty of specific examples. But she has chosen a Rogerian approach to this sticky problem, and this means making her best effort to demonstrate that she understands and honors her supervisor's reasons and values. In practical terms, a Toulmin-based approach might have produced a solid argument, but it could have left the writer out in the cold in terms of getting her supervisor to acknowledge her position on salary increases. When your audience is your opposition, as is frequently the case in Rogerian writing, make the effort to dignify the other view, honor its strengths, and point out shared values; this can indicate that you are less interested in dueling and more interested in a serious, mutually respectful conversation.

 tip 9b

Acknowledge and Validate the Opposition

Put yourself in the frame of mind to build a Rogerian argument by recalling a time in your life when others put you first and listened closely and without judgment to your opinion on a given issue. What might have motivated these individuals? What might motivate you to behave this way with an opponent?

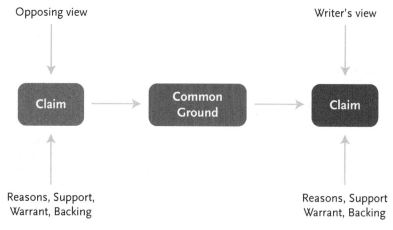

Figure 9.4 The Rogerian argument model

your turn 9e GET STARTED **A Rogerian Argument**

In introducing an issue, what historical context will you provide? What specific information will you use to orient readers to the issue? Answers to these and the following questions will help you start your Rogerian approach.

1. When sides are far apart, a Rogerian approach often works best. Are you working with an issue that is sufficiently controversial to generate distinctly different sides? Explain.
2. What is the claim, what is the warrant, and what are the main reasons for each view on this issue? What beliefs and values do each of the parties hold?
3. What measures will you take to avoid judging or rebutting your opposition? How will you establish and maintain a neutral, objective, fair-minded attitude toward each opposing view and those who hold it?
4. Would each party with a stake in this issue be comfortable with how you present its position? Explain.
5. How will you maintain a neutral tone toward other parties? Explain how your tone calms rather than ignites emotions.
6. What is your claim? Describe your warrant. What are the main reasons and kinds of support you bring to your position?
7. What specific values and beliefs do you share with each party? What values does your audience hold regarding this issue? Establish common ground by describing overlapping values among the opposition, your audience, and your own view.
8. Is your audience likely to accept your claim based both on your accurate, fair-minded presentation of other views and on the reasons and support you build into your position? Explain.

Sample Rogerian Argument

Martin Luther King, Jr. wrote his "Letter From Birmingham Jail" in the margins of a newspaper and on scraps of paper, the only materials he could obtain. This document contains effective examples of Rogerian writing. King aims his letter at white clergymen during a time of racial segregation and profound differences over tactics appropriate in the struggle for racial equality. The paragraphs included below demonstrate King's ability to reach out in positive ways to his opposition. These few paragraphs are part of a long letter to the very clergy who recommended his incarceration: remember that a Rogerian approach is often practical when opposing parties are deeply divided. Note below how the writer finds common ground and uses it to both respect his opposition and deliver his ideas.

PARAGRAPHS FROM "LETTER FROM BIRMINGHAM JAIL"

By Martin Luther King, Jr.

MY DEAR FELLOW CLERGYMEN:

[Paragraph #1] While confined here in the Birmingham City Jail, I came across your recent statement calling my present activities "unwise and untimely." Seldom do I pause to answer criticism of my work and ideas. If I sought to answer all the criticisms that cross my desk, my secretaries would have little time for anything other than such correspondence in the course of the day, and I would have no time for constructive work. But since I feel that you are men of genuine goodwill and that your criticisms are sincerely set forth, I want to try to answer your statements in what I hope will be patient and reasonable terms.

[Paragraph #3] But more basically, I am in Birmingham because injustice is here. Just as the prophets of the eighth century B.C. left their villages and carried their "thus saith the Lord" far beyond the boundaries of their home towns, and just as the Apostle Paul left his village of Tarsus and carried the gospel of Jesus Christ to the far corners of the Greco-Roman world, so am I compelled to carry the gospel of freedom far beyond my own hometown. Like Paul, I must constantly respond to the Macedonian call for aid.

[From Paragraph #31] But though I was initially disappointed at being categorized as an extremist, as I continued to think about the matter I gradually gained a measure of satisfaction from the label. Was not Jesus an extremist for love: "Love your enemies, bless them that curse you, do good to them that hate you, and pray for them which despitefully use you, and persecute you." Was not Amos an extremist for justice: "Let justice roll down like waters and righteousness like an ever-flowing stream." Was not Paul an extremist for the Christian gospel: "I bear in my body the marks of the Lord Jesus." Was not Martin Luther an extremist: "Here I stand; I cannot do otherwise, so help me God." And John Bunyan: "I will stay in jail to the end of my days before I make a butchery of my conscience." And Abraham Lincoln: "This nation cannot survive half slave and half free." And Thomas Jefferson: "We hold these truths to be self-evident, that all men are created equal . . ." So the question is not whether we will be extremists, but what kind of extremists we will be. Will we be extremists for hate or for love? Will we be extremists for the preservation of injustice or for the extension of justice? In that dramatic scene on Calvary's hill three men were crucified. We must never forget that all three were crucified for the same crime—the crime of extremism. Two were extremists for immorality, and thus fell below their environment. The other, Jesus Christ, was an extremist for love, truth and goodness, and thereby rose above his environment. Perhaps the South, the nation and the world are in dire need of creative extremists.

[Final paragraph] I hope this letter finds you strong in the faith. I also hope that circumstances will soon make it possible for me to meet each of you, not as an integrationist or a civil rights leader but as a fellow clergyman and a Christian brother. Let us all hope that the dark clouds of racial prejudice will soon pass away and the deep fog of misunderstanding will be lifted from our fear-drenched communities, and in some not too distant tomorrow the radiant stars of love and brotherhood will shine over our great nation with all their scintillating beauty.

Argument Based on a Microhistory

An argument based on a **microhistory** allows you to comment on a particular part of our past, especially if what you have to say differs from the conventional understanding of a person, event, or place you are studying.

Focus on the Local and Specific

Microhistory is a relatively recent approach in the field of history. Traditionally, history sought to record the accomplishments of a few individuals in positions of power, sometimes called "the history of great men." Or traditional history was focused on military and political histories of a country or culture. Social histories focus on emerging social movements and what caused these movements, and they can include economic, legal, and labor histories. Common to these traditional approaches to history is the attention they give large social and political institutions, group behavior, and, in general, central and mainstream features of a society.

In contrast, a microhistory narrows the scope, focusing on:

- A person, a certain event, or a particular place.
- The margins or fringes of a certain culture or society, the ordinary people and events that typically are considered unimportant and that often are left out of larger histories.
- Precise, or "thick," description of the everyday details of an individual's life, a place, or an event.
- Primary documents and materials created by or connected to an individual, an event, or a place.

- Connecting the microhistory to the larger culture as a way to reveal trends, forces, pressures, and expectations acting on an individual or place.
- Filling gaps created by broadly focused histories so as to acknowledge and honor common people *and* to reveal the effects of economic and political forces on the common people.

Building this kind of argument requires that you work as a historian and then use the microhistory that you prepare in order to deliver an argument. Writing an argument based on a microhistory means that you will:

- Introduce to your audience the subject of your microhistory and the light you hope to shed on its significance.
- Explain your interest in your subject and the questions you hope to answer by compiling your microhistory.
- Provide extensive context for the individual, event, or place you will study. This means accessing as much primary source material as you can—court and public records, diaries and journals, letters and correspondence, articles and information drawn from local newspapers, newsletters, special-interest publications, maps, and in general any materials that clarify the daily realities of your subject.
- Draw conclusions for your audience that reveal how a close study of the individual, place, or event reveals something about the larger culture. This will mean background reading in secondary documents to get a sense of what the culture values and how its rules and regulations affected the lives of everyday people.
- Deliver at or near the end of your argument a claim based on your microhistory.
- Give voice to the questions and uncertainties that remain for you at the end of your argument.

Make Room for Local Histories

Delivering an argument based on a microhistory can be a powerful experience for a writer. It is a chance to collect and analyze primary historical material and then argue a claim based on that analysis. The ideas you bring to the conclusion of your argument as you make sense of the historical information can bring to light some of the challenges everyday people weathered during an earlier time, challenges that often are missing in broader histories. Your research and the conclusions you draw can add to our "public memory" of a certain time and place, and this is no small contribution.

But what role can argument play in a microhistory? Based on the primary materials you're working with and the sense you make of them, you are in a position to make a claim that argues against the generally accepted understanding of a particular time and place in history. For example, if you choose to dig into that box of letters your great-grandmother wrote three generations ago, you may find information that contradicts our general notion of women's roles during your great-grandmother's time. Suppose you learn that your great-grandmother was active in civic life, spoke up at town meetings, and wanted women to be allowed to enter the fields of law, medicine, and finance. You learn that in some letters she wrote to a friend about religion and spirituality, marriage, and food and diet. At the end of your work with these primary documents, you know that your great-grandmother's life differs from our culture's general understanding of women's civic and intellectual lives during your great-grandmother's time. Based on your work with the letters, you are in a position to make a claim that argues against the limited understanding of women's lives three generations ago.

Two additional examples might help clarify the value of forging an argument based on a microhistory. Recently, a student and passionate baseball fan crafted a compelling argument focused on the integration of Major League Baseball in 1947. Mainstream history represents this event as a victory in American race relations, with much of the credit going to an executive with the Brooklyn Dodgers, the team that penciled Jackie Robinson into its starting lineup. The student moved outside this perspective by reading the columns of an African American sportswriter for the black-owned *The People's Voice*, a weekly newspaper published from 1942 to 1947. In these columns, the student uncovered a new perspective, one that told a very different history than the formerly accepted "history." The sportswriter revealed that integrating Major League Baseball was not completely positive: as a result of the integration, the Negro Leagues were dead a few years later, leaving the players and employees for these teams out of work. Having studied this primary material, the student was motivated to claim that integrating Major League Baseball in 1947 was a partial victory only. He supported his claim with evidence from the sportswriter's columns. The opposing point of view in this argument is the more general and common history of baseball's integration.

The second example involves a writer's work with a historical monument erected in 1929 next to what is now a college campus. The monument commemorates a reunion of Civil War veterans and reads as follows:

> GLORIA VICTIS
> IN COMMEMORATION OF THE 39TH ANNUAL REUNION OF THE UNITED CONFEDERATE VETERANS AT CHARLOTTE, NORTH CAROLINA, JUNE 4–7, 1929.
> A STATE AND CITY'S TRIBUTE OF LOVE; IN GRATEFUL RECOGNITION OF THE SERVICES OF THE CONFEDERATE SOLDIERS WHOSE HEROISM IN WAR AND FIDELITY IN PEACE HAVE NEVER BEEEN SURPASSED.
> ACCEPTING THE ARBITRAMENT OF WAR, THEY PRESERVED THE ANGLO-SAXON CIVILIZATION OF THE SOUTH AND BECAME MASTER BUILDERS IN A RE-UNITED COUNTRY.
> VERITAS VINCIT

Language on the monument motivated the student to research events associated with the reunion—a large parade, social activities, reports and editorials in the local newspaper, and so forth—and it motivated the student to understand how ideas grounded in racial inequality could be memorialized. Interestingly, in her research, this writer also learned much about African American political life in the community in 1929, and this information allowed her to think about the monument in much broader terms. She argued that the marker must be contextualized to include differing ideas in the community regarding notions of "civilization" and a "reunited country." Specifically, editorials in the community's black newspaper and references to sermons delivered by African American ministers provided a much different history for the monument, one not grounded in "tribute" and "love."

Work with Primary Materials

A first step in preparing a microhistory is locating **primary materials.** Local and college libraries often hold special collections and archived material. This material can include letters, various other kinds of correspondence, court and legal records, diaries, journals, bills of sale, and business records. Local museums, churches, and historical societies are also depositories for this kind of primary material. Communities always keep records

Hank Frentz/Shutterstock.com

Figure 9.5 Primary documents, like this collection of old photographs, and their interpretation are the center of arguments based on a microhistory. The ways in which these documents argue against common and more general treatments of a historical period can reveal the complexity of our past and steer us away from damaging stereotypes.

of their past in one way or another, and sometimes this information is kept by families and individuals. It may be that members of your immediate or extended family are keeping such records and that some of those records may inspire you to prepare a microhistory and offer a claim based on what you learn. Think of yourself as an archaeologist uncovering neglected arti-facts at the site of a dig. Your job is to describe and make sense of your findings.

There are many excellent, book-length microhistories. All are built on very specific information that reveals more complete pictures of a culture. Subjects of microhistories have been far ranging and include people, prod-ucts, places, and facts that fall outside the scope of mainstream history: the natural ice industry in nineteenth-century North America; the final Civil War battle at Gettysburg in 1863; cadavers; the cockroach; and products including Spam, sugar, coffee, coal, and cotton. Sometimes microhistories consider community institutions whose histories have been overlooked, such as local businesses, social service organizations, hospitals, schools, and government-related agencies. Of course a microhistory that you pre-pare for an assignment will be shorter than book length, but the narrative you piece together and the conclusions you draw can be just as compelling as longer projects.

Subjects and Materials for Microhistories

Subjects practical for arguments based on microhistories can include but are not limited to the following.

Individuals

- A family member or relative
- A member of your community whose life experience is not part of public knowledge
- A local employee, official, coach, clergy, teacher, neighbor, or police officer
- Any other person, living or dead

Events

- An event that affected your family, such as a marriage, a divorce, a hiring or firing, a birth or death, a dispute, or a relocation
- An event in your community, such as a business closing and the result-ing loss of jobs, a celebration, a battle, or a natural disaster

Places

- Neighborhood
- Natural area
- Home

- Factory, warehouse, place of employment
- School
- Church
- Government building

Sources

Primary materials to consider when preparing a microhistory can include:

- Letters
- Journals
- Diaries
- Family histories
- Business records
- Court documents
- Legal documents
- Photographs
- Church records
- Newspapers and newsletters
- Sermons
- City and community histories
- Oral histories

Map an Argument Based on a Microhistory

Following is an outline for an argument based on a microhistory. Note that the structure of this kind of argument differs from Toulmin-based, Middle-Ground, and Rogerian arguments.

COMMUNITY
School-Academic
Workplace
Family-Household
Neighborhood
Social-Cultural
Consumer
Concerned Citizen

TOPIC: Justice

ISSUE: Murder of a Female Slave

AUDIENCE: Members of Writing Class

CLAIM: Evidence like this court transcript suggests that in some areas of the slave South justice was applied across the color line.

Support

- Primary documents: Transcript of 1839 Iredell County, North Carolina Superior Court decision. The transcript recounts the trial of a slaveholder who, with "malice aforethought," murdered his female slave. The transcript is lengthy and full of details about owner–slave relations.
- Secondary documents: Scholarly books and articles about justice regarding slaveholders and slaves.

What the Microhistory Reveals about the Culture

The court records document the court's decision to execute the white slaveholder for murdering his slave. This decision in many ways reveals that some communities delivered justice when and where it was due, regardless of color and status.

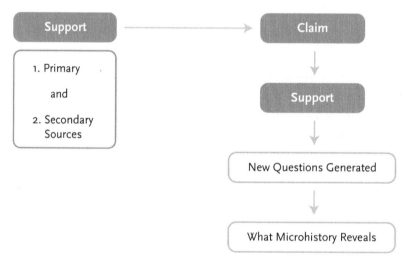

Figure 9.6 The Microhistory model

Claim

Evidence like this court transcript suggests that in some areas of the slave South justice was applied across the color line.

New Questions Generated from the Microhistory

Based on work with these primary documents, findings can move readers away from thinking about justice in the slave South in common and stereotypical ways. New questions might focus on how justice was carried out in a particular community or on a particular plantation, how this kind of information can be incorporated into public school curricula, and what factors from the local culture influenced this court decision.

your turn 9f   **GET STARTED Set Up an Argument Based on a Microhistory**

1. What is the subject of your microhistory? What motivates you to study this subject?
2. What do you hope to learn from this project?
3. What primary source materials will you use as you prepare your microhistory? Where will you find these materials?
4. What secondary sources will you use to establish cultural context, or background, for your subject?
5. What does the larger culture's history seem to value about the time period you are examining? For example, were there acceptable and unacceptable kinds of behavior and attitudes during this time, and does your microhistory contradict these ideas?
6. What does your subject reveal about the culture? For example, if your subject is an individual, how does he or she fit into or not fit into the norms and expectations of the culture? If your subject is an event or place, what does it tell you about how the larger culture functions, about behavior the larger culture approves or disapproves of, about behavior the larger culture encourages or discourages?
7. Based on this close study of your subject and its time period, do you now think differently about this period? Explain.
8. Based on your microhistory, what will you claim?
9. What additional questions do you have about your subject and the time period of your microhistory?
10. How can your argument based on a microhistory make us think more realistically about the period, individual, event, or place that it addresses?

 tip 9c

Think of Microhistory as Archaeological Work

Writing a microhistory means working outside the mainstream. Your work will involve digging into mostly unrecognized corners of our past and bringing to light a person, place, or event. Your job is to uncover, dust off, and interpret the primary materials you identify and review.

The questions in Your Turn 9f are challenging, and because you have made a careful study of your primary documents, you can answer them in order to prepare a sound argument. While the other approaches to argument that are discussed in this chapter—MIDDLE GROUND and Rogerian—devote much attention to support for the claim, an argument based on a microhistory requires that you devote most of your project to support. Bring your claim in at or near the end of an argument based on microhistory, after you establish credibility with readers based on your work with primary source material. A warrant and backing are addressed when you discuss how your subject reveals something new about the culture and what we can learn from your subject today.

The microhistory you prepare will be original and unique to you. While this project likely will be submitted as a class assignment, the work you do and the insights you generate will help fill gaps in our culture's collective memory and widen the window to our past. Furthermore, because your subject in all probability has been left out of conventional histories, you bring in from the margins of a culture an additional perspective that can help us better understand our past and our present.

Sample Argument Based on a Microhistory

In the following microhistory, what this New York City writer considers is the integration of Major League Baseball. The writer's primary material is an extensive archive of columns written by area sportswriters. The writer's claim, appearing in the argument's conclusion, is that while Jackie Robinson and Branch Rickey should be honored as the player and executive who broke the barricades preventing Black ballplayers from entering the Major Leagues, the real heroes of this civil rights victory are the sportswriters because they did the hard work of building support for integration over many years. The idea for the microhistory originated in columns found in family scrapbooks. The writer then accessed research libraries, including the Schomburg Center for Research in Black Culture, which houses many columns written during the run-up to April 15, 1947, the date when Jackie Robinson was penciled into the starting lineup of the Brooklyn Dodgers. The writer's careful research allows him to argue against our limited public memory of this seminal historical event; that is, the research allows the writer to focus attention on the heroic work of these sportswriters, figures all but lost in our overly generalized understanding of Major League Baseball's integration. The first paragraph introduces the writer's project, and the other paragraphs focus on primary materials. Note: For essays that demonstrate correct formatting, please see Appendix A for MLA style and Appendix B for APA style.

Baseball, Integration, And Militant Rhetoric:
The Pioneering Work Of New York City Sportswriters

Jackie Robinson and Branch Rickey are American heroes, and everybody who knows even a little about baseball respects them. They are heroes because they had the courage to cross the color line and integrate our national game. They should always be heroes. But if we want to really understand why Black ballplayers were finally allowed to compete alongside whites, it is essential that we honor the work of sportswriters who fought over many years to convince readers of the moral rightness of integrating the game.

As a nation, we focus our eyes on April 15, 1947, the day when Robinson started at first base for the Brooklyn Dodgers. A 2013 movie, *42*, was made and many books have been written about this day and about Robinson's career, about the regular taunting from opposing players and hostile fans and about his incredible determination and strength to keep going. I probably would have walked away and hoped to take some of my dignity with me.

Making all this possible were mostly Black sportswriters like Joe Bostic, Dan Burley, and Romeo Daugherty, who toiled for Black-owned dailies and weeklies. Perhaps the greatest praise should be heaped on a white sportswriter, Lester Rodney, who began campaigning for integration of baseball in 1936 as sports editor for the *Daily Worker,* the newspaper of the Communist Party (Silber 56). If we want to know about the difficult work of creating social change, we must study the historical columns of these brave sportswriters.

Joe Bostic was sports editor from 1942 to 1945 for the militant *The People's Voice,* a Black-owned newspaper published in Harlem. Bostic often called out the white baseball establishment for its racist practices. He also questioned the presumed superiority of white players and whether or not integration would mean a step up for Black players. In a July 11, 1942 column, he writes, "We're not convinced that the baseball played in the organized leagues necessarily represents the best caliber of ball played per se, and therefore, the Negro players would not be moving into faster company than that in which they were already playing" (Bostic 85). One has to wonder how Bostic flipping the "superiority" mindset might have influenced readers. Bostic also knew that while integration might be a social victory, it would also be a financial defeat for the Negro Leagues, a predominately Black-owned industry.

In what some view as the most aggressive challenge to Major League Baseball's segregationist policy, Bostic arranged a tryout at the Dodgers' spring training camp in April of 1945 for two Negro League players, Terris McDuffie and Showboat Thomas. Bostic appeared at the camp uninvited and knew that he'd cause trouble. He was challenging Dodgers' President Branch Rickey to make practical his contention that he favored integrating the game. Rickey was furious and never spoke to Bostic again. The players were not signed. Bostic wrote about the tryout, embarrassed Rickey, and added a few more soldiers to the march against segregation (Bostic 87).

After reading all of Bostic's baseball columns, I am convinced that he should be in the Baseball Hall of Fame for his efforts. Mostly I see him as a man ahead of his time. He knew that the game would be integrated, especially after Commissioner Landis died, but he wanted the world to know that the Negro Leagues were successful in their own right and that Black players were unlikely to find faster company in white leagues. He also exposed Branch Rickey, a powerhouse in the baseball establishment, for wanting to integrate the game on his terms only. For me, Bostic's militancy distinguished the Negro Leagues and, ultimately, contributed to the work of integrating the game.

Lester Rodney is not exactly a household name, but it should be. Rodney was sports editor for the *Daily Worker* from 1936 to 1958 and spent much of his first decade with the paper working aggressively to promote the integration of baseball. Rodney believed that a Communist critique of a capitalist system could occur on sports pages as well as anywhere, and that these pages were good places to appeal to workers. Rodney was different from most Communist Party hard-liners in that he believed that workers' passion for their teams was genuine and not something manufactured by the system. On a personal level, Rodney describes his drive for integration this way: "I was in it because I wanted the damn ban to end, to bring elementary democracy to the game I loved and to see the banned players get their chance to show they belonged" (qtd. in Silber 97). Rodney's many columns on the issue spurred the *Daily Worker* to conduct petition drives in which more than one million people signed in support of the integration of baseball. Rodney and writers at some Black papers regularly shared information in a concerted drive to build momentum.

Rodney did not hold back in his criticism of American racism. Of April 15, 1947, he writes: "It's hard this Opening Day to write straight baseball and not stop to mention the wonderful fact of Jackie Robinson. You tell yourself it shouldn't be especially wonderful in America, no more wonderful for instance than Negro soldiers being with us on the way overseas through submarine infested waters in 1943" (qtd. in Silber 98).

Sometimes Rodney's columns issued challenges. For example, in an interview Rodney recalls a conversation he had with the great Negro Leagues pitcher Satchel Paige in 1937 in which Paige had suggested that the winner of that year's Major League World Series play an all-star team of Negro League players:

So I say to him, "What makes you so sure you'll win?" And he replies, "We've been playing teams of major league all-stars after the regular season in California for four years and they haven't beaten me yet. . . . Must be just a few men who don't want us to play Big League ball. The players are okay and the crowds are with us. Just let them take a vote of the fans whether they want us in the game. I've been all over the country and I know it would be one hundred to one in favor of such a game" (qtd. in Silber 62).

Like Joe Bostic, Rodney used various strategies to push the integration movement forward. He is a hero, more than deserving of a prominent place in our public history.

Works Cited

Bostic, Joe. "In Re Negroes in Big Leagues." *Black Writers, Black Baseball: An Anthology of Articles from Black Sportswriters Who Covered the Negro Leagues.* Ed. Jim Reisler. McFarland, 2007. pp. 84–86.

Silber, Irwin. *Press Box Red: The Story of Lester Rodney, the Communist Who Helped Break the Color Line in American Sports.* Temple UP, 2003.

Reflect and Apply

Answer the following questions as a way to determine the kind of argument practical to your purpose.

1. Identify a few issues in your personal or public life that seem especially appropriate for middle-ground approaches. If you were to argue on these issues, how would you reconcile their extreme positions with more practical claims?

2. How does the approach to the opposition in Rogerian argument differ from the approach to the opposition in Toulmin-based argument? Reflecting on issues in your life as a student, worker, consumer, and concerned citizen, explain why some issues are appropriate for a Rogerian approach.

3. Regarding your family or your community, what part of history do you want to know more about? Why? What primary documents available to you could lead you into a deeper understanding of an earlier time period?

KEEPING IT LOCAL

THE NARRATIVE that opens this chapter—a writer's burgeoning awareness of how a big utility impacts citizens' daily lives and the writer's task of crafting a middle-ground argument in response—provides a strong lesson in audience awareness. Because the writer aimed at the state Utilities Commission, and not the utility, the general public, or elected officials, the writer could emphasize the commission's dual role to both protect ratepayers and ensure that the utility brings in sufficient profit to continue operating. Had the writer aimed the argument at the utility, then a Toulmin-based approach would have been appropriate because of the writer's concern for ratepayers. Or, had the writer aimed the argument at the Chamber of Commerce, a group representing the interests of local businesses, then a Rogerian approach may have been practical because of business owners' sensitivity to the utility as a business not only providing an essential service but also vulnerable to economic risk. In a middle-ground approach, the writer identified the two extreme positions as (1) the utility's request for regular rate hikes in the midst of a tough economic cycle, and (2) some ratepayers' demands that the utility reduce rates and cross over to renewable energy sources in the next few years. The writer's claim: "The Utilities Commission should rule that yearly rate hikes are unacceptable and mandate an energy portfolio standard that includes increasing percentages of renewable energy sources."

It's important, always, to decide early in your writing process whom you want to influence and inform on an issue. Knowing what an audience values—profit, public service, or both—makes it easier to choose the best approach to your argument. Your choice of approach begins with a sense of your local community: who holds the reins of power, who looks out for everyday people, and where openings for change can be found.

─ ─ ─ ─ ─ ─ ─ ─ ─ ─ ─ ─

When our opinions on an issue differ with others' opinions, we tend to think in "I'm right, and you're wrong" terms. In many ways, that is how we have been trained to think. In everyday life you have choices about your thought process in situations where you differ with others on an issue that's important to you. How will you remind yourself that these choices exist?

Now identify the single most difficult issue in your life, the one you'd most like to avoid. Now that you have learned four ways to approach an issue, which approach to argument would you choose for this tough issue? What would you claim?

CHAPTER 10

Build Arguments

Learning Objectives

By working through this chapter, you will be able to

- define the function of a claim in an argument.
- select the type of claim appropriate to your argument's purpose.
- explain the function of reasons in an argument.
- employ qualifiers to make the claim of your argument believable.
- build a warrant based on your knowledge of your argument's audience.
- use backing to support a warrant in an argument.

The current assignment in your argument class asks you to argue on an issue that affects the local environment. Your teacher advises the class that extensive research will be essential to forge a persuasive argument because environmental issues are usually evaluated in terms of the factual evidence supplied by each side. A brief conversation with your neighbor, who opposes the construction of a nearby fracked gas pipeline, compels you to do some preliminary research, and the issue motivates you to argue a position. The two sides are clear: for and against. Each side supports its position with scientific studies, personal testimony, and a lot of economic data and projections.

To date, opponents of the pipeline have been unsuccessful in their efforts to halt construction, even though protests and public hearings have received substantial media coverage. On the other side, the private utility provider building the pipeline argues that jobs created by the new pipeline are essential to the local economy and that improved technology will limit emissions of methane gas into the air.

All Illustrations by iStock.com/A-digit

COMMUNITY

School-Academic

Workplace

Family-Household

Neighborhood

Social-Cultural

Consumer

Concerned Citizen

TOPIC: Air Quality

ISSUE: Construction of Fracked Gas Pipeline

AUDIENCE: Readers of Local Newspaper

CLAIM: Concerned citizens in our community should be aware that completion of a fracked gas pipeline will create health risks for decades into the future.

With the pipeline's construction already underway, you decide that your argument must generate local awareness of the health risks the pipeline poses to your community. With its extensive circulation, the local newspaper seems to be a practical place to present your argument, especially because twice a week, the paper provides space for editorials that address local issues.

A powerful local issue like this one calls for a practical response. When an argument contains a clear center that an audience recognizes as thoughtful, direct, and fully supported, it presents such a response. In Chapter 8, "Consider Toulmin-Based Argument," and Chapter 9, "Consider Middle-Ground Argument, Rogerian Argument, and Argument Based on a Microhistory," you learned about kinds of argument, that is, approaches to an issue that can serve your purpose. But any of the four kinds of argument treated in these chapters require some or all of the following parts: claim, reasons, support, qualifier, warrant, backing, and reservations. This chapter teaches you how to use each of these parts to build your argument and in this way fleshes out the four kinds of argument discussed in Chapters 8 and 9.

At this point, it may be helpful to think about a complete argument as having two major parts. (See Figure 10.1.) Part one is built around a claim, its support, and the qualifiers that make your argument realistic. Part two is built around a warrant, backing, and reservations, elements that justify your claim. With both parts of an argument, pay close attention to your audience and let your argumentative strategies appeal both to your audience's values and to your audience's reservations.

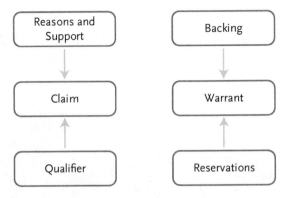

Figure 10.1 The two major parts of a complete argument

How a Claim Functions

The following sections explain why a claim must be the center of an argument. It is the single statement that your readers, including your teacher, refer back to in order to stay focused on your purpose and position in an argument. Unlike a thesis that explains, summarizes, or confesses, a claim is a type of thesis that argues. It identifies an issue, takes a position, and addresses those who hold differing views.

Claim: The Center of Your Argument

A **claim** is the center of an argument and is a kind of thesis. It is your position on an issue, the idea or belief that motivates you to argue. From the perspective of you, the arguer, a claim answers the following questions:

- Where do I stand on this issue?
- What point of view do I want my audience to accept at the end of my argument?
- What is my purpose in delivering this argument?

A claim is also a position you are prepared to defend with reasons and support. The effectiveness of a claim always depends on your ability to convince an audience of its truthfulness. A claim is the single statement that members of your audience, including your teacher, regularly revisit in order to confirm that you remain focused on your claim.

An audience may agree with a claim, it may agree in part with a claim, or it may be skeptical of a claim and require substantial convincing. In all cases, careful study of your audience will put you in a position to craft a claim practical to your purpose. As you begin building an argument, it will be helpful to review the Chapter 2 section titled "Define and Target Your Audience" regarding the importance of aiming an argument at an appropriate audience.

Figure 10.2 In this photo a New York University student is addressing the media during a student-led protest. The setting and her expression reveal three elements of a successful claim: the arguer knows where she stands on the issue at hand, she knows what she wants her audience to accept, and her purpose is clear.

From the perspective of an audience, a claim should answer these questions:

☐ Where does the arguer stand on this issue?

☐ What is the arguer trying to prove?

☐ What are we being asked to accept or consider?

A claim is often most effective when placed at the beginning of an argument, in your introduction or in an early paragraph. But depending on your purpose, sometimes a claim is effective at or near the end of an argument, especially when it is important for you to first fully inform an audience about an issue. Consider the issue below and how the writer builds a focused, clearly worded claim that is aimed at a specific audience.

COMMUNITY

School-Academic

Workplace

Family-Household

Neighborhood

Social-Cultural

Consumer

Concerned Citizen

TOPIC: Discrimination in the Health-care Field

ISSUE: Promotion Practices

AUDIENCE: Director of Hospital Services

CLAIM: Competent, qualified nurses of color in our hospital are often passed over for better-paying positions.

In response to this issue of promotion practices at a local hospital, the arguer has chosen a claim of fact (defined in Table 10.1) as the center of her argument. She makes clear her position, or what she wants her audience to accept, and implies that she wants her claim acknowledged as objective fact in the hospital where she works. In terms of audience, the arguer makes it clear where she stands, and she implies that she intends to prove that this kind of discrimination exists. Then she must sway her audience using convincing support. The arguer plans to target the individual who oversees promotions and disputes as the audience. The arguer's purpose is to make this person aware of her claim of fact. Later arguments on this issue may require different kinds of claims, such as a claim of cause or a problem-based claim, especially if the arguer intends to argue for something to change. This claim is strong because it is direct and because it targets an appropriate audience.

Connect Claim with Purpose

Choose a claim based on what you want to accomplish with an audience. If your aim is to rally an audience to action based on your solution to a current problem, then a problem-based claim would be appropriate. When you determine that confusing or ambiguous language characterizes an issue, you can isolate a key term or word and offer a precise meaning in a claim of definition. If you are motivated to argue an issue on moral grounds, choose a claim of evaluation in which you can center your argument in the particular moral principle in question. When you prove that something is factual that is not regarded as factual by everyone in your audience, a claim of fact forms the foundation of the argument. And when you are compelled to reveal the history of an issue and thus to connect the past with the present, a claim of cause can be effective. Use Table 10.1 to determine the kind of claim that best fits your goals with your audience.

All three kinds of support—logical, ethical, and emotional—can be used effectively in any type of argument. The category "Primary Support," in Table 10.1, identifies the *essential* support required in each kind of claim.

> **your turn 10a** ▸ **GET STARTED Determine Your Purpose before Writing a Claim**
>
> Answer the following questions to determine the kind of claim that fits your purpose in an argument. Use Table 10.1 as a guide.
>
> 1. On what single issue are you motivated to argue?
> 2. What is the audience for your argument? Why, exactly, is this audience a practical target?
> 3. What do you want to accomplish with this argument?

Five Kinds of Claims

Practical arguments require clearly worded claims directed at specific audiences. When your goals with your audience are clear, choose the kind of claim that matches your purpose. Kinds of claims are discussed in the following sections.

Table 10.1 Finding an Appropriate Claim

Purpose of Argument is to . . .	Appropriate Kind of Claim	Essential Support
Prove something as true Prove that something happened	Fact	Logical facts examples credible research
Define Clarify Identify characteristics	Definition	Logical and Ethical facts personal examples credible research
Prove a problem exists Prove a problem needs attention Offer a solution Rally audience to action	Problem-Based	Logical, Ethical, and Emotional facts credible research personal examples emotional example
Make a judgment Prove relevance of a principle	Evaluation	Logical and Ethical personal examples credible research facts
Establish cause and effect Identify relationships Position an issue in history	Cause–Effect	Logical facts credible research

Claim of Fact

A **claim of fact** argues that something is a fact—an event or series of events, a trend, an attitude, or a part of history—that may not be considered a fact by everyone. When you argue a claim of fact, you argue that something is truthful and can be proven objectively in the real world. Your responsibility in this kind of claim is to bring enough support to make your claim believable. Review the following examples of claims of fact.

- Although many local businesses claim to be green, problems with air, water, and waste continue and, in some cases, have gotten worse.
- Despite the complaints of many students about online courses, I gain a lot from these courses: I interact more effectively with my teachers than in the classroom, I get more thorough feedback, and members of my group are more responsible.
- Bailing out big banks helps the banks but not everyday Americans.

In each of these claims, arguers have claimed as facts events that others might dispute. If these claims are to appear truthful to target audiences, arguers must bring in convincing support in the form of powerful reasons, personal examples, and credible research.

your turn 10b PRACTICE **Writing Claims of Fact**

Write a claim of fact in response to each of the following issues.

1. The U.S. military spending is the highest in the world.
2. You and several classmates are confused about an essay assignment.
3. Production of renewable energy is now mandatory in many states.
4. Multinational corporations should be held responsible for poor working conditions in the farms and factories these corporations own.
5. Sentencing juveniles as adults enrages many people across your state.

your turn 10c GET STARTED **Claims of Fact**

Use the following questions to begin work with a claim of fact.

☐ What kind of logical support will you use with your claim? Specifically, what facts, data, and statistics from your research will help support your claim? What examples from real life will you bring in as part of your support?

☐ To gain credibility with your audience, you will need to draw on the work of experts and professionals. Who are these experts, and what makes them credible? Are you careful to avoid using personal beliefs and speculation as part of your logical support?

☐ What, exactly, is the context you provide for your audience on your issue? What is the specific history of your issue? What are the key terms you define as you orient your audience to your issue?

☐ As part of the context you use for your audience, describe the time-line, or chronology, you provide for your issue. What are the important events along your timeline?

☐ What does your audience have to gain by accepting your claim of fact?

☐ What are the strongest lines of support you will use in your argument? Will you place them early in the argument?

☐ What, precisely, are you claiming is or is not a fact?

☐ In addition to your claim, where in your argument will you use qualifiers? How will these qualifiers make your claim more believable?

Additionally, answer the following questions to test the validity of your claim of fact.

☐ Are there clear points of view different from the claim of fact you may work with, and thus does your claim of fact respond to an issue that can be considered legitimate and arguable? Might some people question whether your claim is factual?

☐ Are you prepared to prove your claim with specific information?

If you answer "yes" to these questions, then your claim of fact may be interpreted as valid by an audience.

Claim of Definition

A **claim of definition** defines a word or term that is central to an issue. This kind of claim typically offers a definition that is different from popular understanding or different from a definition associated with a particular point of view or agenda.

Sometimes issues occur because people have different meanings for key words or terms. For example, the word *patriotic* to one person may mean supporting American military presence in Iraq and Afghanistan, but to another person this term may mean opposing our presence in these countries. A claim that offers a precise definition for each key term, a definition that is fully supported with convincing evidence, can be the center of an effective argument and can clarify and bring broader meaning to a confusing or controversial term. Consider the following examples of claims of definition.

- Group work in my online classes has not been about higher education.
- So much of the food I eat, the fuel I expend, and the clothing I wear works against the idea of sustainable living.
- A curriculum based on workforce training alone ignores the ideals of American citizenship.

Popular terms in the above examples—*higher education, sustainable living,* and *American citizenship*—need to be defined. In the first example, the arguer will need to demonstrate how group work in online classes does not fit with the definition of the term *higher education*. In the second sample claim, the arguer has outlined an argument in a way that can define the term *sustainable living* in terms of food, fuel, and clothing. And in the third example, the arguer will need to identify and discuss the ideals implied by the term *American citizenship*. These terms do not mean the same to everyone, and the arguer's task is to bring in convincing support to argue for more precise definitions.

Because easy-to-remember terms and slogans are everywhere in mainstream media, it is important to know who is using them and for what purposes. Often, slogans convey one impression but hide agendas that tilt toward one side of a political or economic spectrum. Slogans like "family values," "change," "health care for all," and "survival of the fittest," to name just a few, are often used to reduce complex issues to catchy, simplified language. The power of an argument grounded in a claim of definition is that it can move beyond this kind of oversimplification by acknowledging the complexity of an issue.

your turn 10d PRACTICE **Writing Claims of Definition**

Write a claim of definition in response to the use of italicized terms in the following statements. Remember that these popular terms have multiple meanings in our culture. Write claims that offer your definitions of the terms.

1. Those who argue for same-sex marriage are only being *politically correct*.
2. Single-payer health care must be aggressively resisted by the U.S. health insurance industry.
3. An *economic bailout* is the only practical way to restore confidence in our banking system.
4. *Free trade* benefits everyone because it lets other countries do business more easily with the United States.
5. In view of last week's protests, the *sexual misconduct* policy at our college needs to be revised.

your turn 10e GET STARTED **Claims of Definition**

Determine whether a claim of definition is appropriate for your purpose by answering the following questions.

☐ What is the word or term you intend to define? Who is your audience?

☐ What context will you bring in to establish this word or term as controversial? What research will you reference in order to establish the word's different meanings, the various agendas these meanings serve, and that the word's meaning is being disputed?

☐ What populations are being affected by this word's various meanings?

☐ How will you argue against popular and dictionary definitions of this word?

☐ Because your job is to replace vague meanings of a word with a precise definition, explain how you will bring in and discuss clear characteristics, examples, and synonyms for the word.

☐ How will you clarify the specific conditions your definition must meet in order to be accepted by your audience?

☐ Does your definition include discussion of what the word or term *is not* as well as what it *is*? Explain.

These kinds of claims should identify a popular and controversial word or term. The support that follows your claim should offer specific explanations for the definition you support. Your ability to defend your definition with compelling support will determine the success of an argument based on a claim of definition.

Problem-Based Claims

Problem-based claims propose solutions to issues. They address issues with answers, with specific suggestions, and with a practical sense for what will work in a given context. This kind of claim responds to a problem with a solution. Sometimes called a "proposal claim" or a "policy claim," the problem-based claim must include a plan to solve a problem, and this plan must be defended by the arguer with plentiful support. Problem-based claims often include words and phrases like "must," "should," and "would benefit from." Review the following problem-based claims, and note how each one offers a specific solution to a problem.

- The state's Public Utilities Commission should hold public hearings across the state in response to an energy company's request for a permit to build another fracked gas pipeiline.
- To serve all our residents, the community's suicide prevention center must agree to work with the general population, not just teenagers.
- Students at my school would benefit from completing a service learning requirement in order to graduate.

The problems that these claims address—that citizens are concerned about the effects of a fracked gas pipeline, that not everyone considering suicide has access to a potentially life-saving resource, and that an education is not complete without some connection to the local community—are met with solutions. The arguer now must follow through on a claim with a set of practical reasons and specific support to make a solution realistic and believable.

> **your turn**   **PRACTICE Writing Problem-Based Claims**
>
> Write a problem-based claim in response to each of the following issues.
>
> 1. A growing debate across the country is whether water should be a publicly owned or privately held resource.
> 2. The Department of Homeland Security, so important after the 9/11 attacks, has faded from public view.
> 3. End-of-grade testing in public schools has some parents crying, "Unfair!"
> 4. Some states' decision to reject federal money for Medicare services will plunge many older people into poverty.
> 5. Many subscribers to social networking sites have mixed feelings about these sites owning materials that subscribers post.

your turn 10g **GET STARTED** **Problem-Based Claims**

Based on the issue you're working with now, answer the following questions to begin work on a problem-based claim.

- ☐ What specific context will you bring in to prove that the problem exists and needs attention

- ☐ Is your audience in a position to act on your claim? Is it clear what you're asking your audience to do?

- ☐ Explain how well you know your audience and why you feel you can engage this audience with emotional examples that inspire action. What does your audience value, and what will motivate your audience to act on your claim?

- ☐ What are the compelling reasons and logical support you will use to prove that your claim is practical? Describe the research you will use to support your plan. What are your strategies to argue for the advantages of your claim and to show how it is more practical than what is in place now?

- ☐ How will you respond to rebuttals that assert that there is too much uncertainty about your claim because it involves a new approach to the problem?

Do your claims propose solutions to problems? Will your audience take your claim seriously because it offers a practical answer to a local problem? It is especially important with this kind of claim to understand when and where an issue began, its history, and why it continues to be unresolved.

Claim of Evaluation

A **claim of evaluation** centers on a judgment you make. It argues that something is practical or impractical, ethical or unethical, fair or unfair, healthy or unhealthy, worth our time or not worth our time, detrimental or beneficial, and so on.

Because an audience naturally will ask how you can make such a judgment, an argument centered in a claim of evaluation insists that you identify the standards and guidelines used to make your judgment. In other words, you must state the reasons you believe that something is good or bad, right or wrong, fair or unfair, safe or unsafe. Then you must support these reasons with examples, the testimony of experts, and appeals to the values of your audience. Review the following examples of claims of evaluation.

- A single-payer, government-funded health-care system is a bad idea for most Americans.

- The lyrics in most hip-hop songs are more socially relevant than the lyrics of 1960s rock songs.
- Lifting the ban on fracking in our state would create unsafe conditions we're not prepared to tolerate.
- The best way to address the problem of increasing traffic congestion is to vote in favor of an increased transit sales tax.

In the first example, the arguer must spell out what is bad about a single-payer approach to health care. With the second claim, the increased social relevance of hip-hop songs must be demonstrated. In the third claim, the term *unsafe* must be broken down into categories that can be supported with specific information. And in the fourth claim, it must be clear why voting for an increased transit sales tax is better than other ways of guarding against future traffic congestion. With all four examples, the effectiveness of each argument depends completely on the arguer's ability to defend an evaluation.

your turn   PRACTICE **Writing Claims of Evaluation**

Write a claim of evaluation for each of the following issues.

1. Arranged marriages, practiced in some Asian and African cultures, involve a marriage arranged by people other than the bride and groom.
2. Civil disobedience, the decision to break the law as a way to engage in political protest, has a long history in the United States.
3. Job outsourcing, as many Americans know, can have profound effects on the local economy.
4. A carbon tax aims to penalize those who pollute the environment with excessive carbon emissions.
5. Supporters of a Voting Rights Act claim that the Act will eliminate voter fraud at the polls.

your turn   GET STARTED **Claims of Evaluation**

Respond to the following questions to get started on a claim of evaluation.

☐ Based on how you want your audience to react to your evaluation, what values do you share with your audience?

☐ What specific context will you bring to your argument?

☐ Given that your claim is grounded in a value or values you hold, are you prepared to support your claim with credible research and evidence grounded in logic and reason? Describe your research and evidence.

☐ What are the standards and guidelines you use to make your evaluation? Describe how you will justify these standards based on the examples you will use.

☐ Regarding your claim and the standards you use, what rebuttals do you anticipate? How will you counter these rebuttals?

☐ Will you compare your evaluation with other, similar claims, and will you contrast your evaluation with other, differing claims? In other words, how will you position yourself as part of an ongoing conversation on your issue?

☐ What emotional examples will you use to inspire and motivate your audience?

Claim of Cause

A **claim of cause** argues that one thing or event sets in motion a chain of events. This kind of claim requires the arguer to recognize connections between events, determine a reasonable cause for events, and demonstrate factual relationships between one event and its effects.

A claim of cause can be a powerful choice as the basis for an argument because you will identify for your audience a pattern of connected events. In most cases, a claim of cause works best when you bring in relevant factual information or when you make realistic comparisons to similar cause–effect patterns. Review the following claims of cause.

- Evidence of global warming has caused widespread local activism across the country, as many Americans now try to limit their use of various energy sources.

- My boss is inconsistent in his comments about customer complaints, and this is causing the company to lose clients.

- The city council's decision to again postpone discussion of homelessness is only increasing the number of homeless in our community.

In each of these examples, the arguer claims that one event is causing another event or chain of events. To convince a target audience of these claims, specific relationships that a certain event has generated must be demonstrated with factual information and/or with realistic comparisons to other cause–effect patterns. A successful argument based on a claim of cause can lead to a later argument centered in a problem-based claim, where you can offer a solution to the problem at hand.

what!?

your turn 10j ▸ PRACTICE **Writing Claims of Cause**

With attention to the italicized words, write a claim of cause that responds to each of the following issues.

1. *Grade inflation*, a cause for concern among students and local employers, seems to continue from one semester to the next.
2. *Recent federal laws that permit new kinds of surveillance and interrogation* are necessary if we want to ensure national security.
3. *Stress in the workplace*, a problem for everyone I know, cannot be discussed during my annual review.
4. *Children and online safety* is now a national topic of debate.
5. The issue of *undocumented workers* never seems to be addressed in our community.

your turn 10k ▸ GET STARTED **Get Started: Claims of Cause**

Answer the following questions to get started with a claim of cause.

☐ What, exactly, is the cause–effect relationship you are claiming?

☐ Because you will argue that one event has caused other events, it is vital that you bring in adequate history for your issue. What is the history of your issue? What are the specific conditions that your audience needs to know in order to establish the cause–effect connections that your argument requires? How far back in time must you go in order to convince your audience?

☐ What are the factual examples you'll bring in to make your cause–effect connections believable?

☐ Based on your research, do others argue for causes different from yours? Describe these other claims. Why is your claim more practical?

☐ Should your audience agree with your claim of cause, how will it benefit?

☐ What values do you and your audience share, and what appeals will you make based on these values?

tip 10a

Know What You Want to Accomplish with an Audience

Many arguments are written to solve problems, and thus problem-based claims are common. But if your aim is to demonstrate that something is unfair or unsafe, then a claim of evaluation is appropriate. Or if you want to reveal that one event causes another, that something is factual, or that clarification is needed for a word or term, then claims of cause, fact, and definition become practical. The key to choosing a practical claim is to identify an audience that is invested in your issue and then create a claim that audience is willing to accept.

Use Reasons to Support Your Claim

Reasons give your claim direction and make it believable. They organize an argument into manageable parts. Plan to devote one or more paragraphs in support of each reason you bring to an argument. Position a reason at the beginning of a body paragraph and follow it with specific support, such as examples from your experience, facts and statistics drawn from your research, and the commentary of experts. Without reasons to direct your audience, an argument lacks structure and becomes only a collection of information.

Use reasons that are immediately relevant to your claim. As you begin to think through your claim, you may jot down some eight to ten reasons that seem appropriate to your argument. But be critical when deciding on the reasons you choose to support. It may be that three or four reasons stand out from the rest based on the support you know you can bring to each reason. Choose reasons that are likely to appeal to the values of your target audience.

Reasons are essential in an argument because they:

Figure 10.3 Similar to this photo in which the speaker is explaining one part of an idea or position he is defending, reasons organize and provide direction for an argument. They link to an argument's claim and alert the reader that specific support will follow.

- Defend your claim.
- Announce the focus of each paragraph in an argument.
- Frame the specific support you bring to an argument.

Review the following issue and the reasons the writer brings to the argument. Note that some reasons are more practical than others based on the specific targeted audience.

COMMUNITY

School-Academic

Workplace

Family-Household

Neighborhood

Social-Cultural

Consumer

Concerned Citizen

TOPIC: Degree Requirements

ISSUE: Service Learning

AUDIENCE: Teachers at My College

CLAIM: Students at my college may benefit from completing a service learning requirement in order to graduate.

REASONS CONSIDERED

- Personal enjoyment
- **Become aware of local service agencies**
- Vary course options
- **Experience serving a population**
- Find a career direction
- Get leadership training
- Become more compassionate
- **Connect classroom and community**
- Volunteer opportunity
- **Works with any subject area**

REASONS FINALIZED

- By fulfilling a service learning requirement, students would become aware of service agencies in the community and why they are important.
- Students would gain hands-on experience serving a specific population in the community.
- Students would be in a position to make connections between what's learned in the classroom and what they learn in a community agency.
- Service learning is appropriate for any subject area.

These reasons answer the question, "Why is my claim important?" They also structure this argument into manageable parts. With a focus on awareness, experience, and connections, each reason is distinct from others and implies that specific support will follow. The arguer's target audience—the school faculty—may pay close attention to these reasons based on their values as educators and whether they feel service learning is appropriate. Faculty unfamiliar with service learning may benefit from the specific support the arguer uses. Of the original ten reasons generated during a prewriting session, four are chosen based on the arguer's knowledge of the audience.

your turn   PRACTICE Writing Reasons

Complete the following sentences to determine the soundness of reasons you plan to use in an argument.

1. My claim is important because . . .
2. I want to use this reason in my argument because . . .
3. This reason should appeal to my audience because . . .
4. Each reason connects directly to my claim because it . . .
5. I plan to delete some reasons from my argument because they . . .
6. Some of the information I plan to bring in to support this reason includes . . .

Build Body Paragraphs around Reasons

The reasons you bring to an argument must be supported, and it is this specific support that forms the bulk of body paragraphs. The vital question you must ask when building a body paragraph is, "Will the support I bring in justify my reason?" As always, knowing your audience and its values will determine the specific support you use. Full discussion of support is covered in Chapter 11, "Support an Argument with Fact (Logos), Credibility (Ethos), and Emotion (Pathos)." For your claim and reasons to be taken seriously, you must use support that an audience finds credible and current. The body paragraphs in the following section are taken from arguments written in recent argument classes. Carefully read the discussion sections that evaluate how reasons and support and defend claims.

COMMUNITY

School-Academic

Workplace

Family-Household

Neighborhood

Social-Cultural

Consumer

Concerned Citizen

TOPIC: Transportation

ISSUE: Red Light Cameras at Major Intersections

AUDIENCE: Readers of the Local Newspaper

PROBLEM-BASED CLAIM: The use of red light traffic cameras should be discontinued on our streets.

Sample Body Paragraph

Red Light Cameras—Pursuing Profit without Process or Purpose

When first considered, red light traffic cameras seem benign. After all, the stated purpose of the cameras is to improve safety on Charlotte streets. *However, red light traffic cameras are a serious concern because they are owned and operated by private companies that are motivated by profit rather than justice.* In July 2003, *The Charlotte Observer* reported that red light traffic cameras extracted $7.4 million over a five-year period from the taxpayers driving in Charlotte. Of that, $3 million went to the city — and nearly $4.5 million went to the private contractor (Whitacre 1A). The American Civil Liberties Union explains that "many red-light camera systems have been installed under contracts that deliver a cut of ticket revenue to the contractor [as in Charlotte]. That creates an obvious incentive to contractors to 'game' the system in order to increase revenue and, in turn, generates public cynicism and suspicion" (Steinhardt 1). Ron Arnone, an employee of Sherman Way and Woodman, a red light traffic camera company in Los Angeles, bluntly states, "I never heard them talk about safety. It was all about finding good locations to make these people [the owners] a lot of money" (qtd. in Goldstein 1). An illustration of this comes from John Irving of Bethesda, Maryland. He was ticketed for running a red light so he went back and timed the yellow light. John found that the camera-patrolled intersection had a yellow light set to 2.7 seconds, while every other yellow light on that stretch of road was 4 seconds ("Tale of the 3-Second Yellow Light" 1). Obviously, the contractor or the government gained by shortening the yellow light as that one traffic camera netted $1 million in 14 months.

The third sentence in the previous body paragraph, the italicized sentence, is a reason. It directly supports the writer's claim that red light traffic cameras should be discontinued. This reason is followed by specific support, both from experts and from people affected by red light cameras. The reason also announces the focus of the paragraph and is followed immediately by logical, ethical, and emotional support.

COMMUNITY

School-Academic

Workplace

Family-Household

Neighborhood

Social-Cultural

Consumer

Concerned Citizen

TOPIC: Energy Dependence

ISSUE: Wind power as a viable alternative to oil and coal

AUDIENCE: Leaders of the Local Construction Industry

PROBLEM-BASED CLAIM: America needs a plan, and the Pickens Plan will benefit our country because the fuels are ready now, it will keep money in our country, and it is environmentally friendly.

Sample Body Paragraph

Pickens Has the Plan for the Future

First, the fuels for this plan are ready now. Throughout the world today there are over 14 million cars on the road fueled by compressed natural gas (CNG) and liquefied natural gas (LNG), and only a handful of them are in the US ("Natural Gas and Propane" 1). There is currently only one CNG-powered car made in the US, the Honda Civic GX. Toyota will be introducing its CNG-powered Camry in November to compete ("Toyota Decides" 2). The technology and the fuel are ready and used throughout the world today, and we are behind the power curve. The Midwest of the United States has the greatest wind energy potential in the world and is what some call the "Saudi Arabia of wind power." Pickens is currently in the process of building the largest wind farm in the world. Once built, it will produce 4,000 megawatts of energy, the equivalent output of four large coal-burning plants combined, and will double our country's wind production ("Pickens Building World's Largest Wind Farm"). The largest solar plant in North America will be finished soon in Nevada. Once finished, it will provide 15 megawatts of energy, 30% of the consumption of the neighboring Air Force base where 12,000 people work and 7,215 people live ("Air Force Embraces" 8). As you can see the potential is there for development of these resources, we just need leadership with the ambition to lead the way.

The reason (i.e., the italicized first sentence) announces to readers that fuels needed to replace oil are available and should be used in the United States. Written in 2007, this text supports the claim that, at that time, the Pickens Plan was needed and that it would benefit our country in terms of our dependence on foreign oil. The writer supports this reason by referencing the potential of planned wind and solar operations. The writer's reason links claim with support.

The various kinds of support needed to make reasons credible and demonstrated in the preceding examples are covered in Chapter 11, "Support an Argument with Fact (Logos), Credibility (Ethos), and Emotion (Pathos)."

 **tip 10b**

Make Sure You Can Defend Reasons
Draft your reasons carefully; make sure you can follow them with logical, ethical, and emotional support. Make a list of reasons you may use in an upcoming argument. Are some grounded primarily in emotion? Are some grounded in stereotypes and hearsay? Delete these from your list and focus on reasons that you are prepared to support.

Use Qualifiers to Make Your Argument Believable

A **qualifier** can make a claim or reason more believable to an audience. It limits a claim or reason to what is reasonable or possible within a given context or set of conditions. Simply put, it can be wise to change words and phrases like those in the left column (in the following table) to qualifiers in the right column.

Table 10.2 Qualifiers

always never absolutely only in all cases	*change to*	usually probably possibly in many cases generally most likely may or might can with few exceptions sometimes

Figure 10.4 Qualifiers are crucial to making a claim or reason believable because they move the arguer away from absolute statements and toward qualified statements that speak to certain conditions. In this photo, a seventh-grade student addresses an audience at a school board meeting, a meeting in which the board announced that more than 400 out-of-district students would be removed from a local school and forced to enroll at other schools.

Qualifiers keep you from making absolute statements and broad generalizations, a habit that can make your argument vulnerable to criticism from the opposition. If you claim, for example, that Macintosh computers are by far the most practical choice for students today, some members of your audience may reject your argument based on the cost of a Mac. A revised, more realistic claim would include a qualifier: "For students who can afford them, Macintosh computers are practical choices." This limits the range of your claim and makes it more likely to be accepted by your audience.

With most issues, steer clear of generalizations and statements that claim certainty. Narrow a claim to what your audience is most likely to accept. When your claim is too broad and you promise too much to an audience, you leave yourself vulnerable to attack.

your turn 10m PRACTICE Writing Qualifiers

Explain why the following claims may not be believable to an audience. Rewrite each claim using an appropriate qualifier.

1. There must be a law that prohibits credit card companies from marketing to college students.
2. Texting in the classroom is always inappropriate.
3. Homeschooling is never a substitute for a local public school with high academic standards.

4. The only way to understand the increasing high school dropout rate is to study the lack of student motivation.

5. Homelessness in our community can be solved with more affordable housing.

6. The boom in green building means that we are reducing the effects of global warming.

7. Low voter turnout in our last local election obviously means that most of us are not interested in the issues that affect our daily lives.

8. Employers have every right to monitor employees' online behavior.

9. It is now clear that success in professional sports is due to steroid use.

10. Because it's so convenient, researching online is more practical than hunting for print sources in a library.

Justify Your Claim with a Warrant

Arguments succeed because they persuade audiences. A claim, the center of an argument, can be convincing to an audience when it is followed by reasons and plenty of support. But a claim requires another line of support—a justification, or warrant—to be successful. A **warrant** justifies a claim, it bridges a claim and its support, and it identifies a value, principle, belief, regulation, or law that an audience finds important. Without a warrant, an argument is rudderless, steering in no particular direction and aimed at no particular audience. In fields like medicine, law, and the sciences, warrants often take the form of justifying evidence in an argument. But for our purpose—constructing practical arguments that address everyday issues—warrants based primarily on values are most appropriate.

In the narrative that opens this chapter, the writer has targeted an audience that may be practical for his argument—readers of the local newspaper—because it is the writer's intention to generate local awareness of health risks from a proposed fracked gas pipeline. Having drafted a claim and gathered support, the writer then must articulate in a warrant common ground that he and his audience share. The writer instinctively may know what this common ground is, but it is his responsibility to put into words precisely the values he shares with an audience. The writer must also include support for his warrant—backing—should he sense that an audience may need proof that his warrant is practical for and relevant to the argument he plans to deliver. Additionally, when a writer anticipates an audience having some difficulty accepting a warrant, he should acknowledge these audience reservations. Just as including a qualifier can make a claim or reason more believable, including possible audience reservations in a warrant can make that warrant more believable—and more practical.

 tip 10c

Peer Edit a Claim and Its Reasons

For an argument in progress, ask a few writers to evaluate your claim and reasons. Ask writers to base their evaluations on whether your claim and reasons are realistic and practical and whether you should add or refine qualifiers. See Chapter 13, "Develop and Edit Argument Structure and Style," for more tips on peer review.

Figure 10.5 Connecting with an audience, especially where audience and arguer are far apart on an issue, means identifying a value or belief that differing sides have in common. Building a warrant on a shared value is a way to make this connection.

Use Your Audience to Construct a Warrant

Think of a warrant as permission from an audience to deliver an argument. If an audience finds your warrant acceptable, it likely will grant you permission to argue. But if an audience rejects a warrant—that is, if it does not share in some way the values, principles, or beliefs you include in a warrant—then permission will not be granted and the remainder of your argument will be regarded as unwarranted. As discussed in Chapter 2, "Explore an Issue that Matters to You," targeting a specific audience and its values is an essential early step in building a practical argument.

A warrant answers the following questions:

- ☐ What values, beliefs, and principles do I share with my audience?
- ☐ Why would an audience grant me permission to deliver an argument?
- ☐ How can I justify my claim and support?

Know What Your Audience Values

Consider the following issues and the claims and warrants that respond to each issue. Note that each argument is aimed at a specific audience. Remember that, in relation to an issue, a target audience will expect you to appeal to its values, beliefs, and principles. Hence, knowing an audience well is an important first step in having an argument accepted.

When you feel that textbook prices at your college are too high and are motivated to speak out on this issue, study your audience carefully. For example, targeting other students via your student newspaper means that you should know what most students value in relation to this issue. This likely includes values of wanting to pursue an education, the importance of a good career, the need to budget money carefully, and a commitment to balance work, family, and school responsibilities. Your warrant should reflect these values and might read like this: "As students with full lives, it's important that we be allowed to pursue our academic and career goals without the inconvenience of overpriced textbooks." Such a warrant identifies and honors audience values and grants you permission to make your argument.

Working with this same issue of textbook prices, suppose you target a different audience—readers of your local newspaper. The values of this audience are in some ways different from those of students at your college. Members of this audience include local employers, alumni of your college, and taxpayers whose money supports the college. Values may include training a local workforce and keeping the college in line with its mission of providing affordable education to local residents. With these values in mind, your warrant might read like this: "Affordable workforce training is essential to our economic future." Because you have acknowledged and plan to honor these values, you are in a position to deliver an argument to this audience.

Should you choose to direct your argument on textbook prices to another audience, this time the president of your college, another set of values would need to be acknowledged. In relation to this issue, the president values the need to maintain a budget, produce trained graduates, and continue her commitment to serving the community. With this in mind, you might craft a warrant like this: "Our college can better serve the community by offering discounts on textbook prices." The message you send to this audience honors its beliefs and professional commitments. That you have taken the time to study your audience puts you in a position to argue in a focused, purposeful way, a way that lets you address your audience from a practical perspective.

---

your turn 10 **GET STARTED** **Determine What Your Audience Values**

Based on the issue you're working with now, determine what your audience values by answering the following questions.

☐ Why is this audience invested in this issue?

☐ What is the history of this audience's connection with this issue?

☐ What values, principles, and beliefs motivate this audience to care about this issue?

Let a Warrant Bridge Claim and Support

A warrant should be a bridge between your claim and support. (See Figure 10.6.) It justifies your position on an issue. With many arguments, it may seem that a warrant will be instinctively understood by an audience, especially an audience you know well, but we strongly urge you to spell out in specific terms warrants in your arguments. As you gain experience building arguments, you may choose to leave a warrant unsaid based on your knowledge of an audience. But at this point, consider it essential to make your warrant a clear, strong statement.

Recently a student writer chose to argue on the issue of the local high school dropout rate and to deliver this argument during a parent–teachers' association meeting. As a prospective teacher and parent, the writer crafted a warrant that identified the value for student success and higher-performing schools she shared with the parents and teachers in her audience. In a nutshell, her argument looked like this:

CLAIM:	Systemic changes in the way our school system is structured are needed to lower the high school dropout rate.
SUPPORT:	Research that featured reasons, examples, data, statistics, and the opinions of experts as to how systemic changes can reduce the dropout rate were included. Attention to principals having more control, a longer school day and year, the need for more courses, and a teacher reward system based on performance were addressed.
WARRANT:	Student success and higher-performing schools are essential to the future good health of our community.

The warrant in this example bridges claim and support. The change the writer wants to see is supported with reasons and examples and then justified by shared values. Identifying these shared values in her warrant means that her audience may be willing to grant the writer permission to deliver her argument. Without shared values and common ground, this audience would be less likely to permit such an argument.

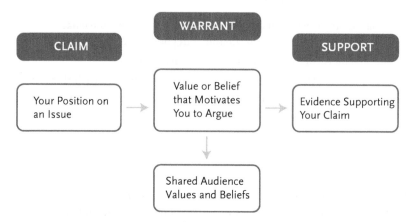

Figure 10.6 A warrant bridges claim and support

your turn 10o **PRACTICE Bridging Claim and Support**

Write a warrant for each of the following examples. Build each warrant based on values, beliefs, and principles the writer may share with the audience.

1. Issue: Requiring Extra Materials for a Class
   Audience: Your College Faculty Senate

Claim: Teachers should not require students to purchase materials
for a class beyond a digital or print textbook.

Support: Reasons may include that requiring additional materials
causes economic hardship for students and that additional materials should be made available through online sources. Specific
support may include examples of how students are inconve-
nienced by having to spend more on a class, such as impact on
individual and family budgets.

Warrant: _____

2. Issue: Road Repair in My Neighborhood
Audience: County Commission
Claim: Road repair in my community is based on economic status.
Support: Reasons may include that wealthier neighborhoods are pri-
oritized above poorer neighborhoods and that wealthier neighborhoods have more political influence. Specific support may
include examples of longstanding problems with roads in poor
neighborhoods and the fact that road problems are addressed
more promptly in wealthier neighborhoods.

Warrant: _____

3. Issue: Legalizing Prostitution in Our State
Audience: Members of Introductory Ethics Class
Claim: Legalizing prostitution will reduce sex crimes in our state.
Support: Reasons may include that legalizing prostitution may reduce
sex trafficking crimes in our state, may reduce rape and sexual
assault, and may improve public health. Specific support can include
extensive data drawn from academic studies, from state crime
reports, and from health-care professionals in the community.

Warrant: _____

Use Backing to Support a Warrant

An analogy may be helpful to begin work with another building block of
practical argument—**backing**. The analogy: support is to a claim as backing is to a warrant. To be convinced of a writer's claim, an audience requires
specific support. Similarly, to be convinced of a writer's warrant, an audience requires a similar kind of support, and this is called *backing*.

Backing answers the following questions:

☐ Why do you believe your warrant is credible?
☐ What specific support can you bring to your warrant?
☐ How will backing your warrant make your argument more convincing?

Let Your Audience Determine the Extent of Backing

Close knowledge of your audience should determine how much backing you bring to a warrant. You may feel that an audience generally is in line with the values stated in your warrant, and this means that backing may be limited to a few facts or examples. However, when an audience may not completely share the values in your warrant, or when an audience may question the relevance of your warrant to the issue at hand, more extensive backing (i.e., more support for your warrant) may be required.

Consider the following arguments and the extent of backing needed to move an audience closer to accepting the writer's claims.

ISSUE:	Supporting the Microcredit Movement
AUDIENCE:	Members of Your Writing Class
CLAIM:	Microcredit is proving to be an ineffective response to poverty in developing countries.
SUPPORT:	Reasons may include that in many cases microcredit loans are not used for entrepreneurial purposes, as intended, but for everyday needs such as food and health care; that this kind of lending traps borrowers in a cycle of borrowing without measurable improvement to earned income; and that repayment officials are often aggressive and threatening. Specific support can be drawn from the increasing number of academic studies and from professional reporting on this issue.
WARRANT:	Institutional and individual lenders should stop wasting their money on microcredit and instead encourage mid-size companies to relocate to developing countries and provide jobs to those who are now impoverished.
BACKING:	Examples of companies building factories and production centers in poor countries and providing jobs are plentiful. Equally effective support for this warrant can include beliefs that compassion for poor people should be grounded in financial common sense and not in fostering economic dependency, and that job security can reduce the need to borrow.
	The target audience for this argument, members of a writing class, may or may not be familiar with the microcredit movement, and the writer's aim is to generate awareness *and* deliver a judgment on this issue. Appropriately, the writer crafts what is both a claim of fact ("is proving to be") and a claim of evaluation ("an ineffective response"). Sometimes kinds of claims overlap, as in this case. Backing for this warrant is effective because the writer emphasizes values of efficiency and avoiding waste, values that this audience more than likely shares with the writer, especially during a period of economic recession.

ISSUE:	Banning Social Networking Sites at Work
AUDIENCE:	Your Employer
CLAIM:	Occasional use of social networking sites should be allowed in the company.
SUPPORT:	Reasons may include that a sense of trust is established between employer and employee when occasional social networking is permitted; that productivity is not affected; and that company security is not compromised. Specific support can include numerous personal examples that demonstrate company loyalty, reference to performance reviews, and professional and academic studies supporting your claim.
WARRANT:	Responsible use of social networking sites is good for the company.
BACKING:	Several studies show that employee retention improved and that security systems were not breached when social networking was allowed. Additionally, many employees at your and other companies claim that the chance to spend 15 to 20 minutes during a work day on Facebook makes for a more comfortable work environment, and some argue that allowing social networking can sometimes create new business contacts.

Because the audience targeted for this argument is the writer's employer, it is important that the writer provide plenty of backing for a warrant that the employer may question. The writer is wise to identify the good of the company as a shared value, but because the employer predictably may not be convinced that spending time away from work while social networking is good for company business, substantial backing should be included in this argument. The writer has chosen to balance academic studies with personal examples from his and others' experience on the job. Improved retention may suggest employee job satisfaction to the employer, and an unhampered security system may relieve concerns about system safety. Examples of new business contacts made possible from social networking may allow the employer to move closer to accepting the writer's claim.

In each of the preceding examples, the writers' target audiences are likely to need some convincing before these arguments are accepted. The backing the writers bring to their warrants validates the values and beliefs on which each argument is built. Without this backing, writers limit an argument's audience appeal.

Make Backing Specific

Backing is most effective when it is specific. Like the support you use with a claim, you should use reasons, facts, examples, statistics, data, and the research of experts to back up a warrant.

Regarding the issue of microcredit and social networking on the job, specific kinds of backing are noted. Note that audiences for these arguments may require substantial backing to make the warrant acceptable. As we know, arguments fail if warrants are not accepted by audiences, and writers of these two arguments must back up warrants with plenty of specific support.

Let's return to the earlier argument where a writer addresses the high school dropout rate, and let's consider effective backing for the warrant, "Student success and higher-performing schools are essential to the future good health of our community." Values embedded in this warrant include concern for student success, higher-performing schools, and the community's economic future. But unlike the audiences targeted for the microcredit and social networking arguments, this audience may need less convincing at the level of the warrant. The writer may know that an audience of parents and teachers, for the most part, share these values; thus, the amount of backing needed for this warrant may be less than what is needed for warrants in the other two arguments, where audiences may require more convincing.

your turn   **PRACTICE Building in Backing to Support a Warrant**

Note the following issues, claims, and warrants. What kind of backing is practical for each warrant? Note that categories in number 4 are blank. Complete this part of the practice based on the argument you are currently building.

1. Issue: Tuition for International Students at Your College
   Audience: College Administration
   Claim: Tuition for international students should be reduced from five times what in-state residents pay to twice what residents pay.
   Warrant: International students should be allowed to pursue college degrees without taking on an unreasonable financial hardship.
   Backing: _____

2. Issue: Online Privacy
   Audience: Friends and Classmates
   Claim: Google and Facebook are invading my privacy.
   Warrant: We should be protected from private companies with large data warehouses that can search our private lives.
   Backing: _____

3. Issue: Arranged Marriages
   Audience: Members of Sociology Class
   Claim: Arranged marriages are a realistic alternative to "love" marriages.
   Warrant: Most successful marriages are built on trust and responsibility.
   Backing: _____

4. Issue: _____
   Audience: _____
   Claim: _____
   Warrant: _____
   Backing: _____

Respond to Audience Reservations to Make a Warrant Believable

Acknowledge in an argument objections an audience may have with your warrant. This move can earn you credibility with an audience because it presents you as thorough and fair-minded. Audience objections to a warrant are called **reservations.** An audience may reserve its full acceptance of a warrant because there may be circumstances in which the warrant is not convincing or morally acceptable.

Responding to audience reservations answers the following questions:

☐ What objections does my audience have about my warrant?

☐ What limits or qualifications can I use to support my warrant and thus make it more acceptable to my audience?

Figure 10.7 Audience reservations should be responded to in ways that acknowledge an audience's objections to the warrant that are based on moral grounds. In this photo, two Pakistani students address the media at Lahore Airport in Pakistan after being deported from England on unsupported allegations of terrorist activity.

In the earlier argument about microcredit, some members of the writer's audience may take issue with the notion that supporting the microcredit movement is wasteful and thus have reservations about the writer's warrant. Specifically, some members of the audience may believe that helping poor people through low-interest loans to be morally sound behavior. Reservations to the warrant that supporting the microcredit movement is wasteful and inefficient might be stated in the following sentences.

- Supporting microcredit in developing countries, especially via loans made by individuals, provides an economic option where others do not exist.
- Microcredit is a way to aid individuals directly without having to encounter formal institutions or governments.

In the earlier argument about social networking on the job, the writer's audience (i.e., the employer) may not completely accept the warrant that responsible use of social networking sites is good for the company. The employer may have reservations about the validity of this warrant, and you should acknowledge similar reservations in your argument. The audience's reservations in this argument might look like this:

- In some companies, employees have been known to spend too much time on social networking sites.
- Some employers are concerned that employee performance will suffer when there is no policy for social networking.

When you include audience reservations in an argument, you demonstrate respect for your audience and confidence in yourself. An audience may accept a warrant only in part, and it is important to validate these reservations. As noted earlier in this chapter, construct a warrant so that the values you share with your audience are clear. Acknowledging the audience's sense of a warrant's limits can make an argument more practical. (Additionally, see Chapter 6, "Work Fairly with the Opposition," for working with the opposition.)

tip 10d

Interview Your Audience

Think of yourself as a journalist and interview your audience to determine its reservations about your warrant. Depending on your audience, the interview can occur in-person during a conversation or through careful research. Record the values your audience holds. Think through the reservations this audience may have based on your warrant.

your turn 10q GET STARTED Acknowledge Audience Reservations to a Warrant

Answer the following questions based on an argument you plan to build.

1. What might prevent my audience from fully accepting my warrant? That is, are there certain conditions in which exceptions to my warrant are valid?
2. Will your argument be strong enough to accommodate your audience's reservations? Explain. How, specifically, will you respond to audience reservations?

Reflect and Apply

1. What is the most pressing issue for you at school, at your job, and as a concerned citizen? What kind of claim seems most appropriate for each issue? Explain.

2. Working with the claims you draft for each issue in question one above, sketch out a warrant for each claim. Anticipate problems an audience may have accepting these warrants. Describe these problems.

3. As this chapter explains, good arguments fit various pieces together. Based on the argument you are working on now, which piece comes to mind first? How will you build the rest of the argument after beginning with this piece?

KEEPING IT LOCAL

THE NARRATIVE that begins this chapter addresses one of many environmental issues before us today. This particular issue, construction of a fracked gas pipeline, has been the focus of several strong arguments in recent years. These arguments were effective because writers matched claim with purpose. In some cases, writers built problem-based claims because their purpose was to argue that construction should stop. Another writer used a claim of cause to explain the health risks the fracked gas pipeline would cause, and another opted for a claim of evaluation, because her purpose was to expose an unfair (in her view) assault on the health of everyday people. Arguments become practical when writers know where they stand on issues and the claim and information they want their audiences to accept. In the matter of the fracked gas pipeline, writers used certain argumentative strategies to dignify and address a matter of great local concern. These individuals believed that many people would suffer from the effects of methane gas emissions, especially children, the elderly, and people with upper respiratory conditions. Their structured arguments allowed them a voice. At this point, construction of the plant continues—as does the regular back-and-forth between opponents and supporters. Politics and professional agendas being what they are, we know that even the very strongest arguments can sometimes have little effect on an audience. But it is essential that you put your best foot forward when you feel strongly about an issue, even when there is no immediate promise of success. This is precisely what these student writers have done. While construction of the plant has not stopped, their voices are now audible and part of an increasingly important conversation in the community and in classrooms. Their voices are clear because they built complete arguments, arguments that included clear claims and justification for their claims.

● – – – – – – – – – – – ●

In order to go public with a claim and a successful argument that addresses an issue of concern, you must include all the elements essential to a sound argument. What is your preferred method of getting started on this process? Contrast the challenge of building an argument with challenges posed by writing assignments in other classes. What are your observations?

CHAPTER 11

Support an Argument with Fact (*Logos*), Credibility (*Ethos*), and Emotion (*Pathos*)

Learning Objectives

By working through this chapter, you will be able to

- identify the types of support that can be used in an argument.
- determine when and where to use each type of support in an argument.

For the past three semesters you have been on the dean's list at your university. This semester, you have worked particularly diligently, even cutting back hours at work, in order to make the president's list. You are extremely upset and confused, then, when you check your grades and see that you have a "D" in your English course. You did not receive comments on your final essay, so you do not know what happened with that assignment.

You've ranted to your friends and cried to your parents, but you have not yet contacted your professor. She has not been very friendly throughout the semester and you are frankly intimidated by her. Instead, you filed an arbitration request, and a meeting has been set for you, your professor, and the arbitration committee. Meanwhile, you gather all of your graded essays, along with your professor's comments, copies of the current essay, and your professor's syllabus. You are hoping that having a moderator between you and your professor will allow you to express your concerns and obtain a grade change.

All Illustrations by iStock.com/A-dig t

273

COMMUNITY

School-Academic
Workplace
Family-Household
Neighborhood
Social-Cultural
Consumer
Concerned Citizen

TOPIC: Grades
ISSUE: Unfair Semester Grade
AUDIENCE: Arbitration Committee
CLAIM: My semester grade in English is unfairly low and needs to be changed.

In Chapter 2, "Explore an Issue that Matters to You," you learned how to focus on the needs and values of your argument's audience. In Chapter 3, "Develop a Research Plan," you discovered some great sources of material that will support your claim. What do you do with all of that material, though? This chapter helps you to decide what to do with the material you've gathered. What kinds of support should be used at various points in your argument? Given what you know about your audience and the type of claim you are making, you'll now learn how to determine which of three kinds of support (factual, emotional, or personal credibility) best back your claim.

Field-Specific Support

As you probably know, people are not easily convinced of anything: they need different kinds of proof before they buy into an idea. Your first step in gathering support for your claim must be to determine what kind of support will be acceptable to your audience.

When looking for evidence to support your claims, you must first determine what types of evidence are appropriate in your field. Will the support that is acceptable in a biology class be acceptable in a political science class as well? Will the types of evidence you need to support your evaluation of new business sites be different from the types of evidence you would supply to the IRS in a dispute of your taxes?

A science class may value observation, results of experiments, and lab reports. Your English teacher would prefer your own ideas and interpretations of a novel shored up by literary theory. A sociology course may value interviews; a business course, case studies. You may want to call attention to the abusive treatment of women in domestic violence relationships using emotionally charged language. This may be appropriate in a women's studies course; however, it may be inappropriate in your

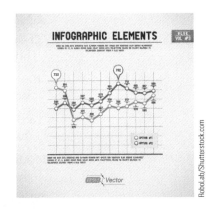
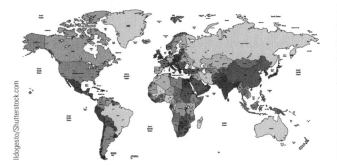

Figure 11.1 An audience needs a variety of proofs before it can believe an argument. The arguer's task is to filter through the support to find the proofs best suited to an audience.

business writing course, for example, in a paper on the costs of domestic violence to the workplace.

It is important to understand your audience, and part of doing so is knowing what type of support it values. For example, if your audience is involved in a particular industry or profession, you can research trade and scholarly journals and read books in the field in order to determine what kinds of evidence the authors use. If you are writing to colleagues about your own field of study, you will improve your chances of supplying the best support for your arguments by asking colleagues, bosses, and professors for guidance.

Find Support for the Physical Sciences

Students in chemistry, biology, physics, engineering, and geology courses look to observation to determine how the world works. Lab reports and literature reviews help these students develop their arguments. Arguments in these courses can use the following as support:

- Results of experiments
- Observation logs

Additional Resources for Writing in the Sciences

"Chemistry Writing Guide." Swarthmore University Writing Center, 2019, https://www.swarthmore.edu/writing/chemistry-writing-guide.

"Health Sciences: Essays." La Trobe University Library, 2018, https://latrobe.libguides.com/writing/health-sciences.

"Lab Reports." The Center for Global Communication and Design, Rensselaer, 2018, https://www.commd.rpi.edu/resources/.

McMillan, Victoria E. *Writing Papers in the Biological Sciences*. 6th ed., Bedford/St. Martin's, 2016.

"Writing in the Sciences: A Handout." University of North Carolina. https://writingcenter.unc.edu/tips-and-tools/sciences.

Many disciplines that call for American Psychological Association (APA) formatting use a similar organization with headings. You will usually have to provide a cover page as well.

Cover pages include a running head and page numbers in the headings. The student name, class number, school name, and date are usually included on the cover page as well.

Visit the Online Writing Lab at Purdue University for a sample APA paper, with a cover page to follow: https://owl.purdue.edu/owl/research_and _citation/apa_style/apa_formatting_and_style_guide/apa_sample _paper.html

---

Sections of a Typical Science Lab Report

The sections for many science and social sciences essays are as follows:

Abstract: Provides a summary of the research.

Introduction: Provides the hypothesis that will be tested.

Materials and Methods: Describe how the research will be conducted, what materials will be used, and how the results will be evaluated.

Results: Explain what was discovered.

Discussion: Explains what the results mean, and often what should be done next or what implications the results imply for future research.

References: Cite sources in the preferred style: APA, CSE, or other style required by the instructor.

Find Support for Education, History, and Social and Behavioral Sciences

For writers in education, the emphasis is often on defining educational problems and suggesting solutions. Students of history, anthropology, and sociology examine how people live, in the past and now. Political science students ask questions about the workings of governments. Economics students try to figure out how economies work. Arguments in these courses can use the following as support:

- Statistics
- Interviews
- Surveys
- Artifacts
- Documentaries
- Primary sources such as newspapers, diaries, photographs, bills of sale, deeds, and advertisements
- Audio and visual documentaries

Sample Social Sciences Essay Excerpt

Joe Student

SOC 202

Central Piedmont Community College

March 15, 2019

Cell Phones and Society

The use of cell phones in today's society increases seemingly by the minute. Many people have their phones physically on or near them constantly. They have become not just a device for calling friends and family, but a multimedia toy with endless functions and features. What used to be used strictly to talk to others has evolved into a miniature computer that delivers countless functions from what used to take multiple appliances. Many people use phones for other functions more than they actually use them to call someone. I would like to know what functions people are using their cell phones for most often.

.....

Cell phones are amazing tools for networking and communicating and a great source for entertainment, but there are certain times when it is inappropriate to use them. Using a cell phone while driving is a huge distraction, which can be extremely dangerous. According to Francescutti (2012), drivers who use cell phones increase their chances of having a collision by four to six times. North Carolina Statute 20-137.4 (2009) states that it is unlawful to "manually enter multiple letters or text in the device as a means of communicating

(continued)

with another person or read any electronic mail or text message transmitted to the device or stored within the device."

The following observations were made at the retail plant nursery named *D– Gardens* in H–, NC. A retail plant nursery is a great location to perform an observational study because it attracts men and women of all different ages and races; although, the people observed were often distracted by the many flowers and garden displays, so they may have been using their phones differently than they would have in another setting. The observations made are just a small sample size as a result of the time constraints of the study. They were only in the nursery for a small portion of their day. The observer for this study was a 25-year-old Caucasian male who works at the aforementioned retail plant nursery. Some of the people observed communicated with the observer.

Although the observer did not conduct any interviews, the questions that would have been asked are as follows: Do you use your cell phone most for talking, texting, the Internet, taking pictures, social media? How many hours per day on average are you away from your cell phone? About how many hours per day do you use your cell phone? Do you ever use your cell phone while driving? What is your favorite function of your cell phone?

While observing, a code was devised to make keeping track of people's actions easier. There were four basic actions observed. Talking on the phone was given then code "T," using the camera was named "C," using the Internet was "I," and texting was given the code "X."

	Gender	Age	Action
Person 1	Male	Middle-Aged	Internet
Person 2	Female	Senior	Talk
Person 3	Male	Senior	Talk
Person 4	Male	Middle-Aged	Camera/Text
Person 5	Female	Middle-Aged	Talk
Person 6	Male	Senior	Talk
Person 7	Female	Senior	Camera
Person 8	Male	Young	Internet/Camera
Person 9	Female	Middle-Aged	Camera
Person 10	Female	Middle-Aged	Camera

Figure 1 Coded observations, from *D– Gardens*

(continued)

References

Francescutti, L. (2012). Cell phone use and driving. In *Encyclopedia of lifestyle medicine and health*. Thousand Oaks, CA: SAGE Publications. Retrieved from http://ezproxy.cpcc.edu/login?qurl=http%3A%2F%2Fsearch .credoreference.com.ezproxy.cpcc.edu%2Fcontent%2Fentry%2Fsag ehm%2Fcell_phone_use_and_driving%2F0.

North Carolina Statute 20-137.4 (2009). *General Assembly Of North Carolina, Session 2009*, https://www.ncleg.net/Sessions/2009/Bills /House/HTML/H9v5.html.

Additional Resources for Writing in the Social Sciences

"Anthropology." University of North Carolina. https://writingcenter.unc .edu/tips-and-tools/anthropology.

"History." University of North Carolina. https://writingcenter.unc.edu /tips-and-tools/history.

Rosnow, Ralph, and Mimi Rosnow. *Writing Papers in Psychology*. 9th ed. Cengage, 2012.

"Sociology." University of North Carolina. https://writingcenter.unc.edu /tips-and-tools/sociology.

Find Sources for the Humanities and the Arts

What counts as support in humanities courses such as literature, art, music, and philosophy? In humanities courses, the emphasis is on interpretation based on close reading, listening, and viewing. Arguments in these courses can use the following as support:

- The actual texts, films, pieces of art or architecture, or pieces of music being studied
- Critical articles published in scholarly journals
- Interviews with authors and performers

Sample Humanities Essay Excerpt

Jane Student

Professor McNair

HUM 212

March 3, 2019

Madonna with the Long Neck as a Mannerist Painting

The Renaissance painter Parmigianino created *Madonna and Child with Angels and St. Jerome*, which is better known as the *Madonna with the Long Neck*. The reason why is not difficult to figure out. The figure of

(continued)

Mary in the painting has not only a really long neck, but also long arms, long fingers, and long toes. Several of the figures are elongated. In fact, elongation is one of the characteristics of a style of painting called mannerism. *Madonna and Child with Angels and St. Jerome* features several characteristics of mannerism.

Contemporary critics are not always enamored with the strange artificial style of mannerism. The article on mannerism at the National Gallery of Art explains several features elongation, convoluted poses, and a setting that invokes anxiety, among other characteristics.

The first feature we see of mannerism in the painting is the elongation. The image of Mary is stretched out to uncomfortable lengths. Her body feels unnatural. Andrew Morrall traces a line of development in the Renaissance of art that is shows a "deliberate and exaggerated ugliness" (80).

Works Cited

"Mannerism." National Gallery of Art. https://www.nga.gov/features/slideshows/mannerism.html.

Morrall, Andrew. "Defining the Beautiful in Early Renaissance Germany." *Concepts of Beauty in Renaissance Art*, edited by Francis Ames-Lewis and Mary Rogers, Routledge, 1998, pp. 80–92.

Additional Resources for Writing in the Humanities

Barnet, Sylvan. *A Short Guide to Writing about Art*. 11th ed., Pearson, 2014.

Barnet, Sylvan, and William E. Cain. *A Short Guide to Writing about Literature*. 12th ed., Pearson, 2012.

Bellman, Jonathan. *A Short Guide to Writing about Music*. 2nd ed., Pearson, 2007.

Corrigan, Timothy. *A Short Guide to Writing about Film*. 9th ed., Pearson, 2015.

Seech, Zachary. *Writing Philosophy Papers*. 5th ed., Cengage, 2009.

your turn 11a **PRACTICE Identifying Field-Specific Support**

What kinds of evidence are acceptable in your field? Make a list of the types of support you can use in your classes or in your job. If you are unsure, ask your professor, your boss, coworkers. You can also ask a librarian to help you find journals in your field. What sources do the authors of the journal articles use to support their arguments?

Use All Three General Kinds of Support

In general, there are three categories of support that can be used in an argument. *Logos*, *pathos*, and *ethos* are the traditional Greek terms given to these categories. Let's begin with *logos*. **Logos**, or support based on facts, refers to the more traditional types of support that we tend to think of first in our writing. For example, if I am arguing that cell phones should be mandatory in every vehicle sold in America, support in the *logos* category could include statistics about how many lives are saved by 911 calls made from cell phones, how much safer it is for drivers to be able to call AAA or towing services from their car, or the time saved by being able to conduct business while driving.

But there are other ways to persuade a reader who may be skeptical about your cell phone argument. **Ethos** is a term that refers to one's authority or expertise on a topic, one's credibility. If, for instance, you own a cell phone yourself, you are in a better position of authority to discuss the advantages of cell phones than someone who doesn't own one. Think about celebrities who provide testimonials for products and services, as shown in Figure 11.2. The audience is supposed to be convinced that, if Ariana Grande uses Brand Q makeup and looks great, then if they use Brand Q, they will look great too. So does this mean that if you don't own a cell phone or wear Brand Q makeup that you cannot write about these products? Of course not. It simply means that you might not have a lot of authority. Always ensure the sources you use to establish your credibility are good and reliable.

The term **pathos** is used to refer to emotional appeal that comes from support such as stories, illustrations, charts, or photos. In our cell phone example, we could use a story of people stranded on the side of the road who used their cell phones to obtain help for their 90-year-old grandmother who was having a heart attack: see how this works? Be careful, though. A story that sounds unconvincing or seems manipulative may backfire. A judicious use of all three types of support will produce the most convincing argument.

Your strongest essays will include combinations of all three types of support. You also need to be able to identify the types of support used in other people's arguments in order to understand the arguments' strengths and weaknesses. If an argument is too loaded with logical support—that is, the argument has lots of facts and figures, statistics, percentages, charts of numbers, and so on—then it will make very little connection with the audience. If an argument depends too heavily on stories and anecdotes, especially those designed to arouse anger or pity in an audience, then emotion has been achieved, but understanding of the topic may be lacking. A healthy combination of all three types of support is your goal.

Vince Bucci/Getty Images for Crest

Figure 11.2 Actor and musician Nick Cannon introduces Crest Whitening Plus Scope Extreme Toothpaste at the launch of a product website.

Good examples of arguments or persuasion using multiple types of support are the commercials that seek donations for children in impoverished conditions. A commercial may begin with a credible spokesperson, usually a recognizable celebrity (*ethos*), telling the audience that for X amount of money they can support a child in Bolivia for a year (*logos*). The ultimate purpose of these commercials, however, is to part people from their money. Although the viewer may find the pitch so far interesting, he is unlikely to open his wallet until an emotional push (*pathos*) is applied. This is the part of the commercial where you see images of barefoot children digging through massive garbage piles searching for food to eat or listless children with distended stomachs too weak to brush away hovering flies. It is the photography that hits us and propels us to act. Let's look at each appeal individually to see how each works in action.

Use Support Based on Facts and Research (*Logos*)

Logical support, or *logos*, is defined as support that appeals to the audience's reason: facts, figures, statistics, and scientific data. When most people think of facts, they think of cold, hard, logical science. They think of logic as a way of pursuing the truth. The large number of television programs featuring detectives, both fictional and factual, attest to the public's belief that crimes are best solved in a logical manner. The true-crime television series *Cold Case Files* presents numerous cases that are solved solely on the basis of physical evidence. In court cases, forensic evidence—such as blood spatter patterns, DNA matches, and bullet matches—is a great persuader of juries.

There is no disagreement that logical, physical evidence is extremely important in solving crimes and arguing before juries. Your arguments, though, may rarely take you into court. What are other types of logical evidence that can be used in argument?

Although we can all agree that facts are important in an argument, sometimes it can be difficult to separate fact from opinion.

Facts and Opinions

What exactly is a fact? The question seems nonsensical until you examine it closely. To Aristotle, a scholar of ancient Greece, it was a fact that women had fewer teeth than men. To the men and women of the Middle Ages, it was a fact that the Earth was the center of the universe and the sun and planets revolved around it. Until a few years ago, the chemical composition of water was factually recorded as H_2O; according to a 2003 study, though, the chemical structure of water could well be $H_{1.5}O$. Pluto was the ninth planet in our solar system; and then it wasn't. And now the debate continues, and it may be reinstated. What has changed? The way that planets are defined as we improve the technology that we have to scan our galaxy may continue to alter our roster of planets.

Figure 11.3 Geocentric model of the universe based on the Ptolemaic system

Figure 11.4 Heliocentric model of the universe based on the Copernican system

A quick Internet search will yield many definitions of the word *fact*. Our favorite is "an indisputable truth." Obviously, this definition is disputable. A fact is only a fact until new facts come to light. Huh? Well, let's look at the "truth" surrounding the structure of the universe in the Middle Ages as an example of how facts change.

CLAIM:	A divine being created the Earth.
SUPPORT:	The Earth is the center of the universe.

The geocentric theory of the universe developed in ancient Egypt and Greece and was the view held until the sixteenth century. Figure 11.3 shows the Earth at the center of the universe and the moon, sun, and other planets revolving around it.

For people who had neither access to space travel nor to the technology to conjecture otherwise, it was common sense that the Earth (created as it was by a divine being) was at the center of all creation. However, in 1543, Nicolaus Copernicus published *De revolutionibus orbium coelestium*, which argued that the universe was actually heliocentric, or sun-centered (see Figure 11.4). What was once a fact, an indisputable truth, was no longer so.

Facts are facts only until new facts come to light. Particularly in the field of science, facts change continually, based on the technology available. In every field, facts are based on the best efforts of scholars and scientists, but facts are understood to be subject to change. The following are all facts:

- The moon is not a planet.
- Memphis is short five inches of rain for 2013.
- The population of Las Vegas is increasing at a rapid pace.

How the facts are interpreted leads to **opinions**:

- Because Memphis's rainfall is currently five inches below normal, the city is experiencing a drought.

What makes this an opinion? Well, it depends on the definition of the term *drought*. Is a designation of drought only made when the number of inches of rain falls below a certain level? Does it also have to do with how many months of low rainfall have been experienced? Some experts may believe that particular conditions justify the label of "drought." Others may disagree about which conditions should be used to make the determination.

When we supply expert opinions from authorities in a field, we are adding evidence that we cannot adequately supply ourselves. We may have an opinion about the lack of rain, but unless we are meteorologists, our assessment of a drought situation will carry little weight. Expert opinion can help us strengthen our arguments. Because expert opinion is gathered from other sources, such as interviews, articles, lectures, and so forth, it should always be credited to the expert and cited properly, whether you paraphrasing or quoting verbatim (see Chapter 4, "Evaluate and Engage with Your Sources").

So what kinds of facts can we use? All of the items in the following list can be interpreted factually. Keep in mind that the line between types of evidence is blurry. An example or a statistic can be included to spark an emotional response (*pathos*) as well as provide valuable logical information (*logos*).

- Images
  - Charts
  - Graphs
  - Photographs
- Statistics
- Scholarly articles
- Physical laws and theories
- Examples

Graphic images such as charts, tables, and photographs may make a stronger point than the metaphorical thousand words, but they are also the easiest to manipulate to the user's advantage. (See Chapter 12, "Enhance Your Argument with Visuals," to learn how you can use graphics effectively and ethically to present facts.) But graphics can be useful to visually organize information for readers, particularly information to which readers will need to refer frequently, for example, the chart of the Wechsler Adult Intelligence Scale sub-scores shown in Figure 11.5.

Statistics

Statistics can be useful to your reader. While they can be very convincing, they can also be confusing. When you select your statistics, be sure that your reader understands what point you are making with them. You can

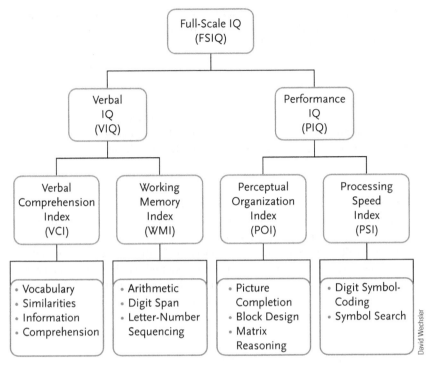

Figure 11.5 The Wechsler Adult Intelligence Scale subscores, an example of an informative graphic

use statistics when you want to compare what happens to one group versus another, as in the following example.

The National Student Clearinghouse tracks the enrollment of students at 97% of all colleges and universities in the United States. According to data from the Clearinghouse, part-time students who attended four year public colleges and universities were far more likely than full-time students to drop out within six years. Of students who attended part time, 70% had neither graduated nor remained in college after six years. In contrast, 76% of full-time students had graduated after six years, with only 20% dropping out and 4% still enrolled.[1] These statistics support the argument that students who are serious about graduating should strongly consider attending full time.

These are **descriptive statistics**. They answer questions such as, "Who did what where and when?" Statistics used to link cause and effect or to make conclusions about a group larger than the group the original research considered are called **inferential statistics**.

[1] Shapiro, Doug, et al. "Completing College: A State-Level View of Student Attainment Rates (Signature Report No. 12a)." National Student Clearinghouse, 2017.

- According to one study, students who do not take their college placement tests and the classes recommended by those tests fail to complete a degree 35 percent of the time.

Two useful books for learning how to use statistics are *Introduction to the Practice of Statistics*, by David S. Moore and George P. McCabe, and *How to Lie with Statistics*, by Darrell Huff and Irving Geis. The Online Writing Lab at Purdue University offers excellent coverage of writing with statistics as well: https://owl.purdue.edu/owl/research_and_citation/using_research/writing _with_statistics/writing_with_descriptive_statistics.html

Tips for Understanding and Using Statistics

Some of the problems that come from using statistics arise from an incomplete understanding of what the statistics indicate. If you are going to use statistics in a paper or report, be certain that *you* understand them and their significance, particularly if they come from a study that you did not conduct, which is usually the case for assigned writing. Do your best to verify that the statistics you have provided are accurate and the sources of the information are reliable by asking the questions in the Understand Statistics checklist and in Tips 11a and 11b.

Understand Statistics

- ☐ Who is the provider of your statistics?
    - ☐ Is the source you are using reputable?
    - ☐ Why is the information being gathered by the source (website, journal, etc.)?
    - ☐ Can you trust the information?
    - ☐ Does the researcher explain the methods and conditions of his research?
- ☐ Who is interpreting the data?
    - ☐ Often you will be relying on statistics not only gathered by someone else but also interpreted by someone else. Who is this person?
    - ☐ Is she respected in her field?
    - ☐ Does she supply contact information so that others can contact her to discuss her findings?
    - ☐ Is her work published in credible publications?
    - ☐ Do you feel comfortable using her interpretation of the numbers, or do you see a very different way of reading them?
    - ☐ Are you detecting serious biases?
- ☐ Explain why you are using the statistics. What is your reader to understand about the subject based on the numbers you are providing? Interpret the statistics for the reader.

☐ Organize your statistics clearly if your material is lengthy. Graphs and tables are a good way to arrange statistics of the same type (time, measurements, people, behaviors, costs, etc.). See Chapter 12, "Enhance Your Argument with Visuals," for more information on creating graphs and tables.

☐ In accord with most style manuals, do not begin a sentence with a numeral, including percentages.

Incorrect: 30.6 percent of students who earned a college degree ...

Correct: We found that 30.6 percent of students who earned a college degree . . .

☐ Don't forget to cite the source of your statistics!

tip 11a

If there is any sort of vagueness or secrecy surrounding the source of your information, it is perhaps not a good source to use.

COMMUNITY

School-Academic

Workplace

Family-Household

Neighborhood

Social-Cultural

Consumer

Concerned Citizen

TOPIC: Smoking Risks

ISSUE: Reducing Smoking on College Campuses

AUDIENCE: Student Senate

CLAIM: Because death from lung cancer is greatest in the Southeast, we must make an effort to reduce exposure to smoke by eliminating smoking from all college campuses.

Discussion

This is a good issue to support with statistical information. Today's college campuses are often quite diverse, and students of varying ages attend college today. The statistics gathered from charts available through *The Atlas of United States Mortality* found at The National Center for Health Statistics (https://www.cdc.gov/nchs/products/othcr/atlas/atlas.htm) indicate that the highest death rates for white males aged 40 from lung cancer were found in the Southeast. The rate determined from a study completed in 1992 was 12 percent. This is the kind of startling statistic that could be very persuasive.

Although this author cites a landmark study, the Atlas has not been revised. Would you still use these figures? Why or why not?

tip 11b

Numbers can be very effective in supporting your argument, but your audience has to know that these numbers can be trusted.

Additional Resources for Gathering and Using Statistics

Driscoll, Dana Lynn. "Writing with Statistics." *Purdue Online Writing Lab.* 8 January 2010. Web. http://owl.english.purdue.edu/owl/resource/672/01/.

"Finding and Using Health Statistics." *U.S. National Library of Medicine. National Institutes of Health.* https://www.nlm.nih.gov/nichsr/stats _tutorial/cover.html.

Kornblith, Gary J. "Making Sense of Numbers." *History Matters: The U.S. Survey Course on the Web.* http://historymatters.gmu.edu/mse /numbers/.

Looking for international, national, state, and local statistics? Try FedStats: http://www.fedstats.gov/regional.html

U.S. Census Bureau. https://www.census.gov.

your turn PRACTICE **Use Statistics**

Examine a set of statistics that you find in an article or on a website by answering the first two question sets in the Understand Statistics checklist. Does the information gathered and interpreted by the researcher or author seem valid based on these questions? If not, why? What is troubling about them?

Scholarly Articles

In Chapter 3, "Develop a Research Plan," you learned how to perform research to find materials that support your claims. In Chapter 4, "Evaluate and Engage with Your Sources," you learned how to document information you have found through your research. The proper use of material from these research sources can go a long way to convince your readers of the strength of your argument. Most of the support you will use in any argument is likely to come from research. Whether you are using questionnaires and surveys; magazine and journal articles; or information from interviews, websites, and documentaries; your goal is to be sure that you are using this information credibly and citing it correctly.

To determine an author's credibility, you can use the Internet to quickly get answers to the questions on the Determine Credibility checklist.

Determine Credibility

☐ Is the author attached to an institute of higher learning or a reputable company? Most people, particularly academics, have web pages affiliated with their institutions. Visit the author's page to learn more about him.

☐ Is the author published in his field? Are his publications regarded well in his field? Check for reviews of published books. Also, make sure that the journals in which he is publishing have a peer review editing policy. This means that reviewers come from within the field and are usually highly respected and knowledgeable themselves.

☐ Does the author use unprofessional language? Does she belittle her opposition or use an aggressive or sarcastic tone of voice?

☐ Does the author include support that you can verify by further research?

Guidelines for Evaluating Support Based on Fact

- Does it answer all the questions you need it to answer?
- Is the information from a reputable source?
- Does more than one source support your findings?

your turn **PRACTICE Determine Author Credibility**

Find two scholarly articles in trade- or field-specific journals. How credible are the journals and the authors? Use the questions in the Guidelines for Evaluating Support Based on Fact to determine if the authors are qualified to write on their subject.

Use Support to Create Credibility (*Ethos*)

There are three things which inspire confidence in the orator's own character—the three, namely, that induce us to believe a thing apart from any proof of it: good sense, good moral character, and goodwill (Aristotle, Rhetoric, Book II, Chapter 1, 1378a: 5–7).

Ethos is the arguer's personality—how he or she is perceived by the audience, specifically in terms of credibility or trustworthiness. Gerry Spence, the famous Wyoming lawyer who is virtually unbeatable in the courtroom, often appears in court wearing cowboy boots and a 10-gallon hat. His tone is down-to-earth, and he plays up his rural persona, or character. He wants his audience, the jury, to associate him with the law and order brought to the Wild West. He gives off an air of being trustworthy and therefore the little guy. This is Spence's character—his *ethos*.

Credibility can be based on one's character. If I am a good person, my argument may be judged to be good as well, even if it has flaws. If I believe what you believe and if I share your values, my argument may be judged as good, even if it is lacking any support. If I am a bad person or if I do not share your values, my lack of credibility in

OJO Images Ltd/Jupiter Images

Figure 11.6 The speaker achieves professional credibility by engaging her audience with handouts, a PowerPoint presentation, and her professional appearance.

your eyes is based on personality, not the support of my argument. Do not underestimate the power of personal credibility. For better or worse, we are judged for our personality as much as for our argumentative strategies.

Although the word *ethos* is related to the word *ethics*, it is not the same thing. It is undeniably important to argue in an ethical manner and not to use one's skill at persuasion for bad ends. *Ethos*, however, is a more general term used to describe the credibility a writer or speaker creates for himself. For example, when I give a lecture on nineteenth-century author Henry James to my American Literature class, my students are convinced of my credibility when they see that I have published articles on James. I have proven that I am worthy of speaking on the subject. If, however, I am teaching a business course and I don't know about TQM (Total Quality Management) or the latest quality control best practices, my students will quickly find all of my lectures on the subject suspect. They will no longer be inclined to consider me an expert.

What about you personally will lend weight to your argument? If you are writing about the dangers of fad diets, for example, what about you will lead your audience to believe your argument? Do you have a history of trying every weight loss gimmick that comes along, or do you have a family member who has that history? Have you lost a great deal of weight by sensible dieting as opposed to following a fad? What about the research you have done on the subject? Have you selected the best arguments? Used the most responsible sources? Arranged your material in such a way that your audience is convinced you know what you are talking about?

Like Gerry Spence, you need to decide how to properly present yourself when you are presenting an argument.

Types of support that create positive credibility:

- **Personal anecdotes.** Do you have a brief personal story that will convince your audience of your connection to the subject of your argument? For example, if you are a believer in cell phone use in cars, perhaps you have an anecdote of a time when a cell phone call saved your or someone else's life.

- **Unbiased consideration of opposing or alternate views.** How you treat any opposing arguments reflects upon your character. Are you negative or sarcastic in discussing alternate views? If so, your tone of voice may damage your credibility with your audience. Being respectful of others' views will help you earn your audience's respect.

- **Strong and careful presentation of support.** If your argument is based on research, be certain that all of your quotations are accurate, that your material is not misrepresented, and that your documentation is clean; sloppy editing and inaccuracies can lead your audience to doubt you and, in turn, your argument.

To increase your credibility, then, you must provide strong evidence retrieved from credible sources, and you must present the evidence without errors in logic or writing, organized in the best way possible.

How you relate to your audience, in writing or speaking, will determine how well your claims and supporting examples are received. If they are well received, you are on your way to persuading your audience. Tone of voice is one way to create a persona readers can relate to and trust. The tone of the writer's voice is related to the point of view being used.

- First person: When a speaker uses *I*, she is relating directly to the audience and discussing the argument as it relates to her.
  - Plus: The audience feels that the speaker has authority or background that makes her an expert or someone who can be trusted to speak on the topic.
  - Minus: The audience may focus on the speaker more than on the topic of the argument.
- Second person: When a speaker uses *you*, and directly addresses her audience, she forges a connection that is based on a direct sharing of information.
  - Plus: The speaker can take on a teacherly or mentoring role.
  - Minus: The speaker can take on a lecturing tone of voice, which can be off-putting to an audience.
- Third person: When a speaker uses *they*, she is focusing on the information at hand and not the audience or her own role in the argument.
  - Plus: The focus is on the argument and nothing personal or anecdotal.
  - Minus: The connection between speaker and audience is weakened by the lack of personal interaction.

Each argument and audience is different, so you will need to do some research to determine which tone of voice is best used in each given situation. In general, academic arguments should be made in the third person with limited personal involvement, unless a professor has authorized first or second person.

Guidelines for Evaluating Support to Establish Credibility

- Does your support make you appear to be an expert on the subject?
- Is all your research well cited and properly formatted?
- Are quotes and paraphrases treated properly?
- If you are using testimonials, do the people who provided them have valid reasons for supporting your ideas?

your turn ➤ **GET STARTED Establish Your Credibility**

Use the "Guidelines for Evaluating Support to Establish Credibility" to review the support you have gathered for your argument.

Use Support to Create Emotion (*Pathos*)

To accomplish your goal of persuading an audience and building the strongest possible argument, use all three types of support. Some writers are often reluctant to use emotion, or *pathos*, in their papers, feeling that to do so is being manipulative or unethical. Other writers use too much emotion, at the cost of providing too little logical support. Aim for balance even as you purposely evoke your audience's emotions. It is also important to know when it would be inappropriate to use emotional appeal. *Pathos* is support that attempts to make a connection with one's audience through anecdotes or graphics that evoke emotion.

The methods you use to evoke an emotional response should be based on your understanding of your audience's values, or what its cultural or historical beliefs are. For example, if you are arguing that children's fashions may be too suggestive and that instituting a school dress code would eliminate this problem, you need to understand what your audience feels about both children's clothing in general and school uniforms in particular.

Before you can select supporting reasons, you need to understand the audience's belief system. What are some of the things parents value in terms of their children?

- Safety
- Cost of clothing
- Comfort
- Individuality
- School performance

COMMUNITY

School-Academic

Workplace

Family-Household

Neighborhood

Social-Cultural

Consumer

Concerned Citizen

TOPIC: Children's Clothing

ISSUE: Children Wearing Suggestive Clothing

AUDIENCE: Parents of School-Age Children

CLAIM: The problem of suggestive clothing worn by school children can be eliminated with the adoption of a school uniform policy.

Discussion

Once you understand what your audience values, it is easier to find reasons that appeal to these values. Then you should determine when and where in your argument an appeal to emotions might work. Yes, parents want their children to be comfortable and they don't want to spend a lot of money on clothing. They may even be somewhat concerned that uniforms or a dress code may stifle creativity and individuality. But of these five values, the two that should stand out as being candidates for emotional support are safety and school performance.

Do you have any statistics about how teenagers perform better when they are not distracted by skimpy skirts or revealing tops? Do you have any scary stories about the dangers to girls wearing suggestive clothing? Statistics that shock and stories that scare are powerful tools in your arsenal of support—as long as you don't overdo it.

Anecdotes

It is often hard for people to connect to big issues until there are individuals to connect with. Individual stories allow an arguer to take an abstract topic and make it concrete and specific. They also help to create common ground with an audience, especially when the audience can identify with, or at least sympathize with the individuals. Persuading an audience is more effective when you can get it on your side.

For example, tax reform is a large, important, yet abstract issue. Making it matter to your audience is easier when you can show how it would affect the lives of ordinary people. On January 24, 2012, when President Obama raised the issue in his State of the Union address, he pointed to Debbie Bosanek, a secretary from Bellevue, Nebraska. She was remarkable for two reasons: one, that she was taxed at a higher rate than her boss, and two, that her boss happened to be Warren Buffett, a billionaire.

Anecdotes, or brief stories, can be used in your argument whenever a good story is needed, but they are particularly well suited to introductions. A good story must have these elements:

- It must be brief. Stories that go on and on will begin to bore the reader. Make it short and to the point, using only those details that are needed to set the scene.

- It must seem real. When a hypothetical story is unrealistic or feels contrived, readers will know that the story has been created to fit the topic.

You can also choose language in telling a story that you know will evoke emotion (sometimes called "loaded language"). Consider this opening from the student argument on fracking that appears in the APA Appendix:

> In Kerns County, California, a cherry orchard is dying. In Washington County, Pennsylvania, a hillside is slipping away. In Shelby County, Texas, a bathtub walks itself down a hallway. In Logan County, West Virginia, a bulldozer plows up the graves of World War II veterans to make a road. In Colorado, a goat gives birth to a head. In Wisconsin, a thousand trucks a day blow by a woman's house, filling it with toxic sand. Her stabling business has been ruined and she fears that her twenty-two month old daughter is at risk.

In addition to using anecdotes, the writer increases the emotion by listing many frightening incidents, and by using colored language designed to register emotionally—words and phrases such as slipping away, ruined, plowing up graves, blowing by a house. The writer also introduces a character most likely to elicit an emotional response: a toddler who is threatened.

Finally, never underestimate the value of humor in establishing an emotional link with your audience. Chapter 12, "Enhance Your Argument with Visuals," provides more insight into using humor effectively to break the ice with your audience and helping you make sometimes complex or abstract issues more relatable.

Photographs

Photographs go a long way to evoke emotion in an audience. Along with emotion-laden stories, images can produce an effect in your reader that a mere presentation of logical facts cannot. The images here are so familiar that they have become **iconic**. An iconic image is one that represents so much more to the viewer than just the contents of the image itself. It has risen above pictorial representation to become symbolic.

Images such as these can evoke strong emotional responses to your argument. For more information on how to use images in an ethical and appropriate manner, see the material on visual arguments in Chapter 12, "Enhance Your Argument with Visuals."

Figure 11.7 A memorial in Sandy Hook, Connecticut, commemorates the victims of the school shooting on December 14, 2012.

Using Humor in Your Arguments

Geeta is in the same Natural Resources and Environment course as Alejo. She is working on an argument in favor of a vegetarian diet.

She has run across figures stating that it takes 2,500 gallons of freshwater to produce one pound of beef. This is because most beef is made by feeding corn to cows, and most of that corn is grown in irrigated fields. Most of that water is lost from the freshwater supplies. In that sense, eating beef is much harder on the water supply than eating vegetables and grains, which are grown and fed directly to us, instead of traveling first through the digestive systems of livestock. In the course of her research, Geeta discovers that the average American eats 100 pounds of beef per year, and she wants to illustrate how much water the average American uses each day by eating beef. She also wants to show that using water by eating beef is a waste because it is unnecessary for health and nutrition. It's like flushing that water down the toilet. Toilets happen to use 1.6 gallons of water per flush. Here was a place for her to use humor in her argument:

> The average American eats 100 pounds of beef per year, and it takes about 2,500 gallons of fresh water to produce one pound of beef. How much water is that per day? To find out, go home and flush your 1.6 gallons-per-flush toilet. Now flush it again. And again. And five more times. By this point, someone else in your household might have become worried. To throw them off your scent, you should probably groan, and speak softly through the door, asking for the name of a good gastroenterologist. Then flush the toilet 40 more times. But wait, you're not done yet. Push that handle another 200 times. No one in his right mind (or bowels) would ever stand there and waste the water it would take to flush the toilet 248 times, right? But that's just what we're doing every day by eating beef.

That illustration could have been created without the humor, and it would still be effective. It's an amazing statistic to say that by eating beef we use the equivalent of 248 toilet flushes every day. However, the humor may help to win the trust of the audience by sounding less preachy than the information would sound without the humor. It also serves to make the blind wastefulness more concrete, clearly showing the ridiculous excesses of human consumption.

Guidelines for Evaluating Support to Evoke Emotion

- Is the emotion you are evoking relevant to the subject?
- Are you being respectful of your audience's ideas and values? Is any humor used culturally appropriate?
- If you are using hypothetical situations, are they brief and relevant?

 **Tip 11c**

When Is Humor Appropriate?
There are times when humor has a place in an argument:

- To make a stressful situation seem less stressful.
- To establish an alliance with the audience indicating that "We are all in this together; I am part of your group; I understand your culture, and I demonstrate this via my use of humor that you understand."
- To make oneself appear to be less threatening or appear to be an insider.
- As a way to bridge the distance between disparate groups or views.
- To avoid confrontation.

 **Tip 11d**

When Is Humor Inappropriate?
There are also times when you should not use humor in an argument:

- To belittle another group's values, beliefs, or customs.
- To enforce negative stereotypes.
- To disguise an attack on an opponent's character (just as we would avoid the fallacy of *ad hominem*—see Chapter 5, "Read Critically and Avoid Fallacies").
- To forge an alliance with an audience in order to feel superior over another group.
- To draw attention away from weak support of your claim.
- To play for laughs with off-color jokes or jokes based on sexual innuendoes, body parts, or body functions.

David Livingston/Getty Images

Figure 11.8 Sgt. 1st Class Charles Shuck and retired military dog Gabe, who completed more than 200 combat missions in Iraq.

your turn   **PRACTICE Determine the Function of Emotion**

- From a daily newspaper, select a story that is not illustrated and that does not include any personal anecdotes. Is the story effective? Why or why not?
- Select a story that seems to need either anecdotes or graphics to elicit emotion. What stories or graphics would you suggest to the author to help him capture the hearts of his readers?
- Some graphics relate to a specific topic so strongly that they can almost replace the written text. For example, Figure 11.8 shows a military dog with over 200 combat missions under its collar. What story does it tell? What emotions does it convey? Can you find other images that are strong enough to convey or even provoke emotion without accompanying words?

Reflect and Apply

1. What sources are you using to guide your writing strategies for your assignment? Are you writing an argument for biology, sociology, education, or English? The expectations for arguments in each of these areas are unique.

2. How are you ensuring that you have separated fact from opinion—your own and those of your selected research?

3. How are you establishing your credibility? Do you have insider knowledge about this issue? If so, how are you incorporating your own expertise with your research while avoiding personal opinion and bias?

4. Explain why you are or are not using sources that elicit emotions. Is an emotional response from your audience appropriate for the field of your assignment? Why or why not?

5. If it is appropriate to create an emotional response in your audience, how are you ensuring that you are not going so far as to manipulate the audience in an unethical manner?

KEEPING IT LOCAL

IN A RESEARCH PAPER, during a work dispute, in court—these are all places where you will be judged on the evidence you bring to the table. Audiences of your peers, your instructors, and even a jury are not persuaded by only one type of support.

Returning to the example that opened this chapter, consider that your grade change could well hinge on the evidence you have brought to the arbitration meeting. Your facts (e.g., past essay grades, professor syllabus, and policies) combined with your credibility (i.e., your academic standing at the university) and comments made by the professor (e.g., derogatory comments), which serve to provoke anger from the committee, may show that your grade was indeed unfairly evaluated.

Your supporting materials along with your own credibility present a package to your audience, whether they are present to listen to your claim or are reading your argument in print. Think about the package you want to present in order to be successful in your argument.

How are you representing yourself and your claim? Have you gathered all the facts, and are you presenting them clearly in charts or graphs, in a well-organized narrative with properly documented sources? Do you know when it is proper, even necessary, to use emotional support? How are you representing yourself physically and vocally?

PART FOUR

How to Take Ownership of Your Argument: A Style Guide

CHAPTER 12 Enhance Your Argument with Visuals

CHAPTER 13 Develop and Edit Argument Structure and Style

All Illustrations by iStock.com/A-digit

CHAPTER 12

Enhance Your Argument with Visuals

Learning Objectives

By working through this chapter, you will be able to

- identify the strengths and weaknesses of visual arguments.
- interpret visual arguments (including graphs, photographs, and ad campaigns).
- implement visual arguments effectively in your writing.

After driving past several gas stations searching for a lower price, you realize that you are wasting gas (and money) and pull into the next station. Because last month's hurricane shut down several major pipelines, gas has been scarce and prices are high. You read an article this morning that extolled the virtues of hydraulic fracturing, known as "fracking," and domestic drilling as alternatives to importing oil. A rebuttal by an environmental activist pointed out the dangers to farm animals in areas where fracking has taken place. Is tapping American oil reserves worth long-term dangers to the food we eat?

All Illustrations by iStock.com/A-digit

COMMUNITY	TOPIC: Environment
School-Academic	ISSUE: Domestic Oil Production
Workplace	AUDIENCE: U.S. Government
Family-Household	CLAIM: There should be no fracking or drilling for oil in the United States because the risk of major impact on the environment outweighs the minor impact on oil supplies.
Neighborhood	
Social-Cultural	
Consumer	
Concerned Citizen	

What Are Visual Arguments?

When we think of visual argument, we most often think about advertisements. It's true that this is the form of visual persuasion that we encounter most frequently. But there are many other forms of visual arguments:

- Tattoos
- Hair styles
- Car models
- Viral videos
- Political cartoons
- Fashion
- Art and architecture
- Photographs

All of these forms, and many others, are arguments. They make a claim, and they support that claim by the images they use, their colors, their layout, and the medium in which they appear.

Visual imagery can be very powerful. Witness the effects of images of the devastation of a natural disaster (Figure 12.1), the horror of war (Figure 12.2), or the pride felt by a winning team (Figure 12.3).

AB Forces News Collection/Alamy Stock Photo

Figure 12.1 Aerial view of the aftermath of Hurricane Maria, the storm that hit Puerto Rico on September 20, 2017.

Popperfoto/Getty Images

Figure 12.2 John Sharpe of Leicester who was a prisoner of War in an internment camp, World War II, September 28, 1945.

Ezra Shaw/Getty Images Sport/Getty Images

Figure 12.3 The Chicago Cubs celebrating their historic 2016 World Series win.

internet activity 12a **Evaluate Web Images**

Visit several news sites on the Internet. How do they use images in their reports? On at least three different websites, identify stories covering the same issue or event. What is different about the way images are used in the three stories? Consider the emotions that are being evoked. Are these emotions appropriate to the news story? How well do the images relate to the storyline?

These sites are the most frequently visited for breaking news:

https://www.cnn.com
https://www.cbsnews.com
https://news.google.com
https://news.yahoo.com
https://www.msn.com
https://www.foxnews.com
https://www.time.com

https://www.nytimes.com
https://news.bbc.co.uk
https://abcnews.go.com
https://www.reuters.com
https://www.worldnews.com
https://www.cbc.ca/news
https://www.ap.org

Understanding and Using Visual Arguments

You can profitably use visual arguments in your own writing when you want to make an emotional impact that will be heightened by the use of images. Photographs, charts, and graphs can also add credibility to the facts you

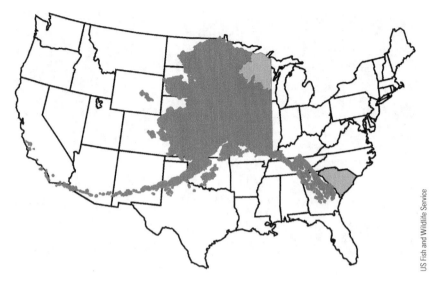

US Fish and Wildlife Service

Figure 12.4 A comparison of the area that is being studied for oil drilling to the state of Alaska specifically and to the United States in general.

are using. You will occasionally be asked to provide an argument based totally on visual elements. More often, however, you will be asked to create arguments that include visual elements that bolster your written support. Other times, you will encounter images that make arguments or that are part of arguments that you need to consider critically.

How do we read a visual argument coolly, without allowing what we see to overly affect our emotions? How do we avoid knee-jerk reactions and instead follow up on the story behind the images? It's not easy. Let's take as an example an argument that many people have forwarded over email in recent years, an argument about drilling in the Arctic National Wildlife Refuge, or ANWR. Reading over this type of email message, it's very easy to agree with the arguer's claim that drilling should be allowed. The photographs are quite convincing (see Figures 12.4 and 12.5). Maybe too convincing ...

The anonymous author of the original email (anonymity is tipoff number one—always be skeptical of authors who don't take responsibility for their work) is asking the audience to compare the land that is earmarked for drill-ing, a small area of the green ANWR region, to the size of the United States. What is being implied? That such a small area is nothing compared with the entire United States. But no one is suggesting that we drill for oil in the entire United States. An either–or fallacy is being set up: either we drill in this one tiny spot or we risk the need to drill everywhere.

Then the author provides another image of Alaska (Figure 12.5) with the exact location of ANWR pinpointed. Again, we're being asked to consider that these 2,000 acres are nothing in comparison to the area that is *not* being drilled.

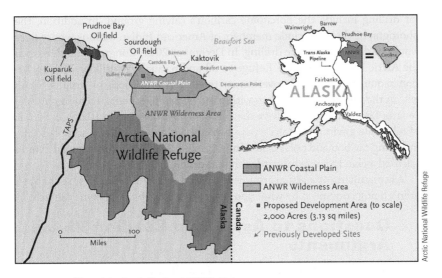

Figure 12.5 Map of the Arctic National Wildlife Refuge.

This very informative map shows the exact location of the drilling and marks the location of other drilling sites. The Kuparuk oil field is the second largest oil field in the United States and is expected to yield 2 billion barrels of oil. It operates on a site that is not part of a wildlife refuge. Although studies indicate that the demands of an oil field would damage the wilderness area of proposed drilling, known as Area 1002, they also indicate that after costs of extracting and producing the oil, between 3.2 billion and 5 billion barrels of oil would reach market. That's a staggering amount. The Kuparuk oil field has been operating since 1981 and is not yet tapped out.

But all of these images, as convincing as they may be in arguing that drilling will not affect the environment, cannot answer the question, "Will the cost and effort required to drill in these areas make us any less dependent on foreign oil?" Some studies indicate that production in the proposed drilling location would not reach its peak until 2030 and would reduce our need for imported oil by only 9 percent.

An argument made by other photographs in the email (see Figure 12.6) is that wildlife would not be affected by the drilling or the facilities needed for production. The animals in these photographs certainly do not look bothered by the facilities. On the other hand, the photos do not tell you that the areas proposed

Figure 12.6 Caribou along the oil pipeline. Kuparuk Oil Field Arctic, AK.

for drilling include the porcupine caribou's calving ground. In addition, the photographs do not include members of American Indian nations whose lives would be disrupted by the drilling. In December 2017, Congress voted to open the Arctic National Wildlife Refuge to oil and natural gas drilling. The legislation requires the federal government to hold two auctions of drilling leases within the refuge's coastal plain within 10 years. Proponents, including Alaska senator Lisa Murkowski, believe that the area holds more than 10 billion barrels of oil, while environmentalists point out the vulnerable animal and plant life, including caribou and polar bears. In December 2018, President Donald Trump released a plan to move forward with that drilling.

As convincing as a visual argument can be, you want to make sure that you aren't being convinced by what you see, rather than by your own research.

Questions to Ask While Reading Visual Arguments

☐ Does the argument target a specific audience?

☐ Is the claim clearly stated in the images, the layout, and/or any included text?

☐ Do you detect any bias or stereotypes based on gender, religion, nationality, economic class, or ethnicity? Are you being asked as a reader/viewer to identify with any of these biases?

☐ What assumptions does the argument make about either the target audience or the claim itself?

☐ Is the argument relying on facts or on emotion to make its claim? Are patriotic or religious icons or symbols used in order to get your attention or to claim affiliation with the reader/viewer?

☐ What is not in the image? Are only certain genders, races, or economic backgrounds included?

your turn 12a ▶ **PRACTICE Read Visual Arguments**

Visit any of these sites and "read" the argument that is being made, using the checklist "Questions to Ask While Reading Visual Arguments."

• The White House https://www.whitehouse.gov/search/?s=photos
• Controversial Benetton Ad Campaigns http://www.benettongroup .com/media-press/image-gallery/institutional-communication /historical-campaigns/
• World War II Army Recruitment Posters (select one) https:// www.archives.gov/exhibits/powers_of_persuasion/powers_of _persuasion_intro.htmlhttps://www.archives.gov/exhibits/powers _of_persuasion/powers_of_persuasion_intro.html

Also, there are a number of websites that house vintage advertisements. These ads have strong arguments that can be read as well.

Let's explore an example of how to read and structure a visual argument. For his Natural Resources and Environment course, Alejo decides to research the environmental effects of drilling in Alaska. The question he wants to answer is, "Do the proposed drilling and fracking offer a solution to the oil problem or cause environmental problems that are not worth the risk?" Before developing a claim, he does some research.

Alejo begins his research at the source. At the ANWR website (https://anwr .org), Alejo watches a video produced by the organization. The video, narrated by a member of the Inuit Nation whose family has always lived in ANWR, provides glimpses of seemingly thriving wildlife alongside photographs of schoolchildren who are benefiting from improvements in the economy that have resulted from oil-related jobs. The site also provides a graph of the number of Alaskans who support the coastal drilling (see Figure 12.7). The writer also cites a 2011 poll of citizens of Karoo, South Africa, where Shell Oil plans to frack. This poll showed that 73 percent of the population is in favor of gas extraction and that 61 percent trust Shell.

The images are very persuasive. However, upon further reading, Alejo learns that the small size of the oil field footprint shown in the video cannot be confirmed using other sources. Also, the video does not discuss the possibility of oil spills or what their environmental effects would be. The video also fails to mention the effects that the massive infrastructure construction would have on the porcupine caribou's calving habits.

Alejo also reads several sources that include images of farm animals suffering from the effects of fracking, including animals dying from chemicals released into the air during the oil extraction process. Another video presents fracking as a clean process with very little disruption to the environment—but again, Alejo's further research reveals that the damage from fracking is often invisible. He develops a claim for his project:

As he continues to research his claim and write his own argument, Alejo must simultaneously read the visual arguments he encounters in periodicals and on websites—maps, photographs, videos, charts, and graphs—and consider creating his own.

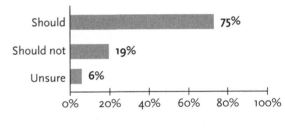

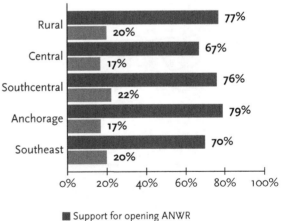

■ Support for opening ANWR
■ Does not support opening ANWR

Figure 12.7 Graphs illustrating the percentage of Alaskans supporting drilling in ANWR.

School-Academic
Workplace
Family-Household
Neighborhood
Social-Cultural
Consumer
Concerned Citizen

TOPIC: The Environment

ISSUE: Domestic Oil Production

AUDIENCE: The U.S. Government

CLAIM: There should be no fracking or drilling for oil in the United States because the risk of major impact on the environment outweighs the minor impact on oil supplies.

Reading Photographs and Illustrations

The words used to describe certain events often evoke emotion, but the power of a photograph is unbeatable. This power, unfortunately, can be abused. Images are often used to convince people that something is real when it may not be, as in photos of Bigfoot and the Loch Ness monster (Figures 12.8 and 12.9).

With digital photography, there are no film negatives to examine, and any image can be retouched to look very different from the original. Image-editing

Figure 12.8 A purported sighting of the legendary creature called Bigfoot.

Figure 12.9 A sighting of another legendary animal, the Loch Ness monster.

programs can be used to fabricate images that trick people into believing events unfolded in a particular way.

Photojournalism is a type of news reporting whose goal is to capture the most evocative images of a news event. Some of these images go on to become icons—enduring symbols—that evoke memories of an event, a time period, a crisis, and so forth. Some examples of iconic images are the extremely memorable photograph of United Airlines Flight 175 crashing into the South Tower of the World Trade Center on September 11, 2001 (Figure 12.10), or the photo of Kim Phuc Phan Thi, a child during the Vietnam War, who was photographed running from a napalm bomb.

Photojournalism also can be responsible for changes in society. In 1890, Jacob Riis' *How the Other Half Lives* exposed the poverty of New York City's slum tenements and included evocative images such as the one shown in Figure 12.11. Images from the

AP Images/CARMEN TAYLOR

Figure 12.10 The horrifying image of *Flight* 175 crashing into the World Trade Center, September 11, 2001.

Jacob Riis/Jacob Riis Picture History/Newscom

Figure 12.11 Jacob Riis photograph of Italian immigrants in a yard on Jersey Street in New York City.

Figure 12.12 A candlelight vigil at Memory Mall at the University of Central Florida commemorating the one-year anniversary of the mass shooting at Marjory Stoneman Douglas High School.

seemingly endless stream of school shootings, whether of students being evacuated or taken away in ambulances, or of student or community vigils, such as the one shown in Figure 12.12, continue to shock readers, reminding them of how wrong things can go in our schools.

Images that appear, or do not appear, in public—American monuments and museums, historical places, and so forth—provide interesting arguments about what is accepted, rejected, glorified, or praised. For example, John C. Barans argues that the portraits chosen for inclusion in the National Portrait Gallery in Washington, D.C., comprise an "acceptable" history of the American people.[1]

internet activity 12b Evaluate Images

Conduct a search of your favorite Internet sites, whether they are related to shopping, cooking, sports, news, religion, or some other topic. Evaluate the images you find there using the checklist, "Questions to Ask While Reading Visual Arguments."

[1]Negotiating the American Identity in the National Portrait Gallery, http://xroads.virginia.edu/~MA98/barans/npg/introframe.htm

Using Photographs and Illustrations in Your Argument

Visual evidence is powerful. Photographs can provide gripping support for an argument. They can show more clearly than words what you are describing. They can be used for both illustration and for manipulation. Your goal obviously is to avoid manipulation. Select your photographs to accomplish what your words may not be able to. We've all seen the "before and after" shots of people who have used a particular diet, piece of exercise equipment, or supplement. The results are often striking and persuasive. You can bet that a reader who sees a photograph of a middle-aged woman who is significantly smaller in her "after" shot is more likely to buy the Fat Blaster Ab Eliminator than a reader who does not see the photograph!

Makeovers have become a staple of contemporary television programming. Programs depicting makeovers of people, houses, and backyards have all become hot, and "before and after" footage is at the heart of the shows. As in the weight-loss example, though, keep in mind that photographs must make a significant impact in order to be persuasive. As mentioned earlier, the line between the types of support (factual vs. persuasive/emotional) is easily crossed. Photos or illustrations of how something works—those in an owner's manual, for example—are clearly factual with no attempt at persuasion. A photograph of Sri Lankan soldiers working to remove oil from a pipeline leak from the beach at Uswetakeiyawa, a coastal town north of Colombo, on September 10, 2018. The spill that started on September 8 was caused by a pipeline leak, officials said, and the oil flow was confined to an approximately 5-km stretch of coastline before the leak was halted and clean-up could begin (see Fig. 12.13).

LAKRUWAN WANNIARACHCHI/AFP/Getty Images

Figure 12.13 A 5-km stretch of Uswetakeiyawa Beach, north of Colombo, Sri Lanka, is covered with cleanup bags from the oil pipeline leak.

Your sources must always be cited; this holds true with images, not only written information. The following checklist will support your efforts to use and label your images correctly.

⬤ Using Photographs and Illustrations

☐ Select the right image for your information. Does the image clearly illustrate the point you are trying to make in the text?

☐ Clearly label the image: what it is and where it was found.

☐ Don't include an image if it does not improve the quality of your argument. You do not want your argument to be cluttered and visually unappealing.

☐ For inclusion in a student paper, permission to use a photograph is generally not needed. For more public purposes, however, you may need to obtain permission. To obtain permission from a publishing house, use the information on the copyright page of the book or consult the publisher's website. When making your request, be sure to include the ISBN (International Standard Book Number; a number publishers use to identify books), which usually appears near the copyright notice or on the back cover of the book.

☐ For permission to use photos and illustrations found in magazines, start with the information found on the credits page or masthead (near the front of the magazine). In some cases, the photographer or artist is not an employee of the publisher, and you may need to obtain permission directly from the photographer or artist. Publishers will often tell you how to contact artists or photographers.

---

your turn 12b ▶ **GET STARTED** **Use Photographs and Illustrations**

Use one of the community topics from Chapter 2, "Explore an Issue that Matters to You," and find images that would support a claim based on your selected topic. Then, answer the following questions:

1. Why did you choose these images?
2. How do the images improve your argument?
3. Who is your target audience?
4. Would your image selection be different if the audience for your claim was different?

Reading Graphs and Charts

Graphs and charts use numbers to illustrate their claims. They can help a reader visualize a claim by showing increases and decreases in anything that can be measured, such as weight loss or presidential approval ratings.

Graphs are particularly convincing when the numbers are dramatic. Look at the graph shown in Figure 12.14. It shows the dramatic rise in both global temperatures (the blue and red bars) and carbon dioxide (the black line). Carbon dioxide is considered a common greenhouse gas because it lets sunlight into our atmosphere but traps the heat energy that the sunlight produces. This graph makes it appear that our modern industrial society has produced unprecedented levels of both carbon dioxide and heat: a pretty scary situation.

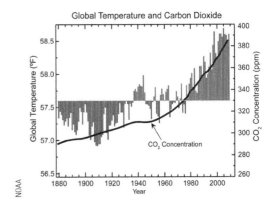

Figure 12.14 A graph showing temperature variation over a 130-year period.

On the other hand, a second graph (Figure 12.15) puts these increases into a much longer timeframe, adding an important context. This graph, like the other one, shows a rise in global temperatures (presented in degrees Celsius, rather than degrees Fahrenheit) and carbon dioxide, but this graph provides a context that makes the current increases look similar to increases that have occurred at other times in the last few hundred thousand years. The recent rise is still significant, but perhaps not as scary because it has happened before. A good student of science would go on to ask, "What about looking at global temperatures for the last few hundred million years?" and "How do the recent increases in carbon dioxide and temperatures compare to the climate, say, when the dinosaurs lived?" If human beings are creating higher levels of carbon dioxide than have ever existed before, the situation truly is scary. A chart showing only the past few decades won't address that important issue.

Graphs can seem difficult to read, and it can also be difficult to tell when their information is misleading. For help, refer to the checklist, "Questions to Ask While Reading Graphs."

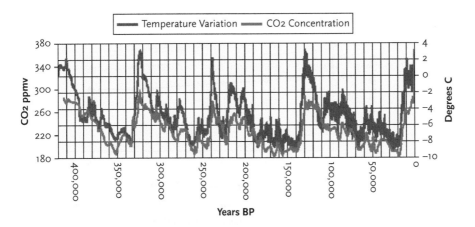

Figure 12.15 A graph showing temperature variation over a longer period of time.

your turn **PRACTICE Reading Graphs**

Find a graph in a newspaper or in a news or science magazine that is geared toward the general public. *USA Today* frequently uses graphs as do *Time, Newsweek, US News and World Report, Scientific American,* and *Discover*. Using the questions in the checklist, "Questions to Ask While Reading Graphs," evaluate your selected graph. If there are problems with the graph, what could be done to correct them?

Questions to Ask While Reading Graphs

- ☐ Are all numbers represented and compared the same way: percentages with percentages, numbers with numbers, and so on?
- ☐ Does the *y*-axis start at 0?
- ☐ Are all objects represented in the same scale?
- ☐ Are both the *x*-axis and the *y*-axis labeled, and does the graph have a title?
- ☐ Is the graph understandable without reading the accompanying text?

Using and Creating Graphs in Your Argument

Graphs and tables are an excellent way to condense a large amount of information into a graphic that is easy to read. Any time you are using a lot of numbers in a paragraph, a graphic may be useful to the reader. Graphs can illustrate weight loss, for example, showing more clearly how much two groups of dieters have lost over a period of time, as shown in Figures 12.16 and 12.17, which were created for an essay arguing the effectiveness of two weight-loss programs.

Here we have one way we could compare the weight loss of two "teams" of dieters. Figure 12.16, a **line graph**, shows the weekly weight loss of dieters

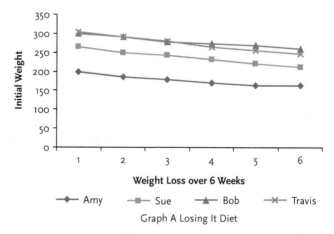

Figure 12.16 A line graph for the Losing It Diet.

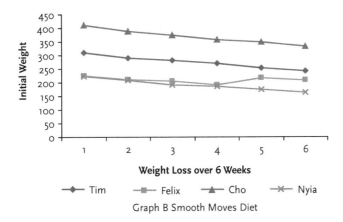

Figure 12.17 A line graph for the Smooth Moves Diet.

on the Losing It diet. Figure 12.17 illustrates the weight loss of dieters on the Smooth Moves diet. As we can see, both groups of dieters lost weight.

But how are these graphs helpful to an argument that one diet is superior to the other? All we can really tell from the two charts is that both teams lost weight. Ultimately, even though these charts are well constructed, labeled properly, and easy to read, they are not useful for comparing the effectiveness of the two diets. A more effective graph for the argument that one diet (Smooth Moves) is superior to the other (Losing It) is the bar graph shown in Figure 12.18.

This graph compares only the total loss for each team, ignoring the weekly ups and downs of individual team members. The **bar graph**, compared with the line graphs, works better to compare the total loss of the two teams—the columns are thicker and have more heft, standing out better and showing the Smooth Moves group's weight loss as more significant than that of the Losing It group.

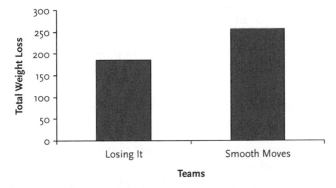

Figure 12.18 A bar graph clearly showing greater weight loss for the Smooth Moves team.

your turn **12d** ▶ PRACTICE **Create Graphs**

You have gathered figures to support an argument that employers are invading workplace privacy at a rate that increases each year. You also note that different kinds of monitoring devices are gaining in popularity among employers. Arrange these figures first in a line graph and then in a bar graph. Which is more effective?

Keystroke monitoring	Internet monitoring	Packet sniffing
2007: 37% 2013: 50%	2007: 28% 2013: 75%	2007: 10% 2013: 78%

Creating Graphs

☐ Select the right graph for your information.

☐ Use the chart function of your word processing program or your spreadsheet program to try different graph types and to create a clear and uniform graph.

☐ Clearly label the components of the graph.

☐ Title the graph fully. In the weight-loss example, a title of "Weight Loss" would not give the reader much information about what he was looking at. Be concise, but provide as much information as the reader needs.

☐ Ensure that you provide sufficient information so that your reader can interpret the graph without the support of the accompanying text.

Reading Advertisements

For every product imaginable, from widgets to wing-dings, there is an advertising team to promote it with a sustained campaign. Many of these ads don't even use words. Other times, the words are secondary to the visuals. Ads are meant to persuade you to buy a product or service. How this goal is accomplished varies from ad to ad. But here are some points to look for as you read an advertisement.

Questions to Ask While Reading an Advertisement

☐ How is information about the product conveyed? Is there any text, or is the entire ad visual?

☐ Who is the target audience for the product? Male or female, rich or poor, young or old?

- ☐ Can you quickly tell what product or service is being advertised?
- ☐ Is the ad part of a larger campaign?
- ☐ What strategy is used to sell the product or service? Bandwagon? Celebrity endorsement? Company credibility? Offers to make you rich, thin, beautiful, insert adjective here ___?
- ☐ Does it appeal primarily with facts, emotions, or credibility?
- ☐ And, finally, do you believe the claims made in the advertisement?

internet activity 12c **Evaluate Advertisements**

Do a search on the Internet to find advertisements or, preferably, an entire ad campaign. Use the questions in the checklist, "Questions to Ask While Reading an Advertisement" to evaluate the ad or ad campaign.

KEEPING IT LOCAL

GAS PRICES REMAIN volatile, going up and down depending on such vagaries as weather, global conditions, and the economy. Some people fume every time they fill up at the pump, arguing that there is no reason we should have to pay so much for imported oil. Reading and listening to the myriad arguments in newspapers, on news programs, on blogs, and at the water cooler can be overwhelming. It is easy to gravitate toward quick and easy photographs, charts, and graphs that seem to make clear solutions such as, "Drill closer to home."

As we are faced with the growing need to search for new sources of energy, be careful as you evaluate the many solutions proposed by various arguments. Don't be a slave to the lure of visual images without evaluating them for their soundness and determining their credibility and the arguer's reason for using them.

Find images that both support and oppose an argument you are developing. How are the images created to stir your emotions? What techniques are used to sway you? Recognizing the appeal of an argument's graphics can empower you to feel more confident in your reaction to and your assessment of the argument itself.

CHAPTER 13

Develop and Edit Argument Structure and Style

Learning Objectives

By working through this chapter, you will be able to

- edit both an argument's structure and its style.
- revise your argument's structure.

Halfway through the dinner shift at the restaurant where you've worked for the last six years, you peer out into the dining room. Sweat is running under your cap, and you've been cooking like mad. But the dining room is only half full. The owner, Robie, is at the cash register having yet another argument with a customer about the use of an expired coupon. Tonight is the night, you decide. You've got to talk to Robie about the decline in his business. In his efforts to keep costs down, he ends up fighting with his customers and driving them away. If he keeps it up, the place will close and you both will be out of work.

Now the restaurant has closed for the night; everything is cleaned and stored in its proper place. The moment is here, but something holds you back. The speech you've been going over in your head is basically a complaint. You imagine rambling, blaming Robie, and in the end convincing him of nothing except that you don't like him. And that's not true—you've become good friends over the years, even though he's your boss. What you really need is a different approach or format for your message—not a rant or a note, but maybe something more formal, like a presentation. And it needs to be well organized, too, with facts instead of accusations. Maybe you could include statistics

TOPIC: Business

ISSUE: Poor Customer Service Driving Away Customers

AUDIENCE: Your boss, Chef and Restaurateur Robeson Barnes

CLAIM: Getting creative with problem customers can improve customer service and increase sales.

from the restaurant industry and some examples—maybe even a case study from someone in Robie's shoes who turned his business around. Although it is late when you get home, now is the time. You begin to lay out your argument.

In this textbook you have learned the terms used to discuss argument: *claim, warrant, data, grounds, support,* and *rebuttal.* However, it is rare to use these terms in an actual argument. In writing your claim, you don't say, "My *claim* for this essay is . . ." Nor do you say, "The *warrants* of my argument are . . ." In fact, you generally will not use the first-person pronoun *I* at all. So how do you make sure that your arguments include the language appropriate to argumentative writing? In this section, you will learn how to introduce the various sections of your argument. The three categories of material that you introduce are:

- The argument itself (your claim)
- The support
- The opposition and your rebuttal of the opposition

Consider Your Argument's Claim

Introduce Your Claim

Your introduction, which you will learn more about later in this chapter, has two parts: the hook, which grabs the reader's attention and sets the claim in context, and the claim itself. It is important that your reader know what type of argument you are making from the first paragraph, so the language you use to introduce the claim must provide a road map for the reader.

- **Is your claim based on causes or effects?**
  - The main cause of acid rain in California is . . .
  - Some contributors to the problem of inflation are . . .
  - To get to the root (basis) of the problem of welfare fraud, we must consider . . .
  - The primary effect of identity theft is . . .
  - The outcomes of a peer-based discipline approach are . . .
  - An increase in global spending produces . . .
- **Is your claim based on an extended definition?**
  - The main point of argument in abortion issues is the *definition* of the term *life*.
  - People don't understand global warming because the term has not been *explained* properly.
  - To clarify the argument about euthanasia, we must *specify* what is meant by the phrase *quality of life*.
- **Is the claim an evaluation?**
  - An *evaluation* of the various solutions to the problem of teenage pregnancy will lead to the most cost-effective method.
  - After reviewing the criteria, we can *judge* the most nearly fair labor practices.
  - Before suggesting that student achievement has increased, educators should *review* the factors that determine student achievement.
- **Are you proposing a solution to a problem?**
  - The *solution* to the problem of overcrowding in schools is . . .
  - To *eliminate* childhood obesity, schools should:
    - *Implement*
    - *Enforce*
    - *Provide*
    - *Put into effect*
    - *Stop/end/cease*
    - *Start/begin/initiate*
    - *Use/employ*
    - *Apply*
- **Does your claim argue that something is a fact?** With a claim of fact, concrete, specific language is important but the specific terms used in the discussion will depend on the subject matter.

When your thesis uses specific terminology to cue the reader to expect a specific type of argument, your argument will be more successful. In the

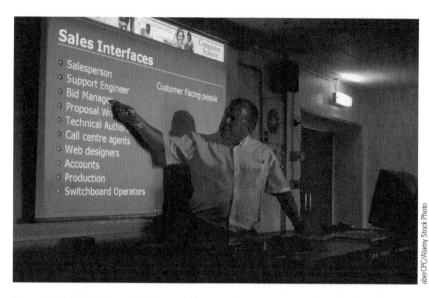

Figure 13.1 Visual presentations can go a long way toward convincing an audience if you are careful to accompany the text with explanations.

case of the restaurant proposal, the claim is that Robie would keep more customers if he learned to stop fighting with them. Stating that explicitly might turn Robie off to the argument. It might be better to soft-sell the idea—not hide it exactly but rather imply it. Turn it into a positive. Maybe even save it for the last slide in your PowerPoint presentation. Something like, "Now you can help your customers and grow your business," sounds much better than stating the claim more frankly, such as, "Robie, you need to quit driving your customers out the doors before you have to close them for good." The checklist titled "Edit Your Claim" provides questions to ask while editing your claim.

your turn 13a GET STARTED Edit Your Claim Introduction

Write a claim for a paper you are currently working on so that it uses language that indicates the type of argument you are making: cause–effect, solution, definition, or evaluation. Alternately, use one of the following issues to develop a claim.

- Street improvement
- Degree requirements
- Academic integrity
- Stress
- Sex education
- Diet or food consumption

Edit Your Claim: A Checklist

☐ Every claim should answer these questions:
  ☐ Where do I stand on this issue?
  ☐ What point of view do I want my audience to accept at the end of my argument?
  ☐ What is my purpose in delivering this argument?
☐ A **claim of cause** should also answer this question:
  ☐ What, exactly, is the cause–effect relationship I am claiming?
☐ A **claim of definition** should also answer these questions:
  ☐ What is the word or term I intend to define?
  ☐ What are clear characteristics, examples, and synonyms for the word?
  ☐ What are specific conditions must my definition meet in order to be accepted by my audience?
☐ A **claim of evaluation** should also answer the question:
  ☐ Have I provided and explained the standards and guidelines I used to make my evaluation?
☐ A **problem-based claim** should also answer the questions:
  ☐ Is it clear what I'm asking my audience to do?
  ☐ Do my claims propose solutions to problems?
☐ A **claim of fact** should also answer the questions:
  ☐ Precisely what information am I claiming as fact?
  ☐ Does this claim of fact respond to an issue that can be considered legitimate and arguable?

State Your Claim

Where should your claim be placed in your argument? Should you come right out and state the claim explicitly, or should you be indirect? **Explicit claims** are made obvious by the writer; they are directly stated.

Mark Lange's editorial "Do You Work in Sales? Thank You." directly states its claim in the title, restates it in the subtitle, and restates it several more times throughout the essay:

Had enough of the recession? Next time somebody pitches you something—whether or not you open your wallet—at least say thanks.

Because economic growth is a story we tell one another. Transactions are its dialogue. And the authors of both are the master storytellers: salespeople.

Before you tune out, consider this: Nothing happens until somebody sells someone something. And no matter what the rest of us do all day, our paychecks and prosperity rely on the efforts of salespeople.

Lange, Mark. "Do You Work in Sales? Thank You." *Christian Science Monitor* 9 September, 2009.

And so on. The writer makes his claim obvious because he believes that everyone should act upon it but that currently, not everyone does. He wants to drive his point home.

Implicit claims are implied but not hidden very deeply. They quickly become obvious to the average reader. Implicit claims are common in professional writing, but they are not recommended to students because of the risk of making an unclear claim. Sojourner Truth uses an implicit claim in her speech "Ain't I a Woman?"

> Well, children, where there is so much racket there must be something out of kilter. I think that 'twixt the negroes of the South and the women at the North, all talking about rights, the white men will be in a fix pretty soon. But what's all this here talking about?

> That man over there says that women need to be helped into carriages, and lifted over ditches, and to have the best place everywhere. Nobody ever helps me into carriages, or over mud-puddles, or gives me any best place! And ain't I a woman? Look at me! Look at my arm! I have ploughed and planted, and gathered into barns, and no man could head me! And ain't I a woman? I could work as much and eat as much as a man—when I could get it—and bear the lash as well! And ain't I a woman? I have borne thirteen children, and seen most all sold off to slavery, and when I cried out with my mother's grief, none but Jesus heard me! And ain't I a woman?

> Then they talk about this thing in the head; what's this they call it? [member of audience whispers, "intellect"] That's it, honey. What's that got to do with women's rights or negroes' rights? If my cup won't hold but a pint, and yours holds a quart, wouldn't you be mean not to let me have my little half measure full?

> Then that little man in black there, he says women can't have as much rights as men, 'cause Christ wasn't a woman! Where did your Christ come from? Where did your Christ come from? From God and a woman! Man had nothing to do with Him.

> If the first woman God ever made was strong enough to turn the world upside down all alone, these women together ought to be able to turn it back, and get it right side up again! And now they is asking to do it, the men better let them.

> Obliged to you for hearing me, and now old Sojourner ain't got nothing more to say.

It isn't until the third paragraph that Sojourner Truth claims that blacks and women ought to be educated, and she only does that with a metaphorical question about measuring cups. Finally in the fourth paragraph, she gives her claim directly, this time by quoting someone who disagrees and using the opposition to give the claim in the negative. Her speech is artful. The audience knew what she stood for: justice and equality for African Americans and women. She didn't need to tell them that; therefore she had some freedom to be artistic and to use rhetorical devices and figures of speech instead of stating her claim explicitly.

Hidden claims are useful when the writer wants the reader to do more of the work. A humorous argument might use irony and never state or even strongly imply the real claim. One example of this is "A Modest Proposal" (1729), in which the explicit claim is that in order to solve the Irish famine, parents should sell their babies as food. Obviously, that's not at all the real claim. Swift is actually arguing that the English and Irish people should step in and work together to solve the problems of poverty and starvation. Swift actually states his true claim toward the end of his essay. Up to that point it remains hidden because until then he is explicitly stating things his country should not do. A good reader understands that Swift isn't really advocating the eating of babies but instead is trying to get people to save the starving and the poor.

> *Therefore let no man talk to me of other expedients: Of taxing our absentees at five shillings a pound: Of using neither cloaths, nor houshold furniture, except what is of our own growth and manufacture: Of utterly rejecting the materials and instruments that promote foreign luxury: Of curing the expensiveness of pride, vanity, idleness, and gaming in our women: Of introducing a vein of parsimony, prudence and temperance: Of learning to love our country, wherein we differ even from Laplanders, and the inhabitants of Topinamboo: Of quitting our animosities and factions, nor acting any longer like the Jews, who were murdering one another at the very moment their city was taken: Of being a little cautious not to sell our country and consciences for nothing: Of teaching landlords to have at least one degree of mercy towards their tenants. Lastly, of putting a spirit of honesty, industry, and skill into our shop-keepers, who, if a resolution could now be taken to buy only our native goods, would immediately unite to cheat and exact upon us in the price, the measure, and the goodness, nor could ever yet be brought to make one fair proposal of just dealing, though often and earnestly invited to it.*

> *Therefore I repeat, let no man talk to me of these and the like expedients, 'till he hath at least some glympse of hope, that there will ever be some hearty and sincere attempt to put them into practice.*

In his essay "On the Decay of the Art of Lying," Mark Twain claims that the art of lying has decayed, that people don't lie nearly so well nowadays, and that the art of lying ought to be restored to its former place of grandeur and perfection. Of course, his hidden claim is that, while we all do lie, we are hypocritical about it and lie to help ourselves and hurt others. In reality, we ought to realize what liars we are and lie only for good, not for evil. Like Swift, Twain can't resist explicitly stating his claim, again toward the end of his argument:

> *Lying is universal—we all do it; we all must do it. Therefore, the wise thing is for us diligently to train ourselves to lie thoughtfully, judiciously; to lie with a good object, and not an evil one; to lie for others' advantage, and not our own; to lie healingly, charitably, humanely, not cruelly, hurtfully, maliciously; to lie gracefully and graciously, not awkwardly and clumsily; to lie firmly, frankly, squarely, with head erect, not haltingly, tortuously, with pusillanimous mien, as being ashamed of our high calling. Then shall we be rid of the rank and pestilent truth that is rotting the land; then shall we be great and good and beautiful, and worthy dwellers in a world where even benign Nature habitually lies, except when she promises execrable weather. Then—But I am but a new and feeble student in this gracious art; I cannot instruct this Club.*

In other arguments, claims may be missing altogether. Stephen J. Dubner's "What Should Be Done About Standardized Tests? A Freakonomics Quorum," which is readily available online, is really a collection of different opinions by experts. In a way, it has no claim of its own except a set of claims made by other, various experts. Readers get to make a decision and formulate their own claims.

Position Your Claim

A good introduction pulls the reader in and reveals the issue or topic at hand. It may also clearly state the arguer's claim. As a student, the safest thing you can do is to clearly state your claim in your introductory paragraph. However, as you get better at arguing and constructing papers, you will develop the skills to keep your reader in suspense by describing the issue but not your take on that issue. At that time, you can trust your readers to wait.

Your introduction can be short—a paragraph, or perhaps even just a sentence or two—or it can take several paragraphs. The introduction to Richard Louv's book *Last Child in the Woods: Saving Our Children from Nature-Deficit Disorder* is an example of a brief, direct approach to an issue, along with a clear statement of the claim. The initial sentence contains the factual claim that underpins his entire ethical argument:

> *If, when we were young, we tramped through forests of Nebraska cottonwoods, or raised pigeons on a rooftop in Queens, or fished for Ozark bluegills, or felt the swell of a wave that traveled a thousand miles before lifting our boat, then we were bound to the natural world and remain so today. Nature still informs our years—lifts us, carries us.*

Dubner, Stephen J. "What Should Be Done About Standardized Tests? A Freakonomics Quorum." *Freakonomics.* 20 December, 2007.

Pressmaster/Shutterstock.com

Figure 13.2 The best logical support in the world may not keep an audience interested. Using suspense and other strategies will ensure that your audience will stick with you until the end of your argument.

He is saying that because children's experiences of nature permanently bind them to the natural world (the factual claim), we need to make sure children experience nature (the ethical claim). As the introduction continues, we get more of a sense of the ethical argument, of what is at stake for children if we do not introduce them to nature in a meaningful way. Later, he discusses how exposure to nature encourages children to cherish and care for the natural world as they grow into adulthood.

> *For children, nature comes in many forms. A newborn calf; a pet that lives and dies; a worn path through the woods; a fort nested in stinging nettles; a damp, mysterious edge of a vacant lot—whatever shape nature takes, it offers each child an older, larger world separate from parents. Unlike television, nature does not steal time; it amplifies it. Nature offers healing for a child living in a destructive family or neighborhood. It serves as a blank slate upon which a child draws and reinterprets the culture's fantasies. Nature inspires creativity in a child by demanding visualization and the full use of the senses. Given a chance, a child will bring the confusion of the world to the woods, wash it in the creek, turn it over to see what lives on the unseen side of that confusion. Nature can frighten a child, too, and this fright serves a purpose. In nature, a child finds freedom, fantasy, and privacy: a place distant from the adult world, a separate peace.*

Louv, Richard. *Last Child in the Woods: Saving Our Children from Nature-Deficit Disorder.* Algonquin Books, 2005.

Often, the first half of a claim is placed in the opening paragraph and the second half of the claim comes later. However, in Thomas J. Hanson's blog editorial "College Graduation Rates–Statistics Tell a Sad Tale," the first part of the claim is located in the first three paragraphs (as shown in the following excerpt), and the second half of the claim comes much later, starting around paragraph 13.

> The results of a first-of-its-kind study recently graced the front pages of the Boston Globe. In "Hub Grads Come Up Short in College," James Vaznis revealed an all too similar refrain regarding college completion rates.
>
> Of the members of the graduating class from Boston high schools for the year 2000 who had gone on to higher education, nearly two-thirds of the class had not earned a college diploma seven years after they had begun collegiate studies.
>
> The findings were particularly troublesome for a city that has touted its steadily increasing college enrollment rates over the last few years. In simplest terms, **Boston does see more high school graduates enrolled in college than does the nation as a whole, but the college completion rate for those students is actually lower than the national average.**

Hanson is arguing that Boston high school students are completing college degrees at a lower rate than the national average, but that isn't his entire claim. The blogger's whole claim is that this problem is best solved not by the traditional solution of shoring up education from kindergarten through 12th grade, but instead by focusing on the education that colleges themselves provide. We see this later in the essay.

> **The state of public education has focused on the K-12 system in recent years.** During that time frame, higher education has earned a free pass. In fact, the general consensus from most folks is that America's colleges and universities represent the best of the educational system in our country.
>
> However, Mark Schneider, the vice president for new educational initiatives at the American Institutes for Research, offers a very contrasting viewpoint. In "The Costs of Failure Factories in American Higher Education," Mark Schneider asks, "If there is virtually universal agreement that American high schools are failing, how do our colleges and universities measure up against such a low benchmark?" Turns out not very well.

Hanson, Thomas J. "College Graduation Rates–Statistics Tell a Sad Tale." Open Education. 20 November 2008.

Hanson says that while the problem is obvious—in fact, that it is "an all too familiar refrain"—the solution is something new. The solution is to examine and improve college education to make it fit student needs better; the rest of the essay goes on to discuss how that might be done. This is really a typical problem–solution essay. The writer merely takes some time to reveal his entire claim.

Another common tactic is to ask a question in the title and let the argument answer it. That way, the reader is hooked in by suspense, at least for awhile. Readers want to read on to find the answer. For other guidelines on writing effective titles, see the section "Supply a Strong Title" later in this chapter.

Still other arguments will hook the reader but leave the claim unstated, perhaps until the conclusion of the argument. Finally, some arguments leave their claim implied throughout, never directly stating it.

How should you introduce your claim to Robie? He is known to be sensitive and to take things personally. That's why he's been arguing with his customers in the first place. Maybe you could start with humor and by agreeing with Robie's views on customer relations. You begin to gather stories of nightmare customers who want something for nothing and take great pleasure in watching retailers dance to meet their needs. Only then will you move to the all important "but." Robie is right, *but* being right isn't always the goal in customer service.

> **your turn 13b** ▸ **GET STARTED Edit Your Claim**
>
> 1. How will your argument benefit if you state your claim explicitly?
> 2. How will your argument benefit if you state your claim only implicitly?
> 3. Would you ever consider hiding your claim?
> 4. How could you hide your claim in a way that is still ethical and serves your purposes?

Introduce Your Counterarguments

As you learned in Chapter 6, "Work Fairly with the Opposition," it is important to present your argument with as little bias as possible. This means respectfully presenting for your reader's consideration counterarguments: opposing and alternate views. Sometimes there is no view directly opposing your own, yet there are lots of alternate views. For example, you may be arguing that a bullying policy needs to be instituted at your daughter's school. There may be no formal objection to this policy, but there may be differing views regarding how the policy should be implemented. A clear and objective presentation of the opposition's case is one sign of a strong writer. There are two ways to introduce counterarguments into your own argument.

- The counterargument is incorrect.
- The counterargument is correct, but . . . (does not completely solve the problem or does not go far enough toward a solution)

The Counterargument Is Incorrect

You may feel that the counterargument is incorrect. You find it mildly inaccurate or wildly wrong. You may be slightly amused by the view, or you may be highly offended. You may find the opposition misleading or downright evil. Regardless of how you feel, the manner in which you present the ideas of others is a mark of your character. A respectful tone of voice and an objective treatment of alternate claims will go a long way to make your argument professional and persuasive. Some structures for introducing a counterargument that you feel is incorrect are:

- No evidence supports X.
- X's example of . . . is incorrect.
- The argument put forth by X is flawed.
- Although X was once a widely held view, recent findings no longer support it.

your turn 13c **GET STARTED Edit the Introduction of Incorrect Counterarguments**

For your own paper, or for the claim you produced in Your Turn 13a, introduce two countering views in an objective way.

The Counterargument Is Correct, But . . .

There are times when the opposition is correct; even in these cases, opposition cannot be wished away or ignored. Because it could be construed as unethical or negligent to suppress alternative claims and their support, you must present them. The goal is to present the material objectively and to state clearly why the view either is not actually relevant to the current argument or perhaps why does not go far enough. In the following examples, the italicized words and phrases introduce the counterargument and the rebuttal.

- *X is a solution* for several problems *but is not suited* to . . .
- *Although X's* example of . . . *may be correct, it does not apply* to . . .
- The argument put forth by *X has some value, but it has largely been discredited* by . . .

- *X* could be a *good* solution *if . . .*
- It is true that *X is the effect for some* people; *however, for this group . . .*
- *Some of the causes X lists* have been noted. *One of these*, though, *does not . . .*

your turn 13d **GET STARTED Edit Your Introduction of Correct Counterarguments**

For your own argument, or for the claim you produced in Your Turn 13a, introduce two valid, countering views. Taking an objective tone, state each view and then rebut it.

Create Strong Introductions

Your introduction is one of the most important sections in your argument. Whether you are producing a report for your boss suggesting a move to a larger site, arguing that your son's high school athletic program needs to set higher grade standards, or writing a research paper for a political science course, your argument needs to include a strong introduction.

The introduction performs two basic functions:

1. It hooks your audience, forcing them to become interested in your topic and to care about its outcome.
2. It provides your audience with your thesis—that is, the claim that you support in the remainder of your argument.

There are many ways to hook your audience. You can tell them a brief story that sets up the claim to come. You can misdirect them, sending them in a direction that is opposite of your true intention. You can set up the conflict explicitly and immediately. The function your introduction absolutely must perform is to get the audience's attention. And you don't have long to do so. Think of how many times you've been in a waiting room somewhere with only a stack of old magazines to entertain you until your name is called. You pick up a copy of *Time* and flip through the pages. You start this article, you start that one. Finally, you settle in to read about the rising crime rate in rural areas. You don't live in a rural area, never even been near a cow. So why did you reject the first two articles but decide to read this one? Probably because the introduction made the subject of rural crime seem interesting. The author provided a hook that drew you in, and you wanted to know more. This is your first job as a writer: make the audience want to learn more. If you don't get their attention from the beginning, all the brilliant reasons and support in the remainder of your argument will never be heard. Let's look at some ways to heighten an audience's interest:

- Anecdote (a brief story)
- Misdirection (fooling the audience for a time)

- Conflict (one thing versus another)
- Suspense (creating anticipation)
- A seeming impossibility (misdirection that generates suspense)

Anecdote

An **anecdote** is a brief story, often a personal memory or experience, that sets the tone for the argument's claim. Anecdotes can be used anywhere in your argument where a good story is needed, but they work especially well to introduce your issue. A good anecdote must have these elements:

- It must be brief. Stories that go on and on will bore the audience. Make your anecdote short and to the point, using only those details that are relevant to your purpose.
- It must seem real. If a hypothetical story is not realistic or feels contrived, an audience can tell.

Marjory Simpson was surprised to see the sheriff's car and ambulance in her neighbor's driveway as she returned from the grocery store. She lifted bags out of her trunk as EMTs wheeled out a gurney covered with a sheet. Moments later, a handcuffed teenager was escorted to the sheriff's cruiser. Jim Stone, the sheriff's deputy, rolled a length of yellow tape around the porch and several trees in the front yard.

Marjory had moved to the small town of Six Acres a year earlier to escape the growing crime rates of Tulsa. This was the second murder in the town since she'd arrived. Maybe she hadn't moved far enough out. It seemed that even in this rural community, crime was on the rise.

How well does this anecdote work as an introduction to the subject of crime in rural areas? First, it is brief, only around 100 words. Second, the story is realistic with no gruesome details thrown in, which might make it seem contrived. A crime scene is described simply, through the eyes of someone who had moved to the country to escape the crime of the big city. Notice, too, the scarcity of details: only a few names, yellow police tape, and bags of groceries—just enough to keep the scene feeling authentic. The claim comes at the end of the paragraph, introducing the issue of rising crime in rural areas, the focus of the argument.

Misdirection

To misdirect an audience is to lead them down one path so that they are temporarily tricked into thinking that the topic or your position is different from the one that is ultimately presented. **Misdirection** gives a bigger punch to the actual claim once it is reached.

A paper I once received from a student began, "Hitler was right." Well, needless to say, that got my attention. Hitler, infamous for being one of the most evil men of all time, was right about something? A nice, polite 18-year-old was agreeing with him? I read further: I was *hooked*, you might say.

"Hitler was right. Our youth are our most important commodity." Okay, I get it. I was led down the path of outrage, tricked just as the author had intended me to be. I was temporarily misdirected from the student's ultimate discussion of the importance of our young people by a quote from Hitler. It worked. The writer had my attention.

Misdirection should have these elements:

- It should lead the audience down an exciting path.
- That path should be false.
- The real situation should be explained quickly so that the audience doesn't feel duped and stop trusting the writer.
- The real situation should also be somewhat interesting.

Arrest rates are skyrocketing. Burglaries are up 25%. Rapes are up 17%. The murder rate has escalated 8% in one decade. Young adults are being incarcerated at a rate that has never been seen. Six Acres, Oklahoma, home to 20,000 inhabitants, is seeing a troubling increase in crime that exhibits no likelihood of slowing.

Initially, the startling statistics lead the audience to believe that the argument is going to be about big-city crime, the likes that are seen in New York or Chicago. The paragraph ends with the seemingly casual mention that it is a small, unknown town experiencing this crime wave. The jolt, and therefore the increased interest level, comes from the unexpected final sentence. The audience wants to know more about these rising levels of rural crime.

Conflict

Use **conflict** when you want to immediately highlight seemingly irreconcilable differences among factions or groups. In argumentative essays, the issue being addressed is often surrounded by conflict. One group wants this, another group wants that. Often, there are many sides an issue. But just as often, there are two groups whose views seem to be lodged at opposite ends of the spectrum. Often the conflict between them seems irresolvable. The introduction is the place to foreground the conflict, establishing the battle lines from the beginning.

Conflict can generate attention and excitement if it has the following elements:

- Two sides the reader cares about—either by liking or disliking at least one side.
- Something at issue that can be decided by a winner and a loser—though it might end up in compromise.
- Some uncertainty as to which side will prevail.

In recent years, many parents have argued that the school districts need to be improved—that is, with the exception of the schools that their own children attend. Surveys indicate that parents with children in magnet programs believe their children's schools are doing fine. They typically fight any changes that school districts want to make in order to improve the school system if those changes threaten the existence or scope of their own schools' programs.

Right away the writer has set up a conflict between parents' concerns about the overall success of their school districts and their concerns that their children's particular schools might be negatively affected by attempts to improve the system. In this case, claims will likely attempt to reconcile the conflict and suggest solutions.

Suspense

Use **suspense** when you want to hold off on presenting the audience with your claim so that you increase anticipation. There are lots of ways of generating suspense, including anecdotes, conflict, misdirection, and seeming impossibilities. But suspense can also be generated by telling only part of a story or leaving out some important piece of information that an audience wants to have. In general, suspense can be created if you:

- Gain the attention of the audience—essentially by promising to reveal something interesting.
- Delay fulfillment of that promise.

It's Friday night, and we are at the Olympics, the Special Olympics, that is. My son is on a relay-race team competing against fourth-graders from all over the school district.

The audience wants to know if the writer's son is going to win. In the remainder of the introduction, this hook, loaded with bait to get the audience's eyes to continue down the page, will need to be followed with a claim. For example, the paragraph can be continued this way:

We want to see his team win, but of course anybody's win is welcome in the Special Olympics, where disabled kids learn that they are not so different from others and can enjoy sports that were once deemed out of their range. Sadly, our anticipation about our son's possible win is small compared to our dread that funds to sponsor the Olympics may be cut. If the government cuts Special Olympics from its budget, this really will be our son's—and other parents', sons', and daughters'—last race.

The hook, and the suspense it generated, has its conclusion in the introduction's final sentence, where the claim is made explicit.

A Seeming Impossibility

One effective type of misdirection is to present an audience with a situation that sounds impossible. Perhaps it sounds too good to be true, too awful to be real, too unlikely to be a mere coincidence, too odd to have been planned. Unlike a standard misdirection, this technique usually involves the audience's understanding that they are purposely being toyed with and kept in suspense, so it isn't necessary to present the real situation as quickly. The solution to the riddle might only come at the very end of a long argument.

Effective misdirection can be created using the following elements:

- Present a highly unlikely claim.
- Resolve the seeming impossibility by explaining the real situation and how it was possible after all.

Perhaps we shouldn't ignore those infomercials for exercise balls, Tai Bo, and diet programs. It seems that looking better not only improves your body but may also save your mind. A new study links overweight, particularly in people who carry extra weight in their midsections, to a higher incidence of Alzheimer's disease.

What seems impossible about this hook is that one's body can size have an effect on the health of one's mind. A normal-weight body, the claim following the hook argues, may be key to avoiding Alzheimer's disease, a disease that attacks the mind. The claim, then is this: to save the mind, mind the body.

Other standard hooks for introductions include the following: using interesting quotations or startling statistics, asking questions that you intend to answer in your argument, and making comparisons, often to show that one side is different in an unanticipated way.

What type of introduction might ease your boss into listening to your argument about his poor customer service? No one wants to face the fact that failure is his or her own fault. You could begin with a few anecdotes of outrageous customer incidents that you have gathered from others. You can show how, in each case, the customer was wrong. Then you can introduce the idea that even wrong customers deserve the best service that can be given. The anecdotes can thus pave the way for Robie to see that he is not alone.

your turn 13e ▶ PRACTICE Edit Your Introductions

Select one of the topics related to the various communities from Chapter 2, "Explore an Issue That Matters to You," and narrow it to a claim. Use three of the following hooks, creating three separate introductions for your claim:

- Anecdote (a brief story)
- Misdirection (fooling the audience for a time)
- Conflict (one thing versus another)

- Suspense (creating anticipation)
- A seeming impossibility (misdirection that generates suspense)

Which approach worked the best? Which seemed the most natural for both the topic and for your writing style?

Write Memorable Conclusions

The conclusion sums up the essay but in a new way. Any piece of writing has to have a conclusion; otherwise, the reader feels cheated. The opening passages of an essay or story make a promise to the reader that what follows will entertain us and/or teach us something. A good conclusion helps to fulfill that promise to the reader. It also offers the reader something memorable to take away from the essay—something to ponder, to come back to later in the day, to argue with.

A good piece of writing will have a really good conclusion—one that doesn't simply repeat the thesis. Nobody wants to read a line that says, "So you see, I told you I would tell you about the dust on television screens, I went ahead and told you about the dust on television screens, and now I am telling you that I told you about the dust on television screens."

The best conclusions do sum up the writing, but they do so by finding a way to reaffirm the claim in some new way. If there is repetition, it is repetition that also includes a difference.

Good conclusions provide a sense of completion and satisfaction, but they can also leave the reader with new questions and with a sense that the topic has life beyond the page, that the issue they've been reading about is not a dead issue.

Good conclusions also give a sense of symmetry and form. They often bring back a theme from the opening by completing an anecdote or showing what has changed or stayed the same. There is even a rare type of conclusion that I call "circling back," which repeats the opening almost word for word, to show the reader how different his or her views are now, after reading, and how much he or she has learned about the topic. In other words, circling back shows readers how far they've come. These four general types of conclusions are very effective:

- Broadening out (A): strengthening
- Broadening out (B): extending
- Opposition
- Circling back

Broadening Out

The most common type of conclusion, by far, is what I call broadening out. It is simply a matter of (A) taking the original claim and showing how it applies more broadly to things beyond the specific topic of the essay, or (B) extending the claim and showing how much deeper it goes or how much more detail is involved. Here are two possible conclusions for the "seeming impossibility" introduction that made the claim that being overweight can lead to Alzheimer's disease. One of the conclusions shows the effects of strengthening; the other shows the effects of extending.

Strengthening

The fact that being overweight can lead to a higher incidence of Alzheimer's disease shouldn't be surprising. If one's body is neglected, the mind is often neglected as well. The switch that controls the gene for Alzheimer's may be kept in the "Off" position with a combination of good physical and mental health. Taking the weight off of the midsection may take the weight off that gene as well, keeping that switch "Off," where it should be.

Extending

The fact that being overweight can lead to a higher incidence of Alzheimer's disease shouldn't be surprising. The link between mind and body has been suggested for years. Many diet books suggest that maintaining a positive outlook can keep the pounds off; self-help books agree that keeping physically fit can lesson feelings of depression. Mind and body work together. Keeping both a healthy mind and a healthy body is a holistic approach to general wellness that other countries, including India and China, have practiced for centuries. Maybe we should take a lesson from them.

In both of these conclusions, the reader is invited to go beyond the basic summary—"there are three factors that connect body weight and Alzheimer's disease"—and to think about how the issues of body and mind can address not only Alzheimer's (strengthening) but also one's holistic health picture (extending).

Opposition

When you use opposition, which is simply the technique of moving from one thing to its opposite, your introduction and conclusion take the theme of the paper in opposite directions. If you start your essay with bitter cold, you could end with comforting warmth. If you start with pollution, you could end with a clean environment, or vice versa. Arguments about problems often end with proposed solutions. Stories about war often begin or end with moments of peace.

In this hook from the misdirection example of an introduction, the author sets up some startling statistics about crime that the reader believes, incorrectly, occur in the city.

Arrest rates are skyrocketing. Burglaries are up 25%. Rapes are up 17%. The murder rate has escalated 8% over a decade ago. Young adults are being incarcerated at a rate that has never been seen. Six Acres, Oklahoma, home to 20,000 inhabitants, is seeing a troubling increase in crime that shows no likelihood of slowing.

The claim, which directly follows this hook, is that these statistics were gathered from rural areas where crime is rising faster than it is in major metropolitan areas. To conclude the argument, the writer can offer a solution to the problem or discuss the good things that still take place in rural areas.

Although "big city crimes" that have come to rural areas are decreasing community members' feeling of safety, people in such towns as Six Acres are fighting back. They have organized crime watches in their neighborhoods—even in neighborhoods that are not clearly established.

In other words, instead of collapsing under the weight of escalating crime and their own fears, residents are fighting back.

Circling Back

The technique of circling back can be very effective. It shows just how far the reader has come in the essay. In one extreme, it can repeat the opening almost word for word, but because the audience has read the body of the essay, audience members realize that the words in the opening mean something quite different than they initially thought. Often, the extent of this change is a measure of how much the reader has learned. It can also be a way of emphasizing a theme of the writing. In the following conclusion, the scene from the "anecdote" introduction is repeated, bringing the reader back to the original scene.

As Marjory watched the deputy stringing the yellow crime scene tape like a garland around the neighbor's driveway, she realized that no distance from the city was going to outdistance crime. It had followed her to this rural spot. Perhaps fighting back was going to be the only way to win this race: running wasn't working.

Now the reader is brought full circle to the essay's beginning. The checklist, "Do's and Don'ts for Creating Successful Conclusions" offers some helpful tips for writing conclusions.

The conclusion for your proposal to Robie is partly written: "here's how your customers can help you grow your business." This will be a strengthening of the argument you have already made. You can sum up the two or three ways of working with customers instead of against them. By accepting all reasonable requests, such as cooking dishes off the menu, accepting expired coupons, and changing the menu to suit customer likes and dislikes, Robie can expect more repeat visits, more money in his pocket, and a secure livelihood for years to come.

Do's and Don'ts for Creating Effective Conclusions

- ☐ Don't introduce new ideas. The conclusion is the place for winding down, not exploring new avenues.
- ☐ Don't use clichéd closers, such as "in conclusion" or "to summarize."
- ☐ Don't simply provide a summary of all your argument's points.
- ☐ Do use one of the previously described techniques to let the reader know you are finished.
- ☐ Do be more creative, for example, directing your reader to think about your paper's topic in terms of what may happen in the future.
- ☐ Do provide a summary of all your paper points. But this time, do so in a different or briefer way, providing a look at the future, a solution, or a final comment.

your turn 13f PRACTICE Edit Your Conclusions

Use the three hooks you created in Your Turn 13e and create conclusions for them, each using a different choice from the list of conclusion types:

- Broadening out (A): strengthening
- Broadening out (B): extending
- Opposition
- Circling back

Your claim is the most important sentence in your argument. You must be clear about your claim, or your reader will not be. Even if you are clear, you need to verify that your claim—the way you have phrased it in your essay—clearly states what you want it to state.

Edit and Organize Your Argument's Support

With your claim solidified and your audience identified, you are ready to review your support and arrange your argument.

Edit Support

You learned in Chapter 11, "Support an Argument with Fact (Logos), Credibility (Ethos), and Emotion (Pathos)," about the three kinds of support and the value of using as many types of support as you can. Let's look at examples of both successful and unsuccessful support. Use these examples as a guide as you edit your own argument.

Support Based on Facts (Logos)

In his article "Beware the Idea of the Student as a Customer: A Dissenting View," Peter Vaill presents a series of miniature logical arguments. Here is one:

> *Education is clearly a service, not a product, and therefore the heavily units-of-product mode of thinking characteristic of business may not hold in a service endeavor. Many businesses, of course, are learning these difficult lessons as well as higher education.*

This approach is effective as long as the reader agrees with his premises and the way his conclusion follows those premises. With his business professor jargon, he sounds like he knows what he's talking about ("heavily units-of-product mode of thinking"); furthermore, the first idea in the passage is presented as if only an idiot would disagree ("education is clearly a service"). The combined effect is that the reader comes to the same conclusion as the author—that education experts are on the wrong track when they think of education as a product.

With regard to your customer-service proposal with your boss Robie, some of your support should be based on facts—perhaps restaurant-industry case studies and research. For example, one study showed that coupons effectively increase visits from regular customers but not visits from new customers. Another study showed that customer wait time affected profits more than food waste. A case study showed the importance of simplicity in menu design. You doubt that your boss will be swayed by studies like these, but if he asks you a question, you can always pull out this information. He might be impressed by your knowledge and interest in the business.

Support to Generate Credibility (Ethos)

Ethos is about credibility, or social norms. It's about the kinds of things we respect and listen to. Who do we listen to and why? Are they experts on a subject? For example, Dr. Mehmet Oz has created a career for himself as a talk show personality. During his regular appearances on the Oprah Show, he addressed health issues of all kinds.

So, who is Dr. Oz and why do people find him so appealing? First, and most importantly, he is a practicing doctor and directs the Cardiovascular Institute and Complementary Medicine Program at New York-Presbyterian Hospital. Second, he has authored or co-authored hundreds of articles on medical issues. The handsome doctor's trim physique also adds credibility to his arguments for healthy eating and exercise. And although Oz's ideas are not accepted by everyone all of the time, he is credible enough to be very influential.

"Beware the Idea of the Student as a Customer: A Dissenting View" by Peter Vaill, University of St. Thomas, 2000.

To move on, then, who are we as authors and why should anyone listen to our views? What is our ethos? Are we experts in our field, as Oz is in his? Do we make wise choices in the research we do and the support we select for our arguments? Do we make arguments that are consistent with the lifestyle we live and the way in which we present ourselves?

Finally, we have to ask ourselves what will seem credible to Robie? The opinions of other chefs? No, because in his opinion he is the equal of any chef. Research studies? Experts in business? Again, no. Robie is stubborn and egotistical, and he thinks he knows what is best. You decide the best credibility you can offer as support will simply be your caring and concern for his business, along with the knowledge and ideas you bring to the table. He won't be threatened by you, and he just might listen.

Emotion-Based Support (Pathos)

In the article "Are Students the New Indentured Servants?" Jeffrey Williams crafts his argument around an analogy sure to generate emotion: today's college students are like the indentured servants of the American past.

> *For the bound, it meant long hours of hard work, oftentimes abuse, terms sometimes extended by fiat of the landowner, little regulation or legal recourse for laborers, and the onerous physical circumstances of the new world, in which two-thirds died before fulfilling their terms.*

Clearly, most college students will survive to pay off their college loans, but the comparison works on an emotional level. The implication is that the "more than four thousand banks" that profit on the college loan system must not care about what happens to these poor indebted students any more than colonial landowners cared about the welfare of their debt-bound servants.

Good emotional support works because it communicates the high stakes involved in an argument. Reading Williams's piece makes a person want to rescue the poor college students from this system of virtual slavery to wealthy bankers. Good emotional support allows the reader to come to that conclusion, which is far more effective than if Williams had come out and said just that.

Emotional support for your proposal to Robie might come from case studies of failed restaurateurs, presented to show your boss the danger of not changing his ways. Or they might come from success stories, tales of restaurateurs who turned things around just in time. You select the latter, deciding that it is more positive but still shows Robie the dangers of staying stuck.

Williams, Jeffrey J. "Are Students the New Indentured Servants?" AlterNet February 5, 2009

your turn 13g **GET STARTED Edit Your Support**

Review the support you've used in your argument. Do you have a combination of logos-, ethos-, and pathos-based support? Does any one type of support dominate? If so, why? If one element is missing, why? Will its exclusion be a problem?

Organize Your Support

You can organize the elements of your argument in many ways. The numbers of the elements below refer to the order of the information. You may use as many paragraphs as you need for each section, although generally one idea to a paragraph is best unless your section has subsections that each need their own paragraphs.

All of these elements tend to be included in effective essays. With regard to the sections of the argument, we recommend that item 1 be followed directly by item 2, and that item 6 be presented last. Items 3–5 can be arranged in any order; decide what works best for your argument.

1. Introduction with Claim
   a. The claim can go anywhere in the introduction, but many writers find that placing it near the end helps lead readers to the essay body.
   b. Beginning the introduction with an attention-grabber like those described in the earlier section, "Create Strong Introductions," works well to draw your readers into your argument.
   c. If you feel the need to justify your warrants, now may be a good time to do so; however, explanation of your warrants can be placed wherever it is needed.

2. Background Information
   If your audience needs a bit of history in order to follow your argument, provide the history right after your introduction. This is also a good place to state why you think the topic is important in the first place, particularly if its importance is in question.

3. Examples Supporting Your Claim
   a. College-length papers usually include between three and five examples supporting their claim. Fewer than three may be kind of skimpy; more than five gets a little long. Base the specific number on the assignment or the needs of the project.
   b. If you feel you must justify your use of these examples, do so as you go.
   c. Counterarguments
   d. Rebuttal of Counterarguments
   e. Conclusion

Three Organization Samples of Body Paragraphs

As you can see, there are many combinations of body paragraphs—just use whatever works best for your particular argument, and make sure all of your bases are covered. Here is an example to support a claim of work discrimination.

Claim: Competent, qualified nurses of color in our hospital are regularly passed over for promotion to better-paying positions.

Let's see how the body elements for this claim can be organized in three different ways. (Note that the number of supporting and opposing examples used here is just for illustration; arguments vary regarding the quantity of support they require.)

Sample Body Arrangement One:

1. Supporting Example One
2. Supporting Example Two
3. Supporting Example Three
4. Counterargument One
5. Rebuttal of Counterargument One
6. Counterargument Two
7. Rebuttal of Counterargument Two

Sample Body Arrangement One:

1. Supporting Example One

   Research indicates that 45 percent of the nurses in hospitals are African American, Hispanic, or Asian American, yet only 5 percent of hospital administrators are people of color.

2. Supporting Example Two

   Of the 50 nurses of color who submitted application forms for the six senior positions available at our hospital in 2012, only 1 was promoted.

3. Supporting Example Three

   Carla Rivera has been a registered nurse for 25 years and recently received the American Society of Nurses' Award for logging 500 hours of community service. She applied for a higher position in her unit and was not even interviewed.

4. Counterargument One

   Hospital administrators say that the 5 percent of administrators who are people of color is one proof that they do promote nurses of various ethnicities.

5. Rebuttal of Counterargument One

   Upon closer examination, it was found that, of these 5 percent, only two positions had been filled from within.

6. Counterargument Two

The hospital also argues that it does not feel that the nurses of color who have submitted applications for higher positions have had the same credentials as their white counterparts.

7. Rebuttal of Counterargument Two

There is a wide range of abilities and backgrounds among the nursing staff, and it is generalizing to state that white nurses have better training or education than their African American, Hispanic, and Asian American colleagues.

For this arrangement, the writer chose to present all the supporting evidence for his claim first, and then he tackled the counterarguments one by one.

Sample Body Arrangement Two:

1. Supporting Example One
2. Counterargument One
3. Rebuttal of Counterargument One
4. Supporting Example Two
5. Counterargument Two
6. Rebuttal of Counterargument Two

Sample Body Arrangement Two:

1. Supporting Example One

Research indicates that 45 percent of the nurses in hospitals are African American, Hispanic, or Asian American, yet only 5 percent of hospital administrators are people of color.

2. Counterargument One

Hospital administrators say that the 5 percent of administrators who are people of color is proof that they do promote nurses of various ethnicities.

3. Rebuttal of Counterargument One

Upon closer examination, it was found that, of these 5 percent, only two positions had been filled from within.

4. Supporting Example Two

Carla Rivera has been a registered nurse for 25 years and recently received the American Society of Nurses' Award for logging 500 hours of community service. She applied for a higher position in her unit and was not even interviewed.

5. Counterargument Two

The hospital also argues that it does not feel that the nurses of color who have submitted applications for higher positions have had the same credentials as their white counterparts.

6. Rebuttal of Counterargument Two

   There is a wide range of abilities and backgrounds among the nursing staff, and it is generalizing to state that white nurses have better training or education than their African American, Hispanic, and Asian American colleagues.

In this second example, the writer examines each supporting example and the corresponding counterargument before moving to the next supporting example and its corresponding counterargument.

Sample Body Arrangement Three:

1. Counterargument One
2. Counterargument Two
3. Rebuttal of Counterarguments One and Two
4. Supporting Example One
5. Supporting Example Two

Sample Body Arrangement Three:

1. Counterargument One

   Hospital administrators say that the 5 percent of administrators who are people of color is proof that they do promote nurses of various ethnicities.

2. Counterargument Two

   The hospital also argues that it does not feel that the nurses of color who have submitted applications for higher positions have had the same credentials as their white counterparts.

3. Rebuttal of Counterarguments One and Two

   Upon closer examination, it was found that, of these 5 percent, only two positions had been filled from within. There is a wide range of abilities and backgrounds among the nursing staff, and it is generalizing to state that white nurses have better training or education than their African American, Hispanic, and Asian American colleagues.

4. Supporting Example One

   Research indicates that 45 percent of the nurses in the hospital are African American, Hispanic, or Asian American, yet only 5 percent of hospital administrators are people of color.

5. Supporting Example Two

   Carla Rivera has been a registered nurse for 25 years and recently received the American Society of Nurses' Award for logging 500 hours of community service. She applied for a higher position in her unit and was not even interviewed.

In this final example, the writer has opted to address the counterarguments first, rebut them, and then concentrate on his supporting examples for the remainder of the essay's body.

When you organize your argument in various ways, you will find that some arrangements work better than others. You may want to start with the opposing sides' arguments and then rebut them so that you can spend the remainder of the essay supporting your claim. Or you may find it more useful to present each of your supporting arguments and the corresponding opposition as you go. By trying different arrangements, you can see what works best for your particular claim and audience.

In your presentation to Robie, your organizational strategy will be based on your desire to win him to your side by first humoring him and then offering him ideas for turning each problem customer into an ally. Unruly families might be happier in the family section, waited upon by Rose, who has four children of her own and can handle just about anything. The too-choosy customer can be satisfied by offering "off-menu" selections with fixed prices designed to reward Robie for his extra efforts. Finally, cheapskate customers might be satisfied by free mini-portions of desserts; Robie hates when desserts go to waste, and once customers taste these unique and sweet creations, some of them will order (and pay for) a full portion.

your turn 13h   **PRACTICE Edit the Arrangement of Your Support**

Develop a claim addressing one of the following topics. Then create three different outlines, each one showing a different organization of body paragraphs, based on one of the preceding examples.

1. Something at work that management seems not to notice
2. Expectations from a teacher in one of your classes

Which organizational strategy works best for your claim and the type of support you are using? Next, label each section to indicate whether it includes support based on facts, support based on emotions, or support based on credibility.

Supply a Strong Title

A really good title will hook the audience. It will probably also reveal the general issue or even the specific topic of the argument. Like introductions, titles build suspense for the audience and draw them into the argument. Types of titles include the following:

- Titles that seem impossible: "Hip-Hop Graffiti Is a Significant American Art Form."
- Titles that represent conflict: "The Kindle's Assault on Academia: Amazon Wants to Corner the Textbook Market: But Don't Think It's Gonna Be Easy"

- Titles that generate suspense, often by leaving the reader wanting to know "how": "Loan Ranger: The Way Americans Pay for College Is a Mess; Here's How to Fix It"
- Titles that mark the beginning of an anecdote, such as the story of a particular family: "A Dad on His Own: A New Baby, a Wife's Death, and . . ."
- Titles that use misdirection: "On the Decay of the Art of Lying"

A less effective but still serviceable title will tell what the issue is, give the specific topic related to that issue, and even present the arguer's claim.

These two titles simply state the claim:

- "Killing the Entrepreneurial Spirit: Government Is Not a Good Investor"
- "Government Initiatives Will Not Reduce Homelessness"

These two titles don't give the claim but do present the issue or topic of the argument:

- "That 'Buy American' Provision"
- "The Potential in Hillary Clinton's Campaign for Women"

A bad title doesn't hook the reader or reveal the issue at hand. Here's a title that does neither:

- "Statement in the Great Trial of 1922"

Don't blame Ghandi for that sub-par title: he didn't write it; he actually gave the statement during a real trial. He had been charged with "bringing or attempting to excite disaffection towards His Majesty's Government established by law in British India."

Titles are sometimes inadvertently misleading:

- "No: Alternatives Are Simply Too Expensive"

Even if we see this title in the context of the environment, a lot of readers might not know the word *alternative* refers to alternative energy sources. That fact isn't mentioned until the sixth paragraph.

- Or titles may have grammatical errors. Here are two examples: "Animal Testing and Their Rights"
- "Is Bank Fees Fair to Customers?"

Before you print out your presentation for Robie, you must work on the title, the first thing he will see. The title should draw him in. What you may be tempted to say is, "Robie, No!" or perhaps, "Quit Killing Customers!" That, however, will only turn him off. Instead, you settle on something innocuous but slightly intriguing: "Three Ways to Fatten the Golden Goose."

your turn 13 ▶ **PRACTICE Edit Your Title to Support Your Claim**

Here are some titles, representing the good, the serviceable, and the unsatisfactory. Can you label which is which? Can you identify the five types of hooks? Can you spot the title that contains its argument's claim and which simply discloses its argument's topic?

1. "Stem Cell Research"
2. "The Consequences of Diesel-Powered Vehicles"
3. "Children Shouldn't Be Tried and Prosecuted as Adults"
4. "Would a Federal Gun Ban Lower Indiana's Crime Rate?"
5. "Space Exploration: Manned or Unmanned?"
6. "Sex Should Be Taught in School"
7. "Thirty-Eight Who Saw Murder Didn't Call Police"
8. "Freedom of the Pulpit"
9. "Student Hits Wall, Leaves"
10. "Gun Control"
11. "Capital Punishment Is Wrong"

Participate Effectively in a Peer Review Session

When you are asked to participate in a peer review session, you are being asked to help a classmate (or work colleague) determine what is working and what is not working in an argument. You are also being asked to listen to feedback about what is and is not working in your own argument. This chapter's guidelines for structure and style can help you identify what is effective and not effective. In this final section, we also provide a flowchart (Figure 13.1) to help you work through the process and make the most of your time as a peer reviewer and as a peer reviewee.

Your Role as a Reviewer

Read the assignment carefully, marking areas of concern that your instructor has assigned you to review. If there are no specific review instructions, mark and comment on the issues and concerns shown in Figure 13.3.

In presenting your findings to your partner:

1. Ask your partner to explain anything that does not make sense to you.
2. Although you may have made written comments on many areas of the argument, pick two or three of the most important problems to discuss rather than pointing out a laundry list of errors.
3. Politely point out errors—don't be a know-it-all.

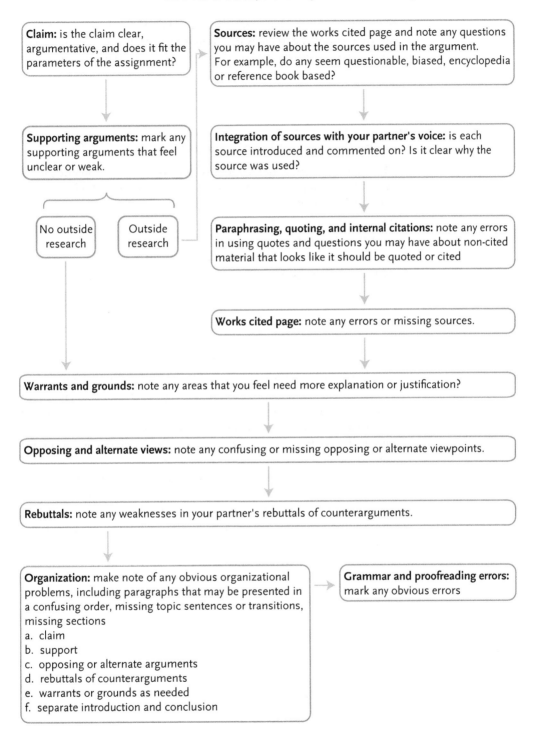

Figure 13.3 Peer review flowchart

4. Ask if there is anything you haven't pointed out that your critique partner would like to know or, as time permits, if your partner would like you to expound on anything you have marked but have not discussed.

Your Role as a Reviewee

When your partner presents his or her observations (or when your partners present their observations), listen carefully and avoid getting defensive.

1. Take notes. If you do not agree with your reviewer's comments, make note of them anyway. Upon later reflection, you may find that your partner has a good point.
2. Listen for patterns. If more than one reviewer gives you the same advice, you probably want to pay attention.
3. Ask for clarification of any confusing comments.
4. List two or three areas you'd especially like to have clarified.

Reflect and Apply

1. How is your argument's introduction setting the scene for your claim? Explain how your conclusion provides closure for your reader.
2. Explain your reasons for selecting the logical, ethical, and emotional support that you have included. How does each type of support increase your audience's understanding and buy-in? If you have not used all three types of support, explain your decision to leave out one or more types.
3. Review the organization of your argument. Using the Peer Review Flowchart, can you identify any sections that are missing or that need shoring up? Explain how you will address problems.
4. Review your title. Explain how it provides a link to your argument's claim.

KEEPING IT LOCAL

You've done the best you can with your presentation to the restaurant's owner, Robie. His reaction? Better than you had anticipated. Although he doesn't agree that bad customers deserve good service, he is impressed by the amount of work that you did to convince him otherwise. He is willing to consider some of your recommendations. For your part, you are pleased that you will be able to maintain your job while you are still in college.

The success of your proposal came from your willingness to edit every facet of your argument, from the claim and its position to the introduction and corresponding conclusion, the types of support you included, and the arrangement of the ideas on the slides. By taking into account your audience and gearing the argument to his needs and values, you have opened the door to a dialogue in which resolutions can be made and changes set in place.

What can you do to ensure that your argument is well-arranged and well-supported? Do you have a friend or classmate you can trust to review your argument and give you good advice? Good arguments are a product of thinking about your own point of view on an issue and then thinking of the best way to present your point of view to others. Are you sure you have done all that you can to persuade your audience?

An Anthology of Arguments

Anthology 1   School and Academic Community

Anthology 2   Workplace Community

Anthology 3   Family and Household Community

Anthology 4   Neighborhood Community

Anthology 5   Social/Cultural Community

Anthology 6   Consumer Community

Anthology 7   Concerned Citizen Community

Anthology 8   Classic American Arguments (Mindtap)

Intersections: Contemporary Issues and Arguments

Anthology 1
School and Academic Community

ABOUT THIS READING

Jennifer A. Mott-Smith is Professor of English at Towson University. She has been teaching college composition courses, with a focus on second language writing, for more than 25 years. She has pursued an interest in plagiarism and source use for the last ten years.

Bad Idea About Writing: Plagiarism Deserves to Be Punished

By Jennifer A. Mott-Smith

"College Plagiarism Reaches All-Time High"
"Studies Find More Students Cheating, With High Achievers No Exception"
Headlines like these from *The Huffington Post* and *The New York Times* scream at us about an increase in plagiarism. As a society, we feel embattled, surrounded by falling standards; we bemoan the increasing immorality of our youth. Plagiarism, we know, is an immoral act, a simple case of right and wrong, and as such, deserves to be punished.

However, nothing is simple about plagiarism. In fact, the more we examine plagiarism, the more inconsistencies we find, and the more confusion. How we think about the issue of plagiarism is clouded by the fact that it is often spoken of as a crime. Plagiarism is not only seen as immoral; it is seen as stealing—the stealing of ideas or words. In his book *Free Culture*, Stanford law professor Lawrence Lessig questions what it can possibly mean to steal an idea.

"I understand what I am taking when I take the picnic table you put in your backyard. I am taking a thing, the picnic table, and after I take it, you don't have it. But what am I taking when I take the good idea you had to put a picnic table in the backyard—by, for example, going to Sears, buying a table, and putting it in my backyard? What is the thing that I am taking then?"

Lessig gets at the idea that, when a person borrows an idea, no harm is done to the party from whom it was taken. But what about loss in revenues as a form of harm? Surely there is no loss of revenues when a student plagiarizes a paper. From Lessig's metaphor we can see that theft, and even copyright infringement, are not entirely apt ways to think about plagiarism.

iStock.com/A-digit

But Lessig's metaphor does not help us understand that, in academic writing, acknowledgment of sources is highly valued. Neither does it reveal that taking ideas and using them in your own writing, with conventional attribution, is a sophisticated skill that requires a good deal of practice to master.

There are at least three important things to understand about the complexity of using sources. First, ideas are often a mixture of one's own ideas, those we read and those we discuss with friends—making it hard or even impossible to sort out who owns what. Second, writers who are learning a new field often "try out" ideas and phrases from other writers in order to master the field. That process, which allows them to learn, involves little or no deceit. And third, expectations for citing sources vary among contexts and readers, making it not only confusing to learn the rules but impossible to satisfy them all.

It is quite hard to separate one's ideas from those of others. When we read, we always bring our own knowledge to what we're reading. Writers cannot say everything; they have to rely on readers to supply their own contribution to make meaning. One difficulty arises when you read an argument with unnamed steps. As a good reader, you fill them in so you can make sense of the argument. Now, if you were to write about those missing steps, would they be your ideas or those of your source?

Writers may reuse the ideas of others, but surely they know when they reuse words, so should they attribute them? Perhaps not. Words are not discrete entities that can be recombined in countless ways, rather, they fall into patterns that serve certain ways of thinking, the very ways of thinking or habits of mind that we try to instill in students.

The fact is that language is formulaic, meaning that certain words commonly occur together. There are many idioms, such as "toe the line" or "cut corners" that need not be attributed. There are also many co-occurring words that don't quite count as idioms, such as "challenge the status quo," "it should also be noted that . . ." and "The purpose of this study is to . . ." that similarly do not require attribution. Those are called collocations. Student writers need to acquire and use a great number of them in academic writing. What this means is that not every verbatim reuse is plagiarism.

Moreover, imposing strict rules against word reuse may function to prevent student writers from learning to write in their fields. When student writers reuse patterns of words without attribution in an attempt to learn how to sound like a journalist, say, or a biologist, or a literary theorist, it is called *patchwriting*. In fact, not only student writers but all writers patch together pieces of text from sources, using their own language to sew the seams, in order to learn the language of a new field.

Because of the complex way in which patchwriting mixes text from various sources, it can be extremely difficult to cite one's sources. Despite this lack of attribution, much research has shown that patchwriting is not deceitful and therefore should not be punished. In fact, some scholars are interested in exploring how writing teachers could use the concept of patchwriting to help student writers develop their own writing skills.

The third reason that it is not always easy to acknowledge sources is that expectations for referencing vary widely and what counts as plagiarism depends on context. If, for instance, you use a piece of historic information in a novel, you don't have to cite it, but if you use the same piece of

information in a history paper, you do. Journalists typically do not supply citations, although they have fact checkers making sure their claims are accurate. In business, people often start their reports by cutting and pasting earlier reports without attribution. And in the academy, research has shown that the reuse of words in science articles is much more common and accepted than it is in the humanities.

In high school, student writers probably used textbooks that did not contain citations, and once in college, they may observe their professors giving lectures that come straight from the textbook without citation, cribbing one another's syllabi and cutting and pasting the plagiarism policy into their syllabi. They may even notice that their university lifted the wording of its plagiarism policy from another institution!

In addition to those differing standards for different genres or fields of study, research has also shown that individual "experts" such as experienced writers and teachers do not agree whether or not a given piece of writing counts as plagiarism. Given such wide disagreement over what constitutes plagiarism, it is quite difficult, perhaps impossible, for student writers to meet everyone's expectations for proper attribution. Rather than assuming that they are trying to pass off someone else's work as their own and therefore deserve punishment, we should recognize the complexity of separating one's ideas from those of others, mastering authoritative phrases and meeting diverse attribution standards.

While most people feel that plagiarism deserves punishment, some understand that plagiarism is not necessarily deceitful or deserving censure. Today, many writers and writing teachers reject the image of the writer as working alone, using (God-given) talent to produce an original piece of work. In fact, writers often do two things that are proscribed by plagiarism policies: they recombine ideas in their writing and they collaborate with others.

Interestingly, the image of the lone, divinely inspired writer is only a few hundred years old, a European construct from the Romantic era. Before the 18th century or so, writers who copied were respected as writers. Even today, rather than seeing copying as deceitful, we sometimes view it as a sign of respect or free publicity.

Today, millennial students often copy without deceitful intent. Reposting content on their Facebook pages and sharing links with their friends, they may not cite because they are making an allusion; readers who recognize the source without a citation share the in-joke.

In school, millennials may not cite because they are not used to doing so or they believe that having too many citations detracts from their authority. In either case, these are not students trying to get away with passing someone else's work off as their own, and, in fact, many studies have concluded that plagiarism, particularly that of second-language student writers, is not done with the intent to deceive.

Despite these complexities of textual reuse, most faculty members nevertheless expect student writers to do their "own work." In fact, student writers are held to a higher standard and punished more rigorously than established writers.

What is even more troublesome is that teachers' determinations of when plagiarism has occurred is more complicated than simply noting whether a

student has given credit to sources or not. Research has shown that teachers let inadequate attribution go if they feel the overall sophistication or authority of the paper is good, whereas they are stricter about citing rules when the sophistication or authority is weak. Furthermore, they tend to more readily recognize authority in papers written by students who are members of a powerful group (e.g., whites, native English speakers or students whose parents went to college). Thus, in some instances, plagiarism may be more about social inequity than individual deceit.

As we come to realize that writers combine their ideas with those of others in ways that cannot always be separated out for the purposes of attribution, that writers often reuse phrases in acceptable ways, that citing standards themselves vary widely and are often in the eye of the beholder, and that enforcement of plagiarism rules is an equity issue, the studies and articles panicking over plagiarism make less and less sense. In looking at plagiarism from the different perspectives offered by collaborative writers and today's millennial student writers, we can see that much plagiarism is not about stealing ideas or deceiving readers.

Unless plagiarism is out-and-out cheating, like cutting and pasting an entire paper from the internet or paying someone to write it, we should be cautious about reacting to plagiarism with the intent to punish. For much plagiarism, a better response is to relax and let writers continue to practice the difficult skill of using sources.

Analyze This Reading

1. Explain how the writer uses law professor Lawrence Lessig to complicate how we think about plagiarism.
2. How does the writer justify her notion that it may be acceptable to use the words of others without citing sources?
3. How do the terms "collocations" and "patchwriting" add momentum to this argument?
4. What is the claim of this argument and where does it occur?
5. How does this argument encourage us to reimagine traditional images of an individual writing?
6. Identify inconsistencies common to writing teachers and how these inconsistencies further complicate the issue of plagiarism.

Respond To This Reading

1. Are you comfortable with plagiarism policies in your classes? If not, how would you improve them?
2. What is your understanding of the term "patchwriting?" Would you be a better writer by patchwriting?
3. Respond to the final sentence in this argument. Should teachers adopt this position? Explain.

AUTHOR'S NOTE AND A QUESTION

This argument originally appeared in a volume where editors requested that writers not use citations in their arguments and essays. Writer Mott-Smith originally

had included 32 in-text citations and agreed to remove all citations. Upon reflection, however, Mott-Smith feels strongly that one citation should remain in the piece so as to rightfully acknowledge an original source. This citation acknowledges writer Malcolm Gladwell's use of Lawrence Lessig's idea in paragraphs 5 and 6 to further complicate Gladwell's argument about plagiarism. The argument can be found via this link: (2004, Nov. 22, "Something borrowed: should a charge of plagiarism ruin your life?" *The New Yorker*, retrieved from http://www.newyorker.com/magazine/2004/11/22/something-borrowed/).

Question: Why might editors have thought that citations were inappropriate for this argument by Mott-Smith?

The Rich-Poor Divide on America's College Campuses is Getting Wider, Fast

Rich, poor take paths even more dramatically divergent than in the past, new data show

By Jon Marcus and Holly K. Hacker

HARTFORD, Conn.—The main dining hall at Trinity College starts you off with a choice of infused water: lemon, pineapple, strawberry, melon. There are custom-made smoothies, all-day breakfasts, make-your-own waffles, and frozen yogurt, along with countless choices of entrees hovered over by white-jacketed chefs.

Sun pours in through windows overlooking the leafy, manicured campus fringed with stately red brick dorms and classroom buildings past which students stroll with their noses in books. A new student center that will include a Starbucks is going up beside the tennis courts. As a college worker clears her dishes, one senior talks over lunch about the job she's already lined up after graduation with the help of an alumna.

Across the city, off an exit from an elevated highway, other students dodge downtown traffic to squeeze into the sluggish elevators in time for the start of their classes at Capital Community College. This campus consists of a concrete parking garage and a onetime department store converted into classrooms and offices.

There's a campaign here to start a food bank for students who can't afford food, even though many work full time. Many also are raising families.

It's a stark view of the reality of American higher education, in which rich kids go to elite private and flagship public campuses while poor kids—including those who score higher on standardized tests than their wealthier counterparts—end up at community colleges and regional public universities with much lower success rates, assuming they continue their educations at all. And new federal data analyzed by the Hechinger Report and the Huffington Post show the gap has been widening at a dramatically accelerating rate since the economic downturn began in 2008.

Once acclaimed as the equal-opportunity stepping stone to the middle class, and a way of closing that divide, higher education has instead become more segregated than ever by wealth and race as state funding has fallen and colleges and universities—and even states and the federal

government—are shifting financial aid from lower-income to higher-income students. This has created a system that spends the least on those who need the most help and the most on those who arguably need the least. While almost all the students who go to selective institutions such as Trinity graduate and get good jobs, many students from the poorest families end up even worse off than they started out, struggling to repay loans they took out to pay for degrees they never get.

Instead of raising people up, "Today in many ways the system is exacerbating inequality," said Suzanne Mettler, a government professor at Cornell University and author of *Degrees of Inequality: Why Opportunity Has Diminished in U.S. Higher Education*. "It's creating something of a caste system that for too many people takes them from wherever they were on the socioeconomic spectrum and leaves them even more unequal."

Or, as Julian Lopez, a student catching up on his homework between classes at Capital Community College, puts it: "There are plenty of smart people here. But everything's about the money. The majority of people who come here, it's because they can't afford to go to more expensive schools. It depends on how much money you have and how much money your parents make."

Because of stagnant household incomes, and because more low-income students are successfully completing high school and being pushed to go to college, the proportion of all students who qualify for federal Pell grants, reserved largely for the children of families with incomes of around $40,000 or less, is up by almost a third since 2008, to 49 percent of undergraduates. But the federal figures show that some of the nation's most elite private universities and colleges—the category that includes such lush green, lavishly equipped campuses as Brown, Columbia, Duke, Georgetown, Yale and Stanford—are taking only a few more of them than the very small percentages they always have, up from 12 percent of their total student bodies, on average, to 15 percent now.

Elite flagship public institutions such as the universities of Oregon, Texas at Austin, Washington, Colorado-Boulder, Maryland, Connecticut, and Georgia Tech do slightly better; there, the proportion of students who are low income has grown from an average of 20 percent to 28 percent. But that's only half the proportion of college students nationally who come from low-income families eligible for Pell grants.

Instead, low-income students are increasingly winding up at for-profit universities such as ITT Tech, Brown Mackie, DeVry, and the University of Phoenix, where the proportion who are low income has jumped from 49 percent to 66 percent since 2008, and where graduation rates are the worst in higher education.

They're also concentrated at regional public universities whose already thinly stretched funding to support them has generally been sliding downward, such as Alabama State, Boise State, Montclair State, the University of Southern Maine, Grambling State, Southeastern Oklahoma State, and others, some 41 percent of whose students now are low income. And 42 percent of students are low income at the hardest-pressed sector of American higher education: community colleges, which spend less per student than many public primary and secondary schools, and where the odds of ever graduating are also comparatively low.

Just as in 2008, only a little more than 10 percent of students are low income at Trinity, for example, which spends two and a half times more per student on instruction than Capital Community College. At Capital, nearly 60 percent of the students are low income—up 12 percentage points since 2008—while the budget for student services has actually declined. So has instructional spending, thanks in large part to cuts in its appropriation from the state. Taxpayer outlays for community colleges nationwide are down almost 5 percent since 2008, and some state financial aid has been shifted to students who go to private colleges and universities.

"There are other things we'd like to provide, but we can't," said Capital's president, Wilfredo *Nieves*.

Only 7 percent of students graduate from the two-year college within even three years, according to the U.S. Department of Education. (The school says another 23 percent transfer.) At Trinity, 86 percent of students finish their four-year degrees within six years.

In part because of disparities like this, students from high-income families are a staggering eight times more likely to get bachelor's degrees by the time they're 24 than from low-income families, up from six times more likely in 1970, according to the Pell Institute for the Study of Opportunity in Higher Education.

"The gap between the haves and the have-nots is just getting bigger," said Laura Perna, chairman of the higher-education division at the University of Pennsylvania Graduate School of Education. "Really it calls into question the American dream. We tell people, just work hard and you'll have these opportunities available. The reality is, if you grow up in a neighborhood in West Philadelphia, your chances are quite different than if you grow up just a few miles away in a family with a quite higher income."

It's not about academic ability. The lowest-income students with the highest scores on eighth-grade standardized tests are less likely to go to selective colleges than the highest-income students with the lowest test scores, according to the Education Trust, which advocates for students who are being left behind in this way. If they do manage to make it to a top school, many do well—at Trinity, for instance, finishing with even higher graduation rates than their wealthier classmates.

Yet more than a fifth of those high-achieving low-income students never go to college at all, never mind to top colleges, the Education Trust says. Only 16 percent find their way to highly selective schools, and fewer than half continue their educations anywhere, compared to nearly all of their wealthier counterparts at every level of ability.

Cost is a principal reason, of course. Average tuition has more than doubled since 1970 when adjusted for inflation, according to the Pell Institute, and income and financial aid have not remotely kept pace. Among other reasons for the huge tuition increases: the pricey arms race in amenities to attract higher-income students, a huge increase in the number of administrators, and other non-academic expenses, all fueled by the easy supply of government-subsidized loans.

In 1975, the maximum federal Pell Grant covered two-thirds of the average cost of college; today, that's fallen to about a quarter. So while a higher education is a strain for even the wealthiest families, who will annually spend an amount equal to 15 percent of their earnings on one, the lowest-income families have to pay, on average, the equivalent of 84 percent of their earnings. This at exactly the time when median family income has increased for the wealthiest Americans but flattened off or fallen for the poorest.

Colleges and universities have their own financial preoccupations. Public universities, for instance, faced with declining state funding, have chosen to not only make up for this by raising their tuition, but by recruiting higher-paying out-of-state students. They and private, nonprofit colleges and universities are offering wealthier applicants billions of dollars in financial aid that once went to lower-income ones, the U.S. Department of Education found. While private colleges and universities often say that they give lots of money in financial aid, they don't specify who's getting it, and the proportion of students who get aid for reasons other than need has doubled in the last 20 years, the department found.

Another of those reasons: Students from schools in higher-income suburbs usually do better on college entrances exams such as the SAT and other measures that make the universities and colleges that accept them look better in national rankings.

"We've almost built this system that isn't set up to open its doors to low-income students," said Angel Pérez, Trinity's vice president of enrollment and student success.

Himself the son of Puerto Rican immigrants, raised in the projects of the South Bronx, Pérez said, "Admitting kids that share my story is riskier these days. Take too many and your average GPA or SAT scores decrease. There goes your *U.S. News* ranking. Admit students who don't have the best stats and you might damage your yield and retention numbers. There goes your Moody's bond rating."

Just returned from a budget meeting to his office in the Trinity admissions building, where applicants find fresh flowers and roaring fires in a waiting room whose floor-to-ceiling windows overlook the leafy campus, Pérez said the college would like to see its proportion of low-income students increase. "But these are conversations that are really, really difficult. Do we all want more low-income students? Sure, but we would go into financial ruin."

It's not just colleges and universities that have shifted their financial aid to more upscale recipients. So have some states, in an effort to stop high-achieving and often high-income students from moving away; 12 states plus Washington D.C. now spend more on so-called merit-based aid than on need-based aid. In 15 states, less than half of taxpayer-funded financial aid now takes financial circumstances into account, the College Board reports.

Some federal financial-aid programs, such as work study, have also been shown to disproportionately benefit wealthier students; nearly one in five work-study recipients—who earn an average of $1,642 each, per academic year, by working in dining halls, libraries, and other places on and off campus—comes from a family whose annual income exceeds $100,000, according to research conducted at Teachers College, Columbia University. And even though only one-fifth of American households earn $100,000 or more per year, and 13 out of 14 of them would have sent their children to college even without them, those families get more than half of $34 billion a

year in politically popular federal tuition tax credits, the Tax Policy Center calculates.

"They already knew since they were little kids that they were going to college," said Jermaine Jenkins, a student at Capital Community College and president of its black student union. "For me, I had to fill out scholarships, I had to keep my grades up. We definitely work harder. It's sad to say this, but that's never going to change."

Even private scholarships from the likes of Rotary clubs and others disproportionately go to wealthier families whose parents and college counselors know to apply for them. Nearly 13 percent of students from families that make more than $106,000 a year get private scholarships, compared with about 9 percent of those whose families earn less than $30,000, according to the Education Department.

"Machiavelli would be proud of how evil this education finance system has become," said Tom Mortenson, a senior scholar at the Pell Institute. "Why are we subsidizing wealthy students? You're just shifting the cost onto students who can't afford it."

In fact, since 2008, lower-income students have seen the amount they pay, after grants and scholarships, rise even faster than it has for their higher-income classmates.

"The United States is—quote, unquote—the greatest country in the world," said Yvonne Duhaney, a student majoring in social services at Capital Community College and the first in her family to go to college, who hopes to continue on to get a bachelor's degree. "Yet if you're not part of that population, the 1 percent, you're not guaranteed to go to college. Some people, even though they want to go to college, they have to worry about putting food on the table."

Meanwhile, families in the top 10 percent of incomes have vastly increased what they spend on such things as test preparation, private schools, and other things meant to give their kids a leg up in admission, according to a report by the Stanford Center on Poverty and Inequality.

"High-income parents have resources they can use for this, and low-income parents have had to cut back," said Sabino Kornrich, a professor of sociology at Emory University who coauthored the report. "We've seen since the recession this inequality of spending become even more pronounced."

Students from higher-income families are far more likely to use the kind of so-called "college enhancement strategies" elite institutions' admissions offices take into account, including community service and extracurricular activities, scholars at New York University reported in November.

Resumé-building may be the last thing on many lower-income students' minds. In many cases the first in their families to go to college, they're often derailed by the complicated process of not only making themselves look good to admissions officers, but simply applying for admission and financial aid.

"If you come from a community where your parents went to college, and it's part of the dinnertime conversation, then it's in your expectations," said Doris Arrington, dean of student services at Capital Community College. "Many of our students don't have that kind of information."

For them, college counselors may not be available to help much either. The average public high school college counselor is responsible for 471 students, according to the National Association of College Admissions Counselors—an average dragged down by the even higher ratio in schools that serve low-income students. That means college counselors in public high schools juggle about twice as many students apiece as is recommended by the American School Counselor Association and almost five times the number counselors in private schools work with.

"Try to be that student and see if you can navigate our complex institutions of higher education," said Estela Mara Bensimon, professor of higher education and co-director of the Center for Urban Education at the University of Southern California.

If lower-income students do manage to overcome these odds and enroll in college, they face still more hurdles. More of them work while enrolled, the U.S. Department of Education reports. Especially on elite campuses, that reinforces a socioeconomic split.

"You can think of it as a luxury cruise," said Laura Hamilton, a sociologist at the University of California Merced and coauthor of *Paying for the Party: How College Maintains Inequality*. "There are the people who are there to enjoy their four-year vacation, and people who are there to serve them. The only interaction that poor students have with wealthy students is picking up their towels at the [campus] gym or washing their dishes in the cafeteria."

For that, along with financial reasons, Hamilton said, lower-income students often quit. "If they even make it to a flagship university in the first place, which is extremely unlikely, a lot of them can't stay there, and a lot of them leave because of the total isolation and segregation," she said.

And where the data show they land—or start in the first place—is at private for-profit schools, open-admission regional public universities, and community colleges like Capital, with vastly lower levels of support than at top schools populated largely by higher-income students.

"There are just fewer ways to fail at more prestigious schools," said Hamilton. "But when you go down the ladder, there's a lot less of that kind of support. The amount of advising and the number of student advisors drop off."

Separate, said Richard Kahlenberg, a senior fellow at the Century Foundation, a nonpartisan think tank, "is rarely equal, and when you look at outcomes, that's true."

While primary and secondary schools that serve the lowest-income Americans get additional federal and, in two-thirds of the states, state aid to help them overcome disparities in funding, he said, "in higher education, we're doing precisely the reverse. We give the fewest resources to the students with the greatest need."

What students in those poorer institutions get is far inferior to what their counterparts at richer schools enjoy. The dropout rate at community colleges is higher than it is at high schools; while 81 percent of students who start in one say they eventually want to transfer and earn at least a bachelor's degree, only 12 percent of them do, the Century Foundation reports.

At Trinity, by comparison, "For me and I know for most students here, my only worry is getting my homework done, because everything else is sort of given to us," said Miguel Adamson, an international studies major, sitting under a tree on the campus working on his laptop. Members of the squash team pass by through arched passageways hung with flyers advertising an

organ recital and internship and study-abroad programs, and another student outfitted in Vineyard Vines apparel stops by to say hello.

"These sorts of schools are places where you can really see the economic divide, especially between people who get a lot of financial aid and people who don't, even by what they're wearing," said Adamson, who went to private school in Washington D.C.

With relatives who are lower-income—including a cousin with whom he has discussed this issue—he has been "more exposed, I think, to what some people are up against," Adamson said. "I would take things for granted and she would yell at me, 'You don't know what the struggles are.'"

Other Trinity students think about this rift, too, said Rose Carroll, a senior political science major from Pasadena, California, who already has a job lined up for when she graduates in the spring, thanks to the help of an alumna.

"We talk about these issues a lot," Carroll said in the dining hall. Like other top colleges, she said, Trinity "is an amazing pocket of intellectual diversity but not economic diversity. Students care about this, but they're not sure how to address it."

And if these realities are evident to the students who attend elite schools, they're glaringly obvious to those who don't. Seventy-five percent of students who go to a community college make their decision based on the price, a national poll by Boston public radio station WGBH found, and an even higher proportion say they'd probably go elsewhere if they could. Two-thirds say that, even with a community college education, it will be hard to rise up into the middle class. (A third of those who dropped out say job responsibilities were the reason, second only to family obligations.)

"The low-income students really want to be somewhere else. If they had a choice, they wouldn't want to be at the parking garage and the old department store. They would want the same opportunity of the students at the private colleges," said Maureen Hoyler, president of the Council for Opportunity in Education.

"We don't need a dual system of higher education where rich people get one thing and poor people get another thing, especially if what they get is kind of a lie. Their chances of really graduating from college are very low. And the burden's all on them—you know, take out loans and then don't graduate."

If they do graduate, these students still are at a disadvantage. They lack the alumni networking advantages that students finishing elite schools get. Research at Northwestern University's Kellogg School of Management finds employers disproportionately prefer graduates from prestigious colleges who have participated in extracurricular activities such as playing lacrosse and squash and who have served in internships—pursuits less likely to have been available to lower-income students.

"If we're going for the same job, they're going to pick the kid from Trinity," Lopez, the Capital Community College student, said with a shrug of resignation.

It's not that universities couldn't take more lower-income students if they wanted to—especially top public universities with high graduation rates but low proportions of such students now—an October report from the Institute for Higher Education Policy found. Only 15 percent of the students at Penn State's main campus, for example, are lower income, but the study showed

that double that proportion would likely qualify for admission. If the university accepted them, some 900 more lower-income students per year would finish there. If the same thing happened at all the universities and colleges that now take fewer lower-income students than they could, the report concluded, 57,500 more of them per year would graduate with bachelor's degrees.

The disinvestment by states, from higher education "is certainly a culprit in this larger stratification that we're seeing, but certainly a leader who's committed so socioeconomic diversity can prioritize it and still have a college that functions and is fiscally sound," said Kahlenberg, of the Century Foundation. "There doesn't appear to be a lot of leadership on this issue."

Among other things, advocates are pushing for private universities and colleges to be required to increase their enrollments of lower- income students in exchange for continuing to receive billions of dollars of tax exemptions.

Mortenson, for one, is not optimistic. Access to an equitable college education "is really crucial to what America is, was, and at least used to stand for," he said. "It clearly doesn't stand for that any more. The data show, in every way you look at it, that we're on the wrong path."

Higher education, said Hamilton, "was once the gleaming star and the centerpiece of the American dream, because it was the mechanism through which you could achieve anything. But the golden period of higher education, when the government really partnered with schools to really create educational opportunities for people regardless of their backgrounds, that moment is gone. It's thoroughly gone."

Leon Lewis hopes that isn't true. A student at Capital Community College studying social work, he wants something better for his three children.

"I want my kids," said Lewis, "to go to a four-year university."

Analyze this Reading

1. The writers claim that funding programs in higher education break America's promise that college is a stepping stone into the middle class. How do they support this claim?
2. Describe how writers use a scholar, Suzanne Mettler, and a student, Julian Lopez, to deliver an important idea.
3. Explain how changes in funding impact low-income students.
4. The writers use the terms "isolation" and "segregation" to evaluate the college experience of many low-income students. Refer to a few examples that support this contention.

Respond to this Reading

1. While this writing is more a report than an argument, its focus on inequality and privilege in American colleges may address to some degree your college experience. Are there issues addressed here that you could build an argument around? Explain.
2. Should a college education be a privilege or a right? If tuition-free college becomes an issue in political elections, what position would you favor? Why?

ABOUT THIS READING

The writer is U.S. Representative for the Fifth Congressional District of Minnesota. His argument appears in *The American Prospect*, a print and digital magazine that, in the words of its mission, aims to "build public support for policies that serve the greater good. We pay particular attention to efforts to renew American democracy and civic life and to revitalize the social movements that can help achieve a more just society."

The Argument for Tuition-Free College

By Keith Ellison

Soaring tuitions and student loan debt are placing higher education beyond the reach of many American students. It's time to make college free and accessible to all.

In 1862, President Abraham Lincoln signed the Land Grant College Act into law, laying the groundwork for the largest system of publicly funded universities in the world. Some of America's greatest colleges, including the University of Minnesota, were created by federal land grants, and were known as "democracy's colleges" or "people's colleges." But that vision of a "people's college" seems awfully remote to a growing number of American students crushed under soaring tuitions and mounting debt. One hundred and fifty years after Lincoln made his pledge, it's time to make public colleges and universities free for every American.

This idea is easier than it looks. For most of our nation's history, public colleges and universities have been much more affordable than they are today, with lower tuition, and financial aid that covered a much larger portion of the costs. The first step in making college accessible again, and returning to an education system that serves every American, is addressing the student loan debt crisis.

The cost of attending a four-year college has increased by 1,122 percent since 1978. Galloping tuition hikes have made attending college more expensive today than at any point in U.S. history. At the same time, debt from student loans has become the largest form of personal debt in America— bigger than credit card debt and auto loans. Last year, 38 million American students owed more than $1.3 trillion in student loans.

Once, a degree used to mean a brighter future for college graduates, access to the middle class, and economic stability. Today, student loan debt increases inequality and makes it harder for low-income graduates, particularly those of color, to buy a house, open a business, and start a family.

The solution lies in federal investments to states to lower the overall cost of public colleges and universities. In exchange, states would commit to reinvesting state funds in higher education. Any public college or university that benefited from the reinvestment program would be required to limit tuition increases. This federal–state partnership would help lower tuition for all students. Schools that lowered tuition would receive additional federal grants based on the degree to which costs are lowered.

Reinvesting in higher education programs like Pell Grants and work-study would ensure that Pell and other forms of financial aid that students don't need to pay back would cover a greater portion of tuition costs for low-income students. In addition, states that participate in this partnership would ensure that low-income students who attend state colleges and universities could afford nontuition expenses like textbooks and housing fees. This proposal is one way to ensure that no student graduates with loans to pay back. If the nation can provide hundreds of billions of dollars in subsidies to the oil and gas industry and billions of dollars more to Wall Street, we can afford to pay for public higher education. A tax on financial transactions like derivatives and stock trades would cover the cost. Building a truly affordable higher education system is an investment that would pay off economically.

Eliminating student loan debt is the first step, but it's not the last. Once we ensure that student loan debt isn't a barrier to going to college, we should reframe how we think about higher education. College shouldn't just be debt free—it should be free. Period.

We all help pay for our local high schools and kindergartens, whether or not we send our kids to them. And all parents have the option of choosing public schools, even if they can afford private institutions. Free primary and secondary schooling is good for our economy, strengthens our democracy, and most importantly, is critical for our children's health and future. Educating our kids is one of our community's most important responsibilities, and it's a right that every one of us enjoys. So why not extend public schooling to higher education as well?

Some might object that average Americans should not have to pay for students from wealthy families to go to school. But certain things should be guaranteed to all Americans, poor or rich. It's not a coincidence that some of the most important social programs in our government's history have applied to all citizens, and not just to those struggling to make ends meet.

Universal programs are usually stronger and more stable over the long term, and they're less frequently targeted by budget cuts and partisan attacks. Public schools have stood the test of time—let's make sure public colleges and universities do, too.

The United States has long been committed to educating all its people, not only its elites.

This country is also the wealthiest in the history of the world. We can afford to make college an option for every American family.

Analyze this Reading

1. This argument opens with reference to the vision of an American president, to some a revered figure who embodies principles of equal opportunity and fair play. What factual information does the writer bring to his argument to demonstrate how this vision is now under attack?
2. Describe the reinvestment program at the center of this argument. How would this program signal a shift in public investment priorities?

3. Describe the emotional appeal the writer deploys in support of public funding for higher education.

Respond to this Reading

1. Do you favor free college tuition? Are there conditions attached to your position? Explain.
2. Identify the rebuttal in this argument. Evaluate how the writer counters the rebuttal.
3. How would your educational and career plans be altered should we move from our present tuition structure to a tuition-free approach?

ABOUT THIS READING

Reporter Katie Reilly is on the staff of *Time* magazine, a weekly news magazine and news website. This reading describes mental health conditions that many college students endure. More a report and a summary than an argument, the reading identifies a number of issues worth arguing about.

Record Numbers of College Students Are Seeking Treatment for Depression and Anxiety—But Schools Can't Keep Up

By Katie Reilly

Not long after Nelly Spigner arrived at the University of Richmond in 2014 as a Division I soccer player and aspiring surgeon, college began to feel like a pressure cooker. Overwhelmed by her busy soccer schedule and heavy course load, she found herself fixating on how each grade would bring her closer to medical school. "I was running myself so thin trying to be the best college student," she says. "It almost seems like they're setting you up to fail because of the sheer amount of work and amount of classes you have to take at the same time, and how you're also expected to do so much."

At first, Spigner hesitated to seek help at the university's counseling center, which was conspicuously located in the psychology building, separate from the health center. "No one wanted to be seen going up to that office," she says. But she began to experience intense mood swings. At times, she found herself crying uncontrollably, unable to leave her room, only to feel normal again in 30 minutes. She started skipping classes and meals, avoiding friends and professors, and holing up in her dorm. In the spring of her freshman year, she saw a psychiatrist on campus, who diagnosed her with bipolar disorder, and her symptoms worsened. The soccer team wouldn't allow her to play after she missed too many practices, so she left the team. In October of her sophomore year, she withdrew from school on medical leave, feeling defeated. "When you're going through that and you're looking around on campus, it doesn't seem like anyone else is going through what you're going through," she says. "It was probably the loneliest experience."

Spigner is one of a rapidly growing number of college students seeking mental health treatment on campuses facing an unprecedented demand

for counseling services. Between 2009 and 2015, the number of students visiting counseling centers increased by about 30% on average, while enrollment grew by less than 6%, the Center for Collegiate Mental Health found in a 2015 report. Students seeking help are increasingly likely to have attempted suicide or engaged in self-harm, the center found. In spring 2017, nearly 40% of college students said they had felt so depressed in the prior year that it was difficult for them to function, and 61% of students said they had "felt overwhelming anxiety" in the same time period, according to an American College Health Association survey of more than 63,000 students at 92 schools.

As midterms begin in March, students' workload intensifies, the wait time for treatment at counseling centers grows longer, and students who are still struggling to adjust to college consider not returning after the spring or summer breaks. To prevent students from burning out and dropping out, colleges across the country—where health centers might once have left meaningful care to outside providers—are experimenting with new measures. For the first time last fall, UCLA offered all incoming students a free online screening for depression. More than 2,700 students have opted in, and counselors have followed up with more than 250 who were identified as being at risk for severe depression, exhibiting manic behavior or having suicidal thoughts.

Virginia Tech University has opened several satellite counseling clinics to reach students where they already spend time, stationing one above a local Starbucks and embedding others in the athletic department and graduate student center. Ohio State University added a dozen mental health clinicians during the 2016-17 academic year and has also launched a counseling mobile app that allows students to make an appointment, access breathing exercises, listen to a playlist designed to cheer them up, and contact the clinic in case of an emergency. Pennsylvania State University allocated roughly $700,000 in additional funding for counseling and psychological services in 2017, citing a "dramatic increase" in the demand for care over the past 10 years. And student government leaders at several schools have enacted new student fees that direct more funding to counseling centers.

But most counseling centers are working with limited resources. The average university has one professional counselor for every 1,737 students—fewer than the minimum of one therapist for every 1,000 to 1,500 students recommended by the International Association of Counseling Services. Some counselors say they are experiencing "battle fatigue" and are overwhelmed by the increase in students asking for help. "It's a very different job than it was 10 years ago," says Lisa Adams Somerlot, president of the American College Counseling Association and director of counseling at the University of West Georgia.

As colleges try to meet the growing demand, some students are slipping through the cracks due to long waits for treatment and a lasting stigma associated with mental health issues. Even if students ask for and receive help, not all cases can be treated on campus. Many private-sector treatment programs are stepping in to fill that gap, at least for families who can afford steep fees that may rise above $10,000 and may not be covered by health insurance. But especially in rural areas, where options for off-campus care are limited, universities are feeling pressure to do more.

At the start of every school year, Anne Marie Albano, director of the Columbia University Clinic for Anxiety and Related Disorders (CUCARD), says she's inundated with texts and phone calls from students who struggle with the transition to college life. "Elementary and high school is so much about right or wrong," she says. "You get the right answer or you don't, and there's lots of rules and lots of structure. Now that [life is] more free-floating, there's anxiety."

That's perhaps why, for many students, mental health issues creep up for the first time when they start college. (The average age of onset for many mental health issues, including depression and bipolar disorder, is the early 20s.) Dana Hashmonay was a freshman at Rensselaer Polytechnic Institute in Troy, New York in 2014 when she began having anxiety attacks before every class and crew practice, focusing on uncertainties about the future and comparing herself to seemingly well-adjusted classmates. "At that point, I didn't even know I had anxiety. I didn't have a name for it. It was just me freaking out about everything, big or small," she says. When she tried to make an appointment with the counseling center, she was put on a two-week waitlist. When she finally met with a therapist, she wasn't able to set up a consistent weekly appointment because the center was overbooked. "I felt like they were more concerned with, 'Let's get you better and out of here,'" she says, "instead of listening to me. It wasn't what I was looking for at all."

Instead, she started meeting weekly with an off-campus therapist, who her parents helped find and pay for. She later took a leave of absence midway through her sophomore year to get additional help. Hashmonay thinks the university could have done more, but she notes that the school seemed to be facing a lack of resources as more students sought help. "I think I needed something that the university just wasn't offering," she says.

A spokesperson for Rensselaer says the university's counseling center launched a triage model last year in an effort to eliminate long wait times caused by rising demand, assigning a clinician to provide same-day care to students presenting signs of distress and coordinate appropriate follow-up treatment based on the student's needs.

Some students delay seeing a counselor because they question whether their situation is serious enough to warrant it. Emmanuel Mennesson says he was initially too proud to get help when he started to experience symptoms of anxiety and depression after arriving at McGill University in Montreal in 2013 with plans to study engineering. He became overwhelmed by the workload and felt lost in classes where he was one student out of hundreds, and began ignoring assignments and skipping classes. "I was totally ashamed of what happened. I didn't want to let my parents down, so I retreated inward," he says. During his second semester, he didn't attend a single class, and he withdrew from school that April.

For many students, mental health struggles predated college, but are exacerbated by the pressures of college life. Albano says some of her patients assume their problems were specific to high school. Optimistic that they can leave their issues behind, they stop seeing a therapist or taking antidepressants. "They think that this high school was too big or too

competitive and college is going to be different," Albano says. But that's often not the case. "If anxiety was there," she says, "nothing changes with a high school diploma."

Counselors point out that college students tend to have better access to mental health care than the average adult because counseling centers are close to where they live, and appointments are available at little to no cost. But without enough funding to meet the rising demand, many students are still left without the treatment they need, says Ben Locke, Penn State's counseling director and head of the Center for Collegiate Mental Health.

The center's 2016 report found that, on average, universities have increased resources devoted to rapid-access services—including walk-in appointments and crisis treatment for students demonstrating signs of distress—since 2010 in response to rising demand from students. But long-term treatment services, including recurring appointments and specialized counseling, decreased on average during that time period.

"That means that students will be able to get that first appointment when they're in high distress, but they may not be able to get ongoing treatment after the fact," Locke says. "And that is a problem."

We're busier than we've ever been

In response to a growing demand for mental health help, some colleges have allocated more money for counseling programs and are experimenting with new ways of monitoring and treating students. More than 40% of college counseling centers hired more staff members during the 2015–16 school year, according to the most recent annual survey by the Association for University and College Counseling Center Directors.

"A lot of schools charge $68,000 a year," says Dori Hutchinson, director of services at Boston University's Center for Psychiatric Rehabilitation, referring to the cost of tuition and room and board at some of the most expensive private schools in the country. "We should be able to figure out how to attend to their whole personhood for that kind of money."

At the University of Iowa, Counseling Director Barry Schreier increased his staff by nearly 50% during the 2017–18 academic year. Still, he says, even with the increase in counseling service offerings, they can't keep up with the number of students coming in for help. There is typically a weeklong wait for appointments, which can reach two weeks by mid-semester. "We just added seven full-time staff and we're busier than we've ever been. We're seeing more students," Schreier says. "But is there less wait for service? No."

The university has embedded two counselors in dorms since 2016 and is considering adding more after freshmen said it was a helpful service they would not have sought out on their own. Schreier also added six questions about mental health to a freshman survey that the university sends out several weeks into the fall semester. The counseling center follows up with students who might need help based on their responses to questions about how they'd rate their stress level, whether they've previously struggled with mental health symptoms that negatively impacted their academics, and whether they've ever had symptoms of depression or anxiety. He says early intervention is a priority because mental health is the number one reason why students take formal leave from the university.

As colleges scramble to meet this demand, off-campus clinics are developing innovative, if expensive, treatment programs that offer a personalized support system and teach students to prioritize mental wellbeing in high-pressure academic settings. Dozens of programs now specialize in preparing high school students for college and college students for adulthood, pairing mental health treatment with life skills classes—offering a hint at the treatments that could be used on campus in the future.

When Spigner took a medical leave from the University of Richmond, she enrolled in College Re-Entry, a 14-week program in New York that costs $10,000 and aims to provide a bridge back to college for students who have withdrawn due to mental health issues. She learned note-taking and time management skills in between classes on healthy cooking and fitness, as well as sessions of yoga and meditation.

Mennesson, the former McGill engineering student, is now studying at Westchester Community College in New York with the goal of becoming a math teacher. During his leave from school, he enrolled in a program called Onward Transitions in Portland, Maine that promises to "get 18- to 20-somethings unstuck and living independently" at a cost of over $20,000 for three months, where he learned to manage his anxiety and depression.

Another treatment model can be found at CUCARD in Manhattan, where patients in their teens and early 20s can slip on a virtual reality headset and come face-to-face with a variety of anxiety-inducing simulations—from a professor unwilling to budge on a deadline to a roommate who has littered their dorm room with stacks of empty pizza boxes and piles of dirty clothes. Virtual reality takes the common treatment of exposure therapy a step further by allowing patients to interact with realistic situations and overcome their anxiety. The center charges $150 per group-therapy session for students who enroll in the four-to-six-week college readiness program but hopes to make the virtual reality simulations available in campus counseling centers or on students' cell phones in the future.

Hashmonay, who has used the virtual reality software at the center, says the scenarios can be challenging to confront, "but the minute it's over, it's like, 'Wow, OK, I can handle this.'" She still goes weekly to therapy at CUCARD, and she briefly enrolled in a Spanish course at Montclair State University in New Jersey in January. But she withdrew after a few classes, deciding to get a job and focus on her health instead of forcing a return to school before she is ready. "I'm trying to live life right now and see where it takes me," she says.

Back at the University of Richmond for her senior year, Spigner says the attitude toward mental health on campus seems to have changed dramatically since she was a freshman. Back then, she knew no one else in therapy, but most of her friends now regularly visit the counseling center, which has boosted outreach efforts, started offering group therapy and mindfulness sessions, and moved into a more private space. "It's not weird to hear someone say, 'I'm going to a counseling appointment,' anymore," she says.

She attended an open mic event on Richmond's campus earlier this semester, where students publicly shared stories and advice about their struggles with mental health. Spigner, who meets weekly with a counselor on campus, has become a resource to many of her friends because she openly discusses her own mental health, encouraging others not to be ashamed to get help.

"I'm kind of the go-to now for it, to be honest," she says. "They'll ask me, 'Do you think I should go see counseling?'" Her answer is always yes.

Analyze this Reading

1. How do extensive statistics and facts at the beginning of the reading prepare readers for the issue of mental health on campuses today?
2. Are colleges keeping up with the demand for mental health services? Explain.
3. Describe some of the innovative treatment programs now available for students seeking to return to college after withdrawing due to anxiety and depression? What are the implicit strengths and weaknesses of these programs?

Respond to this Reading

1. According to the writer, the Counseling Director at the University of Iowa contends that "early intervention is a priority because mental health is the number one reason why students take formal leave from the university." Is this your sense of why most students withdraw from college? Explain.
2. Describe the counseling services available at your college? Are they adequate and accessible? What changes, if any, would you make to these services?
3. According to the writer, today's college experience is stressful due to demanding workloads and pressures to succeed. In your view, are there structural changes in curriculum and campus life that could reduce the stress of college? Explain.

Anthology 2
Workplace Community

ABOUT THIS READING

At the University of Maryland, Gar Alperovitz is Professor of Political Economy and a founding principal of the Democracy Collaborative. Among Alperovitz's research interests are community-based economics in an era of globalization and political change that includes peace as a goal. His books include *America Beyond Capitalism: Reclaiming Our Wealth, Our Liberty, and Our Democracy* (2004) and, with Lew Daly, *Unjust Deserts: How the Rich are Taking Our Common Inheritance and Why We Should Take it Back* (2008). Keane Bhatt authors the blog "Manufacturing Contempt," where the writer analyzes how American media representations are "shaped by money, power, and ideology." This article appeared in *Truthout*, a daily newsletter that, in its own words, "works to broaden and diversify the political discussion by introducing independent voices and focusing on undercovered issues and unconventional thinking."

Employee-Owned Businesses Ignored by Mainstream Media

A bold new threat to the economic status quo brings on a press blackout.

By Gar Alperovitz and Keane Bhatt

Social pain, anger at ecological degradation and the inability of traditional politics to address deep economic failings has fueled an extraordinary amount of practical on-the-ground institutional experimentation and innovation by activists, economists and socially minded business leaders in communities around the country.

A vast democratized "new economy" is slowly emerging throughout the United States. The general public, however, knows almost nothing about it because the American press simply does not cover the developing institutions and strategies.

For instance, a sample assessment of coverage between January and November of 2012 by the most widely circulated newspaper in the United States, the *Wall Street Journal,* found ten times more references to caviar than to employee-owned firms, a growing sector of the economy that involves more than $800 billion in assets and 10 million employee-owners—around three million more individuals than are members of unions in the private sector.

Worker ownership—the most common form of which involves ESOPs, or Employee Stock Ownership Plans—was mentioned in a mere five articles. By contrast, over 60 articles referred to equestrian activities like horse racing, and golf clubs appeared in 132 pieces over the same period.

Although 2012 was designated by the United Nations as the International Year of the Cooperative—an institution that now has more than one billion

iStock.com/A-digit

members worldwide—the *Journal's* coverage was similarly thin. More than 120 million Americans are members of cooperatives and cooperative credit unions, 30 million more people than are owners of mutual funds. The *Journal*, however, devoted some 700 articles to mutual funds between January and October and only 183 to cooperatives. Of these the majority were concerned with high-end New York real estate, with headlines like "Pricey Co-ops Find Buyers."

The vast number of cooperative businesses on Main Streets across the country were discussed in just 70 articles and a mere 14 gave co-op businesses more than passing mention. Together, the articles only narrowly outnumbered the 13 *Journal* pieces that mentioned the Dom Perignon brand of champagne over the same time frame, and were eclipsed by the 40 *Journal* entries that refer to the French delicacy *foie gras*.

Another democratized economic institution is the not-for-profit Community Development Corporation (CDC), roughly 4,500 of which operate in all 50 states and the District of Columbia. Such neighborhood corporations create tens of thousands of units of affordable housing and millions of square feet of commercial and industrial space a year. The *Journal* ran no articles mentioning CDCs in 2012 and only 43 over the past 28 years—less than two a year. Meanwhile, the word *château* appeared in 30 times as many articles, and luxury apartments received 300 times as much coverage over the same period.

Not surprisingly, the growing "new economy movement" championing democratization of the economy has itself received even less coverage, despite growing citizen involvement on many levels. Over the past year, major national, state and other conferences focusing on worker-owned companies, cooperatives, public banking, nonprofit and public land trusts, and neighborhood corporations were oversubscribed, reflecting the growing interest in these forms. The *Journal*, however, gave scant coverage to the movement.

Thousands of other creative projects—from green businesses to new forms of combined community-worker efforts—are also underway across the country but receive little coverage. A number are self-consciously understood as attempts to develop working prototypes in state and local "laboratories of democracy" that may be applied at regional and national scale when the right political moment occurs. In Cleveland, Ohio, for instance, a complex of sophisticated worker-owned firms has been developing in desperately poor, predominantly black neighborhoods. The model is partially structured along lines of the Mondragón Corporation, a vibrant network of worker-owned cooperatives in northern Spain with more than 80,000 members and billions of dollars in annual revenue.

Since 2010 legislation to set up public banks along the lines of the long-established Bank of North Dakota has been proposed in twenty states. Several cities—including Los Angeles and Kansas City—have passed "responsible banking" ordinances that require banks to reveal their impact on the community and/or require city officials to do business only with banks that are responsive to community needs. But municipally led responsible banking initiatives appear to have received no attention in the *Journal*, whereas the newspaper published seven articles this year discussing President Obama's birth certificate.

The limited nature of the coverage can also be seen in particular cases. Recreational Equipment, Inc. (REI) is a highly successful consumer co-op with $1.8 billion in sales for 2011, allowing it to share $165 million of its profits with its 4.7 million active members and 11,000 employees. Organic Valley, a Wisconsin-based cooperative dairy, generated more than $700 million in revenue for nearly 1,700 farmer-owners. From January through October 2012, the *Journal* referred (briefly) to REI in just three articles; Organic Valley rated just one mention. In combination, REI and Organic Valley appear in the *Journal* only as often as the Cavalier King Charles spaniel, a breed of dog that turned up in four entries in the *Journal*'s pages this year.

Further perspective on the coverage is offered in the way in which "hot topics" are presented, and others of greater economic significance played down. Co-ops in the U.S. generate over $500 billion in annual revenues. The global market for smartphones is estimated by Bloomberg Industries at $219 billion—less than half as large. Furthermore, there are 20 million more co-op members than smartphone users in the United States. The *Journal*, however, published over 1,000 print articles that included the terms "smartphone" or "smartphones" from January through October this year—more than five articles for each piece mentioning co-ops (many of which, as noted, were about upscale Manhattan apartments).

The print coverage of the *Journal* was analyzed by the Democracy Collaborative of the University of Maryland through the online database ProQuest. Although the assessment focused on the *Journal*, the nation's preeminent source of news for economic and business affairs, a preliminary review suggests that other national media outlets devote a similarly miniscule proportion of space to the exploding "new economy" sector. This highlights the need for greater media exposure regarding important developments toward a more democratic, sustainable and community-based economy.

Analyze this Reading

1. What is the "new economy" and, according to the writers, why don't more Americans know about it?
2. Why might the writers have focused their research solely on *The Wall Street Journal*? What does their research reveal about this publication?
3. The writers bring in extensive factual support for their claim, especially in the form of specific examples. In fact, little if any emotional or ethical support appears in this article. With this strategy in mind, does emphasizing only one kind of support weaken this argument? Explain.

Respond to this Reading

1. What new economy institutions exist in your community? What cooperatives do you belong to?
2. What does the idea of bringing democracy and worker ownership into the workplace look like to you? How does it contrast or overlap with conditions in your present workplace?

ABOUT THIS READING

Tim Kastelle writes about workforce innovation for the *Discipline of Innovation Blog*. He is on the faculty of the University of Queensland Business School in Brisbane, Australia, and his academic articles appear on *Google Scholar*. This argument was published in *Harvard Business Review*, a magazine devoted to business management strategies across a range of industries.

Hierarchy Is Overrated

By Tim Kastelle

Maybe you've heard the old cliché – if you've got "too many chiefs," your initiative will fail. Every time I hear it, I wonder, "Why can't everyone be a chief?"

For instance, the Second Chance Programme is a group that raises money to help reduce homelessness among women here in Southeast Queensland. It's achieved impressive results since being founded in 2001, and is run by a committee of about ten people. In the early days, a management consultant used the familiar chiefs/Indians line to predict they'd fail.

This kind of thinking assumes:

- You need a hierarchy to succeed.

- The people that do the work are of lower status than those that decide what work to do.

- Organizations that don't follow the norms are likely to fail.

I think that all of these ideas are wrong. Second Chance has certainly been very successful with their flat, nonhierarchical structure. They have achieved a great deal, while keeping their overhead close to $0. If the structure of the management committee was a problem, they would have failed by now.

But maybe this kind of structure only works for not-for-profits?

Nope. About 20% of the world's websites are now on the WordPress platform, making it one of the most important Internet companies. And yet, Automattic, the firm behind WordPress, only employs a couple hundred people, who all work remotely, with a highly autonomous flat management structure. GitHub is another highly successful firm with a similar structure.

So, maybe this structure only works for not-for-profits and software firms with open source platforms?

Well, Valve is a gaming company that makes Half Life, Portal, and many other popular games. Their software is proprietary. And they are famous for not having bosses at all. And 37Signals has a structure that looks a lot like Automattic's, while building software that enables distributed collaboration, such as Basecamp and Ruby on Rails.

Ok, then, flat structures work for not-for-profits and software startups. But you surely can't run, say, a big manufacturing firm like this, can you?

Actually, you can. Take a look at W.L. Gore. Gore is one of the most successful firms in the world. They have more than 10,000 employees, with

basically three levels in their organizational hierarchy. There is the CEO (elected democratically), a handful of functional heads, and everyone else. All decision making is done through self-managing teams of 8–12 people: hiring, pay, which projects to work on, everything. Rather than relying on a command-and-control structure, current CEO Terri Kelly says:

"It's far better to rely upon a broad base of individuals and leaders who share a common set of values and feel personal ownership for the overall success of the organization. These responsible and empowered individuals will serve as much better watchdogs than any single, dominant leader or bureaucratic structure."

They've had challenges in maintaining their structure as they've grown, but the remain one of the most innovative and most profitable firms in the world.

But all of these examples have had flat structures from the day they were founded—you couldn't do something like this in a firm that has been operating for a while with the normal hierarchical structure, could you?

That's exactly what Ricardo Semler and his team at Semco did when he joined the firm in 1983. In the 30 years since, the Brazilian conglomerate has continually worked at distributing decision-making authority out to everyone. One of the firm's key performance indicators is how long Semler can go between making decisions. The time keeps getting longer, while the firm has maintained around 20% growth for nearly 30 years now.

All of these are examples where everyone is a chief. The flat organizational structure can work anywhere. This works best when:

- **The environment is changing rapidly.** Firms organized around small, autonomous teams are much more nimble than large hierarchies. This makes it easier to respond to change.

- **Your main point of differentiation is innovation.** Firms organized with a flat structure tend to be much more innovative–if this is important strategically, then you should be flat.

- **The organization has a shared purpose.** This is what has carried Second Chance through their tough times–their shared commitment to the women they are helping. While the objectives may differ, all of the firms discussed here have a strong central purpose as well.

There is a growing body of evidence that shows that organizations with flat structures outperform those with more traditional hierarchies in most situations (see the work of Gary Hamel for a good summary of these results). But while we are seeing an increasing number of firms using flat structures, they are still relatively rare. Why is this so?

It's not because people haven't heard of the idea. There have been more than 200 case studies of Gore and Semco alone, and I would bet that nearly every MBA program in the world includes at least one case study looking at a firm with this kind of structure. But there are other obstacles:

- **Many people don't believe in democracy in the workplace.** Even people who adamantly oppose small amounts of central planning in government are perfectly happy to have the strategy of even very large firms set by just a handful of people.

- **Even if you do believe in democracy, it can be hard to imagine work without hierarchy.** The "normal" structure is so deeply ingrained, and so widespread, that it can challenging to even think of an alternative in the first place. That's why these case studies are so important.

- **Fear of the unusual.** John Maynard Keynes said, "Worldly wisdom teaches that it is better for reputation to fail conventionally than to succeed unconventionally." Unfortunately, this is still largely true today.

- **It's hard to change organizational structures.** Despite the positive example of Semco, in reality it is very hard to change organizational structures. Even with Semco, it took a financial crisis to trigger the change in thinking. It takes a strong belief in democracy in the workplace along with a resistance to criticism to stay the course and execute such a change.

However, as digital technologies make it easier to work in a distributed manner, and we enter the social era, flat structures will become increasingly common. There are sound business reasons for treating people with dignity, for providing autonomy, and for organizing among small teams rather than large hierarchies.

It's time to start reimagining management. Making everyone a chief is a good place to start.

Analyze this Reading

1. Describe in your own words what a flat workplace structure is and how it differs from more conventional, hierarchical structures.
2. What explanations does the writer offer regarding the difficulty moving into democratic structures in the business world?

Respond to this Reading

1. Describe your work experience in terms of management and decision-making. Is your life as a worker closer to a flat or hierarchical structure? Explain.
2. Research 2 to 3 companies referenced in this writing. Discuss what distinguishes these companies as "flat" and why these features might or might not appeal to you as a worker.
3. Is it reasonable to incorporate some of the approaches to democratically run businesses to the way in which your college operates? Explain.

ABOUT THIS READING

Recently the U.S. Supreme Court ruled in favor of providing constitutional protections to corporations. Many view this as a threat to democracy, as the decision opens the door to unlimited corporate spending in political campaigns among other issues. The following argument appeared in *Synthesis/Regeneration*, a magazine of green social thought. The authors are members of the Women's International League for Peace and Freedom.

Abolish Corporate Personhood (Thinking Politically)

By Jan Edwards and Molly Morgan

Colonies, Constitutions and Corporations

The history of the United States could be told as the story of who is, and who is not, a person under law. Women, poor people, slaves, and even corporations had long been considered persons for purposes of follow-ing the law. This is because early laws were written "No person shall . . ." Corporate lawyers had tried to avoid these laws by claiming corpora-tions were not persons and therefore not required to follow the law. So it was decided that for purposes of following the law, corporations were persons. This allowed corporations to sue and be sued in court among other things. But corporations were not persons with rights in the law, and neither were women, slaves, indentured servants, or poor people. We know some of the ongoing story of human beings' struggle to gain the rights of persons under law, but how did corporations gain these rights?

To understand the phenomenon of corporate personhood, we start by looking at the foundation of U.S. law, the Constitution of the United States of America. This document was written by 55 gentlemen cleverly described by one historian as "the well-bred, the well-fed, the well-read, and the well-wed." Many of them wrote and spoke at length about the inability of the common people to be self-governing.

The word "democracy" appears nowhere in the Constitution. The Constitution only mentions two entities: We the People and the govern-ment. We delegate some of our power to the government in order to per-form tasks we want government to do. In a representative democracy, this system should work just fine.

The problem is that the phrase "We the People" is not defined in the Constitution. In 1787, in order to be considered one of "We the People" and have rights in the Constitution, you had to be an adult male with white skin and a certain amount of property. This narrowed "We the People" down to about 10% of the population. Those who owned property, including human property, were very clear that this was rule by the minority.

So here was the first definition of who gets to be a person in the United States. Ninety percent of the people, including all the immigrants, inden-tured servants, slaves, minors, Native Americans, women, and people who did not own property (the poor), were, legally, not "persons."

Without using the words "slave" or "slavery," the Constitution ensures that even if slaves get to free soil, their status as property remains the same. This is just one of the clauses defining property in the Constitution. It also defines contracts, labor, commerce, money, copyright, and war as the province of the federal government. So the Constitution, the founda-tion of all U.S. laws, was not written to protect people—it was written to protect property. The Constitution does contain some protection for peo-ple in Section 9, but the Bill of Rights is the concentration of rights for "We the People."

Constitutional Fallacies

Most people believe that the Constitution, specifically the Bill of Rights, guarantees our rights to freedom of speech, religion, and press, to peaceably assemble, and so forth. People of all political stripes say this. But the truth is, it does no such thing. Almost all of our constitutional protections are expressed as the absence of a negative rather than the presence of a positive. So the First Amendment, for example, does not say, "All citizens are guaranteed the right to free speech"; it only says, "Congress shall make no law . . . abridging the freedom of speech . . ." The First Amendment just restricts the government from specific encroachments; it doesn't guarantee anything. This was not a concern for the people because they had strong bills of rights in their state constitutions, and at that time, the states had more power than the federal government.

If those rights were actually guaranteed in the Constitution, people could, for example, take the Bill of Rights into the workplace. Anyone who thinks workers have free speech while they are on corporate property should ask the workers or talk to a union organizer. Because corporations are property, and because the Constitution protects property rights above all, most people have to abandon the Bill of Rights in order to make a living.

Another word that does not appear in the Constitution is "corporation." The reason is that the writers of the Constitution had zero interest in using for-profit corporations to run their new government. In colonial times, corporations were tools of the King's oppression, chartered for the purpose of exploiting the so-called "New World" and shoveling wealth back into Europe. The rich formed joint-stock corporations to distribute the enormous risk of colonizing the Americas and gave them names like the Hudson Bay Company, the British East India Company, and the Massachusetts Bay Colony. Because they were so far from their sovereign, the agents for these corporations had a lot of autonomy to do their work. They could pass laws, levy taxes, and even raise armies to manage and control property and commerce. They were not popular with the colonists.

So the writers of the Constitution left control of corporations to state legislatures (10th Amendment), where they would get the closest supervision by the people. Early corporate charters were very explicit about what a corporation could do, how, for how long, with whom, where, and when. Corporations could not own stock in other corporations, and they were prohibited from any part of the political process. Individual stockholders were held personally liable for any harms done in the name of the corporation, and most charters only lasted for 10 or 15 years. Most importantly, in order to receive the profit-making privileges the shareholders sought, their corporations had to represent a clear benefit for the public good, such as building a road, canal, or bridge. When corporations violated any of these terms, their charters were frequently revoked by the state legislatures.

That sounds nothing like the corporations of today. So what happened in the last two centuries? As time passed and memories of royal oppression faded, the wealthy people increasingly started eyeing corporations as a convenient way to shield their personal fortunes. They could sniff the winds of change and see that their minority rule through property ownership was under serious threat of being diluted. States gradually started loosening

property requirements for voting, so more and more white men could participate in the political process. Women were publicly agitating for the right to vote. In 1865, the 13th Amendment was ratified, freeing the slaves. Three years later, the 14th Amendment provided citizenship rights to all persons born or naturalized in the United States, and two years after that, the 15th Amendment provided voting rights to black males. Change was afoot, and so the ruling class responded.

During and after the Civil War there was a rapid increase in both the number and size of corporations. This form of business was starting to become a more important way of holding and protecting property and power. Increasingly through their corporations, the wealthy started influencing legislators, bribing public officials, and employing lawyers to write new laws and file court cases challenging the existing laws that restricted corporate behavior. Bit by bit, decade by decade, state legislatures increased corporate charter length while they decreased corporate liability and reduced citizen authority over corporate structure, governance, production, and labor.

But minority rulers were only going to be able to go only so far with this strategy. Because corporations are a creation of the government, chartered by the state legislatures, they still fell on the government side of the constitutional line with duties accountable to the people. If minority rule by property was going to be accomplished through corporations, they had to become entitled to rights instead, which required them to cross the line and become persons under the law. Their tool to do this was the 14th Amendment, which was ratified in 1868. From then it took the ruling class less than 20 years to shift corporations from the duty side of the line, where they are accountable to the people, to the rights side, where they get protection from government abuse.

The 14th Amendment, in addition to saying that now all persons born or naturalized in the US are citizens, says that no state shall "deprive any person of life, liberty, or property, without the due process of law; nor deny to any person . . . the equal protection of the laws." The phrase about not depriving any person of life, liberty, or property without the due process of the law is exactly the same wording as the Fifth Amendment, which protects people from that kind of abuse by the federal government. With the ratification of the 14th Amendment, the states could no longer abuse people in that way either. These are important rights. They are written in a short, straightforward manner. After the Civil War and all the agony over slavery, the people in the states that ratified the 13th, 14th, and 15th Amendments were clear that they were about righting the wrong of slavery.

That clarity, however, did not stop the railroad barons and their attorneys in the 1870s and 80s. As mentioned before, those who wanted to maintain minority rule were losing their grip. There was real danger of democracy creeping into the body politic. Until the Civil War, slavery was essential to maintaining the entire economic system that kept wealth and power in the hands of the few—not just in the South, but in the North as well. It was the legalization of a lie—that one human being can own another. Slavery was at the core of a whole system of oppression that benefitted the few, which included the subjugation of women, genocide of the indigenous population, and exploitation of immigrants and the poor.

Now that the slavery lie could no longer be used to maintain minority rule, they needed a new lie, and they used the 14th Amendment to create it. Because these rights to due process and equal protection were so valuable, the definition of the word "person" in the 14th Amendment became the focus of hundreds of legal battles for the next 20 years. The question was: who gets to be a person protected by the 14th Amendment?

In the Courts

The watershed moment came in 1886 when the Supreme Court ruled on a case called Santa Clara County v. Southern Pacific Railroad. The case itself was not about corporate personhood, although many before it had been, and the Court had ruled that corporations were not persons under the 14th Amendment. Santa Clara, like many railroad cases, was about taxes. Before the Court delivered its decision, the following statement is attributed to Chief Justice Waite:

> The court does not wish to hear argument on the question whether the provision in the 14th Amendment to the Constitution, which forbids a State to deny to any person within its jurisdiction the equal protection of the laws, applies to these corporations. We are all of the opinion that it does.

The statement appeared in the header of the case in the published version, and the Court made its ruling on other grounds. How this statement appeared in the header of the case is a matter of some mystery and competing theories, but because it was later cited as precedent, corporate personhood became the accepted legal doctrine of the land.

What was it in the 14th Amendment that was so valuable to corporate lawyers and managers? Why did they pursue it so aggressively? At the time, as is still true today, corporations were chartered by state governments, and the 14th Amendment reads "No state shall . . . ." If the word "person" in the 14th Amendment included corporations, then no state shall deny to corporations due process or equal protection of the laws. This allowed corporate lawyers to allege discrimination whenever a state law was enacted to curtail corporations.

This was also the beginning of federal regulatory agencies, so because corporations were now persons under the 14th Amendment, it would be discriminatory not to give them the same rights under federal laws. With the granting of the 5th Amendment right to Due Process (Noble v. Union River Logging, 1893), corporate lawyers could challenge, and the Supreme Court could find grounds to overturn, democratically legislated laws that originated at the federal as well as state levels.

Once corporations had jumped the constitutional line from the "government" side to the "people" side, their lawyers proceeded to pursue the Bill of Rights through more Supreme Court cases. As mentioned above, in 1893 they were assured 5th Amendment protection of due process. In 1906 they were granted 4th Amendment search and seizure protection (Hale v. Henkel). In 1922, they were acknowledged as being protected under the "takings" clause of the 5th Amendment (Pennsylvania Coal Co. v. Mahon), and a regulatory law was deemed to be a "takings."

In 1947, they started getting First Amendment protections (Taft-Hartley Act). In 1976, the Supreme Court determined that money spent for political purposes is equal to exercising free speech, and since "corporate persons" have First Amendment rights, they can basically contribute as much money as they want to political parties and candidates (Buckley v. Valeo).

Every time "corporate persons" acquire one of these protections under the Bill of Rights, it gives them a whole new way of exploiting the legal system in order to maintain minority rule through corporate power. Since 1886, every time people have won new rights, like the Civil Rights Act, corporations are eligible for it too.

Knowing the Enemy

It is important to remember what a corporation is to understand the implications of corporate personhood for democracy. A corporation is not a real thing; it's a legal fiction, an abstraction. A corporation can live forever. It can change its identity in a day. If it's found guilty of a crime, it cannot go to prison.

Corporations are whatever those who have the power to define want them to be to maintain minority rule through corporations. As long as superhuman "corporate persons" have rights under the law, the vast majority of people have little or no effective voice in our political arena, which is why we see abolishing corporate personhood as so important to ending corporate rule and building a more democratic society.

Today the work of corporatists is to take this system global. Having acquired the ability to govern in the United States, the corporation is the ideal instrument to gain control of the rest of the world. The concepts, laws, and techniques perfected by the ruling minority here are now being forced down the throats of people everywhere.

First, a complicit ruling elite is co-opted, installed, or propped up by the U.S. military and the government. Then, just as slavery and immigrant status once kept wages nonexistent or at poverty levels, now sweatshops, maquiladoras, and the prison-industrial complex provide ultra-cheap labor with little or no regulation. Just as sharecropping and the company store once kept people trapped in permanently subservient production roles, now the International Monetary Fund and World Bank's structural adjustment programs keep entire countries in permanent debt, the world's poorest people forced to feed interest payments to the world's richest while their own families go hungry.

A World without Corporations

What would change if corporations did not have personhood? The first and main effect would be that a barrier would be removed that is preventing democratic change, just as the abolition of slavery tore down an insurmountable legal block, making it possible to pass laws to provide full rights to the newly freed slaves. After corporate personhood is abolished, new legislation will be possible. Here are a few examples.

If "corporate persons" no longer had First Amendment right of free speech, we could prohibit all corporate political activity, such as lobbying and contributions to political candidates and parties. If "corporate persons" were not protected against search without a warrant under the Fourth Amendment, then corporate managers could not turn OSHA (Office of Safety and Health Administration) and the EPA (Environmental Protection Agency) inspectors away if they make surprise, unscheduled searches. If "corporate persons" were not protected against discrimination under the 14th Amendment, corporations like Wal-Mart could not force themselves into communities that do not want them.

So what can we do to abolish corporate personhood? Within our current legal system there are two possibilities: the Supreme Court could change its mind on corporations having rights in the Constitution, or, we can pass an amendment to the Constitution. Either scenario seems daunting, yet it is even more difficult than that. Every state now has laws and language in their state constitutions conceding these rights to corporations. So corporate personhood must be abolished on a state as well as a national level.

The good news is that almost anything we do toward abolishing corporate personhood helps the issue progress on one of these levels. If a city passes a nonbinding resolution, declaring their area a "Corporate Personhood Free Zone," that is a step toward passing a constitutional amendment at their state and eventually at the national level. If a town passes an ordinance legally denying corporations rights as persons, they may provoke a crisis of jurisdiction that could lead to a court case. We think both paths should be followed. It was, however, undemocratic for the Supreme Court to grant personhood to corporations, and it would be just as undemocratic for this to be decided that way again. An amendment is the democratic way to correct this judicial usurpation of the people's sovereignty.

We see that corporate personhood was wrongly given. It was given, not by "We the People," but by nine Supreme Court judges. We further see that corporate personhood is a bad thing, because it was the pivotal achievement that allowed an artificial entity to obtain the rights of people, thus relegating us to subhuman status. Finally, because of the way corporate personhood has enabled corporations to govern us, we see that it is so bad, we must eradicate it.

Slavery is the legal fiction that a person is property. Corporate personhood is the legal fiction that property is a person. Like abolishing slavery, the work of eradicating corporate personhood takes us to the deepest questions of what it means to be human. If we are to live in a democracy, what does it mean to be sovereign? The hardest part of eliminating corporate personhood is believing that We the People have the sovereign right to do this. It comes down to us being clear about who's in charge.

Analyze this Reading

1. How do the writers interpret the phrase "We the People" in the Constitution?
2. Describe the status of corporations prior to the American Revolution.
3. What points do the writers make regarding the 14th Amendment and corporations?

4. What is the significance of the 1886 Supreme Court case Santa Clara County v. Southern Pacific Railroad? What is the significance of the 1976 Supreme Court determination?
5. According to the writers, what threats to everyday people do corporations pose?
6. The writers conclude with ideas of what our country would become when corporate personhood is disallowed and with suggestions for what can be done to begin this work. Describe these ideas and suggestions.
7. The writers reach far back into American history to establish context for the issue of corporate personhood. With broad, public issues like this one, why are extensive historical references important? And, have you ever experienced a change in your position on an issue before and after conducting research on it? Explain.

Respond to this Reading

1. What is your reaction to the Supreme Court's recent ruling granting "person" status to corporations?
2. While the writers' position on corporate personhood is clear, they do not make room in their argument for opposing views. Does this affect the argument and its credibility? Explain.
3. In some countries, political campaigns are conducted with public financing only, that is, without the support of corporate donations. How, specifically, would political campaigning in the United States be altered with such a system?
4. With attention to terms like *corporate personhood, democracy, We the People*, and *sovereign right*, what issues occur to you after reading this argument? On what single issue are you motivated to argue?

ABOUT THIS READING

Rich Meneghello, the author of this reading, is a partner at the Portland, Oregon, office of Fisher & Phillips LLP, a law firm that represents the interests of management. The solution to workplace dating that Meneghello outlines below is crafted so as to steer management and ownership clear of any potential lawsuits that may occur due to love relationships among employees. This reading appeared in *The Daily Journal of Commerce*, a newspaper reporting on the building and construction market in Portland, Oregon.

Solutions at Work: When Love Enters the Workplace

By Rich Meneghello

Problem: A recent survey revealed that approximately 40 percent of U.S. workers have dated a fellow employee, and that another 40 percent would consider doing so. Inevitably, most workplace relationships end. Some end badly, and many of those result in lawsuits involving claims of

coercion or retaliation, despite the fact that most of these relationships are completely consensual at the outset. And it's not just the jilted lover who could be your company's next adversary in court. A few years ago a group of California employees uninvolved in a workplace romance succeeded in establishing hostile work environment discrimination based upon favoritism bestowed on those who were romantically linked with a supervisor. This theory of liability will undoubtedly be tested in other states. In response to litigation arising from workplace relationships, many businesses have implemented nonfraternization policies designed to prohibit or discourage workplace relationships. But these "no dating" policies have had limited effect. According to the same survey, 84 percent of U.S. workers either have no idea whether their employer has such a policy or believe it has chosen not to institute one. Clearly, most employers are doing a poor job of making their expectations known to employees on these issues. Additionally, many employers recognize that it is neither possible nor desirable to ban all workplace relationships. First, employers generally prefer not to chaperone employees. Second, most employees consider employer monitoring of personal relationships an invasion of privacy. Finally, and probably most important, outright dating bans simply don't work. Since most workers spend at least one-third of each day in the office, it is hardly surprising that personal relationships will develop. Solution: In response to the limited effectiveness of these policies, many companies have developed Employee Relationship Acknowledgments, otherwise known as "love contracts," in which employees in a relationship make certain disclosures to the employer. A love contract, when properly implemented, can serve as a powerful deterrent to future litigation. With this in mind, any company considering the use of love contracts should be aware of the following:

Essential Elements
Although the precise language will vary, an effective love contract should contain the following disclosures:

- the relationship is consensual and not based on intimidation, threat, coercion or harassment;
- the employees have received, read, understood, and agree to abide by the company's policy against harassment and discrimination;
- the employees agree to act appropriately in the workplace and avoid any behavior that is offensive to others;
- the employees agree not to let their relationship affect their work, or the work of their coworkers;
- neither employee will bestow upon the other any favoritism or preferential treatment;
- either employee may end the relationship at any time, and no retaliation of any kind will result;
- the contact information for the person in the HR department [responsible for handling disputes will be made available] (should either employee feel the relationship is affecting his/her work); and

- the employees have had sufficient time to read the document and ask questions before executing it of their own free will.

What if it's a "contract"? Whether the document is an enforceable contract doesn't matter, and is almost beside the point. The real strength of a love contract lies in the nature of the acknowledgements made. It shows that the employer took affirmative steps to maintain a workplace free from sexual harassment and retaliation, and it serves as powerful evidence that, at least at the time of execution, the relationship was consensual. Finally, it reaffirms that both employees are aware of the existence of a policy prohibiting sexual harassment, discrimination, retaliation, and their obligation to abide by it.

Can it prevent litigation? As with many other steps an employer can take, a love contract can be a strong deterrent to employee claims, but it will not prevent all future litigation arising out of a workplace relationship. What it does do is lay the groundwork for a solid defense should a lawsuit develop. For example, aggrieved employees can still claim they suffered retaliation after a breakup, but a love contract confirming that the relationship began consensually can help support a defense that the perceived post-relationship retaliation was based on personal animosity rather than gender-based discrimination.

Considerations before Utilizing Love Contracts

Although not a concern in Oregon, companies with operations out of state should confirm whether privacy laws of that jurisdiction prohibit or limit employer monitoring of workplace relationships. You should also consider how the idea of a love contract will be presented to a couple, and decide in advance what you will do if one of the participants denies the relationship or refuses to sign the document. Finally, since there is no one way of developing an effective love contract, you should consult experienced labor and employment counsel to draft the appropriate language that meets the particular needs and objectives of your property. Love contracts, when properly implemented and appropriately drafted, will reduce the likelihood of litigation arising from workplace relationships. In the event of litigation, an effective love contract will help lessen the chances of misunderstandings or even lawsuits, and bolster a company's defenses in the event one is filed.

Analyze this Reading

1. Why is workplace dating an issue? Why would employers be motivated to have a policy in place?
2. What prevents employers from banning all workplace relationships?
3. The writer claims that a love contract can provide "solid defense" for an employer should a lawsuit arise from a workplace relationship. What does this mean?
4. In your view, at what kind of audience is this argument aimed? Explain.

Respond to this Reading

1. This solution to workplace dating is written from the perspective of management. In your view, does workplace dating need a solution? If you feel that it does, how might you craft a solution from the perspective of employees?
2. Explain whether the "essential elements" of a love contract outlined above are fair or unfair.
3. Are there important features of workplace dating not covered in the writer's solution? If yes, what are they?
4. In addition to the issue of workplace dating, what other issues concern you in your current job? On which of these issues are you motivated to argue?

Anthology 3
Family and Household
Community

ABOUT THIS READING

This article appeared in *Maclean's, CA*, a weekly Canadian public affairs magazine. Sue Ferguson is Coordinator of the Journalism Program at Wilfrid Laurier University in Waterloo, Ontario, Canada. At *Maclean's* she served as senior writer and associate editor.

Leaving the Doors Open

Interaction between adoptive and birth families isn't for everyone. But when it works, it can give children a greater sense of being loved.

By Sue Ferguson

Emma Sands was just 2 1/2 weeks old when her father decided that he and her mom needed help. "I was scared about how Carrie was handling the baby—she wasn't herself," says Gary Sands (to protect Emma's privacy, all the names have been changed). He picked up the phone and a social worker soon arrived at his door. Carrie, diagnosed with schizophrenia, was admitted to hospital. Sands, who had spent years in and out of jail for petty crime driven by his drug and alcohol addiction, was left to parent by himself. On his wife's return eight months later, things spiraled out of control once again. "One of her friends introduced me to cocaine," says Sands, "and that was it. I was back in crime—lost my job and ended up going to jail." Emma was sent to live with a foster family and, by her first birthday, the foster parents had applied to adopt her.

Emma turned 12 in February. When Sands, now a youth counsellor and in a new relationship, arrived at her Port Coquitlam, B.C., home for the birthday party with his nine-month-old son, she yelled to friends in the basement, "Wanna meet my baby brother?" The poignancy of that moment wasn't lost on Sands—"I was like, wow," he recalls.

This isn't a story of a birth father reuniting with his child. Outside of a few periods, including a two-month stay in a recovery house, he has seen Emma regularly, taking her to swimming lessons and movies. (Carrie has disappeared from both their lives.) In recent months, Emma, who calls 36-year-old Sands "Daddy Gary," has begun to spend the occasional night at his house. Emma's adoptive parents encouraged the relationship from the beginning—taking her to visit Sands in jail and maintaining contact even when, on parole in the early 1990s, he filed, unsuccessfully, for custody.

Open adoptions of this nature are rare. Traditionally, adoption has been shrouded in secrecy, with every effort made to ensure birth parents and adoptive families never cross paths. But judges, says Adoption Council of Canada chair Sandra Scarth, are increasingly reluctant to sever children's

iStock.com/A-digit

ties to their biological parents, believing that giving kids information about their origins is critical to nurturing a healthy sense of self. For the same reason, private agencies now commonly arrange to have birth parents meet and choose the prospective adopters and keep in touch with their child through letters, photos and, in some cases, visits.

But openness is a scarier proposition for families who opt for public adoption. Parents of permanent wards are often scarred by mental illness and addictions, or have abused or neglected their children. And, unless the law clearly spells out the rights of the various parties (as it does in B.C. and Newfoundland), families who arrange open adoptions are taking a leap of faith. "It's hard to tell potential adopters unequivocally" that the birth family couldn't take the child back into their custody at any time, says Nancy Dale, acting associate executive director of the Children's Aid Society of Toronto. The issue is further complicated in Ontario by a law that prevents the over 6,000 Crown wards with access orders—legal provisions for contact between birth parents and the children taken from them—from getting adopted. "If you have an access order," says Dale, "you grow up in foster care. That's the plan." At least, it is for now. Minister of Children and Youth Services Marie Bountrogianni says the government intends to free kids with access orders for adoption when it's in their best interest and hopes to introduce openness legislation by next year, as part of a wider initiative to boost placement rates.

In the meantime, some families are able to work out ad hoc openness arrangements. Two years ago, Patty and Ken Winer, who live in the southern Ontario town of Arkell and already had biological children Kyra, 13, and Brent, 11, adopted Lisa, now 10, and her brother Joseph, 8. They would happily have also taken brother Alan (a pseudonym), now 14, but because of an access order he remains in foster care. With the help of the local Children's Aid Society, however, Alan regularly visits and phones his siblings. He joined the Winers for 10 days at their cottage in Prince Edward Island last July. He's also served as a go-between, delivering letters and Christmas presents from their birth mother—from whom the children were seized by police three years ago (she's permitted to see Alan six times a year)—to his brother and sister. In time, the Winers say, they'll arrange for Lisa and Joseph to visit her. For now, however, the letter to Lisa—which reads in part "I wish for you a happy home . . . I know I am still learning"—helped alleviate Lisa's feeling of responsibility for her biological mother's well-being, notes adoptive mom Patty. It was "tremendously important" to the girl, she adds.

For Ken Winer, openness is just a matter of common sense. "They will go back and see their mom when they're of legal age," he says. "Why put up a brick wall when it's going to have to then be torn down?" He speaks from experience: both he and his sister were adopted. When his sister later contacted her birth parents, he says, "it just about destroyed our family"—an experience he's not anxious to repeat by searching out his own roots. At the same time, he and Patty insist adoptive parents need to have the last word in arranging the terms of contact. Adopting is "just like when you bring your new baby home from the hospital," says Patty. "You want to hold it for yourself, so you can get adjusted. Then as it gets older, you're OK to let go."

Many adoptive parents fear the birth parents are the ones who won't let go. But, notes Scarth, "people haven't been clamouring to get their

children back. In fact, they often fade off into the distance after they're satisfied things are fine with their child." For those, like Gary Sands, who stick
around, it's not always easy. In the early days, he says, "I felt like Emma's
mine, my personal piece of property." But eventually, "through time and
all the heartache," he learned to put her interests ahead of his own. "I'm
amazed at myself," says Sands. "I had to be really understanding of the
adoptive parents." He even signed an agreement limiting contact to super-
vised monthly visits if he started to slip into his old ways again.

As for the kids, rather than feeling abandoned, they can gain a sense of
being loved and valued by more than one set of parents—a principle behind
adoptions within First Nations. Cindy Blackstock, executive director of First
Nations Child & Family Caring Society of Canada, recalls the adoption cer-
emony she attended at Alberta's Yellowhead Tribal Services Agency in 2002.
Elders and family members from the children's and the adoptive families'
bands were all present. "Watching the community step forward to take care
of those five children was the most moving experience in my life," she says.
"It was something to be celebrated—nothing to be ashamed of." Were openness readily accepted in public adoptions, she adds, it might help navigate
the stormy waters of cross-cultural adoptions. "The children wouldn't have
a sense of having to choose."

And, in Emma's case, she hasn't been the only one to benefit. Her adoptive parents, says Gary Sands, "saw me go through a lot of things, show up
in messes, crying. They never closed their door on me"—giving a home, in
effect, to daughter and father.

Analyze this Reading

1. According to the writer, what is motivating a change in traditional attitudes toward adoption?
2. What is an openness arrangement? What risks does it pose?
3. How does the writer address the fear of some adoptive parents that
   birth parents may have difficulty letting go of their biological children?
4. The writer includes compelling examples but little research. How does
   this help or hinder this article?

Respond to this Reading

1. In your view, what conditions should be attached to open adoptions?
2. Were you to write an argument in response to this reading, what
   would you claim and on what value or principle would you build your
   argument?

ABOUT THIS READING

Jewel Kilcher is the author of *Chasing Down the Dawn* (2001), a study of her professional life on the road, and a poetry collection, *A Night Without Armor* (1999).
She is a successful actress, guitarist, and singer-songwriter, having sold more than
25 million albums. This article appeared in *USA Today Magazine*.

Street Life Is No Life for Children

By Jewel

Coming home after school or a day with friends is something most kids take for granted, but for more than 1,000,000 young people living in this country, there is no place to call home. Youth homelessness is a complex issue that often is overlooked in the U.S.—even as we face a growing crisis of teens and children living alone on the streets. Left to fend for themselves, children as young as 11 years old confront such nightmarish scenarios as human trafficking and drug use, often with little understanding or sympathy from the general public. In June, I testified before the House Ways & Means Committee to support bipartisan resolutions designating November as "National Homeless Youth Awareness Month." Setting November aside in this way should help raise much-needed awareness of the issue, while demonstrating to kids on the streets that Congress is listening, people do want to help, and America cares about their futures.

While youngsters often become homeless due to some kind of family breakdown, there is no one cause. Poverty; lack of affordable housing, access to education, and other resources; unemployment among family members; abuse; and mental health issues all can be contributing factors. The issue of homeless youth is complicated further by misperceptions about children and teens who end up on the streets, as many people immediately jump to easy—but wrong—conclusions. For instance, when walking by a teenage girl sitting on a bench in the middle of a weekday, few might consider whether she is homeless. The easier response is to assume that she probably is just some punk kid who ditched school and is hanging around waiting for her friends. Few onlookers go so far as to consider an even darker reality—such as the fact that this girl might be forced into prostitution to make enough money to put food in her stomach.

This also is a population that is very good at making itself "invisible" to adults—since it is adults who so often have endangered or let these teens down in the past. That boy at your son's high school may seem like a nice, average kid, but he may have no home to return to after the school day; the point is, these girls and boys do not live on the streets or become homeless by choice. The sad truth: many of them feel safer there and, despite what many Americans think, this is not an easily "correctable" condition, land of opportunity or not.

I have a personal understanding of the plight of these young people on the margins, because I experienced homelessness firsthand. When I was 15 years old—I am a native of Utah but was raised in Alaska—I received a vocal scholarship to attend Interlochen Center for the Arts in Michigan. It was a time when, for many reasons, I increasingly felt I no longer could live at home—my parents long ago had divorced—and so the change of scenery was exciting, as was the opportunity to be surrounded by music. However, school breaks—like the upcoming Thanksgiving and Christmas recesses—presented an immediate challenge. Unlike my fellow students, the close of class sessions meant I was on my own. I enjoyed performing solo; so, during one spring break, I jumped on a train heading south and subsequently

hitchhiked to Mexico, earning money by singing on street corners. These were my first experiences of life without a safety net, but the harder reality was yet to come. After Interlochen, I moved to San Diego. As a result of a series of unfortunate events and bad breaks, I ended up living in a car. When that car was stolen, along with many of my possessions at the time, I borrowed $1,000 from a friend to buy a van—and that van became home right up until my break into the music industry.

When my story is told in the music press, it can take on a romantic glow, but living in a van was not romantic. I washed my hair in public bathroom sinks. People often would stare at me and make nasty comments. Some would wonder aloud how a "pretty girl" could end up in such a state. Yet, many more simply pretended that I was not there. I was humiliated and embarrassed about my situation and the stigma that was being attached to me. My experience is much like that of other young people fending for themselves, except for the fact that my story has a happy ending. Too many others are not so fortunate. Homeless organizations say that 30% of shelter youth and 70% of street youth are victims of commercial sexual exploitation at a time in their lives when these boys and girls should be finishing up elementary school.

These are just a few of the reasons why I do not believe America's homeless youth population is made up of children who leave home because they want to. Most homeless kids are on the streets because they have been forced by circumstances to believe they are safer alone than in the home they once knew—if that home even exists for them anymore. Others may have reached the end of their economic resources, or those of their family's, and are left trying to climb out of poverty from the disadvantageous position of the streets.

Some researchers estimate that up to 1,600,000 youth experience homelessness each year. Based on the amount of kids turned away from shelters each day, as well as the number of phone calls made to the National Runaway Hotline, those numbers may be even higher. Understand that many homeless kids are running from something, making it difficult to find or count them as part of any single community. What is clear, though, is that life in a shelter or on the streets puts homeless youth at a higher risk for physical and sexual assault, abuse, and physical illness, including HIV/AIDS. Estimates suggest that 5,000 unaccompanied youngsters die each year as a result of assault, illness, or suicide. That is an average of 13 kids dying every day on America's streets.

Anxiety disorders, depression, Post Traumatic Stress Disorder, and suicide all are more common among homeless children. Previous studies of the homeless youth population have shown high rates of parental alcohol or drug abuse. Contrary to many people's misconceptions, however, substance abuse is not a characteristic that defines most youngsters who experience homelessness.

Despite the many challenges faced by homeless kids, there is room for optimism. Statistics show, for instance, that a majority of homeless children make it to school, at least for a period of time. Our education system can become another lifeline for these children in need. If safe shelters, counseling, and adequate support were more available for these kinds of kids and, if

we could put increased emphasis on job training programs, there would be greater opportunities for homeless young people to graduate high school and build the skills they need to go on to live healthy and productive lives.

There are a number of organizations that play a critical role in making a positive, long-term difference in the lives of youth in crisis. StandUp For Kids, for example, is a not-for-profit group founded in 1990 by retired Navy officer Richard L. Koca to help rescue homeless and at-risk youth. With its national headquarters in San Diego, the organization is run almost entirely by volunteers, and has established more than 35 outreach programs in 20 states. Its mission is to find, stabilize, and assist homeless and street kids in an effort to improve their lives. YouthNoise, meanwhile, exists in the virtual world—but is equally powerful at inspiring and uniting young people. It runs the first youth-based social network dedicated to social change. Youth homelessness is one of the many critical issues that YouthNoise and its young members tackle, allowing teens to share thoughts on issues and convert ideas to action in their communities.

However, the government and nonprofit sectors cannot do this work alone. It is equally critical that our corporate citizens step up as well. I accepted the role as the first U.S. Ambassador of Virgin Unite, the Virgin Group's charitable arm created by Sir Richard Branson, in order to help one global brand increase its charitable voice and efforts. Through this role, I joined Virgin Mobile USA and The RE*Generation movement in their efforts to raise awareness of youth homelessness—and to support the direct work of programs like StandUp For Kids and YouthNoise.

Finally, the cliché is true—each person can make a difference, particularly this month as we recognize the very first "National Homeless Youth Awareness Month." There are a host of ways to get involved. By volunteering time, donating clothing or money, or simply by spreading the word, each of us can build a better future for children alone on the streets.

Analyze this Reading

1. As an activist for homeless youth, what projects has the writer pursued? What are the goals of each project?
2. What causes and misperceptions of youth homelessness does the writer identify?
3. How do the writer's personal experiences contribute to this reading? What compelling facts and statistics about homeless youth does she include?
4. What "room for optimism" does the writer describe?

Respond to this Reading

1. What is your understanding of homelessness in your community? Does some of the information the writer brings to this reading sound familiar? Are there features of youth homelessness the writer does not mention?
2. Do you share the writer's optimism regarding the challenges of addressing the problem of youth homelessness? What strategies for working with this issue would you add to what the writer mentions?

3. What are the attitudes toward homelessness in your community? Specifically, what are the views of elected leaders, of the business community, of social justice and faith groups, of your friends and family?
4. Were you to argue for a plan to address homeless students at your college, what would you claim? What support would you bring to your claim?

ABOUT THIS READING

In his book *Last Child in the Woods: Saving Our Children From Nature-Deficit Disorder*, Richard Louv warns that the health of children is endangered as they spend more time indoors and less time in the natural world. Based on his research, Louv claims that obesity and depression in children are in part due to limited physical activity and too much time alone. His ideas have generated interest in and beyond the United States. This reading is the introduction to *Last Child in the Woods*.

Introduction from Last Child in the Woods

By Richard Louv

One evening when my boys were younger, Matthew, then ten, looked at me from across a restaurant table and said quite seriously, "Dad, how come it was more fun when you were a kid?"

I asked what he meant.

"Well, you're always talking about your woods and tree houses, and how you used to ride that horse down near the swamp."

At first, I thought he was irritated with me. I had, in fact, been telling him what it was like to use string and pieces of liver to catch crawdads in a creek, something I'd be hard-pressed to find a child doing these days. Like many parents, I do tend to romanticize my own childhood—and, I fear, too readily discount my children's experiences of play and adventure. But my son was serious; he felt he had missed out on something important.

He was right. Americans around my age, baby boomers or older, enjoyed a kind of free, natural play that seems, in the era of kid pagers, instant messaging, and Nintendo, like a quaint artifact.

Within the space of a few decades, the way children understand and experience nature has changed radically. The polarity of the relationship has reversed. Today, kids are aware of the global threats to the environment—but their physical contact, their intimacy with nature, is fading. That's exactly the opposite of how it was when I was a child.

As a boy, I was unaware that my woods were ecologically connected with any other forests. Nobody in the 1950s talked about acid rain or holes in the ozone layer or global warming. But I knew my woods and my fields; I knew every bend in the creek and dip in the beaten dirt paths. I wandered those woods even in my dreams. A kid today can likely tell you about the Amazon rain forest—but not about the last time he or she explored the

woods in solitude, or lay in a field listening to the wind and watching the clouds move.

This book explores the increasing divide between the young and the natural world, and the environmental, social, psychological, and spiritual implications of that change. It also describes the accumulating research that reveals the necessity of contact with nature for healthy child—and adult—development.

While I pay particular attention to children, my focus is also on those Americans born during the past two to three decades. The shift in our relationship to the natural world is startling, even in settings that one would assume are devoted to nature. Not that long ago, summer camp was a place where you camped, hiked in the woods, learned about plants and animals, or told firelight stories about ghosts or mountain lions. As likely as not today, "summer camp" is a weight-loss camp, or a computer camp. For a new generation, nature is more abstraction than reality. Increasingly, nature is something to watch, to consume, to wear—to ignore. A recent television ad depicts a four-wheel-drive SUV racing along a breathtakingly beautiful mountain stream—while in the backseat two children watch a movie on a flip-down video screen, oblivious to the landscape and water beyond the windows.

A century ago, the historian Frederick Jackson Turner announced that the American frontier had ended. His thesis has been discussed and debated ever since. Today, a similar and more important line is being crossed.

Our society is teaching young people to avoid direct experience in nature. That lesson is delivered in schools, families, even organizations devoted to the outdoors, and codified into the legal and regulatory structures of many of our communities. Our institutions, urban/suburban design, and cultural attitudes unconsciously associate nature with doom, while disassociating the outdoors from joy and solitude. Well meaning public-school systems, media, and parents are effectively scaring children straight out of the woods and fields. In the patent-or-perish environment of higher education, we see the death of natural history as the more hands-on disciplines, such as zoology, give way to more theoretical and remunerative microbiology and genetic engineering. Rapidly advancing technologies are blurring the lines between humans, other animals, and machines. The postmodern notion that reality is only a construct—that we are what we program—suggests limitless human possibilities; but as the young spend less and less of their lives in natural surroundings, their senses narrow, physiologically and psychologically, and this reduces the richness of human experience.

Yet, at the very moment that the bond is breaking between the young and the natural world, a growing body of research links our mental, physical, and spiritual health directly to our association with nature—in positive ways. Several of these studies suggest that thoughtful exposure of youngsters to nature can even be a powerful form of therapy for attention-deficit disorders and other maladies. As one scientist puts it, we can now assume that just as children need good nutrition and adequate sleep, they may very well need contact with nature.

Reducing that deficit—healing the broken bond between our young and nature—is in our self-interest, not only because aesthetics or justice

demands it, but also because our mental, physical, and spiritual health depends upon it. The health of the earth is at stake as well. How the young respond to nature, and how they raise their own children, will shape the configurations and conditions of our cities, homes—our daily lives. The following pages explore an alternative path to the future, including some of the most innovative environment-based school programs; a reimagining and redesign of the urban environment—what one theorist calls the coming "zoopolis"; ways of addressing the challenges besetting environmental groups; and ways that faith-based organizations can help reclaim nature as part of the spiritual development of children. Parents, children, grandparents, teachers, scientists, religious leaders, environmentalists, and researchers from across the nation speak in these pages. They recognize the transformation that is occurring. Some of them paint another future, in which children and nature are reunited—and the natural world is more deeply valued and protected.

During the research for this book, I was encouraged to find that many people now of college age—those who belong to the first generation to grow up in a largely de-natured environment—have tasted just enough nature to intuitively understand what they have missed. This yearning is a source of power. These young people resist the rapid slide from the real to the virtual, from the mountains to the Matrix. They do not intend to be the last children in the woods.

My sons may yet experience what author Bill McKibben has called "the end of nature," the final sadness of a world where there is no escaping man. But there is another possibility: not the end of nature, but the rebirth of wonder and even joy. Jackson's obituary for the American frontier was only partly accurate: one frontier did disappear, but a second one followed, in which Americans romanticized, exploited, protected, and destroyed nature. Now that frontier—which existed in the family farm, the woods at the end of the road, the national parks, and in our hearts—is itself disappearing or changing beyond recognition.

But, as before, one relationship with nature can evolve into another. This book is about the end of that earlier time, but it is also about a new frontier—a better way to live with nature.

Analyze this Reading

1. Often, writers choose to begin serious arguments with an anecdote that attempts to draw in readers emotionally. Is the writer's personal anecdote that opens this argument effective? Does it make you want to read on? Explain.
2. Describe the difference the writer identifies between his childhood and his perceptions of childhood today.
3. In paragraph nine, the writer claims that for children today "nature is more abstraction than reality." With what examples does he support this position?
4. In paragraph 10, the writer refers to historian Frederick Jackson Turner's famous thesis that the American frontier ended with Western expansion. Does the writer return to Turner later in the argument to agree or

disagree with the historian? And does the writer return to his opening anecdote? In your view, is this circling back to earlier references effective? Explain.

5. In paragraph 11, the writer argues that "Our society is teaching young people to avoid direct experience in nature." Does this statement function as a claim of fact for this argument, or should it be analyzed as a reason supporting another claim?

6. What values does the writer bring to his argument? Do these values contribute to an effective warrant?

Respond to this Reading

1. The term "nature deficit disorder" begins with Richard Louv. While not widely accepted as a legitimate psychological condition, does Louv's term have merit? Do you agree with Louv's contention that our dependence on technology occurs at the expense of children interacting with nature? Explain.

2. With what parts of Louv's argument do you disagree? What parts do you agree with?

3. Identify elements of bias or limited perspective you find in this reading.

4. Louv wants us to think about nature deficit in terms of education, recreation, and health. Are there other issues that occur to you in terms of the younger generation and nature? What would you claim for each issue?

ABOUT THIS READING

American Dahr Jamail was an unembedded journalist during the 2003 Iraq Invasion, posting reports on his website, *Dahr Jamail's MidEast Dispatches*. He is also a contributing writer to *Al Jazeera*, among other publications, and a contributing writer for *Truthout*, the daily online news site in which this article appears. His books include *Beyond the Green Zone: Dispatches from an Unembedded Journalist in Occupied Iraq* (2007) and *The Will to Resist: Soldiers Who Refuse to Fight in Iraq and Afghanistan* (2009).

A Morally Bankrupt Military: When Soldiers and Their Families Become Expendable

By Dahr Jamail

The military operates through indoctrination. Soldiers are programmed to develop a mindset that resists any acknowledgment of injury and sickness, be it physical or psychological. As a consequence, tens of thousands of soldiers continue to serve, even being deployed to combat zones like Iraq and/or Afghanistan, despite persistent injuries. According to military records, over 43,000 troops classified as "nondeployable for medical reasons" have been deployed to Iraq and Afghanistan nevertheless.

The recent atrocity at Fort Hood is an example of this. Maj. Nidal Hasan had worked as a counselor at Walter Reed, hearing countless stories of bloodshed, horror and death from dismembered veterans from the occupations of Iraq and Afghanistan. While he had not yet served in Iraq or Afghanistan, the major was overloaded with secondary trauma, coupled with ongoing harassment about his being a Muslim. This, along with other factors, contributed toward Hasan falling into a desperation so deep he was willing to slaughter fellow soldiers, and is indicative of fissures running deep into the crumbling edifice upon which the U.S. military stands.

The case of Pvt. Timothy Rich also demonstrates the disastrous implications of the apathetic attitude of the military toward its own. Not dissimilar from Major Hasan, who clearly would have benefited from treatment for the secondary trauma he was experiencing from his work with psychologically wounded veterans, one of the main factors that forced Private Rich to go absent without leave (AWOL) was the failure of the military to treat his mental issues.

Rich told Truthout, "In my unit, to go to sick call for mental health was looked down upon. Our acting 1st Sergeant believed that we shouldn't have mental issues because we were too 'high speed.' So I was afraid to go because I didn't want to be labeled as a weak soldier."

What followed was more harrowing.

"The other problems arose when I brought my girlfriend down to marry her. My unit believed her to be a problem starter so I was ordered not to marry her, taken to a small finance company by an NCO and forced to draw a loan in order to buy her a plane ticket to return home. They escorted her to the airport and through security to ensure that she left. Once the NCO left she turned around and hitchhiked back to Fort Bragg. Before the unit could discover us, we went to the courthouse and got married. We were then summoned by my Commander, Captain Jones, to his office and reprimanded. He called me a dumb ass soldier and a shit bag for marrying her and told my wife that she was a fool to marry someone as stupid as me. Members of my unit started referring to me as Pvt. Bitch instead of Pvt. Rich. The entire episode caused a lot of strain in our relationship. Unable to cope with all this, I bought two plane tickets and went AWOL with my wife."

Rich was later apprehended when a federal warrant was issued against him. After 11 days in a country jail, he was transported back to Fort Bragg in North Carolina. On August 17, 2008, he was wrongly assigned to Echo Platoon that was part of the 82nd Airborne, whereas his unit was part of the 18th Airborne.

Rich recollects, "I was confused when they assigned me to the 82nd. I was dismissed as a liar when I brought this up with my NCO Sgt Joseph Fulgence and my commander, Captain Thaxton. I ended up spending a year at Echo before being informed that I was never supposed to have been in the 82nd."

At Fort Bragg, he was permitted to seek mental health treatment and was diagnosed with schizophrenia, psychosis, insomnia and a mood disorder. This, however, did not stop his commander from harassing him. His permanent profile from the doctor restricted him from being on duty before 0800 (8 AM) hours, but his commander, Sergeant Fulgence, dismissed the profile as merely a guideline and not a mandatory directive. The soldier was accused of using mental health as a pretext to avoid duty. So, Rich was up every morning for first formation at 0545 (5:45 AM). It wasn't until he refused to take his medication because it made him groggy in the morning that his doctor called his commander and settled the matter. By then, Rich had already been forced to violate his profile for six months.

During this period, his mental health deteriorated rapidly. The combined effect of heavy medication and restrictions on his home visits resulted in his experiencing blackouts that led him to take destructive actions in the barracks. When he was discovered talking about killing the chain of command, he was put on a 24-hour suicide watch that seemed to have served little purpose, because on August 17 he was able to elude his guards and make his way to the roof of his barracks.

"I climbed onto the roof of the building and sat up there thinking about my family and my situation and decided to go ahead and end my suffering by taking a nose dive off the building," Rich explained to Truthout.

His body plummeted through the air, bounced off a tree, and he landed on his back with a cracked spine. The military gave him a back brace, psychotropic drugs and a renewed 24-hour suicide watch, measures as effective in alleviating his pain as his failed suicide attempt.

When Truthout contacted him just days after his failed suicide attempt, a fatigued Rich detailed his hellish year-long plight of awaiting a discharge that never came. "I want to leave here very bad. For four months they have been telling me that I'll get out next week. It got to the point that the NCOs would tell me just to calm me down that I'd be going home the next day. They went as far as to call my wife and requesting her to lie that she was coming to get me the next day. I eventually stopped believing them. I didn't see an end to it, so I figured I'd try and end it myself."

The noncommissioned officers in his barracks thought it was hilarious that Rich had jumped, and he was offered money for an encore that could be videotaped.

At the time he was in a "holdover" unit, comprised mostly of AWOL soldiers who had turned themselves in or had been arrested. Others in his unit had untreated mental health problems like him or were suffering from severe PTSD (post-traumatic stress disorder) from deployments in Iraq and or Afghanistan.

According to Rich, every soldier in his platoon was subjected to abusive treatment of some kind or the other. "It even got to the point when our 1st Sergeant Cisneros told us that if it were up to him we all would all be taken out back and shot, and that we needed to pray to our gods because we were going to pay (for our actions)."

Tim's wife Megan had to bear his never-ending ordeal in equal measure. She witnessed the military's callousness up close. She informed Truthout, "Since February of this year, Tim's unit had been telling him he would be out in two weeks. After two weeks when he asked, they would repeat the same thing. At times he would get excited and start packing his belongings and I would try to figure out how to get him home to Ohio. He would call me crying in relief because he thought we were going to be together again real soon. The military forced me to lie to him too. When he realized they did not

mean to release him he grew very destructive during his black out spells. Eventually he simply gave up on coming home."

Megan first realized there was a problem with the way the military was treating her husband when she noticed him doing and saying things that were out of character for him, like apologizing for not being a good husband and father and being openly suicidal. He had also begun to self-medicate with alcohol, an increasing trend among soldiers not receiving adequate mental-health treatment from the military.

She revealed to Truthout, "He had quit for the girls and me but it seems like he could not handle the stress and needed an escape. This caused a huge problem between us and we began to argue about it. He became severely depressed, pulled away from me, and started to do things he normally doesn't do, such as giving away his money and belongings, and telling the recipients that he wouldn't need those things in hell."

She sensed that her husband would be in trouble if he were to stand up for himself, so she began to advocate on his behalf. Her attempts to do so met with fresh abuse from his commanders. The chain of command banned her from the company barracks and had her escorted off post. The couple was commandeered into Sergeant Fulgence's office where they were chastised. The sergeant referred to Megan as "a bad mother" and "a bitch." When Megan attempted to leave the office in protest, the sergeant ordered her to stay and listen to what he had to say.

This was followed by an encounter with the commander of the platoon, Commander Thaxton. The commander in this case ordered Tim to shut up, and threatened him with confinement. He demanded that Megan explain what kind of mother would bring her child to a new location without a place to live. She tried telling him that the AER loan was for her to come to Fort Bragg since they had lost their house after Tim's arrest and loss of job. Although the paperwork for the loan clearly stated that it was for her travel, food and lodging at Fort Bragg, the commander insisted it was for an apartment. When Tim intervened to say that the $785 would not be sufficient to pay rent and bills, especially since he wasn't being paid his wages and his wife couldn't work because of the baby, and according to Tim, both Sergeant Fulgence and Captain Thaxton "had a nice laugh over that" and dismissed the duo, referring to them as "juvenile dumb-asses."

After Tim returned from being AWOL and was brought up on charges, he went through 706 (a psychology board) that declared him mentally incompetent at the time of his being AWOL. It took a painfully long amount of time for the charges to be dismissed without prejudice. The soldier believes that his superiors deliberately refused to do the requisite paperwork for his clearance and subsequent resumption of his pay.

He told Truthout, "Every time I came on base I got arrested even though I was on active duty again. Then my wife and I got an AER loan for her to come down to Fort Bragg. When she got there and my pay continued to be withheld, the AER money ran out and my wife and child had to sleep in the van we owned. When my unit found out they called the Military Police and ordered me to give custody of my daughter to my father." When Tim refused to do that, they punished him by confining him to the barracks and barring his wife from entering the base. To add insult, the chain of command took away his van keys and said that neither he nor Megan was allowed use it.

The nightmare ended when the military finally released Pvt. Timothy Rich, and by default, Megan. He was discharged and "allowed" to enter the ranks of U.S. citizens searching for jobs and health care. Their traumatic journey to that starting point is what distinguishes them from their civilian counterparts.

Rich's advice to anyone thinking of joining the military today: "Don't join. Everything they advertise and tell you about how it's a family friendly army is a lie."

Sgt. Heath Carter suffered a similar fate at the hands of an indifferent military command. Upon return from the invasion of Iraq, he discovered that his daughter Sierra was living in an unsafe environment in Arkansas under the care of his first wife, who had full custody of the child. Heath and his new wife, Teresa, started consulting attorneys in order to secure custody of Sierra, who also suffered from a life-threatening medical condition. Precisely during this time, the military chose to keep changing Carter's duty station from Fort Polk, Louisiana, to Fort Huachuca, Arizona, then to Fort Stewart, Georgia. Not only did these constant transfers make it difficult for Carter to see his daughter, they also reduced his chances of gaining custody of Sierra. Convinced that this was a matter of life and death for his daughter, he requested compassionate reassignment to Fort Leavenworth, Missouri, about two hours from his first wife's home in Arkansas.

His appeals to the military command, the legal department, chaplain and even to his congressman failed, and the military insisted that he remain at Fort Stewart, Georgia. Having run out of all available avenues, in May 2007 he went AWOL from Fort Stewart and headed home to Arkansas where he fought for and won custody of Sierra, and was able to literally save her life by obtaining needed medical care for her.

However, on January 25 of this year, Carter was arrested at his home by the military police, who flew him back to Fort Stewart where he has been awaiting charges for the past eight months. Being a sergeant, he is in a regular unit and not in a holdover, but that does not help his cause. Initially, his commander told him it would take a month and a half for him to be sent home. Several months later, it was decided he would receive a court-martial.

Carter feels frustrated, "Now I have to wait for the court martial. It's taken this long for them to decide. If we had known it would take this long, my family could have moved down here. Every time I ask when I'll have a trial, they say it is only going to be another two weeks. I get the feeling they are lying. They have messed with my pay. They're trying to push me to do something wrong."

His ordeal has forced Carter to reflect on the wars. He admits that, although his original reason for going AWOL was personal and he had otherwise been proud of his missions, he sees things in Iraq differently today. "I don't think there is any reason for us to be there except for oil."

Yet, both Private Rich and Sergeant Carter were offered deployments to Afghanistan amid their struggles. It is soldiers like these that the military

will use to fill the ranks of the next "surge" of troops into Afghanistan, which at the time of this writing, appears to be as many as 34,000 troops.

The stage is set for more tragic incidents like the recent massacre at Fort Hood.

Analyze this Reading

1. What does the writer claim in the first paragraph? What context does he provide for his claim?
2. What kinds of support does the writer use? Are the cases of Private Rich and Sergeant effective? Explain.
3. While this text is a report and not an argument, would the report have benefited from attention to the conventional elements of argument, such as a warrant, opposing points of view, and reasons? Explain.

Respond to this Reading

1. What is your understanding of how our military personnel are responded to when they express concern about health and sickness? Does it fall in line with the writer's view? Why or why not?
2. Were you a member of a citizens advisory group charged with monitoring veterans affairs in your community, what regulations would you insist on and what resources in the community would you enlist in support?

Anthology 4 Neighborhood Community

ABOUT THIS READING

Barbara Nichols is the author of *The No Lawsuit Guide to Real Estate Transactions*. She is a real estate broker and contractor. Her argument appears in *REALTOR Magazine*, the official magazine of the National Association of Realtors.

Airbnb is Crashing the Neighborhood

By Barbara Nichols

There's a good reason every city has zoning laws. They separate various types of buildings and building uses for the mutual benefit of everyone, so people don't have to live next to a factory or a motel. Most cities also have laws related to the minimum rental period for a single-family house or a multifamily dwelling. In Los Angeles, for example, a residential rental of less than 30 days—called a "short-term rental"—is currently prohibited.

Internet companies such as Airbnb and VRBO pay no mind to such ordinances. They've swamped the market in California and elsewhere with thousands of STR listings, making the rules difficult or impossible to enforce. These rental sites appeal to home owners who need additional income. Then the companies use those owners as examples to coax cities into making STRs legal. Even though there's clear demand on the part of home owners, that doesn't justify the many problems STRs cause for the larger community.

Usually, there's no problem with people renting a room in their home, as long as the lease is longer than 30 days and the home owner is present to monitor the renter's activities. The owner has an opportunity to check the potential renter's credit, employment, and references. However, STR websites are calling this type of preexisting rental the "shared economy" to sell their quite different concept to cities.

These websites claim that home owners should have the right to do whatever they want with their property—but that's a fallacy. When someone has purchased in a single-family or multifamily zone, they have accepted the rules of that zoning. They do not have the right to turn their home into a motel (transient zoning), a restaurant, or a factory to the detriment of everyone else in that zone.

STRs are having a dangerous effect on our housing stock. In L.A., a city desperate for more affordable housing, 11 units of long-term rental housing are being lost daily to STR conversions, according to a report from the Los Angeles Alliance for a New Economy. The report says people are converting rent-controlled units into commercial STR operations, and long-term rent-control tenants are being evicted. The loss of these units in the long-term rental market has driven up total housing costs for L.A. renters by more than $464 million in the last year. (Read more in this *Los Angeles Times* article, "Rental sites like Airbnb aren't as innocuous as they pretend.")

The trend for STRs is away from "shared spaces," where owners are present. Individuals are now purchasing single-family or multifamily units to turn them into STRs—creating a business—to the considerable detriment of their neighbors. Some short-term renters turn these locations into party houses, creating noise, traffic, and a public nuisance. In such instances, neighbors who need a night's sleep to work the next day or who have school-age children are disturbed. In my neighborhood, a home owner leased her property for a year to someone she believed was occupying it, only to learn he listed it on one of the STR sites as a "commercial party house." Some 500 people being charged $125 apiece crammed narrow, winding canyon roads by illegally parking and throwing trash everywhere. When the property owner was alerted, she was shocked and started eviction proceedings.

STRs pose big risks for the home owners who are leasing their properties: Home insurance typically covers only owner-occupied or long-term rental homes. Damage to an STR likely isn't covered. Airbnb seems to have addressed this problem with its "host guarantee" that offers up to $1 million for property damage caused by short-term renters, but owners should read the fine print: Airbnb itself says its policy "should not be considered as a replacement or stand-in for homeowners or renters insurance." Most notably, it doesn't cover liability at all. The fine print also suggests that property owners try to settle with the guest first. If no settlement can be reached, they have to document the damage and submit to a possible inspection. Airbnb won't cover "reasonable wear and tear"—whatever that means—and limits compensation for high-value items such as jewelry and artwork. So, really, how much can a host expect to be protected?

The negative impact of STRs goes far beyond the immediate neighborhoods they're in. Every region has environmental challenges, and short-term renters who are unfamiliar—or unconcerned—with those challenges could pose a big threat. California is in the midst of a severe drought. Imagine if a short-term renter who knew nothing of the threat—or didn't care—threw a cigarette butt over a balcony onto dry brush?

Worst of all, the growth of short-term rentals has pitted neighbor against neighbor, with neighborhood organizations joining forces to fight STRs. Some cities are calling for stricter STR regulations or outright bans, but who will pay for enforcement of these rules? In fairness, STR websites and their customers should pay the bill. Local taxpayers would prefer to see their tax revenue used for better schools, roads, and public transit.

Those who support STRs speak of the financial help it has provided and the interesting visitors they have met. STR hosts say they provide lower-cost accommodations than conventional motels and hotels. Well, hotels and motels pay taxes and employ millions of people. They are required to meet public-safety laws, including fire exits, sprinklers, and habitability. Unregulated STRs are not currently subject to these provisions, and many "hosts" would like to keep it that way.

The real estate industry is caught in the middle of a fight between those who oppose STRs and the property owners and companies promoting them. But practitioners selling real estate should keep this in mind: A

single-family home or condo unit next door to a short-term rental—where the occupants change every few days—will take longer to sell and bring in lower offers. You never know who your neighbors could be, and that's a classic situation of property stigma.

In the future, real estate agents could be required to disclose to a seller or long-term renter the existence of a nearby STR. The California Association of REALTORS® may soon ask its Forms Committee to add a question to the Seller's Property Questionnaire: "Is your home across from or next door to a short-term rental?" If agents fail to disclose nearby STRs they know about, they could open themselves up to a lawsuit by unhappy clients who end up living next door to one.

The real estate industry needs to take a stand to protect residential zoning laws against STRs. Without this protection, property values will decline and cause neighborhood stress and disruption. Real estate agents will have another obstacle to overcome in marketing properties and could expose themselves to liability. Saving our communities and protecting our property values is the mission of our industry. I have worked hard as a real estate broker to pay for my home of 29 years. I did not buy in a transient motel zone and do not believe that the profit motives of these short-term rental companies and a few property owners should be allowed to negatively impact my home's value, peace and quiet, and safety.

Analyze this Reading

1. What context does the writer provide to introduce the issue to readers?
2. What does the writer claim? Where does the claim appear in the argument?
3. Two reasons that support the claim center on "housing stock" and "risk." Describe these reasons.
4. Explain how the writer counters the rebuttal.

Respond to this Reading

1. Do Airbnb and VRBO (vacation rental by owner) companies have a presence in your community? If yes, how do local residents react to short-term rentals?
2. Given the long-standing tension between realtors, like the writer, and owners of short-term rental units, are you sympathetic with one or the side? Explain.

ABOUT THIS READING

A professor of communications at Monmouth University, Eleanor Novek researches the role of communication in racial residential segregation. This reading appeared in *Shelterforce*, a magazine published by the National Housing Institute and devoted to issues in the fields of housing and community development.

You Wouldn't Fit Here

By Eleanor Novek

In *Race in America: The Struggle for Equality*, Patricia J. Williams, a legal scholar, recalls seeing an advertisement for a two-bedroom apartment in Madison, Wisconsin. The landlord agreed to meet her at the address to show the place. Williams, who is African-American, arrived first. "I saw her catch sight of me as I sat on the doorstep. I saw her walk slower and slower, squinting at me as I sat in the sunshine. At ten minutes after three, I was back in my car driving away without having seen the apartment. The woman had explained to me that a 'terrible mistake' had occurred, that the apartment had been rented without her knowledge . . ."

Williams's experience is a common one for people of color in all walks of life. Decades after the passage of federal fair housing laws, housing discrimination and racial segregation are alive and well in the United States. Many communities still operate under a strict "virtual apartheid," and in some parts of the country, racially divided neighborhoods are even more prevalent than they were before civil rights legislation. Extensive regional and national studies have documented that minority home seekers receive less assistance than whites in finding housing that meets their needs and are more likely to be turned down for mortgage loans and home insurance than comparably qualified white applicants. Buyers of all races continue to be steered toward neighborhoods where their own ethnic groups are concentrated.

While many ethnic groups have encountered housing discrimination, no group has experienced the sustained high level of residential segregation that has been imposed on African Americans. Segregation has concentrated African Americans into disadvantaged neighborhoods characterized by higher crime rates, fewer public services, and lower housing values. It has restricted their access to job opportunities, information resources and political influence. Schools in segregated areas are plagued by high dropout rates and severe educational disparities that threaten the life chances of African-American children. Racial residential segregation is a primary cause of urban poverty and inequality in the United States.

Although many forces are responsible for this persistence of racial segregation, the role of communication is often overlooked. Since passage of the Fair Housing Act, polite social interaction is often used to carry the same ugly messages formerly stated directly, with entire conversations conducted as if something other than race is causing the denial of housing. These communication strategies have helped to preserve segregation where the law has tried to dismantle it.

History of Residential Segregation

Scholars track the institutionalization of racial separation to the early 1900s, when large numbers of blacks migrated from the rural South in search of factory jobs. When they tried to settle in the largely white urban areas of the North and the Midwest, they met with exclusion, intimidation and violence.

Whites in some cities boycotted and harassed businesses like boarding houses, hotels, and real estate firms that provided shelter to African Americans. Other whites established suburbs where they used zoning laws and exclusionary deeds to keep out people of color. Responding to these dynamics, real estate agents found it easiest and most profitable to steer home buyers and renters to neighborhoods where people of their own races were already concentrated.

Such steering was soon underscored by federal policies. In the 1930s and '40s, the Federal Housing Administration underwrote mortgages in segregated white neighborhoods, while directing lenders to turn down minority mortgages. Between 1930 and 1960, fewer than 1 percent of all mortgages in the nation were issued to African Americans. In the 1960s, urban renewal plans placed low-income housing projects in minority neighborhoods, concentrating the nation's poorest residents in the same neighborhoods occupied by people of color.

The Federal Fair Housing Act of 1968 outlawed overtly discriminatory market practices like exclusionary deeds, steering and redlining, but it had relatively little effect on established routines among real estate agents and lenders. Over the next two decades, despite increases in income, education and job status for minorities, housing patterns remained segregated. In the 1990s, despite modest changes in newer suburban neighborhoods in the South and West, segregation actually deepened in many cities. Between 1996 and 1998, the U.S. Department of Justice prosecuted more than 80 cases of criminal interference with housing rights, including cross-burnings, shootings and fire-bombings.

Biased Brokers

Such acts of violence are not the primary way that segregation is reinforced in much of the country, however. Real estate sales and rental agents, mortgage lenders and insurers all have significant influence on the choices home buyers make. And despite the Fair Housing Act, race still influences their interactions with their customers.

First, there is direct discrimination. Minority home buyers receive less assistance than whites in finding housing that meets their needs, and are more likely to be turned down or overcharged for home loans and insurance than comparably qualified white applicants. Doug Massey and Nancy Denton describe in *American Apartheid: Segregation and the Making of the Underclass* how racial minority customers are told that the unit they want to see has just been sold or rented, or they are shown only one advertised unit and told that no others are available.

At some real estate offices, Massey and Denton note, minority customers are "told that the selling agents are too busy and to come back later; their phone number may be taken but a return call never made; they may be shown units but offered no assistance in arranging financing; or they may be treated brusquely and discourteously in hopes that they will leave." National studies using matched pairs of testers have documented these actions at real estate firms and mortgage lenders around the country. Many of these abuses originate in the earliest personal interactions between

sellers and buyers, or in the first informational materials home buyers confront.

Less directly abusive, but even more clearly perpetuating segregation is the practice of steering, whereby customers are strongly encouraged, both by what they are shown and by "commentary," to buy or rent in single-race neighborhoods where they "fit in." When consumers want to inspect housing in locations where they would be in a racial minority, some real estate agents try to discourage them through conversation. In Bloomington, IN, an agent warned an Asian woman and her white husband away from a house they wanted to buy because it was not in "a mixed neighborhood." And a white woman in Ocean, NJ was assured by an agent that "this is a great neighborhood—there are none of them here." Real estate salespeople often say they know other agents who discuss the racial makeup of neighborhoods with clients, but they refuse to discuss such practices in detail, fearful of backlash from those agents.

Research demonstrates that white buyers typically hear positive comments from agents praising neighborhoods and schools in mostly white areas, but they hear discouraging comments about neighborhood amenities and schools when a neighborhood's population is more than 30 percent black. Black customers tend to hear little commentary—positive or negative—from agents about predominantly black neighborhoods, but they are invariably warned against buying in predominantly white areas because of the possible "trouble" they would face there.

Advertising Exclusivity

Newspaper real estate ads are a key source of information for home seekers, and they often contain discriminatory messages. The Federal Fair Housing Act forbids references to race, color, religion, sex, handicap, familial status or national origin in real estate advertising, but subtler messages of exclusion in photographs or text often get through. In some real estate markets, for example, the models shown in photographic ads for homes and apartment complexes are all white, and very blonde. Some have described neighborhoods "where Wally and the Beaver would feel right at home," or homes built in "the style of Northern Europe," available only to "a select few" or representing "a return to family values."

These tactics have resulted in individual complaints and lawsuits. Some courts have ruled that using only white models in real estate advertisements sends a discriminatory message to other races. In one study, African-American and white respondents viewed groups of real estate ads with white models only and with a mix of black and white models. Typical responses to the all-white ads included: "Because the 'actors' are perceived to be all Europeans, I would question if African Americans would be welcome here," and "From people pictured on posters, this apartment complex is 'for white only.'"

In 1993, in partial settlement of a lawsuit, *The New York Times* began requiring that real estate ads containing photos of people be representative of the racial makeup in the New York metropolitan area. Some advertisers responded by removing all human figures from their ads. In 1994, the publishers of the *Philadelphia Inquirer* and the *Philadelphia Daily News*

cautioned advertisers not to use "coded" text in ads, including "such words and phrases as traditional, prestigious, established and private community, which, when used in a certain context, could be interpreted to convey racial exclusivity."

Data Labeling

Internet marketing sites and the practice of computer-assisted target marketing have added a new twist to communication about race and real estate. Many residential sales firms, including brands like Century 21 and Re/MAX, have established consumer websites to attract customers, offering prospective home buyers information and advice from mortgage rates to moving tips. Some sites furnish "neighborhood profile" services, where consumers can type in the street address or zip code of a home and receive a description of nearby schools, crime rates, and property values. Or they may offer "neighborhood matching," a service that allows relocating buyers to type in the zip codes of their current neighborhoods and find communities in other cities with comparably priced housing.

The demographic information on Internet real estate sites is provided by marketing services such as Lysias, Taconic Data, CACI Marketing Systems and Claritas. These firms combine demographic data from the U.S. Census with consumer spending research and package the information for easy use by commercial clients. Such firms pioneered "cluster marketing" techniques in the 1980s, analyzing the consumer habits of neighborhoods across the U.S. by zip code and then assigning them catchy nicknames like "Affluent Suburbia," "Mid-City Mix," and "Metro Singles."

However, some of these profiles categorize neighborhoods not only by zip code and consumer behavior, but also by ethnic signifiers. For example, a profile offered by CACI Marketing Systems characterized one zip code as having mostly black residents who had not completed high school and "tend to purchase fast food and takeout food from chicken restaurants." Claritas' online "Hispanic Mix" neighborhood profile is decorated with a cartoon image of a brown-skinned mother shopping at a sidewalk market, and describes residents who are pro basketball fans and use money orders to pay their bills.

MicroVision's middle-income "City Ties" cluster (where residents are said to eat at chicken restaurants, smoke menthol cigarettes, and read *Ebony* magazine) is illustrated by a photo of a smiling black family with three children. Its upscale "Metro Singles" cluster (where residents are said to use sunburn remedies and have dental insurance) is illustrated by a blonde white woman reclining alone on a sofa.

In February 1999, the National Association of Realtors took a stand against the use of racial and ethnic demographic information on members' real estate websites, but a number of firms continue the practice. These techniques have recently come under fire from community groups and citizens. ACORN, a nonprofit fair housing organization, has charged Wells Fargo/ Norwest Mortgage with racial discrimination over the company's Internet real estate site (which has since been taken down). Plaintiffs argued that the website's neighborhood profiles used "overt racial classifications" to discourage people from inspecting or buying homes in predominantly minority areas by exaggerating the desirability of areas deemed white occupied

and the drawbacks of areas classified as minority occupied. The plaintiffs also claim the site's neighborhood matching feature steered residents of predominantly minority zip codes to other minority zip codes, and referred residents of predominantly white zip codes to other white zip codes.

The practices described above are common but hard to track, located more often by anecdotal example than by research. Although they are not as dramatic as acts of violence and not as quantifiable as redlining, they play a significant role in the persistence of housing discrimination. Together, they may be as discouraging to the growth of integrated communities as the easier-to-measure practices of discriminatory pricing, mortgage lending and insurance underwriting. However, these habits that support segregation can be broken by a concerted effort to bring them into the light of day. . . .

First, let's talk about what is going on. The absence of public dialogue is one of the conditions that allow racial discrimination to persist. Most individual home buyers see themselves not as change agents but as consumers whose decisions are merely individual choices that have no broader impact. Community organizations and coalitions play a key role in helping to raise public awareness of segregation and the contemporary problems it creates.

Second, community organizations can strengthen their case by partnering with researchers and journalists to more precisely document the scope of residential segregation in their communities. Academic researchers can teach local groups techniques for tracing social patterns and analyzing their impact in a community over time. Journalists can bring the issue of segregation to public attention. Rather than focusing their stories on individual acts of housing bias involving a few people, news organizations need to cover residential segregation as an issue story, highlighting the social processes and outcomes that affect thousands of people. Such efforts can begin to raise broader public support for changes in policy. Publishers and editors should also assess the racially exclusive advertising practices in their own real estate sections and pressure advertisers to change.

Finally, we must call on public officials at local, state and federal levels to address residential segregation through assertive social programs. Models for these already exist, such as the one developed by the Fund for an Open Society in Philadelphia. This plan calls for the creation of neighborhood enterprise zones dedicated to residential integration. It suggests the creation of mortgage subsidies and tax exemptions for homeowners, and recommends that participating localities be made eligible for dedicated funding for new construction and school support. The Fair Share Housing Center in Cherry Hill, NJ works with residents of Mt. Laurel, NJ to develop low-income housing that would allow some of Camden's inner city residents to afford suburban housing. The South Orange/Maplewood Community Coalition on Race is also testing out some of these ideas.

Segregation is a stubborn problem. Although some communication practices have been used to circumvent fair housing and integration, others can help. Let's talk frankly about the racial makeup of our neighborhoods. Let's document and publicize what is going on. Let's define segregation as a social harm rather than as an inconvenient byproduct of individual preferences. And let's come up with alternatives for viable communities with quality of life for all.

Analyze this Reading

1. What is "virtual apartheid"? According to the writer, what have been its effects?
2. Identify the claim in this argument. What kind of claim is it?
3. What factual information does the writer bring to her treatment of the history of residential segregation?
4. How do the strategies of steering, advertising, and data labeling contribute to residential segregation?
5. What methods for breaking the habits of residential segregation does the writer recommend?

Respond to this Reading

1. What is your experience or the experiences of others you know with racial residential segregation? Are some of the strategies described by the writer for maintaining this kind of segregation familiar? Explain.
2. How does this argument fit with your understanding of other forms of racial segregation?
3. Consider building an argument in response to one feature of racial residential segregation, either as it exists in your community or as it exists in general in America. Of the several features described in this argument, which might compel you to argue? What kind of claim would you build your argument around?

ABOUT THIS READING

James Q. Wilson is Ronald Reagan Professor of Public Policy at Pepperdine University. His books include *Moral Judgment* (1997), *The Marriage Problem: How Our Culture Damages Families* (2002), and *Understanding America: The Anatomy of an Exceptional Nation* (2008, ed. with Peter Schuck). This reading appeared in *Commentary*, a monthly magazine that, in its own words, sees itself as "consistently engaged with several large, interrelated questions: the fate of democracy and of democratic ideas in a world threatened by totalitarian ideologies; the state of American and Western security; the future of the Jews, Judaism, and Jewish culture in Israel, the United States, and around the world; and the preservation of high culture in an age of political correctness and the collapse of critical standards."

Bowling with Others

By James Q. Wilson

Ethnic and racial diversity is an important social characteristic in neighborhoods because, in the long run, it promotes connections between different social groups, reducing ethnocentric behavior. According to political scientist Robert D. Putnam, ethnically integrated neighborhoods help solidify

social solidarity by helping create new, inclusive social identities. In the short term, however, it is difficult for people to adapt to ethnically diverse surroundings. Studies focusing on the impact of diversity on the social well-being of neighborhoods prove that ethnically diverse neighborhoods currently rate consistently below ethnically homogenous neighborhoods. Mixed ethnic groups reveal a lower level of social trust across different groups, resulting in little or no group unity. Forced integration, such as initiatives helping minorities gain access to communities where they have never lived before, are limited in their ability to promote true ethnic integration. Although the legal system should be used to strike down blatantly racist policies, government mandates forcing diversity into neighborhoods will not be successful until families find common ground on their own, based on similar moral values. These values cross ethnic lines, and can form a strong basis for true integration.

In his celebrated book *Bowling Alone*, the political scientist Robert D. Putnam argued that America, and perhaps the Western world as a whole, has become increasingly disconnected from family, friends, and neighbors. We once bowled in leagues; now we bowl alone. We once flocked to local chapters of the PTA (Parent Teacher Association), the NAACP (National Association for the Advancement of Colored People), or the Veterans of Foreign Wars; now we stay home and watch television. As a result, we have lost our "social capital"—by which Putnam meant both the associations themselves and the trustworthiness and reciprocity they encourage. For if tools (physical capital) and training (human capital) make the modern world possible, social capital is what helps people find jobs and enables neighborhoods and other small groupings of society to solve problems, control crime, and foster a sense of community.

Social Capital and Communities

In *Bowling Alone*, Putnam devised a scale for assessing the condition of organizational life in different American states. He looked to such measures as the density of civic groups, the frequency with which people participate in them, and the degree to which (according to opinion surveys) people trust one another. Controlling for race, income, education, and the like, he demonstrated that the higher a state's level of social capital, the more educated and affluent are its children, the lower the murder rate, the greater the degree of public health, and the smaller the likelihood of tax evasion. Nor is that all. High levels of social capital, Putnam showed, are associated with such civic virtues as greater tolerance toward women and minorities and stronger support for civil liberties. But all of these good things have been seriously jeopardized by the phenomenon he identified as "bowling alone."

After finishing his book, Putnam was approached by various community foundations to measure the levels of social capital within their own cities. To that end he conducted a very large survey: roughly 30,000 Americans, living in 41 different communities ranging downward in size from Los Angeles to Yakima, Washington, and even including rural areas of South Dakota. He published the results this year (2007) in a long essay in the academic journal *Scandinavian Political Studies* on the occasion of his having won Sweden's prestigious Johan Skytte prize.

Putnam's new essay takes an in-depth look not at social capital per se but at how "diversity"—meaning, for this purpose, racial and ethnic differences—affects our lives in society. Such diversity is increasing in this country and many others, if for no other reason than immigration, and so Putnam has tried to find out how it changes the way people feel about their neighbors, the degree of their confidence in local government, their willingness to become engaged in community-wide projects, and their general happiness.

When ethnic groups are mixed there is weaker social trust, less car pooling, and less group cohesion.

The ethnic and racial diversity that Putnam examines is widely assumed to be very good for us. The more time we spend with people different from us, it is said, the more we will like and trust them. Indeed, diversity is supposed to be so good for us that it has become akin to a national mandate in employment and, especially, in admissions to colleges and universities. When the Supreme Court decided the (*University of California v. Bakke*) case in 1978, the leading opinion, signed by Justice Lewis Powell, held that although a university was not allowed to use a strict numerical standard to guarantee the admission of a fixed number of minority students, it could certainly "take race into account," on the theory that a racially diverse student body was desirable both for the school and for society at large.

As a result of this and similar court rulings, not only colleges but many other institutions began invoking the term "diversity" as a justification for programs that gave preferences to certain favored minorities (especially blacks and Hispanics). Opponents of these programs on constitutional and civil-liberties grounds were put in the difficult position of appearing to oppose a demonstrated social good. Did not everyone know that our differences make us stronger?

But do they? That is where Putnam's new essay comes in. In the long run, Putnam argues, ethnic and racial diversity in neighborhoods is indeed "an important social asset," because it encourages people to form connections that can reduce unproductive forms of ethnocentrism and increase economic growth. In his words, "successful immigrant societies create new forms of social solidarity and dampen the negative effects of diversity by constructing new, more encompassing identities."

Whatever his beliefs about the positive effects of diversity in the long run, however—not only does he consider it a potentially "important social asset," but he has written that it also confers "many advantages that have little or nothing to do with social capital"—Putnam is a scrupulous and serious scholar (as well as a friend and former colleague at Harvard [University]). In the *short* run, he is frank to acknowledge, his data show not positive effects but rather the opposite. "The more ethnically diverse the people we live around," he writes, "the less we trust them."

Diversity, Putnam concludes on the basis of his findings, makes us "hunker down." Not only do we trust our neighbors less, we have less confidence in local government, a lowered sense of our own political efficacy, fewer close friends, and a smaller likelihood of contributing to charities, cooperating with others, working on a community project, registering to vote—or being happy.

Diversity and improved solidarity have gone hand in hand only in those institutions characterized by enforced authority and discipline.

Of course many of these traits can reflect just the characteristics of the people Putnam happened to interview, rather than some underlying condition. Aware of the possibility, Putnam spent a great deal of time "kicking the tires" of his study by controlling statistically for age, ethnicity, education, income or lack of same, poverty, homeownership, citizenship, and many other possible influences. But the results did not change. No matter how many individual factors were analyzed, every measure of social well-being suffered in ethnically diverse neighborhoods—and improved in ethnically homogeneous ones.

Diversity and Neighborhoods

"Shocking" is the word that one political scientist, Scott Page of the University of Michigan, invoked to describe the extent of the negative social effects revealed by Putnam's data. Whether Putnam was shocked by the results I cannot say. But they should not have been surprising; others have reported the same thing. The scholars Anil Rupasingha, Stephan J. Goetz, and David Frewater, for example, found that social capital across American counties, as measured by the number of voluntary associations for every 10,000 people, goes up with the degree of ethnic homogeneity. Conversely, as others have discovered, when ethnic groups are mixed there is weaker social trust, less car pooling, and less group cohesion. And this has held true for some time: people in Putnam's survey who were born in the 1920s display the same attitudes as those born in the 1970s.

Still, Putnam believes that in the long run ethnic heterogeneity will indeed "create new forms of social solidarity." He offers three reasons. First, the American military, once highly segregated, is today anything but that—and yet, in the Army and the Marines, social solidarity has increased right alongside greater ethnic diversity. Second, churches that were once highly segregated, especially large evangelical ones, have likewise become entirely and peaceably integrated. Third, people who once married only their ethnic kin today marry across ethnic and religious (and, to a lesser degree, racial) lines.

I can offer a fourth example: organized sports. Once, baseball and football teams were made up of only white or only black players; today they, too, are fully integrated. When Jackie Robinson joined the Brooklyn Dodgers in 1947, several teammates objected to playing with him, and many fans heckled him whenever he took the field. Within a few years, however, he and the Dodgers had won a raft of baseball titles, and he was one of the most popular figures in the country. Today such racial and ethnic heckling has virtually disappeared.

Unfortunately, however, the pertinence of the military, religious, or athletic model to life in neighborhoods is very slight. In those three institutions, authority and discipline can break down native hostilities or force them underground. Military leaders proclaim that bigotry will not be tolerated, and they mean it; preachers invoke the word of God to drive home the lesson that prejudice is a sin; sports teams (as with the old Brooklyn Dodgers) point out that anyone who does not want to play with a black or a Jew is free to seek employment elsewhere.

But what authority or discipline can anyone bring to neighborhoods? They are places where people choose to live, out of either opportunity or necessity. Walk the heterogeneous streets of Chicago or Los Angeles and you will learn about organized gangs and other social risks. Nor are these confined to poor areas: Venice, a small neighborhood in Los Angeles where several movie stars live and many homes sell for well over $1 million, is also a place where, in the Oakwood area, the Shoreline Crips and the V-13 gangs operate.

In many a neighborhood, ethnic differences are often seen as threats. If blacks or Hispanics, for whatever reason, are more likely to join gangs or commit crimes, then whites living in a neighborhood with many blacks or Hispanics will tend to feel uneasy. (There are, of course, exceptions: some, especially among the well-educated, prefer diversity even with all its risks.) Even where everyone is equally poor or equally threatened by crime, people exhibit less trust if their neighborhood is ethnically diverse than if it is homogeneous.

Of Putnam's three or four reasons for thinking that ethnic heterogeneity will contribute to social capital in the long run, only one is compelling: people are indeed voluntarily marrying across ethnic lines. But the paradoxical effect of this trend is not to preserve but to blunt ethnic identity, to the point where it may well reduce the perception of how diverse a neighborhood actually is. In any case, the fact remains that diversity and improved solidarity have gone hand in hand only in those institutions characterized by enforced authority and discipline.

Strong families living in neighborhoods made up of families with shared characteristics seem much more likely to bring their members into . . . associational life.

The legal scholar Peter H. Schuck has written an important book on this issue. In *Diversity in America*, he examines three major efforts by judges and government officials to require racial and income diversity in neighborhoods. One of them banned income-discrimination in the sale and rental of housing in New Jersey towns. Another enabled blacks who were eligible for public housing to move into private rental units in the Chicago suburbs. In the third, a federal judge attempted to diversify residential patterns in the city of Yonkers, New York, by ordering the construction of public housing in middle-class neighborhoods selected by him.

Although the Chicago project may have helped minorities to enter communities where they had never lived, the New Jersey and Yonkers initiatives had little effect. As Schuck writes, "Neighborhoods are complex, fragile, organic societies whose dynamics outsiders cannot readily understand, much less control." A court can and should strike down racist public policies, but when it goes beyond this and tries to mandate "diversity," it will sooner or later discover that it "cannot conscript the housing market to do its bidding."

Reducing Segregation

Taking a different approach, Thomas Schelling, a Nobel laureate in economics, has shown in a stimulating essay that neighborhood homogeneity and even segregation may result from small, defensible human choices that

cannot themselves be called racist. In fact, such choices can lead to segregation even when the people making them expressly intend the opposite. Suppose, Schelling writes, that blacks and whites alike wish to live in a neighborhood that is (for example) half-white and half-black. If one white family should come to think that other white families prefer a community that is three-fourths white, and may move out for that reason, the first white family is itself likely to move out in search of its own half-white, half-black preference. There is no way to prevent this.

People who celebrate diversity . . . are endorsing only one part of what it means to be a complete human being, neglecting morality.

Schelling's analysis casts a shadow of doubt on Putnam's own policy suggestions for reducing the disadvantages and stimulating the benefits of ethnic heterogeneity. Those suggestions are: investing more heavily in playgrounds, schools, and athletic fields that different groups can enjoy together; extending national aid to local communities; encouraging churches to reach out to new immigrants; and expanding public support for the teaching of English.

The first recommendation is based on the implicit assumption that Schelling is wrong and on the even more dubious assumption that playgrounds, schools, and athletic fields—things Putnam did not measure in his survey— will increase the benefits of diversity even when age, income, and education do not. The second is empty: Putnam does not say what kind of aid will produce the desired effects. If he is thinking of more housing, Schuck has already shown that providing this usually does not increase diversity. If he is thinking of education, in the 1970s federal judges imposed forced busing in an effort to integrate schools; it was an intensely unpopular strategy, both among those whose children were being bused and among those whose neighborhoods were being bused into.

The third proposal, encouraging outreach by churches, might well make a difference, but how do we go about it? Require people to attend an evangelical church? Would Robert Putnam attend? I suspect not. And as for the final recommendation, teaching English at public expense to everyone, it is a very good idea—provided one could break the longstanding attachment of the education establishment to bilingual instruction.

Shared Values Increase Unity

Whether we should actually seek to transform the situation described by Putnam's data is another question. I do not doubt that both diversity and social capital are important, or that many aspects of the latter have declined, though perhaps not so much as Putnam suspects. But as his findings indicate, there is no reason to suppose that the route to the latter runs through the former. In fact, strong families living in neighborhoods made up of families with shared characteristics seem much more likely to bring their members into the associational life Putnam favors. Much as we might value both heterogeneity and social capital, assuming that the one will or should encourage the other may be a form of wishful thinking.

That is because morality and rights arise from different sources. As I tried to show in *The Moral Sense*, morality arises from sympathy among like-minded persons: first the family, then friends and colleagues. Rights, on the other hand, grow from convictions about how we ought to manage relations with people not like us, convictions that are nourished by education, religion, and experience.

People who celebrate diversity (and its parallel, multiculturalism) are endorsing only one part of what it means to be a complete human being, neglecting morality (and its parallel, group and national pride). Just as we cannot be whole persons if we deny the fundamental rights of others, so we cannot be whole persons if we live in ways that discourage decency, cooperation, and charity.

In every society, people must arrange for trade-offs between desirable but mutually inconsistent goals. James Madison [fourth president of the United States], in his famous *Federalist* Number Ten, pointed to just this sort of trade-off when he made the case for a large national government that would ensure the preservation of those individual rights and liberties that are at risk in small communities. When it comes to the competing values of diversity and the formation of social capital, as when it comes to other arrangements in a democracy, balance is all.

Analyze this Reading

1. What is the writer's view of Robert D. Putnam's position on ethnically integrated neighborhoods? What does the writer claim in response to Putnam's position?
2. What is "social capital"? How does it differ from "physical capital" and "human capital"? In what academic discipline do these terms originate?
3. How does the writer view military, religious, and athletic models of integration next to the neighborhood model proposed by Putnam? What separates the first three models from the neighborhood model?
4. How does the writer use the work of Schuck and Shelling to support his claim?

Respond to this Reading

1. In your view, is the writer fair and open-minded in his many references to Putnam? In your answer, explain how the writer's treatment of Putnam strengthens or weakens the argument.
2. The writer concludes his argument with an idea about shared values and unity. Do you agree with the writer's idea? Explain.
3. "Diversity" is a term regularly used in discussions about many institutions in American life—our schools, workplaces, neighborhoods, and places of worship, among others. From your understanding, why is diversity desirable in our institutions, and from what conditions does this desire originate?
4. Describe your own neighborhood in terms of its diversity—ethnic, racial, and economic—and identify issues that connect to your neighborhood's heterogeneity or homogeneity. What would you argue in response to one of these issues?

ABOUT THIS READING

Writer Noah Smith formerly taught Finance at Stony Brook University and now writes a column for the *Bloomberg Opinion* division of *Bloomberg News*. *Noahpinion* is his blog. *Bloomberg News* covers current financial and business news.

The Poor Don't Deserve Toxic-Waste Dumps in Their Backyards

They're much more likely than other Americans to be exposed to hazardous materials.

By Noah Smith

The American left has a lot on its plate—universal health care, climate change, stagnant wages, wealth inequality and more. But there's one more issue that needs to be added to the list: environmental justice. Poor Americans, especially minorities, are exposed to too many toxins and environmental hazards, destroying their health and harming their opportunities for advancement.

One of the worst hazards is lead. There is now good evidence that banning unleaded gasoline contributed to significant drops in crime and improvement in cognitive performance. But lead pipes and paint still are prevalent in aging urban housing, posing a serious threat to kids—who happen to be particularly vulnerable to its ill-effects. Even small amounts of lead can impair mental performance, and cause other health problems.

But there are plenty of other toxins afflicting Americans' health. Pesticides from agriculture afflict rural communities. Cancer-causing industrial chemicals leak into waterways. Coal mine waste contains mercury, another toxic heavy metal. Gases released by hydraulic fracturing can cause all sorts of health problems. Nuclear waste can leak, causing cancer, brain and lung damage. Arsenic can contaminate groundwater. Landfills hold a huge variety of toxic chemicals. Mining, septic systems, industrial plants, chemical storage, irrigation systems and many other features of an advanced industrial economy all pose toxic risks for people who live nearby.

There's little doubt these toxins drive up the country's health-care bills. But the true cost may go far beyond the health issues. Many of these toxins, especially heavy metals and pesticides, have significant effects on brain development. They are associated with known problems like attention deficit disorder. But they have also been shown to hurt mental functioning in ways not classified as official disorders—reducing learning ability, self-control, emotional well-being and other crucial mental functions. Neurologist David Bellinger estimated in 2012 that heavy metals and pesticides have robbed Americans of a staggering total of 41 million IQ points.

Everyone in America is exposed to these toxins, but some are at much more risk than others. There is a voluminous academic literature across several disciplines, including economics, showing that disadvantaged minorities—in particular, black Americans—are more likely than others to come into close contact with toxic chemicals. The iconic images of

brown lead-filled water gushing from the water pipes in majority-black Flint, Michigan, are an extreme example, but they are emblematic of the environmental hazards faced by similar communities across the country.

This environmental injustice is due to several factors. Black and Hispanic Americans tend to be poorer than other groups, and thus have to rent or buy homes where housing is cheaper—sometimes because of proximity to toxic waste. Poor and minority communities also probably have less political power, and so are less able to prevent toxic chemical plants, mines, landfills or other polluting facilities from locating near them. They're also have less power to compel government to spend money on cleaning up pollution in their neighborhoods.

And finally, some of the difference is due to plain old racial discrimination. A new paper by economists Peter Christensen and Christopher Timmins examined the results of audit studies, in which actors of different races pretend to be prospective house buyers. They found that all else equal, real estate agents systematically steer black buyers toward more polluted neighborhoods. Fair housing laws have been unable to prevent this pervasive form of housing discrimination, which may be covert or even subconscious. But the authors estimate that the difference is great enough to account for 100 percent of African-American mothers' greater likelihood of living near Superfund toxic waste sites.

This environmental injustice almost certainly contributes to many of the social problems that afflict minority communities, from higher crime rates to lower test scores. It also indirectly and directly affects the generally poorer health of black Americans, raising their medical bills and bankruptcy risk. And it reduces mobility for poor minorities, helping maintain the income and wealth gap over generations.

The threat that toxic waste poses to poor and minority Americans should be fought with a multipronged approach. A focused and well-funded national initiative to replace lead pipes and clean up lead paint should be the first order of business. More money for Superfund and other toxic-waste cleanup programs should be a priority, and environmental regulations covering factories, mines, landfills and other dangerous facilities should be enforced more strictly. Needless to say, the current administration is going in precisely the wrong direction on these issues, but environmental cleanup should be a top priority for the next one.

Discrimination also needs to be addressed. The government should crack down on steering of poor minorities toward polluted neighborhoods. And it should more protect poor minority communities from companies and municipal authorities that seek to place toxic facilities in their midst.

Environmental justice might not sound as bold or transformative as universal health care or other big programs now being proposed by the left. But its impact could be no less important for the quality of life enjoyed by disadvantaged minorities and the poor.

Analyze this Reading

1. What does the writer claim in this argument?
2. While logical, ethical, and emotional kinds of support are present, what kind of support dominates? Cite a few examples.

3. What dangers are associated with toxic-waste dumps?
4. According to the writer, what contributes to the presence of toxic-waste dumps in poor and minority communities?

Respond to this Reading

1. Looking at your own community, where are toxic waste sites located?
2. While the writer stops short of accusing large corporations and utilities that produce toxic waste of deliberately locating their operations in poor and minority communities, would you endorse such an accusation if it were applied to your community? How would you research this question?
3. The writer contends that "the current (Trump) administration is going precisely in the wrong direction" in terms of addressing toxic-waste sites in poor communities. If this is the case, what can concerned citizens do to reshape current policy?

Anthology 5
Social/Cultural Community

ABOUT THIS READING

Daniel J. Solove is an expert in privacy law. He is regularly cited in scholarly journals and frequently interviewed by the mainstream media. His 2007 book, *The Future of Reputation: Gossip, Rumor, and Privacy on the Internet*, won the McGannon Award, an honor given to the "most notable book addressing issues of communication policy published during the previous year." This article appeared in *Salon*, a website covering political news and entertainment.

Why "Security" Keeps Winning Out Over Privacy

By Daniel J. Solove

Far too often, debates about privacy and security begin with privacy proponents pointing to invasive government surveillance, such as GPS tracking, the National Security Agency surveillance program, data mining, and public video camera systems. Security proponents then chime in with a cadre of arguments about how these security measures are essential to law enforcement and national security. When the balancing is done, the security side often wins, and security measures go forward with little to no privacy protections.

But the victory for security is one often achieved unfairly. The debate is being skewed by several flawed pro-security arguments. These arguments improperly tip the scales to the security side of the balance. Let's analyze some of these arguments, the reasons they are flawed, and the pernicious effects they have.

The All-or-Nothing Fallacy

Many people contend that "we must give up some of our privacy in order to be more secure." In polls, people are asked whether the government should conduct surveillance if it will help in catching terrorists. Many people readily say yes.

But this is the wrong question and the wrong way to balance privacy against security. Rarely does protecting privacy involve totally banning a security measure. It's not all or nothing. Instead, protecting privacy typically means that government surveillance must be subjected to judicial oversight and that the government must justify the need to engage in surveillance. Even a search of our homes is permitted if law enforcement officials obtain a warrant and probable cause. We shouldn't ask: "Do you want the government to engage in surveillance?" Instead, we should ask: "Do you want the government to engage in surveillance without a warrant or probable cause?"

We shouldn't be balancing the costs of completely forgoing surveillance against privacy. Instead, the security interest should only be the extent to which oversight and justification will make surveillance less effective. In

many cases, privacy protection will not diminish the effectiveness of government security measures all that much. Privacy is losing out in the balance because it is being weighed against completely banning a security measure rather than being balanced against merely making it a little less convenient for the government.

The Deference Argument

Many security proponents argue that courts should defer to the executive branch when it comes to evaluating security measures. In cases where Fourth Amendment rights are pitted against government searches and surveillance, courts often refuse to second-guess the judgment of the government officials. The problem with doing this is that, unless the effectiveness of the security measures is explored, they will win out every time. All the government has to do is mention "terrorism," and whatever it proposes to do in response—whether wise or not—remains unquestioned.

But it is the job of the courts to balance privacy against security, and they can't do this job if they refuse to evaluate whether the security measure is really worth the tradeoff. Deference is an abdication of the court's role in ensuring that the government respects constitutional rights. The deference argument is one that impedes any effective balancing of interests.

The Pendulum Argument

In times of crisis, many security proponents claim that we must swing the pendulum toward greater security. "Don't be alarmed," they say. "In peacetime, the pendulum will swing back to privacy and liberty."

The problem with this argument is that it has things exactly backward. During times of crisis, the temptation to make unnecessary sacrifices of privacy and liberty in the name of security is exceedingly high. History has shown that many curtailments of rights were in vain, such as the Japanese-American internment during World War II and the McCarthy-era hysteria about communists. During times of peace, the need to protect privacy is not as strong because we're less likely to make such needless sacrifices. The greatest need for safeguarding liberty comes during times when we are least inclined to protect it.

The War-Powers Argument

After September 11, the Bush administration authorized the National Security Agency to engage in warrantless wiretapping of the phone calls of Americans. Headquartered in Maryland, the NSA is the world's largest top-secret spy organization. The NSA surveillance program violated the Foreign Intelligence Surveillance Act (FISA), a federal law that required courts to authorize the kind of wiretapping the NSA engaged in. The Bush administration didn't justify its actions on an argument that it was acting legally under FISA. Instead, it argued that the president had the right to break the law because of the "inherent constitutional authority" of the president to wage war.

The war-powers argument is so broad that it fails of its own weight. If the president's power to wage war encompasses breaking any law that stands in the way, then the president has virtually unlimited power. A hallmark feature of our legal system is the rule of law. We repudiated a monarchy in the American Revolution, and we established a nation where laws would rule, not a lone dictator. The problem with the war-powers argument is that it eviscerates the rule of law. The most unfortunate thing is that Congress responded with a mere grumble, nothing with teeth—and not even teeth were bared. The message is now clear—in times of crisis, the rule of law can be ignored with impunity. That's a terrifying precedent.

The Luddite Argument

Government officials love new technology, especially new security technologies like biometric identification and the "naked scanners" at the airport. The security industry lobbies nervous government officials by showing them a dazzling new technology and gets them to buy it. Often, these technologies are not fully mature. Security proponents defend the use of these technologies by arguing that privacy proponents are Luddites who are afraid of new technology. But this argument is grossly unfair.

To see the problems with the Luddite argument, let's look at biometrics. Biometric identification allows people to be identified by their physical characteristics—fingerprint, eye pattern, voice and so on. The technology has a lot of promise, but there is a problem, one I call the "Titanic phenomenon." The Titanic was thought to be unsinkable, so it lacked adequate lifeboats. If biometric data ever got lost, we could be in a Titanic-like situation—people's permanent physical characteristics could be in the hands of criminals, and people could never reclaim their identities. Biometric identification depends on information about people's characteristics being stored in a database. And we hear case after case of businesses and government agencies that suffer data security breaches.

One virtue of our current clunky system of identification is that if data gets leaked, a person can clean up the mess. If your Social Security number is seized by an identity thief, you can get a new one. For sure, it's a hassle, but you can restore your identity. But what happens if your eye pattern gets into the hands of an identity thief? You can't get new eyes. Given the government's existing track record for data security, I'm not sure I'm ready to risk the government having such critical information about me that could cause such lasting and unfixable harm if lost. This isn't Luddism—it's caution. It is heeding the lessons of *The Titanic*. Security proponents just focus on the benefits of these technologies, but we also must think about what happens if they fail. This doesn't mean not adopting the technologies, but it means we should be cautious.

These are just a few of the flawed arguments that have shaped the privacy/security debate. There are many others, such as the argument made by people who say they have "nothing to hide." We can't have a meaningful balance between privacy and security unless we improve the way we debate the issue. We must confront and weed out the flawed arguments that have been improperly skewing the conversation.

Analyze this Reading

1. Which side of the security vs. privacy issue does the writer favor? Refer to two of the arguments the writer analyzes to support your answer.

2. What examples does the writer pull from our history to debunk the "Pendulum Argument?"

3. Describe the "Titanic phenomenon" and how the writer applies it to his position.

Respond to this Reading

1. The security vs. privacy issue in American life has been debated for centuries. For example, American icon Ben Franklin wrote in 1775 that, "They that can give up essential liberty to obtain a little temporary safety, deserve neither liberty not safety." Where do you stand on this issue? With reference to the five arguments the writer condemns, which arguments do you condone? Which do you reject?

2. In 2011 President Obama signed the *PATRIOT Sunsets Extension Act of 2011,* an act that allows for roving wiretaps, investigating a company's business records, and surveillance of individuals, often referred to as "lone wolves," suspected of terrorist activity not connected to terrorist groups. Do you favor this extension act? Explain.

3. In your view, what is the reasonable balance between privacy and security today?

ABOUT THIS READING

Vince Dixon is Data Visualization Reporter for *Eater*, a restaurant guide for numerous major American cities, Montreal, and London. The site also features news and commentary on issues related to the restaurant industry.

The Case Against Tipping in America

The data is overwhelming: Tipping encourages racism, sexism, harassment, and exploitation

By Vince Dixon

When a night at a restaurant or bar finally comes to a close, most Americans engage in an instinctive ritual. They dig into their wallets, fiddle with their smartphone calculators, and then decide how much money to give their server or bartender for a job well done.

Tipping, while practiced around the world, assumes a unique role in America, one to which most diners are obliged, because the United States is one of the only countries that allows businesses to offload the burden of paying workers a fair wage to their customers. And though construed as a fair way to encourage hospitality and reward good service, tipping's roots are in racialized exploitation, while recent data shows that it continues to be, at its core, racist, sexist, and degrading.

For many, it's time for tipping—or at least the wage laws that allow it to penalize servers and diners—to end. Academics and advocacy groups are starting to push to pay servers the same minimum wage as in other fields, rather than having servers rely on the so-called tipped minimum—the low hourly rates (currently set at $2.13, federally) that servers are paid by restaurants in some 43 states—which forces them to rely on tips for a majority of their income.

Until that day, tipping continues to be the source of a power play between workers, employers, and diners. In 2015, Union Square Hospitality Group's Danny Meyer began eliminating tipping at more than a dozen of his restaurants in favor of generally fixed hourly wages, paving the way for other restaurateurs to implement gratuity-free service, with varying degrees of success. (As some have noted, Meyer was not the first restaurateur to do away with tipping, but the shift at USHG is arguably the catalyst for much of the current conversation around going gratuity-free.) Most recently, the Trump administration proposed legalizing tip pools again, which would effectively transfer the ownership of tips from servers to employers, who could then distribute the money as they see fit—opening the door to pocketing tips entirely, as well as other, more subtle forms of wage theft—prompting an outcry in the industry and beyond.

Against this backdrop, Eater analyzed recent data from the U.S. Census and Bureau of Labor Statistics, the Equal Employment Opportunity Commission, the Department of Labor, and academic research and advocacy groups like Restaurant Opportunities Centers United in order to understand the unique impact tipping has on the American dining community. The results are clear: The case against the current tipping system in America is stronger than ever.

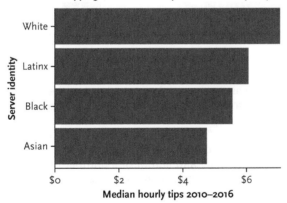

Tipping Reflects and Amplifies Racial Inequality

Server identity (y-axis): White, Latinx, Black, Asian
Median hourly tips 2010–2016 (x-axis): $0, $2, $4, $6

Source: Eater analysis of Current Population Survey data, courtesy of the Integrated Public Use Microdata Series

American travelers brought tipping to the United States from Europe shortly after the Civil War. Once home, they flaunted their newfound European etiquette by offering gratuity to unskilled laborers, many of whom were former slaves and immigrants. The practice spread, and by the early 1900s, some employers saw it as an opportunity to avoid paying wages by encouraging customers to tip workers instead. The Pullman Company, a train service that primarily employed African-American porters in the late 1800s and early 1900s, was notorious for openly underpaying its workers, forcing them to rely on tips.

Despite civil rights battles and a brief ban on tips in some parts of the country, tipping became normalized in America. Many tipped workers,

including restaurant workers, were even excluded from the country's first national minimum wage laws until the mid-1960s, when the first "subminimum" wage—a wage for tipped employees set below the standard minimum wage, now referred to as the "tipped minimum"— was established.

While the unskilled labor force has since diversified, employers of tipped workers can still avoid directly paying them a living wage, and tipped workers of color still suffer disproportionately under the current system. As studies, like one Cornell University report, have shown, some diners let race, gender, and attractiveness impact how much they pay servers: Most dramatically, diners of all races tend to give higher tips to white servers and lower tips to black servers. An Eater analysis of U.S. Census and Bureau of Labor Statistics data (see methodology below) showed that white servers and bartenders across all restaurant types make more in tips than most other racial groups: Between 2010 and 2016, the median estimated hourly tip for white servers and bartenders was $7.06; Latinx (who include people who identify as either black, white, Asian, or multiracial), earned $6.08 an hour in tips; black front-of-house workers made a median hourly tip of $5.57; and Asians earned a median hourly tip of $4.77.

Tipping Encourages Racial Profiling

Servers who admitted acting on racial bias against patrons of color

39%

Servers who witnessed co-worker bias against patrons of color

66%

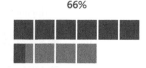

Source: "Quantitative Evidence of the Continuing Significance of Race: Tableside Racism in Full-Service Restaurants," Zachary W. Brewster and Sarah Nell Rusche

Servers have biases too, and tipping unleashes them. A growing body of research shows that racial profiling over expected tips—or a lack thereof— can encourage hostility and flat-out discrimination toward diners of color, especially black diners. "There is a good amount of evidence that indicates that some servers do stereotype," Zachary Brewster, a sociology professor at Wayne State University and author of a number of studies on racial profiling in restaurants, told Eater. "In most cases the form of discrimination is quite subtle."

For instance, servers may provide slower service to black diners—or try to turn the table over more quickly. Brewster's body of research, which includes surveys and interviews with servers, found that in some restaurants, servers actively avoid waiting on black customers because they believe that they would lose out on tips. In some instances, restaurant staff played "games" in which servers tried to stick one another with black tables, or developed code words to warn each other when a black table is seated. This behavior was sometimes allowed by management, Brewster found.

In one 2012 study, Brewster surveyed 200 servers from "bar and grill-" style restaurants. He asked the servers about their perceptions of black diners, and whether they'd seen discriminatory behavior by other employees. Most respondents admitted to providing different levels of service based a

diner's race, or witnessing another server do so, at least "sometimes." In similar studies published by Brewsterand colleagues, servers who admitted to profiling black customers justified their actions by claiming that black patrons demanded more and tipped less. Another study found such sentiments published on online message boards for waiters. (Earlier this month, Applebee's fired employees at a location in Missouri for racial profiling.)

"If I get a good tip from a black person, I'm surprised, or even a decent tip, I'm surprised generally."

Source: "Racially Discriminatory Service in Full-Service Restaurants: The Problem, Cause, and Potential Solutions," by Zachary W. Brewster

Research does show that black diners appear to tip less than white diners—by roughly 3 percentage points—but the reasons are nuanced, Brewster said. One explanation is that African-Americans are generally less familiar with the unwritten rule that a 15 percent tipis the minimum. Other researchers speculate that black diners may have less exposure to dining out growing up—according to the Bureau of Labor Statistics expenditure data, black households spent an average of $2,228 on food away from home in 2016 compared to $3,243 from white households—and thus may be less acquainted with sit-down restaurant norms, he added. Black servers are also underrepresented in front-of-house positions, leading to less familiarity with the direct role that tips play in a server's income. "So they are less likely to learn this tipping norm," Brewster said.

Still, Brewster added, servers often exaggerate the tipping differences between black and white diners in order to justify discrimination. "This exaggeration is a function of racial prejudice and working in a racialized workplace," he said. Prejudice over tipping can also become a cycle that perpetuates itself, as law professor Lu-in Wang described in one report, published in the *Virginia Journal of Social Policy and the Law.* "Some restaurant servers recognize that stereotypes regarding customers' tipping habits can set in motion a self-fulfilling cycle by affecting the service they provide, and in turn, the tips they receive from those customers."

Tipping Widens Opportunity Gaps Between White Servers and Non-White Servers

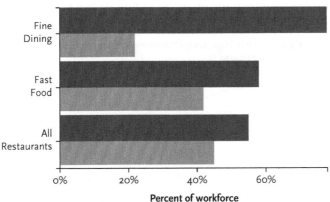

Source: "Racial and Gender Occupational Segregation in the Restaurant Industry," ROC United

One straightforward explanation for why white servers earn higher tips than servers of color is that they are disproportionately employed at fine-dining restaurants—defined by the restaurant worker advocacy group Restaurant Opportunities Centers United as "full-service restaurants with a price point per guest of $40 or more including beverages but excluding gratuity." According to a 2015 study by ROC United, which analyzed U.S. Census Current Population Surveys and surveyed 133 fine-dining restaurants, white people make up 55 percent of all restaurant servers, but comprise 78 percent of the total number of servers in fine-dining restaurants. Additionally, fine-dining servers are more likely to be men: While women make up 52 percent of restaurant workers, they represent only 43 percent of fine-dining front-of-house workers.

People of color are more likely to be employed in "back-of-house" or non-tipped jobs—like dishwashers and line cooks—where they often find it difficult to rise up in the ranks to better-paid tipped positions in the "front of the house," in part because of implicit biases, according to Teófilo Reyes, research director with ROC United. Here's how one restaurant owner described so-called successful employees in ROC United's 2015 report on race and gender in restaurant workplaces:

People who have had really good parenting, where there's been boundaries, and encouragement, and positive feedback, do the best. And people who come from broken homes, and don't understand boundaries, who don't understand punctuality, or make bad choices, or have never really faced consequences for their choices do the worst ... this is very much a performance-based environment.

The report argues that such sweeping generalizations are welcome mats for bias, having an impact on who managers see as being fit for higher-paid jobs, disadvantaging people of color. The resulting lack of representation in tipped and higher-paid restaurant positions inherently discourages people of color from applying for them, according to Reyes. "There's a type of self-selection that occurs if people think they're going to be rejected," he said.

The fine-dining opportunity gap between white men and everyone else has far-reaching consequences: As data from FiveThirtyEight showed last year, on average, workers in casual dining restaurants have to work nine times harder than their counterparts in fine dining to reach the standard minimum wage (turning four tables an hour, versus 0.2 tables).

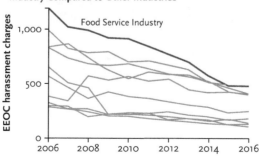

Tipping Fosters High Sexual Harassment Rates in the Restaurant Industry Compared to Other Industries

Food Service Industry

EEOC harassment charges

1,000

500

0

2006   2008   2010   2012   2014   2016

Source: U.S. Equal Employment Opportunity Commission

Sexual harassment in the food industry is pervasive, and tipping plays a role in perpetuating it. A 2014 ROC United study showed that nearly 80 percent of female restaurant workers reported experiencing some sort of sexual harassment from customers at work. The food service industry accounts for more sexual harassment filings (referred to as "charges") with the Equal Employment Opportunity Commission than any other industry, according to EEOC data (many filings are also unassigned to any particular industry, while sexual harassment may be underreported in others).

According to Reyes, one reason is that tipping creates a power dynamic in which servers adopt a mentality that "the customer is always right." In a situation in which servers are actually working for diners and their tips, rather than for their employers' wages, they may be more vulnerable to abuse. That notion is borne out in data showing that women working in restaurants in states with lower minimum wages for tipped employees are twice as likely to report experiencing sexual harassment than those who work in states that have one minimum wage for all workers. Both male and female servers working in tipped minimum wage states report higher rates of sexual harassment—women, for instance, were three times more likely to report being told by management to dress "sexier" or to alter their appearance. As the country moves forward in its discussion about sexual harassment in light of the #MeToo movement, tipping customs expose the industry as one of the most affected industries outside of Hollywood.

Tipping Encourages Worker Exploitation

$39,800,000

**amount of back wages owed to food service workers
(Department of Labor wage data)**

The restaurant industry suffers from an endemic wage theft problem. According to the Department of Labor, the food services industry is one of the biggest violators of wage and labor laws; in 2016, the department found that the industry owed $39 million in back wages.

Wage theft takes many forms: not paying for overtime work, failing to properly distribute tips, and withholding paychecks, among others. Tip-pooling, the practice of collecting and re-distributing tip revenues among the entire staff, has long been contentious, with the debate leading to a ban by the Department of Labor under the Obama administration in 2011. A new tip-pooling proposal under Trump's labor department takes the opposite stance, arguing that employers should be able to collect worker tips and redistribute them as they see fit—to back-of-house workers, for instance. Critics say that the bill, as proposed, will give restaurant owners a legal opportunity to keep tip revenue, rather than actually redistributing it back to workers.

The best way to fix the broken institution of American tipping, Reyes argues, is to pay restaurant servers like any other non-tipped professional. "There are certainly plenty of countries around the world where they look at restaurant workers as professionals, they treat them like professionals, and they pay them a professional wage," Reyes said. "I think we can move to a more professional system."

Some restaurants have already attempted an entirely tip-free system, and the results have been mixed. After Danny Meyer fully eliminated gratuity from his restaurants—a move he called a win for back-of-house staff and diners—40 percent of his longtime front-of-house staff quit. Menu prices were raised, with the additional revenue redistributed in the form of higher base wages for all employees; a lawsuit against Meyer and other restaurateurs alleges that after the switch to a gratuity-free model, money was not fairly distributed between the restaurants and front-of-house staff.

Ultimately, an equitable tipping system will require getting rid of the sub-minimum tipped wage and paying servers, bartenders, and other service employees the standard minimum wage, while allowing them to receive bonuses for exceptional service. However that happens, everyone involved in America's restaurant culture—owners, servers, and diners—will have to play a part.

Methodology

To determine the median hourly tip rate for American servers and waiters by race from 2010 to 2016, Eater looked at Current Population Surveys released by the Bureau of Labor Statistics and the U.S. Census. The surveys are conducted monthly, with 50,000 to 60,000 households queried per month. Eater used data from 2010 to 2016 surveys, filtering responses from servers and bartenders (occupation codes 4040 and 4110), then filtered the results further to show only workers who made an hourly wage and "usually receive overtime, tips, or commissions"—three additional forms of income that the CPS survey refers to as one group. (Also filtered from the results were people who worked more than 40 hours a week, didn't make an hourly wage, and or who provided "non-universe" responses, which indicate that for one reason or another the question did not apply to the respondent.) These filters left a dataset of servers and bartenders receiving hourly pay and some form of additional commission, overtime, or tips, which were assumed to be tips.

The data included the year of the survey, weekly earnings, number of hours worked per week, hourly wage, gender, race, and weights for earnings and wage values. Eater converted the overall weekly earnings and hourly wages to 2016 dollar values using the Consumer Price Index purchasing power formula, then multiplied the reported number of hours worked by the reported hourly wage to determine weekly hourly wages. Eater then subtracted the weekly wage value from the overall weekly earnings value to calculate tips each respondent received. That number was divided by the number of hours each respondent reported working to determine the amount in tips the respondents made per hours worked.

To find the median hourly tip for all respondents, Eater filtered any result that indicated no additional income or tips were made, then calculated the weighted median of the remaining hourly tips (the CPS provides weights for weekly earnings data, indicating the number of people a respondent actually represents, given his or her overrepresented or underrepresented demographic group).

Analyze this Reading

1. When does the practice of tipping begin in the United States? How do employers and wage laws take advantage of this practice?
2. How does tipping encourage racial profiling among some servers? Describe the kind of research the writer uses to support his position on racial profiling.
3. According to the writer, how are people of color disadvantaged in fine-dining restaurants?
4. How does tipping create conditions for sexual harassment in the restaurant industry?
5. Contrast attitudes toward tipping in the Obama and Trump administrations.

Respond to this Reading

1. Have you worked in the restaurant industry? If you have, what rings true about this argument? What points seem questionable?
2. What changes would you endorse with regard to the problem of wage theft in the restaurant industry?
3. As a diner and a consumer, what responsibility, if any, should you bear for the persistent injustices the writer identifies in restaurant culture?

ABOUT THIS READING

Ronald Davis is a retired police chief, was President Barack Obama's Executive Director of the Task Force on 21st Century Policing, and the former Director of the United States Department of Justice, Office of Community Oriented Policing Services (COPS). This opinion piece appears in *HuffPost*, a website devoted to news and opinion, with American and international editions.

My Truth About Being A Black Man And A Black Cop

By Ronald Davis

As more and more shootings of unarmed black men and women are brought to the public's attention, I understand the distrust that many—especially people of color—have against police. As a black man, I've been on the receiving end of profiling and discrimination. As a father to black children, I've had to have "the talk" with them about how to conduct themselves in encounters with law enforcement to make sure they leave with their lives. But I'm also a cop, and I know this job is dangerous and difficult and it comes with its share of fair and unfair scrutiny.

I've spent the last 30 years reconciling these unique and conflicting identities. This effort was not without its struggle. I've tried to change the perspectives of people and officers around me, I've denied that I had differing perspectives of my own, I've tried to balance each identity and fit them into a safe—often false—narrative. All of these efforts failed.

Through these experiences, and those of so many officers and people of color, I've come to realize that the only way to reconcile these perspectives is to accept each experience and the truth they represent, and to allow them to coexist. So, here are my truths.

Real reconciliation can only occur when it starts with the truth, no matter the level of discomfort it may cause. The truth may hurt, but selective ignorance is fatal.

I believe the vast majority of police officers do not engage in police brutality, but when tragedies such as the killing of unarmed black people occur, I question why so many of the victims are people who look like me. I've been racially profiled by the police. I've experienced discrimination in both my personal and professional life. I can't help but to wonder if these shootings, regardless of their legality, stem from implicit bias, our society's fear of black men, racism or a combination.

I see my children, especially my 20-year-old son, in the faces of the young men and women of color who have been killed by the police and who have been victims of police brutality. For black parents, teaching our children "what to do when stopped by the police" is a mandatory course for young people of color in this nation. I can't deny the reality that I have to protect my children from potentially deadly encounters with people whom I respect and who wear the same uniform that I wear.

And while it may be hard for everyday people to understand, I know firsthand the complex, challenging and dangerous nature of being a police officer. As a police chief, I've had to tell a wife that her husband, one of my fellow officers, was shot and killed in the line of duty. I've seen the emotional, physical and mental toll of the job weigh down my fellow officers. It has been an honor working side by side with so many selfless servants dedicated to helping others. I have no doubt that the overwhelming majority of police officers in this country are brave and honorable public servants. But despite this, racial disparities still exist and there's a growing divide between officers and civilians along racial lines.

Yes, we must accept that there are, in fact, some racist police officers. We must also acknowledge that the majority of cops are not racist and they honor the law enforcement profession.

In many ways the varying perspectives I face, and the conflicts they create, are not that different from the diversity of opinions we hear as a nation and the political discourse they have created around black lives and police brutality. In response to these differences, many choose to ignore, deny or try to change differing perspectives and the truths they represent rather than trying to understand varying viewpoints and reconcile our differences.

I tried to do this in my own life, and I've learned we cannot solve the problems we face concerning police and race if we continue to lie to ourselves about the nature of the problem. Real reconciliation can only occur when it starts with the truth, no matter how inconvenient it may be; no matter the level of discomfort it may cause. The truth may hurt, but selective ignorance is fatal.

We must learn the history of policing in this country and the role police have played in enforcing discriminatory laws. The truth is, significant racial

disparities still exist in our policing and criminal justice systems. Many of the systems and practices in policing that exist today were designed in the 1950s and '60s to enforce discriminatory laws and oppress black Americans who are still being and feeling oppressed at this very moment.

Despite the efforts of good officers, the continued use of these draconian operational systems and practices allow structural racism to remain and spread, and it allows racists officers to operate with impunity. And yes, we must accept that there are, in fact, some racist police officers. We must also acknowledge that the vast majority of cops are not racist and they honor the law enforcement profession.

It is a dangerous job and officers face many challenges. The truth is far too many of our communities are plagued by violence that create legitimate dangers for both the police and people we serve. However, it's important to remember that race is not the cause of this community violence. The true cause is institutional racism, societal inequities in education and housing as well as law and order policies that use incarceration as a strategy for keeping the peace.

The shooting of unarmed black men and women, police brutality and racial disparities in the criminal justice system represent a national crisis that requires a national response and presidential leadership.

Blaming the police alone for the inequities of the criminal justice system excuses prosecutors, judges, prison systems, health care disparities, lack of access to mental health services, poor education systems, etc. All of these systems contribute to the crime and violence in our neighborhoods and the over-reliance on police to solve problems that extend well beyond our capacity.

Once we accept even these basic truths, it will become easier to work together rather than remain bitterly divided; to demand accountability from the entire justice system rather than just blame the police; and to develop real solutions to our problems instead of superficial responses to the symptoms.

Both the police and community are accountable for public safety. The police must be held accountable by the community and the community must be willing to hold itself accountable as well.

Such an effort requires all of us to take responsibility for our past and our future. And it requires an all-of-government response. White House press secretary Sarah Huckabee Sanders recently stated these issues are "a local matter." Nothing can be further from the truth. The shooting of unarmed black men and women, police brutality and racial disparities in the criminal justice system represent a national crisis that requires a national response and presidential leadership.

I'm a black man, a black father and a black cop. My struggle has not been to balance these perspectives, but to allow them to coexist. The first step in reconciling these perspectives is to understand that each of these experiences, while different, are valid. Too often we try to either change, ignore or deny the truth. As Nelson Mandela said, "only the truth can put the past to rest." Once we understand, accept and acknowledge the reality each perspective represents, maybe we can move forward to create a new truth—one in which justice is truly blind and all are treated equal under the law.

Analyze this Reading

1. How does the writer establish his credibility? What are the "conflicting identities" he refers to?
2. The writer insists that we learn the history of American policing. Why, in his view, is this important? What examples of this history does he bring in?
3. In addition to policing, what systems should we focus on to fully understand inequities in the criminal justice system?
4. How does the writer respond to Sarah Huckabee Sanders's perspective on community safety?

Respond to this Reading

1. Do you agree that in your community there is a "growing divide between officers and civilians along racial lines?" Bring in local examples to explain your response.
2. The writer urges readers to move away from the notion that race alone causes much community violence. What are the "true causes" he mentions? Discuss this broader perspective in terms of your own community.

ABOUT THIS READING

Writer Jeff Yang's books include *I Am Jackie Chan: My Life in Action* (with Jackie Chan, 1998) and *Eastern Standard Time: A Guide to Asian Influence in American Culture, from Astro Boy to Zen Buddhism* (1997). With Parry Shen and Keith Chow, he edited *Secret Identities: The Asian American Superhero Anthology* (2009). This reading appeared on Salon.com, an online news magazine.

Killer Reflection

Cho and other Asian shooters were portrayed as "smart but quiet" and "fundamentally foreign." What do these stereotypes reveal, and what do they obscure?

By Jeff Yang

Like everyone else, I first reacted to the news of the April 16 shootings at Virginia Tech with shock—visceral and blinding. Sick with horror, but hungry for information, I went through what has become a ritual exercise whenever tragedy or catastrophe strikes—9/11, the tsunami, Katrina. I turned on the television, sorted through the cascade of conflicting details on competing news sites, and began exchanging rapid-fire e-mail and instant messages with friends of every background, from regions around the world. With each new revelation, we shared our common emotions: grief for the victims and their families; rage at the murderer; bitterness at the ready availability of weapons capable of exacting such a devastating toll.

Then came the word that the killer, this faceless stranger responsible for a crime of historic lethality, was Korean American, and the tenor of the messages changed dramatically. Suddenly, most of it was from Asian American friends and colleagues, with a fresh and unique range of concerns. Some expressed guilt, inexplicable and unwarranted, that a child of our community might be responsible for such mayhem: "As a Korean, I do feel partly guilty and responsible," said CeFaan Kim, an associate producer at NY1 News. "Every person I've spoken to who's Korean, and that's a large number, feels the same way. It's a cultural difference, but the fact that our community shares this feeling is simply fact."

Some expressed reluctant empathy: "Ours is not always a forgiving culture," said Jenny Song. "There's a lot of pressure to make it in the top 5 percent—be it schools, jobs, society, etc.; we tend to have an overall closed culture in which you're either 'in' or 'out,' with very little room for those who are a little different or don't fit in with standard norms. I can't help but wonder if there are certain aspects of our culture that may have compounded his feelings. I can't help feel as though this incident is also a wake-up call for Korean society in many ways."

And others wrote words of fear and alarm, decrying the constant representation of the Asian-born but American-raised perpetrator Seung-Hui Cho as a foreigner, pointing to blog postings attacking Asians as an inscrutable, unassimilable threat from within, and noting unconfirmed reports of backlash—a South Korean flag being burned in Fort Lee, N.J.; a Korean American student in Manhattan threatened by white classmates.

"Most of the perpetrators of mass school killings have been white," said Paul Niwa, a journalism professor at Emerson College. "After those shootings, do you think white people felt guilty that the shooter was white? Do you think white people felt that since the shooter was white, that the shooter would give society a bad impression of whites? A shooter can be white and nobody thinks that race played a part in the crime. But when someone nonwhite commits a crime, this society makes the person's race partially at fault."

Reading these comments, I found myself caught in a dilemma. I want to think that race is not a factor in the toxic mix of rage and psychological disturbance that has occasionally discharged as this kind of violence. And, certainly, in most cases it isn't: Teenage angst is colorblind, and the triggers for crimes like these have included parental abuse, schoolyard persecution, romantic obsession—phenomena that exist beyond culture or ethnicity.

But professor Niwa is right: When race enters the equation—when the perpetrator of a crime of this type is black, like "Beltway Snipers" John Allen Muhammad and his ward Lee Boyd Malvo, or Asian, like Cho—it rises to the surface and stays there, prompting inevitable discussions about whether "black rage" or "immigrant alienation" were somehow to blame; whether in some fundamental fashion, color of skin, shape of eye, or nation of origin lie at the seething, secret heart of such tragedies.

There have been two other widely reported school shooting sprees by Asian perpetrators. One of them, the case of University of Iowa exchange student Gang Lu, even served as the inspiration for Chen Shi-zheng's new film, "Dark Matter," which won the Alfred P. Sloan Prize at this year's Sundance

Film Festival. On November 1, 1991, Lu, a promising, Beijing-born physics student, brought a pair of pistols into a department meeting and opened fire, killing five people and paralyzing a sixth, before shooting himself fatally in the head. A *New York Times* article on the film quotes Vanderbilt University physics professor James Dickerson as saying that Asian students are often the victims of "unstated racism" and the preconception that they are smart, hardworking and unlikely to complain. "As a result they wind up as cogs in the research machine and remain isolated from the rest of the community and the culture," says Dickerson. "It's something not widely discussed in the physics community." It then goes on to quote Harvard math professor Shing-Tung Yau on the "high expectation" placed on children by Chinese families. "When they realize that they cannot achieve it, they get very upset," he says. "They also compete among themselves severely."

The other case is that of Wayne Lo, a Taiwanese-born student who moved to Billings, Mont., with his family at the age of 13, then attended Simon's Rock College in Great Barrington, Mass. Accounts of his case—which took place a little over a year after Gang Lu's rampage, on December 14, 1992—carefully use his intelligence (he was accepted at Simon's Rock on the W.E.B. DuBois Minority Scholarship!), his exquisite talent in classical music (he excelled on violin!), and his previous history as a quiet, unassuming individual to counterpoint his bloody rifle attack, which killed two and wounded four others. Here's a typically lyrical quote, from a feature by the *New York Times'* Anthony DePalma: "Only Mr. Lo knows what led him to turn away from the classical music he once loved and instead embrace the violent, discordant music known as hardcore, and a surly group of students who were equally entranced by it. Only he knows how the same fingers that danced with such agility and emotion over the strings of a violin could, as the police say, have pressed the trigger of a semiautomatic assault rifle, shattering the campus silence and ripping through several lives." As with Lu, news reports also emphasized Lo's foreign birth—sometimes implying, sometimes outright stating that Lo's cultural difference may have led to his sense of isolation, of being disrespected, of social exclusion, and ultimately, to his deadly eruption.

The degree to which these paired memes—"smart but quiet" and "fundamentally foreign"—are repeated in the coverage of these two crimes is striking. In Lo's case, it was enough to prompt attorney Rhoda J. Yen to write a paper titled "Racial Stereotyping of Asians and Asian Americans and Its Effect on Criminal Justice: A Reflection on the Wayne Lo Case" for Boalt School of Law's Asian Law Journal, in which she raises the theory that this racial imagery may have tainted Lo's ability to receive a fair trial.

The reporting around Seung-Hui Cho seems to have followed the same through-line: Right here on Salon, Joe Eaton reported one of Cho's high school classmates calling him "a quiet guy, a really, really quiet guy," but also a "'supersmart' student known for his math skills." Most news reports have also referred to him as a "resident alien," a legally proper but semiotically complex term that seems to emphasize difference—while a "legal permanent resident" sounds like someone who belongs in this nation, an "alien" doesn't even sound like he belongs on this planet. It's a word that seems designed to be followed by "invader"—a phrase whose appropriateness is underscored by the pictures of Cho, scowling and fisting guns at the camera, that now stare out from every news site.

There's no excusing Cho's crimes, or those of Lu and Lo before him. All three were guilty of heinous acts, of ruining and ending lives, and merit no apology for what they did. The point of bringing up all three is not to defend them, but to ask whether media and society have too easily conflated them, bundling their individual cases in a convenient packaging that subtly evokes those hoary, oddly contradictory typecasts of the "model minority" whiz kid and invading "yellow peril."

One contributor to the legal group blog De Novo, who actually attended college with Wayne Lo and was close friends with one of his victims, has gone so far as to draw a direct comparison between Cho and Lo. While acknowledging Rhoda Yen's journal article and disavowing any intent to suggest that race was a primary reason for those two slides into murderous violence, "Dave" nevertheless notes that "across the board, college shooters seem to be males under some pressure for success, academic and/or sexual, which would seem to include many Asian males." Dave then admits that this suggestion itself rests on a "model minority" stereotype. And that's a quandary we often find ourselves in when invoking race here—or really, anywhere: It's challenging to talk about it in a complex and constructive fashion, so it's often tossed out, or put into play via crude and simplistic clichés.

Excluding race from the equation entirely eliminates some very real criteria we might use to better understand why acts like this occur, and how to perhaps prevent them in the future. Parental expectations among Asian Americans, particularly within immigrant families, are indeed great; racism and casual discrimination does exist; social isolation may be more likely if you're in a situation where the people around you mostly don't look like you or share your background.

Perhaps most important, there are wide differences between cultures in how mental illness is perceived, with Asian cultures largely rejecting the concept of psychological disorder as a disease—to the point of refusing treatment, ostracizing sufferers, and even suppressing discussion of the topic. Could this attitude, combined with a lack of culturally sensitive counseling, have resulted in the inner turmoil of Lu, Lo and Cho being overlooked or underplayed? "Asian immigrants are not as liberally educated about mental illness as others in the U.S.; they feel it is something strange, something you shouldn't deal with or discuss," says psychiatrist Dr. Damian Kim, who has practiced clinically for 35 years, and who has written a book on mental health for immigrants that is available in both Korean and English. "For them, seeking treatment is an indication that there's something wrong with you."

But focusing on race, particularly using the lens of stereotype, flattens individuality, and obscures other factors that are more meaningful and important. "Pressure for success, academic and/or sexual" isn't in and of itself a reason for someone to go out and commit mass murder. I know hundreds of young Asian males who experienced that kind of pressure as adolescents, who grew up silent, studious and socially awkward; who were perceived as different, to the point of being excluded or taunted; who

had unusual hobbies and obsessions—and who've never shot off anything except their mouths.

I'm one myself. While attending St. Ann's School in Brooklyn, N.Y., back in the mid-'80s, I worked on a student film with my equally weird friends called "Burnout," a horror-comedy that recast our high school as "Sat-An's School," an institution run by a group of diabolical cultists who manipulate a young, misanthropic student to murder his peers and teachers in various silly and bloody ways. We launched the production with the cooperation of faculty and administration, some of whom played themselves. The film was never finished—SATs and parental expectations got in the way.

But I wonder, if I proposed that script as a high schooler today, a quiet Asian American male with few friends and odd interests, would I be automatically dropped into a box marked "potential spree killer"? And if I were tagged with that combination of model minority and yellow peril as a result, if I found myself surrounded by people appalled that a "good, quiet Asian boy" might write a gory slasher flick about a student maniac . . . would that help or hurt?

Analyze this Reading

1. How does the writer respond to the observations of Professor Niwa?
2. According to the writer, how did the media stereotype Seung-Hui Cho and other Asian-born perpetrators? What words and terms does the writer identify as contributing to this stereotyping?
3. How does stereotyping conceal important cultural influences and thus limit more accurate understanding of individuals like Seung-Hui Cho, Gang Lu, and Wayne Lo?'
4. The writer concludes this article with a personal story. Is this movement away from public, objective treatment of the issue into private anecdote effective in terms of engaging the reader? Is this a strategy you can see yourself using in an argument? Explain.

Respond to this Reading

1. Professor Niwa contends that race, and eventual stereotyping, becomes a factor in the media when the perpetrators are not white. Explain why you agree or disagree with this contention. Support your position with examples.
2. What is the danger of racial and ethnic stereotyping? Is it present in your school? What issues exist in your community that warrant discussion about the kind of stereotyping that the writer addresses?
3. Imagine drafting an argument in which you focus on the language of ethnic stereotyping. What terms would you isolate and discuss?

Anthology 6
Consumer Community

ABOUT THIS READING

Writer Judith Simmer Brown is professor of religious studies at Naropa University in Colorado and a Buddhist scholar. This reading appeared in *Contemporary Issues Companion: Consumerism*, edited by Uma Kukathas.

A Buddhist Perspective on Consumerism

By Judith Simmer Brown

Western Buddhism must serve the world, not itself. It must become, as the seventh-century Indian master Shantideva wrote, "the doctor and the nurse for all sick beings in the world until everyone is healed; a rain of food and drink, an inexhaustible treasure for those who are poor and destitute." We can only imagine the kinds of suffering our children will encounter. Even now, we see the poor with not enough food and no access to clean drinking water; we see ethnic and religious prejudice that would extinguish those who are different; we see the sick and infirm who have no medicine or care; we see rampant exploitation of the many for the pleasure and comfort of the few; we see the demonization of those who would challenge the reign of wealth, power, and privilege. And we know the twenty-first century will yield burgeoning populations with an ever-decreasing store of resources to nourish them.

Fueling the suffering is the relentless consumerism which pervades our society and the world. Greed drives so many of the damaging systems of our planet. The socially engaged biologist Stephanie Kaza said that in America each of us consumes our body weight each day in materials extracted and processed from farms, mines, rangelands, and forests—120 pounds on the average. Since 1950, consumption of energy, meat, and lumber has doubled; use of plastic has increased five-fold; use of aluminum has increased seventy-fold; and airplane mileage has increased thirty-three-fold per person. We now own twice as many cars as in 1950. And with every bite, every press of the accelerator, every swipe of the credit card in our shopping malls, we leave a larger ecological footprint on the face of the world. We have squeezed our wealth out of the bodies of plantation workers in Thailand, farmers in Ecuador, and factory workers in Malaysia.

The crisis of consumerism is infecting every culture of the world, most of which are now emulating the American lifestyle. David Loy, in *The Religion of the Market*, suggests that consumerism is based on two unexamined tenets or beliefs:

1. growth and enhanced world trade will benefit everyone, and
2. growth will not be constrained by the inherent limits of a finite planet.

The ground of consumerism is ego gratification, its path is an ever-increasing array of wants, and its fruition is expressed in the Cartesian perversion—"I shop, therefore I am." While it recruits new converts through

iStock.com/A-digit

the flood of mass media, it dulls the consumer, making us oblivious to the suffering in which we participate. Shopping is a core activity in sustaining a culture of denial.

With the collapse of communist countries throughout the world, the growth of consumerism is all but unchallenged. As traditional societies modernize, consumerism is the most alluring path. Religious peoples and communities have the power to bring the only remaining challenge to consumerism. And Buddhism has unique insights which can stem the tide of consumptive intoxication.

How do we respond to all the suffering created by consumerism? How will our children respond? It is easy to join the delusion, forgetting whatever Buddhist training we may have had. But when we return to it, we remember— the origin of suffering is our constant craving. We want, therefore we consume; we want, therefore we suffer. As practitioners, we feel this relentless rhythm in our bones. We must, in this generation, wake up to the threat of consumerism, and join with other religious peoples to find a way to break its grip. We must all find a way to become activists in the movement which explores alternatives to consumerism.

As Western Buddhists, we must recognize the threats of consumerism within our practice, and within our embryonic communities and institutions. From a Tibetan Buddhist point of view, consumerism is just the tip of the iceberg. It represents only the outer manifestation of craving and acquisitiveness. Twenty-five years ago, my guru, the Vidyadhara Chogyam Trungpa Rinpoche, wrote one of the first popular Dharma books in America, *Cutting Through Spiritual Materialism*. Its relevance only increases each year. He spoke of three levels of materialism—physical, psychological, spiritual—that rule our existence as expressions of ego-centered activity. Unchallenged, materialism will coopt our physical lives, our communities, and our very practice.

Physical materialism refers to the neurotic pursuit of pleasure, comfort, and security. This is the outer expression of consumerism. Under this influence, we try to shield ourselves from the daily pain of embodied existence, while accentuating the pleasurable moments. We are driven to create the illusion of a pain-free life, full of choices that make us feel in control. We need 107 choices of yogurt in a supermarket so that we feel like queens of our universe. We go to 24-Plex movie theaters so that we can see whatever film we want, whenever we want. We need faster pain relievers, appliances to take away all inconvenience, and communication devices to foster immediate exchange. All of these create the illusion of complete pleasure at out fingertips, with none of the hassle of pain. When we are ruled by this kind of physical materialism, we identify ourselves by what we have.

But this is just the beginning. On the next level, psychological materialism seeks to control the world through theory, ideology, and intellect. Not only are we trying to physically manipulate the world so that we don't have to experience pain, we do so psychologically as well. We create a theoretical construct that keeps us from having to be threatened, to be wrong, or to be confused. We always put ourselves in control in this way: "As an American I have rights. As a woman, I deserve to be independent from expectations of men in my society. I earn my own salary, I can choose how I want to spend it. As a Buddhist, I understand interdependence."

Psychological materialism interprets whatever is threatening or irritating as an enemy. Then, we control the threat by creating an ideology or religion in which we are victorious, correct, or righteous; we never directly experience the fear and confusion that could arise from facing a genuine threat. This is particularly perilous for the Western Buddhist. In these times, Buddhism has become popular, a commodity which is used by corporations and the media. Being Buddhist has become a status symbol, connoting power, prestige, and money. His Holiness's picture appears on the sets of Hollywood movies and in Apple Computer ads; Hollywood stars are pursued as acquisitions in a kind of Dharmic competition. Everyone wants to add something Buddhist to her resume. Buddhist Studies enrollments at Naropa have doubled in two years, and reporters haunt our hallways and classrooms. Buddhist conferences attract a veritable parade of characters like myself, hawking the "tools" of our trade. Our consumer society is turning Buddhism into a commodity like everything else. The seductions for the Western Buddhist are clear. We are being seduced to use Buddhism to promote our own egos, communities, and agendas in the marketplace.

This still is not the heart of the matter. On the most subtle level, spiritual materialism carries this power struggle into the realm of our own minds, into our own meditation practice. Our consciousness is attempting to remain in control, to maintain a centralized awareness. Through this, ego uses even spirituality to shield itself from fear and insecurity. Our meditation practice can be used to retreat from the ambiguity and intensity of daily encounters; our compassion practices can be used to manipulate the sheer agony of things falling apart. We develop an investment in ourselves as Buddhist practitioners, and in so doing protect ourselves from the directness and intimacy of our own realization. It is important for us to be willing to cultivate the "edge" of our own practice, the edge where panic arises, where threat is our friend, and where our depths are turned inside out.

What happens when we are ruled by the "three levels of materialism"? The Vidyadhara taught that when we are so preoccupied with issues of ego, control, and power we become "afraid of external phenomena, which are our own projections." What this means is that when we take ourselves to be real, existent beings, then we mistake the world around us to be independent and real. And when we do this we invite paranoia, fear, and panic. We are afraid of not being able to control the situation. As Patrul Rinpoche (1808–1887) taught:

Don't prolong the past,
Don't invite the future,
Don't alter your innate wakefulness,
Don't fear appearances.

We must give up the fear of appearances. How can we do this? The only way to cut this pattern of acquisitiveness and control is to guard the naked integrity of our meditation practice. We must be willing to truly "let go" in our practice. When we see our racing minds, our churning emotions and constant plots, we touch the face of the suffering world and we have no choice but to be changed. We must allow our hearts to break with the pain of constant struggle that we experience in ourselves and in the world around us. Then we can become engaged in the world, and dedicate ourselves to a

genuine enlightened society in which consumerism has no sway. Craving comes from the speed of our minds, wishing so intensely for what we do not have that we cannot experience what is there, right before us.

How can we, right now, address materialism in our practice and our lives? I would like to suggest a socially engaged practice which could transform our immediate lifestyles and change our relationship with suffering. It is the practice of generosity. No practice flies more directly in the face of American acquisitiveness and individualism. Any of us who have spent time in Asia or with our Asian teachers see the centrality of generosity in Buddhist practice.

According to traditional formulation, our giving begins with material gifts and extends to gifts of fearlessness and Dharma. Generosity is the virtue that produces peace, as the sutras [Buddhist scriptures] say. Generosity is a practice which overcomes our acquisitiveness and self-absorption, and which benefits others. Committing to this practice may produce our greatest legacy for the twenty-first century.

Analyze this Reading

1. What information does the writer use to describe consumerism in the United States? Why does she connect consumerism with suffering?
2. What are the dangers of physical, psychological, and spiritual materialism? What examples does the writer use to describe these dangers?
3. Early in this reading, the writer claims that "Religious peoples and communities have the power to bring the only remaining challenge to consumerism." What role can Buddhism play?

Respond to this Reading

1. Contrast the values associated with consumerism with values the writer endorses in this reading. How would life be different if the writer's values were to take hold?
2. Some contend that consumerism, and its emphasis on acquisitiveness, is the engine that drives our economy and defines our culture. With this in mind, is it realistic to think that a religious perspective—like Buddhism, Christianity, or Judaism—can alter Americans' need to consume?
3. As a consumer, what issues do you have, especially in terms of your consumption of products and services regarded as essential today? What would you claim in response to the most pressing of these issues?

ABOUT THIS READING

Writer Matt Stannard blogs at *Cowboys on the Commons* and is a member of the Board of Directors of the Public Banking Institute. He is currently Policy Director at *Commonomics USA*. This article, the first in a ten-part series, appears in *Occupy .com*, an online site that defines itself as a "news and media channel amplifying the voices of the global 99%. We use news, analyses, music, video, photography and graphics to heighten awareness and inspire engagement for social, economic and environmental justice."

Seizing the Public Banking Moment

By Matt Stannard

The free market has failed as a governing paradigm of material life. Whatever the case for local markets in their specific context, large-scale competition and hierarchy are destructive, trauma-inducing conditions for people and the planet. For centuries, people have pushed back against those competitive and hierarchical models, advocating and experimenting with more cooperative and ecologically holistic economic visions.

One of those visions is financial democracy: public or community control of the financial system itself. Recognizing that the generation and value of money are artificial, and that how we pay for things is fundamentally a political question, advocates of financial democracy see banking–the power to lend money and to create value through the act of lending–as an enormous power. Such power should be democratic, not autocratic.

Subject to democratic control and administration, where the body politic is committed to egalitarianism and sustainability, banking could do great public good. Public banks can help save the planet from apocalyptic climate change by financing a quick post-carbon transition. They can guarantee employment in communities, facilitate the payment of dividends directly to citizens as a form of universal basic income, and ensure that state and municipal budgets are always healthy.

A network of public banks could help create a network of clean, efficient public transit. Public banking can replace, and thus destroy, every socially destructive banking practice, from the gambling of pensions and public funds in risky investments and complex debt swaps, to predatory payday lending. Assuming we need "money" at all (a debatable question for sure), public banks promise to be the smartest, most sustainable, and most ethical way to manage finance.

The public banking movement has sputtered through the last eight hundred or so years, from medieval and colonial-era church banks, to the Paris Commune's plan in 1871 to have people's banks fund worker cooperatives, to the victory of North Dakota's farmer-socialist Nonpartisan League in the early 20th century. A few countries, notably Germany, have implemented successful public banking policies with positive social effects. America has had more stops than starts, with North Dakota currently being the only state with a (modest and pretty conservative) public bank.

But since the financial crash of 2009 and the Occupy movement of 2011, public banking has gained momentum in over 30 states and dozens of cities. Specifically in the last two years, perhaps in response to the Trump campaign and his presidency's marriage of fascism and finance capital, the public banking movement has scored monumental advances on both the east and west coasts.

The Moment

California is on the brink of a financial revolution that is deeply embedded and shudderingly alive in all corners of that state's huge economy. The cannabis industry has thrown its support (http://www.latimes.com/business

/la-fi-cannabis-bank-chiang-20180130-story.html) behind public banks, and the normally cautious State Treasurer John Chiang has demanded (https:// www.sfgate.com/bayarea/article/John-Chiang-lays-out-plan-to-create-a -publicbank- 12537099.php) a feasibility study for a public bank. Meanwhile, large and diverse groups (https://publicbankla.com/index.php/about/news /54-updates/173-the-growing-movementto-create-city-run-public-banks) in cities including San Francisco, Oakland and Los Angeles have successfully pushed for divestment from big banks like Wells Fargo and the exploration of public banking. Across the state, city councils are passing resolutions, commissioning studies and forming
working groups.

On the other side of the country, the most promising development is the election of New Jersey's new governor, Phil Murphy. Murphy was elected in part because of his promise to create a state-owned bank and he is now the nation's most powerful public official to advocate public banking. Following Murphy's lead, Democratic state senators recently introduced (https://www .politico.com/states/newjersey/story/2018/01/19/codey-and-gill-introduce -murphys-state-bank-proposal-196516) the State Bank of New Jersey Act, which is currently sitting in the Senate Commerce Committee.

Activists in other states are hard at work pushing the agenda. Momentum is growing in New York, where a handful of elected officials over the past few years have committed (http://legislation.nysenate.gov/pdf/bills/2017 /S3172) to the cause, and where one prominent advocacy group is hiring (http://www.neweconomynyc.org/wpcontent/uploads/2017/09/Campaign Organizer2017.pdf) a full-time public banking campaign organizer. In Pennsylvania, the city of Philadelphia has fired Wells Fargo (https:// generocity.org/philly/2018/01/11/jobs-invest-tivoni-devor-pension-fund -publicbank/) and well-organized advocates continue their years-long cam- paign for a state- or city-owned bank. And Massachusetts has just introduced a new public banking bill; like California, the state is looking to public banking to address its cannabis revenue challenges (https://www.americanbanker .com/news/in-massachusetts-a-call-for-a-public-bank-toserve-pot-firm).

Back out west, in Washington, state senators Bob Hasegawa and Patty Kuderer are championing the cause, while in Alaska, representatives Scott Kawasaki and Chris Tuck recently filed legislation (http://www.akbizmag .com/Government/Reps-Kawasaki-and-Tuck-Propose-the-Creationof-the -State-Bank-of-Alaska/) to create a state bank with a mission very similar to the Bank of North Dakota. Another BND-style bill was just introduced (http:// gophouse.org/rep-howrylak-time-nowmichigan-employ-state-run-bank/) in Michigan by state Rep. Martin Howrylak, a Republican.

While most of the proposals around the country are for state-run banks, several municipalities are proposing public banks, too. Cooperative bank- ing is part of the bold solidarity economy agenda in Jackson, Mississippi, a piece of the blueprint (https://cooperationjackson.org/intro/) of Cooperation Jackson. California's movement is propelled in part by a drive for a "network of municipal banks" (http://www.commonomicsusa.org/blog.htm) under a common license. The City of Seattle has committed to spending (https:// hubpublicbanking.org/2018/02/28/seattle-issues-a-rfp-for-apublic-bank -feasibility-study/) $100,000 to study the creation of a public bank, while in

Saint Louis, Board of Aldermen President Lewis Reed recently introduced (https://claytontimes.com/city-of-stlouis-to-look-into-forming-its-own-bank/) a resolution for a task force on public banking.

The Struggle

The road getting here hasn't been easy. There have been setbacks, instances of inertia or outright official rejection. Recent examples include Santa Fe, where a movement with real momentum has been smacked down (https://www.usnews.com/news/best-states/new-mexico/articles/2018-03-21/santa-fe-task-force-plans-to-not-recommend-city-public-bank) by a task force of hostile members, exacerbated by Mayor Javier Gonzales's retreat from his initially enthusiastic support. The state government of Colorado has been unsympathetic to the call for public banking, although demand is growing in both Denver and Boulder.

Meanwhile, the movement for public banking continues unabated in Vermont (https://www.thevermontstandard.com/2018/01/advocates-make-a-case-for-statebank/) despite having the wind taken out of its sails a few years ago. And in Maine, a vocal advocacy group continues to reach out (https://fiddleheadfocus.com/2018/01/12/news/bank-groupawards-aroostook-senators/) to the state's elected officials even after repeated rejection by legislative committees. New Hampshire, Hawaii, Oregon, Illinois and other states have had similar experiences, pushing for public banking legislation that ultimately got exiled in committee – coming close to making a case only to have Wall Street lobbyists generate sufficient noise to confound riskaverse public officials.

In fact, the question of banking reform – and particularly of banking as a public utility – is best seen as an ongoing site of struggle. Right now, the fight is between a solidified status quo propped up by wellfunded think tanks, big bankers, and self-deceiving community bankers on one side, and a growing people's movement on the other. But banking will not cease to be the site of struggle once states and cities begin to establish public financial institutions.

Citizens concerned with economic justice and ecological sustainability will have to fight to keep their new public banks from following North Dakota's example (http://www.yesmagazine.org/peoplepower/north-dakotas-public-bank-was-built-for-the-people-now-its-financing-police-atstanding-rock-20161214), in which the state used the power of its public bank to prop up environmentally destructive energy practices and crush dissent at Standing Rock. Public banking advocates will also have to stay on guard against attempts by private financial firms to "partner" with public banks in ways that distort their priorities.

The Challenge

For now, the challenge for public banking advocates is to remain undeterred and demand the creation of public banks. The experiences of California and New Jersey and the encouraging signs elsewhere suggest that we are closer than we've been in a long time to seeing public banks become a reality. It's also quite possible, on the other hand, that these myriad efforts will still fail

because of pushback and influence from Wall Street bankers, complacent and ideologically fogged-up community bankers, and think tanks like the Cato Institute, armed with badly-researched (http://www.publicbankinginstitute .org/big_banking_interests_push_back_part_two_wall_street_interests _deceive_the_people_about_public_banks) but well-funded arguments.

Therefore, in order not to fail, the movement must gather critical mass. Cities and states with public banking supporters numbering in the hundreds need to gather enough people together to number in the thousands and, ultimately, the tens of thousands. That can only happen if the public banking movement establishes itself as an integral part of a larger movement for economic, social, racial, gender and ecological justice. A transition from Wall Street banking to public banking is a paradigm shift, not merely a policy shift. Only mass movements can shift paradigms.

In other words, it's not enough for public banking to be a good idea. It's not enough to have a few engaged citizens sitting down with elected leaders and convincing them it's a good idea. Politics isn't a debating contest. Being correct isn't enough.

Over the next ten weeks, this series will discuss the way the movement for public banks and cooperative modes of finance have succeeded and failed in the past, and what it's going to take for such a movement to succeed now.

Analyze this Reading

1. What is "financial democracy?" How can public banks act on the principles of financial democracy?
2. Describe current interest in public banking from states and municipalities.
3. What threats are new public banks likely to face?
4. How must the public banking movement proceed in order to avoid failing?

Respond to this Reading

1. Could life change for you if public banks were established in your community and provided realistic alternatives to private banks? Explain.
2. According to the writer, public banking has had limited success in the past 800 years. What conditions exist now, especially in terms of all Americans having access to the essentials of life, that might allow a public banking movement to succeed today?

ABOUT THIS READING

Journalist Andy Kroll is based in Washington, D. C., and is an associate editor at *TomDispatch*, an email publication that makes available articles and opinion from the world press, and is a staff writer at *Mother Jones Magazine*, a nonprofit news organization named after Mary Harris "Mother" Jones, a union organizer and staunch opponent of child labor in the late-nineteenth and early-twentieth centuries and at one time referred to as "the most dangerous woman in America."

How the McEconomy Bombed the American Worker: The Hollowing Out of the Middle Class

By Andy Kroll

Think of it as a parable for these grim economic times. On April 19th, McDonald's launched its first-ever national hiring day, signing up 62,000 new workers at stores throughout the country. For some context, that's more jobs created by one company in a single day than the net job creation of the entire U.S. economy in 2009. And if that boggles the mind, consider how many workers applied to local McDonald's franchises that day and left empty-handed: 938,000 of them. With a 6.2% acceptance rate in its spring hiring blitz, McDonald's was more selective than the Princeton, Stanford, or Yale University admission offices.

It shouldn't be surprising that a million souls flocked to McDonald's hoping for a steady paycheck, when nearly 14 million Americans are out of work and nearly a million more are too discouraged even to look for a job. At this point, it apparently made no difference to them that the fast-food industry pays some of the lowest wages around: on average, $8.89 an hour, or barely half the $15.95 hourly average across all American industries.

On an annual basis, the average fast-food worker takes home $20,800, less than half the national average of $43,400. McDonald's appears to pay even worse, at least with its newest hires. In the press release for its national hiring day, the multibillion-dollar company said it would spend $518 million on the newest round of hires, or $8,354 a head. Hence the *Oxford English Dictionary's* definition of "McJob" as "a low-paying job that requires little skill and provides little opportunity for advancement."

Of course, if you read only the headlines, you might think that the jobs picture was improving. The economy added 1.3 million private-sector jobs between February 2010 and January 2011, and the headline unemployment rate edged downward, from 9.8% to 8.8%, between November of last year and March. It inched upward in April, to 9%, but tempering that increase was the news that the economy added 244,000 jobs last month (not including those 62,000 McJobs), beating economists' expectations.

Under this somewhat sunnier news, however, runs a far darker undercurrent. Yes, jobs are being created, but what kinds of jobs paying what kinds of wages? Can those jobs sustain a modest lifestyle and pay the bills? Or are we living through a McJobs recovery?

The Rise of the McWorker

The evidence points to the latter. According to a recent analysis by the National Employment Law Project (NELP), the biggest growth in private-sector job creation in the past year occurred in positions in the low-wage retail, administrative, and food service sectors of the economy. While 23% of the jobs lost in the Great Recession that followed the economic meltdown of 2008 were "low-wage" (those paying $9–$13 an hour), 49% of new jobs added in the sluggish "recovery" are in those same low-wage industries. On the other end of the spectrum, 40% of the jobs lost paid high wages ($19–$31 an hour), while a mere 14% of new jobs pay similarly high wages.

As a point of comparison, that's much worse than in the recession of 2001 after the high-tech bubble burst. Then, higher wage jobs made up almost a third of all new jobs in the first year after the crisis.

The hardest hit industries in terms of employment now are finance, manufacturing, and especially construction, which was decimated when the housing bubble burst in 2007 and has yet to recover. Meanwhile, NELP found that hiring for temporary administrative and waste-management jobs, health-care jobs, and of course those fast-food restaurants has surged.

Indeed in 2010, one in four jobs added by private employers was a temporary job, which usually provides workers with few benefits and even less job security. It's not surprising that employers would first rely on temporary hires as they regained their footing after a colossal financial crisis. But this time around, companies have taken on temp workers in far greater numbers than after previous downturns. Where 26% of hires in 2010 were temporary, the figure was 11% after the early-1990s recession and only 7% after the downturn of 2001.

As many labor economists have begun to point out, we're witnessing an increasing polarization of the U.S. economy over the past three decades. More and more, we're seeing labor growth largely at opposite ends of the skills-and-wages spectrum—among, that is, the best and the worst kinds of jobs.

At one end of job growth, you have increasing numbers of people flipping burgers, answering telephones, engaged in child care, mopping hallways, and in other low-wage lines of work. At the other end, you have increasing numbers of engineers, doctors, lawyers, and people in high-wage "creative" careers. What's disappearing is the middle, the decent-paying jobs that helped expand the American middle class in the mid-twentieth century and that, if the present lopsided recovery is any indication, are now going the way of typewriters and landline telephones.

Because the shape of the workforce increasingly looks fat on both ends and thin in the middle, economists have begun to speak of "the barbell effect," which for those clinging to a middle-class existence in bad times means a nightmare life. For one thing, the shape of the workforce now hinders America's once vaunted upward mobility. It's the downhill slope that's largely available these days.

The barbell effect has also created staggering levels of income inequality of a sort not known since the decades before the Great Depression. From 1979 to 2007, for the middle class, average household income (after taxes) nudged upward from $44,100 to $55,300; by contrast, for the top 1%, average household income soared from $346,600 in 1979 to nearly $1.3 million in 2007. That is, super-rich families saw their earnings increase 11 times faster than middle-class families.

What's causing this polarization? An obvious culprit is technology. As MIT economist David Autor notes, the tasks of "organizing, storing, retrieving, and manipulating information" that humans once performed are now computerized. And when computers can't handle more basic clerical work, employers ship those jobs overseas where labor is cheaper and benefits nonexistent.

Another factor is education. In today's barbell economy, degrees and diplomas have never mattered more, which means that those with just a high school education increasingly find themselves locked into the low-wage end of the labor market with little hope for better. Worse yet, the pay gap between the well-educated and not-so-educated continues to widen: in 1979, the hourly wage of a typical college graduate was 1.5 times higher than that of a typical high-school graduate; by 2009, it was almost two times higher.

Considering, then, that the percentage of men ages 25 to 34 who have gone to college is actually decreasing, it's not surprising that wage inequality has gotten worse in the U.S. As Autor writes, advanced economies like ours "depend on their best-educated workers to develop and commercialize the innovative ideas that drive economic growth."

The distorting effects of the barbell economy aren't lost on ordinary Americans. In a recent Gallup poll, a majority of people agreed that the country was still in either a depression (29%) or a recession (26%). When sorted out by income, however, those making $75,000 or more a year are, not surprisingly, most likely to believe the economy is in neither a recession nor a depression, but growing. After all, they're the ones most likely to have benefited from a soaring stock market and the return to profitability of both corporate America and Wall Street. In Gallup's middle-income group, by contrast, 55% of respondents claim the economy is in trouble. They're still waiting for their recovery to arrive.

The Slow Fade of Big Labor

The big-picture economic changes described by Autor and others, however, don't tell the entire story. There's a significant political component to the hollowing out of the American labor force and the impoverishment of the middle class: the slow fade of organized labor. Since the 1950s, the clout of unions in the public and private sectors has waned, their membership has dwindled, and their political influence has weakened considerably. Long gone are the days when powerful union bosses—the AFL-CIO's George Meany or the UAW's Walter Reuther—had the ear of just about any president.

As *Mother Jones*' Kevin Drum has written, in the 1960s and 1970s a rift developed between big labor and the Democratic Party. Unions recoiled in disgust at what they perceived to be the "motley collection of shaggy kids, newly assertive women, and goo-goo academics" who had begun to supplant organized labor in the Party. In 1972, the influential AFL-CIO symbolically distanced itself from the Democrats by refusing to endorse their nominee for president, George McGovern.

All the while, big business was mobilizing, banding together to form massive advocacy groups such as the Business Roundtable and shaping the staid U.S. Chamber of Commerce into a ferocious lobbying machine. In the 1980s and 1990s, the Democratic Party drifted rightward and toward an increasingly powerful and financially focused business community, creating the Democratic Leadership Council, an olive branch of sorts to corporate America. "It's not that the working class [had] abandoned Democrats," Drum wrote. "It's just the opposite: The Democratic Party [had] largely abandoned the working class."

The GOP, of course, has a long history of battling organized labor, and nowhere has that been clearer than in the party's recent assault on workers' rights. Swept in by a tide of Republican support in 2010, new GOP majorities in state legislatures from Wisconsin to Tennessee to New Hampshire have

introduced bills meant to roll back decades' worth of collective bargaining rights for public-sector unions, the last bastion of organized labor still standing (somewhat) strong.

The political calculus behind the war on public-sector unions is obvious: kneecap them and you knock out a major pillar of support for the Democratic Party. In the 2010 midterm elections, the American Federation of State, County, and Municipal Employees (AFSCME) spent nearly $90 million on TV ads, phone banking, mailings, and other support for Democratic candidates. The anti-union legislation being pushed by Republicans would inflict serious damage on AFSCME and other public-sector unions by making it harder for them to retain members and weakening their clout at the bargaining table.

And as shown by the latest state to join the anti-union fray, it's not just Republicans chipping away at workers' rights anymore. In Massachusetts, a staunchly liberal state, the Democratic-led State Assembly recently voted to curb collective bargaining rights on heath-care benefits for teachers, firefighters, and a host of other public-sector employees.

Bargaining-table clout is crucial for unions, since it directly affects the wages their members take home every month. According to data from the Bureau of Labor Statistics, union workers pocket on average $200 more per week than their non-union counterparts, a 28% percent difference. The benefits of union representation are even greater for women and people of color: women in unions make 34% more than their non-unionized counterparts, and Latino workers nearly 51% more.

In other words, at precisely the moment when middle-class workers need strong bargaining rights so they can fight to preserve a living wage in a barbell economy, unions around the country face the grim prospect of losing those rights.

All of which raises the questions: Is there any way to revive the American middle class and reshape income distribution in our barbell nation? Or will this warped recovery of ours pave the way for an even more warped McEconomy, with the have-nots at one end, the have-it-alls at the other end, and increasingly less of us in between?

Analyze this Reading

1. What is the "barbell effect" that the writer refers to? How do technology and education figure into this effect?
2. According to the writer, why is it important for the GOP to oppose organized labor?
3. The writer brings to this article two portmanteau words—*McEconomy* and *McWorker*—two words that combine into one. For each portmanteau word, no definition is offered. To what extent is this a risky strategy? Were these words immediately understandable to you? Explain.

Respond to this Reading

1. To what extent do you see workers polarized in your community in terms of income and job security?
2. Explain why labor unions are the best way to restore the middle class. Or, if you disagree with this position, discuss other means by which

more American workers can achieve a path to higher wages and advancement.

3. How do you relate to the term *career*? What conditions would you change, or keep the same, when you think of this term?

ABOUT THIS READING

The issue discussed in this reading concerns Chinese-made products and their safety and quality. Writer Dali L. Yang earned his Ph.D. in political science from Princeton University and is now a professor in the Department of Political Science at the University of Chicago. This reading first appeared under the title "Total Recall" in *The National Interest*, a quarterly journal of international affairs and diplomacy.

Outsourcing Compromises the Safety and Quality of Products

By Dali L. Yang

China once languished, a closed economy with several hundred million people living in abject poverty. Today [2008], it is a major engine for world economic growth. It boasts a rising middle class and the world's largest foreign-exchange reserves. There can no longer be talk about global trade without mentioning the dragon [China], and the American consumer would be hard-pressed to live without goods bearing the "Made in China" label.

For the past year [2007–2008], though, that very label has suffered from some serious image problems. Reports of toxic Chinese-made products have mushroomed: toys covered in lead paint, melamine-tainted pet food, defective tires, toothpaste containing diethylene glycol, contaminated fish and more. There is also talk of unlicensed Chinese chemical companies eager to manufacture and supply fake, subpotent or adulterated drug products. To be sure, the bulk of Chinese exports to the United States are made or assembled to American specifications. Nonetheless, the lengthening list of unsafe goods from China also points to the simple fact that, in their quest for lower costs and higher profits, far too many China-based manufacturers are willing to cut corners at the expense of consumer safety.

Economic Growth Breeds Corruption

At their heart, China's real and exaggerated brand-image problems stem from a unique intersection of the American need for instant gratification and China's poisonous witches' brew of a "post-communist personality" with few moral moorings and an unfailing enthusiasm for getting rich. Too often now, the acquisitiveness so palpable in Chinese society knows no scruples, shifts the costs to others, and is married to opportunism and cunning. Of course, there are many businessmen who have made it big by working hard and honestly, but it's the anything-goes mind-set that rests at the root of many undesirable practices in China: from decadence to all manners of fake certificates, fake products, adulterated food and drinks,

rampant official corruption and sheer disregard for the rights of workers in sweatshops. For many, socialism with Chinese characteristics has a lot in common with the early stage of capitalism Karl Marx described as primitive accumulation.

This phenomenon finds its roots in the Chinese brand of communism from which it was borne and the reforms from which it was shaped. Begun in the 1970s, the proliferation of unruly manufacturers and exporters in China sprang from an environment where the potential for entrepreneurship among peasants and tradesmen was stifled. Technicians were jailed for moonlighting as consultants, and collective farms were enthralled to the party-state. Private business activities were severely punished or suppressed.

But after years of oppression, the government began to allow market-oriented reforms to modernize China's economy. Within a decade, the forces of enterprise were unleashed, but hand in hand with growth came rampant corruption. Reform making and profit making have often meant getting ahead of official policies and bending and breaking existing laws and regulations.

Along with these market reforms came preferential treatment for those of "the Party." China's leaders (and especially Deng Xiaoping) opened the floodgates, allowing government and party agencies, the armed police and even the People's Liberation Army to supplement their budgets with profits that they generated on their own. Here we see the strange melding of the strong party-state that desired a profit with the willingness to bend the rules: government control and unruly capitalism. By the 1990s, the Chinese mentality was then fully transformed. Though the Tiananmen crackdown of 1989 [a pro-democracy movement of university students that was ended by military force] closed the route to political reforms, the raw energy unleashed in China was instead channeled to the pursuit of material wealth. Mammon [riches, material wealth] became the new religion. Business fever took over.

The amazingly quick turn from the asceticism of the Mao era to the cult of Mammon under the leadership of the same Communist Party has landed China in what author Xiaoying Wang termed "a moral wasteland." Indeed, this is the world of doublespeak, with everybody mouthing the rhetoric of the moment as dictated by the party and yet often doing exactly the opposite of what's prescribed. . . .

Product Safety and Quality

It is fitting that one of the most popular books in today's China, written by Li Zhongwu in 1912, highlights how thick skins and cunning were the ingredients for getting ahead in Chinese history.

The reality of this "personality" can be frightening, leading many manufacturers to search for loopholes to slip through to get a leg up due to the relentless pressure for cheaper products. Their goal is to make some quick money, using deceit if necessary. This was apparently the case for suppliers who provided lead paint to the ill-fated toy makers. Likewise, some Chinese suppliers of wheat gluten deliberately added melamine, an industrial chemical, to artificially boost their product's protein reading and thus grade and price. In this situation, Gresham's Law [which states that bad money drives good money out of circulation] prevails; honest firms find it hard to stay in business by competing on price. Even though a fix is available—manufacturers can lower costs and increase profits by improving the efficiency of production processes—oftentimes they just seek to substitute cheaper components. That can be done without sacrificing quality, but that often doesn't happen.

Yet, even with all this finger pointing, we have to keep in mind that the Chinese can't be blamed for all of the safety problems with products manufactured in-country. According to a Canadian analysis of data on toy recalls over the last twenty years, the majority of the recalls involving millions of toys manufactured in China were caused by design defects, with primary responsibility lying with the toy companies. Indeed, a Mattel executive recently admitted that the "vast majority of those products that were recalled were the result of a design flaw in Mattel's design, not through a manufacturing flaw in China's manufacturers." In such cases, the solution for the resultant safety problems needs to come from the (mostly U.S.) toy companies.

Product-quality and safety cases are generally related to the continuing quest by manufacturers to lower production costs.

Unfortunately, the rest of the product-quality and safety cases are generally related to the continuing quest by manufacturers to lower production costs in the face of distributors buying at low prices, a rising currency, and rising labor and raw-material costs. But this unbridled drive to profit, with all its market obstacles and ensuing corruption, has not escaped the Chinese government. Almost from the beginning, it was clear some reining-in was needed. So the contemporary history of economic growth and market expansion is also a history of the modern regulatory state. First steps were put in place—imperfect, but an encouraging start—and all hope for a "morally reformed" China is certainly not lost.

Building the Foundation

No fools they, in the early 1990s, the Chinese leadership took an initial stab at regulation after recognizing the need to build and rebuild the institutional infrastructure for a market economy. No modern economy allows the unbridled pursuit of self-interest, especially when that pursuit causes harm to others. In addition to the obvious internal problems, the collapse of communist regimes in the former Soviet Union and Eastern Europe and, later, the downfall of governments in South Korea and Indonesia during the Asian financial crisis spurred Beijing on even more. The Chinese leadership first reconfigured the tax and fiscal system to strengthen the central government's fiscal capabilities and then revamped the central banking system to enhance financial supervision and promote financial stability.

Of special significance was the divestiture program undertaken amid the Asian financial crisis. In one bold move, the Chinese leadership got the People's Liberation Army, the armed police, the judiciary as well as a host of other party and state institutions out of the business of doing business. This divestiture helped bring rampant smuggling and related corruption under control and was critical to the development of a level economic playing field.

With the passage of time, China's leaders have also undertaken several rounds of government streamlining and restructuring to deal with an

unruly market and rapidly changing socioeconomic conditions. In China, as in other developed nations, a bureaucratic alphabet soup of bodies has emerged to protect the rights of consumers, investors and workers. The advent of a consumer society and growing public awareness, in particular, have pushed safety and quality to the fore of policymaking. And happily, some of these institutions are becoming effective. . . .

While improved regulatory capability—up-to-date product standards, abilities to monitor, test and punish—is a necessity and can go a long way toward the mitigation of product-quality issues, it is generally less effective when dealing with rogue businesses whose intentions are to evade detection and make a quick buck. Shutting down a toxic plant after a scandal is one thing. Using bureaucracies for effective preventive measures is another.

While China has established various regulatory agencies, enforcement has not been optimal.

Cracks in the Mortar

The Chinese government realized that simply creating an array of institutions was not enough—the bureaucracy must also function well, something especially difficult to achieve in developing societies. From poor interagency cooperation to a lack of resources and sheer logistical difficulties, troubles remained. Herein lies the crux of the problem for regulators and consumers in the United States and elsewhere when it comes to the quality of products imported from abroad. While China has established various regulatory agencies, enforcement has not been optimal. Regulatory authority is now fragmented among a multitude of government agencies—each mindful of its own turf and interests—that often fail to work together, especially at the local levels. . . . Failure among the regulators to coordinate and cooperate with each other is believed to have contributed to the deadly milk-powder scandal that came to light in 2004 [when melamine was added to foods to make them appear to have a higher protein content].

Making matters worse, the interests between central and local authorities often diverge. In particular, lower-level authorities may be more tolerant of counterfeiters and other dishonest businesses in their jurisdictions simply because these businesses generate employment and tax revenue. In the words of a *Business Week* reporting team: "Even if Beijing has the best intentions of fixing problems such as undrinkable water and unbreathable air, it is often thwarted by hundreds of thousands of party officials with vested interests in the current system."

Partly to mitigate such divergence, the Chinese government has in recent years promoted the hierarchical integration of regulatory administrations, especially within the provinces. But, as pessimists argue, "China has built a bureaucratic machine that at times seems almost impervious to reform."

China's sheer scale and vast regional disparities present major challenges, too. While the major cities can deploy more personnel, resources and technology to enhance regulatory supervision, this is far from the case in outlying areas, where many of the small businesses, including counterfeiters, are often located.

Last but certainly not least, corruption has plagued some of the regulatory agencies, both in the headquarters and in the localities. Under Zheng Xiaoyu, the former head of the SFDA [State Food and Drug Administration], and his close associates, some pharmaceutical companies were able to obtain a large number of new drug approvals by submitting fake data and bribe money. Zheng was executed for bribe taking and dereliction of duty in 2007.

A history of Chinese regulatory developments in the reform era is thus one about the struggle to curb regulatory corruption and deal with and overcome various institutional flaws. As China's regulatory agencies contend with internal conflicts and cope with external pressures, are we sure they'll be able to effectively address their product-safety and quality problems? . . .

Chinese officials openly express their annoyance at Western media reports they feel exaggerate the magnitude of China's product-safety problems.

Building Better

Sometimes a strong party-state is a very good thing. The successful corrective measures with respect to aviation safety and antidoping in international sports are undoubtedly encouraging. China is able to comply with international rules and norms. Recognizing that China's reputation was at stake, China's leaders took on serious reforms and tough regulatory actions. Unlike in many other developing countries, China, with its Communist Party, has the capacity to get things done when it matters.

Efforts to overcome corruption and cheating in the wake of opening up the Chinese market solved some problems, but created others. Though Chinese officials openly express their annoyance at Western media reports they feel exaggerate the magnitude of China's product-safety problems, they do realize that the reputation of "Made in China" is imperiled— and they care. As Vice Premier Wu Yi noted, bad press had caused "serious damage to China's national image." The government saw the writing on the wall and has taken a new wave of steps to improve watchdogging.

To help fix the problems plaguing regulatory agencies, like fragmentation and poor policy coordination, the State Council established a leading group on product quality and food safety in 2007. The leading group, headed by Vice Premier Wu Yi, is comprised of representatives from fifteen government agencies. And the Chinese government is putting muscle into policy implementation. Building on its long-standing efforts to improve market order, the Chinese government launched a nationwide campaign in August 2007 to investigate and fight the manufacture and sale of fake or substandard food, medicine and agricultural products. By October, the Chinese government had arrested 774 people in the crackdown. As of late November 2007, authorities had also closed down nearly eight thousand slaughterhouses for operating without licenses or for failing to meet government standards. For toy manufacturers blamed for producing toxic products, the Chinese government has suspended their export licenses— the kiss of death for an export business. Foshan Lee Der Toy Co., one of the first to be blamed for Mattel toys containing lead, was shut down. The owner committed suicide.

But most importantly, the Chinese are upgrading quality standards in all areas, from food to pharmaceuticals. They're taking proactive measures to strengthen the monitoring and supervision of production and supply chains for food and manufactures, including implementing monitoring and

inspection programs for wholesale farm-produce markets in all major cities, introducing recall mechanisms for food and more rigorously testing the quality of export products at the border.

In spite of the domestic campaign and crackdown, it is simply impossible for Chinese regulators to achieve full compliance in the domestic market in a short time period. There are hundreds of thousands of firms and families involved in producing food and manufactures. So, the focus of governmental action is, in the words of Wu Yi, "to strengthen the system of supervision and control over product quality, especially relating to *exports.*" This means that, while there will be general improvement, the improvement in the domestic market will likely lag behind that of exports.

The United States and China have reached agreements to strengthen the quality of Chinese exports.

International Expectations

As with aviation-safety regulation and antidoping, the international pressure on China to improve product quality has been accompanied by international assistance. We can hope this collaboration will be as effective. On products ranging from preserved and pet foods and farm-raised fish to certain drugs, medical devices and toys, the United States and China have reached agreements to strengthen the quality of Chinese exports. Whereas previously, authorities would ignore the errant or unlicensed factories until after a product-quality problem had been uncovered, the agreements signed during the Third U.S.-China Strategic [and] Economic Dialogue in December 2007 require Chinese exporters to register with the government and accept inspections to ensure compliance with American standards. This is clearly designed to mitigate counterfeiting and safety problems before the products even leave China.

Western buyers, mindful of the high costs of safety-related recalls, have become more demanding when it comes to quality and safety.

Also as part of the agreements, and as an indication of the growing interdependence between the Chinese and American economies, Beijing has allowed U.S. inspectors to become "embedded" in China to monitor the quality standards of certain Chinese export products, ensuring they meet U.S. quality standards. Stationing U.S. FDA [Food and Drug Administration] personnel abroad helps bridge different regulatory systems. This kind of cooperation is a nascent but significant step toward deep regulatory integration and may also be replicated in other countries. All this highlights the disparity between American and developing-world standards.

Meanwhile, even without the major Chinese government initiatives, the massive recalls would have caused businesses on both sides of the Pacific to modify their behavior. Western buyers, mindful of the high costs of safety-related recalls, have become more demanding when it comes to quality and safety. On the other side, many Chinese manufacturers quickly adopted more rigorous testing and tightened quality standards to keep the orders coming in. Those unable to bear the rising costs and risks have simply exited the market.

It's unlikely that government regulation will be fully effective in the Chinese domestic market, if for no other reason than the sheer number of

businesses that need to be regulated. But when it comes to Chinese exports to developed markets, the message is clear: Beijing will ensure products destined for American markets meet U.S. standards. As Wu Yi said, "China will live up to its responsibilities and obligations when it comes to product quality and food safety." Both government initiatives and market forces will point the way. After all, China's reputation is at stake.

Analyze this Reading

1. According to the writer, what is motivating Chinese manufacturers to compromise product safety? What is the "post-communist personality" the writer attributes to Chinese manufacturers?
2. What have been the effects of the Chinese government's efforts to regulate product quality and safety?
3. What agreements were reached during the Third U.S.–China Strategic Economic Dialogue in December 2007?
4. Why is there a disparity between China's regulation of products destined for export and those produced for internal consumption?
5. A clear strength of this writing is the writer's ability to surround his ideas with broad historical context. Point to 2-3 paragraphs where this broad context occurs.

Respond to this Reading

1. Recalls of products made in China, the United States, and other countries occur because quality and safety are compromised. What values, attitudes, and principles are in play when products are recalled with regard to the parties involved—consumers, manufacturers, and governments?
2. As a consumer, what concerns have you experienced with product safety and quality? How have you responded?
3. Imagine that you are presiding over a meeting of local manufacturers and consumer groups who have been convened to discuss product quality and safety in your community. What goals would you articulate at the beginning of the meeting?

Anthology 7
Concerned Citizen Community

ABOUT THIS READING

This argument is authored by Harry Binswanger, professor of philosophy at the Ayn Rand Institute. In this reading, the author argues that an open immigration system should replace a quota system and takes on the thorny issues of government infringing on individual rights, immigrants stealing jobs from native workers, and the role of immigrants in creating wealth for a country. It originally appeared in *Capitalism Magazine*.

The United States Should Adopt Open Immigration

By Harry Binswanger

This is a defense of phasing-in open immigration into the United States. Entry into the U.S. should ultimately be free for any foreigner, with the exception of criminals, would-be terrorists, and those carrying infectious diseases. (And note: I am defending freedom of entry and residency, not the automatic granting of U.S. citizenship.)

An end to immigration quotas is demanded by the principle of individual rights. Every individual has rights as an individual, not as a member of this or that nation. One has rights not by virtue of being an American, but by virtue of being human.

One doesn't have to be a resident of any particular country to have a moral entitlement to be secure from governmental coercion against one's life, liberty, and property. In the words of the Declaration of Independence, government is instituted "to secure these rights" — to protect them against their violation by force or fraud.

A foreigner has rights just as much as an American. To be a foreigner is not to be a criminal. Yet our government treats as criminals those foreigners not lucky enough to win the green-card lottery.

Quotas Treat Immigrants as Criminals

Seeking employment in this country is not a criminal act. It coerces no one and violates no one's rights (there is no "right" to be exempt from competition in the labor market, or in any other market).

It is not a criminal act to buy or rent a home here in which to reside. Paying for housing is not a coercive act — whether the buyer is an American or a foreigner. No one's rights are violated when a Mexican, or Canadian, or Senegalese rents an apartment from an American owner and moves into the housing he is paying for. And what about the rights of those American citizens who want to sell or rent their property to the highest bidders? Or the American businesses that want to hire the lowest cost workers? It is morally indefensible for our government to violate their right to do so, just because the person is a foreigner.

iStock.com/A-digit

Immigration quotas forcibly exclude foreigners who want not to seize but to purchase housing here, who want not to rob Americans but to engage in productive work, raising our standard of living. To forcibly exclude those who seek peacefully to trade value for value with us is a violation of the rights of both parties to such a trade: the rights of the American seller or employer and the rights of the foreign buyer or employee.

Thus, immigration quotas treat both Americans and foreigners as if they were criminals, as if the peaceful exchange of values to mutual benefit were an act of destruction.

The Rights of the Individual Above All

To take an actual example, if I want to invite my Norwegian friend Klaus to live in my home, either as a guest or as a paying tenant, what right does our government have to stop Klaus and me? To be a Norwegian is not to be a criminal. And if some American business wants to hire Klaus, what right does our government have to interfere?

The implicit premise of barring foreigners is: "This is our country, we let in who we want." But who is "we"? The government does not own the country. Jurisdiction is not ownership. Only the owner of land or any item of property can decide the terms of its use or sale. Nor does the majority own the country. This is a country of private property, and housing is private property. So is a job.

American land is not the collective property of some entity called "the U.S. government." Nor is there such thing as collective, social ownership of the land. The claim, "We have the right to decide who is allowed in" means some individuals—those with the most votes—claim the right to prevent other citizens from exercising their rights. But there can be no right to violate the rights of others.

Our constitutional republic respects minority rights. Sixty percent of the population cannot vote to enslave the other 40 percent. Nor can a majority dictate to the owners of private property. Nor can a majority dictate on whom private employers spend their money. Not morally, not in a free society. In a free society, the rights of the individual are held sacrosanct, above any claim of even an overwhelming majority.

The rights of one man end where the rights of his neighbor begin. Only within the limits of his rights is a man free to act on his own judgment. The criminal is the man who deliberately steps outside his rights-protected domain and invades the domain of another, depriving his victim of his exclusive control over his property, or liberty, or life. The criminal, by his own choice, has rejected rights in favor of brute violence. Thus, an immigration policy that excludes criminals is proper.

Likewise, a person with an infectious disease, such as smallpox, threatens with serious physical harm those with whom he comes into proximity. Unlike the criminal, he may not intend to do damage, but the threat of physical harm is clear, present, and objectively demonstrable. To protect the lives of Americans, he may be kept out or quarantined until he is no longer a threat.

But what about the millions of Mexicans, South Americans, Chinese, Canadians, etc., seeking entry who are not criminal and not bearing infectious diseases? By what moral principle can they be excluded? Not on the

grounds of majority vote, not on the grounds of protecting any American's rights, not on the grounds of any legitimate authority of the state.

Understanding the Nature of Rights

That's the moral case for phasing out limits on immigration. But some ask: "Is it practical? Wouldn't unlimited immigration—even if phased in over a decade—be disastrous to our economic well-being and create overcrowding? Are we being told to just grit our teeth and surrender our interests in the name of morality?"

This question is invalid on its face. It shows a failure to understand the nature of rights, and of moral principles generally. Rational moral principles reflect a recognition of the basic nature of man, his nature as a specific kind of living organism, having a specific means of survival. Questions of what is practical, what is to one's self-interest, can be answered only in that context. It is neither practical nor to one's interest to attempt to live and act in defiance of one's nature as a human being.

Yet that is the meaning of the moral-practical dichotomy. When one claims, "It is immoral but practical," one is maintaining, "It cripples my nature as a human being, but it is beneficial to me"—which is a contradiction.

Rights, in particular, are not something pulled from the sky or decreed by societal whim. Rights are moral principles, established by reference to the needs inherent in man's nature qua man. "Rights are conditions of existence required by man's nature for his proper survival." ([philosopher and author] Ayn Rand)

Every organism has a basic means of survival; for man, that means is: reason. Man is the rational animal, *homo sapiens*. Rights are moral principles that spell out the terms of social interaction required for a rational being to survive and flourish. Since the reasoning mind cannot function under physical coercion, the basic social requirement of man's survival is: freedom. Rights prescribe freedom by proscribing coercion.

"If man is to live on earth, it is right for him to use his mind, it is right to act on his own free judgment, it is right to work for his values and to keep the product of his work." (Ayn Rand)

Rights reflect the fundamental alternative of voluntary consent or brute force. The reign of force is in no one's interest; the system of voluntary cooperation by mutual consent is the precondition of anyone achieving his actual interests. . . .

Work Is Limitless

One major fear of open immigration is economic: the fear of losing one's job to immigrants. It is asked: "Won't the immigrants take our jobs?" The answer is: "Yes, so we can go on to better, higher-paying jobs."

The fallacy in this protectionist objection lies in the idea that there is only a finite amount of work to be done. The unstated assumption is: "If Americans don't get to do that work, if foreigners do it instead, we Americans will have nothing to do."

But work is the creation of wealth. A job is a role in the production of goods and services—the production of food, of cars, computers, the providing of

Internet content—all the items that go to make up our standard of living. A country cannot have too much wealth. The need for wealth is limitless, and the work that is to be done is limitless. . . .

Unemployment is not caused by an absence of avenues for the creation of wealth. Unemployment is caused by government interference in the labor market. Even with that interference, the number of jobs goes relentlessly upward, decade after decade. This bears witness to the fact that there's no end to the creation of wealth and thus no end to the useful employment of human intelligence and the physical effort directed by that intelligence. There is always more productive work to be done. If you can give your job to an immigrant, you can get a more valuable job.

What is the effect of a bigger labor pool on wage rates? If the money supply is constant, nominal wage rates fall. But real wage rates rise because total output has gone up. Economists have demonstrated that real wages have to rise as long as the immigrants are self-supporting. If immigrants earn their keep, if they don't consume more than they produce, then they add to total output, which means that prices fall (if the money supply is constant).

And, in fact, rising real wages was the history of our country in the nineteenth century. Before the 1920s, there were no limits on immigration, yet our standard of living rocketed upward. Self-supporting immigrants were an economic benefit not an injury.

The protectionist objection that immigrants take away jobs and harm our standard of living is a solid economic fallacy.

Welfare and Overcrowding Concerns

A popular misconception is that immigrants come here to get welfare. To the extent that is true, immigrants do constitute a burden. But this issue is mooted by the passage, under the [Bill] Clinton Administration, of the Personal Responsibility and Work Opportunity and Reconciliation Act (PRWORA), which makes legal permanent residents ineligible for most forms of welfare for five years. I support this kind of legislation.

Further, if the fear is of non-working immigrants, why is the pending legislation aimed at employers of immigrants?

America is a vastly underpopulated country. Our population density is less than one-third of France's.

Take an extreme example. Suppose a tidal wave of immigrants came here. Suppose that half of the people on the planet moved here. That would mean an unthinkable 11-fold increase in our population—from 300 million to 3.3 billion people. That would make America almost as "densely" populated as today's England (360 people/sq km vs. 384 people/sq km). In fact, it would make us less densely populated than the state of New Jersey (453 per sq km). And these calculations exclude Alaska and Hawaii, and count only land area.

Contrary to widespread beliefs, high population density is a value not a disvalue. High population density intensifies the division of labor, which makes possible a wider variety of jobs and specialized consumer products. For instance, in Manhattan, there is a "doll hospital"—a store specializing in the repair of children's dolls. Such a specialized, niche business requires

a high population density in order to have a market. Try finding a doll hospital in Poughkeepsie. In Manhattan, one can find a job as a Pilates Method teacher or as a "Secret Shopper" (two jobs actually listed on Craig's List [www.craigslist.org]). Not in Paducah.

People want to live near other people, in cities. One-seventh of England's population lives in London. If population density is a bad thing, why are Manhattan real-estate prices so high?

The Value of Immigrants

Immigrants are the kind of people who refresh the American spirit. They are ambitious, courageous, and value freedom. They come here, often with no money and not even speaking the language, to seek a better life for themselves and their children.

The vision of American freedom, with its opportunity to prosper by hard work, serves as a magnet drawing the best of the world's people. Immigrants are self-selected for their virtues: their ambitiousness, daring, independence, and pride. They are willing to cast aside the tradition-bound roles assigned to them in their native lands and to redefine themselves as Americans. These are the people America needs in order to keep alive the individualist, hard-working attitude that made America.

Here is a short list of some great immigrants: Alexander Hamilton, Alexander Graham Bell, Andrew Carnegie, most of the top scientists of the Manhattan Project, Igor Sikorsky (the inventor of the helicopter), Ayn Rand.

Open immigration: the benefits are great. The right is unquestionable. So let them come.

Analyze this Reading

1. What does the writer claim, and what qualifiers does he attach to his claim?
2. On what value or principle is the claim based?
3. On what grounds does the writer support his contention that quotas treat immigrants like criminals?
4. In paragraphs 9 through 15, the writer makes a moral case for phasing out limits on immigration. Describe this moral case.
5. What objections, or rebuttals, to his argument does the writer anticipate? How does he counter them?
6. This argument concludes with attention to the value of immigrants. How are immigrants valuable?

Respond to this Reading

1. Do you agree with the writer's position on open immigration? Explain.
2. Issues that fall under the topic of immigration are numerous. What immigration issues are current in your community? Describe a recent conversation you had about immigration.
3. What single immigration issue motivates you to argue? What would you claim, and what kinds of support would you bring to your argument?

4. The writer grounds his argument in values of rights, individuality, and property. What values would motivate you to argue on an immigration issue?

ABOUT THIS READING

This reading appeared in writer James L. Dickerson's book, *Yellow Fever: A Deadly Disease Poised to Kill Again.* Dickerson is a former social worker who has authored numerous books and articles on health issues.

Climate Change Could Cause Disease Resurgence

By James L. Dickerson

A 2002 study conducted by researchers at Princeton University and Cornell University concluded that climate warming is allowing disease-carrying viruses such as yellow fever to invade North America. As a result, the researchers warn that yellow fever and other related diseases could become more common as milder winters allow the seasonal survival of more mosquitoes. A warmer climate also could enable mosquitoes to move into areas once protected by cold weather. "In all the discussion about climate change, this has really been kind of left out," said Drew Harvell, a Cornell University marine ecologist and lead author of the study. "Just a one-or-two-degree change in temperature can lead to disease outbreaks."

An Alarming Increase of Disease

The comprehensive two-year study, developed by the National Center for Ecological Analysis and Synthesis, is the first to look at disease in terms of global warming. Said Harvell: "What is most surprising is the fact that climate sensitive outbreaks are happening with so many different types of pathogens—viruses, bacteria, fungi and parasites—as well as in such a wide range of hosts, including corals, oysters, terrestrial plants, birds and humans." Added coauthor Richard Ostfeld, from the Institute of Ecosystem Studies in Millbrook, New York: "This isn't just a question of coral bleaching for a few marine ecologists, nor just a question of malaria for a few health officials—the number of similar increases in disease incidence is astonishing. We don't want to be alarmist, but we are alarmed." Andrew Dobson, a Princeton epidemiologist associated with the study, says the risk for humans is going up: "The diseases we should be most worried about are the vector [insect] transmitted diseases." Even with small temperature increases, he concludes, natural ecosystems are disrupted in such a way as to create more fertile habitats for infectious diseases such a malaria and yellow fever.

Among those individuals not convinced that global warming will bring diseases such as yellow fever into the United States is the CDC's [Centers for Disease Control and Prevention's] Ned Hayes, which, according to one's point of view, is either comforting or highly disturbing. Hayes thinks that a yellow fever epidemic caused by global warming, as opposed to one

caused by terrorists, has little chance of getting a foothold in the United States because of the country's high socioeconomic level and because of the prevalence of window screens and air conditioning. . . .

Not in agreement with Hayes are the researchers who conducted a 1998 study funded by the Climate Policy and Assessment Division of the EPA [Environmental Protection Agency], the National Institute of Public Health, and the Center for Medical, Agricultural, and Veterinary Entomology of the U.S. Department of Agriculture. Using computers to simulate the circulation of the earth's climate, the researchers predicted that rising temperatures will increase the range of a mosquito that transmits the dengue fever virus. All three computer models used by the researchers indicated that dengue's epidemic potential increases with a relatively small temperature rise. At risk are the United States and all other countries around the world that are located in temperate zones, especially those that border on endemic areas where the disease is currently prevalent. "Since inhabitants of these border regions would lack immunity from past exposures, dengue fever transmission among these new populations could be extensive," says Jonathan Patz, lead author for the report and a physician at Johns Hopkins School of Public Health. "Our study makes no claim that climate factors are the most important determinants of dengue fever. However, our computer models illustrate that climate change may have a substantial global impact on the spread of dengue fever."

Global Warming and Mosquitoes

Perhaps the best method of determining the effect of global warming on yellow fever is to examine the effect that warmer temperatures are having on related mosquito-borne diseases such as dengue, malaria, West Nile fever, and encephalitis. If they show signs of increased incidence, then it is only a matter of time before the yellow fever virus makes its reappearance.

Paul R. Epstein, associate director of the Center for Health and the Global Environment at Harvard, feels that those diseases are going to become more prevalent because of the mosquito's sensitivity to meteorological conditions. "Cold can be a friend to humans," he writes, "because it limits mosquitoes to seasons and regions where temperatures stay above certain minimums. Winter freezing kills many eggs, larvae and adults outright . . . within their survivable range of temperatures, mosquitoes proliferate faster and bite more as the air becomes warmer. At the same time, greater heat speeds the rate at which pathogens inside them reproduce and mature. . . . As whole areas heat up, then, mosquitoes could expand into formerly forbidden territories, bringing illness with them."

West Nile Virus

One of the most disturbing developments in recent years has been the arrival of the West Nile virus. In August 1999, tissue samples from a dead crow found in the New York City area and from a horse that died of a central nervous system disease on Long Island, New York, were sent to the National Veterinary Services Laboratories in Ames, Iowa, for identification. Meanwhile, more than two dozen cases of suspicious equine illness were identified in Suffolk and Nassau Counties on Long Island.

By September, the Centers for Disease Control and Prevention was able to identify the infected tissue samples as hosts to West Nile virus, a disease first isolated in 1937 in Africa and the Middle East. It is closely related to St. Louis encephalitis, which is indigenous to the United States and Canada, but, as of August 1999, West Nile virus had never been isolated in tissue samples in North America.

Accompanying the deaths of dozens of horses and thousands of birds in the New York City area was an outbreak of human encephalitis that baffled health officials because it appeared to be a new strain. As the human death toll rose, genetic sequencing studies revealed that humans, birds, and horses were all infected by the same strain of West Nile, one that showed strong similarities to isolates from the Middle East.

Almost right away, the disease, which is spread from animals to humans by mosquitoes, began moving from New York to New Jersey and Connecticut, where 83 cases of West Nile were reported within one year. By 2005 the disease had spread all the way to California, infecting humans in almost every state except Maine, Alaska, and Hawaii. At greatest risk are those people over 50 years of age.

"Yellow fever is transmitted from human to mosquito to human, but with West Nile the reservoir of infection is the birds and possibly some reptiles and you have a different dynamic—humans are sort of incidental," says Dr. Ned Hayes. "You don't get human to human transmission with West Nile. The disease has spread east to west, north to south, going to both Canada and Mexico, but we still don't know what's going to happen in the United States. It is possible it could continue to cause locally intense epidemics in certain parts of the country, and it's also possible it might take a course like St. Louis encephalitis, which flares up after years of dormancy."

Learning from Other Diseases

West Nile is of interest to yellow fever researchers because it demonstrates the speed with which a mosquito-induced disease can spread from state to state within a relatively brief period. Since West Nile can be spread only from animal to human, it is a friendlier disease, epidemically speaking, than yellow fever, which can spread with lightning speed from mosquito to human to mosquito to human. For those concerned about the reemergence of yellow fever in the United States, West Nile's unhindered march across the heartland offers little in the way of comfort.

Malaria is another mosquito-related disease that is raising red flags. Each year the disease kills more than 3,000 people, mostly children. Some scientists predict that, by the end of [the 21st] century, the zone of malaria transmission will increase from one containing 45 percent of the world's population to one containing 60 percent. Malaria has a long history in the United States, but public health measures throughout the country were successful in isolating the disease and restricting it to California by the 1980s. As temperatures have risen since then, the threat has increased the incidence of malaria. In recent years, outbreaks have occurred in Florida, Texas, Georgia, Michigan, New Jersey, New York, and, to the surprise of many, Toronto, Canada.

Similarly, St. Louis encephalitis, a flavivirus related to Japanese enceph-alitis, has shown gains in recent years, with record spikes in the 1990s, which, incidentally, were the hottest years of this century. In the summer of 1999, New York City experienced an outbreak of encephalitis that killed a number of people. Normally, encephalitis, which causes inflammation of the brain, can effectively be treated, but the survival odds are lessened for those with weakened immune systems or for senior citizens.

At the time of the New York outbreak, Dr. Cathey Falvo, director for International and Public Health at New York Medical College, was concerned whether the increased temperatures would allow the disease to survive the winter. Falvo was particularly concerned about the effect that global warm-ing was having on increased incidence of the disease. If global warming continues on its present course, she said, milder winters will result that will not be cold enough to kill the microbes, thus allowing the organisms to still be around when mosquitoes again become active in the spring.

Analyze this Reading

1. What did researchers at Princeton and Cornell find in their study of climate change and disease? Are other researchers the writer refers to in agreement with these findings? Explain.
2. In the writer's view, why are warm temperatures a concern regarding mosquitoes and disease pathogens?
3. In addition to yellow fever, what other diseases does the writer dis-cuss that could become threats in the United States due to warmer temperatures?
4. The writer has limited support of his claim to factual and statistical information and the testimony of experts. Given the issue he's working with, in your view is this a practical strategy, or should the writer have broadened the kinds of support he uses?

Respond to this Reading

1. Discuss why the writer is or is not convincing in the connections he suggests between temperature and disease.
2. In mainstream treatments, climate change and global warming have been discussed chiefly in terms of CO_2 emissions and sea level rise. In addition to the potential for disease outbreak mentioned by the writer, are there other areas of life you believe would be affected?
3. What attitudes to climate change do you encounter in your classes and in your community? What issues within this topic would motivate you to argue?

ABOUT THIS READING

When this argument was published, writer David Howard was a third-year law stu-dent at the University of Texas School of Law. The argument appeared in *Harvard Law and Policy Review*, the official law review of the American Constitution Society for Law and Policy, whose mission is to publish new ideas for connecting law with domestic policy in America.

Automatic Voter Registration: A Rational Solution to an Irrational Problem

By David Howard

Automatic Voter Registration

Voting "is a fundamental matter in a free and democratic society [because it] is preservative of other basic civil and political rights."[1] But before one can vote, that person must first register with the state, often weeks before the election. Voter registration continues to be a contentious issue in the United States, and the current system in many states presents significantly more problems than solutions.

Article I, Section 4 of the Constitution gives the states substantial authority over electoral procedures. As a result, the states have implemented a wide array of varying electoral procedures, making a person's voting rights depend—to a significant degree—on their state of residence.[2] In the past two years, Oregon, California, Vermont, West Virginia, Connecticut, and Alaska have all passed some version of automatic voter registration,[3] while Illinois and New Jersey rejected similar bills in their state legislatures. And there are still many states with antiquated voter registration processes, some of which were specifically designed for the purpose of disenfranchisement.

At one time, voter registration was relatively "straightforward: it would help to eliminate fraud and also bring an end to disruptive election-day conflicts at the polls."[4] Today, some claim voter registration is still necessary, arguing the current lax standards "breeds mistrust and can call the integrity of the whole system into question."[5] This—arguably pretextual—focus on voter fraud filled the airwaves throughout the weeks leading up to the presidential election, and it continues to attract attention, even though the existence of widespread voter fraud has been repeatedly discredited.[6] In fact, there was virtually no evidence of voter fraud this election, except for a women in Iowa voting twice in person for Donald Trump, ironically because she believed the vote was "rigged."[7] Professor Lorraine Minnite put it best: "The claim that voter fraud threatens the integrity of the American election is itself a fraud."[8]

1. Reynolds v. Sims, 377 U.S. 533, 561–62 (1964).
2. Brooke Lierman, *Election Day Registration: Giving All Americans A Fair Chance to Vote*, 2 Harv. L. & Pol'y Rev. 173 (2008).
3. *Automatic Voter Registration*, Nat. Con. of State Leg. (November 29, 2016), http://www.ncsl.org /research/elections-and- campaigns/automatic-voter-registration.aspx.
4. Alexander Keyssar, The Right to Vote: The Contested History of Democracy in the United States 152.
5. John Fund, Stealing Elections: How Voter Fraud Threatens our Democracy 25 (2004).
6. *See, e.g.,* Sami Edge, *No, voter fraud actually isn't a persistent problem*, Wash. Post (September 1, 2016), https://www.washingtonpost.com/news/post-nation/wp/2016/09/01/voter-fraud-is-not-a-persistent -problem/? utm_term=.42b194533f8c; Associated Press, *Studies Contradict Trump Claim That Voter Fraud Is 'Very, Very Common'*, Fortune (October 18, 2016), http://fortune.com/2016/10/18/studies -contradict-trump-claim-that-voter-fraud-is-very-very-common/.
7. Amy Wang, *Trump Supporter Charged with Voting Twice in Iowa*, Wash. Post (October 29, 2016, 10:50 AM),
8. Lorraine C. Minnite, The Politics of Voter Fraud 5 (2007), www.projectvote.org/wp-content/uploads /2007/03/Politics_of_Voter_Fraud_Final.pdf.

Some legal scholars have gone so far as to suggest that allegations of "voter fraud [are] used as a pretext for a broader agenda to disenfranchise Americans and rig elections."[9] For example, the Voter Registrar for Harris County, Texas has in the past deployed resources to purge the voter rolls of people who are believed to be deceased or have not voted in several elections, yet many of these people were actually still alive.[10] There have even been numerous allegations of voter intimidation in Texas, including attempts to prevent voters from registering.[11]

In sum, there continues to be substantial voter suppression—and negligible voter fraud—in many states. This purposeful suppression of the fundamental right to vote is simply un-American, and states should uniformly adopt automatic voter registration to correct this deeply anti-democratic trend.

Why Should All States Adopt This Process?

On Election Day, many Americans either cannot vote because they were unable to register within the required time, or they find their names wrongfully deleted from the voter rolls.[12] The best way to prevent any claim of "voter fraud" and to prevent further barriers to voting is to have the state register eligible voters itself, by passing automatic voter registration reform in each state. Rather than using extensive regulatory efforts and trying to prevent alleged fraudulent voter registration through third parties, states should register every eligible citizen to vote. This process would decrease the chance of third parties affecting the voter registration system while allowing the voter registration system to actually work the way it was intended.[13]

According to the Pew Center on the States: (1) one in four eligible citizens is not registered to vote; (2) one in eight voter registrations in the United States is invalid or significantly inaccurate; and (3) one in four voters wrongly believes their voter registration is automatically updated when they change their address with the Postal Service.[14] This alone causes extensive problems in our electoral system, as eligible voters must register to vote before even casting a ballot.

9. David Schultz, *Less than Fundamental: The Myth of Voter Fraud and the Coming of the Second Great Disenfranchisement*, 34 Wm. Mitchell L. Rev. 483, 486 (2008).

10. Wade Goodwyn, *Many Texans Bereaved Over 'Dead' Voter Purge*, NPR (September 16, 2012), http://www.npr.org/2012/09/16/161145248/many-texans-bereaved-over-dead-voter-purge; Cindy George, *Dispute over 'dead' voters in Harris County is finally resolved*, Houston Chron (September 20, 2012), http://www.chron.com/news/houston-texas/article/Dispute-resolved-over-dead-voter-issue-3879081.php; Lise Olsen, *Texas' voter purge made repeated errors*, Houst. Chron. (November 2, 2012), http://www.chron.com/news/politics/article/Texas-voter-purge-made-repeated-errors-4001767.php.

11. Dale Ho, *The Voter Fraud We Can't Shake*, N.Y. Times (November 3, 2016), http://www.nytimes.com/2016/11/04/opinion/the-strange-career-of-the-voter-fraud-myth.html.

12. *See* Lise Olsen, *Texas' Voter Purge Made Repeated Errors*, Hous. Chron. (November 1, 2012), http://www.chron.com/news/politics/article/Texas-voter-purge-made-repeated-errors-4001767.php; Greg Palast, *The GOP's Stealth War Against Voters*, Rolling Stone (August 24, 2016), http://www.rollingstone.com/politics/features/the-gops-stealth-war-against-voters-w435890.

13. *See* Spencer Overton, Stealing Democracy: The New Politics of Voter Suppression 166 (2006).

14. Pew Center on the States, Inaccurate, Costly, and Inefficient: Evidence that America's Voter Registration System Needs an Upgrade 4-5 (2012), http://www.pewtrusts.org/~/media/legacy/uploadedfiles/pcs_assets/2012/PewUpgradingVoterRegistrationpdf.pdf.

Another practical reason for adopting automatic voter registration—one many states should appreciate—follows from the costs of voter registration reformation. Before the automatic voter registration reform in Oregon, a Pew Center study found Oregon's previous paper-based voter registration system cost the state $7.67 per registration transaction or $4.11 per registered voter in 2008. In contrast, Canada uses modern electronic methods to register voters and spends only 35 cents per voter.[15] Not only would automatic voter and online registration increase access to the fundamental right to vote, but it would also save states a significant sum of money.

How Would Automatic Voter Registration Work?

There is a relatively simple solution that would allow virtually all eligible voters to cast a ballot while maintaining the integrity and accuracy of the voting system: the states must take responsibility for registering every eligible voter. Anytime a citizen came into contact with a state governmental agency, they would be automatically registered through that government agency, and valid voter registration—like citizenship—would eventually become more of an assumption than an aspiration. Automatic voter registration would create two institutional changes to voter registration: (1) eligible citizens would be registered to vote when contacting any government agency unless that person specifically declines, and (2) those departmental agencies would provide the voter-registration information electronically to state election officials. The Brennan Center for Justice at N.Y.U. argues convincingly that this reformation would "boost registration rates, clean up the rolls, save money, make voting more convenient, and reduce the potential for voter fraud."[16] All while protecting the fundamental right—and civic duty—of every American citizen to vote.

As stated above, Oregon, California, Vermont, West Virginia, Connecticut, and Alaska have already passed some version of automatic voter registration, and similar reforms are being proposed in other states with increasing momentum.[17] In California, West Virginia, and Vermont, individuals are registered to vote when they appear at a state agency, and they are given the opportunity to decline registration when in contact with the state's motor vehicle agency. In Oregon, the election agency mails the eligible voter a registration-notification card after their contact with the state motor vehicle agency, and the voter is assigned a "pending" status for 21 days, during which they have the opportunity to decline registration, and if they do nothing, they are automatically registered to vote.[18] Legislatures in both Illinois and New Jersey passed this voting reform, but Governors Rauner

15. Brennan Center for Justice, The Case for Automatic Voter Registration 5 (2016), https://www
    .brennancenter.org/sites/default/files/publications/Case_for_Automatic_Voter_Registration.pdf.
16. *Automatic Voter Registration*, Brennan Center for Justice (September 22, 2016), https://www
    .brennancenter.org/analysis/automatic- voter-registration.
17. *Automatic Voter Registration*, Nat. Con. of State Leg. (November 29, 2016), http://www.ncsl.org
    /research/elections-and-campaigns/automatic-voter-registration.aspx.
18. *Id.*

and Christie vetoed these bills. There have been several national bills proposed in Congress, and a list of the bills introduced has been compiled by the Brennan Center for Justice.[19]

Conclusion

Automatic voter registration will prevent the disenfranchisement of millions of eligible voters, while continuing to protect the integrity of, and trust in, the voting system. Simply put, the states need to take responsibility for registering all eligible voters, by having a state agency transfer all necessary voter registration information to the state's election agency when a citizen comes in contact with a state agency. All states must pass this type of voter registration reform if our electoral system is to maintain its integrity because preventing millions of eligible voters from casting a ballot on the baseless claims of preventing alleged voter fraud does tremendous and irreparable harm to the integrity of our country's elections. This reform would be an important first step toward increasing voter participation in elections, and it will create more accurate voter rolls, reduce the costs on the states, and protect election integrity. It is a simple solution to a complex problem, and one that is desperately needed today.

Analyze this Reading

1. What points does the writer make about voter fraud?
2. What does the writer claim?
3. Identify the reasons used to support the claim? What kind of support anchors each reason?
4. According to the writer's plan, who would take responsibility for maintaining an automatic voter registration system (AVR)? Describe how AVR would differ from traditional voter registration.

Respond to this Reading

1. In your view, what is the writer's warrant, that is, what motivates him to build his argument?
2. Do you favor AVR? Why or why not?
3. In his conclusion, the writer repeatedly uses the word "integrity" to remind citizens of the importance of this issue. Identify other issues common to American citizens that are in need of reform in order to maintain their integrity.

ABOUT THIS READING

When this reading was published, writer David Kelley was director of the Institute for Objectivist Studies, renamed "The Atlas Society" in 2004, an organization devoted to the principles of Ayn Rand, champion of individualism and capitalism. This reading is excerpted from Kelley's book, *A Life of One's Own: Individual Rights and the Welfare State.*

---

19. For the list of bills introduced, see https://www.brennancenter.org/analysis/automatic-voter-registration.

Private Charity Should Replace Welfare

By David Kelley

Charity is the effort to help those in need. But need varies. Sometimes it is brief but intense, the product of an emergency like a hurricane or fire, and the victims need only temporary support to restore their normal, self-supporting lives. Other people are in need as a result of longer term mental or physical disabilities, and a longer term investment is necessary if they are to realize whatever potential they can. Need can arise from sheer bad luck, from factors truly outside the person's control; emergencies are once again the obvious example. At the other extreme, the straitened circumstances in which some people live are entirely their own doing, the result of abandoning responsibility for their lives. Most cases fall in between the extremes; poverty is the result of bad luck and bad choices in various degrees. As Alexis de Tocqueville observed, "Nothing is so difficult to distinguish as the nuances which separate unmerited misfortune from an adversity produced by vice. How many miseries are simultaneously the result of both these causes!"

For that reason, effective charity requires discrimination among cases and the use of measures adapted to the circumstances of the people one is trying to help. This was a central theme of 19th-century philanthropy. Relief workers in that era, especially in America, generally opposed government charity, like the British Poor Law, because it encouraged idleness, teaching the populace that income was possible without work. "Gratuitous aid," wrote New York charity worker John Griscom, produces a "relaxation of concern on the part of the poor to depend on their own foresight and industry." Many of the settlement houses and missions had "work tests"—men were expected to chop wood, women to sew, before they received meals or lodging—as a way of distinguishing freeloaders from people willing to take responsibility for themselves.

Governments find it extremely difficult to draw such distinctions. They simply provide benefits amounting to an alternative way of life for those at the bottom of the economic ladder, with no regard for merit and little regard for circumstance. Though welfare benefits hardly provide a comfortable existence, and benefit levels in some programs such as Aid to Families with Dependent Children (AFDC) had declined in real terms, the package of benefits in many states was more attractive than entry-level work. . . .

None of this is to say that a life on welfare is attractive. The welfare system is demeaning. It imposes on recipients every roadblock and indignity the bureaucratic mind can conceive. The problem is that both the benefits and the drawbacks fall upon the worthy and the unworthy alike. Government programs are unable to draw the distinctions necessary for effective charity because of four factors inherent in their nature as government programs:

1. If welfare is provided by the government in a modern liberal society, it must be construed as a right; it cannot depend on the personal virtues or vices of recipients or their willingness to take responsibility for themselves.

2. Since the state is the agency of coercion, its actions must be governed by the rule of law. Government bureaucrats cannot be given discretionary power to discriminate among recipients on the basis of personal morality or psychology.

3. As the agency of coercion, the government of a free country must also refrain from intruding into the personal dimensions of life, and this precludes the kind of active involvement often required for effective help.

4. Because government programs are bureaucratic and subject to the political process, they cannot have the flexibility to adapt to change, the spirit of innovation, and the diversity of approaches that private agencies have. . . .

Private agencies, by contrast, increasingly recognize the need to replace automatic help with contracts specifying terms that recipients must meet in order to receive help. This is especially true of shelters for the homeless, which deal with the toughest cases: many of the homeless are substance abusers who have been exploiting both public and private agencies—selling food stamps, getting free meals to conserve cash, and so forth—in order to obtain money for drugs and alcohol. At the Center for the Homeless in South Bend, Indiana, those seeking help must agree to abide by a strict set of rules; to receive any aid beyond the minimum, they must work with a case worker to create a plan for becoming self-sufficient. At Step 13 in Denver, those seeking shelter must agree to take Antabuse (a drug that causes sickness if one consumes alcohol) and submit to drug tests; and they can be expelled for disruptive behavior. Above and beyond the specific rationales for those rules, they convey the message that help is conditional, not an entitlement, and that irresponsibility will have consequences. . . .

To be sure, there are fads in private philanthropy, and there is waste. Some charities spend disproportionate amounts of money on fundraising, using the proceeds of one direct-mail campaign to pay for the next one. But there are published standards on fundraising costs that donors can use to compare the organizations soliciting their money, and the better charities far exceed those standards. Government programs, moreover, do not avoid the problem of a "patchwork of services" attributed to the private sector. Despite the existence of hundreds of government programs, some 40 percent of people living below the poverty line receive no government assistance.

Government programs are subject to the political process. Legislative majorities representing diverse interests and viewpoints must come to agreement before any change is possible. Social service bureaucracies are bound by administrative law, which requires complex rules and procedures for carrying out the legislature's intent. Diversity, flexibility, and innovation are the last things one could hope for under such conditions. As is the case with other enterprises run by government, service is slow and unresponsive to customers, wasteful, bureaucratic, and constantly influenced by political considerations. The problems with AFDC [Aid to Families with Dependent Children], for example, had been clear since the 1960s, and every administration since then had promised reform. But it took 30 years to get the first significant change in the program—the reforms of 1996—and even those are partial.

Private agencies, by contrast, can adapt more quickly to changing circumstances and to feedback about the success or failure of their efforts. They can adopt new ideas about how to provide aid most effectively without having to go through the federal budget process or being bound by administrative law. Because private agencies are separate and independent, each can go its own way, experimenting with new approaches without putting other agencies at risk; there is no need to find a single nationwide approach. The welfare reforms of 1996 gave states much more latitude to adopt different ways of providing benefits to the poor, and the states have already begun experimenting with some new approaches. But "the laboratory of democracy" provided by 50 states cannot compare with the experience to be gained through hundreds of thousands of private agencies, from local shelters and youth programs to nationwide charities.

In addition to the greater freedom that private agencies enjoy, they have a much greater incentive to look for solutions that work. Government programs are funded by taxes, and failure rarely results in a program's being cut; failure is more often used as an argument that more money is required. But a private agency must raise funds from donors who contribute voluntarily. Its donors are customers who want to see results and can take their money or their volunteer time elsewhere if an organization is not producing results.

In short, a private system of charity has all the advantages of a free market over government planning. It is now common knowledge that government planning does not work in the commercial realm. Why would we expect things to be different in the philanthropic realm?

The Promise of Private Aid

Despite the advantages of private over public programs for helping the poor, many people have expressed misgivings. One common argument among theorists is that charity must be government run because it is what economists call a "public good." If Person A wants to see Person B's poverty or suffering relieved, A can obtain that value if someone else helps B no less than if A helps B himself. This is one of the features of a public good: nonpayers aren't excluded from benefiting. Each of us thus has an incentive not to help the poor, in the expectation that others will help them, and if we all act on that incentive no help will be forthcoming. The only way out of that dilemma is collective provision, to which individuals are forced to contribute.

But it is irresponsible to want help given without any corresponding desire to help. Some people do behave that way, but not everyone; despite the logic of the public-goods argument, many people are moved by the countervailing logic of the old question: What if everyone did that? In 1995, for example, 68.5 percent of households contributed to charity, giving an average of $1,017. Nearly half the adult population (93 million people) did volunteer work. Volunteers in formal programs gave 15.7 billion hours, or the equivalent of 9.2 million full-time employees, with a value estimated at $201 billion. The poor, moreover, are not an indivisible pool of suffering that must be alleviated as a totality. It is individuals who are poor, and their plight usually makes the strongest claim on family members, neighbors, and others in the community who know them. A great deal of private

charity is local in nature. In helping a given person in my community, I may be conferring unintended value on other community members who know or encounter him, but not on an entire society. Those other community members, moreover, are more likely to know me and thus be in a position to exert social pressure on me to contribute.

But will private, voluntary giving be enough? That is the first question raised whenever the proposal to privatize charity is put forward. The large private charities are often the most vehement in opposing cutbacks in government spending—understandably, since most of them receive a major portion of their funding from government contracts. "Private charity is built on the foundation of government welfare," argues an official of Catholic Charities USA, which gets more than half its funds from government. "We can do what we do because Government provides the basic safety net."

Governments at all levels currently spend about $350 billion on means-tested programs. Charitable giving by individuals, foundations, and corporations came to $144 billion in 1995, but only about $12 billion of that was for human services; another $13 billion was for health, a category that includes some services for the poor. Offsetting this huge disparity is the fact that many people give much more in time, as volunteers, than in money. In the category of human services, the value of volunteer time came to about $17 billion in 1995. Americans also spent 4.6 billion hours doing informal volunteer work—caring for an elderly or disabled person, helping a neighbor—with a value of perhaps $50 billion.

Even so, by the most generous estimates, private giving for the relief of poverty is well under 30 percent of government spending. Since it does not come close to matching government expenditures, how could it possibly replace them? But that hardly counts as an argument against privatization, for three major reasons. The first is that government causes a significant amount of the poverty it aims to relieve have. . . . The package of benefits available to poor mothers typically has a higher value than the money they could earn in an entry-level job. A young mother who has grown up in a welfare family and never completed high school or held a job can easily be sidetracked from the working economy by the welfare system. In addition . . . government regulations such as the minimum wage, occupational licensing, and business restrictions keep the otherwise enterprising poor from helping themselves. Without those barriers to self-reliance, and without the subsidies that undermine the incentives for self-reliance, it stands to reason that many fewer people would be welfare dependents.

Second, a good deal of the money government spends on means-tested programs never reaches the poor. John Goodman of the National Center for Policy Analysis and others, for example, estimated that in 1992 the nonwelfare income of poor people was $94 billion short of the income necessary for them all to live at or above the poverty line. That is less than one-third of the money government spent to lift them out of poverty. The rest goes to the welfare bureaucracy, consultants, and others who administer the system. Of course, it would not be possible simply to send that $94 billion to the poor without some administration, nor would that money eliminate poverty. Poverty is more often caused and sustained by behavioral problems than by strictly financial ones. Still, it is hard to believe that the advantages of private over public aid would not produce a considerable savings.

Third, by nationalizing the charity industry, the government has displaced private spending on the poor. The $300 billion that government spends is taken from the private economy. Some portion of that sum would otherwise be spent on goods and services that create new entry-level jobs, providing opportunities for the poor. And some portion would be contributed to charities. Sixty years of AFDC and 30 years of the Great Society programs have produced the expectation that government will provide an adequate safety net for the poor, and people have shifted their charitable giving to religion, the arts, and other areas. Although it is not possible to quantify this "crowding out" effect precisely, or to predict the amount of private giving that would be shifted to aid for the poor if welfare were privatized, historical research has provided a few hints.

In a detailed study of Indianapolis in the 1870s and 1880s, when government aid was reduced as part of a nationwide reaction against "outdoor relief," Stephen T. Ziliak found that private contributions increased by approximately the same amount. Figures from the 1930s are also illuminating. From 1930 to 1932, as the Great Depression deepened, both government and private spending on poverty relief increased sixfold. After Roosevelt's election, government spending continued to increase rapidly as new programs were introduced, but private spending declined rapidly as people assumed that responsibility had been shifted to the government.

At the same time, private charitable organizations shifted their efforts from poverty relief to other goals. At the New York Association for Improving the Condition of the Poor (AICP), for example, "Many families formerly cared for by AICP have been turned over completely to public relief departments." Thus it is not surprising that charitable giving today goes predominantly to religion and other objects, with human services receiving a relatively small portion. But there is every reason to believe that the proportions would change if government were not already spending so much in this area.

We do not know with any certainty what the result would be of leaving aid to the poor in private hands. We can't predict what ideas people will come up with to solve the problems they observe. One can certainly find grounds for pessimism. In his study of 19th-century Indianapolis, for example, Ziliak found that replacing government spending with private funds had no effect on the average spell of welfare dependence, nor on the number of people finding jobs and becoming self-supporting. Nevertheless, private agencies can provide aid on a conditional basis rather than as an entitlement, and thus more effectively encourage responsibility. They can draw distinctions on the basis of character and psychology, tailoring the help they provide in ways that the government cannot. They can intervene in the personal lives of recipients in ways that get to the root of problems but would be intrusive violations of freedom if done by government workers. And private agencies can be much more flexible, responsive to changing circumstances, experimental, and diverse than government bureaucracies.

Nor can we predict how much aid would be given in a private system, nor in what forms. Our point of departure, morally speaking, is not the needs of recipients but the generosity of donors. It is the donors who set

the terms. Recipients do not own those who support them, and thus do not have a right that must be met, come what may. Those who would privatize poverty relief do not have the burden of showing that all poverty would be dealt with as effectively as it is today by government programs, although . . . that [is] extremely likely. The burden is on those who support government programs to show why they think the poor are *entitled* on altruistic grounds to the aid they are receiving.

Compassion and generosity are virtues, and the charitable help they prompt us to provide the less fortunate is, for most of us, a part of what it means to live in a civilized society. But compassion, generosity, and charity are not the sum of morality, nor even its core; and they are not duties that create entitlements on the part of recipients. The poor do not own the productive, nor are the latter obliged to sacrifice the pursuit of their own happiness in service to the poor. If individuals are truly ends in themselves, then charity is not a duty but a value we choose to pursue. Each of us has the right to choose what weight charity has among the other values in our lives, instead of having the government decide what proportion of our income to take for that end. And each of us has the right to choose the particular people, projects, or causes we wish to support, instead of having government make that decision for us.

Analyze this Reading

1. According to the writer, why are government approaches to charity ineffective?
2. In the author's view, why are private agencies a better approach to poverty? Why do they have a greater incentive to work for solutions? How does he support this view?
3. The writer claims that private charities can replace government welfare programs even though private giving is less than 30 percent of what the government spends. What reasons and support does the writer bring to this claim?

Respond to this Reading

1. The writer concludes with a discussion of poverty in terms of duties and rights. For you, is contributing to poverty relief a right or a duty? Explain.
2. Via your local newspaper archives and government data available online, access information about services to the poor and homeless in your community in terms of both government and charitable sources. What approach to poverty relief dominates? What would you change, if anything?
3. In your own experience as a donor, do you favor charities that attend to local populations, or do you favor broader, international charities, or both? Explain.

PART SIX

MLA and APA Documentation Systems

APPENDIX A MLA Documentation and the List of Works Cited

APPENDIX B APA Documentation and the Reference List

APPENDIX A

MLA Documentation and the List of Works Cited

One of the most important (and possibly tedious) aspects of writing research reports of any type is the documentation. You must supply publication information for every source you use in your writing. This information must appear in a standardized format or style sheet dictated by your company or instructor.

- In the humanities (including fine arts and literature), the most common format is MLA style—that of the Modern Language Association.
- Fields such as sociology, anthropology, education, psychology, and business often require writers to document sources in APA (American Psychological Association) style.
- The Council of Science Editors' manual (CSE) is used for the natural sciences, such as biology and geology.

All of these style sheets are similar in *what* information you should provide for a source, but vary in *how* that information is presented. For example, see how a book is cited for MLA, APA, and CSE side by side:

MLA	APA	CSE
Willoquet-Maricondi, Paula. *Framing the World: Explorations in Ecocriticism and Film.* U of Virginia P, 2010.	Willoquet-Maricondi, P. (2010). *Framing the world: Explorations in ecocriticism and film.* Charlottesville: University of Virginia Press.	1. Willoquet-Maricondi, P. 2010. Framing the world: Explorations in ecocriticism and film. Charlottesville (VA): University of Virginia Press.

The complete guides to MLA and APA can be found on the Internet at a variety of sources. The most reliable source for either style manual is the Online Writing Lab (OWL) at Purdue University:

(MLA) https://owl.purdue.edu/owl/research_and_citation/mla_style/mla
_formatting_and_style_guide/mla_formatting_and_style_guide.html
(APA) https://owl.purdue.edu/owl/research_and_citation/apa_style/apa
_formatting_and_style_guide/general_format.html

MLA Information

Title Page

A paper using MLA format does not need a separate title page. A header with your last name and the page number, flush right, should appear on each page, including the first. Also on the first page of the essay, your name, the instructor's name, the course number, and the date should be typed flush left, double-spaced, in the upper left corner. The title should be centered horizontally on the page. See the Annotated MLA Research Paper written by student Hal at the end of this chapter for details.

In-Text Citation

Whether you quote, paraphrase, or use someone else's ideas in your essay, you have to do two things: (1) acknowledge within your essay that the material comes from a source and (2) include that source on your works cited page.

There are many ways to cite sources within the body of an argument. Passages from Hal's essay demonstrate the various ways.

> North Carolina State Senator Austin Allran believes that the government would save millions of dollars now currently lost to state and federal employees playing Solitaire on their office computers if the games were removed from employees' computers (Jonsson).

In this passage, Hal refers to Senator Allran's beliefs about the wastefulness of employees playing computer games. Because that material was found in Patrik Jonsson's article, Hal has to let the reader know that. In this example, he introduces the statement about Allran and then includes the name Jonsson in what is called a *parenthetical citation*. In parenthesis, before the period, is included the author's name as it appears on the works cited page: (Jonsson). If there had been a page number to include as with PDF copies or print copies of books and articles, that number would be included after the author's name, for example (Smith 23).

> Patrik Jonsson notes that the suggested removal of games like Solitaire from worker's computers "goes straight to the issue of distractions from long days at the office and, more fundamentally, how much of their employees' time and concentration employers can reasonably expect to own."

Since the author of the source is already included in the sentence, then there is no need to include his name again in a parenthetical. In this example, the quote is introduced with the inclusion of Patrik Jonsson's name. Jonsson is the author so Hal did not need to include his name in the citation. As mentioned above, if there were a page number to include, that page number alone would appear in the parenthetical citation (23).

The information in the citation should always appear in the same way it does on the works cited page. Sources with no designated authors can be a bit more challenging.

Here are two samples drawn from a web page. This is the source as it would appear on the works cited page:

"Workplace Privacy." *EPIC: Electronic Privacy Information Center*, 25 July 2006, https://www.epic.org/privacy/workplace/.

In the first, the web page where the information was found is mentioned in the sentence. There is no need for a parenthetical citation.

> A 2006 article, "Workplace Privacy," lists the most frequent types of workplace monitoring, which include phone monitoring and video surveillance.

In sample two, the web page is not mentioned so a parenthetical is necessary. Remember that the information in the citation should appear as it does on the works cited page. In this example, there is no author so the source begins with the title of the web page—that title is what should be found in the citation. Website URLs are never included in the citation.

> Two of the most frequent types of workplace monitoring include phone monitoring and video surveillance ("Workplace Privacy").

General Tips for Writing Works Cited Pages

A list of works cited includes all the sources you have cited in your researched essay. If you consulted a source, but didn't cite from it, the source does not belong on your works cited page.

- Alphabetize sources by authors' last names. If a source does not have a named author, alphabetize by the first word of the title that follows "The" or "A." Do not replace the author's name with the word *anonymous*.
- If there are two or three authors, reverse the first author's name for alphabetizing purposes, but leave the other name(s) in normal order.
  - Davis, John, and Troy Simpson.
- If there are more than three authors, reverse the first author's name for alphabetizing purposes and add et al., which means "and others."
  - Jamieson, Sandra, et al.
- Titles of articles, essays in books, web pages, songs, television episodes, short poems, and short stories are in quotation marks: "Title of Work."
- Titles of magazines or journals, books, websites, podcasts, movies, works of art, television shows, long poems, plays, and novels are italicized: *Title of Work*.
- MLA requires the use of URLs for webpages. However, many scholarly journal articles found in databases include a DOI (digital object identifier). If a DOI is available, cite the DOI number instead of the URL.
- MLA does not require you to include the date when you accessed an online source, but it is often helpful, particularly as Internet sources can disappear. Ask your instructor whether this is required for your particular assignment.

Formatting Issues

It is tempting to use online citation machines to format your works cited for you. Is this such a good idea? Yes and No.

Citation Machines and Database Citations: To Use or Not to Use

There are several websites that can help you in creating citations, such as Citation Machine www.citationmachine.net and EasyBib www.easybib.com. Students use these with some success. In our experience they are time consuming and you must still tinker with format. For example, after filling in the provided form at a citation machine site, a formatted citation is returned, but if the citation is longer than two lines, it will still need to be put in hanging indent in your document, and you will also need to change the underlining to italics. Fairly clumsy. The sites may not always provide accurate citations for all types of sources, particularly the more complex ones.

Most library databases now provide citations for sources. However, they do have errors, particularly in capitalization and italicization. Newspaper titles are particularly prone to errors. But databases are a good place to start.

Using the Hanging Indent Function

It can be time consuming, and sometimes frustrating, to individually format each of your entries in your works cited. It is better to format the page once. Follow these instructions to use a hanging indent, which is required by the MLA and makes it easier for readers to see the break between each entry. Your entries will look like this:

Miller, G. Tyler, and Scott Spoolman. *Environmental Science*. 14th ed., Cengage, 2012.

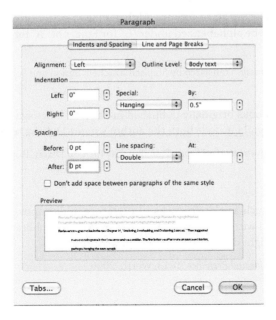

MLA Documentation: Books

Remember that you find the publication information for a book on its copyright page. The publication information should appear in this order in your citation, and you should use the punctuation as shown:

Single Author

Author's Last Name, First Name. *Title*. Publisher, Publication Date.

Wilber, Tom. *Under the Surface: Fracking, Fortunes, and the Fate of the Marcellus Shale*. Cornell UP, 2012.

By Two or More Authors

Deffeyes, Kenneth S., and Stephen E. Deffeyes. *Nanoscale: Visualizing an Invisible World*. MIT Press, 2009.

Two or More Books by the Same Author

Arrange in alphabetical order by title of sources.

Deffeyes, Kenneth S. *Hubbert's Peak: The Impending World Oil Shortage*. Princeton UP, 2009.
—. *When Oil Peaked*. Hill and Wang, 2010.

Book by a Corporate Author

Corporate authors include groups of individuals, such as those of an agency or a committee.

Lifetime Learning, Inc. *Learning Principles of the Lifetime Library*. Lifetime Learning, 2006.

Book with No Author

Some books may not have authors. Alphabetize these by title. The following example would be alphabetized under "E" for Epic, not "A" for anonymous or "T" for The.

The Epic of Gilgamesh. Translated by Stephen Mitchell, Simon and Schuster, 2006.

A Translation

Citations for books originally published in another language and translated into English should include both the author's name and the translator.

Eco, Umberto. *Inventing the Enemy*. Translated by Richard Dixon, Houghton Mifflin, 2012.

Republished Book

Older books, such as classic works of literature, philosophy, or history, are often reprinted without changes. Include the original publication date along with the copyright date for the current publication.

Austen, Jane. *Pride and Prejudice*. 1813. Worth, 2006.

An Edition of a Book

Books of essays or articles often have an **editor**. An editor is the person who compiled the book. There are also **editions** of a book, which means that a subsequent release of the book may have new material. It is important to include all of this information so that your reader can find the correct source you used.

A Subsequent Edition

A book that has been revised or updated is called a *subsequent edition*. It is important to let your reader know which edition of a book you are citing as the material and page numbers will be different in different editions. Cite the book as you normally would, but add the number of the edition after the title.

Nelson, Vaughn. *Wind Energy: Renewable Energy and the Environment.* 2nd ed. CRC, 2013.

A Work Prepared by an Editor

An edition of a book, particularly one that no longer is under copyright protection, is often compiled with notes by an editor. Cite the book as you normally would, but add the editor after the title.

Radcliffe, Ann. *The Mysteries of Udolpho.* Edited by Bonamy Dobrée, Oxford UP, 1980.

An Anthology

An anthology is a collection of works, either of one individual or of many different individuals. An editor compiles the works and often adds notes or an introduction.

McKibben, Bill, editor. *The Global Warming Reader: A Century of Writing.* Penguin, 2012.

A Work in an Anthology

If you are citing a work included in an anthology, list the work and its author first in the citation and then the anthology information.

Essay Author's Last Name, First Name. "Title of Essay." *Title of Anthology,* Editor(s) of the anthology, Publisher, Publication Date. Page number range.

Keeling, Dave. "The Keeling Curve." *The Global Warming Reader: A Century of Writing,* edited by Bill McKibben, Penguin, 2012. pp. 45–46.

If you are citing several works from one anthology, it is not necessary to include all of the publication information each time. If you include complete information for the full anthology (the McKibben entry in the example below), you can refer readers to that entry rather than repeat the information. For the two essays below (Keeling and Oreskes), only the author's name, the title of the essay, the editor's last name, and the page numbers are included.

Keeling, Anne. "The Keeling Curve." McKibben, pp. 45–46.
McKibben, Bill, ed. *The Global Warming Reader: A Century of Writing.* Penguin, 2012.
Oreskes, Naomi. "The Scientific Consensus on Climate Change." McKibben, pp. 75–80.

A Book Available Online (An e-book)

Many books are available to be read online, either through a library service or through sites such as Project Gutenberg.

Author's Last Name, First Name. *Title*. Original Publication date if older. *Source of Access to the Book*. URL.

Muir, John. *Travels in Alaska*. 1915. *Project Gutenberg*. https://www.gutenberg.org /files/7345/7345-h/7345-h.htm.

A Multivolume Work

Some books are published in volumes. The volumes can be individually titled or differentiated only by the volume number. In the first example below, the citation is referring to the entire five volume set. The second example refers to only one volume of the set.

Pausanias. *Description of Greece*. Translated by W. H. S. Jones, Loeb-Harvard UP, 1918. 5 vols.
Pausanias. *Description of Greece*. Translated by W. H. S. Jones, vol. 1, Loeb-Harvard UP, 1918.

If the volume you are using has its own title, cite the book without referring to the other volumes as if it were an independent publication. In the following example, only one volume of Campbell's 4-volume set of books entitled *The Masks of God* is being cited. Each of the four volumes has its own title.

Campbell, Joseph. *Creative Mythology*. Penguin, 1968.

An Introduction, a Preface, a Foreword, or an Afterword

Dawkins, Richard. Introduction. *The Origins of Species* and the *Voyage of the Beagle*, by Charles Darwin, Knopf, 2003. pp. ix–xxx.

Poems or Short Stories

Poems and short stories can be found in collections of the author's work, or in anthologies of works including many other authors. The first example is a citation for Komunyakaa's poem published in a volume of the poet's work. The second example is for the same poem published in an anthology edited by others.

Komunyakaa, Yusef. "Sunday Afternoons." *Pleasure Dome: New and Collected Poems*. Wesleyan UP, 2001. p. 227.
Komunyakaa, Yusef. "Sunday Afternoons." *The Norton Anthology of African American Literature*. 2nd ed., edited by Henry Louis Gates, Jr. and Nellie Y. McKay, Norton, 2004. p. 2531.

Sacred Texts

There are many versions of scriptural works. Provide the title of the work, the editor of that version, any translation information, and the publication information. Alphabetize by the title of the work. NOTE: Do not alphabetize using "The" or "A." The list here is in alphabetical order.

The Bhagavad Gita. Translated by Juan Mascaró. Edited by Simon Brodbeck, Rev. ed., Penguin, 2003.

The Koran. Edited by N. J. Dawood, Rev. ed., Penguin, 2004.

The New English Bible. Edited by Samuel Sandmel, Oxford UP, 1976.

Government Documents

Governments publish a wide variety of documents. These sources are covered in the Primary Sources section in Chapter 3, "Develop a Research Plan."

Documentation: Articles

Documentation gets a little trickier when articles are involved. The publication information can be found in different places and can get confusing. The information you are looking for is author, title of article, title of journal, volume number and issue, year published, page numbers. The publication information is usually at either the top or the bottom of the page.

An Article in a Scholarly Journal

If you have read an article in a print medium, then you should follow this format.

Author's Last Name, First Name. "Title of Article." *Title of Journal,* Volume, Issue, Year, pages.

Tufekci, Zeynep. "Can You See Me Now? Audience and Disclosure Regulation in Online Social Network Sites." *Bulletin of Science, Technology & Society,* vol. 28, no. 1, 2008, pp. 20–36.

Article in a Database

Most college and university libraries (and many public libraries) subscribe to databases of articles that you can read digitally. More and more frequently, you will access articles this way. The only difference in documentation is the addition of that database information and the DOI or permalink. If page numbers are unavailable, skip that information.

Author's Last Name, First Name. "Title of Article." *Title of Journal,* Volume, Issue, Year, pages. *Title of Database.* Link. DOI or permalink.

Weinhold, Bob. "The Future of Fracking." *Environmental Health Perspectives,* vol. 120, no. 7, 2012, pp. A272–A279. *ProQuest,* http://ezproxy.cpcc.edu /login?url=https://search.proquest.com/docview/1028013133?accountid =10008.

Articles Found on the Internet

Another way you can access journal articles is through the Internet. Some journal articles can be found online through sites such as Questia, FindArticles.com, and Google Scholar. Note that sometimes these articles do not include original volume and issue number or page numbers. Include this information if it is available.

McBroom, Matthew, et al. "Soil Erosion and Surface Water Quality Impacts of Natural Gas Development in East Texas, USA." *Water,* vol. 4, no. 4, 2012, pp. 944–58. *ResearchGate,* https://www.researchgate.net/publication/262068903_Soil_Erosion_and_Surface_Water_Quality_Impacts_of_Natural_Gas_Development_in_East_Texas_USA.

Article in a Magazine

The only difference in citations between journal articles and magazine articles is in the way that issues are dated. Journals usually have a volume and issue number; magazines generally don't, but have a weekly or monthly date instead. The first example is of a monthly magazine, the second is a weekly.

Author's Last Name, First Name. "Title of Article." *Title of Magazine,* Day Month Year, pages.

Mooney, Chris. "The Truth about Fracking." *Scientific American,* Nov. 2011, pp. 80–85.

Royte, Elizabeth. "What the Frack Is in Our Food?" *Nation,* 17 Dec. 2012, pp. 11–18.

If you find these articles in a database or on an Internet site, include that information in the same way you do for a journal article.

An Article in a Web Magazine

Author's Last Name, First Name. "Title of Article." *Title of Online Publication,* Date of Publication, URL.

Levy, Stephen. "Eric Schmidt and Jared Cohen on What's Next for the World." *Wired,* 26 Apr. 2013, https://www.wired.com/2013/04/eric-schmidt-and-jared-cohen-on-whats-next-for-the-world/.

Article in a Newspaper

- Most newspapers have the title of the city as part of its name. If not, add the city name in square brackets [ ] after the title. For example, *The Times-Picayune* [New Orleans].
- Some newspapers also have different editions, particularly the larger ones such as *The New York Times.* Identify the edition following the date.
- Most articles in a newspaper are not continuous. An article may begin on page one, but then continue on page three. The way to indicate this is to use the +. This tells the reader that the article continues and the reader can follow the continuations by reading the "continues on page #" note at the end of the article segments.

- Also, in a print edition, refer to the section of the paper where the article can be found (A, B, 1, 2, etc.)
- If you access the article through a database, include the name of the database and the DOI or permalink.
- For documenting historical newspapers, refer to the Primary Sources section in Chapter 3, "Develop a Research Plan."

Author's Last Name, First Name. "Title of Article." *Title of Newspaper* [City, if not given in title], Date, Edition: page numbers. URL.

Schwartzel, Erich. "Survey: Pa. Residents Give Cautious Support for Gas Drilling." *Pittsburgh Post-Gazette,* 15 May 2013, https://www.post-gazette .com/businessnews/2013/05/15/Survey-Pa-residents-give-cautious-support -for-gas-drilling/stories/201305150173.

Documentation: Internet-only Sources

In general, you will probably cite a page from a website most frequently.

Author of Web Page. "Title of Web Page." *Title of Website,* Date Site Was Posted, URL.

Jiménez, Maya. "José Clemente Orozco, *Dive Bomber and Tank.*" *Smarthistory,* 9 Aug. 2015, https://smarthistory.org/orozco-dive-bomber-and-tank/.

Remember that if your search engine directs you to a particular *web page,* you must backtrack to determine the name of the *website* that hosts that page if that information is not on the web page. You should look for any author of the site, the web page title, the date posted if provided, and the URL.

If the search engine directs you to a page and it is not immediately clear what website is hosting that page, you can try deleting everything after a slash in the URL and then keep shortening the URL by increments until you come to the host site.

An Entire Website

Include the website name, the date the site was posted (or last updated), and the date you accessed the material. If there is no posting date, skip it.

Library of Congress. https://www.loc.gov/. Accessed 3 May 2018.

American Rivers. https://www.americanrivers.org/. 2017. Accessed 3 May 2018.

For a course home page:

Instructor name. "Title of Course." *Name of School.* Sponsor of Site. Date of the Course, URL. Date You Accessed the Site.

Walls, David. "The Environmental Movement." *Sonoma State University,* 2018, http://web.sonoma.edu/users/w/wallsd/environmental-movement.shtml. Accessed 10 May 2018.

E-mails

Milton, Suzanne. "Re: *TALTP*." Received by Patricia Bostian, 23 May 2019.

Blog and Discussion Board Postings

Some discussion board forums will only include screen names for authors. Blogs usually have listed authors.

Author's Last Name, First Name (or Screen Name). "Title of Post." *Title of Website*, Organizational Sponsor if available, Date of Publication, URL. Date Accessed.

Walters, Helen. "Why Google Glass Might Actually Be Useful, and Other Tales from Around the Web." *Ideas.Ted.Com*, 14 May 2014, https://ideas.ted.com/why -google-glass-might-actually-be-useful-and-other-tales-from-around-the-web/. Accessed 21 Dec. 2018.

Hal Stevens

Professor Daniels

BUS 321

24 May 2019

Using Work Computers for Personal Business is Not a Problem

A familiar scene plays out in offices everywhere. An employee sitting in his cubicle has just finished a project, grabbed a cup of coffee, and is taking a 15-minute break. He pulls up the Ohio State Buckeyes website to scout next season's potential recruits. Then he plays a game or two of computer Solitaire. A quick check on his personal email account to see if the birthday present he ordered for his wife has been shipped from Sears yet. Break over, the employee returns to his next project. A week later, he is surprised and angered to be called to his supervisor's office and subjected to a reprimand. The subject? Misusing the company's computers. What employees regard as private computer use during personal time turns out to be not so private after all.

In the above scenario, the company has installed new computer surveillance software, which now monitors employees' every keystroke, visits to online sites, and emails—personal or work-related. Is this an invasion of privacy? Is it legal? The answer is a complicated "yes" and "no." Certain kinds of situations are covered by the topic of privacy, others by the legality of the surveillance performed and whether employees are notified of company monitoring policies. Mostly, though, business owners are able to monitor employee computer use at will. Although it is reasonable that companies expect their employees to use company computers for company activity, it is also understandable and desirable that employees have privacy rights at work in regards to their computer usage.

Your last name and the page number should appear in a header on each page, upper right corner. Double-space the entire paper and Works Cited page.

This introductory paragraph serves as a hook to grab the reader's attention and to increase interest in the writer's situation.

Here, after a question, Hal states his claim.

Complete Annotated MLA Research Paper

Stevens 2

France Bélanger and Robert E. Crossler, researchers in the field of information privacy and security, find that little existing research focuses on the issue of electronic privacy of personal information in the workplace. They cite a Pew Internet Project survey, however, that indicates 85 percent of adults find it of the utmost importance to protect their personal information (1017).

The Electronic Privacy Information Center (EPIC) is a clearinghouse that gathers information on workplace privacy. A recent article, "Workplace Privacy," lists the most frequent types of workplace monitoring:

- Phone monitoring
- Video surveillance
- ID tags that can monitor an employee's location (including GPS monitors that can track employees on the road)
- Keystroke loggers
- Email and Internet usage

In an interview I conducted with Gary Hopkins, CEO of Farm Fresh, an Organic Foods wholesale, he indicates that most of his employees do not like their work habits being subjected to monitoring, but there is little that they can do to prevent it. Hopkins says keeping workers on notice with email and Internet monitoring has increased productivity 22 percent in the last year alone.

Currently there are few laws that cover the ever-changing technology of electronic communications, as Nancy Flynn, author of the *e-Policy Handbook*, explains:

> In the United States and many third-world countries, workers have very few privacy protections in law. There are few situations where an employee has a due process right to access, inspect, or challenge information collected or held by the employer. There are a patchwork of state and federal

This paragraph gives background material on the subject of electronic monitoring practices. Some background is usually needed to explain the situation that has led to the controversy about an issue.

Introduction of a long quote that is set off 10 spaces from the margin. If the author had not been introduced before the quotation (as is the case here), the citation would appear at the end of the quote, AFTER the period.

Stevens 3

laws that grant employees limited rights. For instance, under federal law, private-sector employees cannot be required to submit to a polygraph examination. However, there are no general protections of workplace privacy except where an employer acts tortuously—where the employer violates the employee's reasonable expectation of privacy.

One law that would seem to be on the side of employees' privacy is the 1986 United States Electronic Privacy Act (ECPA), which "prohibits reading or disclosure of the contents of any electronic communication not intended for the reader." One important exemption from this act, however, is an employer who owns a company's email system. Several court cases have also sided with employers.

Lothar Determann and Robert Sprague's article comparing advances in European workplace privacy with the lacks in American privacy, points out that in the United States, people have a constitutional expectation of privacy in general, but a low expectation of privacy in the workplace (1022).

Determann and Sprague also explain that employer monitoring has been able to extend its scope to scan emails for viruses and spam and other links that may be harmful to the employees' computers in particular, but to the company network in general. In scanning for harmful activity, workers' log-ons, emails, screen activity, website visits, among other types of information can be accessed (982). Uncomfortable for employees, though, are the monitoring possibilities that extend beyond company security to track Internet access, electronic chats and online sessions, and remote viewing that may not be work-related. Another concern is that with GPS and wireless features, employees who work from home can be monitored as well (982).

Stevens 4

This example is long enough that it warrants its own paragraph. Resist the temptation to cram as much as you can in one paragraph just because it is all on the same topic.

For example, in Smyth vs. The Pillsbury Company (1994), Michael Smyth was fired from his job for sending "inappropriate and unprofessional" comments from his home computer using Pillsbury's email system. The comments to his supervisor "contained threats to 'kill the backstabbing bastards' and referred to the planned holiday party as the 'Jim Jones Koolaid affair.'" Smyth argued that he had a "reasonable expectation of privacy" in sending emails, regardless of content, because Pillsbury's policies on emails was that they would not be monitored or read. The Pennsylvania District Court ruled in favor of the employer saying, "the company's interest in preventing inappropriate and unprofessional comments or even illegal activity over its email system outweighs any privacy interest the employee may have in those comments."

A topic sentence introducing support.

In addition to problems associated with sending email, there are also concerns about employees spending their work time surfing the Internet or playing computer games. North Carolina State Senator Austin Allran, for example, believes that the government would save millions of dollars now currently lost to state and federal employees playing Solitaire on their office computers if the games were removed from employees' computers (Jonsson).

New York City mayor Michael Bloomberg even fired an employee when he saw an in-progress game on the employee's computer. The employee admitted to occasionally playing a game to take a break from exhausting work, but Bloomberg believes that no time should be spent playing computer games during work time (Hu). Patrik Jonsson notes that the suggested removal of games like Solitaire from worker's computers "goes straight to the issue of distractions from long days at the office and, more fundamentally, how much of their employees' time and concentration employers can reasonably expect to own."

Stevens 5

Some proponents of leaving the games on workers' computers argue that they actually increase employee productivity by providing an outlet for stress relief ("2007 Electronic Monitoring"). So although many employees who spend a lot of time staring at computer screens feel that taking a break with a computer game rejuvenates them, employers see the time spent "rejuvenating" as wasteful.

But a far more serious problem is employees using the company's Internet connection to access inappropriate websites. Some employees will visit sites at work that they may not want those they live with to know about, for example pornographic sites, or ones that deal with alternative lifestyles, violence, or drugs. A total of 304 companies participated in the 2019 Electronic Monitoring and Surveillance Survey sponsored by both the American Management Association and the ePolicy Institute. Here are the results of several of the questions about company Internet usage:

- 83 percent of the respondents said that their organization has a written policy governing the personal use of the Internet.
- 16 percent of employers record phone conversations; 84 percent notify employees that their phone conversations are monitored, but only 73 percent notify employees that their voicemails are also monitored.
- 65 percent of companies use software to block inappropriate sites (social networking, pornographic, and entertainments sites top the list).

The survey also indicates that although companies have policies regarding electronic privacy, employees rarely read or otherwise pay attention to the policies.

Another topic sentence introducing support. Notice that the items of support seem to be presented in increasingly important order.

Complete Annotated MLA Research Paper

Stevens 6

Most employees would likely agree that visiting certain sites or spending a significant amount of time surfing the Internet for non-job-related information can be a problem. But what about smaller increments of time that might act as productive breaks? If any email system provided by an employer is subject to monitoring, how much privacy are employees really allowed at work?

An item of qualification. Employees do realize that surfing while working can be a waste of time, but they may question the need for oversight of all activity.

Employers assert that they have a right to know what their employees are doing on company time, particularly with company computers and email systems. Companies worry about loss of productivity. Nancy Flynn notes that employer termination for email and web misuse is increasing: employer terminations for email violations, ranging from violation of company policies and excessive personal use, rose from 14 percent in 2001 to 28 percent in 2007 (182). But for employees who spend enormous numbers of hours at work, using email is one of the best ways to take care of personal business that cannot be done after work, such as making doctors' appointments.

Items of opposition. What are some opposing views? How can they be addressed?

Companies also worry about employees giving competitors access to trade secrets and about charges of allowing a hostile work environment if harassing emails are sent from an office computer (Casilly and Draper 76). Courts mostly side with companies, although occasionally a defendant wins. In *United States vs. Slanina*, the Fifth Circuit Court of Appeals found that because the company by whom Slanina was employed did not have a posted policy about computer usage or Internet monitoring, he "had a reasonable expectation of privacy in his office computer."

It is the issue of reasonable expectations of privacy which poses the largest stumbling block for a solution to workplace privacy

Stevens 7

issues. What seems reasonable to a boss may not seem reasonable to employees.

In 1993, Congress passed the Privacy for Consumers and Workers Act. This piece of legislation doesn't ban electronic monitoring, but states that employees must be given notice that they are subject to monitoring in the workplace (Bockanic and Lynn 64). But how does this work for telecommuting employees? Some of the privacy issues that have not been resolved in the area of monitoring employees who work from home are

- the difficulty of the employer to monitor an employee's work at home without crossing over into the employee's private life,
- the inability to determine when an employee is on "duty,"
- and the inability to differentiate between an employee using the computer and another family member ("Workplace Privacy").

As technology advances, new issues involving the rights of employees to maintain privacy of their electronic lives (email, Internet usage, etc.) will become more tangled. How far can an employer go in scrutinizing their employee's emails? Addressing employees' reasonable expectations of privacy and notifying them of workplace policies are practices already in place for many businesses, but there is no law forcing private businesses to follow these guidelines. The Fourth Amendment guarantees the right of citizens to be safe from unreasonable searches of their "persons, houses, papers and effects" by the government. However, the Internet was not even a faint glimmer of possibility in 18th-century America. Should we add an amendment to the Bill of Rights covering electronic privacy? Maybe that is coming.

Hal's conclusion rounds out the discussion, adding interesting material for the reader to think about without offering new items of support or changes of direction.

Complete Annotated MLA Research Paper

Stevens 8

Works Cited

Bélanger, France, and Robert E. Crossler. "Privacy in The Digital Age: A Review of Information Privacy Research in Information Systems." *MIS Quarterly,* vol. 35, no. 4, 2011, pp. 1017–1036. *ACM Digital Library,* https://dl.acm.org/.

Bockanic, William N., and Marc P. Lynn. "The Privacy for Consumers and Workers Act: Is Privacy Protection on the Horizon?" *Journal of Systems Management,* vol. 47, Jan. 1996, p. 64. *Business Abstracts with Full Text,* search.ebscohost.com/login.aspx?direct =true&db=bft&AN=510389358&site=ehost-live&scope=site.

Casilly, Lisa H., and Clare H. Draper. *Workplace Privacy: A Guide for Attorneys and HR Professionals.* Pike and Fischer, 2004.

Determann, Lothar, and Robert Sprague. "Intrusive Monitoring: Employee Privacy Expectations Are Reasonable in Europe, Destroyed in the United States." *Berkeley Technology Law Journal,* vol. 26, no. 2, 2011, pp. 979–1036. *Berkeley Technology Law Journal,* https://scholarship.law.berkeley.edu/btlj.

Electronic Communications Privacy Act of 1986 (ECPA). 18 U.S.C. § 2510-22. Justice Information Sharing, https://it.ojp.gov /PrivacyLiberty/authorities/statutes/1285.

Flynn, Nancy. *e-Policy Handbook.* 2nd ed. AMACOM, 2009.

Hopkins, Gary. Personal Interview. 20 Oct. 2018.

Hu, Winnie. "Solitaire Costs Man His City Job After Bloomberg Sees Computer." *New York Times,* 10 Feb. 2006, https://www .nytimes.com/2006/02/10/nyregion/solitaire-costs-man-his -city-job-after-bloomberg-sees-computer.html.

Jonsson, Patrik. "Is That a Spreadsheet on Your Screen or Solitaire?" *The Christian Science Monitor,* 18 Mar. 2005, https:// www.csmonitor.com/2005/0318/p01s02-ussc.html.

Stevens 9

"The Latest on Workplace Monitoring and Surveillance." *American Management Association*, AMA, 8 Apr. 2019. https://www .amanet.org/articles/the-latest-on-workplace-monitoring-and -surveillance/.

Michael A. Smyth v. The Pillsbury Company. 914 F. Supp. 97, United States District Court for the Eastern District Of Pennsylvania. 1996. *Internet Library of Law and Court Decisions*, http://www .loundy.com/CASES/Smyth_v_Pillsbury.html.

United States of America, Plaintiff-Appellee, v. Wesley Joseph Slanina. 313 F.3d. 891. United States Court of Appeals, Fifth Circuit. 2002, *CaseText*, https://casetext.com/case/us-v-slanina-2.

"Workplace Privacy." *EPIC: Electronic Privacy Information Center*, 25 July 2006, https://www.epic.org/privacy/workplace/.

APA Documentation and the Reference List

APA Title Page and Abstract

Title Page

A paper written in APA format should have a separate title page. This title page should have the title of the paper, student's name, the school's department and school name, name of the course, professor's name, and date.

Your title should be typed, double spaced, in regular title format (12 pt. Times Roman) and centered in the upper half of the title page. Titles should be no more than 12 words long and may take two lines if necessary.

On subsequent pages, only a page number should appear in the upper right header.

1

Frack(tur)ing the Environment: The Dangers of Fracking

Sabine Ford
Department of Science, Central Piedmont Community College
GEO150: Environmental Issues
Dr. Francis Fielding
October 18, 2019

Abstract

The abstract, a summary of your paper, should highlight the key points of your argument. If you are required to supply an abstract, it should be typed on its own page and follow the title page. Your abstract should be no more than one double-spaced paragraph, between 150 and 250 words. The word *abstract* (not in italics) should be typed and centered at the top of the page.

In-Text Documentation

Whether you quote, paraphrase, or use someone else's ideas in your essay, you have to do two things: (1) acknowledge within your essay that the material comes from a source and (2) include that source on your References page.

There are many ways to cite sources within the body of an argument. We will use passages reproduced in this chapter, from an essay by Sabine Ford, to demonstrate the various ways.

> Howarth, Ingraffea, & Engelder (2011) frighten readers by citing the toxicity of fracking fluid additives, many of which are carcinogens, and which are not only secret, but exempt from the Safe Drinking Water Act.

In this passage, Sabine introduces source material from an article written by Howarth, Ingraffea, & Engelder and includes the authors' names as she does so. After their names, she places the year the referenced article was published (2011). Since their names are mentioned in the text, she does not need to include a parenthetical citation.

> Certainly there is a concern that the enormous quantity of water used during fracking poses a risk to water supplies in drought-prone areas like the Eagle Ford Shale in Texas (Allen, 2013).

In this second example, the author's name is not mentioned in the text, so Sabine has to include a citation with the author's name and the year the source was published separated by a comma. Note that the sentence's period comes after the citation, not before.

If there had been a page number to include as with PDF copies or print copies of books and articles, that number would be included after the author's name also separated by a comma, for example: (Smith, 2013, p. 23).

The information in the citation should always appear in the same way it does on the References page. Sources with no designated authors can be a bit more challenging.

> With oil prices largely unchanged since 2011, and likely to remain so through 2015, and natural gas prices at their lowest levels in more than a decade, the future looks bright (Short-term energy outlook, 11 June, 2019).

Short-term energy outlook. (11 June, 2019). *U.S. Energy Information Administration.* Retrieved from https://www.eia.gov/outlooks/steo/

In this example, there is no author so the source begins with the title of the webpage—that title is what should be found in the citation. The webpage is not mentioned in the text so a parenthetical citation is necessary. Website URLs are never included in the parenthetical citation.

Tips for Writing a Reference List

A **Reference List** is a list of all the sources you have used in your researched essay, the sources from which you have actually cited. If you consulted a source, but didn't cite from it, the source does not belong on your reference list.

- To type your reference list, turn on your hanging indent feature so that all sources will be indented properly without having to use the tab/indent function. Go to the paragraph formatting tool on your computer program.

- Alphabetize sources by authors' last names. If a source does not have a named author, alphabetize by the first word of the article that follows "The" or "A."
- Titles of magazine or journals, books, CDs, movies, podcasts, blogs, works of art, television shows, long poems, plays, and novels are italicized: *Title*.
- Titles of articles, essays in books, songs, television episodes, short poems, and short stories are neither italicized nor in quotation marks.
- For authors' names, include last names and initials. Regardless of the number of authors, reverse all authors' names.
  - Davis, J., & Simpson, T.
- If there are seven or fewer authors, list all names.
- If there are eight or more authors, list the first six names, and three ellipsis points, and add the final name.
  - Davis, J., Collins, P., Gray, L., Clements, H., Simpson, T., Bosch, H., . . . Hunter, B.

APA Documentation: Books

Remember that you find the publication information for a book on its copyright page. Follow the models below for the proper order and marks of punctuation.

Single Author

Author's Last Name, First Initial. (Publication Year). *Title*. Publisher.

NOTE: In the title, the first word of the title and the first word after any colon should be capitalized, as should any proper nouns.

Wilber, T. (2012). *Under the surface: Fracking, fortunes, and the fate of the Marcellus Shale*. Cornell University Press.

By Two to Seven Authors

List all authors' names, up to seven.

Deffeyes, K., & Deffeyes, S. E. (2009). *Nanoscale: Visualizing an invisible world*. MIT Press.

NOTE: The ampersand (&) is used instead of the word "and." Both authors' names are kept in reverse order.

More than Seven Authors

Scientific articles often are written by a team of contributors, sometimes more than seven. In these instances, you should list the first six authors as below. Replace the remaining authors (up to the last one) with ellipses (. . .). Then list the final author.

Zou, M-Q., Zhang, X-F., Qi, X-H., Ma, H-L., Dong, Y., Liu, C-W., . . . & Wang, H. (2009). Rapid authentication of olive oil adulteration by Raman Spectrometry. *J. Agric. Food Chem.*, 57(14), 6001–6006.

Two or More Books by the Same Author

Include the author's name in each entry and arrange by publication date (earliest to latest).

Deffeyes, K. S. (2009). *Hubbert's Peak: The impending world oil shortage*. Princeton University Press.

Deffeyes, K. S. (2010). *When oil peaked*. Hill and Wang.

Book by a Corporate Author

Corporate authors include groups of individuals, such as those of an agency or a committee. If the publisher is the same as the author, use "Author" in the publisher position.

Lifetime Learning, Inc. (2003). *Learning principles of the Lifetime Library*. Lifetime
     Learning, Inc.

Book with No Author

Some books may not have authors. Alphabetize these by title. The following example would be alphabetized under "E" for Epic, not "A" for anonymous nor "T" for The.

The Epic of Gilgamesh. (2006). (S. Mitchell, Trans.). Simon and Schuster.

A Translation

Citations for books originally published in another language and translated into English should include both the author's name and that of the translator.

Eco, U. (2012*). Inventing the new*. (R. Dixon, Trans.). Houghton Mifflin.

Republished Book

Older books, such as classic works of literature, philosophy, or history, are often reprinted without changes. Include the original publication date along with the copyright date for the current publication.

Austen, J. (2006). *Pride and Prejudice*. Worth Press. (Original work published 1813)

An Edition of a Book

Books of essays or articles often have an editor. An editor is the person who compiled the book. There are also editions of a book, which means that a sub-sequent release of the book may have new material. It is important to include all of this information so that your reader can find the correct source you used.

A Subsequent Edition

A book that has been revised or updated is called a *subsequent edition*. It is important to let your reader know which edition of a book you are citing as the material and page numbers will be different. Cite the book as you nor-mally would, but add the number of the edition after the title.

Nelson, V. (2013). *Wind energy: Renewable energy and the environment*
     (2nd ed.). CRC Press.

Editions may also appear as "Rev. ed.," which means "revised edition."

A Work Prepared by an Editor

An edition of a book, particularly one that no longer is under copyright protection, is often compiled with notes by an editor. Cite the book as you normally would, but add the editor after the title.

Radcliffe, A. (1980). *The mysteries of Udolpho*. B. Dobrée (Ed.). Oxford University
     Press. (Original work published in 1794)

An Anthology

An anthology is a collection of works, either of one individual or of many different individuals. An editor compiles the works and often adds notes or an introduction. The abbreviation Ed. indicates that the name listed is an editor, not author.

McKibben, B. (Ed.). (2012). *The global warming reader: A century of writing*. Penguin.

A Work in an Anthology or Edited Book

If you are citing a work included in an anthology, list the work and its author first in the citation and then the anthology information.

Author's Last Name, First Initial. (Publication year). Title of essay. In Editor(s) of the anthology, *Title of anthology* (page numbers). Publisher.

Keeling, D. (2012). The Keeling Curve. In B. McKibben (Ed.), *The global warming reader: A century of writing* (pp. 45–46). *New York, NY:* Penguin.

A Book Available Online (An E-text)

Many books are available to be read online, either through a library service or through sites such as Project Gutenberg (http://www.gutenberg.org). If a DOI is assigned, use it in place of the URL.

Author's Last Name, First Initial. (Original Publication Date). *Title*. URL

Muir, J. (1915). *Travels in Alaska*. http://www.gutenberg.org/ebooks/7345

A Multivolume Work

Some books are published in volumes. The volumes can be individually titled or differentiated only by the volume number. In the first example below, the citation is referring to the entire five-volume set. The second example refers to only one volume of the set.

Pausanias. (1918). *Description of Greece* (W. H. S. Jones, Trans.) (Vols. 1–5). Loeb-Harvard University Press.
Pausanias. (1918). *Description of Greece* (Vol. 1.). (W. H. S. Jones, Trans.) (Vols. 1–5). Loeb-Harvard University Press.

An Introduction, a Preface, a Foreword, or an Afterword

Dawkins, R. (2003). Introduction. In C. Darwin, *The origins of species and the Voyage of the Beagle* (pp. ix–xxx). Knopf. (Original work published 1859)

Sacred Texts

References to sacred texts are cited in-text only, as their sections are usually standardized across editions. In the parenthetical citation, identify the title, version, and section. This first example is from the Qur'an and includes the chapter and verse: (Qur'an 5:3-4). This second example from the Bible includes chapter, verse, and the translation: (Genesis 3:6 King James Version).

Documentation: Articles

Documentation gets a little trickier when articles are involved. In Chapter 3, "Develop a Research Plan," you learned how to find articles in computer databases, and what publication information you need to cite articles properly. The publication information can be found in different places and can get confusing. The information you are looking for is author, title of article, title of journal, volume number and issue, year published, page numbers, and DOI. The publication information is usually at either the top or the bottom of the article. In Fall of 2019, a new 7th edition of *The Publication Manual of the American Psychological Association* (*APA Manual*) will be released. There are a few differences from the 6th edition, two of which are addressed here.

DOI Indicators

Articles found in school library databases provide citations. However, as of this printing, the citations provided by most databases will have inconsistencies with DOIs (document object identifiers) and URLs (uniform resource locators). In the 7th edition of *The Publication Manual of the American Psychological Association* (*APA Manual*), there are guidelines to how to modify citations so that they are most useful to readers.

Let's examine this article found in the *ProQuest* database at my institution's library to see how this can work.

Original Citation provided by the ProQuest database

Koczwara, B., Francis, K., Marine, F., Goldstein, D., Underhill, C., & Olver, I. (2010). Reaching further with online education? The development of an effective online program in palliative oncology. *Journal of Cancer Education, 25*(3), 317-23. doi: http://dx.doi.org.ezproxy.cpcc.edu/10.1007/s13187-009-0037-6 The link, doi:http://dx.doi.org.ezproxy.cpcc.edu/10.1007/s13187-009-0037-6, cannot be made into a hyperlink, and therefore cannot be used to access the article directly.

There are DOI citation formatters that will provide a correct DOI url, such as https://crosscite.org/ but it is useful to understand how to create a DOI url yourself.

Removing the first DOI

Here is that link again: **doi:**http://dx.doi.org.ezproxy.cpcc.edu/10.1007
/s13187-009-0037-6

If the first "doi:" (bolded above) is removed from the beginning of the link, the link can be made into a hyperlink. http://dx.doi.org.ezproxy.cpcc.edu/10.1007/s13187-009-0037-6

However, when the link is clicked, it leads to the logon page for the library where the database is housed (for example, your school library). This may be helpful for those who work at or attend your school, but no one outside the school will be able to access the article.

Modifying the DOI

doi:http://dx.doi.org.**ezproxy.cpcc.edu**/10.1007/s13187-009-0037-6

Modifying the DOI link by removing the first "doi:" from the link and then removing the library identification, "ezproxy.cpcc.edu," (whatever proxy site identifies your school) you will have a hyperlink that can be clicked. http://dx.doi.org/10.1007/s13187-009-0037-6

When the link is clicked, it leads to the publisher of the journal in which the article appears. This allows anyone to access the article, not just readers who have access to your institution's library. For example, clicking on this modified link takes the reader to the Springer website. Springer is the publisher of the *Journal of Cancer Education.*

DOIs and URLs need to be formatted as hyperlinks. Since these links take readers directly to a source, it is no longer necessary to use the phrases "Retrieved from" or "Accessed from" as is shown in bold in this sample from APA 6th.

APA 6th

McAllister, C. (2009). Teaching online: Growth in online education. *Distance Learning, 6*(2), 35-40. **Retrieved from** http://ezproxy.cpcc.edu/login?url=https://search -proquest-com.ezproxy.cpcc.edu/docview/230686706?accountid=10008

APA 7th

McAllister, C. (2009). Teaching online: Growth in online education. *Distance Learning, 6*(2), 35-40. http://ezproxy.cpcc.edu/login?url=https://search-proquest -com.ezproxy.cpcc.edu/docview/230686706?accountid=10008

To create a hyperlink, hit "enter" after the link. It usually turns blue. Do not add a period after the URL, which may interfere with the hyperlink.

Journal Article Found on the Internet or on a Database

Another way you can access journal articles is through the Internet. Some journal articles can be found online through sites such as Questia, the Directory of Online Journals (DOAJ), Google Scholar, or FindArticles.com. If no DOI is included, include the URL. You do not need to include the name of the database.

McBroom, M., Thomas, T., & Zhang, Y. (2012). Soil erosion and surface water quality impacts of natural gas development in east Texas, USA. *Water, 4,* 944–958. https://doi.org/10.3390/w4040944

Howarth, R. W., Ingraffea, A., & Engelder, T. (2011, September 15). Natural gas: Should fracking stop? *Nature, 477,* 271–275. http://www.nature.com/nature /journal/v477/n7364/abs/477271a.html

Article in a Magazine

Author's Last Name, First Initial. (Date including month and day, if available). Title of article. *Title of Magazine, Volume*(issue), Page numbers.

Mooney, C. (2011, November). The truth about fracking. *Scientific American, 305*(5), 80–85.

Magazine Article Found on the Internet

Royte, E. (2012, December 17). What the frack is in our food? *Nation, 295*(25). https://www.thenation.com/article/fracking-our-food-supply/

Article in a Newspaper

Some general tips to follow for citing newspapers are

- Alphabetize articles with no author by first word of the title, excluding "The" or "A."

- You must use p. or pp. for page numbers in citing newspapers. For a single page, use p., for example, p. B2.
- If an article appears on discontinuous pages, list all appearances, for example, pp. B2, B4 or pp. C1, C3–C4.
- Refer to the section of the paper where the article can be found (A, B, 1, 2, etc.).

Author's Last Name, First Initial. (Date, including Month and Day). Title of article. *Title of Newspaper*, Page numbers.

Murawski, J. (2013, 17 May). Wake Co. nuclear plant shut down. *Charlotte Observer*, pp. B1, B3.

Newspaper Article Found on the Internet

NC fracking rule pulled as Halliburton objects. (2013, May 3). *Winston-Salem Journal.* https://www.journalnow.com

A Review (of a book, play, film)

To cite a review, include the abbreviation "Rev. of" plus information about the performance that is being cited before giving the periodical information, as shown in following basic format:

A Review That Includes Its Own Title:

Coppens, J. Y. (2008, May 23). A cloned classic? Not guilty. [Review of the play *Twelve angry men*, Dir. A. Moyers]. *Charlotte Leisure Time*, 15.

An Untitled Review:

Buchanan, M. S. (2013). [Rev. of the book *Ecology and the environment: The mechanisms, marring, and maintenance of nature*, by R. J. Berry]. *Science & Christian Belief, 25*(1), 89–91.

Editorials and Letters to the Editor

To cite a letter to the editor or an editorial, include the words *editorial* or *letter to the editor* after the title.

Doran, W. (2019, June 18). She blew a 0.16 after being pulled over. So why was her conviction just overturned? [Letter to the editor]. Charlotte Observer. https://www.charlotteobserver.com/news/politics-government/article231681048.html

A Government Publication

Cite the author of the publication if the author is identified. Otherwise start with the name of the government agency and any subdivision that served as the corporate author. For congressional documents, be sure to include the number of the congress and the session when the hearing was held or resolution passed. (GPO is the abbr. for the Government Printing Office.)

Brantley, S. R., McGimsey, R. G., & Neal, C. A. (2009). *The Alaska Volcano Observatory: Expanded monitoring of volcanoes yields results* (U.S. Geological Survey Fact Sheet 2004–3084, v. 1.1). http://pubs.usgs.gov/fs/2004/3084/

United States. Cong. Senate. (2007). *Notification to enter into a free trade agreement with the Republic of Korea*. 110th Cong. 1st sess. U.S. Government Printing Office.

A Pamphlet or Brochure

To cite a short printed document, add the source type after the title.

University of Wisconsin, Eau Claire. (2007). *College alcohol inventory* [Brochure].

Dissertations

Dissertations and master's theses may be used as sources whether published or not.

Published Dissertation:

Nduka, U. C. (2019). Hydraulic fracturing and cause-specific mortality: A multicity comparative epidemiological study (Order No. 13428593). Available from ProQuest Central. (2187691937). http://ezproxy.cpcc.edu/login?url=https:// search.proquest.com/docview/2187691937?accountid=10008

Unpublished Dissertation:

Fisk, J. M. (2015). *Fracking and Goldilocks (second order) federalism: Too hot, too cold or just right?* (Unpublished doctoral dissertation). Colorado State University, Fort Collins, Co.

Documentation: Internet-only Sources

In Chapter 3, "Develop a Research Plan," you learned how to gather documentation information from a webpage or website. You should look for any author of the site, the website title, the date posted if provided, and the site's home page address—its URL. There is not always an author for a webpage or site. Sometimes there is no original posting date. Always provide whatever information you can find about the site.

A Page on a Website

Author of Webpage. (Date of Publication). *Title of web page*. Title of Website. URL.

Browder, C. (2011, November 10). *Fracking brings risk, reward to Pennsylvania: Could NC be next?* WRAL. https://www.wral.com/news/local/wral_investigates/video /10365725/

If no author is named, place the page name in the author position.

How hydraulic fracturing works. (2019). https://www.swarthmore.edu/environmental -studies-capstone/how-hydraulic-fracturing-works

E-mails

You do not include e-mails or personal interviews in your References list. They are referenced parenthetically in the body of your argument.

(G. Shearin, personal communication, January 4, 2010).

Blog and Discussion Board Postings

WSJ Staff. (2013, March 26). Big issues: Energy—How to regulate fracking [web log post]. https://blogs.wsj.com/marketbeat/2013/03/26/big-issues-energy-how -to-regulate-fracking/

1

Frack(tur)ing the Environment: The Dangers of Fracking

Sabine Ford
Department of English, Central Piedmont Community College
ENG 112: Writing in the Disciplines
Professor Patricia Bostian
October 31, 2019

Complete APA-Style Research Paper

2

Abstract

The people of the world need energy to power their daily lives. To obtain that energy, various means are used, including fracking. Fracking is a process of fracturing rock formations by using high-pressure liquid. This releases oil and gas deposits, which proponents of the process contend are necessary for the United States to meet its energy needs. However, opponents claim that fracking may be a health and ecological disaster, citing water contamination, air pollution, environmental degradation, noise, silica dust, cancer, industrial and highway accidents, and even earthquakes. Damage caused by fracking is real and commonplace, though so are the benefits. Currently, management of the process is possible, and with safety measures in place, the benefits provided with fracking can outweigh the risks. Thus, with careful management by the energy industry, fracking is a process that should continue because it can be effective as a means of energy exploration for the United States.

Keywords: fracking, fracturing, energy exploration, energy consumption

3

In Kerns County, California, a cherry orchard slowly dies. In Washington County, Pennsylvania, a hillside newly trenched for a pipeline slips toward the creek below. In Wysox, Pennsylvania, water from a faucet bursts into flame. In Shelby County, Texas, a bathtub walks itself down a hallway during an earthquake. In Logan County, West Virginia, a bulldozer plows up the graves of World War II veterans to make a road. In Colorado, a goat gives birth to a head. In Wisconsin, a thousand trucks a day blow by the house of a woman with a 22-month-old daughter, filling the house with toxic sand. What do these incidents have in common? They represent a few out of more than a thousand individual stories of people harmed by fracking (Pennsylvania Alliance for Clean Water and Air, 2013). If these and other stories can be believed, damage caused by fracking is both real and common-place. The question is whether or not that harm outweighs the benefits. If managed properly, it won't. Some have felt the ben-efits of fracking. In Wysox, Pennsylvania, a man adds 40 rooms onto his Riverstone Inn (Browder, 2011). In Williamsport, a carwash business booms, and the owner buys a hot dog truck and sends it out to feed hungry workers. Across Pennsylvania, farmers reinvest, buying tractors and planting orchards (Schaefer, 2012). So, as all of these examples indicate, fracking may be a health and ecological disaster, putting the lives and livelihoods of ordinary Americans at peril. Or, fracking may be a boon to individuals and the nation, reducing the use of dirty coal, while driving down energy prices and turning the United States into a net energy exporter. With fracking, the harm will be mitigated by careful and vigilant management.

Complete APA-Style Research Paper

4

First, what is fracking? High-pressure liquids are pumped into rock formations to fracture them, releasing otherwise unrecoverable oil and gas deposits (How Hydraulic Fracturing Works, 2019). The largest of all such deposits in the United States is the Marcellus Shale, which stretches northeast from Kentucky to Canada.

Is fracking a necessary means of meeting our energy needs? The International Energy Agency reports that coal demands, although decreasing in the United States, is increasing in India and China ("Global Coal Demand," 2018). This means that at least in this country, we are moving from relatively dirty coal to cleaner burning oil and natural gas.

Colorful examples aside, the fears of fracking opponents appear to be valid. Harmful effects that fracking opponents have listed include water contamination, air pollution, environmental degradation, noise, silica dust, cancer, industrial and highway accidents, and even earthquakes. Howarth, Ingraffea, and Engelder frighten readers by citing the toxicity of fracking fluid additives, many of which are carcinogens, and which are not only secret, but exempt from the Safe Drinking Water Act. They also cite the lack of scientific study of environmental dangers, the greater carbon footprint of shale gas relative to conventionally produced natural gas, coal, or diesel oil, and past cases of water supply contamination by leaks and spills of fracking return fluids where deep wells for storage are not readily available. To these they add uncertainties of price and supply, and the crowding out of greener energy technologies as producers rush to take up fracking. In their judgment, "the gas should remain safely in the shale, while society uses energy more efficiently and develops renewable energy sources more aggressively" (Howarth, Ingraffea, & Engelder, 2011).

5

In the counterpoint to this view, Howarth et al. (2011) also emphasize that hydraulic fracturing already happens in nature, that many of the chemicals used are harmless and found in household products, and that the industry is able to manage the real dangers of contamination from fracking return fluids. Water supplies are abundant in some fracking areas, such as the largest—the Marcellus Shale play—and methane, while a potent greenhouse gas, is neither poisonous nor long-lasting. It degrades quickly, and therefore does less long-term harm than carbon dioxide. In this view, with "hydraulic fracturing, as in many cases, fear levels exceed the evidence" (Howarth et al., 2011).

As with most complex issues, there is more than one side. With fracking, the problems are real, but equally real are the benefits, in terms of economic growth, jobs, revitalization of towns and cities, the stability and abundance of energy, the amount of carbon dioxide and other greenhouse gases emitted through energy production, and a reduction in the mercury, acid rain, and smog produced by coal-fired power plants.

There are concerns, however, about the impact on food safety. Many incidents of fracking harm have involved damage to livestock. As Royte (2012) points out, while people may not eat the animals killed by fracking, they very well might eat those animals harmed by it. Once again though, these local incidents are highlighted while other, perhaps broader and more pervasive threats to our food supply go unmentioned. Cooked red meat itself is a carcinogen, and farm animals have often been contaminated by other industrial processes unrelated to fracking. People could be eating animals exposed to all kinds of air, water, and feed contamination.

Complete APA-Style Research Paper

Certainly there is a concern that the enormous quantity of water used during fracking poses a risk to water supplies in drought-prone areas like the Eagle Ford Shale in Texas (Allen, 2013). In 2011, agriculture used about 75 percent of water consumed annually in this country; fracking used roughly 0.3 percent, less than golf courses at 0.5 percent (Jenkins, 2013). Even so, in places where water is scarce, fracking's five million gallons of fresh water consumed per well may drain aquifers and tip the critical balance of supply and demand. In the Eagle Ford Shale play, there has been no difference reported by drillers in groundwater levels, but that doesn't mean that levels won't drop in the future, especially as demand rises with development, and drought conditions worsen, possibly as a result of global warming (Allen, 2013).

Water use in dry areas is not a trivial concern. In the Barnett Shale play, it has accounted for 9 percent of the water used in Dallas, far more than the overall use rate (McBroom, Thomas, & Zhang, 2012). In addition, a study performed in that same area showed that soil erosion and water quality increased as a result of drill pad construction. However, it also showed that when a buffer was used, the effects of both were significantly reduced. That supports the idea that damage that happens locally can be managed or prevented by actions taken locally. It supports the conclusion that the dangers of fracking are real but may be manageable.

On the other hand, Mooney (2011) points out that fracking wells, while usually contained if cementing is done properly, "could connect with preexisting fissures or old wells," through which the new well could contaminate ground water. These accidental connections have occurred multiple times, have taken place unexpectedly, and over a distance of more than 2,000 feet. While this will undoubtedly happen, technology is helping to solve many of the other problems inherent in fracking (Brainard, 2013). Membranes can be used to filter out contaminants from the flowback. A gel made from liquefied gas can take the place of water, increasing production without dissolving natural contaminants into the fluid. Surplus methane, ordinarily vented into the atmosphere or flared—that is burned to produce carbon dioxide—could be captured and converted into fuel or fed to genetically engineered microbes to produce ethanol, eliminating the need to use food crops such as corn. And a new generation of turbines is making power generation from natural gas significantly more efficient.

It is probably safe to say that no industrial process on such a grand scale will ever be completely safe for workers or the environment. Accidents will happen and the environment will be negatively affected. The question is, do the benefits outweigh the damage? So far, critics have not presented evidence that any of the problems are unsolvable, while proponents have cited many fixes and successful preventative measures. Uncertainties do surround fracking, as they do the entire energy industry, but with careful management, the many benefits can be made to outweigh the risks.

Complete APA-Style Research Paper

8

References

Allen, T. A. (2013). The South Texas drought and the future of groundwater use for hydraulic fracturing in the Eagle Ford Shale. *St. Mary's Law Journal, 44,* 487–527.

Brainard, C. (2013, June 4). The energy fix: How to clean up fracking's bad rep. *Popular Science.* https://www.popsci.com/science/article/2013-05/future-energy-oil-and-gas/

Browder, C. (2011, November 10). Fracking brings risk, reward to rural Pennsylvania; could NC be next? *WRAL.* https://www.wral.com/fracking-brings-risk-reward-to-pennsylvania-could-nc-be-next-/10359274/

Global coal demand set to remain stable through 2023, despite headwinds. (2018, December 18). International Energy Association. https://www.iea.org/newsroom/news/2018/december/global-coal-demand-set-to-remain-stable-through-2023-despite-headwinds.html

How hydraulic fracturing works. (2019). Swarthmore University. https://www.swarthmore.edu/environmental-studies-capstone/how-hydraulic-fracturing-works

Howarth, R. W., Ingraffea, A., & Engelder, T. (2011, September 15). Natural gas: Should fracking stop? *Nature, 477,* 271–275. https://www.nature.com/articles/477271a

Jenkins, J. (2013). *Energy facts: How much water does fracking for shale gas consume?* Energy Central. https://www.energycentral.com/c/ec/energy-facts-how-much-water-does-fracking-shale-gas-consume

McBroom, M., Thomas, T., & Zhang, Y. (2012). Soil erosion and surface water quality impacts of natural gas development in East Texas, USA. *Water, 4,* 944–958. https://doi.org/10.3390/w4040944

9

Mooney, C. (2011, November). The truth about fracking. *Scientific American*. https://www.scientificamerican.com/article/the-truth -about-fracking/

Pennsylvania Alliance for Clean Water and Air. (2013, March 12). List of the harmed [web log post]. http://pennsylvaniaalliance forcleanwaterandair.wordpress.com/the-list/

Royte, E. (2012, December 17). What the frack is in our food? *Nation. 295*(25). https://www.thenation.com/article/fracking -our-food-supply/

Schaefer, K. (2012, September 18). The stakes get higher in the fracking debate [web log post]. http://seekingalpha.com /instablog/365869-oil-and-gas-investmentsbulletin/1081001 -the-stakes-get-higher-in-the-fracking-debate

US Energy Information Administration. (2013, May 7). Short-term energy outlook. http://www.eia.gov/forecasts/steo/report /prices.cfm

GLOSSARY

absolute terms   Terms that suggest overgeneralization, for example, "all" or "everyone."

abstract   An abstract is a paragraph-long overview of an argument, essay, or article. It should summarize the writer's claim or thesis and refer to a few important points of support.

ad hominem   This fallacy attempts to mislead an audience by attacking an opponent's character, credibility, or authority instead of focusing on the opponent's argument.

ad misericordiam   This kind of appeal attempts to persuade through pity.

analogy   To argue by analogy refers to seeking similarities in the way similar situations have been addressed.

anecdote(s)   Anecdotes, a kind of support, are real-life episodes drawn from the life of the arguer, or others, that allow a writer to connect on a personal level with readers.

APA   This refers to a style guide for formatting essays and articles developed by the American Psychological Association that is typically used in the fields of social science, business, and education.

attributive phrases or statements   These are short phrases used to introduce quotations and their authors.

backing   Backing is support for a warrant. It elaborates, often through examples, on the values present in a warrant.

bandwagon fallacy   This kind of fallacy claims that something must be true because everyone, presumably, believes it to be true.

bar graph   A kind of logical support, a bar graph is a chart that uses bars to represent data.

bias   Bias refers to the particular viewpoint or slant that an author or a publication leans toward. A writer with a biased point of view often ignores objective fact and risks losing credibility with an audience.

biased language   Includes language that is strongly leaning to a particular direction with no regard for other points of view.

bibliography file   In the course of preparing an argument, a writer builds a bibliography file to maintain a record of all sources that may be used in an argument. For each source, such a file would include publication information, point of access, and notes.

blanket statements   This dangerous fallacy involves a statement that makes an overly general or absolute claim or reason and leaves the arguer vulnerable to attack.

Boolean search   This refers to a method for looking for information with search engines and in databases that combine search terms, or keywords, with the operators AND, OR, and NOT.

broadening out   This is a technique often used near the end of an argument where the arguer extends a claim to demonstrate how it can be applied, or broadened, to issues beyond the focus of a single argument.

causes   Reasons behind why something occurs; backward-looking.

circling back   This refers to a technique of the writer emphasizing, in a conclusion, a claim by referring, or circling back, to the introduction where the claim is first stated.

circular argument   Instead of providing support for a claim, the arguer simply restates a claim in this kind of fallacy.

claim   A claim is the arguer's position on an issue and the center of an argument. It alerts an audience to an argument's purpose and what the arguer wants an audience to accept or consider.

claim of cause   This kind of claim argues that one thing or event causes another event or chain of events.

claim of definition   This kind of claim defines a key word or term in an issue and then brings in reasons and specific support to justify the definition.

claim of evaluation   A judgment or evaluation is made in this kind of claim, as the arguer claims that something is practical or impractical, ethical or unethical, fair or unfair, healthy or unhealthy, worth our time or not worth our time, wasteful or beneficial, etc.

claim of fact   A claim of fact argues that something is a fact—an event or series of events, a trend, an attitude, or a part of history—that may not be considered a fact by everyone.

common ground   Common ground can be created between an arguer, the opposition, and audience when the arguer is careful to recognize shared values and beliefs.

community   The category of "community" is a convenient way to recognize where issues occur in our lives—at school, in the workplace, with family, in the neighborhood, in social-cultural contexts, as a consumer, and as a concerned citizen.

comparisons   Building a comparison in an argument between an idea you're working with and a similar set of circumstances in the past can clarify for readers a claim, reason, or point of support.

conclusion   A conclusion typically is the final paragraph or two in an argument in which the arguer can remind readers of the claim, point out the need for further research, or urge readers to act in response to the issue at hand.

conflict   This is a type of "hook," or way to engage readers, in the introduction that sets up conflicting ideas the writer will resolve in an argument.

consequences (or effects)   This kind of support is used to argue that something has happened or will happen based on past causes or circumstances.

context   The set of circumstances or facts, past and present, that surround a particular event, situation, or issue.

credible   In an argument this term refers to the reputation of the arguer based on his ability to bring in credible research and to prove to an audience that he is qualified to argue on the issue he's working with.

critical reading   Critical reading involves marking terms that are unknown, questioning a text, and investigating the claims made by

the other among other scholarly tasks.

database   A database is a collection of scholarly essays, articles, or other information that can be accessed electronically and then searched. For the purpose of building an argument, academic databases, such as those housed by a college or university, are essential.

deep web   This term refers to material on the Internet that is not searchable by conventional search engines and requires more precise searching, often through websites and private collections.

definition   There are seven kinds of definitions appropriate for academic writing and argument building—scientific, metaphoric, example, riddle, function, irony, and negation. They may be combined to accommodate the arguer's purpose.

definitional equivalence   This occurs when two things—ideas, theories, points of view, etc.—are defined as being the same, whether or not they are the same.

descriptive statistics   This term describes data in terms of who assembled it and in what conditions.

documentation   This is the process of citing the sources used in an argument in both the body of the argument and the end-of-argument reference pages, such as the Works Cited page.

domain extension   The ending element in a web address, or URL (universal resource locator), that indicates the general origin of the site is known as the domain extension. For example "gov" indicates that the site originates within a government-sponsored agency or department; "edu" for sites within an educational setting; "org" for an organization; and "com" reveals that the site is produced within a commercial or business setting.

double standard   A fallacy in which a standard is applied differently to different groups of people.

easy generalizations   A fallacy type that provides shallow generalizations based on stereotypes or inadequate research.

ebooks   Electronic versions of books.

equivocation   When contradictory claims appear in an argument, the arguer has committed a fallacy of equivocation. This kind of fallacy occurs when a word or term has two meanings and the writer intentionally uses the double meaning to deceive or mislead readers.

ethos   This is a Greek term that refers to the credibility of an arguer based on his ability to demonstrate authority or expertise in an argument.

evaluation   Evaluation is an argument strategy that is used when attempting to convince an audience that one thing is better, more efficient, or more feasible than another.

expert opinion   A writer includes expert opinion in an argument when sources include interviews, articles and essays, and lectures by professors, scholars, or recognized experts in a field. This kind of support adds to an arguer's credibility.

explicit claims   Claims that are directly stated by the arguer.

exploratory essay   An essay that allows a writer to explore an issue based on the writer's knowledge of the issue and what research needs to be pursued to build a competent argument is known as an exploratory essay.

facts   Facts are a kind of logical support and include statements and specific information about an issue that generally are regarded as true.

fallacies   Sometimes referred to as logical fallacies, errors in logic, or pseudoproofs, fallacies in an argument, whether accidental or deliberate, are misleading or deceptive statements that draw attention away from the problems in an argument's claim or support. A fallacy does not stand up to investigation based in sound logic or objective fact.

fallacies of choice   This is a category of fallacies that argues readers have limited choices when such limits do not exist.

fallacies of emotion   This is a category of fallacies that relies heavily on emotional appeals at the expense of other types of support, such as logical and ethical.

fallacies of inconsistency   These are fallacies that refer to assertions in an argument that treat ideas and information differently when they should be treated the same. Also refers to ideas and information treated as the same that should be treated differently.

fallacies of support   This category of fallacies makes connections and conclusions that are misleading and cannot be confirmed.

false analogy   A false analogy claims that situations or ideas are comparable when they are not.

false authority   This involves the endorsement of a position by a person not qualified to make the endorsement. While the person may have authority and expertise in another field, the writer incorrectly assumes that an endorsement based on reputation only is appropriate in an argument.

false clue   *See* red herring.

false dilemma/either–or   A fallacy that suggests only two options can occur for any situation.

false testimonial   Similar to a false authority fallacy, a false testimonial involves the endorsement of a position by a person not qualified to make the endorsement.

field-specific support   This refers to support generally regarded as acceptable in a specific field of study.

finding the incongruities in a position   Pointing out the difference between what an opponent says and what she does.

FLOI method   Examining the external elements of a text (table of contents, preface, chapter organization, index, etc.) in addition to the text itself, is a critical reading strategy known as the FLOI method.

glocal   This term refers to a writer making a connection in an argument between local and global contexts.

hasty generalization   This fallacy occurs when an arguer inaccurately generalizes based on a single case or example.

hidden claims   This is used when an arguer chooses to leave a claim unstated, or hidden, and instead wants readers to determine the claim on their own.

HTML document   A file formatted in HTML does not appear as a print document would, missing page numbers, page breaks, and sometimes images or other formatting.

iconic   This refers to an image or object that represents substantially more to the viewer or reader than the contents of the image or object itself.

implicit claims   Claims that an arguer implies but does not state directly.

inferential statistics   Statistics used to draw conclusions about a group of data by linking cause and effect are referred to as inferential statistics.

information overload   Situation that occurs when we are faced with too many sources of information.

introduction   An introduction begins an argument; it is the opening paragraph or paragraphs. In addition to engaging information designed to hook the reader, often a claim and sometimes a warrant appear in an introduction.

issue   An issue is a specific problem or dispute that remains unsettled that occurs within a larger topic and within a precise context, or set of conditions.

jargon   This is specialized language—words, terms, and concepts—originating in a specific field or discipline.

kairos or timeliness   In the context of argument, the Greek term *kairos* means delivering an argument at the optimal time, that is, at a time when there is genuine local or academic interest in an issue.

line graph   This graph uses points connected by line segments to show how something changes over time.

local voices   Local knowledge that makes an argument more focused and immediate.

logos   This is support based on verifiable information, such as facts, statistics, and scientific and scholarly evidence.

material equivalence   This fallacy erroneously claims that erroneously claims that two unequal things, such as facts or ideas, are equal or balanced.

microhistory   An argument based on a microhistory interprets primary documents so as to argue against overly general treatments of a historical period and to establish a layer of history generally overlooked.

Middle-Ground argument   This approach to an issue involves arguing for a practical middle position between two extreme positions.

misdirection   Meant to add suspense in an introduction to an argument, this is a kind of hook that intentionally misleads readers.

MLA   An academic paper formatting guide designed and updated by the Modern Language Association. It is used primarily in the humanities—composition, literature, languages, philosophy, and the arts.

moral equivalence   This fallacy involves the mistake of balancing two unequal facts, ideas, or points of view against each other *morally*, as if they are equally bad or good.

moving from boring to interesting
This prewriting technique is a way for an arguer to make a personal connection with an issue and thus enliven an argument.

newsreaders These are programs that gather and read items from Internet sources, such as discussion groups and RSS (Really Simple Syndication) feeds.

non sequitur This fallacy refers to a statement in an argument that is illogical; that is, a statement that does not connect logically to the statement preceding it.

Occam's Razor A guideline in philosophy and science, Occam's Razor argues that choosing the simpler of two ideas or theories is best. The guideline originates with William of Ockham (1285–1349), a British theologian and philosopher.

opinions Typically, this refers to a personal belief or attitude not based on research or verifiable information.

opposition This term has two meanings in the context of argument. First, it refers to points of view different from an arguer's. Second, it is a kind of conclusion that moves readers in a direction opposite from that in the introduction.

overstatement (hyperbole) This technique exaggerates, or overstates, so as to draw attention to an idea in an argument.

paraphrasing In an argument, paraphrased material occurs when an arguer puts in his own words the ideas of another writer and then acknowledges the source of the borrowed material.

parenthetical citations This is source information, typically author last name and page or paragraph number, placed in parentheses in the body of a text. This information follows quotations or paraphrased information in an argument.

pathos This kind of support appeals to readers' emotions. It can be achieved by using powerful examples, personal experience, and compelling factual information.

PDF document A file format that provides an image of the document that can be viewed as if it is a print document.

plagiarism The use of published material produced by someone else as if it is the writer's; this includes a range of infractions extending from the accidental omission of a citation to passing off an entire essay as one's own.

post hoc, ergo propter hoc Also known as "false cause," this fallacy mistakenly draws a conclusion based on the chronological order in which events occur and ignores other factors that might offer a more accurate explanation.

precedence Refers to the way a situation has been handled in the past.

prewriting This term refers to techniques and strategies used to organize, arrange, and think through ideas for an argument prior to the formal process of drafting an argument.

primary cause This refers to the cause in an argument that results in an immediate effect.

primary materials *see* primary sources

primary sources In terms of argument, primary sources or documents refer to material gathered from the past—letters, journals, photographs, music, artifacts, etc.—that an arguer interprets in support of a claim.

problem-based claims This kind of claim argues for a precise solution to a problem or issue.

qualifier(s) Qualifiers are used primarily to make claims and reasons more believable. Qualifiers move an arguer away from making overly general or blanket statements.

quoting Quoting is using a source word for word rather than paraphrasing the source.

reasons Reasons help organize an argument. They announce the purposes of some paragraphs, link directly to claim, and are followed by specific support.

rebuttal Vital to successful arguments, rebuttals are points of view on an issue different from the point of view of an arguer. Fair, accurate presentation of rebuttals build an arguer's credibility. Rebuttals often are immediately countered by the arguer.

red herring This is a fallacy that diverts attention away from the issue at hand, often by using false or misleading information.

reference list A list of all sources used in an APA format research argument.

reservations This is a statement that recognizes concerns, or reservations, an audience may hold about a warrant in an argument.

Rogerian argument This approach to argument is aimed at building common ground between an arguer and those holding differing points of view on an issue. Highlighting the strengths of other views is a cornerstone of Rogerian argument.

RSS feed (Really Simple Syndication)
These are formats used to publish frequently updated content—such as news, material from blogs, video, and audio—to which Internet users can subscribe.

scare tactics Common in advertising and politics, this fallacy uses emotionally charged language and dramatic examples to frighten and persuade readers. Use of this fallacy typically is part of an agenda—political or economic—among others.

search engines Vehicles for finding material on the World Wide Web, a search engine crawls the Internet for sites that match keywords used in a search.

search string These are keywords or phrases used to find information when using a search engine. Varying search terms can produce more comprehensive results.

secondary causes   Sometimes called peripheral causes, secondary causes are contributing factors to an effect in an argument.

secondary sources   Sources that analyze or explain some aspect of your topic. *See* primary sources.

seeming impossibility   This technique appears in an introduction to an argument and works as a hook for readers, setting up a problem without an apparent solution.

self-effacing humor   This is the use of humor to poke fun at an arguer rather than at the arguer's opponents.

slippery slope (or staircase)   This kind of fallacy presumes that one event will set off a series of succeeding events without providing sufficient explanation.

straw man argument   This fallacy is based on incorrect information, whether the intention is to deliberately misrepresent an opponent's claims or because the facts being used are plainly incorrect.

summary   A synopsis of the original source.

support   Evidence and information used to defend a claim is known as support. Kinds of support include logical (*logos*), ethical (*ethos*), and emotional (*pathos*).

surface web   In the context of Internet searching, this term refers to information gathered using conventional, nonspecific search engines, such as Google, Bing, Dogpile, and Ask.com among others.

suspense   Is used to heighten the tension for a reader as to what the claim will actually be.

target audience   This is the group or individual at whom an argument is aimed; it is the group or individual the arguer intends to persuade so as to accept a position on an issue.

testimonials   A type of fallacy in which an unqualified person endorses a product or stance.

thesis   This statement, often appearing early in a piece of writing, is needed to focus the reader and to identify the writer's main idea or purpose. A thesis may or may not offer a point of view or position.

topic   A topic is a category—such as local politics, transportation, neighborhood security, race relations, or family planning—that contains numerous issues within it. Specific issues and arguments originate in topics.

Toulmin-based argument   This approach to argument is named after Stephen Toulmin (1922–2009), a British philosopher and educator. Toulmin's approach to argument has been adapted as a practical complement to ethics in daily life.

understatement   This is a kind of verbal irony that minimizes, or understates, the seriousness of an issue.

visual argument   A visual argument delivers a claim on an issue visually—through a photograph, video, cartoon, illustration, etc. Support and a warrant often are included to enhance the claim.

warrant   This essential feature of argument refers to a deeply held value, belief or principle that an arguer shares with an audience or opponent.

works cited (page)   A feature of MLA documentation, this is the last page in a written argument using research and lists alphabetically sources used in the argument.

INDEX

A

Absolute terms, 115

Abstract, 86

Ad hominem, 124

Ad misericordiam, 126

Adoptive and birth families, interaction between, 390–392

Advertisements, evaluating, 316–317

Advocacy, expertise valued over, 145–146

Affect versus effect, 165

Aggregators, 65

Airbnb is crashing the neighborhood, 405–407

Analogy, 169

    false, 131–132

Anecdotes, 290, 293–294, 332

Anthology of arguments

    1: School and academic community, 354–373

        keeping up with students seeking treatment for depression and anxiety, 368–373

        punishment for plagiarism, 354–358

        tuition-free college, 366–368

        widening rich-poor divide on college campuses, 358–366

    2. Workplace community, 374–389

        abolish corporate personhood, 380–386

        employee-owned businesses ignored by mainstream media, 374–376

        hierarchy is overrated, 377–379

        love in the workplace, 386–389

    3. Family and household community, 390–404

        interaction between adoptive and birth families, 390–392

        nature-deficit disorder, 396–399

        street life is no life for children, 392–396

        when soldiers and their families become expendable, 399–404

    4. Neighborhood community, 405–422

        Airbnb is crashing the neighborhood, 405–407

        bowling with others, 413–419

        persistence of racial residential segregation, 407–413

        toxic-waste dumps in the backyards of the poor, 420–422

    5. Social/cultural community, 423–440

        Asians as shooters, 436–440

        being a black man and a black cop, 433–436

        case against tipping, 426–433

        "security" versus privacy, 423–426

    6. Consumer community, 441–459

        Buddhist perspective on consumerism, 441–444

        McEconomy and hollowing out of the middle class, 448–453

        outsourcing compromises the safety and quality of products, 453–459

        public banking, 444–448

    7. Concerned citizen community, 460–478

        automatic voter registration, 468–472

        climate change could cause disease resurgence, 465–468

        open immigration, 460–465

        private charity should replace welfare, 473–478

Approaching an argument

    argue with a purpose. *See* Purpose, arguing with

    evaluate and engage with your sources. *See* Sources, evaluate and engage with

    explore an issue that matters to you. *See* Issue, exploring

    read critically and avoid fallacies. *See* Read critically and avoid fallacies

    work fairly with the opposition. *See* opposition, work fairly with

Arguments

    anthology of. *See* Anthology of arguments

    based on microhistory, 228–238

        focus on the local and specific, 228–229

        local histories, making room for, 229–231

        map an argument based on a microhistory, 233–236

        sample, 236–238

        subjects and materials, 232–233

        work with primary materials, 231–232

    building. *See* Building arguments

    definition of, 3–6

    enhancing with visuals, 300–318

        advertisements, evaluating, 316–317

        overview, 300–303

        understanding and using visual arguments, 303–312

        creating graphs, 316

Arguments (*Continued*)
- questions to ask while reading visual arguments, 306
- reading graphs and charts, 312–317
- reading photographs and illustrations, 308–310
- using and creating graphs in your argument, 314–316
- using photographs and illustrations in your argument, 311–312
- four kinds of, 16–19
  - microhistory-based argument, 19
  - middle-ground argument, 18
  - Rogerian argument, 18–19
  - Toulmin-based argument, 17
- middle-ground, 205–219
  - make a middle-ground position practical, 207–208
  - map a middle-ground argument, 209–214
  - recognize where middle-ground arguments are possible, 208–209
  - student-authored, 214–218
- planning, structuring, and delivering argument structure and style, developing and editing. *See* Argument structure and style, developing and editing
  - building an argument. *See* Building arguments
  - consider argument based on a microhistory. *See* Microhistory, argument based on
  - consider middle-ground argument. *See* Middle-ground argument
  - consider Rogerian argument. *See* Rogerian argument
  - consider Toulmin-based argument. *See* Toulmin-based argument
  - explore an issue. *See* Issue, exploring
  - supporting an argument with fact, credibility, and emotion. *See* Support
  - purpose, arguing with. *See* Purpose, arguing with
  - right moment, 46–47

- why they break down, 15–16
  - audience is poorly defined, 15–16
  - there is a lack of balance in the support, 15
  - they contain fallacies, 16
  - they do not fairly represent opposing views, 16
  - they do not persuade an audience, 15
- Argument structure and style, developing and editing, 319–351
  - consider your argument's claim, 320–329
    - edit your claim, 322–323
    - introduce your claim, 320–322
    - position your claim, 326–329
    - state your claim, 323–326
  - create strong introductions, 331–336
    - anecdote, 332
    - conflict, 333–334
    - misdirection, 332–333
    - a seeming impossibility, 335–336
    - suspense, 334
  - edit and organize your argument's support, 339–346
    - edit support, 339–342
    - organization samples of body paragraphs, 343–346
    - organize your support, 342
  - introduce your counterarguments, 329–331
    - the counterargument is correct, but..., 330–331
    - the counterargument is incorrect, 330
  - overview, 319–320
  - participate effectively in a peer review session, 348–350
    - your role as a reviewee, 350
    - your role as a reviewer, 348–350
  - supply a strong title, 346–348
  - write memorable conclusions, 336–339
    - broadening out, 336–337
    - circling back, 338
    - opposition, 337–338
- Articles
  - reading critically and evaluating, 85–90
  - scholarly, 288–289
- Arts and humanities, finding sources for, 279–280

- Asians as shooters, 436–440
- Attributive phrases or statements, 93
- Audience
  - defining and targeting, 10–11, 32–34
  - emotions of, support based on, 38
  - persuading, 15
  - poorly defined, 15–16
  - reservations, respond to in order to make a warrant believable, 269–270
  - using to construct a warrant, 262–265
    - know what your audience values, 262–263
    - let a warrant bridge claim and support, 263–265
- Automatic voter registration, 468–472

B

- Backing, 192, 195, 197, 265
  - to support a warrant, 265–269
    - let your audience determine the extent of backing, 266–267
    - make backing specific, 267–269
- Bandwagon fallacy, 126
- Bar graph, 315
- Bias, 130
  - avoiding, 146–148
  - definition of, 86
- Biased language, 146
- Bibliography file, 60
- Birth and adoptive families, interaction between, 390–392
- Black man and a black cop, being both, 433–436
- Blanket statements, 115
- Books, 75–78
  - take notes and read critically, 90–91
- Boring to interesting, moving from, 30–32
- Bowling with others, 413–419
- Bradbury, Ray, 30–31
- Brainstorming, 29–30
- Broadening out, 336–337
- Buddhist perspective on consumerism, 441–444
- Building arguments, 241–272
  - build body paragraphs around reasons, 257–259
  - claims, five kinds of, 246–255

claim of cause, 253–254
claim of definition, 248–250
claim of evaluation, 251–253
claim of fact, 246–248
problem-based claim, 250–251
how a claim functions, 243–245
claim is the center of your
argument, 243–245
connect claim with purpose, 245
justify your claim with a warrant,
261
overview, 241–243
respond to audience reservations
to make a warrant believ-
able, 269–270
use backing to support a warrant,
265–269
let your audience determine the
extent of backing, 266–267
make backing specific, 267–269
use qualifiers to make your argument believable, 259–261
use reasons to support your claim,
254–256
use your audience to construct a
warrant, 262–265
know what your audience values,
262–263
let a warrant bridge claim and
support, 263–265

C
Cause, 165
claim of, 44, 253–254
definition of, 164
discovering, 164–168
Chain of evidence, 167
Character (yours), support based on,
37–38
Charts and graphs, 312–317
Children, street life is no life for,
392–396
Choice, fallacies of, 114–119
blanket statements, 115
false dilemma/either-or thinking,
116
Occam's razor, misuse of, 116–117
slippery slope (or staircase),
117–119
Circling back, 338
Circular argument, 119–120
Claim, 191, 320–329
defending, 34–36
argue with a purpose, 36

develop a claim, reasons, and
qualifiers, 34–36
definition of, 243
edit your claim, 322–323
evaluating, 181–183
five kinds of, 43–44, 246–255, 323
claim of cause, 44, 253–254, 323
claim of definition, 43, 248–250,
323
claim of evaluation, 44,
251–253, 323
claim of fact, 44, 246–248, 323
problem-based claim, 250–251,
323
how they function, 243–245
claim is the center of your
argument, 243–245
connect claim with purpose, 245
introduce your claim, 320–322
justify with a warrant, 261
position your claim, 326–329
state your claim, 323–326
use reasons to support,
254–256
Climate change could cause disease
resurgence, 465–468
Clustering, 30
College. *See* School and academic
community, contemporary
issues and arguments
Common ground, 219
Concerned citizen community,
contemporary issues and
arguments, 460–478
automatic voter registration,
468–472
climate change could cause disease
resurgence, 465–468
open immigration, 460–465
private charity should replace
welfare, 472–478
Concerned citizen issues, 26
Conclusions, memorable, writing,
336–339
broadening out, 336–337
circling back, 338
opposition, 337–338
Conflict, 333–334
Consequences
definition of, 164
discovering, 164–168
Consumer community, contemporary
issues and arguments,
441–459

Buddhist perspective on
consumerism, 441–444
McEconomy and hollowing out of
the middle class, 448–453
outsourcing compromises the
safety and quality of products, 453–459
public banking, 444–448
Consumerism, Buddhist perspective
on, 441–444
Consumer issues, 25–26
Context, 11
Corporate personhood, abolishing,
380–386
Counterarguments, introducing,
329–331
the counterargument is correct,
but…, 330–331
the counterargument is incorrect,
330
Credible, definition of, 82
Critical reading, 82–83, 111
Cultural/social issues, 25

D
Database
definition of, 65
in libraries, 65–68
Deep web, 60–61
Definition, claim of, 43, 248–250
Definitional equivalence, 129–130
Definitions, using, 157–164
define by example, 162
define by function, 162–163
define by negation, 163–164
define with a riddle, 162
define with irony, 163
define with metaphor
(comparison), 161
define with science (descriptive,
factual), 160–161
Delivering an argument
argument structure and style,
developing and editing. *See*
Argument structure and
style, developing and editing
building an argument. *See* Building
arguments
consider argument based on
a microhistory. *See*
Microhistory, argument
based on
consider middle-ground argument.
See Middle-ground argument

Delivering an argument (*Continued*)
consider Rogerian argument. *See*
Rogerian argument
consider Toulmin-based argument.
See Toulmin-based argument
explore an issue. *See* Issue, exploring
supporting an argument with fact,
credibility, and emotion.
See Support
Descriptive statistics, 285
Developing arguments. *See* Argument
structure and style,
developing and editing
Disease resurgence could be caused by
climate change, 465–468
Document: works cited page,
107–108
Dogmatism, 130
Double standard, 128

E

Easy generalizations, resisting,
139–140
ebooks, 78
Editing. *See* Argument structure
and style, developing and
editing
Education, history, and social and
behavioral sciences, finding
support for, 277–279
Effect, 165
versus affect, 165
definition of, 164
Either-or/false dilemma thinking,
116
Emotion, fallacies of, 124–128
ad hominem, 124
ad misericordiam, 126
bandwagon, 126
scare tactics, 126–127
testimonials and false authority,
125
Employee-owned businesses ignored
by mainstream media,
374–376
Encyclopedias, 54–56
Enhance your argument with visuals,
300–318
advertisements, evaluating,
316–317
overview, 300–303
understanding and using visual
arguments, 303–312
creating graphs, 316

questions to ask while reading
visual arguments, 306
reading graphs and charts,
312–317
reading photographs and illustrations, 308–310
using and creating graphs in
your argument, 314–316
using photographs and illustrations in your argument,
311–312
Equivocation, 130–131
Ethos, 37, 281
use support to create credibility,
289–291
Evaluation, claim of, 44, 181,
251–253
Evidence, chain of, 167
Example, define by, 162
Expertise valued over advocacy,
145–146
Explicit claims, 323–324
Exploratory essay, writing, 183–185
checklist, 184
sample, 184
Exploring an issue. *See* Issue, exploring

F

Fact
claim of, 44, 246–248
and opinions, 282–284
support based on, 37
Fallacies, 16, 110–135
definition of, 111–112
fallacies of choice, 114–119
blanket statements, 115
false dilemma/either-or
thinking, 116
Occam's razor, misuse of,
116–117
slippery slope (or staircase),
117–119
fallacies of emotion, 124–128
ad hominem, 124
ad misericordiam, 126
bandwagon, 126
scare tactics, 126–127
testimonials and false
authority, 125
fallacies of inconsistency, 128–133
definitional equivalence,
129–130
equivocation, 130–131
false analogy, 131–132

inconsistent treatment (from
dogmatism, prejudice, and
bias), 130
material equivalence, 129
moral equivalence, 129
fallacies of support, 119–124
circular argument, 119–120
faulty causality: *post hoc, ergo
propter hoc*, 120–121
hasty generalization and jumping
to conclusions, 120
non sequitur, red herring, and
false clue, 121–122
straw man argument or
argument built on a false
fact or claim, 122–123
identify and avoid, 112–114
overview, 110–111
False analogy, 131–132
False authority and testimonials, 125
False clue, 121–122
False dilemma/either-or thinking, 116
Family and household community,
contemporary issues and
arguments, 24, 390–404
interaction between adoptive and
birth families, 390–392
nature-deficit disorder, 396–399
street life is no life for children,
392–396
when soldiers and their families become expendable,
399–404
Faulty causality: *post hoc, ergo propter
hoc*, 120–121
Field-specific support, 274–280
FLOI method, 90–91
Frank, Thomas, 4
Freewriting, 30
Function, define by, 162–163

G

Generalizations, easy, resisting,
139–140
Global and local contexts, connecting,
13–14
Glocal, 14–15
Government sources, 71–72
Graphs and charts, 312–317

H

Hasty generalization, 120
Hidden claims, 325
Hierarchy is overrated, 377–379

History, education, and social and behavioral sciences, finding support for, 277–279
Hollowing out of the middle class, McEconomy and, 449–453
HTML document, 67–68
Humanities and the arts, finding sources for, 279–280
Humor, using in your arguments, 294–296

I

Illustrations and photographs, 308–310
Immigration, open, 460–465
Implicit claims, 324
Inconsistency, fallacies of, 128–133
    definitional equivalence, 129–130
    equivocation, 130–131
    false analogy, 131–132
    inconsistent treatment (from dogmatism, prejudice, and bias), 130
    material equivalence, 129
    moral equivalence, 129
Inconsistent treatment (from dogmatism, prejudice, and bias), 130
Inferential statistics, 285
Information overload, 112
Internet, 82–90
    critically read material, 82–83
    evaluate articles, 90
    evaluate sites, 83
    read articles critically, 85–89
    take notes, 84–85
Intersections: contemporary issues and arguments. *See* Anthology of arguments
Introductions, creating, 331–336
    anecdote, 332
    conflict, 333–334
    misdirection, 332–333
    a seeming impossibility, 335–336
    suspense, 334
Irony, define by, 163
Issue, exploring, 21–50, 156–186
    argue at the right moment, 46–47
    audience, defining and targeting, 32–34
    choose an issue within a topic, 27–29
    determine what matters to you and why, 23–26

concerned citizen issues, 26
consumer issues, 25–26
family/household, 24
neighborhood, 25
school/academic community, 23–24
social/cultural issues, 25
workplace, 24
discover causes or consequences, 164–168
evaluate your claim, 181–183
getting started, 47–49
overview, 21–22, 156–157
present comparisons, 168–170
pre-think about your issue, 29–32
    brainstorming, 29–30
    freewriting, 30
    mapping, 30
    move from boring to interesting, 30–32
propose a solution, 170–181
    different types of exploration, 173–178
    exploring implementation, 178–181
    exploring the problem, 171–173
stake, defend, and justify your claim, 34–36
    argue with a purpose, 36
    develop a claim, reasons, and qualifiers, 34–36
use definitions, 157–164
    define by example, 162
    define by function, 162–163
    define by negation, 163–164
    define with a riddle, 162
    define with irony, 163
    define with metaphor (comparison), 161
    define with science (descriptive, factual), 160–161
vary the types of support you bring to an argument, 37–45
    examples, 38–45
    support based on audience emotions, 38
    support based on fact, 37
    support based on your character, 37–38
write an exploratory essay, 183–185
    checklist, 184
    sample, 184

J

Jargon, 86
Jumping to conclusions, 120
Justify your claim, 34–36

K

Keyword queries, 61–63

L

Libraries, databases in, 65–68
Line graph, 314–315
Local and specific, focusing on, 228–229
Local context, research process to establish, 10–14
    connect local and global contexts, 13–14
    determine your audience, 10–11
    establish local context for your issue, 11–12
Local histories, making room for, 229–231
Local voices, listening to, 140–141
Logos, 37, 281
    use support based on facts and research, 282–286
    facts and opinions, 282–284
    scholarly articles, 288–289
    statistics, 284–288
Love in the workplace, 386–389

M

Mapping, 30
Material equivalence, 129
McEconomy and hollowing out of the middle class, 449–453
Metaphor (comparison), define by, 161
Microhistory, argument based on, 19, 228–238
    focus on the local and specific, 228–229
    local histories, making room for, 229–231
    map an argument based on a microhistory, 233–236
    sample, 236–238
    subjects and materials, 232–233
    work with primary materials, 231–232
Middle class and the McEconomy, 449–453

Middle-ground argument, 18, 205–219
  make a middle-ground position practical, 207–208
  map a middle-ground argument, 209–214
  recognize where middle-ground arguments are possible, 208–209
  student-authored, 214–218
Misdirection, 332–333
Moral equivalence, 129
Multimedia sources, 72–75

N
Nature-deficit disorder, 396–399
Negation, define by, 163–164
Neighborhood community, contemporary issues and arguments, 25, 405–422
  Airbnb is crashing the neighborhood, 405–407
  bowling with others, 413–419
  persistence of racial residential segregation, 407–413
  toxic-waste dumps in the backyards of the poor, 420–422
Newsreaders, 65
News sites and RSS feeds, 63–65
Non sequitur, 121–122

O
Occam's razor, misuse of, 116–117
Open immigration, 460–465
Opinion
  definition of, 284
  and facts, 282–284
Opposing views, 290
  representing fairly, 16
Opposition, 137, 337–338
  why it matters, 138–139
  work fairly with, 136–153
    avoid bias when you summarize, 146–148
    find points of overlap, 148–151
    listen to local voices, 140–141
    overview, 136–137
    resist easy generalizations, 139–140
    respond to other views, 151–152
    summarizing other voices fairly, 141–145
    value expertise over advocacy, 145–146

why the opposition matters, 138–139
Other views and voices
  responding to, 151–152
  summarizing other voices fairly, 141–145
Outsourcing compromises the safety and quality of products, 453–459
Overlap, finding points of, 148–151

P
Paraphrase, and cite paraphrases, 101–104
Pathos, 37–38, 281
  use support to create emotion, 292–296
    anecdotes, 293–294
    photographs, 294
    using humor in your arguments, 294–296
PDF documents, 65
Peer-edited summaries, 148
Peer review sessions, 348–350
  your role as a reviewee, 350
  your role as a reviewer, 348–350
Photographs and illustrations, 294, 308–312
Physical sciences, finding support for, 275–276
Plagiarism
  avoiding, 105–107
  definition of, 84
  punishment for, 354–358
Planning, structuring, and delivering an argument
  argument structure and style, developing and editing. *See* Argument structure and style, developing and editing
  building an argument. *See* Building arguments
  consider argument based on a microhistory. *See* Microhistory, argument based on
  consider middle-ground argument. *See* Middle-ground argument
  consider Rogerian argument. *See* Rogerian argument
  consider Toulmin-based argument. *See* Toulmin-based argument

explore an issue. *See* Issue, exploring
supporting an argument with fact, credibility, and emotion. *See* Support
Postel, Danny, 105
Post hoc, ergo propter hoc, 120–121
Precedence, 169
Prejudice, 130
Pre-think about your issue, 29–32
  brainstorming, 29–30
  freewriting, 30
  mapping, 30
  move from boring to interesting, 30–32
"Price of Admission, The," 4–5
Primary cause, 165–166
Primary materials, 231
Primary sources, 69–70
  evaluating, 91–95
    checklist, 92
    introduce and comment on sources, 92–95
  finding and using, 69–78
    books, 75–78
    government sources, 71–72
    multimedia sources, 72–75
Privacy versus "security," 423–426
Problem-based claim, 250–251, 323
Public banking, 444–448
Purpose, arguing with, 2–20
  argue about issues that matter to you, 7–10
  argument, definition of, 3–6
  four kinds of arguments, 16–19
    microhistory-based argument, 19
    middle-ground argument, 18
    Rogerian argument, 18–19
    Toulmin-based argument, 17
  overview, 2–3
  reasons why arguments break down, 15–16
    audience is poorly defined, 15–16
    there is a lack of balance in the support, 15
    they contain fallacies, 16
    they do not fairly represent opposing views, 16
    they do not persuade an audience, 15
  recognize where argument is appropriate in real life, 6–7
  research process to establish local context, 10–14

connect local and global
contexts, 13–14
determine your audience,
10–11
establish local context for your
issue, 11–12

Q

Qualifier, 193, 195, 197
definition of, 259
to make your argument believable,
259–261
Quote, and cite quotations, 95–100

R

Racial residential segregation,
persistence of, 407–413
Read critically and avoid fallacies,
110–135
fallacies
definition of, 111–112
identify and avoid, 112–114
fallacies of choice, 114–119
blanket statements, 115
false dilemma/either-or
thinking, 116
Occam's razor, misuse of,
116–117
slippery slope (or staircase),
117–119
fallacies of emotion, 124–128
ad hominem, 124
ad misericordiam, 126
bandwagon, 126
scare tactics, 126–127
testimonials and false
authority, 125
fallacies of inconsistency,
128–133
definitional equivalence,
129–130
equivocation, 130–131
false analogy, 131–132
inconsistent treatment (from
dogmatism, prejudice, and
bias), 130
material equivalence, 129
moral equivalence, 129
fallacies of support, 119–124
circular argument, 119–120
faulty causality: *post hoc, ergo
propter hoc,* 120–121
hasty generalization and jumping
to conclusions, 120

non sequitur, red herring, and
false clue, 121–122
straw man argument or argument
built on a false fact or claim,
122–123
overview, 110–111
Real life, recognizing where argument
is appropriate in, 6–7
Reasons, 191, 194–196, 254–256
Rebuttals, 192–193, 195, 197
Red herring, 121–122
Reference works, encyclopedias, and
topic overviews, 54–56
gather search terms, 55–56
read an overview of your topic, 54–55
Research plan, developing, 52–79
databases in libraries, 65–68
keyword queries, 61–63
news sites and RSS feeds, 63–65
overview, 52–54
primary sources, finding and using,
69–78
books, 75–78
government sources, 71–72
multimedia sources, 72–75
reference works, encyclopedias,
and topic overviews, 54–56
gather search terms, 55–56
read an overview of your topic,
54–55
search engines, using, 57–61
deep web, 60–61
surface web, 57–59
Research process to establish local
context, 10–14
connect local and global contexts,
13–14
determine your audience, 10–11
establish local context for your
issue, 11–12
Reservations, audience, respond to
in order to make a warrant
believable, 269–270
Reviewee, your role as, 350
Reviewer, your role as, 348–350
Rich-poor divide widening on college
campuses, 358–366
Riddle, define by, 162
Rogerian argument, 18–19, 219–228
identify common ground, 221–223
listen closely to the opposition,
219–221
map an argument, 223–226
sample, 227–228

Rogers, Carl, 219
RSS feeds and news sites, 63–65

S

Scare tactics, 126–127
Scholarly articles, 288–289
School and academic community,
contemporary issues
and arguments, 23–24,
354–373
keeping up with students seeking
treatment for depression
and anxiety, 368–373
punishment for plagiarism,
354–358
tuition-free college, 366–368
widening rich-poor divide on
college campuses, 358–366
Science (descriptive, factual), define
with, 160–161
Search engines, using, 57–61
deep web, 60–61
surface web, 57–59
Search string, 61–62
Search terms, 55–56
Secondary cause, 166
Secondary sources, 69
"Security" versus privacy, 423–426
Seeming impossibility, 335–336
Shallow summaries, 146
Shared values, recognizing, 150
Shooters, Asians as, 436–440
Slippery slope (or staircase),
117–119
Social and behavioral sciences,
education, and his-
tory, finding support for,
277–279
Social/cultural community, contemporary issues and argu-
ments, 25, 423–440
Asians as shooters, 436–440
being a black man and a black cop,
433–436
case against tipping, 426–433
"security" versus privacy, 423–426
Soldiers and their families considered
expendable, 399–404
Solution, proposing, 170–181
different types of exploration,
173–178
exploring implementation,
178–181
exploring the problem, 171–173

Sources, evaluate and engage with, 80–109
  books
    take notes and read critically, 90–91
    document: works cited page, 107–108
  Internet, 82–90
    critically read material, 82–83
    evaluate articles, 90
    evaluate sites, 83
    read articles critically, 85–89
    take notes, 84–85
  overview, 80–82
  paraphrase, and cite paraphrases, 101–104
  plagiarism, avoiding, 105–107
  primary sources, evaluating, 91–95
    checklist, 92
    introduce and comment on sources, 92–95
  quote, and cite quotations, 95–100
  summarize, and cite summaries, 100–101
Stake, defend, and justify your claim, 34–36
  argue with a purpose, 36
  develop a claim, reasons, and qualifiers, 34–36
Statistics, 284–288
Straw man argument or argument built on a false fact or claim, 122–123
Street life is no life for children, 392–396
Structure and style of arguments, developing and editing, 319–351
  consider your argument's claim, 320–329
    edit your claim, 322–323
    introduce your claim, 320–322
    position your claim, 326–329
    state your claim, 323–326
  create strong introductions, 331–336
    anecdote, 332
    conflict, 333–334
    misdirection, 332–333
    a seeming impossibility, 335–336
    suspense, 334
  edit and organize your argument's support, 339–346

    edit support, 339–342
    organization samples of body paragraphs, 343–346
    organize your support, 342
  introduce your counterarguments, 329–331
    the counterargument is correct, but..., 330–331
    the counterargument is incorrect, 330
  overview, 319–320
  participate effectively in a peer review session, 348–350
    your role as a reviewee, 350
    your role as a reviewer, 348–350
  supply a strong title, 346–348
  write memorable conclusions, 336–339
    broadening out, 336–337
    circling back, 338
    opposition, 337–338
Structuring and delivering an argument
  argument structure and style, developing and editing. See Argument structure and style, developing and editing
  building an argument. See Building arguments
  consider argument based on a microhistory. See Microhistory, argument based on
  consider middle-ground argument. See Middle-ground argument
  consider Rogerian argument. See Rogerian argument
  consider Toulmin-based argument. See Toulmin-based argument
  explore an issue. See Issue, exploring
  supporting an argument with fact, credibility, and emotion. See Support
Students seeking treatment for depression and anxiety, 368–373
Subjects and materials, 231–233
Summarize, and cite summaries, 100–101

Support, 191–192, 195–196
  edit and organize, 339–346
    edit support, 339–342
    organization samples of body paragraphs, 343–346
    organize your support, 342
  fallacies of, 119–124
    circular argument, 119–120
    faulty causality: post hoc, ergo propter hoc, 120–121
    hasty generalization and jumping to conclusions, 120
    non sequitur, red herring, and false clue, 121–122
    straw man argument or argument built on a false fact or claim, 122–123
  lack of balance in, 15
  using fact (logos), credibility (ethos), and emotion (pathos), 273–298
    field-specific support, 274–280
    overview, 273–274
    use all three general kinds of support, 281–282
    use support based on facts and research (logos), 282–286
    use support to create credibility (ethos), 289–291
    use support to create emotion (pathos), 292–296
  vary the types of support you bring to an argument, 37–45
    examples, 38–45
    support based on audience emotions, 38
    support based on fact, 37
    support based on your character, 37–38
Surface web, 57–59
Suspense, 334

T
Take ownership of your argument: a style guide. See Enhance your argument with visuals; Structure and style of arguments, developing and editing
Target audience, definition of, 32
Testimonials and false authority, 125
Tipping, case against, 426–433
Title, strong, 346–348

Topic, choosing an issue within, 27–29

Toulmin-based argument, 17, 187–204

backing, 192, 195, 197

claim, 191

construct an argument to fit your purpose, 189

mapping of, 194–198

overview, 187–188

qualifiers, 193, 195, 197

reasons, 191, 194–196

rebuttals, 192–193, 195, 197

student-authored Toulmin-based argument, 198–201

support, 191–192, 195–196

terms of, 189–194

warrant, 192, 195, 197

Toxic-waste dumps in the backyards of the poor, 420–422

Tuition-free college, 366–368

V

Visuals, enhancing your argument with, 300–318

advertisements, evaluating, 316–317

overview, 300–303

understanding and using visual arguments, 303–312

creating graphs, 316

questions to ask while reading visual arguments, 306

reading graphs and charts, 312–317

reading photographs and illustrations, 308–310

using and creating graphs in your argument, 314–316

using photographs and illustrations in your argument, 311–312

Voter registration, automatic, 468–472

W

Warrant, 192, 195, 197

backing to support, 265–269

let your audience determine the extent of backing, 266–267

make backing specific, 267–259

bridges claim and support, 263–264

Wechsler Adult Intelligence Scale, 284–285

Welfare, replacing with private charity, 473–478

What matters to you, determining, 23–26

concerned citizen issues, 26

consumer issues, 25–26

family/household, 24

neighborhood, 25

school/academic community, 23–24

social/cultural issues, 25

workplace, 24

Workplace, contemporary issues and arguments, 24, 374–389

abolish corporate personhood, 380–386

employee-owned businesses ignored by mainstream media, 374–376

hierarchy is overrated, 377–379

love in the workplace, 386–389

Y

Your character, support based on, 37–38